ISLAND BATTLES OF THE PACIFIC

Iwo Jima and Okinawa

Red and Black Publishers, St Petersburg, Florida

Excerpted from:
History of U.S. Marine Corps Operations in World War II Volumes I-V; Historical
Branch, G-3 Division, Headquarters, U.S. Marine Corps 1968-1971

Library of Congress Cataloging-in-Publication Data

Island battles of the Pacific : Iwo Jima and Okinawa.
       p. cm.
   "Excerpted from: History of U.S. Marine Corps Operations in World War II, volumes
I-V."
   ISBN 978-1-934941-82-9
1. Iwo Jima, Battle of, Japan, 1945. 2. World War, 1939-1945--Campaigns--Japan--
Okinawa Island. 3. United States. Marine Corps--History--World War, 1939-1945. I.
United States. Marine Corps. History of U.S. Marine Corps operations in World War II.
   D767.99.I9I82 2010
   940.54'25229--dc22

                                                           2010007747

Red and Black Publishers, PO Box 7542, St Petersburg, Florida, 33734
Contact us at: info@RedandBlackPublishers.com
   Printed and manufactured in the United States of America

Contents

Iwo Jima

Chapter 1. Background

The autumn of 1944 saw the Allies poised for a major thrust both in Europe and in the Pacific. On the European Continent, the Allies had liberated almost all of France and stood ready to advance into Germany; in fact, the German western border and the heavily fortified Siegfried Line had already been breached; on the Eastern Front, the Russians had recaptured almost all Russian territory, had driven deep into the Balkans, and were engaged in cutting off sizable German forces in the Baltic countries after an advance into East Prussia. It was evident that Germany, now fighting by herself, having been abandoned by nearly all of her former allies, could stave off the collapse of the Third Reich for only a limited time.

In the Pacific Theater, the year of 1944 had gone badly for the Japanese also. Starting with the American offensive against the Gilberts in November 1943, the inexorable advance across the Pacific had taken American forces 3,000 miles westward by the end of the year. The conquest of Saipan, more than any other reverse, had brought home to Japanese leaders the realization that there no longer was any chance of a Japanese victory. Loss of the Marianas, accompanied by the Battle of the Philippine Sea which all but destroyed Japanese naval aviation, left the Japanese home islands open to American attack. Capture of Peleliu and Ulithi protected the American right flank for a thrust into the Philippines. By late October 1944, American forces had not only gained a foothold on Leyte, but had also inflicted disastrous punishment on the Imperial Navy during the Battle for Leyte Gulf.

The beginning of 1945 saw American forces in possession of most of Leyte and with a solid foothold on Luzon. The enemy naval forces, rendered largely impotent by the reverses they had suffered during the previous year, were no longer able to interfere successfully with American operations in the Philippines, whose liberation had become merely a matter of time.

The Allied advance by early 1945 had carried friendly forces deep into enemy territory in a line extending from an area east of the Kurile Islands southward and westward to a point separating the Mariana and Volcano Islands, thence westward to the Philippines, where the line turned to the southeast and continued southwestward towards New Guinea and Australia. Even though many thousands of enemy troops remained on bypassed islands such as New Britain, Kavieng, Wake, Marcus, and Yap, these erstwhile Japanese strongholds had been so effectively isolated and neutralized by American air power and submarines that they remained merely a nuisance. With the capture of the Mariana Islands during the summer of 1944, the United States had obtained a strongpoint from which the further assaults towards the Japanese home islands could be launched. As an added steppingstone towards the ultimate invasion of Japan, an advance from the Marianas to the Ryukyus appeared logical. It was also considered necessary to secure a foothold in the Nanpo Shoto. The island finally selected for invasion within the Nanpo Shoto was barely more than a speck of dust and volcanic ashes in the Pacific. Little known to the outside world until 1945, its name was destined soon to be on the lips of thousands of men and women throughout the free world and Japan. That island was Iwo Jima.

History and Importance of the Bonin Islands

From the entrance to Tokyo Bay, a chain of islands, known as the Nanpo Shoto, extends southward for about 750 miles to within 300 miles of the Mariana Islands. The Nanpo Shoto consists of three major groups of islands: the Izut Shoto, the Bonin Islands, also known as the Ogasawara Gunto, and the Volcano Islands, known to the Japanese as the Kazan Retto. Among the latter group of islands lies Iwo Jima, located about 670 miles south of Tokyo, 700 miles north of Guam and nearly halfway between Tokyo and Saipan.

Iwo Jima, translated into English, means Sulphur Island, named for the sulphur deposits that extend to the very surface of the island. Iwo's shape has alternately been compared to that of a pork chop, a dripping ice-cream cone, or an elongated sea shell of the type commonly found on ocean beaches of the mid-Atlantic and southern United States. From northeast to southwest, the island measures less than five miles across; the width varies from approximately two and a half miles in the northern part to only one-half mile in the southern portion. Altogether, Iwo Jima occupies less than eight square miles.

There was little about Iwo Jima or the remainder of the Volcano-Bonin Islands to make them attractive to foreigners in search of areas that could be colonized. In the mid-Sixteenth Century a Spanish navigator sighted the Volcano Islands but thereafter Europeans paid little attention to them. As the century drew to a close, a Japanese explorer discovered the Bonin Islands and found them to be uninhabited. They remained this way until the early part of the Nineteenth Century, when an assortment of British and American whaling captains sailed into the waters surrounding the islands. A group of colonists, consisting of Englishmen, Portuguese, Italians, Hawaiians, and an American named Nathaniel Savory, who hailed from New England, set out from Hawaii and settled on Chichi Jima under British sponsorship.

In 1853, Commodore Matthew Perry stopped at Chichi Jima and, impressed by the possible use of the island as a coaling station for U. S. Navy vessels, urged the government to purchase a strip of land on the island on which warehouses could be erected. Congress at the time showed little interest in such a venture, and in the end the project was abandoned.

While none of the European powers showed any interest in the largely barren and forbidding island of Iwo Jima, the Japanese had different ideas. Shortly after Perry's visit to Japan in 1853, the Japanese sent officials and colonists to the Volcano-Bonins. Eight years later, Japan laid formal claim to these islands. By 1891, following increased colonization, all of the islands in the Nanpo Shoto had come under the direct jurisdiction of the Tokyo Prefecture and thus became an integral part of the Japanese homeland. A ban on foreign settlement all but stamped out outside influence in the islands with only one exception: on Chichi Jima, the descendants of Nathaniel Savory and his group still celebrated Washington's Birthday and the Fourth of July; on these occasions they proudly displayed Old Glory, an act hardly in keeping with Japanese policy.

By 1943, Japanese colonization of Iwo Jima had resulted in the settlement of almost 1,100 Japanese civilians on the island. Most of these Japanese were either employed at a sugar mill located in the northeastern portion of the island or a sulphur mine and refinery located in the same general area. The inhabitants of Iwo Jima lived in five villages or settlements scattered over the northern half of the island. The northernmost of these was Kita, located in the north central part of Iwo. The village of Nishi was situated in the northwestern part of the island, while Motoyama, the largest built-up area on Iwo, was located in close proximity to the sulphur mine and refinery. The remaining two villages, Higashi and Minami, were located in the northeastern part of the island.

Only the northern part of Iwo Jima had soil permitting some gardening. Vegetables, sugar cane, and dry grains were raised for local consumption. Rice and all other manufactured consumer items had to be obtained from Japan proper. The inhabitants of Iwo were able to supplement their diet through fishing. In this connection it must be pointed out that one of the most serious impediments to large-scale settlement of the island was the total absence of any source of fresh water, such as a lake or a river. Since the island also lacked wells, water had to be obtained exclusively from rain carefully collected in concrete cisterns. At times, Iwo Jima was supplied with potable water by tankers. Some effort was also made to augment precious water supplies through the distillation of sea water.

While the northern part of the island was hardly designed to become a tourist attraction, the southern half of Iwo Jima was ugly beyond description. Near the narrow southern tip of Iwo, dominating the entire island, stands Mount Suribachi, an extinct volcano, which rises to an elevation of about 550 feet. To the north of Suribachi, inland from the beaches, the ground terraces successively upward to form a broad tableland occupying most of the central section of the island. The area between the northern base of Suribachi and the dome-shaped northern plateau is covered by a deep layer of black, volcanic ash so soft and so much subject to drifting that even walking becomes a problem. Wheeled vehicles cannot negotiate such ground; tracked vehicles can move across it only with difficulty.

The northern plateau consists of several elevations; the highest of these is Hill 382, located just east of Motoyama Airfield No. 2, halfway between Motoyama and Minami; two other hills reach a height of 362 feet. Much of this terrain consists of rough and rocky ground, interspersed with deep gorges and high ridges. Sulphur vapor permeates the entire area with a characteristic smell of rotten eggs. The ground itself is hot in this part of the island; the veils of vapor only serve to accentuate the impression of a ghostly landscape.

The beaches of Iwo Jima from Kitano Point, the northernmost tip of the island, to Tachiiwa Point, two miles to the southeast, are steep and narrow with many rocky shoals offshore. They border terrain that rises sharply towards the northern plateau. Rough and broken ground is typical of all beaches on northern Iwo Jima, in numerous instances with cliffs that drop off sharply towards the water's edge. Beaches along the southwestern and southeastern shores of the island vary in depth from 150 to 500 feet and generally are free from rocks offshore. The terrain would be level, rising gradually towards the interior, if it were not for the existence of sand terraces created by the action of waves. These terraces, which differ in height and width, are undergoing a constant change depending on the surf and winds. Surf conditions at Iwo are unfavorable, even under normal conditions. The island does not possess any anchorage or other inlets to protect ships from the fury of the sea. Steep beaches bring breakers close to the shore, where they can mete out severe punishment to small craft that are inward bound or beached. Winds hitting the shore from the sea serve to increase the fury of the waves.

The climate of Iwo Jima is subtropical with a cool season extending from December through April and a warm season from May through November. Temperatures are moderate, with an average ranging between 63 and 70 degrees during the cool period and 73 through 80 degrees during spring, summer, and autumn. Annual rainfall averages 60 inches, with February the driest month and May the wettest.

The desolation of the island is further accentuated by the sparse vegetation. A few coarse grasses and gnarled trees are engaged in a perennial struggle for survival. An officer in the Imperial Japanese Army, formerly stationed on Iwo, has described it as an "island of sulphur, no water, no sparrow, and no swallow." The only living thing on Iwo, aside from the Japanese, was a bird resembling the American rail, a wading bird related to the cranes, but of medium size.

The above description of Iwo Jima, hardly complimentary in essence, may easily give rise to the question how an island of such poor proportions could assume the strategic importance that both the Japanese and Americans placed on it by the summer of 1944. At least one American, speaking to a Navy Chaplain, expressed the sentiment that "after God got through making the world, he must've took all the dirty ash and rubble left over and made Iwo Jima." Yet the island was destined to witness one of the epic amphibious assaults of World War II, followed by a month-long running battle that cost the assault force heavily in men and equipment and at the same time resulted in the complete destruction of the enemy garrison. The factors that made this otherwise worthless pile of rock and black sand such a prize to friend and enemy alike, require a detailed explanation. Only then can the struggle between 23,000 Japanese and an assault force initially of 60,000 men, combatting each other at closest quarters on this inhospitable island, be readily understood.

Japanese Defensive Preparations In the Bonin-Volcano Islands

Japanese military interest in the Volcano-Bonin Islands first arose in 1914, coincident to the outbreak of World War I. Even though the Japanese home islands were never threatened during that war, which Japan entered on the side of the Allies, a few defenses were prepared on Chichi Jima, an island in the Bonin-Volcano Group about 175 miles north-northeast of Iwo Jima. On 10 August 1920, the Chichi Jima

Branch, Army Fortification Department, was formally established, followed by the construction of fortifications beginning in June 1921. As a result of the Naval Arms Limitation Agreement, concluded on 6 February 1922, work on the fortifications was halted. Since all of the action had occurred elsewhere, the Japanese garrison on Chichi Jima led a peaceful existence and never fired a shot in anger.

During the postwar period and throughout the twenties and thirties, the status of Chichi Jima did not undergo any appreciable change. Though a small garrison remained on the island, no additional installations were constructed. On Iwo Jima, the presence of any military installation was even less conspicuous, though by 1937 a wooden sign had been erected by the Imperial Navy, bearing a legend in both Japanese and English, clearly cautioning the careless trespasser from recording or photographing such installations as he might encounter on the island.

At the time of the Japanese attack on Pearl Harbor an Army force of about 3,700-3,800 men garrisoned Chichi Jima. In addition, about 1,200 naval personnel manned the Chichi Jima Naval Base, a small seaplane base, the radio and weather station, and various gunboat, subchaser, and minesweeping units. On Iwo Jima, the Imperial Navy had constructed an airfield about 2,000 yards northeast of Mount Suribachi. Initially stationed on this field were 1,500 naval aviation personnel and 20 aircraft.

In the wake of the American seizure of the Marshalls and devastating air attacks against Truk in the Carolines during February 1944, the Japanese military leadership was forced to conduct an agonizing reappraisal of the military situation. All indications pointed to an American drive towards the Marianas and Carolines. To counter such a move, it became necessary to establish an inner line of defense extending generally northward from the Carolines to the Marianas, and from thence to the Volcano-Bonin Islands. In March 1944, the Thirty-First Army, commanded by General Hideyoshi Obata, was activated for the purpose of garrisoning this inner line. The commander of the Chichi Jima garrison was placed nominally in command of Army and Navy units in the Volcano-Bonin Islands.

Following the American seizure of most of the Marshalls, both Army and Navy reinforcements were sent to Iwo Jima. Five hundred men from the naval base at Yokosuka and an additional 500 from Chichi Jima reached Iwo during March and April 1944. At the same time, with the arrival of reinforcements from Chichi Jima and the home islands, the Army garrison on Iwo Jima had reached a strength of over 5,000 men, equipped with 13 artillery pieces, 200 light and heavy machine guns, and 4,552 rifles. In addition, the defense boasted 14 120mm coast artillery guns, 12 heavy antiaircraft guns, and 30 25mm dual-mount antiaircraft guns.

The loss of the Marianas during the summer of 1944 greatly increased the importance of the Volcano-Bonins for the Japanese, who were fully cognizant that the loss of these islands would facilitate American air raids against the home islands. Such raids, beyond any doubt, would raise havoc with the entire Japanese war production program, and deal a severe blow to civilian morale.

Final Japanese plans for the defense of the Volcano-Bonins were overshadowed by the fact that the Imperial Navy had already lost most of its naval strength and no longer constituted a major factor in frustrating possible American landings. Moreover, aircraft losses throughout 1944 had been so heavy that, even if war production was not materially slowed by American air attacks, combined Japanese air strength was not expected to increase to 3,000 aircraft until March or April of 1945. Even then, these planes could not be used from bases in the home islands against Iwo Jima because their range did not exceed 550 miles; besides, all available aircraft had to be hoarded for possible use on Formosa and adjacent islands where land bases were available in close proximity.

In a postwar study, Japanese staff officers described the strategy applied in the defense of Iwo Jima in the following terms: "In the light of the above situation, seeing that it was impossible to conduct our air, sea, and ground operations on Iwo Island toward ultimate victory, it was decided that in order to gain time necessary for the preparation of the Homeland defense, our forces should rely solely upon the established defensive equipment in that area, checking the enemy by delaying tactics. Even the suicidal attacks by small groups of our Army and Navy airplanes, the surprise attacks by our submarines, and the actions of parachute units, although effective, could be regarded only as a strategical ruse on our part. It was a most depressing thought that we had no available means left for the exploitation of the strategical opportunities which might from time to time occur in the course of these operations."

Even before the fall of Saipan in June 1944, Japanese planners knew that Iwo Jima would have to be reinforced materially if it were to the held for any length of time, and preparations were made to send sizable numbers of men and quantities of materiel to that island. In late May, Lieutenant General Tadamichi Kuribayashi was summoned to the office of the Prime Minister, General Hideki Tojo, who informed the general that he had been chosen to defend Iwo Jima to the last. Kuribayashi was further apprised of the importance of this assignment when Tojo pointed out that the eyes of the entire nation were focused on the defense of Iwo. Fully aware of the implications of the task entrusted to him, the general accepted. By 8 June, Kuribayashi was on his way to his toughest and final assignment, determined to convert Iwo Jima into an invincible fortress that would withstand any type of attack from any quarter.

The Japanese could hardly have selected an individual better qualified to lead the defense of Iwo Jima. As a member of a Samurai family, the 54-year-old Kuribayashi already had a distinguished military career behind him at the time he received the Iwo assignment.

In the 30 years in which he had served the Empire, the general had seen much of the world. During the late twenties, as a captain, Kuribayashi had spent two years in the United States performing attache duties. In the course of his travels in America, he gained a keen appreciation of American economic power, as expressed in a letter to his wife: "The United States is the last country in the world that Japan should fight. Its industrial potentiality is huge and fabulous, and the people are energetic and versatile. One must never underestimate the American's fighting ability."

Following his travels in the New World, Kuribayashi served in the Japanese cavalry. In August 1936, as a lieutenant colonel, he commanded a cavalry regiment. For the next two years, by then a colonel, he served in the Ministry of War. In 1940, he was promoted to brigadier general and given command of a cavalry brigade. Following the Pearl Harbor attack, he participated in the occupation of Hong Kong as chief of staff of the Twenty-Third Army. In 1943, General Kuribayashi, by then a major general, was recalled to Tokyo, where he commanded the Imperial Guards until his appointment as commander of the Iwo Jima Garrison.

General Kuribayashi arrived on Iwo Jima between 8 and 10 June. As a result, he was on the island when TG 58.1 and TG 58.4, consisting of seven aircraft carriers under the command of Rear Admiral Joseph J. Clark, unleashed their first strike against the Bonins, which resulted in the destruction of 10 Japanese fighters in the air and a possible 70 planes on the ground in two days of operations. In addition, 21 seaplanes were destroyed on Chichi Jima. On 24 June 1944, the American carriers under Admiral Clark again struck at Iwo. This time, 80 Japanese fighters rose to challenge the intruders. When the smoke of battle over Iwo cleared nearly half of the Japanese fighters had been destroyed. One of the Japanese fighter pilots who survived the fierce dogfights over Iwo Jima that day commented: "The loss of forty planes and pilots in a single action staggered me. Equally disturbing was the sight of our inexperienced pilots falling in flames, one after the other, as the Hellcats blasted our outmoded Zeros from the Sky. How much like Lae the battle had been! Except that now the obsolescent planes were Zeros, and the inexperienced pilots were Japanese. The war had run full circle."

The loss of the 40 sorely needed fighters on 24 June was not the only disaster that befell Rear Admiral Teiichi Matsunaga, commanding the Japanese naval forces on Iwo. Not one of 20 torpedo bombers he sent out against the American carriers returned to the island. A third wave of 41 aircraft dispatched against the task force not only failed to inflict any damage on the carriers, but in the process nearly half of the Japanese planes were shot out of the sky.

On the evening of 2 July, Japanese radio monitors on Iwo Jima noted a sudden increase in their adversary's radio traffic. Though the Japanese were unable to decipher the code, the strength of the signals indicated to experienced monitors that an American force was in fairly close proximity to Iwo Jima. Early the following morning, American carrier-based aircraft once again raided the island. While the 40 Japanese fighters remaining on Iwo took to the air to intercept the attacking American planes and soon became engaged in heavy dogfights, a squadron of bombers pounced on the island and bombed the airstrip in five waves. Not a single fighter opposed them, since all of the Zeros had been diverted by the American fighters. At the end of the day it became apparent that once again the Japanese had lost half of their remaining fighters, which left only 20 of the original 80. The air battle over Iwo continued on 4 July. At the end of the day, only nine Zeros, most of them badly damaged, returned to Iwo. This left Japanese aviation on the island with nine damaged fighters and eight torpedo bombers which had somehow escaped the holocaust in their revetments.

On the following day, this remnant of Japanese naval aviation on Iwo was dispatched on a final mission: to seek out the American naval task force and destroy as many carriers as possible. The fighter pilots were admonished to stay with the eight torpedo bombers and avoid combat with intercepting American fighters at all costs. It was made clear to both fighter and bomber pilots that they were engaged in a one-way mission from which they were not expected to return. When the attack force approached Admiral Clark's carriers it proved no match for the intercepting fighters. The slow, sluggish Japanese bombers, heavily loaded with their torpedoes, were shot down one after the other by the attacking Hellcats. One of the few Japanese pilots to survive this action reported that in less than a minute seven of the bombers had been destroyed by American fighters. Late on 5 July, four dispirited Japanese fighter pilots and one bomber pilot returned to Iwo.

In addition to the annihilation of virtually all Iwo-based aircraft, another ordeal was in store for the Japanese garrison. On the day following the unsuccessful bombing mission, a U. S. naval force boldly appeared within sight of the island and subjected the Japanese to a naval bombardment from point-blank range. What it felt like to be on the receiving end of such a bombardment has been recorded by one of the Japanese: "For two days we cowered like rats, trying to dig ourselves deeper into the acrid volcanic dust and ash of Iwo Jima. Never have I felt so helpless, so puny, as I did during those two days. There was nothing we could do, there was no way in which we could strike back. The men screamed and cursed and shouted, they shook their fists and swore revenge, and too many of them fell to the ground, their threats choking on the blood which bubbled through great gashes in their throats. Virtually every last structure on Iwo Jima was torn to splintered wreckage. Not a building stood. Not a tent escaped. Not even the most dismal shack remained standing. Everything was blown to bits. The four fighter planes which had returned from our last sortie were smashed by shells into flaming pieces of junk."

For several days the survivors of the bombardment remained in a state of shock from their ordeal and frantic calls for reinforcements went out in view of what appeared to be an imminent invasion of the Island. When several Japanese transport ships appeared on the horizon, the garrison rejoiced, only to fall into deeper gloom and frustration when American submarines torpedoed these ships before their very eyes. Lookouts posted atop Mount Suribachi scanned the ocean for signs of the approaching invasion fleet, and false alarms were frequent.

Much to the surprise of the Japanese garrison on Iwo, an American invasion of the island did not materialize during the summer of 1944. There was little doubt that in time the Americans would be compelled to attack the island. General Kuribayashi, who had personally witnessed Admiral Clark's second air strike against Iwo, as well as the naval bombardment in early July, was more determined than ever to exact the heaviest possible price for Iwo when the invaders came. Without naval and air support, it was a foregone conclusion that Iwo could not hold out indefinitely against an invader possessing both naval and air supremacy.

As a first step in readying Iwo for a prolonged defense, the island commander ordered the evacuation of all civilians from the island. This was accomplished by late July. Next came an overall plan for defense of the island. Lieutenant General Hideyoshi Obata, Commanding General of the Thirty-First Army, early in 1944 had been responsible for the defense of Iwo prior to his return to the Marianas. At the time, faithful to the doctrine that an invasion had to be met practically at the water's edge, Obata had ordered the emplacement of artillery and the construction of pillboxes near the beaches. General Kuribayashi had different ideas. Instead of a futile effort to hold the beaches, he planned to defend the latter with a sprinkling of automatic weapons and infantry. Artillery, mortars, and rockets would be emplaced on the foot and slopes of Mount Suribachi, as well as in the high ground to the north of Chidori airfield.

A prolonged defense of the island required the preparation of an extensive system of caves and tunnels, for the naval bombardment had clearly shown that surface installations could not withstand extensive shelling. To this end, mining engineers were dispatched from Japan to draw blueprints for projected underground fortifications that would consist of elaborate tunnels at varying levels to assure good ventilation and minimize the effect of bombs or shells exploding near the entrances or exits.

At the same time, reinforcements were gradually beginning to reach the island. As commander of the 109th Infantry Division, General Kuribayashi decided first of all to shift the 2d Independent Mixed Brigade, consisting of about 5,000 men under Major General Kotau Osuga, from Chichi to Iwo. With the fall of Saipan, 2,700 men of the 145th Infantry Regiment, commanded by Colonel Masuo Ikeda, were diverted to Iwo. These reinforcements, who reached the island during July and August 1944, brought the strength of the garrison up to approximately 12,700 men. Next came 1,233 members of the 204th Naval Construction Battalion, who quickly set to work constructing concrete pillboxes and other fortifications.

On 10 August, Rear Admiral Toshinosuka Ichimaru reached Iwo, shortly followed by 2,216 naval personnel, including naval aviators and ground crews. The admiral, a renowned Japanese aviator, had been crippled in an airplane crash in the mid-twenties and, ever since the outbreak of the war, had chafed under repeated rear echelon assignments. More than pleased with finally having been granted a combat assignment, Ichimaru penned a poem which began:

"Grateful to his Majesty for giving me
A chance to fight on the foremost front.
I depart with buoyant heart,
Filled with joy and exultation."

Next to arrive on Iwo were artillery units and five antitank battalions. Even though numerous supply ships on route to Iwo Jima were sunk by American submarines and aircraft, substantial quantities of materiel did reach Iwo during the summer and autumn of 1944. By the end of the year, General Kuribayashi had available to him 361 artillery pieces of 75mm or larger caliber, a dozen 320mm mortars, 65 medium (150mm) and light (81mm) mortars, 33 naval guns 80mm or larger, and 94 antiaircraft guns 75mm or larger. In addition to this formidable array of large caliber guns, the Iwo defenses could boast of more than 200 20mm and 25mm antiaircraft guns and 69 37mm and 47mm antitank guns. The fire power of the artillery was further supplemented with a variety of rockets varying from an eight-inch type that weighed 200 pounds and could travel between 2,000-3,000 yards, to a giant 550-pound projectile that had a range of more than 7,500 yards. Altogether, 70 rocket guns and their crews reached Iwo Jima. As a result of American attacks against Japanese shipping, a number of artillery pieces were lost. Others reached Iwo, but their crews, traveling on other ships, drowned en route. In several instances, guns and crews arrived intact, only to discover that vital optical sights, shipped on other vessels, had been lost. Large shipments of barbed wire, essential for the defense of Iwo, never reached the island; the ships carrying this vital commodity were sunk en route.

In order to further strengthen the Iwo defenses, the 26th Tank Regiment, which had been stationed at Pusan, Korea after extended service in Manchuria, received orders for Iwo. The officer commanding this regiment was Lieutenant Colonel Baron Takeichi Nishi. Like Kuribayashi, he was a cavalryman, had travelled extensively abroad, and in the 1932 Olympics at Los Angeles had won a gold medal in the equestrian competitions. The regiment, consisting of 600 men and 28 tanks, sailed from Japan in mid-July on board the *Nisshu Maru*. As the ship, sailing in a convoy, approached Chichi Jima on 18 July 1944, it was torpedoed by an American submarine, the USS *Cobia*. Even though only two members of the 26th Tank Regiment failed to survive the sinking, all of the regiment's 28 tanks went to the bottom of the sea. It would be December before these tanks could be replaced, but 22 finally reached Iwo Jima. Initially, Colonel Nishi had planned to employ his armor as a type of "roving fire brigade," to be committed at focal points of combat. The rugged terrain precluded such employment and in the end, under the colonel's watchful eyes, the tanks were deployed in static positions. They were either buried or their turrets were dismounted and so skillfully emplaced in the rocky ground that they were practically invisible from the air or from the ground.

For the remainder of 1944, the construction of fortifications on Iwo also went into high gear. The Japanese were quick to discover that the black volcanic ash that existed in abundance all over the island could be converted into concrete of superior quality when mixed with cement. Pillboxes near the beaches north of Mount Suribachi were constructed of reinforced concrete, many of them with walls four feet thick. At the same time, an elaborate system of caves, concrete blockhouses, and pillboxes was established. One of the results of American air attacks and naval bombardment in the early summer of 1944 had been to drive the Japanese so deep underground that eventually their defenses became virtually immune to air or naval bombardment.

While the Japanese on Peleliu Island in the Western Carolines, also awaiting American invasion, had turned the improvement of natural caves into an art, the defenders of Iwo literally developed it into a science. Because of the importance of the underground positions, 25 percent of the garrison was detailed to tunneling. Positions constructed underground ranged in size from small caves for a few men to several underground chambers capable of holding 300 or 400 men. In order to prevent personnel from becoming trapped in any one excavation, the subterranean installations were provided with multiple entrances and exits, as well as stairways and interconnecting passageways. Special attention had to be paid to providing adequate ventilation, since sulphur fumes were present in many of the underground installations. Fortunately for the Japanese, most of the volcanic stone on Iwo was so soft that it could be cut with hand tools.

General Kuribayashi established his command post in the northern part of the island, about 500 yards northeast of Kita village and south of Kitano Point. This installation, 75 feet underground, consisted of caves of varying sizes, connected by 500 feet of tunnels. Here the island commander had his own warroom in one of three small concrete enclosed chambers; the two similar rooms were used by the staff. A communications blockhouse protruded above the ground level. This structure was 150 feet long, 70 feet wide; the roof had a thickness of 10 feet with walls five feet wide. The blockhouse was manned by 70 radio operators who worked in shifts. Farther south on Hill 382, the second highest elevation on the island, the Japanese constructed a radio and weather station. Nearby, on an elevation just southeast of the station, an enormously large blockhouse was constructed which served as the headquarters of Colonel Chosaku Kaido, who commanded all artillery on Iwo Jima. Other hills in the northern portion of the island were tunnelled out. All of these major excavations featured multiple entrances and exits and were virtually invulnerable to damage from artillery or aerial bombardment. Typical of the thoroughness employed in the construction of subterranean defenses was the main communications center south of Kita village, which was so spacious that it contained a chamber 150 feet long and 70 feet wide. This giant structure was similar in construction and thickness of walls and ceilings to General Kuribayashi's command post. A 500-foot-long tunnel 75 feet below the ground led into this vast subterranean chamber.

Perhaps the most ambitious construction project to get under way was the creation of an underground passageway designed to link all major defense installations on the island. As projected, this passageway was to have attained a total length of almost 17 miles. Had it been completed, it would have linked the formidable underground installations in the northern portion of Iwo Jima with the southern part of the island, where the northern slope of Mount Suribachi alone harbored several thousand yards of tunnels. By the time the Marines landed on Iwo Jima, more than 11 miles of tunnels had been completed.

A supreme effort was required of the Japanese personnel engaged in the underground construction work. Aside from the heavy physical labor, the men were exposed to heat varying from 90 to 120 degrees Fahrenheit, as well as sulphur fumes that forced them to wear gas masks. In numerous instances a work detail had to be relieved after only five minutes. When renewed American air attacks struck the island on 8 December 1944 and thereafter became a daily occurrence until the actual invasion of the island, a large number of men had to be diverted to repairing the damaged airfields.

While Iwo Jima was being converted into a major fortress with all possible speed, General Kuribayashi formulated his final plans for the defense of the island. This plan, which constituted a radical departure from the defensive tactics used by the Japanese earlier in the war, provided for the following major points:

In order to prevent disclosing their positions to the Americans, Japanese artillery was to remain silent during the expected prelanding bombardment. No fire would be directed against the American naval vessels.

Upon landing on Iwo Jima, the Americans were not to encounter any opposition on the beaches.

Once the Americans had advanced about 500 yards inland, they were to be taken under the concentrated fire of automatic weapons stationed in the vicinity of Motoyama airfield to the north, as well as automatic weapons and artillery emplaced both on the high ground to the north of the landing beaches and Mount Suribachi to the south.

After inflicting maximum possible casualties and damage on the landing force, the artillery was to displace northward from the high ground near the Chidori airfield.

In this connection, Kuribayashi stressed once again that he planned to conduct an elastic defense designed to wear down the invasion force. Such prolonged resistance naturally required the defending force to stockpile rations and ammunition. To this end the island commander accumulated a food reserve to last for two and a half months, ever mindful of the fact that the trickle of supplies that was reaching Iwo Jima during the latter part of 1944 would cease altogether once the island was surrounded by a hostile naval force.

Opposition to General Kuribayashi's unorthodox defense plan, which reflected changes in earlier Japanese military doctrine, was not long in developing. It must be noted that the defensive form of combat in itself was distasteful to the Japanese, who early in the war had been loath to admit to themselves that the Imperial Army would ever be forced to engage in this form of combat. In fact, "so pronounced was their dislike for the defensive that tactical problems illustrating this type of combat were extremely rare." According to standard Japanese doctrine, the object of the defensive was to inflict on the superior hostile forces such losses by firepower—disposed appropriately on the terrain and behind man-made works—that the initial disparity of forces became equalized to the point of eventually permitting the defense force to go over to the offensive.

As far as the objective in defending Iwo Jima was concerned, General Kuribayashi's plan adhered closely to the prevalent doctrine. It was the manner of execution that aroused the displeasure of some of his subordinates, for during the period following the American capture of Guadalcanal and up until the end of the fighting on Saipan, it had become almost standard procedure for the Japanese to defend the beaches in an attempt to drive the invader back into the sea. Once the position of the defending force on an island had become untenable, a brave *banzai* charge, in which the defenders sought victory in death, usually terminated all organized resistance. Kuribayashi's intent of conserving his manpower and not staking all on a defense of the beaches or futile *banzai* charges was the epitome of the revised Japanese doctrine, already employed at Biak in the Southwest Pacific, to some extent in the Palaus, and very extensively on Luzon in the Philippines.

The most vociferous opposition to General Kuribayashi's plan of defense, strangely enough, came from his own chief of staff, Colonel Shizuichi Hori, a former instructor at the Japanese Military Academy. The latter was strongly supported by General Osuga, commander of the 2d Independent Mixed Brigade. In an unusual display of solidarity between Army and Navy, Captain Samaji Inouye, commanding the Naval Guard Force, sided with the two Army dissidents. According to one source who was stationed on Iwo during the summer of 1944: "Arguments raged in July, August, and September. Arguments were not confined to Iwo command alone, but taken to Tokyo's Army and Navy staffs. In August Tokyo asked Nazi German General Staff's opinion. Germany replied that waterfront repulse was unfeasible under overwhelming American shelling and bombings according to German experience. It was not that German reply was the decisive factor. But anyway, supporters of the waterfront idea gradually dwindled. Kuribayashi made some compromise and the hot arguments ended in September."

Finally, in December 1944, General Kuribayashi decided to restore unity to his command. He dismissed Colonel Hori as chief of staff of the 109th Division and replaced him with Colonel Tadashi Takaishi. General Osuga, commander of the 2d Independent Brigade, was succeeded by Major General Sadasue Senda, an experienced artilleryman who had seen combat in Manchuria and China. Altogether, a total of 18 officers were replaced.

During the final months of preparing Iwo Jima for the defense, General Kuribayashi saw to it that the strenuous work of building fortifications did not interfere with the training of units. As an initial step towards obtaining more time for training, he ordered work on the northernmost airfield on the island halted. In an operations order issued in early December, the island commander set 11 February 1945 as the target date for completion of defensive preparations and specified that personnel were to spend 70 percent of their time in training and 30 percent in construction work.

Despite intermittent harassment by American submarines and aircraft, additional personnel continued to arrive on Iwo until February 1945. By that time General Kuribayashi had under his command a force totalling between 21,000 and 23,000 men, including both Army and Navy units.

General Kuribayashi made several changes in his basic defense plan in the months preceding the American invasion of Iwo Jima. The final stratagem, which became effective in January 1945, called for the creation of strong, mutually supporting positions which were to be defended to the death. Neither large scale counterattacks, withdrawals, nor *banzai* charges were contemplated. The southern portion of Iwo in the proximity of Mount Suribachi was organized into a semi-independent defense sector. Fortifications included casemated coast artillery and automatic weapons in mutually supporting pillboxes. The narrow isthmus to the north of Suribachi was to be defended by a small infantry force. On the other hand, this entire area was exposed to the fire of artillery, rocket launchers, and mortars emplaced on Suribachi to the south and the high ground to the north.

A main line of defense, consisting of mutually supporting positions in depth, extended from the northwestern part of the island to the southeast, along a general line from the cliffs to the northwest, across Motoyama Airfield No. 2 to Minami village. From there it continued eastward to the shoreline just south of Tachiiwa Point. The entire line of defense was dotted with pillboxes, bunkers, and blockhouses. Colonel Nishi's immobilized tanks, carefully dug in and camouflaged, further reinforced this fortified area, whose strength was supplemented by the broken terrain. A second line of defense extended from a few hundred yards south of Kitano Point at the very northern tip of Iwo across the still uncompleted Airfield No. 3, to Motoyama village, and then to the area between Tachiiwa Point and the East Boat Basin. This second line contained fewer man-made fortifications, but the Japanese took maximum advantage of natural caves and other terrain features.

As an additional means of protecting the two completed airfields on Iwo from direct assault, the Japanese constructed a number of antitank ditches near the fields and mined all natural routes of approach. When, on 2 January, more than a dozen B-24 bombers raided Airfield No. 1 and inflicted heavy damage, Kuribayashi diverted more than 600 men, 11 trucks, and 2 bulldozers for immediate repairs. As a result, the airfield again became operational after only 12 hours. Eventually, 2,000 men were assigned the job of filling the bomb craters with as many as 50 men detailed to each bomb crater. The end of 1944 saw American B-24 bombers over Iwo Jima almost every night while U. S. Navy carriers and cruisers frequently sortied into the Bonins. On 8 December, American aircraft dropped more than 800 tons of bombs on Iwo Jima, which shook the Japanese up but did very little real damage to the island defenses. Even though frequent air raids interfered with the Japanese defensive preparations and robbed the garrison of much badly needed sleep, progress of the work was not materially slowed.

Despite the air raids, which became a daily occurrence in December, and increasing isolation from the homeland, morale remained high among members of the Iwo garrison. Japanese national holidays, such as the birthday of Emperor Meiji on 11 February, were celebrated with rice cake and an extra ration of sake. At the same time, the Iwo Jima defenders, gathered in small groups near their battle stations, listened to a Tokyo broadcast in which a song, especially dedicated to the defense of Iwo, was released to the public. Many of the men wore white headbands, similar to the ones worn by kamikaze pilots, to demonstrate their determination to die in defense of the island. Inside the pillboxes, for all to see and burn into their minds, were copies of the "Courageous Battle Vow, " which pledged all to dedicate themselves to the defense of Iwo, and to fight to the last with any and all weapons at hand. The pledge appropriately ended with the following words: "Each man will make it his duty to kill ten of the enemy before dying. Until we are destroyed to the last man, we shall harass the enemy by guerrilla tactics."

As early as 5 January 1945, Admiral Ichimaru conducted a briefing of naval personnel at his command post in which he informed them of the destruction of the Japanese Fleet at Leyte, loss of the Philippines, and the expectation that Iwo would shortly be invaded. Exactly one month later, Japanese radio operators on Iwo reported to the island commander that code signals of American aircraft had undergone an ominous change. On the 13th, a Japanese naval patrol plane spotted 170 American ships moving northwestward from Saipan. All Japanese troops in the Benin Islands were alerted and occupied their battle positions. On Iwo Jima, preparations for the pending battle had been completed, and the defenders were ready.

Chapter 2. Offensive Plans and Preparations

Preliminary planning for the seizure of an objective in the Volcano-Bonin Islands began as early as September 1943, when the Joint War Plans Committee, a planning agency of the Joint Chiefs of Staff, advocated such a move. However, because of impending military operations in the Gilberts, Marshalls, and Marianas no further preparation for any operations against the Bonins were made until the summer of 1944. The successful completion of the Saipan operation in July brought the continuation of operations in the Central Pacific into sharper focus. In a conference held in Washington by top echelon U. S. military leaders from 13-22 July 1944, the senior members of the Joint War Plans Committee presented to the Joint Chiefs the possible courses of action in continuing the war against Japan. Plans for the bombing of the Japanese home islands figured prominently in these discussions. In this connection, the use of the Marianas as a base for long-range bombers was again discussed, as well as the need for seizing the Bonins to facilitate such air operations.

In the course of a visit to Hawaii in mid-July 1944, Admiral Ernest J. King discussed with Admiral Chester W. Nimitz some of the decisions which the Joint Chiefs had reached. He apprised Nimitz of the fact that the Army Air Forces had been ordered to set up four B-29 groups in the Marianas for long-range bombing. In time, 12 groups of B-29s were to be based in the Marianas. In this connection, King brought up the desirability of establishing bases in the Bonins to furnish fighter escorts for the B-29s. With operations in the Carolines and the Philippines scheduled within the next few months, both naval commanders felt that no forces should be diverted to the Bonins at this time. Nevertheless, King instructed Nimitz to prepare plans for an assault against the Bonins, although he considered such an operation unwise unless it was shortly followed by an invasion of Japan.

Planning for an amphibious assault against the Bonins was inextricably interwoven with the development of the B-29 long-range bomber of the U. S. Army Air Forces, and for this reason an explanation of the development and characteristics of this aircraft appear warranted. The B-29 had its origin in 1939, when General H. H. Arnold, then Chief of the Army Air Corps, ordered the experimental development of a four-engine bomber with a range of 2,000 miles. As eventually developed, the B-29 or "Superfortress" had a wing span of slightly more than 141 feet, a length of 99 feet, and four Wright engines with turbo-superchargers developing 2,200 horsepower each at sea level. The giant bomber was armed with a dozen .50 caliber machine guns and a 20mm cannon mounted in the tail. The B-29 had a service ceiling of 38,000 feet and near that altitude had a maximum speed of 361 miles per hour. Without a load, the aircraft was estimated to have a range of 4,400 miles; it could move 3,500 miles when carrying a bomb load of four tons.

During the latter half of 1944, about 100 B-29s operated from airfields in China under the Army Air Forces XX Bomber Command. This command, for all practical purposes, constituted an experimental organization, designed to serve as a prototype for similar units to be activated later. Its mission was three-fold: to test the B-29 under combat conditions; to formulate and refine a tactical doctrine; and to perfect the administrative structure to support the B-29 strikes. By mid-October 1944, China-based B-29s had flown a total of 10 missions against a variety of industrial targets ranging from Bangkok in southeast Asia to Manchuria and the home islands.

Meanwhile, the progress of the American offensive in the Central Pacific had resulted in the capture of the Marianas. Preparations got under way for a sustained bomber offensive against the home islands by Marianas-based B-29s. It was anticipated that the first airfield in the Marianas capable of accommodating the big B-29s would be operational by October 1944. In connection with the initiation of very long-range bombing of the Japanese home islands from B-29 bases in the Marianas, the Volcano-Bonin Islands, situated halfway between the Marianas and Tokyo, assumed major strategic importance. As part of this island group, Iwo Jima appeared the logical choice for invasion because it was the only island suitable for the construction of airfields of sufficient size to handle the new Superfortresses. In this connection, it was not intended to use Iwo as a base or staging area for the B-29s, but as a forward air station from which fighters could fly escort missions for the big bombers. At the same time, crippled B-29s limping back from raids over Japan would be able to make emergency landings on the island instead of ditching into the Pacific. Even while the battle for Saipan was in full swing, 500 of the giant bombers were ready for combat.

As increasing attention focused on bases in the Marianas, the strategic importance of the B-29 bases in China waned. As early as September 1944, General Arnold had seriously considered transferring the XX Bomber Command to a more profitable site. Japanese gains in China ultimately forced the abandonment of the B-29 bases and transfer of the B-29 combat groups and their supporting units to the Marianas.

In July 1944, the Army Air Forces advised the Joint Staff Planners that Iwo was a potential base for fighter planes, since Tokyo would be within the range of P-51 Mustangs based on Iwo. On 12 August, the Joint War Plans Committee recommended the seizure of the Volcano-Bonins, listing as major reasons their availability for bases from which fighter cover could be provided to support the air effort against Japan; denial of these strategic outposts to the enemy; furnishing air defense bases for American positions in the Marianas; and providing fields for staging heavy bombers against Japan.

In a study of naval personnel requirements prepared by the Joint Planning Staff in late August 1944, a list of projected operations included an assault against the Volcano-Bonin Islands with a target date of mid-April 1945. It was estimated that three divisions would be required for these operations. While planning an invasion of Formosa, Admiral Nimitz also was attracted to the Volcano-Bonin Islands. In September 1944, he informed Lieutenant General Holland M. Smith, Commanding General, Fleet Marine Force, Pacific, that the 2d and 3d Marine Divisions should be retained in the Marianas as an area reserve for Formosa. In addition, they were to make up the bulk of the landing force once an attack was mounted against Iwo Jima.

By this time, key service commanders were beset by serious doubts with respect to a major operation against Formosa. Lieutenant General Millard F. Harmon, Commanding General, Army Air Forces, Pacific Ocean Areas, advocated that Formosa be bypassed in favor of the Volcano-Bonins and Ryukyus. His superior,

Lieutenant General Robert C. Richardson, Jr., Commanding General, Army Forces, Pacific Ocean Areas, likewise failed to see any advantage in seizing Formosa and expressed himself in favor of advancing through the Nanpo Shoto. Admiral Nimitz felt that the capture of Formosa could serve a useful purpose only if it was a preliminary step towards subsequent landings on a coast of China, where recent Japanese military gains made such a move of questionable value.

Despite an increasing rejection of Formosa as an invasion target by the military leaders concerned, Admiral King, Commander in Chief of the U.S. Fleet, consistently adhered to the projected operation against that island, at least until early October 1944. However, on 11 and 12 July, when Admirals King and Nimitz visited Saipan, King asked Admiral Raymond A. Spruance what objective he would recommend for his next operation. Spruance replied that he would like to take Okinawa.

Admiral Spruance has described his participation in the early planning and the final change of objectives in the following words: "After the completion of the Marianas Operation I turned my command over to Admiral Halsey on 28 August 1944 and returned to Pearl Harbor early in September. On reporting to Admiral Nimitz, he advised me that my next operation would be the capture of Formosa and Amoy. I said that I thought Iwo Jima, followed by Okinawa, would be preferable, but was told that the orders from Cominch called for Formosa."

Following this conversation, Admiral Spruance went on leave. He was about to return to Pearl Harbor during the latter part of September, when he was ordered to attend a conference between Admiral King and Admiral Nimitz which was to be held towards the end of the month at San Francisco. Admiral Spruance recalled the focal points of this meeting as follows: "At this Conference Admiral Nimitz presented a paper – prepared, I believe, by Captain Forrest Sherman, U.S.N., head of Fleet War Plans Division – recommending the substitution of Iwo Jima and Okinawa for Formosa and Amoy. The reason for this change was that Lt. Gen. S. B. Buckner, U.S.A., Commander 10th Army, who was to command the Landing Force for Formosa, said that he had insufficient Service Troops for an objective so large as Formosa; but that he could take Okinawa. Admiral King, after considerable discussion, was convinced of the necessity for the change and so recommended to the JCS who approved it."

The Joint Chiefs of Staff lost little time in issuing a new directive on 3 October ordering Admiral Nimitz to provide fleet cover and support for General MacArthur's forces in the occupation of Luzon, scheduled for 20 December 1944; to occupy one or more positions in the Nanpo Shoto, with a target date of 20 January 1945; and to occupy one or more positions in the Nansei Shoto by 1 March 1945.

Subsequently, delays encountered in operations in the Philippines affected planning for the Iwo Jima and Okinawa Operations, which were designated DETACHMENT and ICEBERG, respectively. Target dates had to be readjusted to 19 February for the Iwo operation, and to 1 April for the invasion of Okinawa.

On 7 October Admiral Nimitz and his staff issued a staff study for preliminary planning, which clearly listed the objectives of Operation DETACHMENT. The overriding purpose of the operation was to maintain unremitting military pressure against Japan and to extend American control over the Western Pacific. In American hands, Iwo Jima could be turned into a base from which we could attack the Japanese home islands, protect our bases in the Marianas, cover our naval forces, conduct search operations of the approaches to the Japanese home islands, and provide fighter escort for very long-range operations. Three tasks specifically envisioned in the study were the reduction of enemy naval and air strength and industrial facilities in the home islands; the destruction of Japanese naval and air strength in the Bonin Islands, and the capture, occupation, and subsequent defense of Iwo Jima, which was to be developed into an air base.

On 9 October, General Holland Smith received the staff study, accompanied by a directive from Admiral Nimitz ordering the seizure of Iwo Jima. This directive designated specific commanders for the operation. Admiral Spruance, Commander, Fifth Fleet, was placed in charge as Operation Commander, Task Force 50. Under Spruance, Vice Admiral Richmond Kelly Turner, Commander, Amphibious Forces, Pacific, was to command the Joint Expeditionary Force, Task Force 51. Second in command of the Joint Expeditionary Force was Rear Admiral Harry W. Hill. General Holland Smith was designated Commanding General, Expeditionary Troops, Task Force 56.

It was not accidental that these men were selected to command an operation of such vital importance that it has since become known as "the classical amphibious assault of recorded history." All of them had shown their mettle in previous engagements. One chronicler of the Iwo Jima operation put it in the following words: "The team assigned to Iwo Jima was superb – the very men who had perfected the amphibious techniques from Guadalcanal to Guam. Nearly every problem, it was believed, had been met and mastered along the way, from the jungles of Guadalcanal up through the Solomons, and across the Central Pacific from the bloody reefs of Tarawa to the mountains of the Marianas."

For General Smith, who was 62 years old, the Iwo Jima operation was to be his last. In mid-October 1944, Smith issued a letter of instruction designating Major General Harry Schmidt, Commanding General, V Amphibious Corps, as Commander of the Landing Force, Task Group 56.1. General Schmidt, 58 at the time, was a veteran of nearly 26 years of military service, who had commanded the 4th Marine Division during the invasion of Roi-Namur in the Marshalls and during the Saipan operation in the Marianas. His experienced staff, headed by Colonel William W. Rogers, was responsible for the preparation and execution of all Landing Force plans for the operation. When completed, plans for the execution of the landing had to be submitted by the commander of the landing force to General Smith for the latter's approval. on 20 October 1944, VAC received a directive from FMFPac, assigning troops to the corps for training, planning, and operations. Initially, the corps was to be ready in all respects for combat by 15 December.

The major units assigned to the Landing Force were the 3d, 4th, and 5th Marine Divisions. The 3d Marine Division had already distinguished itself on Bougainvillea in the Solomons and on Guam in the Marianas. While planning for Operation DETACHMENT was in progress during the late autumn of 1944, the division was still reorganizing on Guam after the heavy fighting for that island and was actively engaged in rounding up or dispatching Japanese that continued to infest the island. At the age of 47, the division commander, Major General Graves B. Erskine, was one of the youngest generals in the Marine Corps with a well-established reputation for toughness. Joining the Marine Corps Reserve in 1917 as a second lieutenant, Erskine had distinguished himself in France during World War I. Following the war, he had seen service in Haiti, the Dominican Republic, Nicaragua, and China.

At the time of the Pearl Harbor attack, he served as Chief of Staff of the Amphibious Corps, Atlantic Fleet. In 1942, he was assigned as Chief of Staff of the Amphibious Corps, Pacific Fleet, under Holland Smith, who was then a major general. After taking part in the amphibious training of Army troops for the Kiska and Attu operations in the Aleutians, Erskine became Deputy Corps Commander and Chief of Staff of the V Amphibious Corps when it was organized in 1943. He had an active part in planning the seizure of Tarawa and accompanied the assault forces which took Kwajalein, Saipan, and Tinian. When the Fleet Marine Force, Pacific, was organized after the capture of Saipan, General Erskine became Chief of Staff of that organization. Promoted to the rank of major general in October 1944, he assumed command of the 3d Marine Division at that time.

The 4th Marine Division, commanded by Major Clifton B. Cates, also had seen considerable action. During the invasion of Roi-Namur in the Marshalls, it had been the first Marine division to go directly into combat from the United States. In less than a year's time, the division had taken part in three landings. In addition to the Roi-Namur operation, the 4th had also made assault landings on Tinian and Saipan. The forthcoming invasion of Iwo Jima would be the division's fourth landing in less than 13 months.

General Cates had assumed command of the division on 12 July 1944, when General Schmidt became the Commanding General of the V Amphibious Corps. Cates already had a long and distinguished Marine Corps career behind him, having served in France during World War I as a company grade officer. During his 20 months of service with the 6th Marines he had been wounded in action twice and had earned the Navy Cross, in addition to other decorations. At Guadalcanal early in World War II, he had commanded the 1st Marines, one of the two assault regiments that landed on the island.

In contrast to the 3d and 4th Marine Divisions, the 5th Division had not seen combat as a unit prior to the Iwo Jima operation. Organized at Camp Pendleton, California, on 11 November 1943, the division was commanded by Major General Keller E. Rockey. Like his counterparts in the 3d and 4th Marine Divisions, General Rockey had seen combat action at Chateau Thierry in 1918. Even though the 5th Marine Division had no previous combat experience, nearly half of the men comprising the unit had served with other combat units. In speaking of the division after the end of World War II, General Rockey made the following comment: "From its earliest days to the hour of its disbandment, I found the 5th to possess and maintain a high standard of military performance and an esprit exceptionally fine. And when the 5th Division entered combat, it acted from the first hour like a unit of veterans. It fought that first fight with the utmost vigor, courage, and intelligence."

At the time that final plans and preparations for operation DETACHMENT were being made, the 3d Marine Division was still stationed on Guam, following the recent recapture of that island. As commander of VAC, General Schmidt had also located his command post on that island. The 4th Marine Division, upon completion of operations on Saipan and Tinian in the Marianas, had returned to its permanent camp site on Maui in Hawaii. In August 1944, the 5th Marine Division had moved from California to Hawaii, where it underwent final training. The close proximity in which the 4th and 5th Marine Divisions found themselves in Hawaii during the latter part of 1944 was to have a favorable effect on joint planning between the divisions. When General Schmidt moved VAC headquarters to Pearl Harbor on 13 October, the major planning staffs concerned with Operation DETACHMENT, except for the 3d Marine Division, now were functioning close to each other, a circumstance that resulted in better coordination of efforts.

Of the three divisions scheduled to participate in DETACHMENT, the 3d Marine Division was the only one still actively engaged in military operations during the planning phase for Iwo Jima. Even though Guam had been officially declared secure by 10 August 1944, Marines continued to round up or annihilate stragglers until mid-December. The situation on Guam was not without effect on the planning for Iwo Jima and resulted in one of the changes in the basic operations plan. As General Holland Smith was to reminisce at a later time, with reference to the status of the 3d Marine Division: "It had been proposed to hold the division in reserve, alerted at Guam. On further study, I considered it much sounder for this division to arrive with the other troops in the target area on D-Day, available as a floating reserve. This decision proved sound because we ran into a larger garrison and far stronger defenses than we had anticipated."

General Schmidt issued the first blueprint for Operation DETACHMENT on 19 October 1944, to be used as a guide by subordinate commanders. On the following day, General Smith directed him to have the VAC ready for Operation DETACHMENT by 15 December.

During the two remaining months of 1944, VAC evolved tactical and logistical plans in joint conferences with all commanders concerned. As increasing intelligence became available, alternate plans were drafted and changes were incorporated into the original plan. All commanders issued tentative drafts of their respective operation plans, and continual adjustments were made to achieve maximum support with the forces available and to organize the most effective assault force possible. Planning remained flexible right up to D-Day, which itself was postponed twice because the naval forces required for the invasion of Iwo Jima were still engaged in the Philippines. As a result, on 18 November D-Day was postponed to 3 February 1945; on 6 December, an additional postponement to 19 February became necessary.

When Admiral Spruance assumed command of all forces assigned to the Central Pacific Task Force on 26 January, CinCPOA Plan 11-44 was in full effect. Designated for the beach assault were the 4th and 5th Marine Divisions, less the 26th Marines, which was to be held in Landing Force reserve. For training purposes prior to the operation, the 26th Marines would remain with the 5th Division. The 3d Marine Division was to stage on Guam and would remain as reserve on board ship in the objective area until D-day plus 3.

The VAC scheme of maneuver for the landings was relatively simple. The 4th and 5th Marine Divisions were to land abreast on the eastern beaches, the 4th on the right and the 5th on the left. When released to VAC, the 3d Marine Division, as Expeditionary Troops Reserve, was to land over the same beaches to take part in the attack or play a defensive role, whichever was called for. The plan called for a rapid exploitation of the beachhead with an advance in a northeasterly direction to capture the entire island. A regiment of the 5th Marine Division was designated to capture Mount Suribachi in the south.

Since there was a possibility of unfavorable surf conditions along the eastern beaches, VAC issued an alternate plan on 8 January 1945, which provided for a landing on the western beaches. However, since predominant northerly or northwesterly winds caused hazardous swells almost continuously along the southwest side of the island, it appeared unlikely that this alternate plan would be put into execution.

The eastern beaches over which the landings were to be made extended for about 3,500 yards northeastward from Mount Suribachi to the East Boat Basin. For purposes of organization and control of the invasion force, these beaches were divided into seven 500-yard segments, which, from left to right, were designated as Green, Red 1 and 2, Yellow 1 and 2, and Blue 1 and 2. The 5th Marine Division, landing over Green, Red 1, and Red 2 beaches, was to advance straight across the island, which at this point formed a narrow isthmus, until it reached the west coast. At the same time, it was to hold along the right, while part of the division wheeled to the south to capture Mount Suribachi. The 4th Marine Division had the specific mission of moving into the center of the isthmus, while its right flank swerved to the north to seize Motoyama Plateau, the high ground above the East Boat Basin. Unless this vital ground to the north of the invasion beaches and Mount Suribachi to the south – terrain features which overlooked the beaches and permitted the enemy to fire at the exposed Marines at will – were quickly seized, the landing force could be expected to take very heavy casualties.

Once the southern portion of Iwo Jima had been secured, the two divisions could join in a combined drive to the north. At this time, the 3d Marine Division, initially in Expeditionary Troop Reserve on board ships near the beachhead, could be disembarked and landed to assist in maintaining the momentum of the VAC attack.

The detailed scheme of maneuver for the landings provided for the 28th Marines of the 5th Marine Division, commanded by Colonel Harry B. Liversedge, to land on the extreme left of the corps on Green 1. On the right of the 28th Marines, the 27th, under Colonel Thomas A. Wornham, was to attack towards the west coast of the island, then wheel northeastward and seize the O-1 Line. Action by the 27th and 28th Marines was designed to drive the enemy from the commanding heights along the southern portion of Iwo, simultaneously securing the flanks and rear of VAC. As far as the 4th Marine Division was concerned, the 23d Marines, commanded by Colonel Walter W. Wensinger, was to go ashore on Yellow 1 and 2 beaches, seize Motoyama Airfield No. 1, then turn to the northeast and seize that part of Motoyama Airfield No. 2 and the O-1 Line within its zone of action. After landing on Blue Beach 1, the 25th Marines, under Colonel John R. Lanigan, was to assist in the capture of Airfield No. 1, the capture of Blue Beach 2, and the O-1 Line within its zone of action. The 24th Marines, under Colonel Walter I. Jordan, was to be held in 4th Marine Division reserve during the initial landings. The 26th Marines, led by Colonel Chester B. Graham, was to be released from corps reserve on D-Day and prepared to support the 5th Marine Division.

Division artillery was to go ashore on orders from the respective division commanders. The 4th Marine Division was to be supported by the 14th Marines, commanded by Colonel Louis G. DeHaven; Colonel James D. Wailer's 13th Marines was to furnish similar support for the 5th Marine Division.

The operation was to be so timed that at H-Hour 68 LVT (A) 4s, comprising the first wave, were to hit the beach. These vehicles were to advance inland until they reached the first terrace beyond the high-water mark. The armored amphibians would use their 75mm howitzers and machine guns to the utmost in an attempt to keep the enemy down, thus giving some measure of protection to succeeding waves of Marines who were most vulnerable to enemy fire at the time they debarked from their LVTs. Though early versions of the VAC operations plan had called for tanks of the 4th and 5th Tank Battalions to be landed at H plus 30, subsequent studies of the beaches made it necessary to adopt a more flexible schedule. The possibility of congestion at the water's edge also contributed to this change in plans. In the end, the time for bringing the tanks ashore was left to the discretion of the regimental commanders. Company A of the 5th Tank Battalion attached to the 27th Marines was scheduled to land on the Red Beaches at the prearranged time of H plus 30 minutes.

In the event that the landings took place on the western beaches of Iwo, the alternate plan made provision for a company of the 24th Marines, reinforced by a platoon of armored amphibians from the 2d Armored Amphibian Battalion, to seize Kangoku Rock, a 600-yard-long island lying about 2,200 feet northwest of Iwo Jima. The island could be used as an artillery site and for this reason a contingency plan was prepared to land the 105mm howitzers of 4/14 there.

Intelligence Planning

The scheme of maneuver for the Iwo Jima operation, as well as the preliminary planning, was largely based on available intelligence. Enemy documents seized on Saipan during the summer of 1944 gave a fair indication of enemy strength in the Volcano-Bonin Islands. Captured Japanese maps, supplemented by aerial photographs obtained by U.S. Navy carrier pilots during the air strikes of June and July 1944, were utilized in the preparation of situation maps and beach studies. During the planning phase for the operation, pilots of Navy Photographic Squadrons 4 and 5 and the Army Air Forces 28th Photographic Reconnaissance Squadron flew 371 sorties. Liberators of the Seventh Air Force obtained additional photographic coverage of the island in the course of their bombing missions.

Significantly, during the preparatory phase, representatives of the 3d, 4th, and 5th Marine Divisions, the Commander, Amphibious Forces, Pacific, and VAC combined their efforts in preparing a Joint Situation Map which was completed on 6 December 1944. Representative officers from Navy and Marine units were ordered to report to Photographic Interpretation Squadron 2, based on Guam, in late January 1945. There, the most recent photographs were available. On the basis of the most current information then available, a final enemy installations map was prepared that was to play a major part in the pre-D-Day naval and aerial strikes, as well as during the actual assault phase.

Between 29 November and 2 December 1944, the submarine USS *Spearfish* conducted a reconnaissance off Iwo Jima. Approaching as close to the island as he could without being detected, the submarine commander gave a running account of the view that presented itself to his eyes as he watched through his periscope. This commentary was transcribed. So close did the submarine approach the shore of Iwo that at one point the skipper spotted a cave going into the base of Mount Suribachi "with a dejected looking individual sitting in the entrance sunning himself." Additional observations included construction work at various parts of the island, an armored car in motion, and various earthworks and block houses on different parts of the island. The submarine reconnaissance failed to discover any guns or emplacements on the slopes of Mount Suribachi itself, nor could individual pillboxes be identified, though a number of caves were visible.

Beach studies indicated that movement over the loose sand would be difficult for wheeled vehicles; tracked vehicles were not expected to bog down. Partially buried gasoline drums, observed at the edge of the water both on the eastern and western beaches, gave rise to considerable speculation. It was thought that these drums might be wired for electrical ignition, so that burning gasoline would run out over the water to check landing craft, or that they would ignite at the moment the amphibious tractors or tanks reached land to raise a wall of fire before them. It was also possible that the drums had been converted into mines, equipped with pull-type detonators, with attached trip wires, which would ignite when either personnel or tanks came into contact with the wire.

In any case, Marines were warned to expect the widespread employment of antitank mines and obstacles, combined with "close quarter attack units" using hand-placed charges. No change in Japanese artillery tactics was anticipated. Even though the presence of a large number of artillery pieces on the island was a foregone conclusion, there was no reason to believe that the Japanese would employ massed fires in larger than battery concentrations.

From a thorough study of aerial photographs and a captured map showing the scheme of the enemy's defense, it was known that the Japanese had established an elaborate defense in depth. Gun positions were sited to place withering fire on the selected beaches; defensive works such as pillboxes, blockhouses, antitank trenches, and mines were located where they could repel the American advance once the invasion force had landed. Numerous antiboat gun positions as well as coast defense guns were discovered. Unless these guns were neutralized, it was more than likely that the enemy would use them to fire on the leading waves and transport areas of the invasion force.

Planners for the invasion of Iwo Jima further deduced from documents captured on Saipan that the enemy would adhere to his older tactics of attempting the destruction of the invasion force before an adequate beachhead had been established. The most likely time for this counterattack was considered the early morning of the day following the initial landing.

Further study of aerial photographs and captured documents indicated that Iwo had probably been divided into four defense sectors with one infantry battalion manning each sector. Since the Japanese were believed to have nine infantry battalions on the island, this would leave five battalions to be held in reserve. Photographs taken in January 1945, as the invasion date was drawing closer, indicated that the number of field fortifications, pillboxes, and covered artillery positions was increasing despite intensive aerial bombardment. A most significant development noted in these photographs was the construction of a line of defense across the island from a point near Hiraiwa Bay on the northwest coast to high ground north of the East Boat Basin.

During the period from 3 December 1944 to 10 February 1945, it was noted that the number of enemy coast defense guns on the island increased from 3 to 6; the number of dual purpose guns rose from 16 to 42. Automatic antiaircraft guns showed an increase from 151 to 203, and covered artillery positions rose from 39 to 67. There was a decrease in openly emplaced artillery, antitank and antiboat guns, and machine guns, but in the words of the Expeditionary Troops G-2, Colonel Edmond J. Buckley, the apparent reduction in observed machine guns could be offset by the heavy increase in field fortifications, including blockhouses and pillboxes. The blockhouses could contain fixed artillery, and, in numerous instances, their construction was such as to permit mobile artillery pieces to be wheeled into them. It also appeared likely that each pillbox was equipped with one or more machine guns, whose presence could not be ascertained by aerial observation.

Prelanding reconnaissance had shown that the Japanese had established numerous antiboat gun positions, as well as coast defense guns. It was imperative that these guns be neutralized. Such neutralization, of course, depended upon the ability of the invasion force to detect targets and destroy them by naval gunfire and aerial attack prior to H-hour.

Even though planners of the Iwo Jima invasion were generally correct with reference to the enemy's intentions and capabilities, their intelligence estimate erred in two important respects. First among these was an underestimation of enemy strength on the island. Intelligence officers had estimated that the Iwo garrison numbered between 13,000 and 14,000 troops. Names and background of Japanese commanders in the Bonins were known, though the intelligence estimate mistakenly assumed that General Kuribayashi exercised overall command of the Volcano-Bonin Defense Sector from his 109th Division Headquarters on Chichi Jima, and that a Major General Osuka was in charge of the defense of Iwo Jima. Information on the Japanese naval guard and air base units on Iwo was lacking.

The second serious shortcoming of preinvasion intelligence was the mistaken assumption that the enemy defensive tactics to be expected on Iwo Jima would conform to tactics employed in earlier operations. In describing Japanese capabilities, the intelligence estimate voiced the following expectations: "The enemy may be prepared to attempt small local counterattacks prior to the establishment of our beachhead in order to annihilate our forces at the beach. His doctrine specifies that the enemy must not gain a foothold on shore and that in order to combat this all troops must be prepared to attack with the mission of splitting our forces and destroying them by local counterattacks."

At the latest, the enemy could be expected to throw all available reserves against the beachhead prior to dawn on D plus 1.

In addition to their task of accumulating and analyzing all information available to them about the enemy's strength, capabilities, and dispositions during the planning period, American planners were faced with the formidable problem of maintaining complete secrecy with reference to the movement of such a large force as was to take place in the Iwo Jima assault. This was not an easy undertaking in view of the tremendous size of the force assigned to capture and develop the island. Admiral Turner's command alone consisted of 495 ships, including, among others, 4 command ships, 8 battleships, 12 aircraft carriers, 19 cruisers, 44 destroyers, 43 transports, 63 LSTs, and 31 LSMs. The addition of Task Force 58, together with supply and auxiliary ships, brought the invasion fleet to more than 800 vessels. The Marine assault troops numbered 70,647 officers and men. This force was further augmented by Marine and Army garrison units, as well as three Army amphibian truck companies in the assault phase, and Navy personnel assigned to shore duty, bringing the total of the expeditionary force to 111,308 men. If one further adds the crews of Turner's ships and of Task Force 58, more than 250,000 men on the American side were involved in the Iwo operation.

Intelligence officers had a few bad moments on 22 December 1944, when a Pearl Harbor newspaper printed two pictures of Iwo Jima under aerial attack. The pictures bore a startling resemblance to pictures and maps of "Island X," which VAC had issued for training purposes. In order to prevent the Japanese from learning of the assembly and destination of the invasion force, General Schmidt recommended a counterintelligence diversion. Word was spread in the bars and hotels of Honolulu that the command would shortly depart for an attack on Formosa. Whether the diversion had any effect in deceiving the enemy could not be determined.

A serious breach of security occurred on 14 February 1945, while the invasion convoy was en route to the objective. In the course of a radio transmission, someone in the vicinity of Saipan was overheard making the following statement: "We are going to Iwo Jima. It's a Jap island not far from here. The B-29s bomb it from here every day. It's about 600 miles from Japan. We'll make it hot for them Japs when we get there. We're leaving for there in the next day or so."

Such a breach of security was more than enough to make experienced intelligence officers quake in their boots. The intelligence officer of Amphibious Group 2 reported the incident to VAC. There is no indication that this information ever reached the Japanese, though under different circumstances this compromise of vital information could have had disastrous consequences.

Logistics and Administration

Another major responsibility accruing to the staff of the VAC was logistical planning, which had already begun even before VAC staff officers reached Pearl Harbor on 13 October. Special staffs of FMFPac conducted preliminary conferences and executed logistical planning for the assault on Iwo Jima. As in other areas, logistics required the harmonious teamwork of different levels of command, and between the armed services.

The Quartermaster, U. S. Army Forces, Pacific Ocean Areas, was responsible for supplying rations (Class I) to all personnel taking part in the operation, as well as clothing, special equipment, and supplies (Class II), and ammunition (Class V), for participating Army troops. Fuel and lubricants (Class III) were to be supplied by the Navy's Service Force, Pacific. The Supply Service, FMFPac, was to furnish ammunition (Class V) and special supplies, and equipment (Class IV) for the Marines. The latter supplies were to be distributed initially by the 6th Base Depot in Hawaii and the 5th Field Depot on Guam.

Administrative planning, including service and support to the VAC Landing Force, was the responsibility of the G-4 Section, V Amphibious Corps. Prescribed levels for Class I supply were two days' rations for the assault troops plus a 30-day backup supply. Water was to be carried in cans, drums, or other organizational equipment at the ratio of two gallons per man per day for five days. Class II and IV supplies were to be stockpiled for 30 days. Ammunition for ground forces (Class V) was to be provided in quantities of seven units of fire (U/F) for artillery, mortars, and antiaircraft guns, and five units of fire for all other types of weapons.

Special preloads on LSTs were made to provide a balanced initial supply of rations, fuel, and ammunition for the assault troops. These supplies were loaded in LST tank decks and were designed to provide initial priority combat supplies close in to beaches on D-Day and D plus 1. A total of 38 LSTs were to be preloaded at Pearl Harbor, Hilo, and Guam prior to the embarkation of the assault units. In addition, 42 2½-ton Amphibian Trucks (DUKWs) were to be preloaded at Pearl Harbor with assorted small arms and mortar ammunition, rations, fuel, medical supplies, and flamethrower fuel. These vehicles were scheduled to provide an early replenishment supply on the beaches on D-Day.

Resupply plans and preparations were performed by the Marine Supply Service. Initial resupply ships were to be loaded at Oahu with 30 days Class I, II, and IV supplies and 15 days Class III supplies (except for aviation gasoline) for two reinforced Marine divisions and for all garrison troops estimated to be located on Iwo Jima at D plus 35. Class V was to be loaded in this shipment on board one ammunition ship at the rate of 9 U/F for one Marine division, 7 U/F for one 155mm howitzer battalion, 8 U/F for one Army heavy antiaircraft battalion, 4 U/F for one

Army light antiaircraft battalion, and 90 tons of engineer and Chemical Warfare Service demolitions.

The Commander, Forward Area, Central Pacific was instructed to hold available in the Marianas for shipment on call in an emergency, a stock of 30 days supplies of Classes I, II, III, and IV and two units of fire for one reinforced Marine division and one reinforced Army division. Supplies were to be provided by the Commanding General, Pacific Ocean Areas, the Commanding General, FMFPac, and ComServPac. ComAirPac was to maintain a 45-day stock of aviation supplies, except for Class V, in floating storage in the forward area for Navy and Marine aircraft employed in that area. Aviation supplies at Guam and on Roi-Namur were to be held available for emergency shipment. ComGenPOA was to maintain a 45-day stock of aviation supplies in floating storage in the forward area for Army aircraft. ComServPac was to provide the necessary storage if space and facilities assigned to ComGenPOA proved inadequate. ComServPac was to shift Service Squadron 10 to Ulithi to furnish support to fleet units and emergency supply for land-based forces. Elements of the above squadron were to be located in the Marshalls and Marianas for support of small task forces.

Pre-packaged supplies were stockpiled by the VAC Air Delivery Section on Saipan for emergency deliveries by air. If needed, the Commander, Expeditionary Troops, could draw from similar stockpiles in Hawaii and elsewhere in the Marianas. For the Iwo Jima operation, VAC organized the 8th Field Depot, commanded by Colonel Leland S. Swindler, The depot was designed to serve as the nucleus of the shore party organization; the depot commander had a dual designation as Shore Party Commander of the Landing Force, in which capacity he was responsible for coordinating the activities of the division shore parties.

Since Iwo Jima was not surrounded by reefs, all types of landing craft could proceed directly from the transport area to the beachhead without becoming involved in time-consuming transfer operations that had been characteristic of many previous landings in the Central Pacific. This circumstance led VAC to authorize subordinate units to mount up to 50 percent of their supplies on pallets.

Planners of the Iwo operation were aware of the fact that the soft volcanic ash along the beaches, as well as the steep terraces en route inland, would impede the movement of wheeled vehicles. To insure a steady flow of supplies from the beaches inland, runner sleds were improvised that could be loaded with needed items and pulled inland by tracked vehicles. Another improvisation designed to overcome the soft sand or volcanic ash was the use of Marston matting at the beaches. Even though this material was originally used for the construction of airfield runways, it likewise could be employed to great advantage in bridging strips of sand along the beaches that would otherwise be impassable.

In addition to the large variety of supplies and equipment normally used for an amphibious operation, VAC employed two items for the first time. One was the two-wheeled Clever-Brooks 3½-ton amphibian trailer, the other the M-29C light cargo carrier, subsequently known as the "Weasel." This boat-like, tracked vehicle resembled a miniature LVT without ramps. The amphibian trailers reached the three assault divisions during November and December 1944. The Weasels arrived in November and were subjected to extensive tests which revealed that the cargo carriers were capable of excellent performance under conditions anticipated at Iwo.

Three Arrny and two Marine DUKW companies were assigned to VAC for the operation, as were the 31st and 133d Naval Construction Battalions. In addition, a

Marine engineer battalion, a topographic company, an Army bomb disposal company, and the 62d Naval Construction Battalion were attached to VAC and placed under operational control of the Corps engineer. These units would be responsible for clearing minefields, bomb disposal, road construction and maintenance, water supply, and the restoration of airfields on Iwo Jima. Following the beach assault, and as soon as conditions permitted, the 62d Naval Construction Battalion was to begin to ready Motoyama Airfield No. 1 for observation and fighter aircraft. Target date for completion of this assignment was D plus 7. The 31st Naval Construction Battalion was to restore Airfield No. 2 for use by the B-29 bombers. Making the latter field operational for this purpose involved not only restoration of facilities that were already in existence, but called for extension of existing runways to 7,000 feet to accommodate the giant aircraft. Airfield No. 2 was to become operational at D plus 10.

In view of the size and scope of the impending operation, the handling and evacuation of casualties required special planning. Initially, it was assumed that seizure of the objective would require 14 days. It was estimated that five percent of the assault force would become casualties on each of the first and second days; three percent on the third and fourth days; and one and one-half percent on each of the remaining 10 days. It was further estimated that 20 percent of all casualties would be dead or missing.

For the evacuation of casualties from Iwo Jima, two hospital ships, the *Samaritan* and the *Solace*, were assigned, as well as the auxiliary hospital ship *Pinckney*, and LSTs 929, 930, 931, and 1033. These LSTs, especially equipped to handle casualties close to the beach, were to be stationed 2,000 yards offshore and serve as evacuation control centers. There, the casualties would be logged, given additional emergency treatment, and transferred to other ships for further care. One of the LSTs was equipped with a blood bank.

As in so many other instances of operations in the Pacific Theater, the adaptation of existing equipment to a new use was due to the efforts of one individual who not only conceived the idea but also had to sell it at the right time and place. In this instance the conversion of LSTs for the evacuation of casualties was the brainchild of Lieutenant Commander George J. Miller, Medical Corps, USNR, who prepared blueprints of the LSTs showing the plan of operating tables, beds, and other equipment. In December 1944 he presented his idea to several high ranking naval medical officers who initially vetoed it. In the end, the persistent lieutenant commander was able to sell the idea to an even higher ranking personage who immediately recognized the merit of the plan and gave his unqualified approval of it.

In addition to the hospital ships and the specially converted LSTs, long range dispositions had to be made from Iwo Jima for the reception of casualties. In addition to the hospitals that were to be set up on the island itself, once the situation following the landings had stabilized to some extent, 5,000 beds were available in hospitals on Saipan and Guam. Air transportation of casualties was scheduled to begin as soon as airstrips were ready to accommodate transport planes.

These preparations only give a bare outline of the time and effort required to bring logistics and administration into line with the operational planning. At least one account has briefly summed up the diverse items involved and the thought that had to be given to their transport and storage: "It was necessary to think of everything – pencils, blood, toilet paper, 'this item,' said the orders, 'will be stowed under tarpaulin at the rear of all landing vehicles to protect it from spray': matches, gasoline, socks, bullets, wooden crosses (preprinted), water, welding rods, garbage cans, splints, food, spark plugs, blankets, flares, dog food, maps, holy water, smoke pots, paint, shoelaces, fingerprint ink, batteries, rock-crushers, bulbs, cigars, asphalt machines, carbon paper. The Fifth Division alone carried 100 million cigarettes and enough food to feed Columbus, Ohio, for thirty days."

Ships began loading as early as November, every parcel stenciled, weighed, sized, and stowed in a particular spot. Marked photos showed where the cemetery would be located, orders specified the exact depth of burial and space between bodies (3 feet from centerline to centerline of body, fifty bodies to a row, 3 feet between rows.) The graves registration team would land on D-Day, equipped with its own bulldozers to bury the bodies exactly 6 feet deep. Then men would mound each grave with a special wooden form.

Nor was the multiplicity of supplies all that the planners had to consider; there was one more commodity whose importance transcended all others. This was the flow of men towards the scene of action to replace those who would become casualties. During the last months of 1944, long before the first Marines were scheduled to hit the beaches of Iwo Jima, the complex machinery of administration was already set in motion when six replacement drafts embarked from the United States to join VAC. Each draft was composed of about 1,250 officers and men. Each of the three Marine divisions slated to participate in the operation received 2,500 replacements, some of whom were incorporated into the divisions before they left their staging areas. The bulk of the replacement units was kept intact; their personnel were assigned to shore parties, to be employed on the beaches until they were needed to replace combat losses.

Launching an amphibious operation on the scale of the contemplated assault against Iwo Jima required far more than merely assembling men and materiel and shipping them to the objective. The real planning effort had only begun at the point when the objective had been decided upon and the means to seize it were being made available. The efforts of various arms and services had to be combined until the gigantic machine of war functioned as an instrument of precision. Each man, each weapon, each unit, every ship, tank, and airplane had a very definite part in the scheme of things. In this respect, an assembled invasion armada can be likened to an orchestra. The finest musicians, well skilled in their profession and equipped with the best instruments that money can buy, still must learn to work with one another. Few among the audience are aware of the tremendous effort that went into writing the score, the seemingly endless rehearsals, the continuous and often painful planning and rehoning that must take place before all meshes into an integrated whole.

It is no different with the orchestra of war. A plan is made, followed by the assembly of men and supplies. Only then can the vital and difficult process begin of forging the whole into an instrument of such power and precision that it continues to function even in the face of the most adverse conditions that climate, weather, and enemy opposition can impose. When the curtain rises, the spectator is awed by the booming of the big naval guns, the columns of dirt and smoke rising over the objective from naval shells or aircraft dropping their lethal cargo, as rockets swoosh towards the target. Once this orchestra has begun to play, any flaw still remaining can be measured in the lives of assault troops who are separated from the enemy bullets and shells by no more than a few cubic feet of air, often protected only by the thickness of a uniform.

The forging of the precision instrument of war, under way months before Marines went ashore on Iwo, determined in large measure how many men of the landing force would go on to seize the objective and return home; the number whose fragile and mangled bodies would be carried off Iwo for salvage and repair; and those destined to remain on the island forever.

Chapter 3. The Preliminaries

In his capacity as Commanding General, VAC Landing Force, Major General Harry Schmidt was directly responsible for the preparation and training of all units placed under his command for the Iwo Jima operation. Such training, in addition to a routine program, not only featured the participation of VAC units in tests and demonstrations of new types of amphibious equipment such as the Clever-Brooks amphibian trailer and the M-29C cargo carrier (Weasel), but also familiarized personnel with new weapons and techniques scheduled for employment during Operation DETACHMENT. Division training programs stressed attacks against fortified positions; the reduction of pillboxes; detection, marking, and removal of mines; and the employment and coordination of supporting arms.

During the last two weeks of November, the 4th Marine Division carried out amphibious maneuvers on Maui, and a field exercise on the division level. Two command post exercises followed. The 5th Marine Division conducted training exercises at Camp Tarawa on Hawaii Island. At Hilo, the men practiced the embarkation and debarkation of troops and loading and unloading of equipment onto LSTs. The artillery battalions of the 13th Marines went to Maume beach for special loading exercises with DUKWs, LSTs, and LSMs. Using the big amphibious trucks, the artillerymen learned how to load and unload their howitzers and practiced moving in and out of the great jaws of the LSTs, causing at least one Marine to comment: "This reminds me of Jonah and the whale."

Within the 5th Marine Division, the 28th Marines, scheduled to spearhead the assault, received special training.

Each battalion of that regiment conducted exercises that involved landing on beaches resembling those of Iwo, right down to soft volcanic ash. The maneuvers also included the envelopment of a hill that could pass for a fairly close duplicate of Mount Suribachi. Without those in the ranks being aware of it, elements of the division actually executed the scheme of maneuver called for in the Iwo operations plan. The division conducted three command post exercises in Hawaii, including one problem calling for the coordination of air, naval gunfire, and artillery support.

On Guam, the men of the 3d Marine Division trained for the impending operation in accordance with the mission assigned to them. Training stressed the phases a reserve unit had to pass through upon landing and moving up into the interior of the island. Since the division was not scheduled to take part in the amphibious assault, no assault landing exercises were conducted. The 3d Division was to utilize the shore party facilities of the two assault divisions preceding it ashore.

The replacement drafts did not join their divisions until late November. Even though the replacements had received basic individual training in the United States, they had to learn basic small unit tactics and had to exercise in them before qualifying as combat ready. Since the men were to serve with shore parties prior to being assigned to combat duty, they also had to be initiated into cargo-handling duties.

Owing to the advanced state of training in the divisions and the high level of experience of their Marines, VAC training directives were concerned with refinement of combat techniques and provision for supervision and support of divisions and corps troops. Otherwise, training was left to the divisions. A late delivery of DUKWs caused some delay in training the newly activated amphibian truck companies with their vehicles. Considerable retraining was required to familiarize tank crews and maintenance personnel with the operation and servicing of new M4A3 Sherman tanks.

Upon the conclusion of amphibious exercises, the Hawaii-based assault forces began staging on 24 December 1944; by 9 January, all troops had embarked. Individual units proceeded to Oahu, where they assembled with other elements of the Joint Expeditionary Force for rehabilitation. This period lasted from 19-26 January 1945. During this time, all men received some liberty ashore and took part in supervised recreation.

From 27 December 1944 to 8 January 1945, the 4th Marine Division moved on board its transports off Maui. The 5th Marine Division loaded at Hawaii from 25 December to mid-January. The men of the 3d Marine Division on Guam were not scheduled to begin embarkation for another month. Final rehearsals for the remainder of the landing force were held in the Marianas during the second week of February. Also participating in these rehearsals were aircraft and ships of the Amphibious Support Force (TF 52), commanded by Admiral Blandy, and the Naval Gunfire and Covering Force (TF 54), under Rear Admiral Bertram J. Rodgers. The final exercises had the primary aim of testing coordination between the attack force and the supporting arms. Shore fire control parties actually landed on Tinian and tested communications in connection with a simulated bombardment. Sea conditions made it impractical to boat the troops during that part of the exercises conducted on 12 February; on the following day, however, the troops debarked, waves were formed, and landing craft were taken to within 300 yards of the beaches on the west coast of Tinian.

On 15 February, the combat-loaded LSTs (tractor groups) departed for the target area; during the afternoon of the following day, Transport Squadrons 15 and 16, carrying the landing force assault troops moved out, screened by cruisers and destroyers. On the same day, ships carrying the 3d Tank Battalion, corps engineers, naval construction battalions, one corps artillery and two U. S. Army antiaircraft artillery battalions left Guam. On 17 February, Transport Squadron 11 departed Guam, carrying the 3d Marine Division as Expeditionary Troops Reserve. During the voyage to Iwo Jima, RCT 26 was released from Corps Reserve to the 5th Marine Division. RCT 21, which was embarked in Transport Division 32, left Guam on the evening of 16 February, to be released from Expeditionary Troops Reserve to Corps Reserve when it reached Iwo in midmorning of 19 February.

As the invasion fleet silently moved towards the objective, Admiral Turner's flagship, the USS *Eldorado*, carried a distinguished passenger, who on 15 February had boarded the ship with such little fanfare that a large number of the crew initially was unaware of his presence. It was James V. Forrestal, Secretary of the Navy, intent on witnessing the imminent operation as an observer. Dressed in khakis without insignia of any kind, he might easily have been mistaken for one of the civilian war correspondents on board the command ship.

The Japanese were aware of the armada's departure from Saipan almost as soon as it had gotten under way. Whether the fleet was spotted by an enemy aircraft or submarine has never been clearly established, though at least one source credits a naval patrol plane with having reported on 13 February that 170 ships were moving northwest from Saipan. As a result, all Japanese troops in the Volcano-Bonins were placed on a state of alert.

The reaction to the news that an American invasion force was moving towards the Bonins or the Volcano Islands was nothing short of explosive in the home islands, where emotions had already been whipped to a fever pitch: "Uniformed schoolboys stormed into Perry Park at Kurihama, near Yokohama, the site where Commodore Perry had come ashore nearly a century before to reopen Japan to the Western world. The boys, rallying under the banner of the Imperial Rule Assistance Youth Corps, rushed the granite shaft and in a frenzy of patriotism toppled it to the ground and spat upon it."

No such hysteria gripped General Kuribayashi and his Iwo Jima garrison. The Japanese defenses on the island had progressed as far as they ever would. In the time available to fortify the island, all that could possibly be done had been accomplished. Filled with great fighting spirit, reverence for the Emperor, and determination to drive the invaders back into the sea, the enemy sat in his dugouts and waited.

Preliminary Air and Naval Bombardment

Actually, the battle for Iwo Jima had opened long before the first ships of the American invasion fleet hove into view off the island. Following the first large-scale carrier raid of June 1944, regularly scheduled air strikes against the target began in August. Air operations against Iwo passed through two stages. First, there was the strategic phase prior to 16 February 1945, carried out mainly by Marianas-based B-24 bombers of the Seventh Air Force.

Beginning on 8 December, and continuing for 74 consecutive days, the bombers rained death and destruction on the Volcano-Benin Islands. Iwo Jima received special attention. Marine PBJs (B-25 medium bombers) of VMB-612 participated in this bomber offensive from early December 1944 until the last days of January 1945. Operating from the Marianas under the Army Air Forces VII Bomber Command, the Marine aviators flew night missions over the Volcano-Benin Islands with special emphasis on the disruption of enemy shipping, since it was known that the Japanese, vulnerable to American air attack during the daytime, were making a frantic effort to rush supplies to Iwo and nearby islands at night.

As of 31 January 1945, all air missions were executed in accordance with the Iwo Jima Air Support Plan. During the last three weeks preceding the invasion, B-24s from the Marianas flew 30 sorties a day or more against the island. The overall purpose of the bombing was to neutralize the airfields and installations on Iwo, destroy gun positions and fixed defenses, and unmask additional targets. Initially, the land-based missions against Iwo were executed under the Commander, Task Force 93, Lieutenant General Millard F. Harmon, USA. As the invasion date neared, the bomber raids were conducted in accordance with requests from the Commander, Joint Expeditionary Force.

Beginning 16 February, air attacks against Iwo increased in frequency until a daylight attack hit the island at least once every 24 hours. In addition, Iwo was exposed to night harassing missions and fighter sweeps. Photographic reconnaissance flights attempted to obtain a last-minute picture of enemy defenses prior to the invasion.

At numerous times prior to D-Day, aerial photographic reconnaissance attempted to estimate the effectiveness of both aerial and naval bombardment of the target with particular emphasis on the study of selected target areas which had been the subject of specific strike requests. Among the last of these studies was one submitted to the Chief of Staff (G/S) of VAC on 9 February 1945. The first paragraph of this report poignantly stated: "Photographic coverage of Iwo Jima to 24 January 1945 indicates that damage to installations resulting from bombing strikes between 3 December 1944 and 24 January 1945 was, on the whole, negligible. These strikes have apparently not prevented the enemy from improving his defensive position and, as of 24 January 1945, his installations of all categories had notably increased in number. The island is now far more heavily defended by gun positions and field fortifications than it was on 15 October 1944, when initial heavy bombing strikes were initiated."

This information was corroborated in a special memorandum submitted by the G-2 to the C/S on 13 February. This memorandum compared the enemy's static defenses between 3 December 1944 and 10 February 1945, and noted significant increases in the number of heavy weapons and field fortifications, particularly blockhouses and pillboxes.

A further evaluation of the constant bombing indicated that it was not altogether ineffective: the destruction of aircraft on the ground and the temporary neutralization of the Iwo airfields was accomplished. On the other hand, gun emplacements, blockhouses, pillboxes, shelters, and other strong points proved far less vulnerable owing to the thorough preparation of such installations against attack from the air and naval gunfire. The rugged terrain with its countless caves afforded excellent protection from high level bombing.

Even the bomber attacks against the Iwo Jima airfields could not prevent their use by the enemy for any appreciable length of time. In evaluating the effectiveness of the air strikes, the Army Air Forces had to concede "that at no time were all of Iwo's strips rendered inoperational and no single strip was out of service for a whole day: the destructive Christmas raid on Saipan was run the day after a heavy air-sea bombardment of Iwo."

As D-Day for Operation DETACHMENT approached, the Army Air Forces stepped up the assault against Iwo. Between 1 and 16 February, Seventh Air Force bombers flew 283 daylight sorties, dropping 602 tons of bombs and 1,111 drums of napalm; in the same period, B-24s flew 233 night snooper missions, dropping 504 tons of bombs. On 12 February, 21 B-29s of the 313th Bombardment Wing dropped 84 tons of bombs on carefully pinpointed gun emplacements on Mount Suribachi as well as on antiaircraft positions and radio and radar installations elsewhere on the island. Again results were disappointing because the bombers flew at moderately high altitudes and frequently released their bombs by radar because of cloudy weather. In any case, the bomber crews found it extremely difficult to score square hits on the cleverly concealed and deeply dug-in targets. Napalm was dropped for the purpose of burning off the camouflage, but this method was unsuccessful, partly because of inaccurate drops and partly because the rocks and ashes used as cover would not burn.

In view of the failure of the bombing assault to inflict crippling damage on the Japanese on Iwo, the preliminary naval gunfire bombardment of the island, a vital and indispensable prelude to the operation, was bound to grow in importance. The very nature of an amphibious assault against a strongly fortified enemy bastion, largely devoid of the element of surprise, made it mandatory for the preliminary gunfire to eliminate a sizable portion of the enemy defenses. Without this shore bombardment, the very success of the assault could become imperiled or severe casualties could result among the Marines slated to go ashore. It was in this vital realm of naval gunfire support that Marine and Navy leaders of the Iwo expedition failed to achieve complete accord; the former, represented by General Holland Smith, had seen in previous assaults what fire from an enemy not sufficiently subdued could do to Marine assault waves nearing the shore of a well-defended island.

General Smith's anxiety increased the closer D-Day approached. This experienced Marine leader compared Iwo to a worm that became stronger the more it was cut up, for the island seemed to thrive on the American aerial bombardment. The leader of the expeditionary troops was to recall his feeling of what was ahead: "My own study of early air photographs indicated that a situation of an incredible nature existed on the island. It was plain that Iwo Jima had fortifications the like and extent of which we had never encountered. Mindful of Tarawa, where most of the fortifications were above ground and were still standing when the Marines landed, my opinion was that far more naval gunfire was needed on an island five times the size of Tarawa, with many more times the number of defenses, most of them deep under ground. I could not forget the sight of Marines floating in the lagoon or lying on the beaches at Tarawa, men who died assaulting defenses which should have been taken out by naval gunfire. At Iwo Jima, the problem was far more difficult. If naval guns could not knock out visible defenses, how could they smash invisible defenses except by sheer superabundance of fire?"

General Smith and his staff were in agreement that the softening up of Iwo Jima would have to be preceded by an especially lengthy period of intense naval gunfire. The type of guns, as well as the amount and type of ammunition required to do a thorough job, hinged on the intelligence on the kind and number of targets. Based on such intelligence, the number of ships to be employed in the bombardment force could be computed with some degree of accuracy. The guaranteed destruction of a target required visual identification by a spotter on board ship or in the air, followed by precision adjustment. In addition to competence in surface gunnery, the men directing this shore bombardment required special training and experience. On the basis of previous operations at Tarawa, Guam, Saipan, and Peleliu, Marine planners knew that the process of preliminary gunfire could not be hurried.

As early as September 1944, the staff of VAC, supported by members of Fleet Marine Force, Pacific, had begun the preparation of detailed planning for the naval gunfire required for the assault on Iwo Jima. This planning was carried out under the direction of Lieutenant Colonel Donald M. Weller, who had been designated Naval Gunfire Officer for both VAC and FMFPac. Since, even at this early stage of the planning effort, it was known that Iwo Jima represented one of the most heavily fortified strong points on earth, Marine planners stipulated that a force of battleships and cruisers would require 10 days to reduce point targets on the island that could bring direct fire to bear on either of the two landing beaches then under consideration. On 24 October 1944, VAC submitted to Admiral Turner its naval gunfire requirements, which called for a preliminary bombardment force of seven battleships, seven heavy cruisers, and two light cruisers.

Meanwhile, Admiral Turner's gunnery officers had also worked on the naval gunfire requirements for Operation DETACHMENT. Their conclusions differed materially from those of the Marines. In this respect, the naval officers' viewpoint was influenced by a number of factors that unintentionally were to work to the disadvantage of the Marine assault force. Foremost among these was the consideration that the initial surface bombardment had to be closely coordinated with the first carrier attack against Tokyo by the Fast Carrier Force (TF 58). Admiral Spruance initially had planned that a carrier strike on Tokyo was to coincide with the opening of the prelanding bombardment of Iwo Jima. Once the naval bombardment started, all tactical surprise at Iwo would be lost. The longer the prelanding bombardment continued, the more it became likely that enemy aircraft from the home islands would interfere with the landings. A two-day carrier strike against Japan would detract enemy attention from Iwo. At the same time, naval aviation could strike a blow at the enemy's aircraft manufacturing plants, which thus far had escaped crippling damage from landbased aircraft. Sustained air attacks would be required to reduce enemy aircraft production. Admiral Spruance observed, nevertheless, that he could see no object in combatting these aircraft around the perimeter if accurate bombing could wreck the factories that produced the enemy planes. As a result, carrier aircraft were to be employed against a strategic, rather than a tactical objective.

Somewhere in the course of the naval planning process, the air strike against Honshu began to loom ever larger in importance until what had started out as a diversionary maneuver began to turn, in the minds of the naval planning staff, into the major attraction. More and more emphasis was placed on the importance of the naval air strike against Japan; the imminent assault on Iwo gradually began to recede further into the background. Naval planners, in reaching their own conclusions as to what could be made available by way of preliminary gunfire, had to consider limitations on the availability of ships, difficulty in replenishing ammunition, and a tight schedule that made it necessary to launch and complete the Iwo operation with all possible dispatch to avoid any delay in the assault on Okinawa, which was to follow closely at the heels of Operation DETACHMENT.

The two widely varying viewpoints of Marine and Navy naval gunfire planning staffs soon found their expression in the times recommended for preliminary naval gunfire by the Navy commanders and those of the Marine landing force. The initial VAC request for naval gunfire not only asked for a minimum of 10 days' bombardment, but also stipulated that D-Day be made dependent on "the successful prosecution of the destruction of enemy defensive installations."

Marine Corps naval gunfire requirements, strongly endorsed by General Holland Smith, were forwarded to the Commander, Amphibious Forces, Pacific Fleet. The expectation was that the Navy would generally concur with what was considered a carefully prepared and reasonable estimate of the naval gunfire required to ensure the quick seizure of the objective with a minimum of casualties. To the surprise and consternation of Marine planners, Admiral Turner informed VAC on 15 November that "a methodical and thorough bombardment would be instituted by the Amphibious Support Force on Dog minus three."

Faced unexpectedly with a reduction of the vital naval gunfire support from 10 days to 3, General Schmidt had a special staff study prepared, consisting of detailed tabulations, and an appended interpretation and evaluation of these very detailed statistics. As a concession, the study pointed out that the overall time for preliminary fires of all types, including support of Underwater Demolition Team (UDT) and minesweeping operations, as well as the systematic preparatory missions, should not be less than nine days.

Admiral Turner countered the VAC recommendations with a letter that praised the Marine planners and at the same time dashed icy water on any hopes that VAC would receive anything approaching the nine days of naval gunfire. In Turner's words: "the preliminary Naval Gunfire Estimates for the assault of Iwo Jima given in the basic letter are much the best such analysis ever submitted to this command. It is desired not only to meet the wishes expressed in the letter as far as limitations of ships, ammunition, and time permit, but also to furnish even more support than asked for, up to the limit of naval capabilities."

Attached to the basic letter were comments supporting the naval viewpoint. Once again, the efforts of VAC to obtain what it considered a minimum amount of naval gunfire preparation had been thwarted. Nevertheless, General Schmidt was not yet ready to accept the inevitable. By way of another proposal, this one a severe compromise, he asked that the preliminary bombardment begin on D minus 4.

In this request, the Commanding General, VAC, was strongly seconded by General Holland Smith, who pointed out that from lessons learned in previous operations and from continued study and analysis of Operation DETACHMENT, he considered four full days for the preliminary bombardment the absolute minimum necessary for success. General Smith went on to warn that unless the strong Japanese defenses were destroyed or at least neutralized, casualties far beyond any heretofore suffered in the Central Pacific had to be expected; in fact, the success of the entire operation might be jeopardized.

On 30 November, it appeared that Admiral Turner was willing to go along with four days of naval gunfire, provided both that the Commander Fifth Fleet agreed, and that the fast carrier strike force could deliver its blow against Japan on D minus 4. Upon being apprised for the recommended extra day of naval gunfire, Admiral Spruance disapproved the request. The rejection was based on three reasons. First, Spruance insisted that the initial surface bombardment had to coincide with the initial carrier attack upon the Tokyo area. Second, the Commander, Fifth Fleet, thought that the situation on Iwo Jima differed from that previously encountered on Saipan for the reason that by D-Day the enemy personnel and fixed defenses at Iwo would have been under heavy shore-based air attack for a considerable period of time. According to Spruance, this prolonged air bombardment, which was not undertaken at Saipan, had to be considered at least as effective as the recommended additional day of ship bombardment. Third, the admiral pointed out that there would be no early opportunity for replacement of naval ammunition, a large proportion of which had to be saved for support on D-Day. There was a limit to the quantity of ammunition available for pre-D-Day bombardment and no advantage was seen in delivering that quantity in four days rather than in three.

Still, the last word on the subject of naval gunfire support had not yet been spoken, and during the first week of January the Marines tried again. On the 2d, General Schmidt once again pleaded for an extension of the preliminary bombardment period. On this occasion, he suggested that either the time allotted for the preliminary bombardment be increased or the fire be concentrated against the main landing beaches, leaving other parts of the island for later. Once again, General Holland Smith supported the VAC request adding that since the overall time element was an important factor in the capture of Iwo Jima, a preliminary bombardment of sufficient time would actually reduce the duration of the operation. Smith reiterated that the effects of the horizontal bombing attacks on the objective had thus far been negligible and that the final result of the air offensive against the island could not be expected to measure up to the benefits derived from an additional day of naval bombardment. The Commanding General, FMFPac, warned that only an adequate, methodical preliminary bombardment could reduce the island defenses to a point where a quick capture was assured. The preliminary bombardment then planned not only would increase the overall time necessary to complete the operation, but also would require an unnecessary expenditure of lives during the initial assault phase.

In his memoirs, General Smith conceded with some bitterness that his warning did not fall on fertile ground: "Limited, against our better judgment, to only three days' preliminary bombardment, there seemed nothing to do but make the best of the situation . . . Thus we were defeated – a group of trained and experienced land fighters, our full realization of the necessity for naval gunfire based on many previous island operations – again overridden by the naval mind. Finding ourselves in this dilemma, we had tried our best to enlighten the high command, feeling that our judgment would be respected, but naval expediency won again."

Even while the duration of the preliminary naval bombardment was still under discussion, the force required to deliver this fire was being organized. The Amphibious Support Force (TF 52), commanded by Rear Admiral Blandy, consisted of a Gunfire and Covering Force (TF 54) under Rear Admiral Rodgers; a Support Carrier Group (TG 52.2) under Rear Admiral Calvin T. Durgin; a Mine Group (TG 52.3), commanded by Rear Admiral Alexander Sharp; an Underwater Demolition Group (TG 52.4), commanded by Captain B. Hall Hanlon; Gunboat Support Units One and Two (TUs 52.5.1 and 52.2.2), headed by Commander Michael J. Malanaphy; and an Air Support Unit (TU 52.10), under Captain Elton C. Parker.

The limitation of the preliminary bombardment to three days placed a heavy burden on the support ships of TF 54, whose mission it was to knock out or neutralize the most powerful and menacing enemy defenses prior to D-Day. There were no less than 724 Type A and B priority targets to be destroyed during 16, 17, and 18 February. The mission was to be executed by 6 battleships, 4 heavy cruisers, 1 light cruiser, and 16 destroyers. The battleships were the *Tennessee, Idaho, Texas, New York, Nevada,* and *Arkansas;* the *Chester, Salt Lake City, Tuscaloosa,* and *Pensacola* made up the heavy cruiser force; the light cruiser was the *Vicksburg.* The *Arkansas, Texas,* and *Nevada* were veterans of the Normandy invasion in June 1944; the *New York* had seen previous service during the invasion of North Africa in 1942. Two new battleships, the *North Carolina* and the *Washington,* each equipped with 16-inch guns, were the most powerful ships initially slated to take part in the preinvasion bombardment. They were withdrawn, however, to take part in the strike of Task Force 58 against Tokyo.

On board the AGC *Estes* were Admiral Blandy and his staff, responsible for all operations against Iwo during the preassault period. Lieutenant Colonel Weller was also on board the *Estes,* heading the Marine gunfire team. Marines under his command were stationed on board each ship participating in the preassault firing. The bombardment plan incorporated lessons learned in the European and Pacific Theaters of Operations. Iwo Jima had been divided into numbered squares and each square was assigned to a specific ship. Every target was numbered, and on board the *Estes* was a master card index which consisted of a card with appropriate information for each target. Carrier pilots, with special training as gunfire spotters, were ready to take to the air from the carrier *Wake Island* to act as eyes for the bombardment ships.

An elaborate radio net had been set up to coordinate the efforts of the various gunfire teams. Since area bombardment had been found wasteful and inefficient in previous operations, all fire support units had been ordered to fire only when specific targets could be identified and the effects of the shelling could be observed from the air.

Early on 16 February, just as Admiral Mitscher was launching his planes against the Japanese homeland, Admiral Blandy's bombardment fleet appeared off Iwo Jima in plain view of the Japanese garrison. Aware of the approach of the invasion force, General Kuribayashi had on the previous night dispatched to Tokyo an urgent request for the Imperial Japanese Fleet to come out and engage the American forces. The reply to his urgent plea was negative; the Imperial Fleet would not come out now, but on 1 April, when it would sally forth and push the Americans back all the way to the mainland.

The shore bombardment began at 0800, with support vessels following the minesweepers. It became apparent almost at once that prevailing weather conditions precluded the execution of scheduled firing. A low ceiling made it impossible for observers and spotters to perform their duties. Each ship fired in its assigned sector only when the weather permitted. On those infrequent occasions, intensive antiaircraft fire from the island forced observation planes to maintain an altitude above 3,000 feet, too high for an accurate assessment of the effects of the naval gunfire.

Despite the unfavorable weather, the air offensive against Iwo continued on D minus 3, though on a vastly reduced scale. Eight Navy fighters attacked Airfield Number 1 with rockets, while other carrier aircraft attacked gun emplacements on Mount Suribachi. During the afternoon, 42 B-24 bombers arrived from the Marianas, but by this time the overcast had thickened, so Admiral Blandy ordered them back home with their bombs still aboard. Altogether, on 16 February, carrier aircraft from Rear Admiral Calvin T. Durgin's Support Carrier Group (TG 52.2) flew 158 sorties. Until the airfields on Iwo were secured, carrier-based aircraft would have to furnish all the close air support for the combat troops ashore.

During the afternoon of the 16th, little more was accomplished as far as the destruction of primary targets on Iwo Jima was concerned. During one tense moment, the pilot of one of the spotter planes from the *Pensacola*, an OS2U Kingfisher, reported that there was a Zero on his tail. To everyone's surprise, the much faster Zero missed the slow moving target, and as he roared by, the pilot of the spotter plane fired into the Japanese fighter's tail, causing the plane to crash. The appearance of this Zero marked the only aerial opposition the Japanese offered throughout the day.

During the late afternoon, members of UDT 13 proceeded in small boats to Higashi Rock, about 1 ½ miles off the eastern beaches, where they placed a marker which flashed at two-second intervals, to be used as a guide for the assault troops. The Japanese observed the men on the rock and fired at them, but failed to inflict any casualties. Their mission completed, the frogmen withdrew. At 1800, the bombardment ships sailed further out to sea for the night. An undetermined number of the several hundred priority targets on Iwo had been destroyed by the first day's bombardment. Poor visibility precluded an accurate assessment of the results. It was not an auspicious beginning for the Marines.

Six hundred miles to the north, Admiral Mitscher's Fast Carrier Force had also gone into action on the 16th. From a launching position only 60 miles off the Japanese mainland, TF 58 unleashed its carrier planes against the Tokyo area in the early morning hours, specifically against aircraft plants that previous Army Air Forces B-29 raids had failed to obliterate. Despite a low ceiling and bad weather, the carrier pilots, in two days of pounding the Japanese homeland, inflicted heavy damage on enemy war plants. In addition, TF 58 claimed 341 enemy planes shot down, 190 destroyed on the ground, at a cost of 60 aircraft lost in combat and 28 operationally. When weather conditions deteriorated on 17 February and temperatures dropped so low that a considerable number of guns of carrier aircraft froze, Admiral Mitscher cancelled further strikes. After recovering its planes, TF 58 began retiring towards Iwo Jima during the afternoon of the 17th, a day sooner than had been planned. During the night from 17-18 February, destroyers of TF 58 en route to the landing force objective destroyed several small enemy picket boats and rammed a fourth. In passing Chichi Jima and Haha Jima to the north of Iwo, carrier planes attacked the airfield on the former and destroyed several small vessels offshore. TF 58 approached Iwo Jima during the afternoon of the 18th and prepared to lend direct support to the landings scheduled for the morning of the 19th.

The activities of Admiral Blandy's bombardment force off Iwo Jima on 17 February were to be of decisive importance, particularly in view of the fact that little damage on the Japanese defenses had been inflicted by the shelling of the previous day. All indications were that the second day of the prelanding bombardment would be more successful than the first, for the morning's weather had brought clear skies and excellent visibility. The schedule for 17 February called for fighter sweeps against Chichi Jima, minesweeping off Iwo Jima, and beach reconnaissance by Underwater Demolition Teams, closely supported by the large ships, destroyers, and LCI gunboats. During the early afternoon, B-24s were slated to give the island another going over.

Shortly after 0800, a dozen minesweepers approached to within 750 yards of the island, searching for mines and obstacles and probing the reefs and shoals. The tiny wooden vessels drew small arms fire from Mount Suribachi, but refused to be deterred from their mission. No mines or shallows were discovered. At 0840, the battleships *Nevada*, *Idaho*, and *Tennessee* moved to within 3,000 yards from shore to provide close support for the UDT team operations scheduled for 1100 that morning. The three vessels opened fire at almost point blank range. It quickly became apparent that the Japanese did not intend to take this bombardment lying down, and the covering fire support vessels drew heavy fire from enemy shore batteries. First to receive a hit was the *Tennessee*, which had four men injured shortly before 0900, though the ship itself suffered no damage.

Around 0930, the *Pensacola* came close in under the cliffs of the east coast of Iwo in order to provide cover for the minesweepers. Even though the Japanese had received specific orders to hold their fire, the temptation for one gun crew of having such a juicy target pass within 1,500 meters of its gun proved too much; the enemy gunner opened fire at the heavy cruiser with the 150mm gun. The first round was 50 yards short. The *Pensacola* took immediate evasive action, but by this time the Japanese had the range and in a matter of three minutes scored six hits on the vessel. The shells wrecked the combat information center, set fire to a plane on the starboard catapult, punctured the hull, and killed 17 and wounded 120 of the ship's crew. Among the dead was the executive officer. Despite the heavy damage and the extensive casualties, the Pensacola continued to fire as she withdrew to extinguish the fire and repair damage. She continued to carry out her mission, ceasing fire from time to time while casualties were being operated on and given blood transfusions.

Shortly before 1100, nearly 100 UDT swimmers headed for the island. The hazardous mission of these daredevil frogmen was to check beach and surf conditions, look for underwater obstacles both at the approaches to the landing beaches themselves and on the beaches, and to destroy any such impediments while in plain view of the enemy. As the swimmers neared the island, they came under heavy mortar and small arms fire. Covering them were 12 LCIs, stationed about 1,000 yards offshore, from where they directed a steady barrage of rockets and 40mm gunfire against the beaches. This fire, and particularly the launching of the rockets, presumably led the enemy to believe that an assault against Iwo Jima was under way. In any case, contrary to the orders they had received to hold their fire until the assault force had landed, Japanese heavy artillery to the north of the eastern beaches and at the foot of Suribachi opened fire on the lightly armored gunboats. In the course of this uneven contest, which continued for 45 minutes, the LCIs absorbed a severe pounding. An official report noted: "The personnel of these little gunboats displayed magnificent courage as they returned fire with everything they had and refused to move out until they were forced to do so by material and personnel casualties. Even then, after undergoing terrific punishment, some returned to their stations amid a hail of fire, until again heavily hit. Relief LCI (G)s replaced damaged ships without hesitation."

During the furious though unequal exchange of fire, all of the 12 gunboats were hit. The Japanese damaged LCI 474 so badly that the crew had to abandon the ship; when it capsized later, friendly shells sent it to the bottom. Intensive fire from destroyers and fire support ships, and a smoke screen laid by white phosphorus projectiles, were used to cover this operation. Fire support ships took on board casualties from the LCI's as they withdrew. Altogether, 7 men had been killed and 153 wounded in the LCIs; the destroyer *Leutze* also had received a direct hit which killed 7 and wounded 33. Only 6 of the 12 gunboats, LCIs 438, 449, 450, 466, 457, and 469 made it back to Saipan under their own power.

By 1220 all of the frogmen, with one exception, had been recovered; the fate of the missing man was to remain unknown. The members of the four UDT teams had accomplished their mission. Their reconnaissance had disclosed that there were no underwater or beach obstructions or minefield. Beach and surf conditions were found to be favorable for a landing. In fact, some of the swimmers actually had crawled out of the water to collect soil samples for examination on board ship.

While the badly damaged LCIs were withdrawing out to sea, the *Nevada* delivered a heavy and concentrated counterbattery fire against the enemy artillery positions until 1240. At the same time, the battleship *Tennessee* and two others, the *Idaho* and the *Nevada*, put down a smoke screen along the entire eastern beach area to cover the withdrawal of the frogmen. The smoke screen also obscured the view of supporting destroyers and battleships, which experienced difficulty in picking out enemy weapons because of the smoke screen over the water and the dust kicked up by shells bursting on the island.

The work of the UDTs was not completed with the exploration of the eastern beaches; a reconnaissance of the western beaches was scheduled for the afternoon of the 17th. As elements of the UDTS were preparing for the second reconnaissance, heavy bombardment ships began to pound top priority targets on the east coast. The heavy enemy fire from hitherto unsuspected positions had brought home to officers conducting the preliminary bombardment the fact that a large amount of damage remained to be inflicted on the enemy installations. Admiral Blandy revised ammunition allotments upward to permit heavier concentrations of fire against the eastern beaches, particularly those areas sheltering the recently spotted enemy coast defense guns. Admiral Rodgers, commanding the Gunfire and Covering Force (TF 54), recommended to Admiral Blandy that all available fire power be brought to bear against top priority installations around Mount Suribachi and on the high ground north of the eastern beaches. This recommendation was approved, and for the remainder of the 17th, Fire Support Units One and Two, including the *Nevada, Idaho, Tennessee, Vicksburg,* and *Salt Lake City* executed close range fire missions against those areas.

The UDT reconnaissance of the western beaches got under way at 1615, under the protection of three battleships and a cruiser. Once again, the swimmers drew Japanese automatic weapons and rifle fire, but on this occasion there were no casualties and at 1800 the frogmen, having completed the reconnaissance, returned to their APDs. One mine was discovered and destroyed. No minefield or water obstacles blocked the approach to the western beaches. Both beaches and surf conditions were thought to be suitable for landing. Twenty-two Marines from the reconnaissance companies of the 4th and 5th Marine Divisions had accompanied the UDT teams on both beach reconnaissance exploits. Upon completion of these missions, the Marines returned to their units on board command ships at sea. The intelligence collected by the reconnaissance men provided assault unit commanders with current information about the area they were soon to encounter.

As a result of good weather throughout 17 February, aviation also carried out destructive raids on Iwo Jima during the day. Carrier pilots flew a total of 226 sorties, not counting search and patrol missions. The main targets of these attacks were dual-purpose guns and antiaircraft automatic weapons around the airfields and beach areas. Napalm dropped by eight Navy fighters during the day had only limited success. Some of the bombs did not release; others failed to ignite upon hitting the ground. In any case, there was little left to burn on Iwo. The Japanese did not remain passive in the face of the continuous air attacks, for heavy antiaircraft fire met the attacking planes. A force of 42 Army Air Forces B-24 bombers dropped bombs from an altitude of 5,000 feet, scoring hits in the target area. As far as could be ascertained, however, this bombing inflicted little or no known damage to enemy installations.

Late on the 17th, it became apparent that the Japanese really believed that they had repulsed an invasion of Iwo earlier that day. Radio Tokyo reported that the American landings had been frustrated and that five warships, including a battleship, had been sunk.

In a similar vein, Admiral Soemu Toyoda, Commander in Chief of the Combined Fleet, sent the following message to Rear Admiral Ichimaru on Iwo: "Despite very powerful enemy bombings and shellings, your unit at Iwo coolly judged the enemy intentions and foiled the first landing attempt and serenely awaits the next one, determined to hold Iwo at any cost. I am greatly elated to know that, and I wish you to continue to maintain high morale and repulse the enemy, no matter how intense his attacks, and safeguard the outer defenses of our homeland."

Even as the Japanese were rejoicing at the thought of having driven an assault force back out to sea, the top echelon of the American invasion force met in Admiral Blandy's cabin on board the *Estes.* The atmosphere was not a joyful one, for only one more day remained, and two days of bombardment had inflicted comparatively little damage on enemy installations on shore. In fact, following two days of heavy shelling, the Iwo defenses looked more formidable than ever. In Blandy's presence, Commander W. P. Chilton, the gunnery officer, and Lieutenant Colonel Weller, representing the landing force, discussed what should be done. Weller urged that on the last day remaining, all available fire-power be brought to bear against the defenses commanding the beaches. Admiral Blandy approved this recommendation at once.

According to the modified plan drawn up on the evening of 17 February, four battleships, the *Tennessee, Nevada, New York,* and *California,* as well as the heavy cruiser *Chester,* were to concentrate their entire armament of 5-, 8-, and 14-inch guns in a blanket bombardment of the landing areas. The ships received permission to fire all unexpended ammunition, except that needed for D-Day, provided the weather permitted it.

Promptly at 0745 on the morning of the 18th, Admiral Rodgers ordered his Gunfire and Covering Force to "close beach and get going." These ships immediately moved to within 2,500 yards offshore and opened fire. In line with Blandy's special order, the *Tennessee* and *Idaho* were to concentrate their fire against the batteries sited at the foot of Mount Suribachi, as well as against the coast defense guns emplaced on the rim of a quarry about 400 yards north of the East Boat Basin. In executing this vital mission in somewhat less than five hours, the *Tennessee* expended a total of 333 rounds; the *Idaho* fired 280 rounds during the same period of time.

Unfortunately, the weather on 18 February was not nearly so favorable as on the preceding day. Visibility, only fair throughout most of the day, was reduced to poor during the frequent light rains on D minus 1. Despite the handicap imposed by poor observation, the massive bombardment was having its effect. When the last day of the preparatory fire ended shortly before 1830, vital enemy installations had sustained massive damage. Among 201 major targets in the main landing area, 11 coast defense guns, 22 out of 33 five inch dual-purpose guns, 16 of 20 large blockhouses, and nearly half of the 93 pillboxes had been destroyed or heavily damaged.

While Iwo was receiving a final going over by the bombardment group, Seventh Air Force bombers arrived over the island after a long flight from the Marianas. Once again the weather failed to cooperate, and the air strike had to be cancelled. Naval aviators of the Support Carrier Group, commanded by Rear Admiral Calvin T. Durgin, flew 28 sorties against positions flanking the landing beaches. These were the last of 612 sorties flown by carrier planes against ground targets on Iwo Jima prior to D-Day. Only three of the naval aircraft fell victim to enemy ground fire, and their air crews were rescued.

Late on 18 February, a low-flying enemy plane was to strike a brief but vicious blow against the invasion force. At 2130, the *Blessman* (APD-48) was hit by an enemy bomb which exploded in the troop space above the forward fireroom. In addition to serious material damage, 2 of the courageous frogmen of UDT 15, who had emerged from the hazardous beach reconnaissance missions of the previous day unharmed, were killed, and 20 were wounded. The crew of the *Blessman* suffered 11 wounded. This attack on the evening of 18 February was the only action by enemy aircraft to inflict any damage on American units at or near Iwo during the preinvasion operations.

All that remained now before Marines would hit the Iwo beaches the following morning was the execution of the D-Day fire in preparation for the landings. This pre-H-Hour bombardment would be the Navy's final opportunity to pound the enemy defenses before the assault. In fact, when the heavy support units withdrew from Iwo on the evening of the 18th, the softening-up phase had already come to an end. On the eve of D-Day, Admiral Blandy sent this message to Admiral Turner: "Though weather has not permitted complete expenditure of entire ammunition allowance and more installations can be found and destroyed with one more day of bombardment, I believe landing can be accomplished tomorrow as scheduled if necessary. I recommend, however, special attention before and during landing to flanks and East Coast of island with neutralizing fire and white phosphorus projectiles immediately available if required."

The final night before the landings was one of deep soul-searching for General Holland Smith, who found that "the imminence of action and the responsibility for the most appalling operation we had yet undertaken weighed heavily." This veteran Marine commander was filled with apprehension by the gravity of the coming battle. Weeks earlier, Smith recalled, when the Navy had overruled the Marines' request for nine days of preparatory gunfire and then withdrew two of the 16-inch gun ships to provide antiaircraft fire for Task Force 58, Admiral Spruance had told him: "I regret this confusion caused in your carefully laid plans, but I know you and your people will get away with it." Smith realized even then that any curtailment in the duration and volume of preparatory naval gunfire would be paid for with the lives of many Marines. Years later, the general was to recall: "I felt certain we would lose 15,000 men at Iwo Jima. This number was the absolute minimum calculated in our plans made at Pearl Harbor, although some of my officers wistfully predicted a lower figure. So far as the Marines were concerned, we had made every preparation humanly possible to capture the island as expeditiously and as economically as possible. We were to land 60,000 assault troops, and the estimate that one in every four would be dead or wounded never left my mind.

"I was not afraid of the outcome of the battle. I knew we would win. We always had. But contemplation of the cost in lives caused me many sleepless nights."

As night descended upon Iwo Jima and its surrounding dark waters on the evening of the 18th, the preliminary bombardment phase came to an end. Early on the 19th a new phase, the assault, would begin. The invasion of Iwo Jima would take place without modification of the carefully laid plans.

Chapter 4. D-Day on Iwo Jima

Pre H-Hour Bombardment
Early on 19 February, the assault ships of Task Force 53 under Admiral Hill arrived off Iwo Jima and joined Admiral Blandy's Amphibious Support Force. As dawn rose over Iwo Jima, more than 450 ships of the Fifth Fleet lay offshore, the largest armada ever assembled thus far for a military operation in the Pacific Theater.

Included in Admiral Hill's Attack Force were the troop ships carrying the 4th and 5th Marine Divisions, The huge vessels headed towards the transport area about 10,000 yards offshore. On board the ships, 50,000 Marines ate a hearty breakfast and went topside for a glance at the island which they would shortly assault. There was little to see. Almost totally obscured by the darkness, the island appeared as a shadowy mass of land, dominated by Mount Suribachi which "gave thousands of straining eyes aboard ship only periodic glimpses of its sharp, vertical-cone."

It was apparent by early morning that the landing force would encounter favorable weather. The sea was relatively smooth and surf conditions were satisfactory. The sky was clear; visibility was virtually unlimited, and the temperature was 68 degrees. Wind velocity was eight to ten knots from the north.

Promptly at 0640, the heavy support ships launched the pre-H-Hour bombardment, as Admiral Rodgers' Gunfire and Covering Force hurled tons of high explosives into the island. This was the last chance to silence the heavy enemy guns that dominated the boat lanes and beaches, and the gun crews of the *North Carolina, Washington, New York, Texas, Arkansas,* and *Nevada,* turned-to with grim determination. As shell bursts flicked flame, smoke, and chunks of Iwo into the air, it appeared as if the bombardment were intended to blow the very island out of the sea. Even the dead crater of Mount Suribachi seemed to come to life as it steamed from successive hits along its lip. Blasts, following one another in close succession, rocked the beaches, the airfields, and the northern portion of Iwo with its numerous hills and gullies.

In addition to the heavy gunfire ships, the gunboat and mortar support groups participated in the preparatory fire. The latter groups consisted of 42 LCI gunboats. Twelve of the LCIs were armed with 4.5-inch rockets and 40mm guns; 18 carried 4.2-inch mortars, and 9 were equipped with 5-inch rocket launchers. The LCIs joined the bombardment by the big ships at 0730 and, throughout the morning, expended nearly 10,000 rockets and large quantities of mortar ammunition while showering the slopes of Mount Suribachi and the high ground to the north of the beaches with rocket and mortar fire.

At the same time, initial preparations for boating the assault force got under way. LSTs and troop transports eased into the areas assigned to them and prepared to discharge their cargo of troops and equipment. The transports lowered the landing craft, which circled as they waited to be boarded by the Marines. On the tank decks of the LSTs, the engines of the LVTs were started, and Marines took their places in the vehicles assigned to them to await the launching signal. The signal was given at 0725; less than half an hour later, 482 amtracs were churning the water, ready to carry eight battalions into battle.

The prelanding bombardment proceeded exactly as scheduled. A few minutes after 0800, the naval guns lifted their fire and 120 fighters and bombers of TF 58 swept over the island in two waves. The aircraft concentrated their attack against the slopes of Mount Suribachi, the landing beaches, and the high ground to the north of the landing beaches. Following the bombing and strafing by the first wave, the second arrived over the island and unleashed napalm, rockets, and machine gun fire against the defenders. Included in the second wave were 24 Marine F4U Corsairs under the command of Lieutenant Colonel William A. Millington, commanding VMF-124 on board the *Essex.*

The squadron commander led his flight over Iwo Jima to attack the flanks and high ground along the landing beaches. From H minus 45 to H minus 35, the planes remained over the island and launched their attacks in accordance with a plan previously worked out between Millington and Colonel Vernon E. Megee, Commander of the Landing Force Air Support Control Unit and Deputy Commander, Aircraft, Landing Force. Prior to the mission, Megee had admonished the fighter squadron commander to "go in and scrape your bellies on the beach" and that is precisely what Millington proposed to do.

While these air strikes were under way, the gunfire support ships moved closer to the shore and assumed positions from which they would deliver the final neutralization fire. A strike by 44 Army Air Forces bombers had also been scheduled prior to H-Hour, but over half of the Liberators failed to complete the trip from the Marianas; only 15 arrived to drop 19 tons of 100-pound bombs on the eastern defenses of Iwo.

At 0825, the naval bombardment resumed. Since only a half hour remained before the first assault wave would hit the beaches, all available fire was directed against the landing sites. As the last phase of the pre-assault bombardment got under way, air bursts were employed to annihilate any Japanese that might be caught out in the open. The naval gunners subsequently shifted to impact rounds as time for the approach of the first assault wave grew near. During the final 15 minutes of the bombardment, the naval vessels offshore blasted the invasion beaches with everything they had. The thunderous roar of the 16-inch guns was supplemented by the sharper bark of the 5- and 8-inch guns of the destroyers and cruisers. Rocket craft unleashed their fire, and mortar boats shelled inland to a depth of about 1,000 yards. As the assault troops approached the shore, the naval bombardment shifted ahead to provide the mightiest preinvasion shelling thus far experienced in the Pacific Theater. In less than 30 minutes, more than 8,000 shells smashed into the beach area.

In other amphibious assaults in the Pacific Theater, naval gunfire had sometimes lifted too far inland when the troops came ashore. This lack of adequate fire close to landing areas had resulted in heavy casualties early in the operation, notably at Saipan. In order to prevent this situation from arising at Iwo Jima, VAC recommended the use of a rolling barrage reminiscent of the massive artillery concentrations of World War I. Such a barrage had to be precisely timed to keep the fire just ahead of the advancing troops; infantry commanders had to exercise maximum care to keep their men from advancing faster than the scheduled time for lifting the barrage forward. The rolling barrage was to be delivered by the 5-inch batteries, whose gunners were to maintain a 400-yard margin of safety ahead of the friendly troops. If, for any reason, the attack bogged down and did not move forward as rapidly as anticipated, certain prearranged fires were to be repeated.

Only minutes remained to H-Hour. None of the officers responsible for the preliminary bombardment could fathom the effect of the damage inflicted on the enemy defenses; at best they could hope that the naval bombardment and the aerial bombing and strafing had seriously diminished the enemy's ability to frustrate the imminent landings. The Marines about to hit the hostile beaches would be the first to know for certain how strongly the enemy could still react to their amphibious assault.

The Amphibious Assault

For the Marines in the assault waves, D-Day had started with the traditional meal of steak and eggs. Shortly after 0800, while naval shells were rocking Iwo, the amphibian tractors carrying eight Marine battalions to the Iwo beaches were churning in the water. A line of departure had been established about two miles offshore and parallel to the beach. At each end of this line, a control vessel was stationed to mark its boundaries. A central control vessel occupied the middle of the line. Along the line, at regular intervals, small vessels marked the boat lanes. The assistant division commanders, Brigadier General Franklin A. Hart for the 4th Marine Division, and Brigadier General Leo D. Hermle for the 5th, stationed themselves at each end of the line of departure as observers.

Boated and circling, the first three waves were ready to cross the line of departure by 0815. It was from here that the Marines watched the island take a severe pounding from the naval shelling and cheered as the supporting aircraft unloaded their lethal cargo over the island. The men approaching Iwo Jima were fully aware of what lay ahead; there had been no attempt at concealing the fact that a tough and costly battle awaited them. Men of the 4th Marine Division were going in with the prayer of their commander, General Cates, that as many of them as possible might be spared. General Schmidt felt that it would be a bitter but short fight.

The men in the assault waves hoped that the Navy could come up to its expectation of knocking out all defenses on the beaches, as well as most other targets further inland. Their mood varied from incredulity that any of the defenders could survive the heavy naval bombardment to skepticism born out of past experience. Many Marines remembered how many of the Japanese had survived similar bombardments on Tarawa, Guam, and Peleliu. There was also some wishful thinking; smaller islands in the Volcano-Bonins had been known to sink into the ocean, and there was hardly a Marine in the convoy who did not hope that Iwo might put on such a disappearing act under the weight of the explosives pouring upon it.

At precisely 0830, the central control vessel dipped her pennant, releasing the first assault wave. Sixty-eight LVT-(A)s of the 2d Armored Amphibian Battalion, commanded by Lieutenant Colonel Reed M. Fawell, Jr., crossed the line of departure and headed for the beaches. While hundreds of naval shells whistled overhead, the first wave followed the gunboats that poured rockets and 40mm shells into the beach before turning right and left respectively to positions from where they continued to support the flank battalions.

The operations plan had allowed 30 minutes for each assault wave to travel the 4,000 yards from the line of departure to the beaches. Following the first, successive waves crossed the line at 250- to 300-yard intervals. The second assault wave, consisting of 1,360 Marines in LVTs, crossed the line of departure two minutes behind the first wave. Eight more waves formed behind the first two, to be landed at five-minute intervals. The plan called for 9,000 men to be ashore in somewhat less than 45 minutes.

When the leading wave had reached a point 400 yards offshore, the naval bombardment shifted to the interior of the island and to the flanks. At the same time, Lieutenant Colonel Millington's fighters streaked down in magnificent strafing which continued relentlessly as the LVT's approached the beaches. In accordance with their orders, the pilots, who earlier that morning had executed the napalm and rocket strike against Iwo, now hit the beaches in daring low-level attacks. Just as the first wave came ashore, the planes shifted their strafing runs about 500 yards inland.

The ship-to-shore movement of the assault waves was carried out according to schedule. The first wave landed between 0859 and 0903; the second and third waves came ashore at two-minute intervals. The defenders remained strangely silent as the first assault troops approached the beaches, and the initial waves were not subjected to any enemy antiboat fire during the final approach to the objective. For some of the Marines, a small sliver of hope began to emerge that the heavy bombardment had reduced the enemy to impotence.

Up to the point where the first LVT's emerged from the water and ground forward, the entire maneuver had been executed with parade-ground precision. For the incoming Marines, the only indication of the enemy's presence on the island thus far had been confined to the air. One moment, a 5th Marine Division observation aircraft was circling lazily overhead; the next, enemy antiaircraft fire scored a direct hit and the small airplane spiralled into the surf. The first tractors had no sooner reached the beach and commenced heading inland than it was discovered that the 15-foot terrace directly behind the beach blocked their fields of fire. The height and steepness of the terrace was the first unpleasant surprise that the Marines were to encounter on Iwo. A second one was not long in coming. As the Marines of the 4th and 5th Divisions swarmed from their vehicles, it became evident that the composition of the volcanic sand was not what had been expected. Instead of sand with sufficient consistency to support at least tracked vehicles and men on foot, Marines of the landing force, many of them weighted down with more than 100 pounds of weapons and other gear, found themselves floundering in a sea of soft volcanic ash that all but precluded their ascending that 15-foot seawall. Almost immediately, the Marines sank up to their ankles into the loose ash that tugged at their feet and made all forward movement a strenuous undertaking.

Some of the amphibian tractors never slackened their speed upon reaching the beaches but pushed their way straight inland, up the first terrace and beyond it until they had advanced between 50 and 75 yards. Those LVT's failing to negotiate the incline headed back out to sea, where they turned around and fired inland. At 0907, the third wave of 1,200 men went ashore, followed about five minutes later by another 1,600 men of the fourth wave. Successive assault waves followed closely behind the first ones. There still was no organized enemy opposition though a few isolated artillery and mortar shells began to fall in the surf as the later waves neared the shore. Except for a number of land mines, the beaches were found clear of man-made obstacles.

The eight battalions of the 4th and 5th Marine Divisions that landed abreast on the southeastern shore of Iwo Jima were 1/28, commanded by Lieutenant Colonel Jackson B. Butterfield, and 2/28, commanded by Lieutenant Colonel Chandler W. Johnson, on Green 1; 2/27, under Major John A. Antonelli, on Red 1; 1/27, under Lieutenant Colonel John A. Butler, on Red 2; 1/23, commanded by Lieutenant Colonel Ralph Haas, on Yellow 1; 2/23, under Major Robert Davidson, on Yellow 2; 1/25, headed by Lieutenant Colonel Hollis U. Mustain, on Blue 1; and 3/25 under Lieutenant Colonel James Taul, on the southern edge of Blue 2.

As the men headed inland, the Japanese gradually came to life. The first among the landing force to feel the enemy reaction were the men of Major Davidson's 2/23 on Yellow 2 in the 4th Division sector. A moderate amount of mortar fire hit the beach within two minutes after the first wave had landed. Within 15 minutes, Marines on the Yellow and Blue beaches were reporting heavy enemy mortar fire. To the south, on the Red Beaches and Green 1, 5th Division Marines started to advance inland against initially light opposition. By 0930, 1/28 had moved 150 yards inland. Ten minutes later, the battalion reported receiving heavy mortar fire from the left flank. By the time the advance had covered 300 yards, the men were sprinkled, showered, and ultimately deluged by mortar and artillery fire from Mount Suribachi, as well as from the high ground to the north of the landing beaches. The loose, slipping sand offered poor cover; foxholes filled in almost as fast as a man could shovel, and urgent requests for sandbags began to fill the air waves. By 0935, Green 1 and the Red Beaches were on the receiving end of a heavy mortar barrage. Marines moving inland drew intense machine gun and rifle fire from well concealed pillboxes, blockhouses, and caves as soon as they left the protective cover of the first terrace.

While the Marines advancing into the interior of Iwo were being swamped by enemy fire that was still increasing both in volume and accuracy, congestion among the additional waves along the shore began to mount. The Japanese meanwhile had begun to concentrate their fire on LVTs and landing craft on and near the beaches. Enemy mortars and artillery soon scored numerous direct hits on the hapless vessels. Jeeps and trucks emerging from those landing craft that had been fortunate enough to survive the trip ashore rolled out on the beaches only to become bogged down in the treacherous volcanic ash even before they had cleared the ramp. Many of the small craft, their bows pinned to the beach, broached and swamped.

Despite the enemy fire, congestion at the water's edge, and initial confusion accompanying the landings, men and supplies continued to pour ashore. Within an hour and a half from the time that the Marines of the first wave had set foot on the island, all of the eight assault battalions were ashore. At 1005, three LSMs carrying 16 tanks of Lieutenant Colonel Richard K. Schmidt's 4th Tank Battalion hit the Yellow Beaches. The tanks encountered considerable difficulty in getting ashore. Even then, their troubles were far from over, and three tanks struck mines less than 150 yards in from the water.

While the naval barrage was still providing cover, the four newly landed Marine regiments prepared to reorganize and begin the push inland. From north to south these regiments were the 25th Marines, commanded by Colonel John R. Lanigan, and the 23rd Marines under Colonel Walter W. Wensinger, both belonging to the 4th Marine Division. The 5th Marine Division was represented by the 27th Marines, led by Colonel Thomas A. Wornham, and the 28th Marines under Colonel Harry B. Liversedge.

The Advance Inland

As troop strength built up ashore, the time had come to put the basic plan of attack into effect. Along the northern part of the beachhead, the 25th Marines was to advance towards a quarry just north of the East Boat Basin, which formed the eastern anchor of the O-1 Line denoting the objectives to be seized by the end of D-Day. This line, bisecting Motoyama Airfield No. 2, curved across the center of the island to the western shore at a point approximately 1,200 yards west of the airfield. Moving inland from the Yellow Beaches, the 23d Marines was to advance across the northern portion of Motoyama Airfield No. 1 towards Airfield No. 2. To the 27th Marines fell the task of advancing inland in a northwesterly direction, slicing across the southern tip of Airfield No. 1 and then pivoting more to the north, to reach a point west of Airfield No. 2. The 28th Marines had the mission of isolating Mount Suribachi and assaulting this formidable obstacle. To this end, the 1st Battalion, landing at H-Hour, was to cut across the narrow neck of the island, a distance of only 700 yards. The 2d Battalion was to advance about 350 yards inland, then turn southward towards Mount Suribachi.

At 0935, 2/28 started to land on Green 1 behind 1/28. Its mission was to take up positions facing Mount Suribachi, protecting the left flank of the landing force. By this time, heavy mortar and artillery fire was enveloping the beaches, making reorganization of the companies difficult.

As the 1st Battalion launched its 700-yard sprint for the western shore with Companies B and C abreast, accurate enemy small arms fire from concealed positions began to rake the advancing Marines. It soon became evident that the advance would prove costly. The intensity of the enemy fire all but precluded a coordinated movement. Men advanced in small groups, heedless of security to their flanks; some units were temporarily pinned down by an enemy who remained largely invisible. Between the bursts of artillery and mortar shells all around them, the Marines strained to get a glimpse of the defenders. What they saw was not reassuring, for halfway across the island a maze of mutually supporting blockhouses and pillboxes extended across the entire front.

In a situation where movement threatened to bog down in the heavily fortified area, the courage of individual Marines kept the attack rolling. Among the first to distinguish himself was Captain Dwayne E. Mears, commanding Company B. Armed with only a pistol, the company commander personally assaulted a pillbox that was retarding the advance of his company. Despite a wound that later proved to be fatal, Captain Mears continued to attack successive enemy positions until he became too weak to move. On the right, Captain Phil E. Roach led the advance of Company C across the island, carefully maintaining the same rate of progress as Company B. While assaulting a heavily fortified position, Captain Roach also became a casualty. Many men who found themselves separated from their platoons during the dash across the island formed small groups that continued to advance independently, thus helping to preserve the momentum of the attack.

The success of the 28th Marines' attack owed much to the support provided by the 60mm mortars which maintained continuous fire against groups of Japanese that had been flushed out of their emplacements. This fire kept the enemy on the run and out in the open, where he presented a visible target to the advancing riflemen. Lieutenant Richard H. Sandberg, commanding Company A's mortar platoon, spotted an enemy 90mm mortar squad and concentrated his fire on the Japanese until they were forced to abandon their weapon. Even more remarkably, in the heat of the engagement this platoon leader was observed firing a 60mm mortar with amazing accuracy, though it was without a base plate. Before noon, Lieutenant Sandberg became a casualty and had to be evacuated.

At 1035, elements of Company B reached the western shore of Iwo. Enemy fire had inflicted so many casualties and made control so difficult that only the platoon leader, Lieutenant Frank J. Wright, and four men of the 1st Platoon, Company B, made it all the way across the island. Lieutenant Wesley C. Bates, leading the 2d Platoon, and six of his men reached the western beach around 1100 and joined forces with Lieutenant Wright.

Even though elements of the 1st Battalion had now crossed the island, bypassed enemy positions continued to offer fierce resistance. Company A, which had landed in 1/28 reserve and faced south towards Mount Suribachi to protect the battalion's left flank, was now relieved by 2/28 and joined the remainder of the 1st Battalion in mopping up. Because of the heavy casualties 1/28 had sustained, Colonel Liversedge requested the release of 3/28, the division reserve, to his control. General Rockey granted this request. The battalion, boated and prepared to land on any 5th Division beach, received the order to land at 1210. Ten minutes later the first boats crossed the line of departure. As the leading wave approached the shore, heavy fire from Mount Suribachi and the high ground north of the landing beaches was directed at the boats. This unit suffered many more casualties during the ship-to-shore movement than had the 1st and 2d Battalions. Shortly after 1300, all elements were ashore, though it was not until late afternoon that the battalion was able to edge its way into the line. Following a naval gunfire preparation, and with adequate air support, the 2d and 3d Battalions were to jump off jointly at 1545 to attack south towards Mount Suribachi.

For such an attack, the support of armor was necessary. Company C of the 5th Tank Battalion was therefore ordered to land in direct support of the 28th Marines. This company had 14 Sherman M-4 tanks, two flametanks, one tankdozer, and one retriever. When they landed on Red One Beach about 1130, the tanks found it rough going because soft sand and storm terraces made exit difficult and the first terrace was mined. By the time additional elements of the 5th Tank Battalion got ashore, the beach was congested by stranded wheeled vehicles disabled by enemy fire. The increasing concentration of men and equipment in a restricted area was beginning to cause considerable confusion.

An eyewitness had this to say about Company C's arrival on Iwo Jima: "An infantryman picked up one of the first tanks to land and started to guide him off the beach; the route he used was marked with white tape. When the tank reached the top of the first terrace, he was guided to the right, across the tape and immediately struck a horn mine. One casualty was suffered, the driver having both legs broken, the remainder of the crew was badly shaken up. The interior of the tank was so badly damaged no attempt was made to repair it. Later it was turned into spare parts."

Altogether, eight of the battalion's tanks were unable to get off the beaches. Five threw tracks, one hit a mine, one stuck in the sand, and one stalled. Even less fortunate were other supporting arms units, such as the regimental rocket section of RCT 28 which landed during the morning. Enemy artillery smashed three of the four truck-mounted rocket launchers immediately after landing. When the remaining launcher finally got into action and opened fire, a terrific explosion rocked the target area bringing loud cheers from Marines nearby.

The tanks of Company C eventually exited the beach by a road between Red Beach 1 and 2, arriving in the zone of action of 1/28 about 1400. Lieutenant Colonel Butterfield's battalion at the time was pinned down, suffering casualties from Japanese fire coming from pillboxes and blockhouses bypassed earlier. It was decided to use the entire tank company in cleaning up the area. Because of minefield and tank traps, the tanks advanced in a column which came under antitank fire immediately after moving out. Armor piercing shells penetrated the turrets of two tanks, each of which suffered three casualties. Shortly thereafter, the enemy scored a hit on a third tank, rendering the turret inoperative. The tankers ultimately knocked out the hostile gun. This completed their mission with 1/28.

About 1600, the tanks formed up to support 2/28 and 3/28 in the planned attack towards Mount Suribachi but enemy fire was so heavy that the attacking battalions could not get into their proper positions. The 3d Battalion, commanded by Lieutenant Colonel Charles E. Shepard, Jr., was unable to get into jumpoff positions alongside the 2d Battalion. The tanks of Company C had moved out about 200 yards when it was observed that the troops on the right were not moving. By the time the 3d Battalion did get on line, it was considered too late to launch the attack, and Shepard's men began to dig in for the night.

Shortly before 1700, 2/28 launched an attack of its own, supported by tanks of Company C. By 1730, the battalion had advanced only 150 yards and even this slight gain, obtained at the cost of many casualties, had to be relinquished when 2/28 was ordered to fall back and tie in with the 3d Battalion for the night. The tanks of Company C thereafter found themselves in the unusual role of remaining forward of the lines, firing at pillboxes and covering the infantry units as they prepared for the night. Company C was released from this assignment about 1845. One tank, bogged down in a shell crater, had to be abandoned after the crew removed the gun mechanism and destroyed the radio. The company withdrew to a point about 300 yards from the front lines and dug in for a first night marked by almost continuous mortar fire.

At the same time that the 28th Marines was advancing inland from Green Beach, Colonel Wornham's RCT 27 was preparing to advance inland from Red 1 and 2, where 2/27 and 1/27 had landed abreast. On the left, 2/27 pushed inland, initially meeting only scattered resistance. Both battalions advanced rapidly against stiffening resistance, bypassing numerous enemy positions along the way. By 1130, 1/27 was infiltrating the southern end of Motoyama Airfield No. 1 and consolidating along the western edge of the field. Company C had passed the field and occupied a line extending for about 250 yards from its southwestern part to the northwest. The 2d Battalion was generally abreast of the 1st, maintaining contact with it. The 27th Marines also was receiving its share of enemy mortar and artillery fire, and casualties mounted as the advance continued. Among those wounded at this time was the executive officer of the regiment, Colonel Louis C. Plain, who was hit in the arm and subsequently evacuated.

The support of armor was needed to overcome the stubborn enemy resistance, so Company A of the 5th Tank Battalion was attached to 1/27. Earlier that morning, this company had been the first tank unit ashore, landing on the Red beaches at 0925. In attempting to get off the beaches, four tanks broke their tracks in the loose sand; the engine of another Sherman malfunctioned so that it could no longer move. The remaining tanks finally found a way off the beach and proceeded towards Motoyama Airfield No. 1. With their support, 1/27 was somewhat better able to reduce the strongly defended enemy positions, although the presence of armor in the front lines proved a mixed blessing to the hard pressed Marines who found that the Shermans attracted enemy antitank fire. Even with tank support, however, the 1st Battalion was unable to make any significant advance for the remainder of the day.

It was a different story with Major Antonelli's 2d Battalion, hell-bent on driving to the opposite side of the island. Moving inland from Red Beach 1, the battalion ran into heavy fire from light machine guns and rifles; progress was further impeded by the enemy's use of hand grenades.

About 50 yards inland, the battalion encountered its first pillbox, one of many carefully camouflaged in this area. In accordance with their orders to cross the island as quickly as possible, Companies E and F bypassed many enemy installations, eliminating only those directly in their path. Assault teams equipped with flamethrowers and hand grenade-throwing riflemen neutralized the Japanese inside while engineer teams blew up the pillboxes with explosive charges.

Leading a machine gun platoon of 1/27 past the southern end of Motoyama Airfield No. 1 was Gunnery Sergeant John Basilone, known as "Manila John" and famous for his exploits on Guadalcanal in October 1942 that had won him the Medal of Honor. On Guadalcanal he had thwarted a Japanese assault by alternately firing two machine guns and a pistol. His presence on Iwo Jima was his own choice; he had previously turned down a commission in favor of remaining an enlisted man. As Manila John rushed for the west coast of Iwo, a few steps ahead of his men, a mortar shell suddenly burst close behind him, mortally wounding this great fighting Marine and four of his men.

Although the 1st Battalion, 27th Marines could not advance to the north, 2/27 was able to push its attack westward and seized the cliffs overlooking the west coast by mid-afternoon. The regimental reserve, 3/27 under the command of Lieutenant

Colonel Dorm J. Robertson, had landed at 1130 and, moving up behind 2/27, assisted in mopping up positions bypassed by the 2d Battalion.

Despite heavy Japanese shelling of the entire beachhead on D-Day, additional units arrived on shore throughout the day. At 1500, 1/26, commanded by Lieutenant Colonel Daniel C. Pollock, completed its landing and moved into an assembly area about 300 yards inland from Red Beach 1. Shortly thereafter, the battalion was attached to the 27th Marines and ordered to take up defensive positions behind 2/27. Company B, 5th Tank Battalion, began landing on Red Beach 1 at 1300. As in the case of the armor that had landed earlier, the tanks encountered trouble in getting off the beach, but by 1600 they had reached the western side of the island, where they were attached to the 27th Marines.

Meanwhile, the 26th Marines, under Colonel Chester B. Graham, had spent most of the day on board ship in corps reserve. Just before 1000, General Schmidt released the regiment, less the 1st Battalion, to its parent division; the 21st Marines of the 3d Marine Division became the corps reserve. The 26th Marines was ordered to proceed to the line of departure shortly after 1100, but the crowded condition of the beaches and limited space inland precluded a landing until late afternoon. It was 1730 before Colonel Graham's regiment finished coming ashore over Red Beach 1. The regiment moved into on assembly area just south of Motoyama Airfield No. 1, where it took up defensive positions.

The four artillery battalions of the 13th Marines, commanded by Colonel James D. Waller, were also preparing to go ashore. Reconnaissance parties sent to the beaches as early as 1030 had discovered that the previously selected battery positions were still in enemy hands. As a result, 3/13, under Lieutenant Colonel Henry T. Waller, did not reach the island until 1400. Half an hour later, 2/13, commanded by Major Carl W. Hjerpe, went ashore, to be followed at 1645 by 1/13 under Lieutenant Colonel John S. Oldfield. Major James F. Coady's 4th Battalion reached Iwo between 1930 and 2000. The darkness and enemy fire took their toll of 4/13. Three DUKWs swamped; their cargo, consisting of two guns and badly needed radio equipment, was lost.

Major Hjerpe's 2d Battalion had been scheduled to land on Red Beach 2, but just as the first DUKWs approached the shore, they were hit by a heavy enemy barrage. One 105mm howitzer was destroyed by enemy fire; another was slightly damaged. The landing of 1/13 took place under more favorable conditions. One hour after landing, despite the same beach conditions that had slowed up the other battalions, the first battery was in position and ready to fire, a state achieved by the entire battalion at 2245. Last to go ashore, 4/13 was able to emplace eight howitzers by 0440 on D plus 1; two of the 105s and other equipment did not reach the position until later in the morning because their access road was blocked by crippled LVTs.

Landing four artillery battalions on beaches that were still exposed to incessant enemy fire was a hazardous undertaking. When the DUKWs of the Marine 5th and the Army 471st Amphibian Truck Companies reached the beaches with their cargo of 75mm and 105mm guns, they found it difficult to negotiate the deep sand. The wheeled vehicles could not get over the steep terrace behind the beaches until bulldozers and LVTs were pressed into service to pull them over the crest. Inland, the cargo was unloaded amidst heavy mortar and machine gun fire, while many furiously working artillerymen used their helmets and whatever else they could lay hands on to dig gun pits.

The arrival of the artillery on Iwo Jima underscored the fact, if any such emphasis was required, that the Marines had come to stay. To the men pinned down by heavy enemy fire, the presence of friendly artillery had additional implications:

The 13th's guns got over the south beaches somehow, and up the terraces. Within thirty minutes the crack of artillery, clearly recognizable to the foot soldiers, gave heart to the men on both fronts. Sergeant Joe L. Pipes' "Glamor Gal" was first to fire on Suribachi. At about the same instant, Sergeant Henry S. Kurpoat's 75 let go from behind Yellow 2, firing north.

They never settled the argument over which gun fired first, and it really didn't matter. Other guns were right behind them. The Marines shouted as the shells went over them. DUKWS of the Army's 471st Amphibian Truck Company, their drivers pressing ashore through the wreckage, landed the field pieces of the 13th Marines in a steady column.

Most of the artillery managed to get ashore. From that time on, the Japanese no longer had it all their way, though they retained the capability of inflicting major punishment on the assault force for some time to come.

The experience of the 13th Marines is typical of what was accomplished on D-Day and of the difficulties all Marines were to encounter on Iwo Jima. The 3d Battalion, going ashore at the northern end of Green Beach, went into position close to the water's edge. Within 20 minutes, one section of the 105mm guns was registered; by 1745, all guns were in position and ready to support the 28th Marines.

Throughout D-Day, reinforcements poured ashore as the organizational component of the landing force began to build up. At 1430, General Hermle went ashore with the ADC group and a headquarters reconnaissance party and established an advanced 5th Division command post. The assistant division commander, the first American general officer to set foot on the island, crossed Motoyama Airfield No. 1 while it was still under heavy enemy fire and gained first-hand information from units in the front lines.

The picture that presented itself to the observer at the beaches during the afternoon of D-Day was not a pretty one:

At the water's edge amtracs, LCMs and LCVPs were hit, burned, broached, capsized, and otherwise mangled. The loose, black volcanic cinders slid past the churning tires of wheeled vehicles, miring them axle-deep; the steep terraces blocked egress from the beach and extensive minefields took a heavy toll. Debris piled up everywhere.

Wounded men were arriving on the beach by the dozen, where they were not much better off than they had been at the front. There was no cover to protect them and supplies of plasma and dressings ran low. The first two boats bringing in badly needed litters were blown out of the water. Casualties were being hit a second time as they lay helpless, under blankets, awaiting evacuation to ships.

A similar situation prevailed on the 4th Marine Division beaches. There also, men's feet sank to the ankles in the loose, coarse, volcanic ash and jeeps sank to the hubcaps. Trucks could not operate at all, and supplies had to be manhandled from the water's edge to the front. On the congested beaches, the enemy laid down a sustained fire along the water's edge that at times caused heavier casualties among Seabees and engineers and in evacuation stations than those suffered by combat units. One account likened operating in such terrain to "trying to fight in a bin of loose wheat."

While 5th Division Marines struggled for the southern portion of Iwo Jima, fierce action developed on the northern beaches, where General Cates' 4th Division had gone ashore. Precisely at H-hour, Colonel Walter W. Wensinger's 23d Marines had landed on the Yellow beaches with two battalions abreast. The 1st Battalion, commanded by Lieutenant Colonel Ralph Haas, landed over Yellow 1; the 2d Battalion, under Major Robert H. Davidson, landed to the right over Yellow 2. As in the 5th Division sector to the south, RCT 23 encountered little initial resistance until the two assault companies reached the second terrace. At this point, they began to draw heavy and accurate fire from the front and flanks, where the enemy was very much alive and firmly entrenched in pillboxes, ditches, and spidertraps. Squarely astride the regiment's front were two huge blockhouses and 50 pillboxes. Even though the blockhouses had sustained massive damage from the pre-landing bombardment, they still afforded cover for the enemy. Before an advance inland could get under way, the formidable enemy obstacles had to be eliminated, a task requiring the employment of armor.

Shortly before 1000, Company C of the 4th Tank Battalion was dispatched from the line of departure for Beaches Yellow 1 and 2, in three LSMs, carrying a total of 16 tanks. The first tank to leave LSM 216 bogged down after getting off the end of the ramp. Discharge of the armor from the remaining landing ships proceeded more smoothly, but after moving inland less than 150 yards from the water's edge, three tanks were immobilized by mines or the terrain. After attempting for half an hour to recover the tank that had bogged down just off the ramp, LSM 216 withdrew to the line of departure. At 1100, another attempt was made to land the tanks, this time on Yellow 1, but none succeeded in getting ashore. Instead, LSM 216, having received a number of hits, proceeded to the hospital LST to discharge casualties. At 1245, LSM 216 finally succeeded in landing its tanks on Yellow 1. These tanks proceeded inland, but were unable to locate a route to the hard pressed 2/23. Nor was such a route ever found on D-Day.

Thus, only 1/23 received any tank support on 19 February, and due to difficult terrain and heavy enemy resistance, this support was relatively ineffective. Colonel Wensinger eventually requested that two tank retrievers be landed to assist the assault tanks which were in trouble along the beach. Some progress was made, but the nature of the terrain and heavy mortar and artillery fire from the flanks severely hindered retrieving operations.

RCT 23 had to fight its way forward with limited armored support. A hail of shells and small arms fire took a heavy toll of casualties. It was generally agreed that of all the unpleasant beaches on Iwo that day, those of the 4th Division were the hottest. At 0930, 1/23 reported that its forward elements had advanced 250 yards inland. Continued progress was slow. Ten minutes later, 2/23 sent word that it had advanced inland a similar distance, but that its leading elements were pinned down by machine gun fire from pillboxes to its front and flanks.

At noon, 1,/23 had advanced 500 yards further inland to within 200 yards of Airfield No. 1. The advance of the 2d Battalion, still meeting intensive resistance, was lagging. In fact, 2/23 had made only 250 yards since its earlier report. The absence of tank support for the 2d Battalion was beginning to make itself felt; at the same time, it became apparent that such support would not be available for some time. In view of this situation, the regimental commander decided to land 3/23, the reserve battalion, commanded by Major James S. Scales. The battalion received orders at 1300 to land along Yellow 1 Beach, move 200 yards inland, and support the attack of 2/23 with 81mm mortars.

Upon going ashore, the reserve battalion came under very heavy mortar and artillery fire. Fortunately, none of the landing craft received direct hits during the approach to the beach. Once they had come ashore, it was a different story; enemy shells could not help but hit something on the congested beaches, and casualties and destruction of materiel caused serious disorganization. More trouble for the landing force on the beaches was in the offing, and for a time it appeared as if nature had joined hands with a stubborn and determined enemy to thwart the invasion of Iwo. At the same time that the intensity and accuracy of enemy fire on the beaches reached a climax, the surf began to rise. As LVTs bogged down or were hit, the congestion and confusion on the beaches grew immeasurably. But no real trouble developed until the arrival of the LCVPs. As the light boats hit the beaches, the surf broke over them, broaching some and swamping others. Other boats, some already disabled, piled in behind the first ones and were soon hurled on the beach by the waves.

Despite this combination of unfavorable surf and deadly resistance, Marines continued to advance inland, though often every yard gained was paid for in blood. In the zone of attack of RCT 23, tanks finally reached the front lines during the afternoon. The left flank of 1/23 had advanced to the edge of Airfield No. 1 shortly after 1400, but heavy antitank fire forced the armor to beat a hasty retreat behind the revetted edge of the field. In order to get 3/23 off the congested beaches, Colonel Wensinger ordered the battalion to pass through 1/23 and carry the attack across the airfield. This order was partly carried out despite casualties and confusion, and, by 1700, 3/23 had reached the airfield boundary. The 2d Battalion derived little benefit from the arrival of armor in its zone of attack, where enemy mines, the soft volcanic ash, and accurate enemy fire precluded effective tank support. By 1730, Company F was barely able to reach the apron of Airfield No. 1, and there halted its advance for the remainder of the night.

As a result of the heavy resistance encountered by the 23d Marines, General Cates shortly after 1400 committed two battalions of the division reserve, the 24th Marines, commanded by Colonel Walter I. Jordan. The 1st and 2nd Battalions were to be attached to the 25th and 23d Marines respectively. At 1615, 2/24, under Lieutenant Colonel Richard Rothwell, was ordered to land on Yellow Beach 2 to relieve 2/23. Shortly before 1700, the battalion landed and moved inland about 700 yards to the front line. By 1800, it had relieved 2/23 and dug in for the night just short of the airfield, tying in between 2/23 and 1/25.

Among all of the Iwo beaches, the one most exposed to enemy fire was Blue Beach 1, the northernmost of the invasion beaches, located right below a cliff that was held by the enemy in great strength. It was the unenviable task of the 25th Marines to secure the Blue Beaches. The regiment, under Colonel John R. Lanigan, landed two battalions abreast over Blue Beach 1 and the southern edge of Blue Beach 2. As on the remaining beaches, the first waves, landing shortly after 0900, reported only light enemy fire until the troops disembarked and moved approximately 25 yards from the LVTs, when they came under very heavy machine gun, mortar, artillery, and rocket fire.

At 0935, 1/25, commanded by Lieutenant Colonel Hollis U. Mustain, reported that the battalion was still under heavy fire of all types but had moved inland 300 yards. Half an hour later, 3/25, under Lieutenant Colonel Justice M. Chambers, reported that elements of the battalion had moved 350 yards northeastward along the beach and that the battalion's left flank was inland 400 yards and in contact with 1/25. The continuous, well-aimed enemy fire caused some disorganization along the beach and the men sought cover in large bomb craters along the shore. Casualties were heavy. By midafternoon, Company K had lost eight officers; Company L had lost five by 1630, and Company I lost six.

At 1020, Company A, 4th Tank Battalion, which had been attached to 3/25, went ashore on Blue Beach 1. Almost at once the enemy concentrated the fire of his mortars, artillery, and antitank guns on the tank landing ships (LSMs). All three of the LSMs were hit and damaged while unloading. The enemy fire could not prevent the LSMs from landing, but caused a delay in launching the tanks. After having discharged the tanks, the LSMs retracted from the beach. A tank dozer cut a road from the first terrace inland from Blue Beach 1, but became a total loss when it hit a mine and turned into a sitting target for Japanese mortars and artillery.

The remaining tanks formed a column and gingerly proceeded inland for about 100 yards. At that time, the column came to a halt when it encountered an enemy minefield. Though immobilized for the time being, while engineers cleared the mines, the tanks supported the Marine riflemen with their 75mm guns, which fired on enemy positions and pillboxes behind the beach and in the cliffs to the north.

Meanwhile, the withering enemy fire had inflicted very heavy casualties on the 25th Marines, which doggedly continued its advance against a continuous mortar barrage and intense rifle and machine gun fire both from the front and the flanks. By noon the attack of the two assault battalions had become so channelized that a 100-yard gap had opened between 1/25 and 3/25. At this time, Colonel Lanigan decided that it was imperative for RCT 25 to seize the high ground northeast of Blue Beach 2. To this end, he ordered Lieutenant Colonel Lewis C. Hudson to land 2/25, which constituted the regimental reserve, on Blue Beach 1. The battalion was to attack in a column of companies astride the boundary between 1/25 and 3/25, seize the high ground to the northwest near a quarry, and assist the advance of 3/25.

By 1400, 2/25 had moved one company into the line between the other two battalions and a coordinated attack to the north got under way. From the very outset, the regimental attack moved slowly because of heavy enemy resistance. The 3d Battalion advanced for about 300 yards along the beach, then headed for the quarry about 400 yards north of the East Boat Basin. On the battalion's left, elements of 2/25 and 1/25 advanced 100 yards, but were driven back by intense small arms fire. By 1730, casualties and disorganization of 3/25 had assumed such proportions that Colonel Lanigan requested and received permission to commit one company of 1/24. An hour later, 2/25 and 3/25 had seized the high ground on top and inland of the quarry, but this advance had been paid for with extremely heavy casualties. At 1900, Lieutenant Colonel Chambers reported that the combat strength of 3/25 had diminished to only 150 men.

In order to compensate for the heavy losses his regiment had sustained on D-Day, and because the Japanese were expected to counterattack along the right flank of the regiment, Colonel Lanigan requested from division the use of one company of 3/24, the division reserve, which was in position directly behind 3/25. This request was denied, but the regimental commander received permission to use one more company of 1/24. As a result, Company B of 1/24 was attached to 3/25. Units began digging in at 1700 and firm contact was established along the front of RCT 25 except on the left flank where a 75-yard gap remained. This gap was covered by fire and observation during the night. In the course of the evening, the depleted 3/25 was

---

relieved by 1/24 and took up defensive positions to the rear of 1/24. The relief, which took place under occasional enemy fire, was not completed until close to midnight.

The last battalion of the 24th Marines to go ashore was 3/24, under Lieutenant Colonel Alexander A. Vandegrift, Jr. The battalion landed before 1900 and moved inland a short distance from Blue Beach 2. All of the 4th Marine Division's infantry battalions were now ashore, and Marines were busily making preparations for an enemy counterattack they felt sure would develop during their first night ashore.

As in the 5th Marine Division sector on the southern beaches, additional units reached Iwo on the northern beaches during D-Day. With most of the infantry ashore, the time had also come for the artillery regiment of the 4th Division, under Colonel Louis G. DeHaven, to land on the island. Reconnaissance parties from the artillery battalions had already debarked early in the afternoon in order to select positions for their batteries. In doing so, they faced difficulties similar to those encountered by the 13th Marines on the southern beaches. The front lines had advanced more slowly than planned; no routes had been cleared to enable the DUKWs to carry artillery pieces inland. One of the first members of the reconnaissance teams to become a casualty was Lieutenant Colonel Robert E. McFarlane, commanding the 3d Battalion.

At 1405, General Gates ordered 1/14 under Major John B. Edgar, Jr. to land in direct support of the 25th Marines; Major Clifford B. Drake's 2/14 was to lend direct support to RCT 23. Upon hitting Blue Beach 1, the DUKWs of the 4th Amphibian Truck Company with their cargo of 75mm Pack Howitzers of 1/14, became immobilized at once. They quickly bogged down and settled in the volcanic ashes. Bulldozers attempting to get the DUKWs mobile again tugged and strained, but more often than not cables snapped and towing cleats sheered. One howitzer was lost when the DUKW in which it was loaded sank immediately after being discharged from its LST. Nevertheless, by 1715 the 1st Battalion had succeeded in getting 11 howitzers into position after wrestling them up the terraces by hand. Half an hour later, all batteries of 1/14 were registered and ready to fire.

An even more difficult feat was to get the 105mm howitzers of 2/14 ashore. Because of the increased weight of these guns, it proved impossible to manhandle them up and over the terrace. The only feasible expedient was to keep each howitzer in the DUKW and then attempt to get the loaded DUKWs over the terrace. Surf conditions, the slippery sand, and continuous enemy fire combined to make this movement a miserable undertaking that took hours to complete. None of the DUKWs received a direct hit, though several casualties resulted from near misses.

Shortly before dusk, all 12 howitzers of Major Drake's 2/14 were in position near Yellow Beach 1.

The 3d Battalion, under Major Harvey A. Feehan, was ordered to launch its DUKWs shortly after 1500. At this time, for unknown reasons, several DUKWs could not be started and more than an hour elapsed before all of the vehicles were in the water. Because of the congestion ashore and approaching dusk, Colonel DeHaven decided that the 3d and 4th Battalions were to delay going ashore until the following day, and 3/4 was reembarked on board the LST. During the reembarkation, a howitzer and a DUKW were lost when the amphibian truck's motor failed as it headed back up the ramp.

As D-Day on Iwo Jima came to an end, Marines all along the VAC front lines braced for a major Japanese counterattack they felt sure would come before the night was over. The carnage which had taken place on the island on D-Day differed from anything the Marines had encountered elsewhere in the Pacific Theater during World

War II. Despite the enemy presence, which made itself felt everywhere and continuously on the island, and to which the numerous dead and wounded could attest, few of the men who had landed on Iwo that day had actually seen a live Japanese. No prisoners had been taken that first day, and only an occasional enemy corpse was visible.

Nevertheless, a steady flow of American casualties from the front to the beaches underscored the ferocity of the enemy resistance. Along the surf line, the litter of war continued to pile up in an almost unimaginable jumble: smashed landing craft surged upward and forward with every wave, crashing headlong into trucks, crates, and bodies at the edge of the water. Nearby, the wounded were gathered in small groups sitting or lying, just as exposed to the incessant enemy shelling as anyone else on the island and even more helpless in the face of it. For the remainder of D-Day, and into the night, boats approached Iwo Jima, loaded with reinforcements and supplies; having unloaded these, they took on a new cargo: the wounded, for whom surgeons would be waiting in transports and hospital LSTs especially prepared for this purpose.

First Night on Iwo Jima

As D-Day on Iwo Jima came to an end and darkness descended over the island, Marines could take well justified pride in having seized a solid foothold on a heavily fortified bastion, where both the advantage in terrain and troop disposition rested with the defending garrison. Even though the advance nowhere came near to reaching the O-1 Line, VAC had succeeded in getting six infantry regiments and six artillery battalions — nearly 30,000 men and thousands of tons of equipment — ashore.

From General Holland Smith down through the ranks, it was generally believed that according to their earlier tactics, the Japanese would throw all the manpower they had against the vulnerable Marines during their first night ashore. The enemy was known to have a large reserve force of infantry and tanks available for such an all-out counterattack. None of the intelligence personnel of VAC could suspect at the time that General Kuribayashi planned to conserve his manpower and would find other means to decimate the Marines that were crowded into the narrow beachhead.

The burden of battle was not only borne by the Marine assault units who had gone ashore on D-Day. Throughout the day, the supporting arms of the Amphibious Support Force had done all they could to assist their hard pressed comrades in arms. Carrier pilots of TF 58 and the escort carriers of TF 52 flew missions as long as daylight prevailed; airborne observers and spotters kept a continuous vigil over the target area. More than 600 aircraft flew 26 missions in the course of the day, including strikes prior to H-Hour, dropped 274,500 pounds of bombs, not including more than 100 napalm bombs. Offshore, naval guns continued to shell enemy positions on Iwo in response to Marine requests. Gunfire support ships shelled enemy gun emplacements on the high ground north of the beaches and did their best to destroy the concealed enemy mortars whose fire was causing so many casualties on the beaches.

The heavy enemy fire on the beaches, as well as unfavorable surf conditions, precluded the landing of all but highest priority cargo on D-Day. In order of importance, this cargo was limited to ammunition, rations, water, and signal equipment. Once this equipment had been unloaded on the beaches, the shore party teams could do little more than stack the supplies. LVTs and Weasels carried these supplies inland and returned with a cargo of wounded.

As night fell, most of the transports and other vessels retired from Iwo, but some of the command ships, preloaded LSTs, and hospital LSTs remained behind. The work of stacking supplies on the beach and terraces continued after nightfall. Offshore, mortar boats concentrated their fire against the enemy positions on the high ground overlooking the 4th Marine Division beaches. Bulldozers continued hauling vehicles inland, and whenever possible, pulled equipment out of the sand. Under cover of darkness, critical items, especially 81mm ammunition, were brought in. The 81mm shells that had been handcarried ashore with these mortars had lasted for only one hour after the mortars opened fire. With the 81mm mortars out of ammunition, the assault battalions lost the services of a large portion of high trajectory weapons support during most of the violent action on D-Day .

While the Marines anxiously awaited the big *banzai* charge that would finally bring the enemy out into the open, General Kuribayashi cannily began to employ his plan which would destroy the Americans and their supplies on and near the beaches without his risking many of his own men. In short, his plan consisted of a few attempts at infiltration, while at the same time stepping up the fire of his deadly artillery and mortars against the crowded American beachhead. As the night progressed, the rain of enemy shells mounted in intensity, as did the number of American casualties.

By 2300, the enemy shelling of the Yellow and Blue Beaches had become so heavy that both beaches were ordered closed. Elsewhere, it proved to be a sleepless night for most of the Marines on Iwo. On the southern beaches, a few vessels still attempted to bring in cargo, as runners crawled in and out of command posts, bearing reports and orders. Other men were shuffling around in the darkness looking for their units and their equipment. Because of the disorganization of units, it proved impossible at this time to obtain an accurate account of D-Day casualties, though it was known that they were heavy. It was to be determined later that 501 Marines had died on this first day of the invasion; 1,775 had been wounded in action; an additional 47 died of wounds, and 18 were missing in action; 99 of the assault force suffered from combat fatigue.

Despite the heavy casualties, on the evening of D-Day VAC still rated the combat efficiency of the assault force as very good to excellent. As the day ended, the 5th Marine Division had established a beachhead approximately 1,500 yards wide and 1,000 yards in depth, dividing the enemy forces in the northern and southern part of the island and effectively isolating Mount Suribachi. The 4th Marine Division had reached a line extending northward and inland from Blue Beach 2 for about 200 yards on low ground, then from the Quarry on top of the ridge for about 300 yards, then south across the low ground which led off the beach towards Motoyama Airfield No. 2, and from there to a line which was roughly a projection of the main runway of Airfield No. 1. It was clear that the landing had been successful. The Marines were dug in and occupied positions that were difficult but tenable. Supplies were scanty but sufficient for immediate needs.

As the night progressed, there was movement of all kinds on and around Iwo Jima. Offshore, transports carrying the 3d Marine Division were arriving in the reserve area 80 miles southeast of the island. Amidst the steady thumping and crashing of the enemy artillery and mortar shells deluging the 30,000 Marines that had gone ashore, there was stealthy movement as some of the enemy, their guns near Mount Suribachi rendered useless by American air and naval bombardment, moved through the lines and headed for northern Iwo. The enemy had lost a good part of his artillery, and within three hours after H-Hour, all of the heavy guns on the slopes of Mount Suribachi had been silenced.

There were several enemy attempts at infiltration. Shortly after 2300, a barge carrying 39 Japanese approached the west coast of Iwo and prepared to land them. The enemy was spotted by alert riflemen of 1/28, who picked the Japanese off one by one as they tried to get ashore, until all had been killed. On the east coast of Iwo a member of a naval construction unit had a strange experience. He was watching a log in the surf which the current bore south along the shore. Suddenly, the log made a sharp turn. The Seabee fired 13 rounds and at dawn found a riddled Japanese body at the water's edge.

What it felt like to be a member of the VAC assault force during that first eerie night on Iwo Jima has been graphically described as follows: "Bunched in foxholes along the perimeter, the Marines took turns on watch, fighting to stay awake, waiting, waiting for the crazy *banzai*. Now and then, shouting and ragged fire broke out in hysterical patches as the rocks and bushes seemed to move in the eerie light of the star shells. Still the rush didn't come."

Japanese artillery kept pounding the American positions. Shortly after midnight, the enemy scored a direct hit on the command post of 1/23 on Yellow Beach 1, killing Lieutenant Colonel Haas and the regimental operations officer, Captain Fred C. Eberhardt. Minutes later, one of the giant spigot mortar shells, which many Marines first thought to be a P-61 night fighter because of the peculiar sound it made while passing over, came wobbling down from the north and exploded on one of the Green Beaches near Mount Suribachi. Around 0400, the 25th Marines ammunition and fuel dump went off with a terrifying roar. Two full boatloads of 81mm mortar shells, gasoline, and flamethrower fuel exploded, caving in foxholes for yards around.

Initially, these disasters were attributed to lucky enemy hits on these vulnerable targets. It remained for a Japanese postwar history to clear up this point. According to the Japanese version: Instead of all-out desperate banzai charges, Kuribayashi organized small packs of prowling wolves – three or four in a pack – which sneaked in at night to enemy depots or concentration of fuel and ammunition and attacked with demolition charges and hand grenades. This new tactic again proved quite successful at the nights of February 19 and 20. For instance, heaps of 81mm mortar shells of the 4th Marine Division blew up at the southern coast; flamethrower fuel and gasoline at the same coast also burned.

As dawn rose over the island on 20 February, less than 24 hours had passed since the first Marines hit the Iwo beaches. A newspaper correspondent, looking at the scene surrounding him, made this comment: "The first night on Iwo Jima can only be described as a nightmare in hell. About the beach in the morning lay the dead. They died with the greatest possible violence. Nowhere in the Pacific have I seen such badly mangled bodies. Many were cut squarely in half. Legs and arms lay 50 feet away from any body. All through the bitter night, the Japs rained heavy mortars and rockets and artillery on the entire area between the beach and the airfield. Twice they hit casualty stations on the beach. Many men who had been only wounded were killed."

It appeared that General Kuribayashi's strategy was paying off. There had been no *banzai* that first night; but from dusk to dawn Japanese shells had steadily killed off Marines on the congested beaches at no cost to the enemy. As the new day dawned, it would be up to the tired Marines to strip the enemy of his excellent observation posts and firing positions, their only means of eliminating the deadly fire in which the entire landing force was engulfed.

Chapter 5. The Struggle for Suribachi

Securing the Base

Dawn on 20 February saw VAC Marines engaged in two distinct operations. One was the capture of Mount Suribachi whose forbidding slopes glowered down on the Americans on the exposed ground beneath. The other was a prolonged drive to the north, intended to seize the vital airfields and eliminate all enemy resistance.

The story of the capture of Suribachi is basically that of the 28th Marines. After landing on D-Day, Colonel Liversedge's men were facing southward, prepared to tackle the mountain, while the remainder of the 5th Division and all of the 4th had wheeled to the right to complete the capture of Airfield No. 1, and then continue the advance to the northeastern part of Iwo.

The assault on the extinct volcano promised to be difficult. To some of the Marines, gazing at the mottled, bare mountain, "Suribachi resembled the head of a fabulous serpent, with fangs ejecting poison in all directions from its base." Between Colonel Liversedge's men and the base of Suribachi lay a wasteland of broken rock and stubble. This wasteland, guarding the one approach to the volcano, was studded by hundreds of caves, pillboxes, blockhouses, bunkers, spider traps, mines, and every other conceivable defense. It was in the slow and costly approach to the mountain that many Marines were to die or be wounded.

On the mountain itself, 1,600 Japanese were occupying well-camouflaged defensive positions with orders to hold out to the very end. That the Marines had cut the southern portion of Iwo off from the northern part on D-Day had little effect on General Kuribayashi's dispositions and plans. The wily enemy commander had foreseen that the island defenses would be split early in the operation. In relation to his overall defensive plan, Mount Suribachi was but one of several semi-independent defense sectors capable of resisting the American assault with their own resources.

Colonel Liversedge's plan of attack was for the 28th Marines to surround the base of the mountain, maintain a steady pressure on enemy positions that could be identified in the cliffs, and seek out suitable routes to the summit. The regiment was to advance towards Suribachi with the 2d Battalion on the left, the 3d on the right, and the 1st in reserve. H-Hour was 0830, 20 February.

At first light, carrier planes attacked the mountain with bombs and rockets. Napalm was dropped at the foot of the slopes, since most of the enemy fire seemed to come from that area. A destroyer stood offshore close to the west coast to support the advance of the 3d Battalion; a minelayer stood off the east coast to assist 2/28. The weather had changed for the worse; a light rain was falling and it had turned chilly. Four-foot waves were pounding the beach and the wind from the south was rising.

As Colonel Liversedge's men waited to jump off, they felt far from rested. The exertions of the previous day had been followed by a night of continuous enemy bombardment. The sense of gloom and foreboding felt by many men on the morning of D plus 1 was due not only to lack of sleep and the weather, but to the nature of the objective. Mount Suribachi itself imposed a mental hazard on the assault troops similar to that faced by the Allies in Italy a year earlier when they suddenly found themselves confronted by Mount Cassino. The impact of such a terrain feature, known to be held in strength by the enemy, can be formidable. As one account of the Iwo operation was to report: "On this day, and increasingly as days went by, Suribachi seemed to take on a life of its own, to be watching these men, looming over them, pressing down upon them. When they moved, they moved in its shadow, under its eye. To be sure, there were hundreds of eyes looking at them from the mountain, but these were the eyes of a known enemy, an enemy whose intent was perfectly clear. In the end, it is probable that the mountain represented to these Marines a thing more evil than the Japanese."

The assault of the 28th Marines against Suribachi began on schedule, preceded by a bombardment of the mountain by destroyers, rocket gunboats, and artillery. This bombardment destroyed a few enemy emplacements and at the same time unmasked many concrete structures buried in the scrub and rocky ground leading to the base of Suribachi. It soon became evident that the caves on the lower slopes and at the base of the mountain were as formidable as its pillboxes and blockhouses. The caves had from two to five entrances with interconnecting tunnels. Prior to the invasion they had served as air raid shelters and living quarters. They were linked with supply and command caves containing food, water, and ammunition. From the entrances to the caves, 6-inch guns, protected by five foot walls, pointed down the island.

Almost immediately, the advancing Marines came under heavy fire from small arms, mortars, and artillery. Working against the success of the attack was the lack of needed tank support. The 5th Tank Battalion had been scheduled to support RCT 28. Even though eight tanks were available, no fuel or ammunition was at hand. The tankers finally salvaged some from disabled tanks and divided it up. During this redistribution, the enemy put a heavy mortar barrage on the vehicles, forcing them to move to another position. Almost immediately, the mortar fire shifted to the new position. This occurred three times; there was no place where the tankers could move that was not under direct enemy observation.

During the morning, the Marines advanced only 50 to 70 yards. Support from aircraft and ships helped, as did the artillery support from 3/13. However, even the best efforts of these combined arms failed to neutralize enemy fire, particularly that coming from the well-camouflaged pillboxes hidden in the scrub around the base of the mountain. Once the Marines advanced into these formidable enemy defenses, they would be too close for support from aircraft and artillery. Assault demolition teams, using flamethrowers and explosive charges, would have to do the job. Once again, the continuation of the advance depended on the skill and bravery of the individual Marine.

At 1100, the tanks were finally ready to support the advance. The 37mm guns and 75mm half-tracks of the regimental weapons company were also moved up in support. In the face of bitter enemy resistance, only split-second teamwork by every unit could gain any ground. The procedure employed was for infantry and tanks to take each pillbox under fire, while a flamethrower team worked up to one of the entrances. After several bursts of flame had been squirted at the fortification, the remainder of the assault squad closed in to finish the job with grenades. Once the occupants had been eliminated, engineers and demolition teams blasted the positions to ensure that they would not be reoccupied by the Japanese after nightfall. Whenever the rugged terrain permitted, flamethrowing tanks were employed against the pillboxes.

By 1700, RCT 28 had laboriously moved 200 yards closer to the objective, at the cost of 2 officers killed and 6 wounded, and 27 men killed and 127 wounded. The advance had taken the Marines of 2/28 and 3/28 close to the base of the mountain; in the course of the afternoon, they had closed off nearly 40 caves with demolitions. As the men prepared to dig in for the night, they found themselves surrounded by the debris of the heavy enemy coastal guns which the naval bombardment had smashed prior to and during D-Day. Moving towards Mount Suribachi along the western shore of Iwo, 3/28 killed 73 of the enemy. The Japanese corpses presented an encouraging sight in an operation where, thus far, little had been seen of the enemy, dead or alive.

As the 28th Marines pressed their assault, the enemy situation on Suribachi steadily deteriorated. The American naval and air bombardment on D-Day had knocked out all of the 140mm guns. Inside the mountain, the commander of the Suribachi Sector, Colonel Kanehiko Atsuchi, pondered his mounting casualties and dispatched a message to General Kuribayashi asking the latter's permission to go out and seek death through a *banzai* charge, rather than sitting it out in his present position. Shortly thereafter, the advancing Marines found and cut the buried cable linking Suribachi with the northern sector. Colonel Atsuchi never received a reply from the island commander, either because communications were now disrupted or simply because General Kuribayashi felt that his sentiments regarding the outdated *banzai* charge were sufficiently well known to his subordinates to require no repetition.

Some postwar Japanese sources, emphasizing that Atsuchi was actually in charge, have implied that the island commander was not happy with having entrusted Atsuchi, then 57 years old, with command of the crucially important batteries on Suribachi. One of the Japanese officers, initially stationed on Iwo, who was familiar with the enemy command organization, later was to refer to the Suribachi Sector commander as "a poor superannuated amateur," adding "that it was the Army's mistake to send such an aged and rusted character to Iwo, who was simply a misfit for leading many people." Other accounts were somewhat more charitable towards Atsuchi. In any case, there can be no doubt that a *banzai* attack was precisely what General Kuribayashi did not want. He much preferred to force the Americans to fight for the mountain foot by foot, and to inflict heavy losses as a price for seizing the strongly defended elevation.

Loss of telephone communications with the command post in the northern part of Iwo did not mean that Atsuchi's men had been abandoned by their comrades. As darkness fell, the Japanese on Suribachi fired white and amber flares as a signal that artillery and mortar support were desired from the northern sector. For the second night in succession, artillery and mortar fire from Suribachi and northern Iwo pounded the Marine positions. American guns, ashore and afloat, answered this barrage, as the din of battle echoed and resounded well into the night.

As on the eve of D-Day, the men of the 28th Marines veered into the darkness, ever watchful for signs of an enemy counterattack. Tired eyes strained to the south in an effort to detect enemy activity, but for the second night the expected counterattack failed to develop. Division orders for D plus 2 called for a continuation of the 28th Marines attack towards Mount Suribachi. Despite enemy artillery and mortar fire, the tired men tried to obtain what little sleep they could get in anticipation of the rigors that awaited them on the following day.

On the morning of 21 February, the rough weather of the previous day showed no signs of abating. The wind had risen to 19 knots from the northeast and six-foot waves were pounding the landing beaches. Since the distance between the forward elements of the 28th Marines and the base of Mount Suribachi was still significant for air strikes, naval gunfire, and artillery support, the combined force of air and artillery was again brought to bear against the Japanese before the Marines jumped off.

Prior to the scheduled jumpoff at 0825, 40 aircraft struck at the enemy with bombs and rockets, and, strafing within 100 yards of the forward Marine lines, concentrated against an area inaccessible to tanks. This was the closest air support thus far provided and possibly the last, since another day's advance would bring the men too close to their objective.

The 1st Battalion was assigned a one-company front on the regimental right. When the regiment jumped off for the attack at 0825, the units and boundaries assigned to it were identical to those of the previous day. Once again, the tanks were unable to meet H-Hour because of delays in rearming and refueling, and the attack had to get under way without them.

Under cover of fire from warships and land-based artillery, the 1st Battalion attacked towards Mount Suribachi along the west coast. Because the terrain there precluded effective employment of tanks, their absence at the beginning of the attack was immaterial. On the left, it was a different story; even with naval gunfire support no gains were made until the tanks arrived. By 1100, the attack gained momentum when armor, 37mm guns, and half-tracks mounting 75mm guns, as well as rocket detachments, joined in pounding the enemy positions. By noon, the 1st Battalion had reached the western base of Suribachi.

During the advance it became apparent that the enemy was particularly vulnerable to the heavy explosive blast of the rockets and retaliated by concentrating his fire on the rocket launching trucks, which were unprotected by armor-plate. When caught in such a concentration of fire, the crews withdrew to cover and ran up singly to load the rocket platform. When the order to fire was given, one Marine would scamper forward, dive under the truck, then reach his arm around the side to push the firing button. The resulting explosion when the rocket hit the target usually meant that the Marines had one less enemy position to contend with.

Advancing in the center, the 3d Battalion encountered heavy resistance from the same positions that had blocked the advance on the previous day. Nevertheless, the attack of this battalion also was gaining momentum by 1100. Within the hour, an enemy counterattack struck the front of 3/28; this action failed to halt the advancing Marines, and by 1400 the forward elements had reached the foot of Mount Suribachi. There, 3/28 spent the remainder of the day.

The attack of the 2d Battalion down the eastern shore also got under way slowly. At first, there was little resistance and for a few moments, the hulking natural fortress remained quiet, but enemy reaction was not long absent. First came the crack of rifles and the chatter of machine guns. The chatter turned into a heavy clatter and bullets began to snap and whine around the advancing Marines. Some of them found their mark. Then the Japanese began firing their deadly mortars. Some of the Marines could see the high arc of the mortar rounds. Soon the area was blanketed by roaring funnels of steel and sand. The noise and fury increased until the hearing of the attacking Marines was numbed and their thinking impaired. It seemed as if the volcano's ancient bowels had suddenly come to life and the men were advancing into a full-scale eruption. One of the Marines, speaking of the holocaust, was to remark later: "It was terrible, the worst I can remember our taking. The Jap mortarmen seemed to be playing checkers and using us as their squares. I still can't understand how any of us got through it."

Not all of the attacking Marines did get through the lethal curtain of fire, but there were enough of them to carry the advance forward. The feelings of these men, as they faced what seemed to them almost certain death, were expressed by one of their number who lived to tell about it: "We were now part of a real hell-bent-for-leather attack, the kind the Marines are famous for. But there was nothing inspiring about it. None of our ex-raiders shouted "Gung Ho!" . . . and none of our southerners let go the rebel yell. We felt only reluctance and enervating anxiety. There seemed nothing ahead but death. If we managed somehow to make it across the open area, we'd only become close-range targets for those concealed guns. I myself was seized by a sensation of utter hopelessness. I could feel the fear dragging at my jowls.

"It is in situation like this that Marine Corps training proves its value. There probably wasn't a man among us who didn't wish to God he was moving in the opposite direction. But we had been ordered to attack, so we would attack. Our training had imbued us with a fierce pride in our outfit, and this pride helped now to keep us from faltering. Few of us would have admitted that we were bound by the old-fashioned principle of 'death before dishonor,' but it was probably this, above all else, that kept us pressing forward."

Two uncommon acts of heroism, among many, were to occur during the day, indicative of the caliber of the men who had gone ashore on Iwo Jima. The first one was unpremeditated, nor was there time for lengthy thought. It took place in 2/28 when Private First Class Donald J. Ruhl deliberately threw himself on a hand grenade that had landed next to him and his platoon guide, Sergeant Henry O. Hansen, sacrificing his own life in order to save the sergeant. The second involved the rescue of two Marines who lay wounded for more than 24 hours at the eastern base of Mount Suribachi. A hospital corpsman had been keeping them alive by creeping up to them and treating their wounds under fire. One of the wounded was breathing through a glass tube in his neck. Since evacuation by land was out of the question because of enemy fire, a group of Marines, headed by Staff Sergeant Charles E. Harris, manned a raft, landed it on the rocky shore in a heavy surf, and succeeded in evacuating both men under the noses of the enemy. Both casualties survived the ordeal.

By evening of 21 February, the 28th Marines occupied a line which formed a semicircle just north of Mount Suribachi. The 1st Battalion was halfway around the mountain on the western shore; 2/28 had advanced an equal distance along the eastern base of the mountain; the 3d Battalion was squarely facing the volcano in the center of the semicircle. During this third day ashore, the 1st Battalion had advanced 1000 yards, the 2nd Battalion 650 yards, and the 3d, 500 yards. These gains were made at a cost of 34 Marines killed and 153 wounded. Due to these heavy additional casualties, by evening of 21 February the combat efficiency of the 28th Marines had declined to 75 percent.

Much of the success of the day's advance had been due to the tank support available on D plus 2. Altogether, seven tanks supported the advance towards Mount Suribachi. Two of them were put out of action by the enemy and one by the terrain. One ran over a mine, one was hit by antitank fire, and one broke a track. About 1630, after the advance halted for the day, the tanks were released. To avoid any delay when the attack resumed on the following morning, the tanks were rearmed and refueled before dark. Despite the damage sustained by the three vehicles, the tankers engaged near Mount Suribachi had suffered no casualties on this third day of the invasion.

As the afternoon of 21 February wore on, a cold rain began to fall on Iwo, greatly increasing the discomfort of the Marines holding positions around the base of Suribachi. Behind them, and all around them were the remnants of the main defenses guarding the volcano. Some of the pillboxes and bunkers had been crushed like matchboxes by naval gunfire; others had been seared black by napalm flames. The entire area was pervaded by the smell of death and burned flesh, where flamethrowers had done their deadly work. The expenditure of flamethrower fuel had reached such proportions that a temporary shortage developed — overcome only when versatile Weasels carried additional supplies to the front lines.

In the gathering dusk, many Marines could clearly hear the enemy talking inside the mountain. They succeeded in killing a large number of Japanese by pouring gasoline down the fissures and setting it aflame. Inside the volcano, Colonel Atsuchi was dying from a shell fragment wound incurred during the day. His last order was that a squad of men attempt to break through to General Kuribayashi's headquarters to report the situation on Suribachi. Many of the enemy felt extremely bitter at their own lack of air support while American aircraft filled the sky. Nevertheless, enemy morale remained unshaken and nearly all were determined to go down fighting.

Actually, air support for the Japanese garrison on Iwo was closer at hand than anyone, friend and foe alike, might have suspected. At dusk, as the Marines were digging in for the night, the enemy made one effort from the air. About 50 kamikazes had left an airfield near Tokyo early in the day and, after refueling at Hachijo Jima in the Bonins, headed towards Iwo Jima. Each member of the Special Attack Unit had but one objective: to hurl his aircraft and himself at the invasion fleet that was gathered around Iwo.

Radar equipment on the *Saratoga*, about 35 miles northwest of the island, picked the aircraft up when they were still 100 miles away, but they were first mistaken for friendly planes. At 1700, interceptor aircraft reported that the approaching formation was Japanese and that they had downed two of the intruders. Shortly thereafter, two kamikazes struck the *Saratoga* and set her on fire. These fires had barely been put out when another Japanese plane grazed the flight deck and crashed overboard, its bomb blowing a hole in the flight deck. Nevertheless, shortly after 2000, the *Saratoga* once again was able to recover planes. Losses were 123 killed and missing and 192 wounded; in addition, the carrier lost 36 planes by burning and jettisoning, and six by water landings in the choppy seas. The *Saratoga*, once her fires had been extinguished, limped back to Pearl Harbor for repairs.

Another carrier, the *Bismarck Sea*, was in position 20 miles east of Iwo when, shortly before 1900, a kamikaze hit the ship square abeam. Gassed planes on board caught fire and ammunition exploded in the rapidly spreading blaze. As a 22-knot wind fanned the fires, it became necessary to abandon ship. Following a tremendous explosion, the *Bismarck Sea* turned over and sank. Many of the men who had gone overboard were picked up by the escort vessels; others succumbed to the cold waters. Altogether, 218 men of the *Bismarck Sea* were lost, out of a crew of 943 officers and men.

Other ships attacked by the kamikazes were the escort carrier *Lunga Point*, which fought off four torpedo bombers without loss; the net tender *Keokuk*, set afire, losing

17 men killed and 44 wounded; and LST 477, carrying artillery for the 3d Marine Division. The LST was struck a glancing blow by a kamikaze, which failed to do any major damage. None of the Japanese pilots survived the attack.

As 21 February came to an end, the hospital ship *Samaritan* sailed from Iwo Jima to Guam. Her cargo consisted of 623 seriously wounded Marines. The care given to these wounded was in stark contrast to the little attention the Japanese received from their own medical personnel. Japanese defense plans for Iwo Jima had made no provision for the evacuation of any wounded. Those Japanese who were wounded either crawled back or were carried to aid stations behind the lines. There, they might be placed in niches in the walls of tunnels, where their comrades would look after them as best they could. Some of the Japanese bound up their wounds and remained with their units, either to fight again if physically able or else perform other work behind the lines.

For the Marines dug in around the base of Mount Suribachi, another restless night was in the offing. The rain was still coming down, increasing their discomfort. Some of the Japanese inside the mountain were moving around and talking, but no *banzai* charge developed. Enemy artillery and mortar fire continued to fall in the area, though its effect was not as deadly as during the preceding night. The enemy confined himself to two attempts at infiltrating the American lines in the 28th Marines sector. Men of the regiment's 81mm mortar platoon killed some 60 Japanese in front of 2/28 during one of these efforts. Company C accounted for 28 more who, in accordance with Colonel Atsuchi's final orders, attempted to infiltrate north along the western beaches.

The following morning, 22 February, began with all the earmarks of a miserable day. The cold, hard rain had turned Iwo's loose soil and cinders into a sloshy gumbo. At 0800 the enemy scored a mortar hit on the regimental CP which killed the regimental surgeon, Lieutenant Commander Daniel J. McCarthy. The rain, driven from the southeast by a strong wind, not only caused great discomfort to the Marines, but the wet volcanic ash clogged automatic weapons, which could fire only single rounds. Nevertheless, the 28th Marines continued their attack at the foot of Mount Suribachi. Because of the bad weather and the Marines' proximity to the mountain, no air support was available, and artillery support was severely curtailed. Once again, it became the task of individual Marines to pick a path through the rubble, blasting and burning their way through the enemy defenses. The Japanese within the mountain and isolated pillboxes around the base still resisted with heavy mortar and small arms fire.

Once again, seven tanks of Company C, 5th Tank Battalion, supported the attack of the 28th Marines. Two were attached to 2/28 to work around the east side of Suribachi; three were sent to 1/28 to advance around the right, and two remained in support of 3/28 in the center. The heavy rainfall that continued throughout the day severely limited the operation of the tanks. At one time during the afternoon, the rain became so heavy that the crews, unable to see where they were going, had to be guided by men on foot.

Poor weather and enemy resistance to the contrary, 22 February marked the day on which Mount Suribachi was neutralized and surrounded. The men of 3/28 cleared out the base of the north face of the volcano during the day and sent a patrol around the west coast down to Tobiishi Point, Iwo Jima's southernmost extremity. There, the men of 3/28 encountered a patrol from 2/28 which had advanced down the east coast. By 1630, the 28th Marines halted operations for the day. One sergeant of

Company I who scrambled part way up the north face of Mount Suribachi reported seeing no Japanese. He asked whether he should continue up the mountain, but Colonel Liversedge felt that it was too late in the day, and the final advance to seize the mountain was delayed until the following morning.

By the end of D plus 3, the fight for Mount Suribachi was virtually over. Substantial numbers of the enemy, perhaps 300 in all, still occupied caves and other places of concealment within the volcano. But in the course of the 28th Marines' advance, hundreds of the enemy had been killed, and the pernicious power of the fortress was now broken. As Marines, shivering from the cold and wetness, huddled at the foot of Suribachi, the enemy survivors within debated whether they should stay or attempt to fight their way north. Only half of them decided to remain and fight it out. The remainder crawled out into the murky darkness and tried to make their way north through the American lines. Most of them fell victim to accurate fire from alert Marines, determined to halt any infiltration. About 20 of the enemy made it across the lines and reached General Kuribayashi's headquarters near Motoyama in the northern part of the island where they were reassigned.

For the Marine survivors of the drive to Mount Suribachi, the final act in the drama was about to open. The time had come to start climbing. On the evening prior to that venture, no one could guess what the following day would bring.

Seizing the Heights

Friday, 23 February, marked the day on which the Marines climbed to the top of the craggy 550-foot rim of Mount Suribachi. The steep slopes of the mountain fortress all but precluded a converging ascent from various directions. When it was discovered that the only practical route to the crater lay up the north face of the mountain, in the zone of the 2d Battalion, Lieutenant Colonel Johnson became directly involved in planning the climb. The battalion commander's decision was to send several small reconnaissance patrols to the top before ordering a platoon-size combat patrol to make the ascent.

At 0800, Sergeant Sherman B. Watson of Company F led a four-man patrol up the mountain. On top of Suribachi this patrol encountered a battery of heavy machine guns with ammunition stacked alongside around the rim of the crater. There was no sign of the enemy, The bald, gray rock was now surrounded by silence; the caves and underground chambers seemed devoid of life. Uprooted blockhouses and pillboxes offered mute testimony to the destructive power of the heavy naval guns; most of the tunnels on the slopes were closed and smoking. Unaccustomed to the silence, the men wondered why they drew no fire. They slid and scrambled down Suribachi to report to the battalion commander.

Even before the first reconnaissance patrol returned from its climb, Lieutenant Colonel Johnson dispatched two three-man patrols from Companies D and F at 0900 to reconnoiter other suitable routes up the mountain and probe for enemy resistance. None drew any fire. While the small reconnaissance patrols were still executing their mission, Colonel Johnson assembled the combat patrol that was slated to seize Mount Suribachi in force and hoist the American colors over the mountain. The 3d Platoon, Company E, was selected for this mission. The Company executive officer, 1st Lieutenant Harold G. Schrier, led the patrol. A member of the patrol was to recall later: "The 25 men of the 3d Platoon were by this time very dirty and very tired. They no longer looked nor felt like crack combat troops. Although they had just had a relatively free day, their rest had been marred by a chilling rain. They hardly yearned for the distinction of being the first Marines to tackle the volcano. But the colonel didn't bother to ask them how they felt about it."

Lieutenant Schrier assembled the platoon at 0800 and bolstered its thin ranks with other men of Company E until it totalled 40 men. Before starting the ascent, he led the men back around the base of Suribachi to battalion headquarters just northeast of the base. Johnson's final orders were simple and to the point: the patrol was to climb to the summit, secure the crater, and raise the flag. As the patrol prepared to move out, the battalion commander handed Schrier a folded American flag that had been brought ashore by the battalion adjutant, 1st Lieutenant George G. Wells. The flag, measuring 54 by 28 inches, had been obtained from the *Missoula*, the transport that had carried 2/28 from its staging area to Iwo Jima.

Forming an irregular column, the patrol headed straight for the base of Suribachi. They moved at a brisk pace at first. When the route turned steep and the going became more difficult, the patrol leader dispatched flankers to guard the vulnerable column against surprise attack. The men, heavily burdened with weapons and ammunition, climbed slowly, stopping occasionally to catch their breath. At times, the route became so steep that they moved upward on their hands and knees. Along the way, they passed close to several cave entrances, but the caves appeared deserted and no resistance developed. The only Japanese encountered were the dead. Friendly eyes were observing the patrol's laborious ascent: Marines near the northeast base of Suribachi and men of the fleet, who, cognizant of the drama unfolding before them, were watching through binoculars.

Higher and higher the patrol picked its way, avoiding heavily mined trails and keeping men out on the flanks to thwart any enemy ambush. Within half an hour after leaving battalion headquarters, the patrol arrived at the rim of the crater. There, Schrier called a halt while he sized up the situation. He spotted two or three battered gun emplacements and several cave entrances, but no sign of the enemy. He signalled the men to start filing over the rim. As the patrol entered the crater, the men fanned out and took up positions just inside the rim. They were tensed for action, but the caves along the rim and the yawning floor below remained silent.

While half the patrol deployed around the rim, the remainder pressed into the crater to probe for resistance. Part of their mission had been executed. It now remained for them to locate something to serve as a flagpole. Scouting along the rim of the crater, a couple of men located a 20-foot section of pipe. Lashing the flag to one end, they thrust the other into soft ground near the north rim. At 1020, the Stars and Stripes rose over the highest point of the island, where it fluttered in a brisk wind. Small though it was, the flag was clearly visible from land and sea, proof that Suribachi had fallen.

Far below, on the sandy terraces and in foxholes, still exposed to deadly fire from enemy artillery and mortars in the north of Iwo Jima, exhausted and unshaven men openly wept, while others slapped each other on the back and shouted. Out at sea, ships' whistles, horns, and bells rang out in jubilation. On deck of the hospital ship *Solace*, badly wounded Marines raised themselves on their elbows to look up at the tiny speck on the summit.

Not far from the CP of the 28th Marines, a group of men stood on the beach near the surf. They had just stepped ashore from a Higgins boat to become fascinated spectators of the most dramatic moment of the Iwo operation. Deeply moved by the sight was Secretary of the Navy Forrestal, accompanied by General Holland Smith and an assortment of Navy and Army personnel including two admirals. Turning towards General Smith, Forrestal said gravely: "Holland, the raising of that flag on Suribachi means a Marine Corps for the next 500 years."

Atop the mountain, the men of Lieutenant Schrier's patrol had little time for rejoicing. The sight of the American flag waving over Suribachi was too much for the remnants of Colonel Atsuchi's garrison to take lying down. Sergeant Louis R. Lowery, a Marine photographer, had just clicked the shutter of his camera, taking pictures of the flag raising on the rim of the crater, when two Japanese charged out from a cave near the summit. One of the Japanese, running towards the flag and waving his sword was promptly shot down. The other heaved a hand grenade at the Marine photographer who escaped injury or death by vaulting over the rim and sliding about 50 feet down the mountain before his fall was broken. His camera was smashed, but the negatives inside remained safe, The second Japanese was also killed. Other Japanese, frenzied by the sight of the American flag, started to emerge from caves near the crater and met the same fate.

Three hours later, a larger flag, almost twice the size of the first one, was raised over Mount Suribachi. It was the raising of this second flag, obtained from LST 779, that resulted in photographer Joe Rosenthal's picture of the flag raising that became perhaps the most famous photograph of World War II and that has since served as an inspiration to countless Americans.

Proportionate to the elation of Americans at the fall of Suribachi, the Japanese on Iwo Jima and elsewhere felt great consternation. Upon receiving the news of the fall of the volcano, one Japanese staff officer, once himself stationed on Iwo, but subsequently reassigned to Chichi Jima, later recalled that "he was bursting with emotion." Equally shocking to this officer was the fact that the mountain fortress had fallen in only three days. According to the Japanese timetable, Suribachi was to have been held for at least two weeks.

For the remainder of the afternoon, 2/28 continued to mop up on and around Mount Suribachi. Marines annihilated enemy snipers and, together with the engineers, blasted shut a large number of cave entrances. Many Japanese were sealed in and though undoubtedly some later managed to dig their way out of these tombs, an unknown number succumbed from their wounds or were asphyxiated. A few Japanese who survived the fall of Suribachi managed to get back to their own lines in the northern part of Iwo where they faced yet another ordeal. As the survivors from Suribachi entered the Japanese lines, the following incident took place, to be remembered long after by a Japanese petty officer who survived the operation: "I remember a very dramatic scene I saw February 24, 1945. A Navy lieutenant, whose name I don't recollect, and several of his men – all blood stained wearing torn uniforms, reached the command post and said they broke through the enemy encirclement of Suribachi and managed to reach the command post for a report. When I showed the lieutenant up to Captain Inouye's desk, Inouye became furious and bellowed: 'Why did you come, you son of a bitch? Wasn't your assignment to hold that fortress at any cost? Shame on you to come here. Shame, shame, shame! Don't you know what shame is? I tell you that you are a coward and deserter!' His aides tried to calm the Captain down. But Inouye was madder and howling more profanity, and finally said: 'Under any military regulations, a deserter is executed summarily. I shall condescend myself to behead you.'

"So the Captain drew his sword and pulled it up. The wounded lieutenant knelt down silent, immobile. Presently, the aids clung to the captain and physically wrested his sword away. Inouye burst into tears, mumbling: 'Ugh, ugh, Suribachi's fallen! Suribachi's fallen!' The aides took the lieutenant away to the sick bay for first aid treatment."

While the reinforced platoon of Company E scaled Suribachi, part of the same company patrolled down around the eastern end of the island until it made contact with elements of 1/28 advancing down the west side. Temporary contact between patrols in this area had already been made on the previous day. The two patrols met near Tobiishi Point at 1015, just a few minutes before the first flag raising. There was no enemy resistance, though a mine killed two men of 1/28.

To garrison the summit of Mount Suribachi during the coming night, 40 men from Company E remained on the crest; the rest of the regiment occupied positions around the base of the mountain. During the night, 122 Japanese were killed trying to infiltrate the American lines. Many of them had demolitions tied to their bodies and probably were trying to blow up Marine command posts and artillery positions along with themselves.

During one predawn breakthrough attempt early on 24 February, 30 grenade-throwing Japanese assaulted the command post and aid station of 1/28. Personnel of battalion headquarters, corpsmen included, used whatever weapons were at hand to kill the infiltrators while protecting wounded Marines who lay helpless on stretchers amidst the turmoil.

There were to be no easy victories on Iwo Jima, and the cost of seizing Mount Suribachi was high. The operation from D plus 1 to D plus 4 cost the 28th Marines 519 casualties. Of these, 3 officers and 112 men were killed and 21 officers and 354 men were wounded. These figures do not include the 385 casualties sustained by the regiment on D-Day.

It proved impossible to obtain an accurate figure of Japanese killed on and around Suribachi, though 1,231 enemy were counted and hundreds more were sealed inside caves and blockhouses. Except for a handful of men that succeeded in getting through to northern Iwo, the entire garrison of Mount Suribachi was virtually killed to a man. In the days following the fall of the fortress, an occasional Japanese might succeed in digging his way out of a cave or tunnel that had been blasted shut, only to be shot by the alert Marines stationed on and around the mountain for the purpose.

Working together with the infantry, members of the 5th Engineer Battalion had destroyed 165 concrete pillboxes and blockhouses, some with walls 10 feet thick. They had blasted 15 strong bunkers and naval gun positions; destroyed thousands of enemy shells, grenades and land mines; and had sealed 200 caves, some of them three stories high and equipped with heavy steel doors. In addition, the supporting troops evacuated several hundred wounded Marines and bulldozed 1,500 yards of roads and tank paths up to the crater.

Immediately after it was secured, Mount Suribachi was put to practical use. The 14th Marines rushed echo and flashranging equipment to the top in order to spot Japanese artillery and fortifications in the northern end of the island from this vantage point, which thus was turned into a vital observation post. Colonel Liversedge's regiment remained in corps reserve in the Suribachi area for the next five days, picking off occasional enemy survivors, salvaging arms and equipment, and training new replacements.

As vital and dramatic as the capture of Mount Suribachi was, it marked but one step in the conquest of the stubbornly defended island. A grim and deadly battle was being fought to the north. Few Marines at this stage suspected the strength of the enemy defenses and the cost to be exacted in advancing to the northern end of the island. For the Marines on Iwo, the capture of Suribachi marked the end of a beginning; for General Kuribayashi's well entrenched main force it was the beginning of the end.

Chapter 6. Drive to the North

Capture of Airfield No. 1

While the 28th Marines was engaged in the epic assault on Mount Suribachi during the first four days of the invasion, a bloody slugging match involving the main body of General Schmidt's VAC was developing to the north. The battalions in line for the offensive were, from west to east, 1/26, 3/27, 3/23, 2/24, 1/25, 2/25, and 3/25. Two companies of 1/24 were attached to the latter battalion. The seven battalions were deployed along a 4,000-yard front extending from the western shore just north of Mount Suribachi northeastward across the southern end of Airfield No. 1. From there, the line followed the eastern fringes of the field and then pivoted sharply to the east, meeting the coast at the East Boat Basin.

It had already become evident on D-Day that, despite extensive naval gunfire and air support, numerous enemy positions had survived the preliminary bombardment completely unscathed. At this juncture, the depth of the enemy defense system on the island was still a matter of conjecture. The dramatic drive of the 28th Marines towards Mount Suribachi had initially captured the limelight; but it was in the central and northern part of Iwo that General Kuribayashi had concentrated the bulk of his forces. The wily enemy commander had left nothing undone to make his defenses in the northern and central sectors impregnable. In this, he was aided by the topography of the island, for the entire area comprised a weird looking array of cliffs, ravines, gorges, crevices, and ledges. Jumbled rock, torn stubble of small trees, jagged ridges, and chasms sprawled about in a crazy pattern. Within this maze, the enemy sat deeply entrenched in hundreds of carefully constructed positions, ranging from blockhouses to bunkers, pillboxes, caves, and camouflaged tanks. All fields of fire were well integrated.

One of the reasons for the failure of American naval gunfire and aircraft to neutralize or destroy an appreciable number of enemy positions prior to the landings was the masterful use of camouflage by the enemy. So skillfully had the Japanese hidden their positions that American ships and aircraft failed to detect them. Even those that were spotted and became targets of American naval gunfire and bombs frequently escaped major destruction because of their structural strength.

In the northern part of Iwo Jima, just as in the south, the first night ashore proved to be a restless one. Damage and casualties to the 1/23 command post on Yellow 1, as well as the explosion of the 25th Marines ammunition dump during the early morning hours, have already been recounted. Elsewhere, it was a similar story. At 0230, about 500 Japanese formed in front of the 27th Marines but were dispersed by artillery fire from the 13th Marines. Shortly after 0700, the enemy scored a mortar hit squarely on the command post of 2/25 above Blue Beach 1. The battalion commander, Lieutenant Colonel Lewis C. Hudson, Jr., the executive officer, Major William P. Kaempfer, and the operations officer, Major Donald K. Ellis, were badly wounded. The commander of Company B, 4th Tank Battalion, who had stopped by to obtain further details about the impending attack, scheduled to be launched within the hour, was killed. The executive officer of 3/25, Lieutenant Colonel James Taul, took over the command of the 2d Battalion.

The initial objective of the assault on D plus 1 was to seize the O-1 Line extending eastward from Iwo's west coast to the southern tip of Airfield No. 2, whence it curved southward in the form of a horseshoe and continued generally east to the coast northeast of the East Boat Basin. In order to reach the O-1 Line, VAC units would have to complete the northward pivot from west to east, which had already begun on D-Day. Units along the left flank of VAC and those in the center were to sweep across Airfield No. 2 and straighten the sagging portions of the line until they had advanced generally abreast of the 25th Marines, with 1/24 attached, which occupied the hinge position on the right.

For many of the Marines preparing to jump off on the morning of D-plus 1, daylight brought with it a most depressing sight. At least one observer was to record: "It was not until the next morning, when Marines along the airfield could look back on the beach, that the full extent of our losses was apparent. The wreckage was indescribable. For two miles the debris was so thick that there were only a few places where landing craft could still get in. The wrecked hulks of scores of landing boats testified to one price we had paid to put our troops ashore. Tanks and halftracks lay crippled where they had bogged down in the coarse sand. Amphibian tractors, victims of mines and well-aimed shells, lay flopped on their backs. Cranes, brought ashore to unload cargo, tilted at insane angles, and bulldozers were smashed in their own roadways.

Packs, gas masks, rifles, and clothing, ripped and shattered by shell fragments, lay scattered across the beach. Toilet articles and even letters were strewn among the debris, as though war insisted on prying into the personal affairs of those it claimed.

And scattered amid the wreckage was death. An officer in charge of an LCT had been hit while trying to free his boat from the sand and was blown in half; a life preserver supported the trunk of his body in the water. Marines, killed on the beach, were partially buried under the sand as the tide came in. Perhaps a hand stretched rigidly out of the sand, and that was all.

In the face of all this death and destruction, the battle continued and, following an intensive artillery, naval gunfire, and air preparation, the VAC attack to the north jumped off as scheduled at 0830. Along the 1,000-yard front in the 5th Division zone of attack, Colonel Wornham committed 1/26 and 3/27 abreast, keeping 1/27 and 2/27 in reserve. General Rockey had designated the 26th Marines, less 1/26 which had been attached to RCT 27, as division reserve, standing by in positions near the southwestern tip of Airfield No. 1.

The advance of 1/26, commanded by Lieutenant Colonel Daniel C. Pollock, and 3/27, under Lieutenant Colonel Dorm J. Robertson, soon was seriously slowed down by numerous enemy pillboxes and land mines; even more deadly was the well-aimed enemy mortar and artillery fire and particularly a heavy concentration of air bursts from Japanese antiaircraft guns fired from their minimum angle of elevation. West of the airfield, Colonel Wornham's men had to move through relatively open terrain that offered neither cover nor concealment from an enemy who enjoyed both excellent observation and fields of fire. Supported by Companies A and B of the 5th Tank Battalion, the 5th Division Marines moved forward steadily, taking heavy losses as they advanced. At 1800, when Colonel Wornham ordered the two battalions to halt and consolidate, the advance had gained 800 yards. However, 1/26 on the left had to pull back about 200 yards to more favorable ground for night defense. As D plus 1 came to a close, the two 5th Division battalions dug in along an east-west line extending from the northwestern edge of Airfield No. 1 to the west coast. For the night, 2/27 backed up 1/26 while 1/27 dug in behind 3/27 to provide a defense in depth.

For the attack on D plus 1, the 4th Marine Division committed two regiments abreast. On the left of the division zone of attack, the 23d Marines, with 2/24 attached, jumped off at 0830 and almost immediately encountered intense enemy machine gun, mortar, and artillery fire. In attempting to pinpoint the source of this fire and silence it, Colonel Wensinger's men temporarily lost contact with Lanigan's 25th Marines. Even though the terrain in this area was unfavorable for the employment of armor, a reinforced platoon from Company C, 4th Tank Battalion was able to support the advance of the 23d Marines. By noon, an aggressive attack had carried past the northern fringes of Airfield No. 1. This thrust breached an important portion of the Japanese defensive system and at the same time reduced a number of well-concealed pillboxes and infantry strongpoints. The attacking Marines also had suffered severe casualties. Movement, both on the airfield flats and on the slopes from the beaches, was almost entirely under enemy observation, and the Japanese made the most of their favorable situation.

During the afternoon, the 23d Marines continued the advance. However, minefields and increasingly rough terrain all but precluded effective armored support. The enemy directed deadly rocket, artillery, and mortar fire against the advancing Marines, and after the morning's gains little more ground was taken for the remainder of the day. Altogether, in crossing the airfield, Colonel Wensinger's men had advanced roughly 500 yards. At 1630, the reserve of the 23d Marines, consisting of 1/23 and 2/23, moved forward to positions along the seaward edge of the airfield to form a strong, secondary line of defense. The 23d Marines linked up with the 27th Marines on the left and the 25th Marines on the right before nightfall.

The attack of Colonel Lanigan's 25th Marines on D plus 1 was to be carried out by three battalions abreast. On the left, 1/25 under Lieutenant Colonel Hollis U. Mustain, was to make the main effort; the 2d Battalion in the center, commanded by Lieutenant Colonel James Taul, was to seize the high ground directly to its front and, after taking it, give fire support to 1/25. On the extreme right flank, the attached 1/24 under Major Paul S. Treitel, was to remain in place until 1/25 and 2/25 could come abreast. Because of heavy casualties sustained on D-Day, 3/25 was pulled out of the lines and held in regimental reserve.

The 25th Marines jumped off on schedule. Tanks of Company B, 4th Tank Battalion, supported the attack, but the exceptionally rough terrain made this support practically worthless. In addition, each time that a tank reached a firing position, it immediately attracted accurate enemy mortar and artillery fire. Crossfire from enemy machine guns mounted in concealed emplacements, combined with a heavy volume of well-aimed rifle fire, seriously interfered with the advance of Colonel Lanigan's regiment and inflicted heavy casualties.

In discussing the advance on D plus 1, a survivor of the Iwo battle later was to remark: "There was no cover from enemy fire. Japs deep in reinforced concrete pillboxes laid down interlocking bands of fire that cut whole companies to ribbons. Camouflage hid all the enemy installations. The high ground on every side was honeycombed with layer after layer of Jap emplacements, blockhouses, dugouts, and observation posts. Their observation was perfect; whenever the Marines made a move, the Japs watched every step, and when the moment came, their mortars, rockets, machine guns, and artillery, long ago zeroed-in—would smother the area in a murderous blanket of fire. The counterbattery fire and preparatory barrages of Marine artillery and naval gunfire were often ineffective, for the Japs would merely retire to a lower level or inner cave and wait until the storm had passed. Then they would emerge and blast the advancing Marines."

The deadly effectiveness of the enemy fire was not limited to the front lines. At 1100, Japanese artillery scored a direct hit on the aid station of 1/25, killing six Navy corpsmen and wounding an additional seven. It was apparent that General Kuribayashi had so sited his artillery that all the beaches and routes into the interior of the island were covered. Japanese gunners could search out various supply dumps, evacuation stations, and command posts at will. Normally, LVTs had the task of bringing supplies to the front lines. In the zone of attack of the 25th Marines, however, even these versatile vehicles were unable to get through and work details from units in reserve had to manhandle critically needed materiel.

Colonel Lanigan's Marines continued to press the attack throughout the afternoon of D plus 1, but progress was woefully slow. At 1600, the exhausted men were cheered by the arrival of friendly aircraft which, it was hoped, might lend some impetus to the advance. This joy, however, soon, turned into terror when .50 caliber machine gun bullets, rockets, and bombs from a friendly air strike hit men of Company B, 1/24, standing upright on the southern slope of the quarry about 400 yards inland from the eastern shore. This strike, neither called for nor controlled by 1/24, was delivered without a preliminary run and placed on the front lines despite the fact that yellow frontline marking panels had been displayed prior to and during the attack. In consequence of this error, 1/24 suffered five killed and six wounded. As if attempting to advance under heavy enemy fire and being strafed, bombed, and rocketed by friendly aircraft were not enough, the hapless company also was shelled by naval gunfire and found friendly artillery registering on its positions. This misguided naval gunfire, consisting of two complete salvos fired by an unidentified cruiser, landed in the front line of 1/24 and resulted in approximately 90 casualties.

By 1800, 1/25 and 2/25 had made gains of 200-300 yards. The left flank of 1/25, on the other hand, had been unable to move at all throughout the day because of extremely heavy fire received from the left front in the zone of action of the 23d Marines. At 1800, orders were issued to all units to consolidate, dig in, and establish firm contact with each other.

As night descended over bitterly contested Iwo Jima on 20 February, the capture of Airfield No. 1 had been completed and the 4th Division front had advanced between 200 and 500 yards. For these gains, the Japanese had exacted a heavy price. As the second day ended, the 5th Marine Division had lost 1,500 men killed and wounded and the 4th Division about 2,000. The first prisoners, a total of three, had been taken during the day, but two of them died. A total of 630 enemy dead had been counted, but it was assumed that many others had been killed.

Early on D plus 1, General Schmidt had ordered the corps reserve, the 21st Marines, commanded by Colonel Hartnoll J. Withers, to boat and prepare to land on order. The regiment began debarking before noon, in rain and rough water. Dozens of men missed the drop into the bobbing boats and after they had been fished out, the boats went to the rendezvous area. There the LCVPs circled for six hours, the Marines cold, wet, and miserable. The congestion at the beaches, which was steadily increasing, combined with a rising surf that made landing conditions hazardous, precluded their landing. In the end, General Schmidt ordered the regiment back to its transports to be landed later when conditions had improved.

At the same time, on D plus 1, there was a desperate need for artillery, whose landing could not be postponed. As a result, the 4th Marine Division landed the 3d and 4th Battalions of the 14th Marines during the day. Shortly after 1000, 3/14 had launched all of its DUKWs, but the landing was delayed by enemy fire. Finally, in midafternoon, the amphibian trucks carrying 3/14 began to land over the southernmost portion of Yellow 1. The battalion's 105mm howitzers moved into positions prepared by the 3/14 reconnaissance party just inland from the boundary separating Yellow 1 and Red 2. Around 1730, the howitzers opened fire and reinforced the fires of the 1st Battalion of the division artillery.

The landing of the 105s of 4/14 turned into a disaster. The first DUKW to emerge from LST 1032 remained afloat only for a moment. Then waves surged over the side, the engine stopped, and the DUKW sank, taking the 105 down with it. Seven more DUKWs waddled out of the LST and sank in succession. As a result, a total of eight 105s were lost, as well as a dozen officers and men. It was subsequently determined that motor failure of the DUKWs was caused by water in the gasoline, and by insufficient freeboard resulting from extremely heavy loads and choppy water. Thus, 4/14 had lost 8 out of 12 howitzers before firing a round on Iwo Jima.

The disaster for Lieutenant Colonel Youngdale's battalion did not end here. The remaining four DUKWs headed for the beach late in the evening and two of them broached at the surf line while attempting to go ashore at 2230. Out of a dozen DUKWs and howitzers, only two finally made it to shore. The guns, having gone into position, began firing northward into the inky darkness.

In order to offset the critical artillery shortage, some of the big 155mm howitzers also were ordered to land. In late afternoon, LST 779 forced its way through the wreckage littering Red Beach 1 and discharged Battery C of the 2d 155mm Howitzer Battalion. Despite extremely difficult beach conditions, the four howitzers were hauled up the steep bluffs by tractors and were in position by 1840 in the 5th Marine Division sector near the west coast. The two remaining batteries of Major Earl J. Rowse's battalion were not landed for another two and four days respectively. Even those artillery battalions that did make it ashore encountered unusual problems from the very outset. Before the 28th Marines put the Japanese artillery on Mount Suribachi out of action, artillerymen firing to the north received enemy fire from the south that proved more troublesome than enemy rounds from the front.

Advance Towards the O-1 Line

At the cost of heavy casualties, the Marines at the end of D plus 1 controlled nearly one-third of Iwo Jima and occupied a two mile-wide beachhead extending along the landing area and 2,000 yards up the southwest coast. Motoyama Airfield No. 1 was completely in American hands. Marine lines stretched in an east-west direction from the west coast opposite the end of the airstrip, past the end of the airfield, with a slight curve to the quarry. Just beyond that point the line curved at right angles to face east with the right flank resting on the shore along the ridge facing the East Boat Basin. The O-1 Line had not yet been reached at any point, but positions were well knit and more artillery and serviceable tanks were available for support. Even though enemy resistance on 20 February was even heavier than that encountered on D-Day, both Marine divisions were holding the ground they had seized.

Beach conditions remained extremely difficult throughout the day, both because of a high surf and the continuous enemy artillery fire. The shore party battalions were raked by artillery, mortar, and small arms fire as they desperately attempted to clear the beaches and unload incoming landing craft. They stacked supplies well above the high-water mark, but gear piled up there faster than it could be moved inland. In order to cope with this crisis, the entire logistical plan of establishing shore-party dumps had to be abandoned. Without pausing on the beaches, incoming amtracs – the only vehicles that could climb the terraces and reach firm ground unassisted – waddled up the slopes into the front lines, where they delivered ammunition, rations, and water directly to the combat units. The tractors freed weapons and vehicles that had bogged down and hauled supply-laden DUKWs over the terraces, thus enabling the latter vehicles to move supplies right up to the front lines. In addition to the vehicles shuttling back and forth between the beaches and the lines, Marine working parties handcarried ammunition forward in order to alleviate critical shortages.

In view of the overall situation, it became apparent to Generals Smith and Schmidt at the close of D plus 1, that the strength of enemy resistance dictated the necessity of employing the 3d Marine Division, still afloat, before long. The requirement of furnishing food and ammunition to an additional 20,000 Marines would impose an added strain on available beach facilities, but the dwindling combat strength of the two Marine divisions already on the island left no other choice. As a result, the 21st Marines of the 3d Marine Division were again ordered to land on D plus 2, to be placed at the disposal of General Cates.

The night of 20-21 February was punctuated by loud explosions as the Japanese exchanged artillery fire with the Americans. At the same time, U.S. Navy gunfire support ships and LCIs mounting 4.2-inch mortars delivered counterbattery and harassing fire. Early in the evening, around 2000, a group of Japanese was observed massing opposite the 27th Marines. Immediate fire by the 13th Marines and attached corps artillery killed a number of the enemy and dispersed the rest. Shortly before 0500, about 100 Japanese attempted to pierce the lines of the 4th Marine Division in the 1/25 sector, but were driven off with heavy losses.

As 21 February dawned, 12 destroyers, 2 cruisers, 68 aircraft, and 33 howitzers took turns at battering the enemy-held portion of Iwo before VAC resumed the attack on D plus 2. At 0810, both the 4th and 5th Marine Divisions jumped off. On the left flank of VAC, the 27th Marines met immediate and violent resistance from the enemy's main defensive positions, which consisted of a belt of caves and concrete-and-steel emplacements. This defense system had a depth of a mile and a half and extended from the west coast to the east coast of Iwo. It featured innumerable pillboxes and around 1,500 caves.

The terrain in the 27th Marines' zone of advance was suitable for the employment of armor; elements of the 5th Tank Battalion moved forward just ahead of the infantry. By 1340, 1/26 on the left and 3/27 on the right had advanced nearly 1,000 yards and had reached a point just south of the O-1 Line. Because of the relative speed of the advance and heavy enemy shelling, a sizable gap had developed by this time between the 4th and 5th Marine Divisions. Company B, 1/27 was committed from regimental reserve to fill this gap between 3/27 and the 23d Marines. Under continuous enemy fire, the 5th Marine Division spent the remainder of the afternoon reorganizing, evacuating casualties, and consolidating its lines. In the course of the afternoon, General Rockey and his staff came ashore and established their headquarters near the southern end of Airfield No. 1.

At the same time that the 5th Marine Division jumped off on D plus 2, the 23d and 25th Marines continued their attack. The 23d, with 2/23 on the left and 2/24 on the right, slowly pushed forward with 1/23 and 2/23 following at a 600-yard interval. Almost immediately, the advancing Marines encountered severe mortar, machine gun, and artillery fire, as well as a number of minefields. The advance through the minefield and against numerous pillboxes was very time-consuming and costly. Engineer units went forward to remove the mines. The only significant advance made was on the left flank in the 23d Marines zone of advance, where slightly defiladed areas permitted local and restricted envelopment. But even the progress of the 23d Marines averaged only slightly more than 100 yards during the entire day. After reestablishing contact with the 27th Marines on its left, the 23d dug in for the night shortly before 1800.

On the extreme right, the 25th Marines attacked with 1/25, 2/25, and 1/24 in line, and 3/25 in reserve. Even though the enemy had laid minefields in front of the 25th Marines, the terrain here was so rocky and irregular that the enemy had not been able to mine all avenues of approach. Tanks of Company A, 4th Tank Battalion, supported the advance of 1/25 and 2/25, while tanks of Company B fired on pillboxes and dugouts on the cliff facing 1/24, driving the enemy from the heights of the quarry and cliff areas. Howitzers of 1/14 placed counterbattery and supporting fire across the regimental front. Resistance in the center of the regimental zone gradually weakened and fair progress was made on the right along the shore of the East Boat Basin. Altogether, the 25th Marines gained from 50-300 yards in the course of the morning. Casualties were heavy throughout; at 1000, while checking his frontline positions, Lieutenant Colonel Hollis U. Mustain, commanding 1/25, was killed by enemy shellfire. The battalion executive officer, Major Fenton J. Mee, assumed command.

The irregular advance of units over difficult terrain caused a serious gap to develop between the 1st and 2d Battalions, 25th Marines; in midafternoon Colonel Lanigan committed his 3d Battalion between the two. Since all units were under heavy enemy fire, 3/25 encountered major difficulty in moving into the line. By 1700, the move had been accomplished and the regiment consolidated for the night. Similarly, in order to fill a sizable gap between the right flank of the 5th Marine Division and the left flank of the 4th, 1/27 was moved into position along the 5th Division's right flank. Lines of General Rockey's division had to be extended about 400 yards into the 4th Division zone of attack.

Throughout the day, the two-divisional advance towards Airfield No. 2 received effective air and naval gunfire support. More than 800 aircraft flew direct support missions with a total of 32 strikes carried out by 14-20 planes each. Eleven destroyers stood by offshore to provide direct support and illuminating fires for VAC; 1 destroyer, 2 LCI mortar support units, and 2 cruisers fired deep support missions. Naval gunfire and artillery air spotters continued to use carrier-based aircraft, since Airfield No. 1 was still unable to accommodate VMO units.

A pressing need for reinforcements made it necessary to land more troops on Iwo as soon as possible. Improved beach and landing conditions on the morning of D plus 2 finally permitted the 21st Marines of the 3d Marine Division to come ashore. The regiment, commanded by Colonel Hartnoll J. Withers, was ordered to land at 1130 over the Yellow Beaches; it was to be attached to the 4th Marine Division to assist in the capture of Airfield No. 2. Colonel Withers landed his battalions throughout the afternoon of 21 February. Despite a heavy surf, the regiment did not incur any casualties and by 1800 all three battalions and the regimental command post were ashore. After being attached to the 4th Marine Division, RCT 21 assembled near the edge of Airfield No. 1.

Shortly after noon, the assistant commander of the 4th Marine Division, Brigadier General Hart, also went ashore in order to report on beach conditions and select an appropriate site for the division command post. Finding the beaches under heavy fire and littered with the debris of the invasion, General Hart recommended that division headquarters remain afloat at least until 22 February. The assistant division commander also recommended, after consultation with the regimental commanders, that the 21st Marines, instead of relieving the 25th Marines as previously planned, would relieve the 23d Marines on D plus 3. His recommendation was approved.

As 21 February drew to a close, VAC held a very irregular line which passed between the two airfields. When units consolidated their positions for the night, a total of eight battalions was facing the enemy across the island. The slow Marine advance during D plus 2 had forced the Japanese back yard by yard. Once again, for the gains made in the course of the day, VAC Marines had paid with heavy casualties. During the first 58 hours ashore, the landing force had sustained more than 4,500 casualties, and combat efficiency of the 4th Marine Division had been reduced to 68 percent.

The night from 21-22 February proved to be a bad one for men of the landing force, who felt extremely uncomfortable in the cold drizzle. Within the overall scope of General Kuribayashi's prohibition of any major *banzai* charges, the Japanese did all within their power to make their unwanted guests as miserable as possible.

At dusk, enemy aircraft attacked American shipping offshore and scored hits on the outer ring of the warships surrounding Iwo Jima. Taking advantage of the commotion resulting from the sudden air attack, the enemy executed local counterattacks and infiltration against both the 4th and 5th Divisions. Along the left front of VAC, an enemy counterattack in undetermined strength hit the 27th Marines at 2100. No penetration resulted from this attack, which was stopped within the hour. At 0245, the exhausted men of Colonel Wornham's regiment repulsed an attempted infiltration. An hour later, the enemy tried his luck once again, and at 0400, RCT 27 reported 800 enemy massing in front of its lines. As the long night finally ended, the regiment's lines were still intact, though an undetermined number of the enemy had managed to infiltrate.

It also proved to be a restless night for Marines of the 4th Division. Shortly before midnight, an enemy force of about 200 men massed on Airfield No. 2 and headed for the lines of 3/23. Before this attack could get organized, the enemy was hit by naval gunfire and artillery and was forced to withdraw.

During the long night, the 25th Marines reported that an enemy aircraft had bombed Blue Beach behind its lines. Almost as steady as the rain was the volume of enemy mortar and artillery fire that covered the Marine front lines, beaches, and rear areas throughout the night.

D plus 3 was, if anything, even worse than the three days that had preceded it. A cold, heavy rain pelted the island, coating Marines and their weapons with a sort of grayish paste on top of the layer of volcanic ash they had already acquired. The front lines of VAC, on the morning of 22 February, bent back in the form of a horseshoe in the center of the 3,400-yard line, where elements of the 23d Marines still were 1,200 yards short of the O-1 Line. Fatigue and heavy casualties both had left their imprint on the men in the lines, and the three days and nights of incessant, nerve-shattering action were beginning to have an adverse effect on combat efficiency. Without rest or sleep, subsisting solely on a diet of K rations and water, occasionally supplemented by unheated C rations, the men were beginning to show a marked drop in morale.

In order to provide added impetus for the attack on this fourth day of the operation, both Generals Rockey and Cates decided to relieve some of the frontline units, notably the 23d and 27th Marines. Along the left flank of VAC, the 26th Marines under Colonel Chester B. Graham moved out at daybreak with the mission of relieving the 27th Marines and continuing the attack to the north. Once RCT 26 had passed the lines, 1/26, which previously had been attached to RCT 27, was to revert to its parent regiment. The 27th Marines reserve, 2/27, would become attached to the 26th Marines.

At 0500 the 21st Marines prepared to relieve RCT 23 with the attached 2/24. Upon being relieved, the 23d Marines, less two mortar platoons, was to be held in VAC reserve near the northeastern edge of Airfield No. 1. The mortar platoons were to remain in position to support the attack of RCT 21. The 25th Marines, with 1/24 attached, was to remain on the 4th Division right, while the 24th Marines, less 1/24, would continue in division reserve.

The relief of the 27th Marines took place in a heavy downpour of rain, which turned the ground into gumbo. Mortar fire, coming from the higher ground ahead and in the center of the island, fell as steadily as the rain, and both combined to create confusion and disruption. The 26th Marines, with 2/27 attached, passed through the lines of the 27th Marines with the mission of attacking to the northeast, following the western contour of the island. At the same time to the right, the 21st Marines moved in on the left of the 4th Marine Division.

The zone of attack of the 5th Division extended from the western beaches to a formidable terrain obstacle which ran from northeast to southwest down the west center of the island, curving west across the division's front near Airfield No. 2. This obstacle was a bluff almost 100 feet high, whose slopes dropped almost vertically towards the American lines. The high ground above the bluff provided the enemy with perfect observation into the division area and enabled him to effectively block any advance from both the front and the right flank.

At 0835, following preparatory naval gunfire and air strikes, both divisions jumped off. In the zone of attack of the 5th Marine Division the 26th Marines attacked with three battalions in the line. Almost immediately, the advancing Marines drew heavy fire from the front and right flank. Enemy shells and bullets were no respecters of rank; around 0940, Lieutenant Colonel Tom M. Trotti, commanding 3/26, and his operations officer, Major William R. Day, were killed by a mortar shell. Captain Richard M. Cook, commanding Company G, took over until noon, at which time Major Richard Fagan, the division inspector, assumed command. Despite heavy losses, the 26th advanced for about 400 yards. In the course of the day, the weather turned from bad to worse. Rain was falling in torrents and visibility became extremely poor. Because of the heavy rain, no air support could be made available. The poor weather even handicapped the tanks, whose drivers could see but a few yards ahead.

During the afternoon it became apparent that the attack by 3d Division Marines against the bluff itself had stalled, leaving the 26th Marines exposed to heavy fire from the front, the right flank, and the right rear. In addition, the Japanese were beginning to launch several thrusts against the regiment's left flank and center. As if to mock Colonel Graham's drenched and dispirited Marines, Japanese artillery and mortars on the bluff directed heavy fire into the 26th Marines' lines. At 1400, the exhausted and severely mauled Marines were forced to relinquish the 400-yard gain they had made earlier in the day and pulled back to the line of departure. Japanese mortar and artillery fire harassed the men for the remainder of the afternoon during the withdrawal and continued after the Marines had occupied defensive positions for the night.

In the sector occupied by the 4th Marine Division, things had gone little better during D plus 3. At 0500, the 21st Marines began the relief of the 23d. The newly arrived 3d Division Marines faced very rough going from the outset. In the heavy downpour and continuous enemy fire, the relief of the 23d Marines required nearly six hours. Even before the relief was completed, Colonel Withers committed his 1st and 2d Battalions, commanded by Lieutenant Colonel Marlowe C. Williams and Lieutenant Colonel Lowell E. English, respectively, against an intricate network of mutually supporting pillboxes on the high ground between the two airfields. The 3d Battalion, under Lieutenant Colonel Wendell H. Duplantis, remained in reserve.

As the 21st Marines advanced northward, with 1/21 on the right and 2/21 on the left, it had to push its attack uphill against mutually supporting pillboxes and bunkers with mined approaches. These pillboxes were well protected on the flanks and only direct hits by large caliber weapons appeared to have any effect on them. In the taxiways between the airfields, bunkers blocked the advance, and the area adjoining the runways of Airfield No. 2 was dotted with pillboxes that were covered with sand and often protruded only a foot or so above the ground. This was the beginning of the enemy main line of resistance. The restricted nature of the area and the excellent defensive system precluded any maneuver but a frontal assault.

Bad weather and a well-entrenched enemy who took full advantage of the terrain with prearranged fire, presented the 21st Marines with an exceedingly brutal introduction to Iwo Jima. By afternoon of D plus 3, 2/21 had advanced 250 yards in places; 1/21 had gained about 50 yards. Casualties had been out of all proportion to the gains made. Lieutenant Colonel Williams was wounded by a mortar shell but refused evacuation until nightfall, at which time he turned command of 1/21 over to the battalion executive officer, Major Clay M. Murray. At about 1700, the attack halted for the day and all units began to prepare positions for the night.

To the right of the 21st Marines, the 25th, with three battalions and the attached 1/24 in the line, was to have attacked on D plus 3 in order to straighten its regimental front in conjunction with the advance of the 21st Marines. Once the lines had been straightened out, both the 21st and 25th Marines were to launch a coordinated drive to the north to seize the O-1 Line. Failure of the 21st Marines to make any sizable gains had an adverse effect on operations of the 25th Marines, which was unable to launch a full-scale attack. Nevertheless, in the course of the morning, 1/25 advanced about 200 yards, only to find its left flank completely exposed. As a result, the advance had to be halted until the battalion could tie in firmly with the 21st Marines. In the center of the 25th Marines line, the 3d and 2d Battalions found themselves marking time. The only cheerful note for the day was sounded when 3/25 requested and received rocket support against a hill some 800 yards northwest of the quarry. Two salvoes fired against enemy positions on this hill drove about 200 Japanese from their emplacements. Caught out in the open by well-placed machine guns of 3/25, a large part of the enemy force was wiped out.

Around 1530, the Japanese struck back. While leaving his forward observation post, Lieutenant Colonel Chambers was severely wounded by enemy machine gun fire, when a bullet struck his left collarbone. Since Lieutenant Colonel James Taul, the battalion executive officer, had assumed command of 2/25 on 20 February, when the commander of 2/25 had been wounded and evacuated, Captain James C. Headley assumed command of 3/25.

The 2d Battalion of the 25th Marines, meanwhile, remained largely stationary during the day. Even so, it took its share of casualties. In midmorning, the Japanese laid a heavy and accurate mortar barrage on the battalion lines; an attempted enemy counterattack was quickly smashed. At 1830, Japanese were observed moving towards the battalion lines. Before an attack could get under way, infantry heavy weapons fire and artillery support from the 14th Marines dispersed the Japanese.

At the right end of the VAC lines, 1/24 spent most of the day in mopping up along the east coast above the landing beaches. Major Treitel's men blasted caves and pillboxes in an attempt to reduce the heavy enemy mortar and sniper fire originating in the bluffs around the quarry. In its operations during D plus 3, the battalion fared better than the 25th Marines on its left and casualties were comparatively light. At 1700, the battalion consolidated its positions and established contact between units.

The ferocious battle raging between the airfields took its toll not only of men but also materiel. Thus, at the end of D plus 3, the 4th Tank Battalion reported that 11 of its tanks had been destroyed and 8 were under repair, leaving 28 operational. The 5th Tank Battalion reported 34 tanks operational, 4 under repair, and 13 destroyed.

Even though the advance towards the north of Iwo had made little headway during 22 February, the command organization and activities on the Iwo beaches became somewhat better coordinated. Headquarters of the 9th Naval Construction Brigade, commanded by Captain Robert C. Johnson, CEC, USN, was set up ashore, and initial work was started on preparing Iwo to serve as a giant aircraft carrier. In the course of the day, burials began in the Fourth Division cemetery halfway between Yellow 1 and Airfield No. 2.

Burials in the 5th Division cemetery, located just south of the airfield, had already commenced during the afternoon of D plus l. Provision was made for those Marines who died on board ship to be buried at sea, provided that this took place in water more than 100 fathoms deep.

Evacuation of the numerous casualties became a critical problem on D plus 3 because of poor beach conditions, LST 807 voluntarily remained on the beach under fire and acted as a hospital ship during the hours of darkness, while the remaining LSTs withdrew for the night. As darkness descended over the battle area, a steady stream of casualties arrived on the 807, where doctors performed emergency operations in the wardroom. Before morning, more than 200 casualties had been treated on the LST; of this number only 2 died.

At sundown on 22 February, Task Force 58 set sail for its second raid against Tokyo. On board the *Indianapolis*, Admiral Spruance accompanied this strike force. A task group of this fast carrier force, TG 58.5, consisting of the *Enterprise*, two cruisers, and Destroyer Squadron 54, remained at Iwo to provide night fighter protection. The departure of TF 58 materially reduced the availability of aircraft for direct ground support; overall responsibility for providing this type of support for the Marines ashore now fell on the small carriers of the carrier support force under Admiral Durgin, in addition to its mission of conducting air searches for survivors, providing anti-submarine and combat air patrols, and strikes against nearby Chichi Jima. As a result, the close air support for Marines fighting on the ground would henceforth have to be curtailed due to the shortage of aircraft.

Marines, shivering from wetness and cold in the front lines, faced another restless night. The Japanese began to probe the American lines shortly after dusk. Following an extremely heavy mortar and artillery barrage around 1800, a strong enemy force attacked the northernmost lines of the 26th Marines and succeeded in driving back the outposts. The enemy counterattack was brought to a halt after heavy casualties had been inflicted upon the attacking force. During the early morning hours, enemy swimmers, who had infiltrated across the western beaches into the 5th Division area, had to be eliminated. Similarly, in the zone of action of the 4th Marine Division, there was sporadic enemy activity throughout the night. Around 0500, an estimated 100 Japanese attempted to infiltrate the lines of 2/25 and 3/25. Even though these enemy efforts were thwarted, the intermittent firing served to keep the weary Marines from getting some much-needed sleep. In addition to all this activity, Japanese artillery continued to hit friendly positions along the corps front, inflicting further casualties and adding to the sense of uncertainty.

Despite the continuous harassment by enemy infantry and supporting arms, VAC plans called for the continuation of the attack on 23 February. The objective for D plus 4 was to be the O-2 Line. Jumping off at 0730, the 4th Marine Division was directed to make the main effort on its left against Airfield No. 2. Since the strongly defended bluffs on the far left of the 4th Division's zone of advance dominated all of western Iwo, VAC authorized the 5th Marine Division to advance beyond the boundary separating the two divisions if such an advance promised to neutralize or eliminate these prominent obstacles.

At 0730 on 23 February, the VAC attack continued in the direction of Airfield No. 2 and the O-2 Line. The 26th Marines, with 2/27 attached, moved forward against very heavy fire from the front and the right flank. After advancing for about 200 yards against bitter opposition, the regiment found the ground untenable and withdrew to its jumpoff positions. Shortly before noon, enemy artillery scored a direct hit on the command post of 2/26. The battalion commander, Lieutenant Colonel Joseph C. Sayers, was wounded and had to be evacuated. Major Amedeo Rea, the battalion executive officer, assumed command. For the remainder of D plus 4, the 26th Marines attempted to advance, but it was driven back each time by heavy enemy fire. At the end of the day, the battalions dug in for the night in about the same positions they had occupied during the preceding night.

In the center of the VAC line, where the 4th Marine Division with the attached 21st Marines was to make the main effort against Airfield No. 2, events took a similar turn. Because of the importance of this airfield General Kuribayashi had assigned the 145th Regiment commanded by Colonel Masuo Ikeda to defend this vital objective. This regiment was considered the best Japanese outfit on Iwo Jima; its 47mm antitank guns were sited to fire straight down the runways. In fact, the Marines were now encountering the enemy main defense line, which began in the west at the rocky cliffs to the north of the western beaches, stretched east across the island to skirt the southern end of Airfield No. 2, and terminated in the cliffs at the northern end of the eastern beaches. This line was organized in depth with all types of heavy weapons within and behind it, capable of delivering fire upon both the isthmus and beach areas. It was also heavily organized with a series of mutually supporting pillboxes, bunkers, blockhouses, tunnels, and other dug in positions. In addition, all approaches to the airfield were mined; enemy dead, saki bottles, helmets, and ammunition dumps were found booby trapped.

It became the lot of the 21st Marines to advance into this cauldron of enemy fire. Typical of the fighting which this regiment was to see at the approaches to Airfield No. 2 on D plus 4 were the experiences of some of the members of this unit:

Major Clay Murray, taking over 1/21 for his first day, figured that if he could find the weakest point and destroy it he could then knock off the supporting positions one by one. He lifted the telephone to give an order and a machine gun burst smashed the phone in his hand. Two bullets tore through his left cheek and out his open mouth, taking five teeth with them, and the rest of the burst sheared the knuckles of his left hand and ripped open his left ear. Major Robert H. Houser became 1/21's third commander in two days.

Private First Class George Smyth, 18, of Brooklyn, had never seen such Japanese. They were six footers, and they never retreated. Smyth's buddy fell beside him, a pistol bullet through his head, dead center. It came from a captured Marine. On the other side, a Japanese came down with his sword, both hands grasping the hilt. The Marine put up his right hand to ward off the blow, and his arm was sliced down the middle, fingers to elbow. As Smyth ran forward, a Japanese disappeared before him into a hole. Smyth dropped at the hole to finish him off, but the Japanese was already rising from a tunnel behind him. Smyth turned just in time to kill him. The ground was giving Ikeda's men every advantage, and they were using them all.

In the end, 1/21 was unable to make any gains for the day and had to consolidate for the night in its jumpoff positions. The 2d Battalion, now commanded by Major George A. Percy, had already become engaged in a sharp firefight at daybreak and, as a result, did not jump off until 0935. The heavy curtain of enemy fire prevented any advance until a second artillery preparation had neutralized some of the known targets on Airfield No. 2. The assault companies reached the southwest approaches to the airfield, but every effort to get troops onto the field itself failed, despite heavy support from naval gunfire and a rocket barrage. Finally, some of the advance elements succeeded in crossing the lower end of the northeast-southwest runway following an air strike, only to be driven back later by heavy machine gun and direct antitank fire. The 21st Marines consolidated its lines for the night at the southern edge of the field. For all practical purposes, gains for the day were nil, though the regiment had sustained heavy casualties.

On the right flank of the 4th Marine Division zone of attack, the 24th Marines, now in line with three battalions abreast, was to make the only sizable gains for the day. Advancing against moderate to heavy enemy resistance, Colonel Jordan's men gained as much as 300 yards. Since units along the regiment's left flank failed to advance, the regiment halted around 1500 and dug in for the night.

Even though two air strikes, artillery, and naval gunfire had supported the VAC attack on D plus 4, gains made for the day remained negligible. Before the morning attack opened, the *Idaho* had fired 162 rounds of 14-inch fire within 400 yards of the Marine lines; the *Pensacola* fired 390 rounds of 8-inch ammunition, all apparently without seriously affecting the enemy's power to resist. Discouraging as this tenacious enemy defense was to the frontline troops, there was a brighter side to the picture along the beaches, where, almost imperceptibly, order was beginning to emerge out of chaos. More exits from the beaches were being opened, permitting a steady flow of supplies inland. On 24 February, 2,500 rounds of 81mm mortar ammunition, of which there had been a critical shortage, were brought ashore, as were 25 tanks of the 3d Marine Division. When an eastward shift of the wind made it apparent that Iwo's eastern beaches would have a high surf on the following day, preparations were made to shift the unloading of cargo to the western beaches in the 5th Division sector for the next few days.

At the same time that supplies were coming ashore at a more steady pace, the command organization on Iwo Jima also became more stabilized. During the morning of D plus 4, General Cates came ashore and established his command post just east of the northwest-southwest runway of Airfield No. 1. Now that the headquarters of both the 4th and 5th Marine Divisions had been set up on the island, General Schmidt made an inspection of activities ashore while an advance party of the VAC Landing Force under the corps chief of staff made preparations for the establishment of a command post. In the course of a meeting between General Schmidt and the division commanders it became apparent that more pressure against the enemy would have to be applied if any appreciable progress was to be made on the following day. In consequence, an intermediate objective south of the O-2 Line was established. The new line roughly corresponded at both ends with the O-1 Line; however, in the center it protruded nearly 800 yards to include all of Airfield No. 2. On 24 February, a concerted attack was to be launched against the bluffs that stood squarely in the center of the VAC line. The assault was to be preceded by the heaviest concentration of aerial bombardment, naval gunfire, and artillery that could be mustered. Tanks of the 3d, 4th, and 5th Marine Divisions were to support the main effort. Lieutenant Colonel William R. Collins, Tank Officer of the 5th Marine Division, was charged with responsibility for coordinating the armored support. At the same time, the remainder of the 3d Marine Division, except for the 3d Marines, was to land and move into position, prepared to take over the center of the VAC line on the following day.

As D plus 4 drew to a close, one phase of the Iwo Jima campaign had ended. The Stars and Stripes had been hoisted above Mount Suribachi; Task Force 58 had already pulled out on the previous day, and Secretary of the Navy Forrestal departed for Guam during the late afternoon of 23 February. The Marines of VAC had established a solid foothold ashore, and there no longer was any chance for the Japanese on the island to dislodge them. Yet the most bitter and bloody part of the campaign was just about to begin. No one knew this better than the Japanese who, poised in their massive defenses, somberly awaited the American onslaught. During the night from 23-24 February, Admiral Ichimaru cabled to Admiral Toyoda his apologies for not having annihilated the Marines at the water's edge, adding: "Real battles are to come from now on. Every man of my unit fully realizes the importance of this battle for the future of the nation and is determined to defend this island at any cost, fulfilling his honorable duty."

Even as the Japanese naval commander was composing this message, small groups of Japanese once again attempted to infiltrate the lines of both the 4th and 5th Marine Divisions. In the 5th Division sector the enemy attempted to infiltrate both from the north and the south. In addition, the enemy shelled the rear areas and beaches during the night, thus assuring another miserable night for the Marines, who were dug in as best they could on the fringes of the enemy's main defense line.

On Saturday, 24 February, Iwo Jima resembled a giant beehive as the strong winds of the previous day diminished and moderate wind and surf under partly cloudy skies favored the unloading of men and supplies. On the beaches, a steady stream of men, machines, and supplies was pouring ashore, heedless of sporadic enemy mortar fire that was still hitting the beaches. At 1000, General Schmidt landed and assumed command ashore; shortly after noon, the VAC command post opened near the western beaches. On Airfield No. 1, men of the 31st Naval Construction Battalion began the hazardous job of restoring the field. With riflemen covering them, they had to crawl up the runways on hands and knees, probing for mines and picking out shell fragments. Hidden Japanese still sniped at the Seabees and enemy artillery occasionally shelled the runways, but the work continued without interruption. By midafternoon, the 9th Marines, commanded by Colonel Howard N. Kenyon, and Headquarters, 3d Marine Division, had come ashore. General Erskine established his command post at the northern tip of Airfield No. 1, preparatory to taking over the central zone of action on the following day.

On the northern front D plus 5 got under way with a terrific bombardment of enemy positions just north of Airfield No. 2 from air, ground, and sea. Beginning at 0800, the *Idaho*, stationed off the western beaches, began to hurl 14-inch salvoes at the heavily fortified area abutting the field; standing off the eastern beaches, the *Pensacola*, still bearing the scars of her previous duel with enemy artillery on Mount Suribachi, was firing her heavy guns against enemy positions lying east of the *Idaho's* target area. This destructive naval bombardment continued for more than an hour. At 0845, howitzers of the VAC artillery joined the bombardment in conjunction with the division artillery, which laid down a powerful preparation directly in front of the VAC line. At 0900, the naval bombardment ceased as aircraft from the escort carriers arrived over Iwo Jima to saturate the target area with bombs and rockets. Following the powerful preparation, VAC opened its attack at 0910 with the 26th Marines on the left, the 21st Marines in the center, and the 24th Marines on the right.

The Corps attack order had placed the axis of the main effort in the zone of action of the 5th Marine Division. For all practical purposes, however, tanks advancing on Airfield No. 2, in the zone of advance of the 21st Marines, were to deliver the main stroke. Once this attack had gained impetus, the combined force of infantry, armor, and artillery was to be brought to bear against the enemy. The concentration of overpowering force at one point, in accordance with the maxims of war, could produce significant results.

It was evident from the outset that the success or failure of the day's operation would hinge largely on the performance of the tanks of the three Marine divisions, which had been placed under the overall control of Lieutenant Colonel Collins. The approach of the tanks to the front lines ran into considerable difficulty almost from the outset. The original plan for the employment of armor had stipulated that the 5th Division tanks, followed by those of the 3d Division, were to proceed to Airfield No. 2 by way of the westernmost taxiway which led from Airfield No. 1 to the second field. Tanks of the 4th Marine Division were to head for No. 2 airfield over the eastern taxiway. This plan proved impossible to carry out when Company A, 5th Tank Battalion, which spearheaded the advance along the western route, ran into horned mines, buried aerial torpedoes, as well as heavy antitank fire. The first tank in the column struck a mine and was disabled. Shortly thereafter, the second tank in line, which had proceeded some distance beyond the first, ran over a buried aerial torpedo which demolished the vehicle and killed four members of the crew. In the midst of the confusion resulting from the explosion of the aerial torpedo, heavy artillery and mortar fire immediately hit the remaining tanks in the column, four of which were put out of action momentarily, though two of them were repaired under fire. Since the enemy had effectively blocked their route of advance, the remaining tanks returned to the bivouac area and prepared to advance on Airfield No. 2 by way of the eastern taxiway. There, the advancing armor also encountered mines and spent most of the morning in clearing a lane. Eventually, a dozen tanks reached the fringes of Airfield No. 2 and, having arrived there, opened fire on enemy emplacements to the north of the field.

Because of the delayed arrival of the supporting armor, the 26th Marines did not jump off until 0930 when, with three battalions abreast, it advanced, making the main effort on its right in coordination with the assault by the 21st Marines. Progress was slow, and many tanks fell victim to mines and accurate enemy antitank fire. For the men of the 21st Marines, who were denied the expected armored support during the early part of the day, the going was extremely rough, and the regiment had to advance into intense enemy fire. Shortly after 1000, both Companies I and K lost their commanding officers in a matter of minutes. Nevertheless, and despite high casualties, the advance continued. By noon, elements of Company K, 21st Marines, had crossed the field and were attacking enemy positions on an elevation just north of the junction of the two runways.

It was rough going for the attacking Marines of 3/21 all the way, as they charged across Airfield No. 2 and uphill against a well-defended belt of interconnected pillboxes, trenches, tunnels, and antitank gun positions. Twice they were driven off the ridge, but they attacked again. Once within the enemy positions, the Marines assaulted Colonel Ikeda's men with rocks, rifle butts, bayonets, knives, pistols, and shovels. Around noon, just as it appeared that the ridge had been secured, heavy artillery fire began to hit the forwardmost elements of 3/21 and the attack ground to a halt. Nevertheless, a gap had been made in the enemy line and through this gap tanks, bazookamen, mortarmen, and machine gunners were now able to advance.

The attack of 2/21 encountered considerable difficulty in moving towards Airfield No. 2 in its zone of advance. The arrival of supporting armor at 1000 proved to be a mixed blessing, since the armor attracted a heavy volume of artillery and mortar fire that pinned down the assault companies. When the supporting tanks tried to advance over the runways, Colonel Ikeda's antitank guns soon put a stop to this effort. Nevertheless, by inching northward around the end of the runway, elements of 2/21 were nearly abreast of the 26th Marines on their left shortly after noon. This advance served to erase the deep bulge which the enemy positions had previously made into the Marine lines.

At 1330, as soon as the 21st Marines had consolidated the morning's gains, a second deadly preparation of naval gunfire and artillery, similar to that which had preceded the jumpoff in the morning, rained down on the Japanese positions north of Airfield No. 2. As aircraft joined in the preparation, the 26th and 21st Marines launched a coordinated tank-infantry attack against the high ground to the north of the airfield. Once again, vicious hand-to-hand combat broke out. By 1415, Companies I and K of 3/21 had occupied the high ground across the east-west runway and tied in with each other. The supporting tanks now were able to operate on the western half of both runways, from where they directed their fire against enemy gun emplacements and pillboxes. The enemy responded with heavy antitank fire and mortar barrages. The latter did little damage to the tanks, but proved extremely detrimental to the infantry advancing alongside the armor. By the time the attack halted in late afternoon, the most forward elements of the 21st Marines had to withdraw to the southern edge of the east-west runway. Companies I and K of 3/21, on the other hand, were determined to hold their hard-won positions north of the airfield and remained in place. Badly needed supplies for these men had to be brought up after dark across the airfield.

At the same time that the 21st Marines swept northward across the airfield during the afternoon, the 26th Marines, with 2/26 and 3/26 abreast, also jumped off. Colonel Graham's men moved forward without significant difficulty over the ground directly in front of the regiment until they pulled abreast of the forward lines of the adjacent 21st Marines. From that point on, they drew continuous fire from cave positions to their right front. As the Marines approached, the Japanese on the high ground lobbed down grenades on the exposed assault force. The Marines retaliated with flamethrowers and white phosphorus grenades. By 1600, 3/26 had advanced about 400 yards beyond the forward lines of the 21st Marines and secured for the day. The 1st Battalion, 26th Marines, was pulled out of reserve and moved up to positions along the foot of the ridge line on the right boundary which the 5th Marine Division shared with 2/21. As in the case of the 21st Marines, RCT 26 had paid for the day's advance with heavy losses. The enemy did not spare the stretcher bearers who were forced to run a gantlet of fire as they attempted to carry wounded Marines to the rear, and losses among these men were heavy.

The most difficult fighting and terrain, with the least gains on D plus 5 fell to Colonel Jordan's 24th Marines on the very right flank of the VAC line. Following the thunderous preparation prior to H-hour, the 24th Marines, with 2/25 attached, jumped off. Both 2/24 and 3/24 attacked alongside the 21st Marines towards Airfield No. 2. Initially, the two battalions made good progress and by 1100, 2/24 was approaching the eastern end of the east-west runway.

At this point the advancing Marines found themselves confronted by a nondescript hill which ran along the southeast edge of the east-west runway. For lack of a better name, in accordance with military custom, this otherwise insignificant elevation was designated as Charlie-Dog Ridge, so named after the map grid squares in which it was located. To the southeast, a spur of this ridge culminated in a semicircular rise of ground soon to become infamous as the "Amphitheater." There, the Japanese had constructed some of the most formidable defenses on the island. The approach to this terrain feature from the south came squarely under the guns emplaced on the ridge. To the east, the route led across a weird series of volcanic outcropping and draws.

Just before 1130, as the Marines were preparing to assault Charlie-Dog Ridge, only 150 yards from the eastern end of the east-west runway, the enemy on the ridge fired at point-blank range with heavy machine guns, rifles and antitank guns. At the same time, 2/24 and 3/24 were hit by antiaircraft airbursts and mortar and artillery fire that stopped them cold. The 24th Marines was approaching the core of General Kuribayashi's central island defense system, featuring Hill 382, highest elevation on northern Iwo just beyond the airfield, as well as the Amphitheater, Turkey Knob, and Minami village. A sensitive enemy nerve had been exposed, and the Japanese reacted accordingly. Once the pinned-down men had taken the measure of what confronted them, they called for support from the 105mm howitzers of the 14th Marines and brought fire from their 81mm and 60mm mortars to bear against the firmly entrenched enemy. While these weapons peppered the enemy positions, Marines of 2/24 were able to move four machine guns into positions offering a clear field of fire on some of the enemy emplacements on Charlie-Dog Ridge. At the same time, men of the weapons company moved a 37mm gun close to the front and succeeded in knocking out a number of enemy emplacements.

Under cover of this barrage, the Marines were able to inch their way forward. For the remainder of the afternoon, assault squads, burning and blasting their way to the top of the ridge, led the way, followed by the remainder of Company G. As elsewhere along the VAC line, casualties were heavy; at 1500, the mortars of 3/24 fired 80 white phosphorus smoke shells to screen the evacuation of wounded. Shortly after 1600, just as it appeared that all the enemy resisting on Charlie-Dog Ridge could be mopped up before nightfall, the Japanese unleashed a tremendous mortar barrage which drove 2/24 and 3/24 off the ridge that had been taken at such heavy cost. One of the mortar shells exploded in the command post of 3/24, killing three men and wounding the battalion commander, Lieutenant Colonel Alexander A. Vandegrift, Jr., the son of the Commandant. Wounded in both legs, the battalion commander had to be evacuated and the battalion executive officer, Major Doyle A. Stout, assumed command.

On the right of the 24th Marines, the 1st Battalion had also jumped off for the attack on D plus 5. However, from the very outset, the progress of 1/24 was seriously impeded by the broken terrain, which prevented the battalion from playing any part in the main effort taking place to its left. Instead, Major Treitel's men crept and crawled forward, while an unseen enemy, operating from cleverly concealed emplacements and caves, poured a steady stream of fire into the attack force. In its attempt to keep the advance from bogging down altogether, 1/24 had the assistance of five LVT's which had been attached to the regiment for fire support. Three of the vehicles went up the coast road a short distance beyond the East Boat Basin and fired on targets designated by infantry commanders; the remaining two fired inland from the water, giving the hard pressed infantry all possible support. At 1700, Colonel Jordan ordered all units of his regiments to consolidate for the night. During the day, the left flank of RCT 24 had advanced about 500 yards; the center approximately 50 yards, and the extreme right flank about 100 yards, thus straightening the line in the regimental sector.

On the whole, 24 February had been a gruelling day for all VAC units. As the day closed, General Schmidt was able to report that gains of 200 to 1,000 yards has been made in the attack and that the VAC objective had been reached on both flanks. The price for the gains made in men and materiel continued to be very heavy. Since D-Day, the enemy had destroyed 32 friendly tanks. As D plus 5 ended, American casualties on Iwo Jima had risen to 7,758, an increase of 5,388 since the end of D-Day. During the five-day drive to Airfield No. 2, 773 Marines had died; 3,741 had been wounded, of whom nearly 300 subsequently were to succumb to their injuries; 5 were missing, and 558 were suffering from combat fatigue. The combat efficiency of the 4th Marine Division at the end of the day had been reduced by casualties and battle fatigue to an estimated 60 percent. The 5th Marine Division with a total of more than 3,000 casualties, had fared little better. The 26th Marines, in particular, had sustained very heavy losses. By evening of D plus 5, Colonel Graham's regiment had lost 21 officers and 332 enlisted men.

Nevertheless, the Japanese were beginning to feel the impact of the VAC assault. Late on 23 February, the commander of the 309th Independent Infantry Battalion had already reported to Major General Sadasue Senda, commanding the 2d Mixed Brigade, that communication to all units had been severed, and that his command post had been surrounded for the last three days and harassed by hand grenades and flamethrowers through the entrance. "Nevertheless," the battalion commander concluded, "the fighting spirit of all men and officers is high. We shall continue to inflict as much damage as possible upon the enemy until we are all annihilated. We pray for final victory and the safety of our country".

The defenses of Iwo Jima were correctly formulated in a 4th Marine Division intelligence report which concluded that "lack of a large scale enemy counter-attack to date was an indication of conservation of forces for a continued stubborn defense in depth." Since the enemy had a sizable force left, an eventual counterattack could not be discounted. In fact, since the high ground held by the Japanese now was jeopardized, a counterattack by a large enemy force was a dangerous probability. In any event, the enemy was certain to continue his harassment of the invasion force with artillery and through air attacks launched from nearby islands. The scales of battle had not yet tilted fully in favor of the American assault troops. It was clear to all involved that much heavy fighting lay ahead before all of Iwo Jima was conquered.

Chapter 7. 3d Marine Division Operations on Iwo Jima

Advance in the Center

By the end of the first week on Iwo Jima, VAC had made important gains, though far more slowly than had been anticipated. The key to seizing the remainder of the island north of the two completed airfields was the flat, high ground in the center of northern Iwo, commonly known as the Motoyama Plateau. The plateau itself was relatively level and unmarked by ravines. To the east and west, the ground was broken, descending to the shore in a very irregular pattern of gullies, canyons, and arroyos. The extensive shelling this part of the island had received prior to and since the landings had done nothing to improve the terrain, which was beginning to look like a lunar landscape. Cliffs, often with a sheer drop down to the waterline, were characteristic of the coast along the northwestern, northern, and northeastern shore of the island.

The frontal assault northward from Airfield No. 1 towards the second airfield had thrown the Marines squarely against the most heavily fortified part of the island. There was no way to bypass this area. On the west coast, the 5th Marine Division was confronted with one ridge after another. In each instance, men fought their way up the slope and over the top, only to run into another ravine with another ridge beyond. To the east, the 4th Marine Division was attempting to maneuver on a battlefield devoid of all cover. Where trees once had grown, all that remained was shattered rock, tangled brush, and defiles running to the sea. In the midst of this desolation, three terrain features stood out, each a formidable obstacle in itself: Hill 382, highest elevation in northern Iwo; a bald knob designated as Turkey Hill, and the southeastern extension of Hill 382, known as the Amphitheater.

Since an advance up either coast did not appear promising, the only way for VAC to take the remaining two-thirds of the island was to go up the high ground in the center. Since, from D plus 6 onward, the three Marine divisions on Iwo Jima fought jointly but in clearly defined areas, the narrative henceforth will deal separately with the day-to-day progress of each division as it forged a laborious trail across the island.

Fully aware of the limitations imposed upon the assault force by the terrain, General Kuribayashi had established his most elaborate defenses across Motoyama Plateau, right in the path of the 3d Marine Division. A detailed description of the plateau, therefore, appears in order: ". . . dangling ledges, and eaves carved by nature as well as the Japanese. Fissures of steam spewed from cracks in the ground, and evil-smelling sulphur fumes vied with the repulsive odor of decomposing bodies. Everywhere were Japanese defenses, grottoes, bunkers, blockhouses, pillboxes, deep caves, antitank ditches and walls, minefields, and a profusion of flat-trajectory antitank guns, dual purpose automatic antiaircraft weapons, and small arms, all backed by lethal mortars and rockets firing from reverse slopes." At a loss for words to describe this devil's playground, correspondents and officers writing their action reports sometimes recalled a Goya sketch or Dore's illustrations for Dante's Inferno.

In the midst of this rubble, Major General Sadasue Senda had deployed his 2d Independent Mixed Brigade, consisting of the 310th, 311th, and attached 315th Independent Infantry Battalions, plus an artillery and an engineer battalion. The top of Hill 382 harbored remnants of a thoroughly demolished radar station; on the far bluff of the Amphitheater, cave mouths and tunnel entrances could be seen, yet not a single gun barrel was visible. But, according to one account, "at every turn and fold in the rock were crosslanes of fire for machine guns and mortars, automatic weapons and rifles, light artillery, and rapid-fire cannon. Behind them were the men, some with sabres or pistols, bamboo lances, and sacks of grenades, waiting."

Since there was no way to bypass the strongest enemy defenses on the Motoyama Plateau, an advance into this veritable hornets' nest became unavoidable. The enemy had to be driven from the high ground in the center of Iwo Jima to permit opening up the western beaches. VAC was working under a tight deadline to clear the beaches, get the airfields back into operation, and unload with all possible dispatch so that ships could be made available for Operation ICEBERG, the invasion of Okinawa, now only five weeks away.

The same urgency applied to driving the Japanese from the high ground in the northeastern portion of the island, which enabled the enemy to place observed fire on VAC reserve areas and rear installations. Even though the Japanese had interfered with the American buildup on Iwo Jima, they had not done so to the extent that they were capable. Probably, they feared that such activity, if carried too far, would expose their guns and mortars to aerial observation, and that these mainstays of the defense would fall victim to American artillery and naval gunfire.

One of the problems facing General Schmidt at the end of D plus 5 was maintaining control of his advance up the island. Fresh in his mind was his experience on Saipan, where the 4th Marine Division had advanced so rapidly that at one point it was left with a 3,000-yard gap on its flanks. Similarly, on Iwo Jima, if one division advanced significantly beyond the others, troops for flank security would have to be made available, and the exposed division could expect to receive fire from every direction. Even though the VAC commander was aware of the necessity of executing a frontal assault across the center of the Motoyama Plateau, he was determined, for the time being, to push the VAC front forward all along the line in what may appear to have been "a partial violation of the military principles of mass and economy."

In any case, as of 25 February, General Schmidt still favored a coordinated advance across the island. Since the 4th and 5th Marine Divisions, which had thus far borne the brunt of the fighting, were already seriously depleted in men and materiel, General Schmidt decided to commit the 3d Marine Division for the assault against the enemy's main defenses in the center of the island. Of the 3d Division's three infantry regiments, the 3d, 9th, and 21st Marines, the latter had already been landed and attached to the 4th Marine Division on 21 February. Three days later, the 9th Marines, commanded by Colonel Howard N. Kenyon, had gone ashore, together with division headquarters, leaving only the 3d Marines afloat. Attached to the infantry were units of the 12th Marines, the 3d Tank Battalion, the 3d Pioneer Battalion, and the 3d Engineer Battalion.

By the end of D plus 5, three battalions of the 9th Marines had moved into assembly areas ready to join in the attack. Elements of the 12th Marines, under Lieutenant Colonel Raymond F. Crist, Jr., also came ashore on the 24th, followed by more batteries on the following day. It was 1 March before all of the 3d Division artillery had been landed. Several factors were responsible for the slow debarkation of the artillery. Foremost among these were the lack of landing ships and adverse beach conditions. Having anticipated that his troops would be employed piecemeal, General Erskine had decentralized his artillery while combat loading. Most of the men and equipment of the 3d Division were embarked in attack transport and cargo vessels. It had been planned to put them ashore as needed in landing craft, DUKWs, and amphibian tractors borrowed from the 4th and 5th Marine Divisions.

Participation in the drive to the north by the 3d Marine Division could not wait until all of the division artillery had come ashore. As a result, only one battery of the 12th Marines, and 1/14 in direct support and 4/13 in a reinforcing role, would be available on the morning of D plus 6.

As of 0700, 25 February, the task of clearing the critical central portion of the Motoyama Plateau fell to General Erskine and his 3d Marine Division. The division's route of advance lay across Airfield No. 2, through the remains of Motoyama Village to Airfield No. 3, which was still largely unfinished. As soon as the 21st Marines was returned to its parent division, General Erskine passed the 9th Marines through the 21st to continue the attack, while the latter unit went to the rear to rest and reequip. On D plus 6, the line of departure for the 9th Marines skirted the southwest edge of Airfield No. 2, protruded across to the high ground due north of the center of the field, and then receded to the southern edge, where the regiment tied in with the 4th Division. On the left, 2/9, commanded by Lieutenant Colonel Robert E. Cushman, Jr., faced heavily defended positions along a line of bluffs that extended northward from the western edge of the airfield and the high ground just north of the east-west runway. On the right 1/9, under Lieutenant Colonel Carey A. Randall, was face to face with a low but strategically placed hill subsequently to become known as Hill PETER.

Preparations for the 3d Marine Division attack on D plus 6 were similar to those of the previous day. A battleship and two cruisers fired for 20 minutes before the jumpoff. The naval bombardment was followed by a 1,200-round preparation fired by the VAC artillery. More than half of these shells hit the enemy in front of the 3d Marine Division, where the main effort was to be made. Carrier planes pounded the enemy positions with 500-pound bombs just prior to the jumpoff.

As soon as the attack got under way at 0930, both the 1st and 2d Battalions of the 9th Marines moved out, with 2/9 making the main effort. Lieutenant Colonel Cushman's men almost immediately drew heavy fire from enemy emplacements to their front and left flank and made little progress. The 1st Battalion made some headway and one platoon actually advanced to the base of Hill PETER, but was unable to hold the position. Since the main effort was to be made on the left, 26 tanks from Companies A and B, 3d Tank Battalion, under Major Holly H. Evans, had been attached to the 2d Battalion. Prior to the attack, Lieutenant Colonel Cushman had weighed the idea of having his infantry ride the tanks across the airfield. In view of the heavy enemy mortar and machine gun fire, this idea had to be abandoned, and the tanks moved out across the airstrip 200 yards ahead of the infantry. Almost immediately, the three leading tanks were hit by enemy antitank fire; two of them flamed, the third was immobilized. The heavy enemy mortar fire directed against the tanks did little damage to the vehicles but inflicted heavy losses on the infantry following in their wake. As the agonizingly slow advance of the 2d Battalion continued, nine tanks were knocked out before some of the enemy installations could be destroyed.

By 1400, the situation had reached a comparative stalemate. Both assault battalions had made slight gains, the biggest one being made by 1/9, which in five hours of bitter fighting had advanced 100 yards. The battalions were now separated by a sizable gap which had developed during the intense fighting. As a result, at 1430, the 3d Battalion, commanded by Lieutenant Colonel Harold C. Boehm, was ordered to pass through the right of 2/9 and attack to the north until it had bypassed the center of resistance that had thwarted the advance of 2/9. Once this had been accomplished, 3/9 was to effect a junction with the 26th Marines of the 5th Marine Division.

As soon as 3/9 began its advance, it started to receive a hail of rifle and automatic weapons fire from the front and the left flank. At the same time, the mortar and artillery fire increased in volume and accuracy. Casualties mounted with alarming speed. Unless the high ground to the battalion's front was quickly seized, the attack was in danger of bogging down. As the Marines crept ahead, the Japanese adjusted their artillery to keep pace with the advance. Within minutes, the two commanders of the assault companies were killed; many more officers and men became casualties. By 1700, losses had become so heavy that units were beginning to show signs of disorganization; the riflemen could not penetrate the curtain of fire thrown up by the enemy and some of the ground previously seized was being ceded. Despite the confusion of battle, Lieutenant Colonel Boehm succeeded in reestablishing contact with adjacent units, so that shortly after 1900 the situation had again stabilized and contact existed between all units along the regimental front. As D plus 6 came to a close, the 9th Marines had gained little ground, but, at any rate, the line had moved north of Airfield No. 2 at all points except for the extreme right tip. The regiment had seized a foothold on the rising ground north of Airfield No. 2 from where, on the following day, the attack could be continued.

Three additional batteries of the 3d Division artillery came ashore during 25 February and were ready to fire by 1700, The newly arrived units were organized into a provisional battalion under 1/12, and 1/14 was relieved of supporting the regiment. Additional help for the 9th Marines during the day had been furnished by the 21st Marines, which had fired heavy machine guns, 37mm guns, and light mortars at the stubborn enemy defenses. The 81mm mortars of the 21st Marines also had been attached to the 9th Marines during the day, but reverted to control of the parent regiment in late afternoon.

At 0800 on 26 February, the 9th Marines resumed the assault, following a 45-minute artillery preparation, The 1st and 2d Battalions attacked abreast, with 3/9 and newly attached 3/21 in reserve. The men of Colonel Kenyon's regiment knew that they were now up against the enemy's main defenses. In front of the regimental zone of attack, Hill PETER and 225 yards to the northwest, Hill OBOE, formed the most important obstacles to the advance.

Once again, the 1st and 2d Battalions bore the full brunt of the day's fighting. At the cost of heavy casualties, slight gains were made in the high ground beyond Airfield No. 2. The 3d Battalion remained in position, returning to regimental reserve after the attack jumped off. For the remainder of the day, 3/21 occupied a defensive position just north of the east-west runway. Several aircraft were on station throughout the day and executed four missions for the ground troops. Tanks were also available to support the assault. Naval gunfire was employed against deep targets spotted by aircraft; infantry units called for supporting fire against suspected gun and mortar positions. The effects of this support could not be accurately gauged by the assault units, for enemy resistance continued unabated. With respect to the air support received during this critical phase of the operation, the 3d Marine Division had this comment: "The number of planes on station daily for support of three divisions was eight fighters and eight torpedo bombers, a decidedly inadequate number. An average of two and a half hours was required before a mission could be executed. . . . Support aircraft, like artillery, should not be frittered away in the execution of piecemeal missions but should be employed in mass in support of the main effort of the ground forces."

In his operation order for 27 February, General Schmidt ordered the 3d Marine Division to continue the assault. The corps artillery was directed to devote half of its fire in support of this main effort, while the remaining 50 percent was to be equally divided between the 4th and 5th Marine Divisions.

At 0800 on D plus 8, the 3d Marine Division continued its attack, which was preceded by a 45-minute artillery preparation in which corps artillery fired 600 rounds. Once again, the 9th Marines, with the 1st and 2d Battalions abreast and 3/9 and 3/21 in reserve, jumped off. The 1st Battalion on the right immediately encountered devastating enemy mortar, artillery, and small arms fire from well concealed emplacements on and around Hills OBOE and PETER. On the left, 2/9 made an initial advance of approximately 150 yards. The increased employment of armor, particularly in the 2/9 zone of advance, aided the attack materially, even though 11 tanks were knocked out. The infantry, using flamethrowers and rocket launchers to good advantage, made small gains throughout the morning. The 2d Battalion finally reached the base of Hill OBOE, while 1/9 took the top of Hill PETER and began working down the northern slope. At this point, 1/9 was pinned down by fire from well-concealed enemy positions on the reverse slope of the hill. Heavy fire from Hill OBOE also caused the advance of the 2d Battalion to grind to a halt.

Just as it appeared that the remainder of the day would pass without any major gains being made, the unexpected occurred. Following a 10-minute preparation by the entire 3d Division artillery, reinforced by the corps artillery, 1/9 and 2/9 jumped off in a coordinated attack. This time, the coordination of all arms brought results, and the Japanese, stunned by the massed artillery fire, were temporarily unable to halt the Americans. Following the preparation, the 2d Battalion moved forward rapidly for a distance of 700 yards. The 1st Battalion overran Hill PETER, continued down the reverse slope and drove up to the crest of Hill OBOE. Now that most of the enemy fire from the two important hills had been silenced, Lieutenant Colonel Cushman's 2nd Battalion moved forward rapidly for approximately 1,500 to 1,700 yards. For the first time since the beginning of the attack, the lines of 2/9 now were abreast of those of the 1st Battalion.

Thus, after three days of ramming headlong into the main enemy defenses, the 9th Marines had scored a major advance. All of Airfield No. 2 and the commanding terrain to the north were now in American hands, even though enemy troops, many of them bypassed in their caves, continued to offer stubborn resistance. Mopping up operations in the area would require two more days, but General Erskine's men were now coming out on the Motoyama Plateau, with relatively level terrain ahead. As D plus 8 came to an end, yet another phase of the heavy fighting for Iwo Jima had been brought to a close, at least in the 3d Marine Division zone of advance. In summing up the overall results of this phase, the 9th Marines listed gains of 800-1,200 yards. Beyond that, the regiment stated that highlighted in this fighting were: "the skill, determination and aggressiveness displayed by our troops; the unprecedented tenacity and defensive resourcefulness displayed by the enemy (in the left of the 2d Battalion 77 large pillboxes were counted) ; the decisive aid rendered infantry troops by tanks; and finally, the excellent coordination of all supporting units with infantry maneuvers."

Advance To Motoyama Village

On Wednesday, 28 February, the 3d Marine Division continued its drive to the north. The last day of February marked the tenth day since the Marines first had stormed ashore on Iwo Jima. Optimistic forecasts to the contrary, somewhat less than half of the island had been taken thus far. No one ashore doubted that fighting of the utmost severity still lay ahead.

Since the 5th Marine Division on the left also had made gains during the last days of the month, the center and western portion of the VAC front now was approaching the O-2 Line. As a result, in his operation order for 28 February, General Schmidt established an O-3 Line. This line started on western Iwo about 1,000 yards south of Kitano Point, then curved southeastward, generally following the northern and northeastern contour of the island until it reached the eastern shore just north of the eastern terminus of the O-2 Line near Tachiiwa Point.

Before dawn on D plus 9, the 21st Marines, with the 3d Tank Battalion and the 81mm mortar platoons of RCT 9 attached, relieved the 9th Marines. Enemy snipers and machine gunners interfered with these movements, but by 0815 the relief was essentially completed and the 9th Marines passed into division reserve.

Following a 30-minute preparation by the division artillery, reinforced by corps artillery, the 21st Marines continued the attack at 0900 with the 1st Battalion on the left and 3/21 on the right; the main effort was to be made by 1/21. The artillery preparation was followed by a seven-minute rolling barrage which lifted 100 yards every minute to extend 700 yards beyond the front lines. The 1st Battalion advanced about 500 yards when it was stopped by hostile mortar and small arms fire. On the right, 3/21 also made good progress, closely following the barrage and, within a half hour after the jump-off, had gained 400 yards. As the morning wore on, elements of 3/21 became intermingled with 4th Division troops near the division boundary.

Shortly after launching its attack, Company I of 3/21 was to have an eerie experience. As the men moved forward in the wake of the rolling barrage: "Company I was confronted with tanks rising from the earth. These were Colonel Nishi's tanks, flushed at last from what had appeared to be hillocks. They churned forward, throwing off mounds of dirt, shrubbery, and rocks, and firing rapidly. The Marines faltered in shock before the heavy fire, and for moments the battle teetered. Captain Edward V, Stephenson, who had fought at Guam with great valor, rushed forward and rallied his company. Massing flamethrowers and bazookamen, he led a counterattack that smashed the tanks. Three were destroyed on the ground, and planes caught two more of them with 20mm fire."

Now there were only three tanks left out of the 22 which Colonel Nishi had been able to obtain the previous December, all of which had been carefully dug in. Shortly before noon, the attack bogged down all along the 3d Division front. At this time, 3/9 was attached to the 21st Marines and by VAC order, 4/13 reverted to the 5th Division control, after having been attached to General Erskine's division for several days.

At 1300, following a five-minute preparation by the corps and division artillery, the 1st and 3d Battalions of the 21st Marines launched a coordinated attack. The 1st Battalion bogged down almost at once, but 3/21, following closely behind an artillery barrage, advanced rapidly and seized the remnants of Motoyama Village and the high ground overlooking Airfield No. 3. The advance of 3/21 created a gap between the left of the 3d Battalion and the right of 1/21; into this gap, 2/21 was committed at 1530 with orders to attack. Following a five-minute preparation, the battalion moved out in an attempt to outflank the enemy positions which were holding up the advance of 1/21. Because of the heavy fire it received as it moved up to the line of departure, 2/21 was unable to launch its attack on time and consequently did not closely follow the rolling barrage. As a result, only small gains were made. At 1700, when the assault troops halted for the night, units held a winding but continuous line across the division front.

As night fell over the battle-scarred island, it appeared that the 3d Marine Division had burned and blasted its way through the center of the Japanese main line. To either side of the 3d Division, however, neither the 4th nor the 5th had kept pace with General Erskine's men. As a result, the VAC operation order for 1 March made a change in the quantity of supporting fires that would be made available. The lion's share of artillery support no longer would go to the 3d Marine Division; instead, the corps artillery henceforth was to divide its fires equally among the three divisions.

General Erskine believed that this division, in breaking through the enemy's main defenses in the center of Iwo Jima, had not received all of the neutralizing support it should have had. In commenting later on the Iwo Jima operation, he stated: "that the zone of action assigned this division was the most suitable for making the main effort as it extended along the high ground in the center of the island. Had the bulk of all supporting weapons been allotted to this division instead of being more or less equally distributed between all three divisions, it is believed that penetration would have been effected sooner at less cost."

By morning of 1 March, all battalions of the 12th Marines were ashore. For the remainder of the operation, until the 3d Marine Division reached the northeast coast, Erskine's modus operandi remained the same. He brought all the fire power available to him to bear against the enemy. Neutralization furnished by his own guns and by the corps artillery, when available, enabled him to push forward. As soon as he sensed a weak spot in the enemy defenses, he exploited the situation by committing reserves at the flanks and through the gaps that were created as his two assault regiments moved forward. The advance across Motoyama Plateau did not leave room for any additional maneuver.

The tactics employed by General Erskine during this critical phase of the operation have been explained as follows: "Erskine's zone of action was sufficiently narrow and his reserve sufficiently deep to permit him to employ these tactics more readily than could the other division commanders who were operating on wider fronts and across more difficult terrain. Cates and Rockey were equally competent, but the Third Division was in the pivotal position."

These tactics saw Erskine's men advance across the second airfield and up onto the Motoyama Plateau, through the stench of the sulphur refinery, and beyond the shambles that was Motoyama Village. No longer could the Japanese sit atop the central ridge and place observed fire on every inch of lower Iwo. The Third Division had cut its way through the main line of resistance into the guts of Iwo Jima. The evening of the 28th found these Marines looking down on the third airfield. It was believed that penetration to the coast would be easy, and the final airfield was quickly overrun, but then the secondary line of resistance was struck, and again the assault slowed and halted.

At 0830 on 1 March, the 21st Marines continued the assault with 2/21 and 3/21 abreast, the latter making the main effort. Once again, the attack was preceded by a heavy artillery preparation. The 12th Marines fired a 15-minute preparation in support of the attack, reinforced by VAC artillery. Direct support destroyers fired a half-hour preparation from 0800 to 0830, deepening the fire of the 12th Marines. The heavy artillery preparation was followed by a rolling barrage which lifted 100 yards every eight minutes for 300 yards. The 1st Battalion remained behind on the left flank to mop up the enemy pocket that the regiment had bypassed on the previous day.

As the two battalions jumped off, the 2d Battalion, which had attacked to the north on 28 February, pivoted on its right and advanced towards the northeast. Initially, both battalions made good progress, particularly 2/21 which was receiving effective tank support. As a result, the 21st Marines was moving well ahead of elements of the 5th Marine Division to the left. In order to protect the left flank of 2/21 and seize the left boundary of the division's zone of action, at the same time encircling the enemy pocket, 3/9 was committed in support of 1/21 in the course of the morning.

The 3d Battalion, 9th Marines, advanced against light resistance and prior to 1500 had arrived at the division's left boundary. By this time 1/21, attacking generally north to mop up the pocket of resistance to its front, had eliminated it and also had reached the boundary of the division to the left of 3/9. By VAC order, at 1500, the boundary between the 3d and 5th Marine Divisions was adjusted to shift the position held by 1/21 to the 5th Division sector. The latter division was ordered to extend to the northeast and relieve 1/21.

In mid-afternoon, 2/21 and 3/21 were unable to advance further in view of effective enemy opposition. After having broken through the center of the first line of resistance, Marines of General Erskine's division now had to advance into even more nightmarish terrain whose outstanding features are described below: "Beyond the low-lying final airfield, the ground rose again sharply into a saddle, and then fell off to the sea. The high points of the saddle were two additional hill masses of almost identical height, which represented the northwestern and southeastern corners of the Motoyama tableland. These terrain features were intermingled with caves and bunkers in deep criss-crossing crevices, and were studded with huge sandstone boulders, many outcroppings, and defensive weapons of all calibers and types. Their height gave the enemy full observation of the Marines to the east of the third airfield, and Erskine found it impossible to snake between them. The job was all the more difficult since there were no feasible ridge lines which could be followed onto their summits. On the contrary, just to the northwest of the right point of the saddle, commanding direct approaches to the high ground in the center, was a third heavily fortified hill, almost as high as the other two."

The three hills were situated in such proximity that the two on the right fell into the zone of advance of the 3d Division, while a portion to the left was just beyond the division boundary. Since the capture of this high ground was deemed essential for the further advance of General Erskine's division, it was shifted from General Rockey's zone to that of the 3d Marine Division. Even so, the Japanese would be able to delay any advance on General Erskine's left until the 5th Division had been able to pull up alongside. The center of the secondary line of resistance thus would have to be broken by a frontal assault against the southeastern hill mass.

Several days were to pass before this second line could be cracked. In the meantime, General Erskine, "his available infantry substantially weakened by the furious fighting of late February," had little choice but to continue the assault. Thus, at 1545 on 1 March, he decided to launch a coordinated attack with both regiments abreast, while the 9th Marines took over a portion of the zone of action of the 21st Marines, with 3/21 and a tank company attached. The 3d Tank Battalion, less one company, was to remain attached to the 21st Marines. The attack actually got under way at 1645, the 9th Marine passing 1/9 through 3/21, which took up a reserve position in the vicinity of Motoyama Village. The 2nd Battalion, 9th Marines, went into reserve.

The afternoon attack was preceded by a five-minute preparation fired by the division artillery and direct support destroyers, followed by a rolling barrage. Enemy resistance remained heavy, particularly in front of the 9th Marines, and little ground was gained. When lines were consolidated shortly after 1800, General Erskine had contact with both adjacent divisions. Even though the afternoon attack had brought little gain, some progress had been made during the day, and the 21st Marines, in the course of the morning, had advanced 500 yards to deepen the breach in the heavily fortified enemy defense line. On the evening of 1 March, the two 3d Division regiments faced northeast from positions about 600 yards east of Motoyama Village, along a line running north across the western portion of Airfield No. 3.

The peculiarities of the terrain within the 3d Marine Division's zone of attack dictated some changes in the division boundary. While Hill 362B did not physically block the advance of the 21st Marines, the division left flank was completely exposed to it. The decision to attack this hill was made on the evening of 1 March and permission to do so was obtained at that time. This decision departed from convention in that in attacking and seizing the hill, 3/9 which was still attached to the 21st Marines, would attack north across the division boundary to seize the ground vital to the division's progress.

On the morning of 2 March, the 3d Marine Division continued its attack with the 21st Marines and the 9th Marines abreast. The 21st Marines attacked with 3/9 attached on the left and 1/21 on the right, while the 9th Marines attacked with 2/9 on the left and 1/9 on the right. The attack, which jumped off at 0800, followed a 15-minute artillery and naval gunfire preparation. Again, a rolling barrage preceded the assault units. Tanks, using direct fire, participated in the advance.

Almost immediately, the 9th Marines ran into heavy small arms, mortar, artillery, and antitank gun fire. The supporting tanks were able to destroy one enemy gun and several emplacements; at the same time, it was becoming apparent that Colonel Kenyon's men were facing an exceptionally strong and well organized enemy position.

The 21st Marines, advancing in a column of companies, made only small gains before the attack bogged down by heavy machine gun and antitank gun fire from Airfield No. 3. Only 3/9, supported by tanks firing directly on emplacements, was able to move forward. By 1300, 3/9, advancing against strong enemy resistance, had secured a foothold on the rising ground in front of Hill 362B. By this time, the battalion had advanced beyond the units on its right and left regardless of flank security. Using 60mm and 81mm mortars, the Marines slowly moved up to a ridge that would serve as the final jumpoff position for a direct attack on the final objective.

As a result of heavy enemy resistance, the attack came to a standstill in early afternoon. A new assault, following a powerful artillery preparation, was launched at 1530. Eight artillery battalions took part in this preparatory fire. As had become customary by this time in 3d Marine Division attacks, the original preparation was followed by a rolling barrage. But even with such powerful support, the infantry was unable to score any notable gains. At 1730, the commanding officer of 2/21, Lieutenant Colonel Lowell E. English, was wounded, and the executive officer, Major George A. Percy, took over command. In tying-in for night defense, one company of 2/21 had to be pulled back a short distance from its exposed position. A slight withdrawal also became necessary for 3/9 to more favorable night positions.

As D plus 11 drew to a close, there had been some significant progress on the division left, but little gain elsewhere. The attack of 3/9 had driven a 700-yard salient into the enemy lines, and the battalion had occupied positions on the lower slopes of Hill 362B. At the same time, 2/21 had advanced northeast along the left boundary. However, the 9th Marines had gained almost nothing against the enemy stronghold in the right of the 3d Division zone of advance. In their exposed positions, the 3d Division Marines were to spend a restless night. Throughout the hours of darkness, the enemy remained very active in the broken terrain in front of the 21st Marines. Since Airfield No. 3 was still covered by enemy fire, it was not possible to occupy a continuous line.

During the night 2-3 March, luck played into the hands of the 3d Marine Division. An enemy sketch of the defensive area facing the division, particularly the zone of action of the 9th Marines, fell into General Erskine's hands. This map had been captured by the 21st Marines and was immediately forwarded to the division command post, where it was translated. The captured sketch bore out the belief that the 9th Marines was in contact with a strongly organized enemy position, if there had been any doubt left. General Erskine now hoped that he might find a soft spot in the enemy defenses, through which a wedge could be driven, somewhere between the enemy holding up the 9th Marines and the strong enemy defenses near Hill 362B.

The VAC operation order for 3 March called for elements of the 5th Marine Division to relieve 3d Division units near Hill 362B by 1000. In line with this relief, General Erskine planned to adjust the boundary between his regiments so that the zone of attack of the division was again equally divided. In consequence, the 21st Marines once again would be attacking northeastward.

At 0800 on 3 March, the 3d Marine Division resumed the attack with the same formation but with a new boundary between the regiments. The assault was preceded by a 10-minute preparation by the division artillery and direct support destroyers, followed by a rolling barrage. Almost immediately, the 9th Marines drew such heavy fire that it was unable to advance. In the zone of action of the 21st Marines, 3/9 maintained its position while waiting to be relieved by elements of the 5th Division. This relief was accomplished in the course of the day, but the maneuver was complicated by the fact that both the relief force and 3/9 became embroiled in time-consuming fire fights with the enemy.

In the zone of action of the 21st Marines, 2/21 advanced slowly under heavy fire and shortly before noon secured a foothold on Hill 357. At this time it was believed that no major resistance remained in front of 2/21, though it was still receiving heavy fire from the high ground to its left in the zone of action of the 5th Marine Division. General Erskine decided to change the direction of attack by assigning a new boundary between regiments in order to attack the flank of the enemy defensive area opposite the 9th Marines. Accordingly, an attack to the southeast was launched at 1500 with the main effort on the left.

At this time, 1/21 was pulled out of reserve and moved to the rear of 2/21 with orders to launch a drive towards the southeast with the mission of seizing Hill 362C. At the same time, 2/21 was to advance northeastward to the O-3 Line. The 3d Battalion was to remain in 9th Marines reserve, but could not be committed without General Erskine's specific permission.

The afternoon assault followed a five-minute artillery and naval gunfire preparation. The 1st Battalion, 21st Marines, initially made rapid progress and advanced for about 250 yards to its front. The 2d Battalion seized the high terrain on Hill 357 along the eastern edge of the Motoyama Plateau, but was unable to continue its drive because of heavy flanking fire from hills in the 5th Marine Division zone of action. The movements of 1/21 were facilitated by a platoon of tanks attached to the 21st Marines which, from positions in the vicinity of Motoyama Village, effectively supported the battalion's attack by placing direct fire on targets in front of 1/21.

In resuming its attack during the afternoon of 3 March, the 9th Marines once again ran into a stone wall and no gains were made. In an attempt to make some progress, Colonel Kenyon committed tanks singly and in small groups in the broken terrain. The armor did what it could and, in fact, reduced a number of enemy emplacements and some guns. Nevertheless, the tanks were unable to breach this enemy position sufficiently to permit an advance by the infantry. The Japanese emplacements, cleverly hidden in the chaotic jumble of torn rocks, could not be detected, because enemy artillery, mortars, and small arms firing from these positions were using smokeless powder as a propellant. In addition, the heavier weapons were not as active as they had been on previous days, but the fire from antitank guns and machine guns was devastating.

At 1800, the attack halted and the assault battalions consolidated for the night as best they could. In the zone of action of the 21st Marines, 2/21 and 1/21 made physical contact, but an open flank remained on the right of the 21st adjoining the 9th Marines. The gap was 250 yards wide and covered by fire. It would not take the combat-wise Japanese long to note the existence of this gap and take advantage of it.

Most of the action in the 3d Division zone of attack on D plus 12 had taken place in the northern half of the zone, where the 21st Marines had seized nearly all of the high ground northeast of the airfield. Beyond that, they had launched a drive to the southeast to envelop the enemy to the south. The 9th Marines, having made little headway, remained in substantially the same positions it had occupied all day.

At this point, an assessment of the situation from the Japanese point of view appears in order. In seeking to block General Erskine's drive to the sea, the Japanese resisted at every hill, rise, and rock. Every fold in the earth was cut with trenches and tank traps and covered by mortar and machine gun fire. Artillery had been sited across the unfinished runways of Airfield No. 3, and the roads and edges of the field were strewn with mines. From Hill 362B, north of the airfield, the fire came straight down into the flanks of units moving east. As one account of the battle was to sum up the situation: "The enemy was making a last organized stand, and doing it well. This was Kuribayashi's order. He had estimated that losses on both sides had been about equal until the end of February. He felt these early days of March to be the crucial ones and believed that if he could apply enough force, possibly even a counterattack, the Americans might fall back, or at least halt. If not victory, he would buy time, which is all he really hoped for."

During the night of 3-4 March, General Kuribayashi decided that the time was ripe for a limited counterattack. How the Japanese learned of the existence of the gap between the 21st and 9th Marines is not clear, but at approximately 0300, 4 March, an estimated 200 enemy troops attempted to infiltrate the eastern end of Airfield No. 3 between 2/9 and 1/21. After a sharp fire fight, the brunt of which was borne by the left company of 2/9, the enemy was repulsed with 166 casualties; 2/9 also had heavy losses. Reports indicated that some of the enemy infiltrators had succeeded in crossing the lines and were observed moving along the airfield. Patrols were sent to intercept this enemy force and 3/21, which ordinarily would have moved out for the attack at dawn of 4 March, was directed to remain in place and continue patrolling until after daybreak, when the situation could be clarified. Around dawn, patrols of 3/21 killed two or three of the enemy and the situation was found to be under control.

The VAC attack on 4 March had been scheduled to jump off at 0815. General Erskine initially had issued orders for 3/21 to be released to the 21st Marines. The battalion was to have moved prior to daybreak, passing through 1/21 and continuing the attack to the southeast to seize Hill 362C. In view of the confusion caused by the enemy infiltration, General Erskine had to secure permission from VAC to delay the 3d Division attack until 3/21 could complete its mopping up and get into position to attack. The battalion started to move shortly before 0700, at which time it reverted to its parent regiment. In crossing the area to the northwest and north of Airfield No. 3, the battalion drew heavy fire from enemy mortars and small arms. Extremely poor visibility further delayed and hindered preparations for the passage of lines, so that 3/21 did not reach its positions until 1100.

Forty minutes later, the division attack jumped off, again preceded by an artillery preparation and a rolling barrage. The same scheme of maneuver used on the previous day was employed, except that 3/21 passed through 1/21. Once again, the 9th Marines was unable to penetrate the enemy positions to its front. Similarly, the 21st Marines encountered heavy resistance, including direct fire from artillery pieces that were difficult to locate; little progress was made. Still unable to advance because of hostile flanking fire from the high ground to its left in the zone of action of the 5th Division, 2/21 suffered heavy casualties.

In the course of the morning, elements of the 5th Marine Division relieved 3/9, which, together with 1/21, withdrew to reserve positions near Motoyama Village. One company of 1/21 was employed to cover the gap between the 9th and 21st Marines when lines were consolidated for the night. At 1800, the units dug in with assault battalions just east of Airfield No. 3 and Motoyama Village. All of the assault battalions of the 3d Marine Division were tied in with each other, as well as with 5th Division units on the left and the 4th Division on the right.

Late in the afternoon of D plus 13, a welcome dispatch from VAC reached the exhausted troops of all three Marine divisions. Except for limited adjustment of positions, no attacks were to be launched on 5 March. Instead, present positions were to be held and one battalion of each regiment was to be rested, reorganized, and prepared to resume the assault on the following day, when all three divisions were to launch a coordinated attack.

On 5 March, the 3d Marine Division held an irregular line with 2/21, 3/21, 1/9, and 2/9, while the other two divisions spent the day receiving replacements and equipment to strengthen their tired and depleted units for the attack on 6 March. Two companies of the 21st Marines were pulled back from their positions on the line to rejoin the 1st Battalion in an assembly area north of Airfield No. 2. The men of 3/9 remained in position as division reserve between the northeast-southwest runway and Motoyama Village.

The day of rest and rehabilitation passed without any major ground action, though artillery duels took place and naval guns continued their harassing fires throughout the day. One air strike was conducted in the area of Hill 362C. It appeared as if even the Japanese welcomed a respite, as shown by their lack of aggressiveness. On their part, the men of VAC also were badly in need of a rest. Their condition on 5 March has been described in the following words: "All were tired and listless, their key personnel were largely casualties, and it was little short of miraculous that they could advance at all. Some gained comfort and a much-needed lift from a powerful drink called 'Suribachi Screamer,' sick bay alcohol and fruit juice. But even where units were pulled back in corps or division reserve, there was only relative quiet and rest, because night infiltration and minor counterattacks were constant; and day and night, Japanese appeared from overrun caves and tunnels, necessitating mopping up of seized ground."

In military operations enemy opposition often surpasses all expectations. According to this maxim, after seeing most of its carefully scheduled and supported attacks frustrated day after day, VAC may have tended to overestimate the extent of the resistance of which the enemy on Iwo Jima was still capable. Actually the position of the Japanese during the first week of March was far from reassuring. According to at least one account: "The fact was the island defenders were in a bad way. Most of their artillery and tanks had been destroyed, and 65 percent of the officers had been killed. On Saturday, March 3, General Kuribayashi estimated that he had 3,500 effective left. Communications had broken down to the point that General Senda was virtually isolated in the east. Captain Inouye still commanded a small remnant of sailors near Airfield No. 3. Admiral Ichimaru was in the north, in touch with Kuribayashi but no longer having effective control over Inouye. In the northern corner of the island, no organized force remained – only small groups of survivors of individual units, acting locally and almost independently. Spirit was still strong, however, and in no unit was there the thought of surrender."

VAC orders called for a resumption of the attack on 6 March. Since any further advance by 2/21 was dependent directly on the progress made by the adjacent 5th Division, the 2/21 attack was to be coordinated with that of General Rockey's men. The advance of 2/21 was so timed that the battalion would move out at 0800, one hour ahead of the remainder of the 3d Division, which would launch its assault in conjunction with that of the 4th Division. Except for the staggered timing, no other changes were made in the previous scheme of maneuver.

At 0600 on 6 March, 3/9 was attached to the 21st Marines in preparation for the attack. For ten minutes prior to the jumpoff of 2/21, three battalions of the 12th Marines, three battalions of the 14th Marines, and one battalion of the corps artillery laid down a heavy preparation, which was further supplemented by naval gunfire. However, no sooner had 2/21 attacked than it became apparent that the artillery preparation had been totally ineffective. The advance bogged down almost at once in the face of heavy enemy mortar and small arms fire coming from the high ground in the zone of action of the 5th Marine Division.

Prior to the jumpoff of 3/21 and the 9th Marines, three battalions of the 12th Marines and one battalion of the corps artillery fired two five-minute preparations, which were further supplemented by naval gunfire which continued for an hour and a half. A rolling barrage was also fired in support of the attack. Nevertheless, despite all this expenditure of ammunition, results remained negligible. As soon as the remainder of the 3d Division attacked at 0900, it drew such heavy fire from enemy small arms, mortars, artillery, and antitank guns that any advance was all but out of the question.

A second push was ordered for 1440, again preceded by a heavy artillery preparation. This time 1/21, having passed through 3/21, was able to score some gains against continued bitter enemy resistance, slowly advancing for 200 yards before lines were consolidated at 1800 for the night. Once again. the progress made was completely out of proportion to the ammunition and effort exerted, During the two preparatory fires on the morning of 6 March, 11 artillery battalions had expended 2,500 rounds of 155mm howitzer ammunition and 20,000 rounds of 75mm and 105mm shells. In addition, a battleship and cruisers had fired an additional 50 rounds of 15-inch and 400 rounds of 8-inch ammunition. Carrier-based aircraft had bombed and strafed the Japanese positions, all apparently without eliminating the enemy's power to resist.

There was one bright note on this otherwise very discouraging day. During the bitter fighting, two platoons of Company G, 3/21, fought their way to the top of a ridge. Before enemy fire drove them off, they were able to get a glimpse of the sea, just 400 yards away. It was an inspiring view, for it indicated to the weary Marines just how far they had come, despite all adversities. It also served as a distant promise that there would be an end to the ordeal all of them were undergoing.

Drive to the Sea

On the evening of 6 March it was apparent that the Japanese positions on northern Iwo would not yield to the tactics that had been thus far employed. At the same time, General Erskine was keenly aware of the heavy losses that were draining the offensive strength of his division. As a result, despite the known risk inherent in such an operation, he ordered an attack against Hill 362C under cover of darkness. It was hoped that employment of the element of surprise would yield results where all other conventional means had failed. Instead of attacking at 0730 on the morning of 7 March, as specified in VAC orders issued late on 6 March, General Erskine requested and received permission to jump off at 0500. The 21st Marines was to make the main effort. Its objective was to seize Hill 362C, while the 9th Marines was to advance for about 200 yards in the darkness as a diversionary measure. Actual seizure of Hill 362C was to be executed by Lieutenant Colonel Boehm's 3/9, which was attached to the 21st Marines.

In reconstructing the events leading to this attack and the preparations made, Lieutenant Colonel Boehm later was to comment: "The order for the attack on Hill 362C, received verbally over the telephone from Colonel Eustace Smoak, executive officer of the 21st Marines, was simply to attack at 0500, using the present front lines of 1/21 as a line of departure, maintain maximum secrecy and silence, and seize the hill. My complaint that I had never seen the ground was countered by the assurance that Major Bob Houser, CO 1/21, would give me all the details on the lay of the land to the front, point out the objective, etc. etc., 'Don't worry about a thing, Houser's been observing the ground all afternoon, he'll give you all the dope.'

"I had my company commanders meet me at the K Company CP, which was nearest 1/21's disposition, briefed them, then took them to the 1/21 CP. Major Houser accompanied us up to a point about the center of his lines, pointed to a hill mass about 300 yards to the front and said that was Hill 362, my objective. I told him it didn't seem possible that his position was so close to the hill. He assured me that it was, and his company commanders determinedly agreed, so we went back a short distance and, under cover, consulted a map. He confidently indicated the position of his front lines and, although highly skeptical, I had no alternative but to accept his description as an accurate picture."

There was a good chance that the surprise attack would succeed. As a rule, during previous World War II operations in the Pacific Theater, Marines had not carried out night attacks. Aside from night patrols, Americans had not ventured in front of the lines after dark on Iwo Jima. To prevent the enemy from learning of the proposed attack, special precautions had to be taken. No mention of the attack was made in any radio traffic, nor was the assault to be preceded by any artillery preparation, except for white phosphorus shells fired around the objective five minutes before the jumpoff. The men were ordered to move as quietly as possible. No one was to fire until it became certain that the enemy had discovered the main body of the assault force.

The assault companies moved out of their assembly areas at 0320 for the line of departure. A light rain was falling throughout the night, and the darkness that engulfed everything on the island was broken only by the naval gunfire illumination, which ceased before the attack was launched.

Minutes before H-Hour, the situation at the 3d Marine Division command post was tense. Even though there was a good chance that surprise would be achieved, there had been no opportunity for Lieutenant Colonel Boehm's battalion to carry out any detailed prior reconnaissance. In the inky darkness, his men would be stumbling into the unknown. The risks inherent in the venture were only too apparent. The atmosphere prevailing at General Erskine's command post during these crucial minutes has been recaptured as follows: "In the Division CP, the staff checked watches; it was 0430. Every few minutes someone would look outside through the foul and rainy weather. If a burst of fire or a stray round was heard, faces tensed. At 0450, the illumination slacked and ceased. Five more minutes, and there followed the familiar crack and swish of an outgoing harassing concentration from the artillery. You could set a watch by the 12th Marines. Then at King-hour, a starshell burst. Hadn't all illumination been checked? Get the naval gunfire officer! It was a 4th Division ship, he reported, and lunged to the field phone and radio. Meanwhile, word came back that the attack had jumped off. Still no sound. Were they moving at all? Had the steaming earth swallowed them?"

It had not. At 0500, the assault companies climbed out of their holes and silently headed southeastward towards Hill 362C assumed to be 250 yards away. The surprise attained was total and 3/9, catching the enemy asleep in his emplacements, took a heavy toll with flamethrowers and automatic weapons. Shortly after 0530, a Japanese machine gun came to life. It was quickly silenced by a flamethrower, and

Lieutenant Colonel Boehm's battalion continued its slow but determined advance towards the objective. By this time, sporadic enemy resistance was making itself felt, but still the advance continued.

Shortly before daybreak, around 0600, 3/9 reported that it had taken Hill 362C. Japanese were being killed out in the open with flamethrowers as they stumbled out of their caves. The battalion had advanced 400 yards with no resistance whatever for the first 40 minutes, and only a smattering of it afterwards. Just when it appeared that complete success had been attained, the light of day revealed a somewhat different and sobering picture. It became apparent that on the basis of the instructions received from 1/21 the preceding evening, 3/9 had captured Hill 331 instead of Hill 362C. The real objective still lay 250 yards ahead. Apparently, the battalion's jump-off positions had been somewhat further back than anyone had realized.

Determined to strike while the iron was still hot, Lieutenant Colonel Boehm called for artillery support and continued to press the attack against the real objective. By this time, the element of surprise had been lost. Jumping off at 0715, 3/9 savagely slashed its way forward from Hill 331 towards 362. The advance progressed over broken and treacherous ground, which exposed Lieutenant Colonel Boehm's men to fire from the front, the flanks, and the rear. Bitter fighting continued throughout the morning, and in approaching the objective, Marines had to eliminate caves and bunkers one by one with flamethrowers, rockets, and demolition charges. At 1330 3/9 reported that it had captured the objective. This report proved correct, and a major obstacle in the path of the 3d Marine Division's advance was thus eliminated. In outlining the activities of 3/9 on 7 March, the battalion commander was to make this comment: "Most notable in the night attack was the fact that, although nearly all the basic dope was bad, the strategy proved very sound, since it turned out that the open ground taken under cover of darkness was the most heavily fortified of all terrain captured that day, and the enemy occupying this vital ground were taken completely by surprise (actually sleeping in their pillboxes and caves). . . . It should be kept in mind, however, that a stroke of luck went a long way toward making the attack a success."

While 3/9, as part of the 21st Marines, was to make the most spectacular gains for the day, the remainder of the 9th Marines was to see some of the most bitter fighting of the Iwo operation. While 3/9 was attacking southward towards Hills 331 and 362C, 1/9 and 2/9 attacked eastward, also in the general direction of Hill 362C. By daybreak the 9th Marines, with the 2d Battalion on the left and the 1st Battalion on the right, had advanced about 200 yards. However, at first light of day the enemy, consisting of Baron Nishi's 26th Tank Regiment, awoke to the presence of the intruders and put up a fierce opposition. The 2d Battalion, which had already advanced into the enemy fortifications, began to draw heavy fire from the front, flanks, and rear. For all practical purposes, the two battalions were cut off and casualties were heavy.

By midmorning it became apparent that the 9th Marines could not break through the resistance it faced from the front, and General Erskine shifted the regimental boundaries so that the advance of the 21st Marines would pinch out the 9th. Around noon, 1/9 regained some freedom of movement and attempted to establish contact with elements of 3/9 atop Hill 362C. This attempt which, if successful, would have caught Baron Nishi's men in a giant vise, failed. Instead, elements of 2/9 were themselves surrounded and unable to move in any direction. Tanks sent forward in support of 2/9 were unable to get through, though they did relieve some of the pressure on the surrounded units. At dusk on 7 March, elements of 2/9 were still pinned down.

It would be 36 hours before two companies of Lieutenant Colonel Cushman's battalion would be able to extricate themselves from the encirclement.

Just about that length of time would be required before the first Marines of the 3d Division reached the coast. It would not be an easy advance for the men of 2/21, 1/21, and 3/9 who would continue the drive for the sea, while Marines of 3/21 and 2/9 would continue to chip away at a stubborn pocket of enemy resistance that still showed no sign of disintegrating.

On the morning of 8 March, D plus 17, the men of the 3d Marine Division resumed the attack, this time with conventional tactics. The attack was preceded by a 10-minute artillery preparation. Destroyers offshore supported the division and corps artillery with a half-hour bombardment. Once again, a rolling barrage was employed. The 21st Marines jumped off with the 1st and 2d Battalions abreast, 1/21 on the right. The advance of 2/21 had to be coordinated with that of the adjacent 5th Marine Division.

This time, the Japanese were wide awake and the 21st Marines received heavy flanking fire from the sector of the adjacent division, as well as from the zone of action of the 9th Marines, whenever an attempt was made to move down to the cliff overlooking the beach. Nine tanks from the 3d Tank Battalion supported 2/21 as best they could by shelling caves and pillboxes in the rugged terrain over which the battalion had to advance. To the right of 2/21, the 1st Battalion was making slow progress and by evening had advanced 300 yards through what was believed to be the final organized enemy defenses before the coast was reached.

In the zone of action of the 9th Marines, 3/9 attacked eastward from Hill 362C, passing 3/21, which had been attached to it, and moving through the right of 1/9. The intermediate objective of 3/9 was the edge of the plateau overlooking the beach; the final objective was the beach itself. Despite tenacious enemy resistance, the battalion advanced some 400 yards beyond Hill 362C towards the beach. At times it appeared that, despite the ferocity of the battle, enemy resistance was less organized and assumed the dimensions of a "last ditch" fight. In order to assist the battalion in its drive through the broken terrain, in which sandstone buttes abounded, a destroyer fired into the draws that led down to the sea; an air strike also was directed into the same general area. By late afternoon, 3/9 had seized the intermediate objective and was ordered to hold up the advance on the high ground.

Meanwhile, the attack of the remainder of the 9th Marines had bogged down in the inaccessible terrain in which the Japanese had holed up. Remnants of Colonel Nishi's force were making their last stand here, fighting from caves and emplacements in the sandstone with all they had. The materiel at their disposal was still formidable: well concealed antitank guns, and dug-in tanks, equipped with 37mm and 47mm guns. As a result, no coordinated advance was possible. Small teams of men, rushing from one standstone butte to another, fought Indian style, blasting away at the enemy defenses here and there, but nowhere could the pocket be dented.

The following day, 9 March, saw the continuation of the 3d Division drive to the sea. Once again, 3/9 jumped off following the customary preparation and advanced towards the beach. While still very much in evidence, enemy resistance was becoming more sporadic. By late afternoon, 3/9 had penetrated down to the beach, both 3/9 and 1/21 dispatching patrols to the water's edge. In support of the two battalions, an air strike was directed against an obstinate enemy pocket in the zone of action of the 5th Division. In addition, a destroyer offshore, with the 3d Division naval gunfire officer on board, fired on caves and enemy positions in the beach area.

Once again, the 9th Marines, with 3/21 attached, hit a stone wall of resistance. Even though tank support was available, the terrain severely limited the employment of armor. The enemy was not slow to take advantage of this situation. He first fired a number of air bursts over one of the tanks in order to disperse the infantry. Once this had been accomplished, he dispatched a demolition detachment under cover of a smoke screen which put the tank out of action with a demolition charge and a Molotov cocktail. Neither 2/9 nor 3/21 were able to score any sizable gains during the day.

Ever since the 3d Marine Division had entered the fight for Iwo Jima and begun its drive through the center of the island, General Erskine had been deeply disturbed by his losses and their adverse effect on his division's combat efficiency. He strongly felt that some of these casualties could have been avoided and subsequently made this statement: "Infantry battalions were now definitely beginning to feel the presence of the large number of replacements, manifested by a sharp drop in combat efficiency. These men were found to be willing but very poorly trained, especially in basic individual conduct. The faulty teamwork, resulting from lack of small unit training, was also a definite hindrance to the operation of the infantry battalions. Many needless casualties occurred in these replacements because of a lack of knowledge of the proper use of cover and concealment." The situation described by General Erskine resulted from an organizational innovation employed for the first time in the Marianas and subsequently on Iwo Jima. Six replacement drafts, totalling 7,188 officers and men, all of them recent arrivals from the United States, had been attached to the three divisions. It had been planned to feed these replacements into the combat units as warranted by casualties, in hopes that such a steady flow would guarantee a high degree of combat efficiency. Prior to being channeled into the combat units, these men were to supplement the shore party, thus serving a dual purpose. The basic thought behind this procedure may have been sound, but: "unfortunately, this plan did not work out nearly so well as had been hoped. Like most replacement drafts, these had been sent overseas with inadequate combat training, the idea being that they would complete this in the field. But the necessity of mastering shore party duties prevented this, with the result that most of them had to be broken in during actual battle by the units into which they had been incorporated. This was hard on all hands, and there were times during the later stages when it appeared that progress was being hindered rather than helped by the presence of the new men."

In reviewing the handling of replacements during the Iwo Jima operation, the former VAC chief of staff was to comment:

"1. These replacements were the only ones available. VAC could do nothing about additional training.

2. If not used for shore party duty, separate troops would have been required for that, necessitating additional shipping.

3. Shore party requirements should be reduced as the advance continued. In fact some pioneers were used later as frontline troops.

4. Duty with the shore party in itself necessitated some training in self protection, which should have proved useful at the front."

In any case, by the evening of 9 March, General Erskine had achieved his primary mission, which was to break through to the northeastern shore of the island. The initial approach to the beach had been made by elements of Company A, 21st Marines, who were later joined by 3/9. By nightfall the 3d Division Marines held nearly 800 yards of shoreline, thus cutting the area still in enemy hands into two separate sectors. At the northern tip of the island, near Kitano Point, General Kuribayashi would continue to offer stubborn opposition. This last vestige of enemy resistance would be eliminated only after protracted fighting by elements of both the 3d and 5th Marine Divisions. Upon reaching the northeast coast after their arduous and costly advance through the center of Iwo, elated 3d Division Marines sent back a canteen filled with sea water to General Schmidt, marked "for inspection, not consumption."

Another milestone in the prolonged battle for Iwo Jima had been reached. In the words of one historical narrative: "Not as dramatic an incident as the flag raising on Suribachi, this was far more significant. The enemy in the bulge of the island was split, and Americans controlled the terrain approaches from the Motoyama tableland down the deep ravines to the cliffs and to the sea."

General Kuribayashi and the remnants of his garrison still held one square mile in the north of the island, determined as ever to sell their lives as dearly as possible. Small though tenacious pockets of resistance remained in the southeastern portion of Iwo. But an end to the terrible slaughter was finally in sight.

Chapter 8. Airfield Development and Activities Behind the Lines

Reconstruction of the Airfields

While three Marine divisions were inching their way northward against tenacious resistance, an equally difficult battle was being fought to the rear of the combat troops. Aside from the Japanese who, particularly during the early days of the operation, were able to blanket any part of the island with artillery and mortar fire, the biggest enemy was the time factor. The basic premise on which the entire operation had been planned was to secure the two southernmost airfields on the island as quickly as possible, and it was for this purpose that Marines up front were hourly giving their lives. Unless the airfields could be quickly put into operation, the sacrifice of these Marines would serve little, if any, purpose.

On D plus 5, men of the 31st Naval Construction Battalion, commanded by Lieutenant Commander Dominick J. Ermilio, began work on the southern airfield. This job initially had been assigned to the 133d Naval Construction Battalion under Lieutenant Commander Raymond P. Murphy, but the battalion had suffered such heavy casualties on D-Day that it was still undergoing reorganization four days later. While, to the north, the battle for Airfield No. 2 was in progress, the Seabees, with riflemen covering them, were crawling up the runway of No. 1 Airfield on hands and knees, probing for mines and picking up the most jagged shell fragments that could wreak havoc with the rubber tires of aircraft.

Throughout the day, the Seabees and elements of the VAC 2d Separate Engineer Battalion, commanded by Lieutenant Colonel Charles O. Clark, sifted the dirt on the runways, often under enemy sniper and artillery fire. By late afternoon of 25

February, the engineers had filled, bladed, and rolled 1,500 feet of the north-south runway of Airfield No. 1, which was then ready for use by small aircraft. This was the scene that took place at the airfield on the following day: "Down on Airfield No. 1 the first planes came in, two little OY-1s of the 4th Division (VMO-4), their wheels kicking up spurts of dust as they touched down. Dirty engineers and Seabees lined the runway and cheered as the little spotter planes rolled to a stop. The Grasshoppers (Stinson Sentinels), or 'Maytag Messerschmitts,' stayed only a few minutes and then took off again, to fly over Turkey Knob and the Amphitheater to spot targets for the 4th Division. As they left, the first of the 133d Seabees' rollers and scrapers climbed up onto the runway. After a week of fighting, and heavy casualties, and reorganization, the 133d was ready to start on the job it had come for. Once the first spotter aircraft had flown in from the escort carrier *Wake Island*, others followed in rapid succession. By 1 March, 16 planes of VMO-4 and -5 had reached the island. Since the airstrip was still under enemy artillery and mortar fire, many of the small planes sustained damage which had to be patched up in frantic efforts. Of the seven aircraft which VMO-4 brought ashore, six eventually were so badly damaged that they had to be surveyed after the end of the operation."

Completion of the first 1,500-foot strip of Airfield No. 1 was but the initial step in the restoration of the entire field. The 2d Separate Engineer Battalion was charged with the reconstruction of the north-south and northwest-southeast runways, while the 62d Naval Construction Battalion, commanded by Lieutenant Commander Frank B. Campbell, was responsible for rebuilding the northeast-southwest runway. Quarries available on the island yielded an excellent sand-clay fill that could be used for the construction of roads and was widely utilized in rehabilitating and extending Airfield No. 1. In fact, it was the use of this material that had made possible the early completion of the short strip for the land-based observation planes.

Good progress was made in restoring the airfield, except for the hours of darkness and those times when the enemy took the field under fire. On the last day of February, Airfield No. 1 invited emergency landings by carrier aircraft. This offer was promptly accepted by a damaged torpedo bomber. From this time on, the popularity of the airfield among carrier pilots rapidly increased. By 2 March, a 4,700-foot runway had been completed and the first air transport, a R4D of Air Evacuation Squadron 2, departed with 12 wounded Marines on board. Noting increased activity on the newly restored airfield, the enemy concentrated his artillery fire on the strip. For the remainder of the day, the field remained inoperative, but subsequent evacuation flights became an almost daily occurrence without any further serious enemy interference.

A new milestone was reached during the afternoon of 4 March, when a B-29 bomber, returning from an air attack against the Japanese homeland, made a forced landing, refueled, and continued on its return flight. This was only the first of hundreds of the giant B-29s which were to make emergency landings on the island for the remainder of the war.

As early as 28 February, planes of the Army Air Forces 9th Troop Carrier Squadron had dropped more than 9,000 pounds of supplies near the western beaches. Beginning 1 March, airdrops were made over the southern airfield. The cargo dropped consisted of badly needed 81mm mortar shells, medical supplies, radio gear, and mail. Work on the two short runways was completed on 4 March. On this date, the first Marine transport, a R5C, piloted by Lieutenant Colonel Malcolm S. Mackay, commanding VMR-952, landed on the island. The aircraft, carrying 5,500 pounds of badly needed mortar shells and ammunition from Guam, had stopped at Saipan before continuing the flight to Iwo. Once Airfield No. 1 had become operational, a variety of aircraft could be brought into the island. The value of Iwo Jima was further enhanced when, on 12 March, the 5,800-foot strip was completed. By this time, landings and takeoffs on Airfield No. 1 had become a daily occurrence.

In addition to the aircraft using the southern airfield for bringing in supplies and evacuating the wounded, fighter planes were needed to assist the ground forces fighting on Iwo. Their mission was both an offensive and a defensive one. On the one hand, the fighters had to give the closest support possible to Marines fighting on the ground. Their second mission, of no less importance, was to make continuous sweeps over Japanese islands in the vicinity of Iwo to preclude any reinforcement of the Iwo garrison, and at the same time to eliminate any Japanese air power still remaining in the Bonins. Above all, the enemy had to be prevented from interfering with the progress of the Iwo ground operation or with the numerous supply ships standing by offshore.

During the first two weeks of the Iwo Jima operation, Colonel Vernon E. Megee acted as the Commander, Landing Force Air Control Unit. In this capacity, he came ashore on 24 February but did not assume control of support aircraft until 1 March, at which time he also became Commander Air, Iwo Jima. The establishment of these functions ashore greatly facilitated coordination and control of fire support for VAC, particularly since Colonel Megee, using forward observers, developed a system of close air support controlled from VAC Headquarters. This proved to be a very busy time for the representative of Marine aviation, who was to reminisce later: "You see, I had a dual status there really. In fact, I stayed Commander there even – let me see, we were supposed to have an Air Force Brigadier for that job but he never showed up until a couple of weeks after the landing and during the interim I was the Air Commander, Iwo Jima. . . . And I had air defense responsibility and the logistical responsibilities during that time so I was like the proverbial paper hanger with the itch." On 6 March, Brigadier General Ernest Moore, USA, arrived on Iwo to assume his duties as air commander. With him came an initial complement of 28 P-51 Mustang fighters and 12 P-61 Black Widow night fighters of the 15th Fighter Group. On 8 and 9 March, the forward echelon of VMTB-242 arrived from Tinian. This squadron, commanded by Major William W. Dean, began to fly air defense missions around Iwo Jima day and night. Based on the southern airfield, the bomber squadron also relieved carrier aircraft of antisubmarine patrol missions. After 23 days of well executed and strenuous operations, the Support Carrier Group departed from Iwo.

On 11 March, 15 of the Iwo-based P-51 fighters launched their first attack against nearby Chichi Jima. This was only the first raid of many to follow. Throughout the assault and occupation phase, Army Air Forces bombers based in the Marianas conducted day and night raids against Haha and Chichi Jima with two raids being directed against enemy positions on Iwo Jima in general support of our forces. Aircraft from the Support Carrier Group, while it was still in the Iwo area, in addition to their numerous daily local commitments, also flew several strikes against Haha and Chichi Jima. Once the southern airfield became operational, an increasingly large number of B-29s sought refuge on the island while returning from raids over Japan, often in a precarious condition. By 14 March, D plus 23, 24 of the giant bombers had made emergency landings on the island, often under the very noses of the enemy still holding out in northern Iwo.

Even as Airfield No. 1 was becoming operational and the number of aircraft using its facilities increased, first steps were under way to restore the second airfield. Since the field, shortly to become known as the Central Airfield, was still under enemy fire during the latter part of February and early March, little could be done by way of actual reconstruction. As a first step, an abundance of mines and booby traps, which the enemy had left behind, had to be cleared, an unenviable task that was handled by the 2d Bomb Disposal Company, a Marine unit specializing in the removal of mines and duds. The company had already performed a similar job creditably at the southern airfield before restoration could get under way. By 16 March, the Central Airfield had been restored to a point where it also became operational. It featured one strip graded to 5,200 feet, another to 4,800 feet. As the assault phase on Iwo Jima came to a close, attention turned to the execution of plans for the development of the island as an important air base. To this end, once the objective was secured, a naval construction brigade was organized and additional construction units were employed. Original plans for the development of Iwo Jima had called for three airfields and installations to accommodate the garrison. The fields were to be designed to handle up to 90 B-29s daily, as well as five groups of escort fighters. The Central Airfield was to be utilized for staging Superfortresses en route from the Marianas to Japan. Airfields No. 1 and 3 were to serve fighters and smaller bombers. Alternate plans, however, were more ambitious than the earlier ones and eventually it was anticipated that the Central Field would be turned into one huge complex featuring two B-29 strips, two fighter strips, and a combat service center. It was finally decided that once the island was secured, the North and Central Fields would be combined, covering more than four square miles, just about half of the surface of the island.

In rebuilding the Iwo Jima airfields, the engineers ran into complex and exasperating problems. Because of the recent volcanic origin of Iwo, laying out the runways or putting in subsurface gasoline lines became a very difficult undertaking when steam pockets or sulphur laden crevasses were encountered. Construction of runways on the volcanic rock also posed a major problem and it became necessary to put the naval construction units on a schedule of two 10-hour shifts daily.

By mid-July, the first B-29 runway had been paved to its full length of 9,800 feet. The second strip had been graded to 9,400 feet by the end of the war but was never resurfaced. The old runway, running from west to east, became a 6,000-foot fueling strip. The fighter strip on Number 1 Airfield was eventually paved to 6,000 feet and was equipped with 7,940 feet of taxiways and 258 hardstands. The rough terrain in the area of the northern strip delayed construction, so that by the end of the war it had been paved to 5,500 feet for the use of fighters; in addition, some 10,000 feet of taxiway had been graded. Two large tank farms and facilities at each field took care of the supply of fuel.

The utilization of Iwo Jima as a fighter base was to be greatly affected by the overall war situation, The reduction of enemy air strength in Japan proper proceeded so rapidly during the late spring and early summer of 1945 that in time fighter escorts from Iwo were no longer required for the B-29s. Nevertheless, some 1,191 escort sorties were to be flown from Iwo, as well as 3,081 strike sorties against enemy targets in Japan. The primary use to which the airfields on the island were put was as an intermediate landing point, particularly for big B-29s in distress. By the time the war came to an end, about 2,400 of the giant bombers had made emergency landings on Iwo runways, involving a total of 25,000 airmen.

Logistics, Rear Installations, and News Coverage

A combination of enemy fire, deep volcanic ash, and heavy surf resulted in grave supply problems during the Iwo Jima operation. The early phase, in particular, became a nightmare for the Navy beach parties and the Marine shore parties. In the days following the initial landings, the main emphasis was on meeting the urgent requirements of the combat troops. The supplies brought ashore in LVTs and DUKWs often were sent directly inland without any rehandling on the beaches. For the first five days, until roads capable of supporting wheeled vehicles could be utilized, LVTs, DUKWs, and the versatile Weasels took care of transporting the bulk of supplies from the beaches to the inland dumps.

The landing of ammunition and supplies took place under extremely difficult conditions. Heavy swells caused extensive broaching of landing craft. With each wave, boats were picked up bodily and thrown broadside of the beach, where succeeding waves swamped and broached numerous landing craft. Other craft in succession hit the wrecks already beginning to pile up on the beaches until considerable wreckage had accumulated. The LSTs and LSMs sent to the beaches once the beachhead was secured also had great difficulty in keeping from broaching. Tugs were in constant attendance to tow them clear. Since unloading continued day and night, the beach parties had to work around the clock.

In order to facilitate getting supplies to the combat troops, Marston matting and armored bulldozers were utilized on the beaches. The matting was of tremendous value in overcoming the obstacle created by the soft volcanic ash on the landing beaches. The armored bulldozers, equipped with steel plates to protect both the driver and the machine, were employed on the beaches to level sand terraces and carve out exits. When fighting shifted to the northern part of the island, several bulldozers were used to cut roads through the rocky gorges characteristic of northern Iwo, notably in the 5th Marine Division zone of advance.

In discussing the value of the Marston matting and the armored bulldozers, the Commander of the Attack Force Beach Party Group, Captain Carl E. Anderson, USNR, pointed out that these two items of equipment "contributed materially to the success of the landing and the moving of heavy equipment off the beaches, which could not have otherwise been accomplished without almost insurmountable hardship." The pioneer battalions were the basic component of their respective division shore parties. The 133d and 31st Naval Construction Battalions provided equipment operators and cargo handlers for the 4th and 5th Marine Divisions. In addition, the Army's 442d and 592d Port Companies, assigned to the 4th and 5th Divisions respectively, and Marine service and supply units were given special tasks within the shore party organizations. Invaluable service was also rendered by the three Army DUKW companies which, like the port companies, were Negro units. Replacement drafts furnished the largest source of labor for ships platoons and shore details, though their subsequent integration into the depleted combat units left much to be desired. As of D plus 3, units of the 8th Field Depot went ashore and were assigned to assist the divisional shore parties, which were becoming depleted from casualties and fatigue.

There were slow but steady signs of progress. On D plus 6, the day that General Erskine launched his drive up the center of Iwo, engineers of the 5th Marine Division began the operation of the first water distillation plant on the west coast. Cognizant of the geological characteristics that were peculiar to the island, the engineers drove intake pipes into the natural springs. The water emerging from the ground was so hot that it had to be cooled with sea water. One of the first amenities of civilization, the hot shower, thus became a welcome arrival on the island.

On the same day, the VAC Shore Party assumed control of all shore party activities, a further indication that the situation on the beaches was stabilizing. The general unloading of cargo ships on the eastern beaches now got under way. As large quantities of supplies began to reach the shore, it soon became evident that additional beaches on the west coast of the island would have to be utilized. Preliminary surveys had indicated that conditions on the west coast were suitable for beaching LCTs and smaller craft. By D plus 8, beach exits and roads had been constructed on western Iwo. Simultaneously, a number of beaches, designated as Purple, Brown, White, and Orange, were established.

The Japanese, increasingly compelled to watch the beehive of activity along the eastern shore in helpless frustration, saw an opportunity to interfere with operations on the western beaches. On 1 March, an ammunition resupply ship, the *Columbia Victory*, was approaching the west coast with a cargo of artillery ammunition when mortar fire from Kama and Kangoku Rocks, as well as northwestern Iwo, bracketed the vessel. One shell exploded so close to the ship that it wounded one man and caused light damage to the vessel. Anxious eyes were watching the Japanese artillery fire, including those of Generals Holland Smith and Schmidt, who viewed the action from VAC headquarters on the west beach. More than the loss of a ship was involved. If the *Columbia Victory's* cargo of ammunition blew up, the entire west coast of Iwo could go with it, along with thousands of Marines working on the beaches. Keenly aware of the danger, the cargo ship reversed course and, miraculously evading additional near misses, headed back out to the open sea. As a result of enemy interference, the western beaches could not be opened until D plus 11, when Purple 2 went into operation. By 3 March, all assault shipping had been unloaded and retired from Iwo Jima, and Garrison Force Zero began to discharge its cargo. This element consisted of troops of the garrison force, commanded by Major General James E. Chancy, USA. The Zero echelon had been embarked in additional shipping to arrive at the objective on call after the assault ships, but prior to the first echelon garrison ships. General Chancy, together with his staff and elements of the Army's 147th Infantry Regiment and men of the 7th Fighter Command, had already gone ashore on D plus 8 as the advance echelon of Army ground and aviation troops that would play an important part in garrisoning the island. Meanwhile, the Army 506th Antiaircraft Battalion, having landed on D plus 6, was firing its 90mm guns at Kama and Kangoku Rocks off the west coast, from which the enemy had harassed the Columbia Victory. Men of the 5th Marine Division advancing up the west coast had already become the target of mortar and rocket fire from these islets.

While the Marines in the front lines were pitting their bodies against a cruel and remorseless enemy, the battle to save lives was being waged with equal devotion in the rear. American skill at improvisation, coupled with determination and medical know-how, were destined to save many lives. On Purple Beach on the west coast, a Navy evacuation hospital opened on the evening of D plus 6 with a capacity of 200 beds. At the 4th Marine Division hospital, located at the northern tip of the southern airfield, 17 doctors, operating in four surgical teams, worked around the clock. The Army's 38th Field Hospital, consisting of 22 officers and 182 enlisted men, came ashore on 25 February. Working together with the Navy medical facilities, it was to make a major contribution in providing medical care to the wounded in the days to come. Hospital facilities on Iwo were further supplemented when the 5th Marine Division Hospital went into operation at the southern tip of Airfield No. 1.

In order to provide the best possible care for the wounded, time was of the essence. This applied particularly to the availability of blood at the company medical aid stations. Blood plasma had been used in earlier operations, where its life-saving capabilities had already become legend. On Iwo Jima fresh whole blood, recently drawn on the west coast of the United States, packed in ice and airlifted directly to the scene of action, was used with excellent effects. Initially, whole blood was flown in by seaplane to a base established near Mount Suribachi at the southeastern tip of Iwo. Use of the seaplane base continued until 8 March, at which time it was decommissioned and the seaplanes, which had also been used to conduct rescues at sea, were returned to Saipan.

Once the southern airfield became operational, whole blood was flown into Iwo by casualty evacuation planes. Up to D plus 25, a total of 960 pints had been flown in. Additional supplies of blood plasma were obtained from the hospital ships. Before the Iwo operation came to a close, the Landing Force had used up 5,406 pints of whole blood. The total used for the care of the Iwo casualties up to this date amounted to 12,600 pints.

Before the Iwo Jima operation ended, Army and Marine air transports, consisting of C-46s and C-47s, airdropped 78 tons of supplies and delivered another 40 tons by air freight. The cargo planes involved were from the Army Air Forces 9th Troop Carrier Squadron and Marine VMR-253, -353, and -952.

On D plus 9, the hospital LSTs, which thus far had provided emergency treatment for the wounded, were released and left the area, fully loaded with casualties. At this time, shore-based medical facilities took over the task of caring for the wounded. Serious cases were subsequently evacuated directly from the beach to hospital ships and transports. By D plus 14, more than 9,500 casualties had been evacuated to rear areas by transports and hospital ships, not counting another 125 evacuated by air. Plans called for the evacuation of the wounded to Saipan, where 1,500 beds were available, and to Guam, which had beds for 3,500. From the Marianas, the casualties were to be transported to Hawaii by such surface ships as were available and by air as the condition of the men permitted.

Part of the activities carried on in the rear involved the collection and burial of the dead. This task was performed by service troops, often under extremely hazardous conditions, since the dead were in close proximity to the front lines. Carrying parties often became the target of enemy small arms and mortar fire. The ever present specter of death on Iwo Jima was to give rise to this description by a veteran of the battle: "As the struggle in the dust of Iwo Jima, in the rocks and ravines, continued night and day, the act of war became a monotony of horror, a boredom of agony and death; it became a way of life, a task, a burden, a work that was repetitious, galling to the body and mind. Death was so commonplace as to be without interest to the living, for the living were resigned to it. They no longer expected to survive. Fear was not of death, but of mutilation. And there was no end to this; no end to mutilating wounds."

Because of the heavy casualties during the Iwo operation, burial of the dead posed a special problem. Disposition of the dead was the responsibility of the 4th Marine Division burial officer, Captain Lewis Nutting, who occupied a dual position as VAC burial officer. Headquarters personnel, and especially members of the division band, performed this sad but necessary duty, which in time became a never-ending chore, as outlined here: "All day long, men carried litters to the field and placed them in neat rows. Two men passed along the rows, taking fingerprints, if the right index finger remained. Other men picked up one dog tag from each body, leaving the other for burial. If there were neither hands nor dog tags, and often there were not, the teams tried to establish identification by means of teeth, scars, tattoos, birthmarks, clothing stencils, jewelry, or uniform marks. Sometimes there was so little left that it was necessary to ascertain which section of the battlefield the body came from in order to determine to which unit the man had belonged."

When a row was ready, the bodies were wrapped in blankets or ponchos and placed in a trench. The bulldozer covered them with 6 feet of Iwo Jima sand, and a grader spread clay on top to keep it from blowing away. The sounds of battle off to the north were ignored. Since D plus 3, Captain Nutting's unit had suffered five casualties of its own. Even in the cemetery there was no security.

The Japanese, on their part, appeared reluctant to abandon their dead on the field, presumably not for sentimental reasons but in order to keep the advancing American forces from becoming aware of the true extent of the enemy losses. As a result, frequently under cover of darkness, Japanese carrying parties sneaked into the battle area and removed the dead. Where the disposition of bodies proved impractical, the enemy burned his dead or buried them in pillboxes.

As the campaign progressed, the efficiency of the landing force organization increased. Improved coordination of air, naval gunfire, and artillery was achieved through the VAC artillery officer, Colonel John S. Letcher, who already had worked out detailed guidelines back in Hawaii with the 4th and 5th Marine Divisions. In close teamwork with members of the Landing Force Air Support Control Unit and the corps air and naval gunfire officers, Letcher screened requests for supporting fire with members of the three division artillery regiments. Some of the members of this coordinating group continued to function on board the *Auburn* even after corps headquarters had gone ashore on 24 February. On the other hand, Colonel Letcher left the *Auburn* at 1430 that date and half an hour later went ashore, where he remained until the operation had ended.

Along with the demands of the situation, there were changes in the organization of the shipping that stood by off Iwo Jima. A new type of logistic vessel, the small craft tender, was introduced here. This vessel was a self-propelled barracks ship, later designated as the APB. Two of these vessels were employed at Iwo Jima on an experimental basis. Actually, the vessels were LSTs converted to meet the needs of the numerous small craft employed around the island with insufficient endurance for long voyages and long periods at objectives. In order to effectively support the small craft, the converted LSTs each carried about 225 tons of frozen and dry provisions, 120,000 gallons of water, and about 235,000 gallons of fuel; they had berthing facilities for 40 transient officers and 300 men, a sick bay for 14 patients, and messing arrangements for 750 men on a round-the-clock basis. The ships serviced by these tenders at Iwo included destroyers, destroyer escorts, destroyer minesweepers, landing ships, minelayers, patrol and landing craft, minesweepers, submarine chasers, and rescue tugs. From 19 February through 7 March, the two APBs refueled and rewatered 54 vessels and reprovisioned 76.

The above does not by far represent the total accomplishment of the two vessels, whose performance was to lead to the following observation: "Perhaps the best thing of all was the way the tenders mothered the landing boats and their crews. Many of these were caught at the beach when their own ships moved out of sight. Many were temporarily disabled, some lost. These tenders berthed a total of 2,500 officers and men, and fed 4,000 on the scale of one man, 1 day. It was a great help to a tired and hungry boat crew to have a place to eat and sleep." The tenders did not carry landing-craft spares or repair facilities. The principal part of the maintenance and repair work at Iwo was done by 3 landing ships (dock), 3 repair ships, 1 diesel repair ship, and 1 landing-craft repair ship. The job was no small one, totaling work on 30 landing ships (tank), 3 destroyers, 5 attack transports, 1 net ship, and numerous landing boats. It has been said that every small boat used in landing on beaches had sustained damage of some sort, many of them more than once. The LSDs worked 24 hours a day on repairs. The divers of the repair ships practically lived in diving suits from sunrise to 10 or 11 o'clock at night clearing propellers and doing underwater repair and salvage work.

An account of developments on and around Iwo Jima would not be complete without mention of the 3d Marines. This regiment, commanded by Colonel James A. Stuart, constituted the Expeditionary Troops Reserve. As early as D plus 9, 28 February, both Generals Schmidt and Erskine had requested commitment of this reserve to lend impetus to the lagging drive up the center of the island. This request was made at a time when the landing force already had sustained crippling casualties, and the loss of manpower, coupled with exhaustion of the men, was beginning to seriously impair the combat efficiency of all three Marine divisions committed on Iwo Jima. Despite the energetic efforts on the part of VAC to get the 3d Marines landed, General Holland Smith felt compelled to repeat the argument of Admiral Turner, Commander of the Joint Expeditionary Force, that the number of troops already ashore was sufficient to complete the capture of the island and that the employment of an additional regiment would only add to the congestion. This contention was to be strongly disputed by the VAC operations officer who was to make this comment: "It was my considered opinion while on Iwo Jima, having visited all parts of the island in our hands, and keeping in close touch with the situation, that the 3d Marine Regiment could have been landed without in any way overcrowding the island. Commitment of this well trained and experienced regiment would have shortened the campaign and saved us casualties."

The pros and cons of committing the 3d Marines were to spark a controversy that has remained unresolved more than two decades later. Members of the landing force still consider with bitterness that "commitment of a fresh regiment at that time would have cheered up the exhausted troops ashore and would have permitted the final capture of Iwo Jima in much less time and with far fewer casualties." According to one analysis of the situation: "The consequences of using battle replacements rather than landing the infantrymen of the Third Regiment and shortening the fronts of the units in the line are, in retrospect, evident. Completing the assault was delayed. Key personnel in the front lines were unduly exposed, and casualties relative to the resistance encountered began to increase both among regular infantrymen and among the battle replacements."

In almost all respects, the conversion of Iwo Jima into an American military base was influenced by the small physical size of the island. There were no buildings, roads, wooded areas, fields, or streams. But above all, there was little room in the rear area, such as there was. Always close to the front lines and never more than two or three miles to the rear, the airfields, gun positions, supply dumps, and troops occupied virtually every inch of the island.

The lack of space in the rear had its effect as much on the location of medical facilities as it did on the headquarters of the three divisions operating on the island and VAC headquarters. The medical organizations dispersed their units into such areas as were allotted "and with the help of the ubiquitous bulldozer literally dug themselves a place on the island." Portable plywood operating rooms were set up in holes in the ground and covered with tarpaulins to keep out the dust and cold. The engineers built roofs over sunken water reservoirs which made good operating rooms. Ward tents were set up in airplane revetments or simply in long trenches bulldozed in the ground. The electric lights went in, the field surgical units were set up, the blood bank moved ashore, and by the time the transports left, a system of excellent surgical facilities was in operation.

In his memoirs, General Holland Smith recalled his impression of the command posts on Iwo Jima which he had occasion to inspect: "I went ashore every second day, calling on Harry Schmidt at V Corps Headquarters, or on Rockey, Cates, and Erskine at their Command Posts, and going forward to watch the progress of the fighting. None of these Command Posts was the Hotel Splendide the invading general seizes for himself and his staff in fictional war. Cates' post, overlooking the sea near the fortified quarry, was a knocked-out Japanese pillbox, where the smell of decomposing enemy dead, buried in the ruins, grew more loathsome every day. Erskine, just south of Motoyama Airfield Two, occupied an abandoned Japanese gun emplacement, with a tarpaulin slung over a 4.7-inch dual purpose gun. Over on the left, Rockey had a ramshackle place up against a cliff, where the Japanese had been flushed out recently."

Supply of the landing force was a highly complex operation. Thus, the average daily expenditure of artillery ammunition right up to the final phase of the campaign, exceeded 23,000 rounds daily. Enough ammunition of various types was unloaded across the beaches to fill 480 freight cars, plus enough food to feed the entire city of Columbus, Ohio, for an entire month. Expressed in definite numbers, for the naval bombardment alone the total of ammunition actually expended came to a staggering 14,650 tons. This amount was divided into 2,400 rounds of 16-inch, weighing 2,280 tons; 5,700 rounds of 14-inch, 3,640 tons; 1,440 rounds of 12-inch, 520 tons; 11,700 rounds of 8-inch high capacity, 2,020 tons; 8,400 rounds of 6-inch high capacity, 440 tons; 152,000 rounds of 5-inch high capacity, 4,160 tons; 17,700 rounds of 5-inch star, 300 tons; 12,000 rounds of 5-inch, 270 tons; 10,000 rounds of 4-inch, 145 tons; and 70,000 rounds of 4.2 mortar, 875 tons.

In addition to ammunition, an amazing quantity of fuel and other items were to be required for the capture of the five-mile long island. These included: 4,100,000 barrels of black oil, 595,000 barrels of diesel oil, 33,775,000 gallons of aviation gasoline, and 6,703,000 gallons of motor gas; plus about 28,000 tons of various types of ammunition; 38 tons of clothing; more than 10,000 tons of fleet freight; more than 7,000 tons of ship supplies of rope, canvas, fenders, cleaning gear, and hardware; approximately, 1,000 tons of candy; toilet articles, stationary, and ship's service canteen items; and about 14,500 tons of fresh, frozen, and dry provisions. General Holland Smith himself was to remark later "that the amount of effort that had gone into the capture of the barren island was staggering. The Navy had put more ammunition on Iwo Jima than anywhere else in the Pacific. Marine artillery expended 450,000 shells and we used huge quantities of mortar shells, grenades, and rockets."

Closely connected with the expenditure of ammunition by shore-based artillery and naval gunfire was the Air Support Control Unit, in charge of the combat air and antisubmarine patrol. The unit was composed of Marine and Navy officers and Marine enlisted technicians and operators. Here the cramped space available on Iwo Jima was an advantage. In this case, the unit was located only 75 feet from the Landing Force Command Post. As a result of this proximity, troop requests for air support could be handled much more expeditiously than before.

For the coordination of artillery fire and air strikes, a brief of each air strike was broadcast over the Corps Artillery Fire Direction Control Net. Each air strike was given a number and information obtained on number and type of aircraft, direction of approach and retirement, minimum altitude, and other pertinent data. Each artillery battalion thus was able to control its fire so that it did not interfere with strikes. A complete cessation of artillery fire became necessary only once or twice when aircraft delivered a low-level napalm attack.

Progress in developing the island did not stop with the construction of new facilities. In some instances, the very shape of the island had to be changed to meet the requirements of the new occupants. Even Iwo's most outstanding landmark, Mount Suribachi, was to be affected by these changes. The Army garrison troops planned to get various trucks housing radar, weather, and navigational equipment for the coming assault against the Japanese home islands on top of the mountain. Before such plans could be realized, it became necessary to construct a road to the top, a project that had never been realized by the Japanese. On D plus 15, construction of a two-lane road, 35 feet wide, got under way, winding its way up and around the mountain for nearly a mile. Early the following morning, the first bulldozer drove into the crater at the top of Suribachi. The Japanese, a number of whom were still living inside the mountain after surviving the battle for Suribachi, were powerless to interfere with the road construction. They stole out of their caves only at night in search of food and water and were methodically eliminated when spotted.

In the midst of the multitude of supporting headquarters and units operating on the island, there was a special complement of men, neither wholly military or civilian, whose job it was to photograph the action on the island or write about it. They were representatives of American and Allied news services, radio networks, and local newspapers. The news reporters were given the widest possible latitude in covering the operation and thus could be found among the invasion force, in the landing boats, and occasionally in the foxholes.

In addition to the accredited civilian correspondents, each of the military services had its own news writers and photographers, including a special Navy film crew which recorded the entire operation on color film. Radio teletype equipment was set up on the beaches for the benefit of the press, and a Navy floatplane was made available to carry copy, photographs, and newsreels directly to Guam, where this material was processed and flown back to the United States. Another precedent was established when, on D plus 7, Admiral Turner and General Holland M. Smith were interviewed on Iwo Jima in a live broadcast while the battle was still raging on the island.

The events on the battlefield received wide coverage and distribution in American newspapers and magazines. None of the ferocity of the fighting was withheld from the American public. As casualties mounted and the full impact of the cost in lives expended to secure the island began to hit home, plaintive voices arose to question the need for such a bloodletting. Then as now, sincere and serious-minded Americans, appalled witnesses to the savage fighting they could not stem, groped for a way out, at least a more inexpensive way to subdue the enemy. Among the expedients suggested was the employment of toxic gas.

The Case for and Against Chemical Warfare

Unknown to the public at large, the employment of chemical warfare agents in the Pacific Theater had already undergone active consideration while the Iwo operation was still in the planning stage. Through collaboration with the Office of Strategic Services, forerunner of the Central Intelligence Agency, a special report had been compiled on the subject of gas warfare on Iwo Jima. Its primary feature was the recommendation that Japanese transmitters on the island be jammed. Once the enemy's communications had been rendered inoperable and he was isolated, the entire island was to be inundated with gas. In late June 1944, the director of Research and Development, OSS, had made a special trip to Hawaii to discuss the project with Admiral Nimitz.

The difficulties of employing gas warfare were twofold, both technical and moral. During the early part of World War II, the United States had thought of the use of toxic gases only as a retaliatory measure. In this connection, the 100-pound mustard-filled bomb was considered by chemical warfare officers as the most suitable munition for retaliation. The peak stock of this item attained in the Pacific Theater in July 1944 was 15,244 bombs with 541.2 tons of toxic filling. In the words of a chemical warfare service officer: "This supply was token only. If, for example, this entire supply had been used on Iwo Jima, which had an area of seven and one-half square miles, it would only have contaminated a little more than half, or four and one half square miles. Considering the vapor effect of mustard and the fact that the entire island would not have been regarded as a target, the stock would have been sufficient for one contamination. In the opinion of most chemical officers one contamination would have been enough to end all enemy resistance on the island. The question of resupply for other objectives would then arise."

The second difficulty in employing chemical warfare against the Japanese could be found in the attitude of most of the nation's civilian and military leaders. In fact, military reluctance to use this weapon had its origin in the experiences of the American Expeditionary Forces in World War I. In connection with the possible employment of toxic gas on Iwo Jima, General Holland Smith made this comment: "I am not prepared to argue this question. Certainly, gas shells smothering the island, or gas introduced into caves and tunnels would have simplified our task, but naturally the use of this prohibited weapon was not within the power of a field commander. The decision was on a higher level. It was in the hands of the Allied Powers, who alone could authorize its use in a war which would have assumed even more frightful proportions had gas been allowed."

In the end, it was the Chief Executive of the United States who had a final voice in approving or disapproving the entire plan. Regardless of their divergent political views, both Herbert Hoover and Franklin D. Roosevelt in the years between the two world wars had been in favor of eliminating gas as a military weapon. In 1937, when vetoing a bill that would have changed the designation of the Army Chemical Warfare Service to that of Chemical Corps, the President had expressed his views on this subject in no uncertain terms:

"It has been and is the policy of this Government to do everything in its power to outlaw the use of chemicals in warfare. Such use is inhuman and contrary to what modern civilization should stand for."

One of the official Army histories dealing with chemical warfare has pointed out in this connection that "gas warfare had no advocates in high places." While this may have been true during the early years of World War II, there is some evidence that, as of early 1945, the atmosphere in Washington has begun to shift in favor of chemical warfare. Another reason for increased American readiness to accept initiation of chemical warfare towards the final phase of the war may be found in the extremely heavy American casualties sustained in the Western Pacific. None other than General of the Army George C. Marshall was to testify after the war had ended that "following the terrible losses at Iwo Jima, he was prepared to use gas at Okinawa." It is interesting to note that, at the same time that American views towards the employment of gas offensively became more aggressive, the Japanese policy shifted in the opposite direction. With the loss of the Marianas in the spring and summer of 1944, the home islands had suddenly become extremely vulnerable to American chemical attack. In the firm belief that the United States would not initiate gas warfare, and since Japanese ability to retaliate was in any case too low, Japan, in mid-1944 "decided to discontinue production of toxic agents and to recall all stocks of gas munitions from the hands of troops in the field. Thus, in mid-1944, the Japanese started a policy of disarmament. Readiness spiraled downward until hostilities ended."

Thus we are faced with the strange spectacle of a hostile nation, pledged to fight to the death, and confronted by an immense military machine, dismantling its limited chemical warfare apparatus as operations reached their climax. Stranger still, Japanese reasoning apparently was based on the declared policy of the United States not to initiate gas warfare. The Japanese failed to consider that, given different time and circumstances, such a policy might be subject to change.

With present knowledge, not available to Allied planners in 1944, it becomes clear that by the time the Iwo Jima operation got underway, Japan was no longer in a position to retaliate with chemical means in response to Allied action, with one minor exception. All that prevented the employment of gas on Iwo Jima was the President's aversion to gas warfare. Even though the United States had not signed any international instrument outlawing such warfare, national policy clearly limited the conditions under which toxic gas might have been introduced. In consequence of this policy, heavy casualties to the contrary, Marines would continue to assault Iwo Jima with rifle, hand grenade, and flamethrowers until all resistance had been overcome. In a matter of roughly three weeks from D-Day, Iwo Jima had been transformed from a strongpoint in the Japanese defense system to an important American air base of strategic and tactical importance to the overall air offensive against Japan. The capture and development of the island denied its use to the enemy and at the same time it served as an emergency haven for aircraft returning from raids against Japan. In American hands, Iwo Jima represented an advance base for search and reconnaissance. It further provided a base within fighter range of Japan. Furthermore, the island could be utilized as a staging point for bombers, permitting greater bomb loads in lieu of gasoline, though the island was not much used for this purpose. Iwo Jima could also become a refueling stop for short-range aircraft en route to bases closer to Japan yet to be seized before the general assault against the Japanese homeland got underway later in the year.

This, then, was the significance of the fiercely contested island. This is why General Kuribayashi had decided to adopt those tactics that would prove most costly to the invasion force and that would cause the most delay in the conversion of the stronghold to American use. After three weeks of bitter fighting, his intention has been partially realized as far as taking a toll in American lives was concerned. But, just behind the front lines, bulldozers were shifting earth, changing the very landscape of the island; communications were humming, and heedless of tenacious Japanese holed up in the northern part of the island, the task of reconstruction was proceeding at an ever-increasing pace.

Chapter 9. The 5th Marine Division Drive On the Left

Advance up the West Coast

As the battle for Iwo Jima neared its climax, the full force of three Marine divisions was employed to reduce the main enemy defenses near the Central Airfield. General Erskine's drive up the center of the island to the northern shore has already been narrated. In addition to the men of the 3d Marine Division who fought and died at such landmarks as Hills OBOE and PETER, Motoyama Village, and Hill 362C, Marines of the adjacent 4th and 5th Divisions were making similar sacrifices to the east and west respectively. In the sectors of the latter two divisions the landmarks may have varied in some respects. They were to bear names like Hill 362A, 362B, Nishi Ridge, and Bloody Gorge. Men of the 4th Division would suffer at places appropriately named the Meat Grinder, the Amphitheater, and Turkey Knob. For all of them the enemy remained the same: fanatical, utterly devoted to his mission, bent on the destruction of the invaders who had dared violate sacred Japanese soil. An attack by the 5th Marine Division on 24 February had resulted in sizable gains by the 26th Marines, which by the end of the day advanced 400 yards north of the 3d Division elements on its right. The gains were made at a heavy cost; 21 officers and 332 enlisted men became casualties on D plus 5. In order to give the 9th Marines a chance of straightening the lines, the 26th Marines was ordered to remain in place on 25 February.

On the morning of D plus 6, the 5th Marine Division held a line extending for 1,200 yards from west to east. From the left to right, 2/27 held the cliffs overlooking the western beaches; the center of the line, protruding into enemy territory, was held by 2/26; to the right of this battalion, the line slanted southward, held by 3/26 with one attached company of 1/26. It had become evident by this time that the high ground in the zone of action of the adjacent 3d Marine Division exerted a paramount influence on the further advance of the 5th Division. No major progress could be expected until General Erskine's division had driven the enemy from this high ground in the center of the island.

While the 26th Marines consolidated its positions on 25 February, the adjacent 9th Marines of the 3d Division attacked northward along its joint boundary with the 5th Marine Division. On this day, the 9th Marines failed to make any noteworthy gains, and the situation along Colonel Graham's right flank remained substantially unchanged. Throughout the day, heavy enemy fire from the right front raked the positions occupied by the 26th Marines, greatly interfering with supply and evacuation. Nevertheless, the men of the 5th Division were to get one break during the day. Around 1500, one of the spotter planes reported enemy artillery moving north along a road following the contour of the island on northern Iwo. Three batteries of the 13th Marines immediately adjusted on the target and fired nearly 600 rounds. At the end of this fire mission, the observer reported that three artillery pieces had been destroyed, several prime movers were burning, and an ammunition dump was ablaze. This was the only time during the Iwo Jima campaign that the enemy ever offered such a choice target. Hereafter, Japanese artillery deployed to new firing positions only at night.

On D plus 7 General Rockey's division resumed the attack. Following a 45-minute artillery and naval gunfire preparation, the 26th Marines jumped off in the main effort. Almost immediately, the attack ran into heavy resistance. The enemy poured fire from small arms, machine guns, and mortars into the ranks of the advancing Marines. At the same time, heavy artillery and mortar fire from the northern part of the island hit the assault troops. As the Marines closed with the enemy, hand grenade duels ensued.

During the advance, the nature of the terrain underwent a subtle change. Thus far, General Rockey's division had been operating in soft, sandy, and open terrain. As the 26th Marines moved northward, the level ground gave way to heavily fortified cliffs. Essentially, the 5th Marine Division now entered a difficult complex of ridges. In each case, the attack had to be carried up one slope, across the top, and then down into another ravine beyond. Above the ridges, there loomed a major enemy bastion, Hill 362A, just south of Nishi Village. This terrain feature impressed the advancing Marines because its sinister presence overshadowed all other obstacles in the area. The hill was rugged and rocky, devoid of all vegetation on its southern slopes. To the north, as yet unseen by the Americans advancing from the south, there was a sheer drop of about 80 feet. The Japanese had exploited this formidable obstacle to the utmost. The entire hill bristled with caves of varying sizes, many of them serving as mortar and machine gun emplacements. The elevation enabled the enemy to observe western Iwo all the way south to Mount Suribachi, and thus exposed to his view all American activity in the front lines, as well as on the western beaches. Despite fierce enemy resistance, the 5th Marine Division attack on 26 February moved steadily towards Hill 362A, still about 800 yards away, whose very prominence made it a natural objective. The three battalions in the main effort were the 2d and 3d Battalions, 26th Marines, commanded respectively by Major Amedeo Rea and Major Richard Fagan, and 2/27 under Major John W. Antonelli. Because of heavy automatic weapons fire from an enemy strongpoint consisting of pillboxes and caves, the advance of 2/26 was so slowed that in two hours gains of only 50 yards were registered. Tanks of Company B, 5th Tank Battalion, took a hand in the fighting. At 1000, Company F of 2/26, thus far held in reserve, was committed. With the support of armor, the infantry launched a spirited attack against the stubborn enemy position. The efforts of this company were quickly crowned with success. For the first time since 2/26 had come ashore, the battalion came face to face with the usually elusive and unseen enemy. In the resulting pitched battle, the Japanese came out second best. Those of the enemy who sought to flee were killed out in the open. Catching the ordinarily well entrenched enemy for once in such a vulnerable position greatly boosted the morale of the Marines engaged in this action, "for no man likes to fight something he cannot see, and the sight of running Japs was, if nothing else, reassuring."

Advancing on the right and supported by tanks of Company A, 5th Tank Battalion, 3/26 gained about 100 yards, smashing fortifications as it went along and destroying numerous guns in the ravines that led down from the plateau perpendicular to the route of advance. Gains made by the adjacent 9th Marines helped 3/26 in its forward movement. To the left of the 26th Marines, 2/27 initially made rapid progress, gaining 400 yards during the first two hours. For the remainder of the day, the battalion stayed in place in order to permit 2/26 to come abreast. The terrain in the zone of advance of 2/27 precluded the employment of tanks. Instead, 20 LVT's of the 2d Armored Amphibian Battalion, under Lieutenant Colonel Reed M. Fawell, Jr., supported the battalion attack from the sea. The 75mm fire from the armored amphibians knocked out several enemy caves, but in the choppy seas their fire began to endanger friendly troops and, as a result, they were ordered to cease fire. When action halted on the evening of 26 February, the lines of the 5th Marine Division still formed an arc whose apogee extended some 400 yards into enemy territory. Gains for the day amounted to roughly 300 yards, Most important of all, the day's advance had netted the 26th Marines two Japanese wells, the last ones believed to be under enemy control. Henceforth, the Japanese would have to rely on such water as they had been able to store or on rainfall.

Enemy reaction to the loss of this vital resource was not long delayed. Following a rainy afternoon, the skies cleared. In bright moonlight, a company-size force of Japanese assembled and started to move down the west coast, presumably with the intention of recapturing the two vital wells. Men of the 26th Marines spotted a sizable enemy force heading for one of the wells near the cliffs south of Hill 362A. The Japanese represented a splendid target in the moonlight. Both artillery and naval gunfire racked the enemy force and dispersed it before it reached any of the wells.

In another incident during this restless night, at the observation post of Company D, the company commander, Captain Thomas M. Fields, and a member of his staff observed three Japanese walking boldly within 25 feet of them with picric acid satchel charges. The two officers routed the enemy with hand grenades, killing one of the intruders. This was only one example of the enemy's boldness in approaching or penetrating the American lines. Marines up front could never be sure of who or what was approaching them in the darkness. One of the early incidents which occurred on D plus 2, involved the compromise of the password "Chevrolet" in the area then occupied by Company F, 2/26. A sentry challenged a moving figure, who gave the correct password. Not satisfied with the pronunciation of "Chevrolet," the sentry repeated his challenge. Once again the password was mispronounced. The sentry fired and killed the intruder, who the next morning was identified as Japanese.

Confrontations of this type tended to increase the vigilance of Marines on Iwo Jima. At times, such alertness was carried to the extreme and, a few nights later, resulted in a humorous incident involving the same company. During the night of 25-26 February, Company F, 2/26, seized a Navajo Indian, who was mistakenly identified as Japanese. His poor English, made worse by a bad case of fright, made his position precarious for a while. Fortunately, he escaped physical harm; his ordeal ended when he was finally identified by another Navajo Marine. At 0630 on 27 February, the 27th Marines, with 1/26 attached, relieved the 26th Marines. Ninety minutes later, following a half-hour preparation by the 13th Marines, reinforced by corps artillery, Colonel Wornham's men jumped off with 2/27 on the left, 1/27 in the center, and 3/27 on the right. The 1st Battalion, 26th Marines, remained in regimental reserve. Shortly before the jumpoff, truck-mounted launchers of the 3d Rocket Detachment showered the area directly in front of the lines with a heavy barrage of 4.5-inch rockets, then pulled back before the enemy could retaliate. At the same time, naval gunfire was brought to bear against Hill 362A, followed by carrier aircraft which bombed and rocketed the hill.

Moving forward in the center, 1/27 gained 200 yards before running straight into a heavily defended cluster of pillboxes. A half-track was able to knock out one of these strong points with its 75mm gun before its crew was hit by well-aimed small arms fire. A decision to move up 37mm guns for support could not be implemented because no suitable positions could be found. Consequently, the task of reducing the formidable obstacle once again fell to small flamethrower-demolition teams who would reduce one pillbox after another in the slow, dangerous, but time-proven method.

During the afternoon, when the company advancing on the left of the 1st Battalion encountered a heavily fortified area, the call went out for tanks. The arrival of a flamethrower tank, in particular, was eagerly awaited. When it finally reached the scene of action, accompanied by other armor, it received a mortar hit and was disabled before it had a chance to take part in the engagement. Nevertheless, the remaining Shermans lent effective support. They fired with everything they had and then moved forward in concert with the infantry. In the course of this advance, several more enemy pillboxes, as well as a dug-in tank, were put out of action. Once the momentum of the attack had been regained, the Marines moved forward for an additional 200 yards until they halted shortly after 1900.

Advancing on the left of the 27th Marines, the 2d Battalion faced not only a determined enemy, but extremely difficult terrain. The cliff on the high ground adjacent to the west coast beaches was honeycombed with caves and emplacements, most of them sheltering mortars and machine guns. In such terrain the employment of tanks was out of the question; furthermore, the few existing routes of approach were heavily mined. Once again, the full burden of the attack fell on small infantry and demolition teams, each one advancing more or less independently, taking its losses as it eliminated one enemy strongpoint after another. Of necessity, such a movement is slow and extremely exhausting, yet steady gains were made and by late afternoon, 2/27 had advanced 500 yards.

On the right of the division line, 3/27 moved against a ridge which guarded the approach to Hill 362A, Company G launched a frontal assault against this ridge and was promptly thrown back. A group of 30 men attempting to outflank this position was initially repulsed; a second try appeared more promising. As the Marines advanced up the slope they were hit by a hail of hand grenades thrown by the enemy from the reverse slope. Ten Marines were killed on the spot, including Gunnery Sergeant William G. Walsh, who dived on a hand grenade which landed in a hole where he and several of the men had taken cover. As other elements of the company reached the scene, the enemy was driven from the reverse slope, and the ridge remained in friendly hands. As D plus 8 came to a close, the 5th Marine Division had gained roughly 500 yards through the heart of the enemy main line of resistance in some of the heaviest fighting in which any Marine unit on Iwo Jima was to take part. Losses throughout the day had been heavy, some units being harder hit than others. In one instance, Company A, 1/27, occupied a ridge only to discover that it was exposed to heavy enemy rifle and machine gun fire. The company suffered additional casualties from enemy hand grenades, thrown from bypassed positions in the flanks and rear. For all practical purposes, the Marines of Company A on top of the ridge were cut off. The 1st Platoon, in particular, was hard hit. By the time the company was relieved by Company B, 8 men had been killed and 50 wounded. While the Company

A losses were unusually heavy, they serve as an indication of the 5th Marine Division's losses since D-Day. By noon of D plus 8, the division had sustained 32 officers and 530 men killed, 134 officers and 2,360 men wounded, and 2 officers and 160 men missing in action, a total of 168 officers and 3,058 men.

The 5th Marine Division had now reached the O-2 Line across its entire zone of advance, though the lines on the evening of D plus 8 were not perfectly straight. Not all of the action occurred in the front lines. Continuous vigilance was required to clear the enemy out of the previously captured ground. Japanese kept appearing seemingly out of nowhere. Only later was it determined that they could move at will through a carefully constructed system of tunnels. As a result, before a day's attack could get under way, some mopping up remained to be done in the rear area. Despite the gains made by the 27th Marines on 27 February, an even more difficult operation awaited 5th Marine Division units on the following day.

The Assault on the Hill 362A

On the morning of D plus 9, the last day of February, the 5th Marine Division was squarely up against Hill 362A, the highest elevation on western Iwo. The hill loomed forbiddingly above the Marines huddled at its approaches. Around the base of this hill mass, rocky outcrops dominated every approach. The Japanese had fortified each one of these rocky spurs,which afforded excellent fields of fire. For the attack on 28 February, the 27th Marines had been ordered to seize an intermediate objective between the O-2 and O-3 Lines. Initially, the mission of taking Hill 362A had been entrusted to 3/27, while 1/27 was to simultaneously attack an irregular line of ridges extending from the objective down to the western beaches. During the night, 1/26 had relieved 2/27 and was committed along the left flank of the regiment along the beaches. Following a 45-minute preparation by artillery, naval gunfire, and rockets, and supported by carrier-based aircraft, the 27th Marines jumped off at 0815 for what was to develop into one of the bloodiest encounters on the island.

From the outset, the enemy offered stubborn resistance all along the regimental front. Advancing in the center and on the right of the regimental line, 1/27 and 3/27 encountered some of the heaviest small arms fire yet directed against them. The 1st Battalion called for and received tank support as it had on the previous day, but the terrain in the zone of advance of 3/27 precluded the employment of armor, and the battalion had to rely strictly on its own fire power. Advancing gingerly across 200 yards of difficult terrain, the two assault battalions reached the foot of the hill around noon.

At this point, the attack began to bog down. In accordance with General Kuribayashi's orders, the Japanese remained in their positions and fought to the bitter end. Those who were bypassed continued to fire into the rear of the advancing Marines. At such close range, the enemy snipers were extremely effective and inflicted heavy casualties on the assault force. In the course of the afternoon, several patrols from 3/27 probed the defenses on the hill itself, seeking for a way to seize it. A patrol from Company I actually made it up the southwest slopes to the crest of the hill around 1630. However, since cohesion between 1/27 and 3/27 had been lost, the patrol had to be recalled in late afternoon and Company I pulled back about 100 yards, where it tied in with elements of the adjacent 21st Marines on the left of the 3d Marine Division.

Far from being content with halting the Marine advance, 50-100 enemy troops sallied forth from positions on Hill 362A during the late afternoon and counterattacked the 3/27 lines. The brunt of this blow fell upon Company H, which engaged in desperate hand-to-hand fighting with frenzied Japanese before the latter were driven off.

By nightfall, men of the 27th Marines were still stalled at the foot of Hill 362A, which towered above them, seemingly as impregnable as ever. After a day of extremely bitter action, which had cost numerous casualties, the overall regimental gain had been about 300 yards. To the left, 1/26 had sent out advance detachments along the beaches, but the northward movement of any large body of troops was seriously impaired by the enemy's possession of the adjacent high ground. The night from 28 February to 1 March turned out to be a very quiet one for the exhausted 5th Division Marines in the front lines. Four listening posts had been established by 2/26 along the beaches to frustrate any enemy intentions of landing reinforcements on the island. Each listening post had been augmented with one dog and its handler from the 6th War Dog Platoon. Eventually, things became so quiet that even the dogs found it difficult to remain awake. Elsewhere on Iwo Jima, it was a different matter. In the southern part of the island, in the vicinity of Mount Suribachi where they had been positioned ever since that elevation was captured, the 28th Marines was preparing to move north to join the 15th Division drive. At midnight, the enemy began shelling the positions of the corps artillery and those of the 13th Marines. This bombardment continued at some length. Shortly after 0200, the 5th Marine Division ammunition dump blew up with a tremendous roar, blazing fiercely for the remainder of the night. At least 20 percent of the division small arms ammunition supply was lost in the conflagration, along with large quantities of heavier ammunition. One of the exploding shells landed in the corps artillery fire direction center but caused no casualties, though it did wreak havoc with the telephone wire.

In the course of the operation, VAC Headquarters itself came under fire a number of times from mortars and artillery. This shelling resulted in several casualties. On at least two occasions, all work in the operations tents of the various staff sections came to a stop and officers and men piled together on the ground as shells landed nearby.

In the midst of the commotion caused by the exploding ammunition dump, the island's air alert system went off. The nerves of personnel in the southern part of the island were further strained when exploding white phosphorus shells were mistaken for gas shells and someone gave the gas alarm at 0300. Within ten minutes, the gas alarm was cancelled; not so the air alert, which continued until 0430.

As it turned out, there was some substance to the air alert. No enemy planes appeared over Iwo Jima during the night, but shortly before 0300 an enemy aircraft, skimming in low over the water, dropped a torpedo near the destroyer *Terry* a few miles north of Kitano Point. The destroyer took evasive action and barely avoided getting hit by the torpedo. However, a few hours later, while passing the northernmost point of Iwo Jima, the ship came under fire from enemy shore batteries, which scored hits on the main deck and forward engine room. Eleven destroyer crewmen were killed and 19 wounded before the *Terry*, assisted by the *Nevada* and *Pensacola*, made good her escape. In addition to the loss in lives, the ship had suffered substantial damage. Another vessel, the destroyer *Colhoun*, anchored off the northeastern coast of Iwo to repair damage sustained in a collision, took several hits from enemy shore batteries which wrecked a torpedo tube, exploded the air flask of a torpedo, and caused other extensive damage. One man was killed and 16 were wounded in the course of this action. At 0630 on 1 March, the 28th Marines, with the

5th Tank Battalion and 3/27 attached, moved forward through the 27th Marines in order to continue the attack on Hill 362A. Between 0745 and 0830, the objective and surrounding area received a heavy shelling from all four battalions of the 13th Marines and the corps' 155mm howitzers. Off-shore, a battleship and two cruisers joined in the bombardment. The volume of fire was such that it was deemed best, in the interests of coordination, to exclude aircraft from the preparatory fire. They would have ample opportunity to support the attack later in the day.

Shortly before 0900 the 28th Marines jumped off with the 1st, 2d, and 3d Battalions from right to left. The attack moved ahead slowly under heavy enemy mortar and small arms fire. To Colonel Liversedge's men, the dogged defense of Hill 362A was reminiscent of the action at the base of Mount Suribachi. The scheme of maneuver called for 1/28 and 2/28 to attack around the right and left of Hill 362A respectively and link up on the north side of the hill. Meanwhile, 3/28 was to advance up the west coast to the left of 2/28.

By 1030, both the 1st and 2d Battalions had reached the top of the ridge and the ridgeline running east and west of Hill 362A. As they attempted to advance beyond the crest, they discovered that a steep drop of nearly 100 feet into a rocky draw confronted them. To make matters worse, heavy fire from small arms, automatic weapons, and mortars hit the advancing Marines from the adjacent ridge to the north, subsequently to become known as Nishi Ridge. The draw itself ran parallel to the ridge line and was bisected by an antitank ditch that ran perpendicular to the hill. Covering the ditch were cleverly constructed positions in the face of the steep cliff, inaccessible from the top. Beyond the antitank ditch and the draw, the ground leveled off for about 200 yards before again rising sharply to form Nishi Ridge.

In order to keep the attack moving, Lieutenant Colonel Jack B. Butterfield, commanding 1/28, sent his reserve, Company A, around the right of Hill 362A. This maneuver proved unsuccessful and the company came under such withering fire, accompanied by a shower of grenades, that it was stopped short in its tracks. During this assault the company commander was killed. A similar attempt by Company B to get into the draw proved equally unsuccessful, and the company commander was wounded. In this jumble of rock, both companies suffered heavy casualties. Among these was Corporal Tony Stein of Company A, who had already made a name for himself on D Day. He set out with 20 men to clear the ridge of snipers. Only seven men returned from this mission. Among the men of Company B killed near the base of Hill 362A this day were three who had raised the American flag on Mount Suribachi; one of them had taken part in the first and the two others had participated in the second flag raising. Throughout the day, 10 regular tanks and 2 flame tanks of Company C, 5th Tank Battalion, gave all possible support to 2/28 to the extent that the terrain permitted, with fire on the cliffs and the high ground to the front. Shortly after noon, two platoons of tanks spearheaded an attack along the left flank of the battalion; subsequently, one platoon was withdrawn and shifted to the right of the zone of action of 2/28, just north and west of Hill 362 A. Even with the support of tanks, 2/28 proved unable to advance. The battle raged hot and heavy at close quarters; in one instance, one of the tanks bogged down, surrounded by 30-40 Japanese, some of them occupying a cave only 10 feet from the tank. Fighting as infantry, the tank crew was able to make a harrowing escape after disabling the gun and radio.

For the remainder of the afternoon of D plus 10, the 1st and 2d Battalions, 28th Marines, remained stalled along the crest of Hill 362A and at the base of the hill, where the enemy still held out in caves. In the course of the afternoon, the boundary of General Rockey's division was extended about 200 yards to the east to facilitate the advance of the adjacent 3d Marine Division. As a result, General Rockey committed 3/26 on the right of the 28th Marines. Shortly before 1900, 3/26 relieved 1/21 and established contact with 3/9 on the right and 1/28 on the left. At the same time, 2/26 displaced forward as 28th Marines reserve.

While the 1st and 2d Battalions, 28th Marines, were making little progress in the extremely difficult and well defended terrain, 3/28 was making a steady advance with two companies abreast near the west coast. The battalion moved forward against moderate resistance until its assault elements on the left were ahead of those on the right, at which time they drew heavy fire from the right front. The battalion had gained about 350 yards and since the regimental attack to the right had stalled, 3/28 halted its advance. By the end of 1 March, Hill 362A and a rocky ridgeline extending to the west coast had been seized. In all, elements of the 5th Division held a 1,000-yard front, which was exposed to heavy artillery and mortar fire from positions to the north. In order to obtain better observation over the northwestern coast of Iwo Jima, artillery observers were placed on board an LCI which cruised up and down the northwest shore. This expedient was successful and several enemy positions were located and silenced.

At the end of 1 March, the 5th Marine Division had taken a total of 12 prisoners; it was estimated that 3,252 of the enemy had been killed in the 5th Division area of responsibility. Casualties sustained by the division to this date were 48 officers and 952 men killed, 161 officers and 3,083 men wounded in action, and 2 officers and 47 men missing. The capture of Hill 362A and the ridges on either side of it in a one day operation had cost the 28th Marines alone 224 casualties. While General Rockey's men were engaged in reducing Hill 362A, the adjacent 3d Marine Division had penetrated the enemy defense system in the center of the island and had pivoted to the northeast. This move threatened to open a widening gap between the 3d and 5th Marine Divisions. As a result, for 2 March, General Schmidt directed the 5th Marine Division to make the main effort on the right while maintaining contact with General Erskine's men. In order to carry out the newly assigned mission calling for an expansion of his boundaries, General Rockey committed the 26th Marines to the right of the 28th. For the continuation of the 5th Division attack on D plus 11, the fire of the 13th Marines was augmented by half of the corps artillery fires.

At 0800 on 2 March, the 26th Marines jumped off along the division boundary with 3/26 in the assault. As the battalion moved forward, a gap arose on the left, and Companies D and F of 2/26 were committed to regain contact with 1/28. In the zone of advance of the 26th Marines the Japanese made maximum use of cleverly concealed positions, whose approaches were mined. Progress was correspondingly slow. Even though the terrain did not favor the use of armor and abounded in antitank obstacles, 3/26 requested tank support, and tanks from Company A, 5th Tank Battalion, spearheaded the attack.

Companies D and F of 2/26 were in the midst of blasting their way into and through the enemy defenses when the battalion had to shift to the right to close a new gap that had developed between the 3d and 5th Divisions. In executing the shift, the two companies had to disengage under heavy fire; they were further harassed by mortars and minefield. A solid line was finally formed in late afternoon just before nightfall. In order to fill the void created when the two companies of 2/26 were shifted to the northeast, it became necessary to commit 1/26.

When fighting came to an end on D plus 11, 3/26 had gained 500 yards. Responsible for these gains to a large measure were the division engineers, who moved alongside the assault units to clear minefields and open supply roads in the rear. In front of the 26th Marines, the enemy had mined the approaches to his pillboxes and permanent fortifications; without the help of the engineers, the advance of Colonel Graham's regiment on D plus 11 would have been doomed to failure. In the left of the 5th Division zone of advance, the 28th Marines jumped off at 0800 with its three battalions employing the same scheme of maneuver as on the previous day. The 1st and 2d Battalions were to attack around both sides of Hill 362A and join on the north side for a coordinated assault against the next elevation 200 yards to the north. This obstacle, extending westward from the plateau almost to the water's edge, was squarely in the path of the 28th Marines. Beyond were the stark remains of what had once been a small hamlet called Nishi. From it, the elevation took its name: Nishi Ridge. As the two battalions jumped off, they encountered undiminished resistance. Every time the Marines moved into the depression north of Hill 362A, they drew heavy fire from both the front and the rear. Tanks from Company B, 5th Tank Battalion, tried to give effective support, but were severely limited in their movements by the antitank ditch extending across their front.

As a result, the 28th Marines made only little progress. The 13th Marines gave all possible support to the infantry, concentrating its fire on enemy mortar positions identified from the air and through forward observers. Finally, elements of the regimental weapons company succeeded in setting up three .50 caliber machine guns to cover the caves that honeycombed the northern slopes of Hill 362A. Friendly mortar fire saturated the defile in front of the infantry.

Eventually, armored bulldozers of the 5th Engineer Battalion got close enough to the antitank ditch to fill in a portion of it. This permitted the tanks to move out and advance for 200 yards until the terrain narrowed and precluded any further forward movement. Caught in this type of cul de sac, the tank crews fought with the enemy at closest quarters. At 1400, tanks of Company C relieved those of Company B, which was beginning to run out of ammunition. En route to the front lines, the tanks of Company C, including a flame tank, blasted and burned enemy positions in the steep northern face of Hill 362A, from which the enemy was still firing into the rear of the advancing infantry.

The enemy made numerous attempts to destroy the supporting armor with satchel charges. Apparently, the appearance of tanks in close support of the infantry in terrain that all but precluded the effective employment of armor confounded the Japanese. One of the officers on General Kuribayashi's staff was to make the following comment on this subject: "When American M-4 tanks appeared in front of Osaka Yama (Hill 362A), Lieutenant General Kuribayashi was very anxious to know how to dispose of this tank. Even our 47mm antitank gun could not destroy it, and at last came to the conclusion that bodily attacks with explosives was the only way to destroy it."

Actually, the Japanese island commander may have overestimated the structural strength of the M-4 tank, which was indeed vulnerable to 47mm antitank fire. Nevertheless, the Shermans were indispensable on Iwo, and without them the assault might have failed. Ideally, a tank with heavier armament and a lower silhouette, as well as improved traction, would have been more desirable, but at the time of the Iwo Jima operation only the Shermans were available to the Marines engaged in the assault.

While the tanks were keeping the enemy to the rear occupied, Company E, 2/28, charged across the exposed terrain north of Hill 362A to the foot of Nishi Ridge. Enemy reaction to this move was immediate and, in the words of the regimental report, "All Hell broke loose" as the Japanese fought back from the cliff line to the north, from Hill 362A, and from a blockhouse in front of and to the east of Hill 362A. Combined with the heavy enemy artillery and mortar fire was a counterattack by a large group of Japanese against 1/28. This attack was repulsed with 129 Japanese killed. Losses among the Marines of 2/28 also were beginning to mount. Shortly after 1400, Lieutenant Colonel Chandler W. Johnson, commanding 2/28, was hit squarely by an artillery shell as he was inspecting the front lines. The battalion commander was killed instantly and the battalion executive officer, Major Thomas B. Pearce, Jr., assumed command. For the remainder of the afternoon, reserve units mopped up in the vicinity of Hill 362A, whose northern face was giving the advancing Marines infinitely more trouble than the southern slopes had.

While bitter fighting was raging along the center and eastern portion of the division line, 3/28 was advancing along a narrow front near the west coast. Movement in this area was seriously impeded by numerous caves and heavy enemy artillery and mortar fire. The caves were attacked and slowly neutralized with 37mm guns, heavy mortars, and demolition charges; a total of 68 were blasted during the day. At 0900 and again around noon, shells falling within the battalion zone of advance gave off a green-yellowish gas which induced vomiting and caused severe headaches to some of the men exposed to it. A brief gas scare resulted until it became apparent that only those men in the immediate proximity of a shell burst were affected; symptoms lasted only for a short time. In the end, the ill effects were ascribed to the presence of picric acid fumes.

At 1700, VAC ordered the lines to be consolidated for the day. In the 5th Division zone of advance, fighting continued until nightfall, some of it at very close quarters. For the night, 5th Division Marines were generally dug in at the base of Nishi Ridge; on the far right, the 2/26 lines extended to the northeast along the division boundary where they tied in with 3/9 near Hill 362B. The biggest advance for the day had been made by the 26th Marines, which had gained 500 yards. There were indications that the regiment was moving into a different type of defensive position than had been previously encountered. There were fewer concrete fortifications and more rock barriers and tank ditches. Even though the enemy was resisting as fiercely as ever, he was abandoning some of his equipment. Items captured on D plus 11 were a generator truck found behind one ridge and a large searchlight behind another.

As night fell, the enemy made several attempts to infiltrate the 5th Division lines. About 50 Japanese sallied forth near Hill 362A and some of this force succeeded in getting into the Marine positions. Once the Marines became aware of their presence, bitter hand-to-hand fighting ensued, in the course of which knives, sabers, pistols, and hand grenades were liberally used. The alertness of the Marines in dealing with the infiltrators led General Kuribayashi to report that "the lookout of American forces has become very strict and it is difficult to pass through their guarded line. Don't overestimate the value of cutting-in attacks." On the evening D plus 11, the battle of Hill 362A was over, but an even bigger challenge was to confront General Rockey's men for the following day: the capture of Nishi Ridge and Hill 362B.

Nishi Ridge, Hill 362B And Beyond

On the morning of D plus 12, the 5th Marine Division resumed the attack with basically the same formations it had employed on the previous day. From the very outset, both the terrain and enemy resistance combined to make it a difficult day. The 26th and 28th Marines were to make the main effort. In the path of the 28th Marines lay a series of gorges and ridges; in front of the 26th Marines the terrain was heavily mined; in addition, from strongly held Hill 362B, the enemy was able to sweep the area with fire. New roads would have to be dozed out before tanks could move in to support the advance. The attack jumped off at 0745. Supported by 75mm half-tracks, 37mm guns, and a reinforced tank platoon, 1/28 and 2/28 in the regimental center moved out and almost immediately ran into heavy mortar and small arms fire. As the two battalions inched forward, the men soon came to close grips with the enemy and numerous hand grenade duels were fought. Within two hours after the jumpoff, Nishi Ridge had been seized and the battalions prepared to move into the rugged terrain beyond. As the advance gained momentum, the 28th Marines swept down from Nishi Ridge into the remnants of Nishi Village, and by late afternoon had reached a point about 200 yards beyond, despite mounting casualties, for enemy resistance never slackened. At the close of the day, when the fury of the battle receded, 1/28 made further gains which brought it ahead of the other two battalions. Since morning, 1/28 had gained 500 yards, while 2/28 had scored gains of only 150 yards, as had 3/28 along the coast. By far the most spectacular fighting and resultant gains were made in the zone of advance of the 26th Marines. The mission assigned to the 26th Marines for D plus 12 had been to advance northeastward to relieve elements of the 3d Marine Division near Hill 362B. The line of departure for 2/26 and 3/26 formed an inverted horseshoe with 3/26 on the left and 2/26 on the right. The two battalions moved out rapidly, even though both began taking casualties almost at once. Company B of the 5th Tank Battalion supported the 2d Battalion by covering the left flank of Company F. Just as it had done on D plus 7 when first committed in the assault, this company smashed into the enemy defenses with great force and aggressiveness. Since, at the outset, the terrain was comparatively level and thus favored the employment of armor, the company commander was able to radio instructions to the armor through a tank liaison man assigned to the command post of 2/26. The assault swept on for about 300 yards before the open terrain changed into the deep gorges and rock formations characteristic of northern Iwo Jima. In these rocky badlands the battle continued, frequently man against man. The Japanese fiercely contested the advance behind every rock and boulder but could not stop it. In some of the most bitter fighting of the entire operation, every weapon at hand was brought into play. By the time the forceful advance came to a halt, Company F had advanced more than 600 yards to the high ground to its front. Even then, the Japanese grimly contested every foot of the freshly seized ground, and numerous hand grenades continued to harass the Marines from cleverly hidden caves and gullies whose presence had hitherto been unsuspected. But the enemy was mortal, and bazooka shells accurately fired into such defensive positions usually eliminated this resistance in short order.

The 600-yard advance of 2/26 eliminated the horseshoe and for all practical purposes, straightened the line. With the severe threat to its left flank gone, 3/26 was able to launch an advance of its own, which resulted in a 200-yard gain. While Company F was tackling the enemy at close quarters, Companies D and E launched an attack northeastward along the division boundary in order to seize Hill 362B and relieve 3/9. The relief was completed by 1430 and the two companies, from positions just southwest of the hill, prepared for the assault.

When it came, at 1600, the battle for the hill proved to be a bloody one. Using rocket launchers, flamethrowers, demolitions, plus a goodly amount of sheer courage and will, the two companies forced their way to the top. The southern and western slopes of the hill were honeycombed with caves and pillboxes, each of which required an individual assault. By the time the crest of the hill was reached, both company commanders and many of their men had become casualties.

The advance made by the 5th Marine Division on 3 March was almost spectacular under the conditions in which the battle was fought. The cost of seizing this ground was correspondingly high. On D plus 12, the 26th Marines alone had 281 casualties. Total losses for the 5th Marine Division on 3 March were 9 officers and 127 men killed or dead of wounds, and 15 officers and 357 men wounded. As of D plus 12, total casualties for the division since D-Day numbered 4,960 officers and men.

As the fury of the battle receded on the evening of D plus 12, the 5th Division lines extended from the west coast at a point roughly 200 yards north of Nishi Village along the northern edge of Motoyama Plateau to the crest of Hill 362B. All along the front, the casualty rate had reached alarming proportions and it became necessary to send men from headquarters and weapons companies into the line as riflemen to bolster the tired and depleted units. Not all of the 5th Marine Division men were able to get much rest that night. In the sector of the 28th Marines, there were relatively few attempts at infiltration. It was another story in the 26th Marines area, where the enemy infiltrators appeared more aggressive and crowded the 26th Marines throughout the night. Almost all of the nearly 100 would-be infiltrators were killed.

Following an artillery preparation and rocket barrage, the 5th Marine Division resumed the attack on the morning of D plus 13. As the men jumped off in the same formation they had employed on the previous day, they were hit by intensive fire from small arms and mortars. Once again, the Marines advanced into terrain dotted with interconnected caves. The lines were now so close to each other that artillery support could be used only on special occasions. Because of a low cloud ceiling, the air support which had been scheduled for the day had to be cancelled.

The low clouds soon gave way to intermittent showers, which did little to lift the morale of the men who were still exhausted in spirit and body from the rigors of the preceding days' combat and lack of sleep caused by the continuous Japanese infiltration attempts of the previous night. The rugged terrain seriously limited the use of 75mm half-tracks and 37mm guns. With Japanese lurking all around them, the crews of these vehicles felt progressively more exposed to enemy fire. Beyond that, the enemy was beginning to take a toll in vehicles with mines, skillfully emplaced in the few avenues of approach available to the supporting armor.

Perhaps the biggest difference between the success attained on D plus 12 and the fighting on the following day was the fact that the attacks were not closely coordinated. Once again, the brunt of the battle was borne by small detachments, moving more or less haphazardly against those enemy caves and pillboxes that were unmasked. As a result, only small gains were made, even though in this jungle of rocks the bravery of the individual Marine continued undiminished. As on the previous day, losses were heavy and many of the combat units were operating at half strength or less. The enemy was noticeably more aggressive in the daytime than he had been before, and the 26th Marines beat back several counterattacks executed in company strength. Nowhere did the Japanese succeed in breaking through the 5th

Division lines, but the counterattacks served to take additional steam out of the drive of the fatigued Marines, and net gains for the day remained practically nil. As one account of the day's operations put it, "The only successful move, in fact, was made by Division headquarters which moved from its original location near the eastern beaches to a position north of Airfield No. 1 on the west side of the island. At about this time, General Kuribayashi shifted his headquarters from the center of Iwo Jima to a large cave in the northwestern section of the island, between Hiraiwa Bay and the ruins of Kita Village, where he prepared to make his final stand. General Schmidt's order to his three divisions that 5 March was to be utilized for reorganization, resupply, and preparations for the resumption of the attack on the following day reached 5th Division units during the afternoon of 4 March. At a time when physical strength and fighting spirit were beginning to flag, this order was more than welcome. Logically, the day of rest would be used, above all, to funnel replacements into the depleted ranks of the frontline units. The exigencies of combat had already necessitated sending some men with specific and critical skills, such as demolition personnel and bazooka or flamethrower operators, into the lines prior to 5 March. On the whole, except for small emergency details, replacements were sent forward when the combat battalions were out of the lines. Replacements, no matter how willing and well trained, always tended to present something of a problem before they were wholly integrated. The reasons for this were outlined in the following report: "Reports from infantry units indicate that the average replacement, upon being assigned to a rifle unit and immediately subjected to the type of fierce fighting encountered, was initially bewildered and terrified resulting from a mental attitude of his being 'alone,' and not knowing his leaders and companions on the battlefield. This lack of a sense of security, even when among battle-experienced troops, was brought about by his separation from contact with those with whom he had previously trained and not yet having become assimilated into a fighting team. Those who did not readjust themselves quickly had a high percentage of casualties since in their bewilderment they usually carelessly exposed themselves."

For the resumption of the attack on 6 March, General Rockey directed 1/26 to relieve 1/27 and ordered the 27th Marines into reserve. At the same time, the 28th Marines was to reorganize so that 3/28 would take over the sector of 2/28. This would leave all three battalions of the 26th Marines in the line, the 28th Marines holding a front with 3/28 on the left and 3/27 on the right, and the 27th Marines, less the 3d Battalion, in reserve.

In accordance with VAC orders, combat activity by 5th Division units was limited to local attempts to straighten the lines during the morning. Throughout the day, artillery and naval gunfire were brought to bear on suspected enemy positions, and carrier aircraft flew 18 missions. Within the 26th Marines sector, a few tanks engaged in reducing caves and other strong points that were directly menacing the front lines. Those tanks not actually engaged with the enemy received badly needed maintenance in the bivouac areas.

Despite general inactivity on the part of the Japanese infantry, the 5th Division suffered casualties through enemy action even on this day of rest. One of the tanks operating near the 26th Marines lines ran over a mine and was disabled, another was hit by enemy antitank fire. Japanese mortars continued to harass the Marines throughout the day, particularly when the enemy observed troop movements near Road Junction 338 northwest of Motoyama Village. Even though this junction was situated in the 3d Marine Division area, it constituted a supply road for the 26th

Marines and other 5th Division units. A particularly unfortunate incident occurred shortly after the relief of 1/27 by 1/26. The 1st Battalion, 27th Marines, was in the process of moving to an assembly area in the vicinity of Road Junction 338 when an enemy shell hit the jeep carrying the battalion commander, Lieutenant Colonel John A. Butler, who had been observing the relief. The battalion commander was killed, and two other men in the vehicle were wounded. Later that afternoon, Lieutenant Colonel Justin G. Duryea, the operations officer of the 27th Marines, took over command of 1/27.

While all three Marine divisions on Iwo remained in place and prepared to continue the assault, several important changes occurred to the rear, indicative of what had been accomplished and how much remained to be done. At the foot of Mount Suribachi, the 133d Naval Construction Battalion put into operation six portable water distillation units. The processed water was sent to the front and there was enough to furnish three canteens per day per man, a vast improvement over what had been previously available. As early as 3 March, the situation from a naval viewpoint had become relatively quiet. Unloading and evacuation progressed favorably over both the eastern and western beaches. It thus became possible for all of the assault shipping including the Defense Group and the Joint Expeditionary Force Reserve to retire to rear areas.

On the morning of D plus 15, it was business as usual for all three assault divisions on Iwo. The only change from the norm was that the heaviest artillery barrage thus far fired preceded the attack. Shortly before 0700, 11 artillery battalions, a total of 132 guns ranging from 75mm to 155mm in caliber, unleashed a tremendous bombardment of enemy positions in northern Iwo, followed by a rolling barrage. Offshore, a battleship, two cruisers, three destroyers, and two landing craft added their fire to that of the land-based artillery, which in little more than an hour expended 22,500 shells, some of them falling within 100 yards of the Marines waiting to jump off. At pretimed intervals, carrier planes strafed, rocketed, and bombed the enemy positions. The portion of the island still in Japanese hands literally rocked under the punishment being meted out, and it appeared that little could withstand such an extensive pounding.

As soon as they jumped off at 0800, the Marines of the 5th Division, as well as those of the two remaining divisions, discovered to their dismay that the barrage had done little to soften up enemy resistance. When the artillery fire lifted, the Japanese, little the worse for wear, contested the advance of General Rockey's men from prepared bunkers, pillboxes, and caves. Marines attempting to advance north from Hill 362B immediately drew heavy rifle, machine gun, and mortar fire interspersed with white phosphorus shells. It was almost as if the heavy bombardment had never happened. The broken terrain all but precluded close tank support and, instead of a big push, the advance could be measured in yards. The vigorous drive to the O-3 Line that had been envisaged could not materialize under such conditions and the attack soon bogged down. By the end of the day, the 26th and 27th Marines had gained between 50 and 100 yards; the 28th Marines' advance bogged down altogether. The only progress made could be measured, not in yards, but in the number of enemy caves and emplacements destroyed. Engineers operating with the 28th Marines were able to seal off numerous caves. As in preceding days, the Japanese harassed the advance from the front, flanks, and rear. Casualties were correspondingly heavy. The type of vicious close-in fighting the Marines were engaged in during this period was reflected in the nature of the casualties evacuated to the rear. In the words of one observer: "At the Fifth Division hospital, Lieutenant Evans was noticing a change in the type of wounds coming in. They were bad ones, from close range sniper or machine gun fire. The earlier wounds, mostly from mortar bursts, had been numerous and ragged, but not so penetrating. The whole blood was being used as little as twelve days after it was given on the West Coast, but often it could not help." After the heavy volume of artillery fire on 6 March, expended with such little effect, VAC limited the use of ammunition, particularly for harassing missions. In his orders for 7 March, General Schmidt directed the 5th Marine Division to seize the high ground overlooking the sea with the main effort to be made in the northeastern portion of the division zone of action. Within this zone, the main effort was to be carried out by the 27th Marines, while the 26th and 28th Marines were to execute limited objective attacks.

The Drive To The Sea

Just as General Erskine's division on the right jumped off for a surprise attack without an artillery preparation early on 7 March, so the 26th Marines, less 2/26 in VAC reserve, duplicated the maneuver on a minor scale. Jumping off 40 minutes prior to H-Hour without an artillery preparation, 1/26 and Company H, 3/26, set about to reduce the stubborn enemy defenses that had thwarted the regiment's advance on the previous day. After overcoming moderate resistance, the battalion reached a 30-foot knoll just north of Nishi Village. As Marines wearily surrounded this hill, enemy fire all but ceased. The sudden stillness was broken only when demolitions men blasted and closed one cave entrance, while machine gunners made short work of several of the enemy who rushed out of a rear entrance. Marines of Company H ran towards the top of the hill in a suspicious silence that was most unnatural for Iwo, until about 40 had gathered on the crest. Then the unbelievable occurred: "The whole hill shuddered and the top blew out with a roar heard all over the island. Men were thrown into the air, and those nearby were stunned by the concussion. Dozens of Marines disappeared in the blast crater, and their comrades ran to dig for them. Strong men vomited at the sight of charred bodies, and others walked from the area crying. The enemy had blown up his own command post, inflicting forty-three Marine casualties at the same time. All that remained of the ridge was a mass of torn, twisted, and burning rock and sand. Smoke emerged from a ragged hole so large that it might well have harbored a good sized apartment building. Many of the men, not directly injured by the blast but stunned by the concussion, were staggering around in a daze." It remained for the commander of Company H, Captain Donald E. Castle, to gather the remnants of his men and lead them in a renewed attack.

Meanwhile, 3/26 had also jumped off and almost at once ran into such heavy resistance that continuous fighting at close range, which lasted until nightfall, produced a gain of only 150 yards. Once again, even this meager advance had to be paid for with heavy casualties.

The 5th Marine Division main effort on D plus 16 was made by 2/27, supported by a company of 1/27. Following a 15-minute preparation by a battery of the 13th Marines, the battalion jumped off for an attack that was coordinated with elements of the 21st Marines operating beyond the division boundary. The objective was a stretch of high ground squarely astride the regimental zone of advance. Initially, good progress was made until the forward elements entered a draw directly in front of the first of a series of ridges. At this point, enemy machine gun fire, coming from two directions, raked the exposed men, who sought in vain to pinpoint the well-camouflaged positions. Casualties mounted as a 37mm gun was arduously manhandled to a forward position, from where it engaged the hidden machine guns with undetermined results.

Throughout the day, fighting raged at close quarters, each side making generous use of hand grenades. In the end, the overall gain for the 27th Marines on D plus 16 was 150 yards, similar to the ground seized by the 26th. Even such a limited advance, executed against a firmly entrenched enemy force that contested every foot of ground with knee mortars, grenades, and deadly accurate sniper fire, was a major accomplishment. The task of the Marine infantrymen might have been greatly eased had tank support been available. As it was, the broken terrain was altogether impassable for armor. During the afternoon, platoon-sized elements of 2/27 attempted to outflank some of the enemy positions, only to be caught by heavy flanking fire that all but isolated them from the main body. A withdrawal became possible only with the help of a smoke screen. Fighting continued throughout the afternoon and individual enemy caves were assaulted and taken. But there was no way of telling how many hidden tunnels led into these caves, or how long it would take the enemy to restock them with new men and weapons after the Marine assault squads had moved on. The only sign of progress of the 5th Marine Division on 7 March occurred on the division's left wing. There, in the zone of advance of the 28th Marines near the west coast, 3/28 and 3/27 dispatched combat patrols before the main body launched a general attack. These patrols moved out at 0900, met with little resistance, and reported this fact back to the regiment. One hour later, without any special artillery preparation, the main body moved out. There was scattered resistance, but not enough to delay the forward movement as 3/28 and 3/27 struck out in a northeasterly direction. In this instance, the extremely difficult terrain proved to be much more of an obstacle than the sporadic resistance encountered. In order to maintain the momentum of the attack, numerous caves were bypassed, to be mopped up later by 1/28 and 2/28. Mortar and rocket fire was directed well ahead of the advancing Marines; additional fire support came from a destroyer offshore.

By 1530, the two battalions had advanced about 500 yards over and through rocky gorges in terrain that was passable only for men on foot. Included in the ground taken this day was Hill 215, located about 500 yards northeast of Nishi Village, only 750 yards from the northern shore. The relative absence of enemy resistance in this sector was to be the most surprising development of the day's operations. In addition to making the longest advance yet in the 5th Division zone, the attacking units killed nine of the enemy in this area and captured one. According to the battalion action report, "a little further advance might have been made, but the positions for the night would have been weak, so the defenses were laid out in the area indicated."

From the time the advance halted for the day until dusk, all three battalions of the regiment dug in for the night in the vicinity of Hill 215, while some of the Marines were engaged in mopping up in the immediate vicinity of the hill. In the midst of this activity, few Marines paid much attention to the fact that a stiff breeze had begun to blow from the north towards the American lines. This nonchalance changed to near-panic when this ill wind was found to be "bringing with it eye-smarting sulphur fumes and smoke from a burning enemy ammunition dump." Unit commanders, always alert to the possibility of the enemy's employing poison gas, sounded an alert which brought hundreds of gas masks into use. The alarm soon passed, however, and CT 28 went on with its reorganizing. The 5th Division advance on D plus 16 had moved the lines forward from 500 yards in the west to 150 yards along the boundary with the 3d Marine Division, where resistance had been the stiffest. In support of the day's operations, naval gunfire had played a significant part. Following the tremendous expenditure of ammunition by the shore-based artillery on 6 March, VAC had restricted the use of the corps 155mm howitzers to "deliberate destructive fires against known enemy targets." The resulting gap in artillery support had been taken up by naval gunfire. All naval gunfire control parties received instructions to expend 500 rounds per ship. On the basis of data furnished by the corps intelligence section, the 5th Division intelligence officer, Lieutenant Colonel George A. Roll, assigned target priorities. Additional support was obtained through air strikes, even though the shrinking enemy perimeter and the proximity of the lines made such support a rather risky undertaking. Altogether, 119 carrier aircraft flew 147 sorties. The employment of napalm bombs was somewhat less than successful: of 40 carried, 7 failed to release; of the 33 released, 7 failed to ignite. An additional 67 500-pound bombs, 170 100-pound bombs, and 426 rockets were not subject to technical failures, but no estimate as to their effectiveness against a well dug-in enemy could be obtained.

The night of 7-8 March was characterized by relatively light enemy activity, though it was far from quiet. In the zone of action of the 5th Marine Division, the Japanese kept things lively with small arms and knee mortar fire and hand grenades. Enemy patrols probed the Marine lines at various points. The only determined attempt at infiltration occurred in front of 1/26, where approximately 25 Japanese tried their luck. The attempt ended in dismal failure when the enemy, tripping flares in his stealthy approach, became a good target and was mowed down by the alert Marines.

The operations order issued by General Schmidt for D plus 17 was simple and to the point. Instead of naming phase lines to be reached in the coming day's assault, the VAC commander directed all three divisions "to capture the remainder of the island." For General Rockey's division, these orders meant that the main effort would continue to be made on the right by the 27th Marines, advancing to the northeast coast along the division boundary parallel to the movements of the adjacent 3d Marine Division.

The terrain over which the 27th Marines was to advance featured a series of interconnected caves and tunnels. All approaches to these defenses were heavily defended. Colonel Wornham planned to meet this challenge by having trails bulldozed into enemy terrain, over which the infantry could advance into close proximity of the enemy. Once there, Marines could reduce the Japanese fortifications at close range with time-proven methods. As added insurance, tanks would support the infantry advance over the newly bulldozed trails. At the first glint of dawn, prior to the jumpoff of 2127 scheduled for 0750, Shermans of the 5th Tank Battalion slowly crawled forward from their bivouac area over a previously reconnoitered route. In the rough, unfamiliar terrain, the tanks moved slowly and did not reach the front until 0930. Meanwhile, 2/27 had launched its assault on schedule, but little progress was made until the tanks arrived. The armor immediately commenced cleaning out pillboxes and emplacements, permitting the infantry to move in close to caves in order to seal them. The enemy opposed the Marines with accurate small arms fire, grenades, and mortar fire. Despite this opposition and the heavily mined terrain, elements of 2/27 by 1030 had gained 100 yards. Company E, 2/27, reported killing 75 Japanese during the first two hours.

On the battalion left, Companies D and F attempted an advance without tank support and were soon halted by heavy machine gun and mortar fire. A 15-man crew from Battery B, 13th Marines, manhandled a 75mm pack howitzer and 200 rounds of ammunition close to the lines to provide badly needed fire support. This unorthodox employment of artillery raised the eyebrows of the 1/13 intelligence officer, impelling him to leave this statement for posterity: "We thought this morning that this battalion had done everything it was possible for an artillery unit to do. We had landed under machine gun, artillery, and mortar fire; gone into position at night; repelled Jap pre-dawn counterattack on D plus 1; fired countless counterbattery missions; had snipers in our position area; participated in regimental missions; fired T.O.T. missions; had our observers on land, on sea, and in the air, and we hauled ammo all night. But today we detached No. 4 Baker and sent it forward to knock off some Jap pillboxes. A report came back that their fire on pillbox was very effective. This was a new twist but the same result—Japs destroyed." The infantry received additional support from rocket launcher crews who blasted the Japanese in their holes and buried them alive. Despite the punishment doled out to the enemy, neither company made much progress, and gains were limited to less than 100 yards.

In the center of the division line, the 26th Marines failed to make even that much progress. With 1/26 and 3/26 still in the assault, Colonel Graham's men found themselves facing a complex system of pillboxes and interconnected caves among the debris that was all that had remained of Kita Village. In the midst of such forbidding defenses, the regimental attack barely got off the ground and, at the end of another exhausting day, the regiment was still in substantially the same position it had occupied prior to the jumpoff. A gain of 400 yards laboriously carved out by 1/26 during the day had to be relinquished at dusk because it was untenable. The 28th Marines on the division left nearly equaled the previous day's advance. Moving along the coast against initially weak enemy resistance, 2/28 actually advanced another 500 yards. Once again, opposition became more stubborn on the regiment's right where 1/28 gained a respectable 300 yards. Both battalions covered the initial 100 yards before serious resistance developed, both from the front and the rear.

Within the limitations imposed by the terrain, the attached 75s and 37mm guns of the weapons company supported the regiment, as did the 81mm mortars. Ahead of the advance, naval gunfire attempted to neutralize enemy positions near the coast, while carrier planes struck twice at Hill 165, one of the last significant obstacles separating the 5th Division Marines from the northern shore. For these carrier aircraft, 8 March was the last day of support for the ground forces. Effective 9 March, such close support would become the responsibility of the Army Air Forces.

The violent battle of attrition raging in the craggy terrain of northern Iwo on D plus 17 was to have more than its share of personal drama in the informal setting of war. Tragedy struck within the setting of Company E, 2/27, which in the course of the morning had already scored an advance of 150 yards through engineer-tank-infantry teamwork. Only a jumble of rocks separated the Marines of Company E from the sea, but hidden behind every crag and in every crevice was an enemy determined to block any and all egress by the advancing Marines to the sea just east of Kitano Point.

As bitter close fighting raged in this inaccessible area, one man began to stand out among the rest of Company E. He was 1st Lieutenant Jack Lummus, a former gridiron star at Baylor University, now determined to overcome the final obstacle barring his men from the sea. Rushing forward at the head of his platoon, the lieutenant was knocked down by an exploding grenade. He got to his feet, shook off some of the dust, and rushed an enemy gun emplacement. A second grenade exploded, knocking him down again and shattering his shoulder. Undaunted, the platoon leader got up, rushed a second enemy position and killed all of its occupants. As his men watched, Lummus continued his rush. When he called to his platoon, the men responded, now moving forward with a deadly purpose. As the attack gained momentum, the entire company began to move, hesitantly at first, then with growing speed and assurance.

Lummus was still at the head of his men, viciously slashing at the enemy in his path, when the incredible happened: "Suddenly he was in the center of a powerful explosion obscured by flying rock and dirt. As it cleared, his men saw him, rising as if in a hole. A land mine had blown off both his legs, the legs that had carried him to All-American football honors at Baylor University. They watched in horror as he stood on the bloody stumps, calling them on. Several men, crying now, ran to him and, for a moment, talked of shooting him to stop his agony.

"But he was still shouting for them to move out and the platoon scrambled forward. Their tears turned to rage, they swept an incredible 300 yards over impossible ground, and at nightfall they were on a ridge overlooking the sea. There was no question that the dirty, tired men, cursing and crying and fighting, had done it for Jack Lummus. Lieutenant Lummus died later that day and was subsequently awarded his country's highest decoration. Even in death his triumph over the enemy and the slaughter that was Iwo Jima was complete. His devotion to duty and personal sacrifice had supplied the impetus for the wild charge. A mixture of love and compassion for their leader, mixed with anger and frustration, had supplied the spark to an explosive mixture which set off a reaction that, for all practical purposes, was the American equivalent of the traditional enemy *banzai* charge."

Throughout D plus 17, tanks of the 5th Tank Battalion supported the infantry assault units as best they could. Tanks of Company B, backing up 2/27, advanced into an important enemy bivouac area replete with ammunition dumps, motor vehicles, and trailers. In the course of this advance, tankers observed at least 100 of the enemy killed, many of them wearing U. S. Marine uniforms. Eleven regular tanks and two flame tanks of Company C, 5th Tank Battalion, moved out in support of 2/28 but soon were unable to keep up with the infantry advance when the engineers, who were checking the road for mines, were pinned down by sniper fire. As a result, tank support was limited to four rounds of 75mm and half a load of flame fuel in this area for the entire day. At about 1300, one platoon with a flame tank was dispatched to the center of the division zone of advance to support 1/26. Even though the area allegedly had been checked by the engineers, two of the tanks hit mines causing considerable damage to both. These tanks had to be abandoned after the guns and radio had been disabled.

As fighting came to a close on the evening of 8 March, the 5th Marine Division had slashed deeply through the enemy lines and was within reach of the northern shore. It had rained intermittently throughout the day and the men were utterly exhausted. However, the enemy was in little better shape, as indicated by the following report submitted by General Kuribayashi on the day's action: "Troops at 'Tamanayanla' and Northern Districts are still holding their position thoroughly and continue giving damages to the enemy. Their fighting situation believing their country's victory looks god-like." Two hours later, the Japanese commander conceded: "I am very sorry that I have let the enemy occupy one part of the Japanese territory, but am taking comfort in giving heavy damages to the enemy." On the evening of D plus 17, the 5th Marine Division stood within reach of victory, but more than two weeks of bitter fighting over the island's most treacherous terrain in northwestern Iwo would be required before Japanese resistance within the division zone of action was broken. During 9 and 10 March, there was no forward movement, and General Rockey's men, with extreme exertion, were able to extend the division left flank about 40 yards. At this point, the 28th Marines came under intensive fire from the high ground that extended southeast from Kitano Point. This fire brought the drive to the northeast to an abrupt halt in front of a long, low ridgeline overlooking a deep gorge. This canyon was to become the final enemy pocket of resistance on Iwo Jima, where General Kuribayashi and the remnants of his garrison would fight to the bitter end. In the northeastern portion of the island, between Tachiiwa Point and Minami, in the 4th Marine Division sector, a second pocket, occupied mostly by naval personnel, would soon become depleted following a reckless *banzai* charge. By noon of D plus 18, within sight of the sea to the north, General Rockey's Marines still faced an uphill battle in some of the worst ground on Iwo. There, the ridges and gorges were so steep as to be almost impassable even for men on foot. As in more accessible areas, caves and dugouts abounded. This phase of the fighting, in the face of undiminished enemy opposition, is referred to in the official records as "a battle of attrition." For a number of days to come, the advance could be measured in feet instead of yards.

As on the previous day, another human drama, again involving the 27th Marines, was to be enacted in the front lines on 9 March. During the early afternoon, Lieutenant Colonel Duryea, commanding 1/27, and Major Antonelli, commanding the adjacent 2d Battalion, went forward to check their lines. They were headed back to the rear when "Duryea called to his runner, who was sitting on a rock, and the youngster replied 'I'm coming, Colonel.' He took one step and was blown to bits. He had set off the detonator of a 6-inch naval shell buried in the ground to catch a tank. A huge fragment of the shell tore off Duryea's left arm at the elbow and another smashed his left knee. Antonelli fell, blinded by sand. Duryea, still conscious, could not see his left leg, doubled under him and thought he had lost it. Thinking an attack was under way he shouted to the others, 'Come here, come here. Don't go away.' He tried to roll over to get the pistol under his right hip, but could not. A captain ran to get corpsmen, and they bundled Duryea and Tony Antonelli into stretchers. Duryea's left leg dangled off the side, and a bullet pierced it, breaking it." With the two battalion commanders out of commission, the executive officers of the two battalions, Major William H. Tumbelston and Major Gerald F. Russell, assumed command. The detonation had also wounded the company commander and another officer of Company E, as well as the intelligence officer of 2/27. Major Antonelli, despite his eye injuries and a broken eardrum, refused evacuation until he had issued orders for the resumption of the attack. Subsequently, the indomitable battalion commander walked out of the division hospital and returned to his unit until Colonel Wornham personally ordered him to return to the hospital. The following day, Antonelli was back at the battalion command post, where he remained during the daylight hours for another week until Colonel Wornham requested his evacuation from the island to prevent further injuries. Aside from routine operations on 9 March, two developments occurred. One was indicative of progress made in developing Iwo Jima as an air base. The other showed to what extent the combat units had been depleted. During the difficult fighting along the north coast, Army Air Forces P-51s went into action for the first time, strafing and bombing the enemy-held gorges in precision attacks that drew admiration from the Marines on the ground. Nevertheless, this impressive air support failed to break enemy resistance or morale, and the results remained inconclusive.

At noon of 9 March, General Rockey decided to bolster the dwindling combat strength of his infantry units by sending personnel from the supporting arms to the front. On the morning of 10 March, 100 men of the 13th Marines joined 3/28 as riflemen. About the same number reinforced 3/26. The 11th Amphibian Tractor Battalion furnished 55 men for 3/27 and slightly more than 100 men from the 5th Motor Transport Battalion joined 1/28.

While the Marines were still able to reinforce their frontline units, such expedient was denied to General Kuribayashi. In the narrow strip of coast separating the 5th Division from the sea, the northern pocket had been compressed into an area less than one square mile in size. Caught in this pocket were General Kuribayashi and his division headquarters, elements of the 2d Battalion of Colonel Ikeda's 145th Infantry Regiment, remnants of the Command Battalion, 17th Independent Mixed Regiment and a conglomeration of stragglers from other units. Altogether, Japanese Army and Navy strength in northern Iwo came to approximately 1,500 men.

At 0800 on 10 March, the 5th Marine Division continued its attack against enemy opposition that was undiminished in ferocity. On the division left, the 28th Marines made an advance of 200 yards before it was stopped by fire from a ridge running generally southeastward from Kitano Point. The 26th Marines gained roughly 100 yards in almost impossible terrain. The 27th Marines destroyed numerous enemy caves and pillboxes in close-in fighting, but progress was minimal. By the end of D plus 19, after another day of heavy and costly fighting, the lines of the 27th Marines were substantially the same as they had been that morning.

Throughout the day, the 5th Marine Division attack was supported by shore-based and naval gunfire, as well as air strikes. Once again, the effectiveness of this support could not be accurately gauged by the exhausted Marines on the ground. It was obvious by this time that it was becoming increasingly difficult to make effective use of these supporting arms because of the rapidly diminishing area held by the enemy. At the same time, the bombs and heavy gunfire directed in heavy concentrations against a shrinking pocket were bound to hurt the enemy. This is best confirmed by the messages emanating from General Kuribayashi's headquarters on the evening of 10 March. Beginning on a fairly confident note, the Japanese commander reported that, "even though American attacks against our northern districts are continuing day and night, our troops are still fighting bravely and holding their positions thoroughly." Changing to a more plaintive note, General Kuribayashi continued: "200 or 300 American infantrymen with several tanks attacked 'Tenzan' (northern Iwo in the 5th Division sector) all day. The enemy's bombardments from one battleship or cruiser, 11 destroyers and aircraft are very severe, especially the bombing and machine gun firing against Divisional Headquarters from 30 fighters and bombers are so fierce that I cannot express nor write here. Before American forces landed on Iwo Jima, there were many trees around my Headquarters, but now there are not even a grasp of grass remaining. The surface of the earth has changed completely and we can see numerous holes of bombardments." In its two-week drive up the coast of western Iwo Jima between 25 February and 10 March, General Rockey's division had covered about 3,000 yards from the vicinity of the Central Airfield to a line that ran from West to east across the base of the northern tip of the island. In the course of this advance the division had sustained more than 4,000 casualties.

Indicative of the severity of enemy opposition is the minute number of prisoners taken by D plus 19. Altogether VAC had seized 111 prisoners since D-Day. Of this figure, only 67 were Japanese, the remainder consisting of Korean labor troops. At the same time, 8,073 enemy dead had been counted in the 5th Marine Division sector. On the evening of 10 March, no one could guess how much more blood would be shed before the battle for Iwo Jima was over.

Chapter 10. The 4th Marine Division Drive on the Right

Advance into the Meat Grinder

The first six days of the Iwo Jima operation had taken the 4th Marine Division to the eastern portion of the Central Airfield and Charlie-Dog Ridge, which had been secured at heavy cost on 24 February. As of D plus 6, it became the division's mission to seize and hold that part of Iwo that lay east of the Central Airfield and to the south of Hill 362C. The ruggedness of the terrain over which General Cates' Marines would have to advance equalled or outdid that encountered by the 3d and 5th Marine Divisions. As might be expected, the enemy had made maximum use of the natural terrain features by digging caves, constructing blockhouses, and tunnelling between ridges until the entire area was honeycombed with defense installations rivaling every other sector on the island. Among a large number of nondescript ridges and canyon-like depressions, the following stood out and formed cornerstones of the main line of defense in the northeastern part of the island: Hill 382, just east of the Central Airfield (Nidan Iwa to the enemy), situated about 250 yards northeast of the east-west runway. About 600 yards south of Hill 382, just west of the remains of Minami Village, was an unsightly elevation which was to become known as "Turkey Knob." Even though its height was not impressive, it sheltered a large communications center made of reinforced concrete. The top of this hill afforded an unobstructed view of the entire southern portion of the island. To the southwest, the high ground gave way to a depression soon to become infamous as the "Amphitheater." On the evening of D plus 5, units of the 4th Marine Division held a line, facing east, extending from the Central Airfield southward to the coast to the vicinity of the East Boat Basin. From their lines, the men could see Hill 382, the highest point in northern Iwo, second in size only to Mount Suribachi. The hill was readily identifiable from the remnants of a radar station, where the skeleton of a radio tower pointed starkly skyward. The Japanese had hollowed out a sizable portion of the hill, which was bristling with field pieces and antitank guns. The guns themselves were housed in concrete emplacements, often protected by as many as 10 supporting machine guns. Some of Colonel Nishi's tanks, mounting 47mm and 57mm guns, backed up these formidable defenses.

The concrete blockhouse on Turkey Knob was so soundly constructed as to make it virtually immune to bombing and naval gunfire. The Knob dominated a broad, rocky area of a deceptively innocent appearance, the Amphitheater. Prior to the naval bombardment, this area had been covered by heavy vegetation and resembled a slight depression in rolling terrain. The true extent and cohesiveness of this major enemy defensive area had not as yet revealed itself to the 4th Division Marines. To them, it looked just like a slight hollow in rolling terrain, though in reality "the Amphitheater was a veritable large scale booby trap, containing three tiers of deep prepared positions facing their advance."

The failure of the advancing 4th Division units to be aware of what awaited them on the rocky, cave-studded terrain of northeastern Iwo Jima was not due entirely to a lack of intelligence. Observers had studied the terrain in the zone of advance of the division from battalion observation posts, from a vessel close to the shoreline, and from one of the reconnaissance planes of VMO-4. A detailed intelligence report compiled on the basis of such observation noted: "The volcanic, crevice lined area is a tangled conglomeration of torn trees and blasted rocks. Ground observation is restricted to small areas. While there are sundry ridges, depressions, and irregularities, most of the crevices of any moment radiate from the direction of Hill 382 to fan out like spokes generally in a southeasterly direction providing a series of cross corridors to our advance and eminently suitable for the enemy's employment of mortars. The general debris caused by our supporting fires provides perfect concealment for snipers and mortar positions. From the air, caves and tracks are observed everywhere, but the enemy's camouflage discipline is flawless and it is the rarest occasion that an Aerial Observer can locate troops." The enemy force charged with the defense of the Meat Grinder, which consisted of Hill 382, Turkey Knob, and the Amphitheater combined, was the 2d Mixed Brigade under Major General Sadasue Senda. This force consisted of five infantry battalions, an artillery battalion, an engineer battalion, and a field hospital. Prior to D-Day, the 2d Mixed Brigade Engineers had consolidated the three terrain features into a closely integrated defense system, complete with extensive communications and electric lights. Marines of the 4th Division, preparing to move into northeastern Iwo, faced the most extensive and powerful defenses on the island.

In the course of 25 February, General Gates' men prepared to advance into the eastern bulge of Iwo Jima. Early on D plus 6, the 21st Marines which had been attached to the 4th Division, reverted to General Erskine and the boundary between the 21st and 24th Marines became the left boundary of the 4th Division. At the same time, the 23d Marines reverted from VAC reserve to the 4th Division and prepared to attack after passing through the left of the 24th Marines. Plans for the assault on D plus 6 called for 3/23 to move out with 1/23 following 600 yards behind. The 2d Battalion, 23d Marines, was to remain in reserve. In the adjacent sector, the 24th Marines, with 2/25 attached, was to continue the advance with 3/24 on the left and 1/24 on the right. The 2d Battalion, 24th Marines, was to become regimental reserve as soon as it had been relieved by 3/23. The 25th Marines, less 2/25, was to remain in division reserve. The division main effort was to be made on the left, where the 23d Marines was to maintain contact with the adjacent 3d Marine Division.

The attack jumped off at 0930. Almost immediately, Colonel Wensinger's 23d Marines, advancing in a column of battalions, encountered heavy mortar and machine gun fire from pillboxes, bunkers, and caves. Progress was accordingly slow. Enemy antitank guns and mines, as well as unfavorable terrain, made it impossible to move armor to the front in the 4th Division zone of advance. The adjacent 3d Division was requested to permit tanks of the 4th Tank Battalion the use of an approach route leading through 3d Division terrain to the Central Airfield. Permission was granted shortly before 1300. Once the Shermans had taken up firing positions along the left boundary of the 23d Marines, they were able to lend effective support to the infantry, destroying antitank weapons, pillboxes, and enemy machine gun emplacements. Once these defenses had been eliminated, an armored bulldozer of the 4th Engineer Battalion was able to clear a route of advance for the tanks in the zone of action of the 23d Marines. Throughout the day, 3/23 continued to meet heavy resistance as it gained a foothold on the high ground at the northeastern edge of the Central Airfield and pushed eastward along Charlie-Dog Ridge. Heavy and accurate enemy mortar fire that blanketed the runways of the airfield made it extremely difficult for Colonel Wensinger's Marines to maintain contact with the adjacent 9th Marines. The 24th Marines, with 2/25 attached, made only little progress on 25 February, slowed by difficult terrain, mortar fire, and interlocking bands of fire from automatic weapons in pillboxes, bunkers, and caves. Prior to the jumpoff, artillery, naval gunfire, and carrier aircraft attempted to soften up the Amphitheater and Minami Village. While the air strike was in progress, 81mm mortars fired 200 rounds into this area. Offshore, LVT's of the 2d Armored Amphibian Battalion attempted to support 1/24, but rough seas soon made their withdrawal necessary.

Enemy resistance in front of 3/24 came from the Amphitheater, while 1/24 found its advance contested by strong enemy defenses to its front. Five tanks of Lieutenant Colonel Richard K. Schmidt's 4th Tank Battalion eventually got into position to support the attack, but the rough terrain severely limited the movement of armor. Having gained roughly 100 yards, the two battalions were halted by heavy enemy fire that took a steady toll among officers and men. Among those mortally wounded in the course of the morning was the commander of Company A, 1/24. The battalion intelligence officer was wounded and evacuated.

For the remainder of the afternoon, neither regiment made any significant gains. An air strike against the high ground facing 3/24 in the early afternoon temporarily reduced the volume of the enemy mortar fire and enabled Major Stout's men to move forward a few additional yards. In midafternoon, 2/24, which had spent most of the day in regimental reserve, was ordered to relieve 1/24 on the regiment's right. This relief, ordered at short notice, was executed without casualties.

On the evening of D plus 6, the 4th Marine Division was poised for the attack into the enemy's strongest line of defenses in the division's zone of advance. At this stage, even before the division had launched a direct assault into what came to be called the Meat Grinder, its combat efficiency had already been reduced to an estimated 55 percent by casualties and battle fatigue. Yet General Cates and the men under his command were unflagging in their determination to see the difficult job through. In commenting on the limited gains of 25 February, the division sized up the situation as follows: "The combination of terrain skillfully employed to the best advantage by the enemy, terrain unsuited for tank employment, the locations of installations in areas which were defiladed from our artillery, and the stubborn fight to-the-death attitude of the defenders had temporarily limited the advance of this Division; but the Division prepared to continue the attack." At 2200 on D plus 6, the rear command post of the 4th Marine Division closed on the USS *Bayfield*. In the course of the evening, support ships fired night missions. During the night, there was little activity in the 4th Marine Division sector. A small enemy patrol attempted to infiltrate into the 3/24 area, but all of the Japanese were either killed or dispersed. The enemy fired sporadically into the division sector with rockets, mortars, and artillery. The 4th

Division attack on the morning of 26 February was preceded by a coordinated preparation fired by the corps and division artillery and naval gunfire support ships. Following the shelling, the 4th Marine Division resumed the attack at 0800 with five battalions abreast. Once again, on the division left, Colonel Wensinger's 23d Marines attacked with 1/23 on the left and 3/23 on the right. On the division right, Colonel Lanigan's 25th Marines, which had relieved the 24th Marines earlier that morning, advanced at 0830 with all three battalions. The half hour delay in the jumpoff of the 25th Marines was caused by the necessity of returning 2/25 from 24th Marines' control and moving the battalion to the line of departure.

The division attack encountered the same difficulties that had stymied its progress on 25 February. Enemy resistance from well organized and mutually supporting positions continued undiminished. In front of the 23d Marines, the enemy occupied a maze of pillboxes, bunkers, and caves. All avenues of approach were protected by successive minefields, which made it almost impossible to commit armor in support of the infantry. On the other hand, enemy tanks dug in on the slopes of Hill 382 had a clear field of fire into the advancing Marines. One of the enemy medium tanks, armed with a 57mm gun, occupied a stationary position in a crevice, from where it could fire at will along the entire length of the main runway of the Central Airfield. Three 47mm antitank guns were emplaced in the northern portion of Charlie-Dog Ridge, which also afforded an unimpeded field of fire at the same runway.

Despite bitter opposition, Colonel Wensinger's Marines continued to push the attack throughout the day. Elements of 1/23, commanded by Lieutenant Colonel Louis B. Blissard, drew heavy and accurate fire not only from Hill 382, but also from the adjacent 3d Division zone, where the enemy still occupied strong positions to the north of the Central Airfield. To the right of 1/23, the 3d Battalion, commanded by Major James S. Scales, met equally heavy fire, but managed to fight its way forward, eliminating well-emplaced and dug-in pillboxes and blockhouses through the use of flamethrowers, rockets, and demolition teams.

By late afternoon, the 23d Marines had gained about 300 yards and seized the southwest slopes of Hill 382. This advance partially denied the use of this vital hill to the enemy. At 1700, the regiment was ordered to consolidate, but one hour later Major Scales' men were still engaged in close combat with the enemy and vicious fighting at close quarters continued until well into the evening. In addition to receiving fire from the front and flanks, the Marines occupying precarious positions on the slopes of Hill 382 also drew scattered sniper fire from the rear, which did little to ease the minds of the exposed Marines. When heavy enemy mortar and rocket fire began to hit the southwestern slopes in the afternoon, it became necessary to withdraw all units to the foot of Hill 382. The 25th Marines was to find the going equally rough on D plus 7. Following a rolling artillery barrage, Colonel Lanigan's regiment, with 3/24 attached, jumped off with 1/25, under Major Fenton J. Mee on the left, 2/25 under Lieutenant Colonel James Taul in the center, and 3/25 commanded by Captain James C. Headley, on the right.

Initially, the advance of 1/25 and 3/24 into the Amphitheater proceeded slowly but steadily against enemy small arms fire. After an advance of about 150 yards, the terrain became extremely difficult. At the same time, Japanese machine guns and mortars unleashed such a deluge of fire from well prepared and camouflaged positions near Minami Village that the men were effectively pinned down. Tanks of Company A, 4th Tank Battalion, attempted to reduce enemy pressure on the infantry but succeeded only in drawing additional artillery and mortar fire which resulted in the destruction of two Shermans just east of the airfield. In the jumbled terrain, artillery forward observers were unable to direct effective counterbattery fire against the enemy. Two spotter aircraft from VMO-4, which had just reached the island, made an attempt to spot the bothersome enemy mortar and artillery positions from the air, but this effort was also unsuccessful due to skillful enemy camouflage.

With the left and center of the 25th Marines pinned down, Company C of 1/25 made an attempt at 1400 to send a platoon, supported by three Shermans, around the right flank to envelop enemy defenses on Turkey Knob. This attempt ended in dismal failure when the Japanese became aware of the maneuver and shifted their mortar fire. The barrage caught the men out in the open and killed several, including the platoon leader. The survivors of this ill-fated platoon were able to withdraw only under cover of a smoke screen.

Along the division right flank, 3/25 made a slow but steady advance against heavy machine gun and rifle fire from the high ground on the left and caves and pillboxes to the front. As Company L slowly moved forward, Company I, supported by two medium tanks and by LVT's offshore, was systematically mopping up near the East Boat Basin. In the wake of Company L's advance followed Company K, using demolition charges and flamethrowers on every position that might possibly shelter enemy troops that had been bypassed.

As D plus 7, 26 February, came to a close, the 4th Marine Division held a very irregular line somewhat resembling the wings of a seagull. On the left, the 23d Marines had gained roughly 200 yards. In the center of the division line, where 1/25 was directly in front of Turkey Knob and the Amphitheater, gains were at best 75 yards. The most progress for the day had been made by 3/25 on the right which by late afternoon had seized a line of cliffs east of the East Boat Basin for an overall gain of nearly 500 yards. One more accomplishment accrued to 3/25: in mopping up the area near the East Boat Basin, the battalion wiped out the last nest of snipers that had interfered with shore party activities on the beaches below. Even though the unloading was still carried on under the muzzles of the enemy artillery, and rockets from northern Iwo still were capable of hitting any point on the island, at least the bothersome sniper fire had been eliminated. The 4th Marine Division intelligence report for D plus 7 outlined the severity of the resistance that the division had encountered, particularly in front of Hill 382 and Turkey Knob, and noted "that the enemy is now fighting to the death in pillboxes, foxholes, and trenches . . . and is not retreating as he apparently formerly had done."

The enemy unit to which this report referred was the 309th Independent Infantry Battalion. On D-Day, this battalion had been stationed near the Southern Airfield and since then it had fought a delaying action, gradually withdrawing northeastward under superior pressure. On D plus 7, the attack by the 23d Marines had severely mauled the battalion and pushed it southeastward, where it found itself in the path of the 25th Marines' advance. As a result, when the day ended, the battalion had been for all practical purposes annihilated.

After a day of exhausting action, 4th Division Marines were in for a restless night, Enemy mortars and artillery kept both the division's front and rear areas under steady fire, paying special attention to the division artillery positions. Beyond any doubt, the accuracy of the enemy fire was aided by bright moonlight which emerged after an afternoon of intermittent rain. Less accurate, but equally disturbing to the peace of mind of 4th Division Marines, were the huge rockets wobbling over their positions and exploding far to their rear. In the midst of this bedlam, there was small arms fire from the enemy side.

Small groups of Japanese attempted to infiltrate all along the division perimeter. Around 0530, the sound of tank engines was heard in front of the 23d Marines and there were indications that the enemy was preparing to counterattack. An artillery preparation into the presumed enemy assembly area restored silence. Offshore, support ships furnished harassing fires and illumination. Aside from the enemy probes, no major attack developed and it was assumed that the artillery barrage had dispersed the possible counterattack. Indicative of the bitterness of the action that continued through the long night is the fact that in the area in front of 1/25 alone, 103 enemy dead were counted after daybreak.

Dawn on 27 February, D plus 8, marked the beginning of the second day of the concerted 4th Division assault into the Meat Grinder. The lineup of units for the attack was substantially the same as on the previous day. From left to right, the five battalions committed were 1/23 and 3/23, and all three battalions of the 25th Marines. The 24th Marines, except for the 3d Battalion which was still attached to the 25th Marines, continued in regimental reserve.

The assault was preceded by a 45-minute preparation of the corps and division artillery. Even though, at this particular time, the corps artillery was giving priority to supporting General Erskine's 3d Division, Colonel Letcher, commanding the 1st Provisional Field Artillery Group, ordered his 155mm howitzers to expend 300 rounds as part of the preparation. For the remainder of the day, the corps artillery was authorized to fire up to 25 percent of the general support missions for General Cates' division. The 4th Division objective for D plus 8 was capture of Hill 382 and advance to the O-2 Line. Following a thunderous artillery preparation, the 4th Division attacked at 0800. On the division left, the two battalions of the 23d Marines resumed the assault on Hill 382. While 1/23 attacked northeastward in order to envelop the hill from the north, the 3d Battalion resumed the assault up the southwestern slopes. Since the Japanese atop the hill enjoyed a perfect view of the American lines, smoke was employed to screen the reorganization and movement of frontline companies in the 3d Battalion area. The enemy was not deceived, however, and almost immediately, the advancing Marines came under such severe fire that forward movement was all but impossible. Nevertheless, throughout the morning, 3/23 launched repeated assaults up the southwestern slopes of the hill without making any substantial headway. Strong and determined enemy resistance from the high ground effectively pinned Major Scales' men down. Two of Colonel Nishi's tanks, emplaced in the recesses of Hill 382, further added to the volume of the enemy fire. A new technique resorted to by the Japanese at this time was firing rifle grenades in volleys, which took a further toll of casualties among the exposed Marines.

By noon, the Japanese were still fully in control of the hill. The 1st Battalion, 23d Marines. was slowly gaining ground to the northwest of Hill 382. Once he had bypassed the objective from the north, Lieutenant Colonel Blissard, the battalion commander, planned to attack up the reverse slope. Both battalions, but especially 3/23, had sustained losses that had reduced them to little more than company strength; some of the companies had shrunk to platoon size, Nevertheless, the assault continued. In order to assist 3/23 in its frontal assault, 2/14 fired a 30-minute preparation beginning at noon, against Hill 382. Following this barrage, the exhausted men of 3/23 jumped off. This time, some progress was made, as Marines threw grenades and satchel charges into the caves and other strongpoints still held by the obstinate defenders. Once the Marines had advanced within striking distance of the two tanks, they were able to finish them off with bazooka fire. Slowly and painfully, the assault force fought its way up the hill.

Additional support for Major Scales' men arrived in two forms. First, shortly after 1400, Lieutenant Colonel Blissard's battalion, having bypassed the hill, commenced an attack up the reverse slope. Secondly, almost at the same time, engineers with a tank dozer began to carve out a path over which some of the Shermans could come within striking distance. Once they had gone into position, the supporting tanks took the Japanese on the higher reaches of Hill 382 under effective fire. This badly needed support, arriving at a crucial time, reversed the situation. The Japanese on the hill found themselves virtually cut off. The deadly fire of the Shermans forced them to stay under cover. As Major Scales' men approached the top of the hill, they discovered that the top had been hollowed out and that it contained a solid wall of artillery and antitank gun positions. Here, among the ruins of the radar station, the men of 3/23 came to grips with the Japanese in vicious close combat in which no quarter was asked or given. Just when it appeared that the Japanese would be driven off, a heavy artillery and mortar barrage hit the advancing Marines. With darkness approaching, 3/23 still had not gained a solid foothold on top of Hill 382, and rather than risk an envelopment during the night, 3/23 was ordered to consolidate on ground that would permit solid contact with adjacent units to the left and the right. As a result, Major Scales' men withdrew from the hill and spent the night in practically the same positions from which they had launched their attack on the morning of D plus 8.

Progress on 27 February was little better to the right of the 23d Marines, where the 25th Marines, with 3/24 attached, jumped off at 0800. On the regimental left, the advance of 1/25 hinged on the progress made by 3/23. If the latter succeeded in seizing the crest of Hill 382, 1/25 was to advance north through part of the 3/23 zone of attack, then pivot southeastward to envelop Turkey Knob while 2/25 was to attempt an envelopment from the south. When it became evident by 1500 that the advance of 3/23 was progressing much more slowly than anticipated, Major Fenton J. Mee, commanding 1/25, ordered the battalion forward, even though Hill 382 still had not been taken. The attack, supported by tanks and preceded by a rocket barrage, initially gained 150 yards across open terrain but came to a halt before cover on the far side could be reached when heavy mortar and antitank fire, as well as intense machine gun fire, hit the assault force. In addition to inflicting heavy casualties on the infantrymen, the Japanese also succeeded in putting two of the three tanks supporting the attack out of action and damaging the third. Shortly after 1700, it had to be conceded that the commanding ground which formed the day's objective could not be reached before nightfall, and the battalion pulled back to its jumpoff positions.

In the regimental center and on the right, 2/25 and 3/25, attacking due east, gained between 200 and 300 yards. After having reached ground that was favorable for night defense, both battalions were ordered at 1600 to halt for the day. Since it was still considered possible that the enemy might attempt a flanking attack from the sea, elements of 3/25 were held in reserve near the East Boat Basin with the specific mission of defending that area against any further attack from the ocean.

As D plus 8 ended, an analysis of the progress made that day showed clearly that the gains made were minimal. Summing up the situation at Hill 382, the 4th Division noted with some disgust that "it was envisaged that the capture of this terrain freak would be a costly and a time-consuming job."

The Battle Of Attrition

For 4th Division Marines, the night from 27-28 February proved to be a restless one. Throughout the darkness, both the front and rear areas came under heavy mortar fire. For a while it appeared that the enemy had singled out the division command post for special punishment, and no less than 15 heavy shells hit the CP prior to 2200. At the same time, the enemy fired on the beach area with either 20mm or 40mm automatic weapons. Offshore, ships of Task Force 54 furnished normal harassing and illumination fires. The enemy probed various sectors in the 4th Marine Division lines, but no counterattack developed. Shortly before 0100, the 23d Marines reported that enemy cargo parachutes were dropping into the enemy lines about 400 to 600 yards ahead of them. Strangely enough, none of the enemy planes had been picked up by the American radar on and around Iwo Jima. Nevertheless, the visual sightings were sufficient to spur American artillery into vigorous action. Concentrated artillery and naval gunfire into the drop zone, though unobserved, was expected to have resulted in the destruction of most of the supplies that had been airlifted to General Senda's 2d Mixed Brigade, elements of which were still holding the crest of Hill 382. The cargo received by the Japanese that night consisted of medical supplies and ammunition, dropped with paper parachutes from planes based elsewhere in the Bonins. Some of these supplies, still attached to the flimsy parachutes, were recovered several days later when Marines entered the drop zone.

Objectives for the continuation of the attack on the last day of February, D plus 9, remained unchanged though some of the regimental boundaries within the 4th Division underwent a slight change. On the left, the 23d Marines was to continue the assault on Hill 382; in the center, 1/25 and 2/25 were to continue their envelopment of Turkey Knob, while 3/25 along the coast was to advance to the O-2 Line.

At 0815, following a 45-minute artillery preparation, the assault battalions of the 4th Marine Division jumped off. On the left, the 23d Marines, reinforced with one company of the 24th Marines, resumed the attack with 1/23 on the left and 2/23 on the right after the latter battalion had relieved 3/23. The 2d Battalion, under Major Robert H. Davidson, attempted an advance into the area between Hill 382 and Turkey Knob, while 1/23 again assaulted the hill from the east. Following the jumpoff, 2/23 advanced about 200 yards before it came under increasingly heavy mortar and automatic weapons fire from concealed bunkers and pillboxes. The 1st Battalion likewise drew fire from automatic weapons and mortars, which brought its advance to a virtual standstill. The 3d Battalion spent most of the morning reorganizing and did not start its push up the southwestern slopes of Hill 382 until later in the afternoon. As a result, the only battalion of the 23d Marines to make any appreciable gains in the course of the morning was 2/23. At 1300, following a 10-minute preparation, 1/23 launched a coordinated attack with the 21st Marines of the adjacent 3d Marine Division. This joint venture resulted in a 300-yard advance of 1/23 near the division boundary. Other elements of 1/23, attacking Hill 382 from the east, destroyed two of Colonel Nishi's dug-in tanks and continued the ascent to a point where they could take the enemy on top of the hill under fire. By midafternoon, Hill 382 was virtually surrounded; the noose around the Japanese was further tightened when two companies of 3/23 were committed to reinforce the lines of the two assault battalions.

Despite the punishment he was taking, the enemy atop Hill 382 continued to fight as if nothing out of the ordinary were happening around him. In addition to resistance coming from the hill itself, the Marines of the encircling force drew heavy mortar, rocket, and artillery fire from enemy positions hidden in the jumbled rocks to the east of the hill. Behind the American lines, the supporting weapons did all they could to support the attack of the infantry against Hill 382. In addition to firing preparations before the jumpoff, the 14th Marines shelled the area ahead of the infantry in an attempt to silence enemy small arms and automatic weapons. Corps and division observers teamed up in an effort to pinpoint as many as possible of the cleverly hidden enemy mortar, artillery, and rocket positions, a slow and time-consuming process that did not always produce immediate results.

The difficult terrain, combined with Japanese expertise in mining the approaches to the front lines and the excellent marksmanship of the enemy antitank gun crews, severely curtailed the use of tanks in close support of the infantry. Nevertheless, individual tanks were able to move forward to deliver overhead fire, which was helpful but still lacked the volume necessary to be really effective. Finally, it was decided that the 4.5-inch rockets of the 1st Provisional Rocket Detachment might provide the massed firepower needed. Initially, whenever the rocket trucks went into action, they invariably attracted immediate counterbattery fire from the enemy entrenched on the dominating heights blessed with the advantage of unlimited observation. In order to compete effectively at such a disadvantage, the rocket launcher crews employed hit-and-run tactics. Rocket trucks would whip into position, fire their launchers, and take off to predesignated assembly points in the rear with all possible speed. If a particularly intensive barrage was desired, six trucks and launchers would fire once, reload with rockets carried on the vehicles, fire a second salvo, and then head for the rear. In this way, a double ripple of 432 rounds could be delivered in somewhat less than five minutes.

By late afternoon of 28 February, it became evident that despite the deteriorating situation of enemy troops on the crest of Hill 382, capture of this objective would not be completed in the remaining hours of daylight. As a result, the 23d Marines remained active well into the night in an attempt to consolidate its lines for night defense. The 1st Battalion, in particular, found it extremely difficult to close the gap on the left with the 21st Marines. This was finally accomplished under sniper fire from enemy pockets that has been bypassed in the adjacent 21st Marines' zone of advance during the day. Gains made by the 23d Marines on D plus 9 totalled about 300 yards on the left and 200 yards on the right. As Colonel Wensinger's regiment vainly struggled to complete the capture of Hill 382 on D plus 9, the adjacent 25th Marines faced its own ordeal in its drive to seize Turkey Knob, the Amphitheater, and the area separating the Knob from the east coast. At 0815, the regiment, with 3/24 attached, jumped off in the same formation it had maintained on the previous day. Two companies of the 1st Battalion, plus one company of 3/24, were to attempt an envelopment of Turkey Knob from the north, while another company was to advance along the low ground southwest of the Knob and attack eastward around the Amphitheater until it could link up with the northern pincers.

Following the usual preparation, elements of the 1st Battalion moved into the wooded area just north of Turkey Knob and advanced some 50 yards. At this point, the enemy unleashed a tremendous mortar and artillery barrage; heavy machine gun fire from the front and the left flank began to rake the Marines. Prompt counterbattery fire called for by observers with the 1st Battalion failed to silence the enemy batteries. By noon, the situation of 1/25 in the woods had become critical and the battalion was suffering heavy casualties. Nevertheless, Major Mee, the battalion commander, ordered his men to hold the woods in order to enable the southern pincers to complete the envelopment of Turkey Knob. As Company B, which was to make the envelopment, started its encircling movement, supported by two Shermans, the enemy on the high ground east of the objective started to shower the force with hand grenades, at the same time raking them with accurate machine gun fire. One of the tanks soon hit a mine and was disabled; the other managed to pull back.

As the fury of the enemy fire increased and casualties mounted, the attack of Company B stalled. By 1645 it was readily apparent that continuation of the attack in the face of such heavy enemy resistance during the limited daylight remaining would serve no useful purpose, and both pincers of 1/25 pulled back to their respective starting positions. In the fading daylight, two tanks made their way forward to a point northwest of Turkey Knob and from this vantage point opened fire against the enemy communications center atop the hill. The 75mm shells, to all appearances, did little damage to the concrete structure and the shelling was ineffective.

To the right of 1/25, the 2d Battalion attempted to extend its left flank to support the advance of the southern pincers of 1/25. To this end, it had to seize the high ground directly to its front. Enemy fire, most of it coming from pillboxes to the left of the battalion zone of advance, pinned down the infantry. The difficult terrain made it impossible for the Shermans and halftracks to give close support to the infantry. The attack soon stalled. At noon, the battalion commander, Lieutenant Colonel Taul, decided to improvise in order to get the attack moving again. He requested and received permission to have a 75mm pack howitzer rushed forward, to be used as a direct assault weapon. A DUKW was used to transport the howitzer to a position just behind the front lines. There, the gun was dismantled and the various pieces were gingerly hand-carried into the zone of advance of 2/25, where the piece was carefully reassembled. Once this feat had been accomplished, the pack howitzer pumped 40 rounds at the concrete structure atop Turkey Knob. Most of the shells bounced harmlessly off the thick concrete walls and did little, if any, damage to the communications center. However, it was not altogether a wasted effort, for the battalion reported that while "the direct result to the enemy was not readily apparent, the morale effect on the men of this battalion was of considerable value because after the howitzer was fired our lines advanced approximately 75 yards by 1900." Two hours later, under cover of darkness, the pack howitzer was again disassembled and returned to its parent organization. On the right of the 25th Marines' zone of advance, 3/25 jumped off on the morning of D plus 9 at the same time as the other battalions of the division. Moving eastward roughly parallel to the east coast, the battalion had gained about 100 yards by 1000. At that time, the advance of the adjacent 2d Battalion began to bog down, and 3/25, which was pacing itself by the progress of the unit on its left, also halted the attack. Since 2/25 on the left failed to make any further progress for the day, neither did 3/25. At 1800, units of the 25th Marines were ordered to consolidate for the night.

In summing up the results of the clay's operations, the 4th Marine Division felt that, even though the enemy was still clinging to the crest of Hill 382 and Turkey Knob, the day's limited advance had outflanked these enemy strongpoints. The feeling was that 4th Division Marines could henceforth bypass the Amphitheater and continue the drive along the east coast of Iwo Jima. Despite the small gains made on D plus 9, the division intelligence officer felt that the central defensive core of resistance had been cracked. He affirmed the possibility of an enemy counterattack, but assumed that the Japanese would be least likely to mount any major counterattack in the zone of action of the 4th Division because of the difficult terrain.

Events were to prove this forecast only 50 percent correct. Throughout 28 February, the assault battalions had received a variety of assistance from the supporting arms. Offshore, gunfire support ships furnished call-fire missions, while smaller craft fired mortars in support of 2/25 and 3/25. During the afternoon a destroyer approached the east shore and began shelling enemy positions on the high ground in front of the 2/25 zone of advance. Air support extended to the entire 4th Division sector, though half of the napalm bombs dropped in front of the 25th Marines in the course of the morning failed to ignite. A second strike, this time in support of the 23d Marines, took unduly long to be executed. When the aircraft did arrive, they went into action against the wrong target area. The night from D plus 9 to D plus 10 turned out to be another restless one for Marines of the 4th Division. The enemy concentrated his artillery fire against rear installations of the 5th Marine Division and scored several lucky hits on the ammunition dumps of that division. The resulting explosions coming from the rear did little to reassure the men of any of the three divisions. Some enemy mortar and artillery fire also fell in the 4th Division area, causing further disruption of sleep. Alert Marines of 3/23 frustrated several enemy attempts to infiltrate their lines, and 29 enemy dead were found in front of the lines on the following morning. Around 2200, the 25th Marines noticed that the enemy in company strength was massing for a counter attack near the coast in the 3/25 area. Naval gunfire and shore-based artillery promptly fired on and dispersed this assembly.

Division orders for 1 March called for continuation of the attack against Hill 382 and Turkey Knob. Beginning at 0530, the 24th Marines was to relieve the depleted units of the 23d, with 2/24 relieving 1/23 and 1/24 taking over the 2/23 sector. The relief was completed by 0630 without major incident and, following a 45-minute naval gunfire and corps artillery preparation, the attack against the key enemy defenses resumed. For 10 minutes prior to H-Hour, set for 0830, the division artillery blasted enemy positions in the division zone of advance.

On the division left, the 24th Marines jumped off, with the 2d Battalion, commanded by Lieutenant Colonel Richard Rothwell on the left and 1/24, under Major Paul S. Treitel, on the right. Almost immediately, 2/24 was hit by heavy artillery and mortar fire. In order to keep his battalion from getting bogged down, Lieutenant Colonel Rothwell requested supporting fire. Shortly after 0930, carrier aircraft dropped napalm about 600 yards in front of 2/24. The aerial assault was followed within the hour by a fire concentration against the same area by the corps artillery; this fire was followed by naval gunfire. This counterfire had a salutary effect and enemy opposition diminished to the extent that elements of the battalion, in the course of the afternoon, were able to make gains of 150 yards.

While part of 2/24, notably Company F, was engaged in attacking northeastward along the boundary with the 3d Marine Division, at times even crossing the boundary, the gains made by General Erskine's men on 1 March exceeded those of the 4th Division and, in consequence, a gap developed along the boundary. Colonel Walter I. Jordan, commanding the 24th Marines, at 1430 had to commit two companies of 3/24 into the gap in order to regain contact with the 3d Division along the left flank. Somewhat farther to the south, the battle for Hill 382 continued with undiminished fury. The reduction of the battered strongpoint fell to Company G, 2/24, which assaulted the hill with flamethrowers, bazookas, grenades, and whatever else was at hand. Just as elements of the 23d Marines had previously fought their way to the top to engage in close combat with the defenders, only to be driven off, so it was with the determined Marines of Company G, 2/24. The viciousness of the fighting that ensued has been depicted in these words: "At one time, Company G of 2/24 was astride the top, but still there was no quarter. The attackers fought with rifles and grenades, with flamethrowers and satchel charges. Still the defenders would not give up, even though their own fire fell on them from the ridges further east." These were the men from Kumamoto in Kyushu, a historic battlefield of the 1877 Civil War, and they would not give up. Not even when Major Kenro Anso died, burned from head to foot by a flamethrower. He led the 3d Battalion, 145th Regiment, in defense of the hill. So great was his inspiration that at his death he was promoted two full ranks to colonel. As the afternoon wore on, the battle for control of the hill continued without letup. While hand grenades flew back and forth, assault squads were blowing cave entrances, and flamethrowers were incinerating such Japanese as showed themselves. Lieutenant Colonel Rothwell, escorted by his company commanders, appeared on the scene in order to conduct a personal reconnaissance, select positions for the coming night, and make plans for the attack on D plus 11. Despite heavy fire that was coming from nearly every direction, the reconnaissance party completed its inspection and the battalion commander left the hill unscathed. As the day ended, the remnants of Major Anso's battalion clung to the crest of Hill 382, still full of fighting spirit despite the loss of their commander.

Along the southern slopes of the hill and near its base to the southeast, the fighting on D plus 10 waxed just as bitterly as it did at the top. Here, 1/24 was attempting an envelopment of Hill 382 from the south against heavy fire coming not only from the top of the hill but also from a patch of woods directly in front and the high ground beyond. As men of the 1st Battalion inched ahead, two tanks attached to Company C provided covering fire. Just before noon, the company commander was wounded and casualties mounted to a point where smoke had to be employed to screen evacuation of the wounded.

Following a heavy artillery and mortar concentration, and led by a new commander, Company C resumed the attack at 1300. Within minutes, the new commander was wounded and had to be replaced. Despite all enemy opposition, the company continued its dogged advance and by 1700, when it began to consolidate its positions, it had seized some of the high ground to the southeast of Hill 382. The biggest gains for the 24th Marines on D plus 10 were to accrue along the 4th Division boundary, where 2/24 made an advance of 400 yards to the east. To the right, the dogged attack of 1/24 to the high ground southeast of Hill 382 culminated in a gain of 200 yards. This forward movement, flanking Hill 382 from two sides, all but surrounded the enemy atop the hill, though this made little, if any, difference to Japanese determined to die there. Of added importance to the further advance of the 24th Marines was the fact that from the high ground southeast of Hill 382, Company C was able to look down on the ruins of Minami Village. Thus it appeared that the day's advance had served not only to outflank most of Hill 382, but a portion of Turkey Knob and the Amphitheater as well.

To the south, the 25th Marines, attacking in the same formation employed in previous days, also was in for a hard day's work. The regiment's plan was ambitious: to execute a double envelopment of Turkey Knob, supported by two companies of 3/23 which relieved elements of 3/24 that had been attached to 1/25 for the past two days. As the 1st Battalion moved out, supported by the companies of 3/23, it crossed an open area prior to entering the woods to its front. Upon reaching the edge of the woods around 1000, 1/25 encountered the same conditions that had halted the advance on the previous day. Once again, Major Mee's men were hit by heavy mortar, artillery, and machine gun fire, which caused the advance to bog down. Despite counterbattery fire and aerial spotting, it proved impossible to put the enemy mortars out of action, nor were the aerial observers able to spot to the cleverly concealed enemy artillery positions.

Fighting for the woods raged throughout 1 March, as Marines of 1/25 pressed the attack. It was an unequal contest with the enemy possessing the advantage of cover, concealment, commanding terrain, and superior fire power. In the end, the assault units of 1/25 had to pull back to their jumpoff positions. As the tired men began their withdrawal the enemy, in a final gesture of defiance, subjected them to a heavy mortar and rocket barrage, which caused additional casualties. The withdrawal was accomplished with the help of a smoke screen, which also made it possible to evacuate the casualties. Shortly after 1600, the Japanese added insult to injury by subjecting Colonel Lanigan's command post to a severe shelling.

Since the remaining two battalions of the 25th Marines were pacing themselves in relation to gains to be made by the 1st Battalion, they remained more or less in place when it became apparent that the attack of 1/25 had bogged down. Nevertheless, 2/25 did succeed in gaining 100 yards along its left. For the most of the day, the division reconnaissance company was attached to 2/25 in order to mop up the rear area. From the 3/25 area, a tank was able to destroy two enemy machine guns, but no additional ground was taken. Indicative of the artillery support furnished to the 25th Marines by 1/14 on D plus 10 are the following figures. The battalion fired 4,640 rounds for 135 missions, of which 94 were harassing, 31 were aimed at targets of opportunity, 6 were for preparation, and 4 were fired at miscellaneous targets. The figures listed above do not include the defensive fire, which 1/14 started at 1640, and harassing fires which continued throughout the night. As D plus 10 came to a close, the 4th Marine Division could book only very limited gains for itself. After five days of continuous assault into the Meat Grinder, all three of the mutually supporting cornerstones of the enemy defense system, Hill 382, Turkey Knob, and the Amphitheater were still in enemy hands, and, with the exception of Hill 382, firmly so. With the heaviest assaults still ahead, the combat efficiency of the 4th Division on the evening of 1 March remained at 55 percent.

The night from 1-2 March passed with few untoward incidents, except in front of 2/24, where small groups of the enemy made various attempts at infiltration, keeping the battalion in a general state of unrest. All of the 4th Division units came under sporadic enemy mortar and artillery fire that hit the lines and rear area in a seemingly haphazard fashion. By way of response, the corps and division artillery replied to each enemy salvo with immediate counterbattery fire, the results of which could not be readily determined.

Early on 2 March, General Cates' division again resumed the battle of attrition in the Meat Grinder. Though none of the weary 4th Division Marines was aware of it that morning, the final battle for the Meat Grinder was about to begin. The main effort was to be made by the 24th Marines against Hill 382, while farther south the 23d and 25th Marines were to assault the Amphitheater and Turkey Knob from the north and south. If the heavy enemy fire against Hill 382 from these two staunch bastions of the enemy defense system could be eliminated, the hill itself could be taken.

Following a 25-minute artillery preparation fired by the corps artillery from H-Hour minus 30 to minus 15, and again from minus 10 to H-Hour, the assault resumed. On the morning of D plus 11, there was one change in the preparatory fires.

Precisely at H-Hour, 0800, the division artillery unleashed an intensive preparation, followed by a rolling barrage.

On the division left, the 24th Marines with 3/24 on the right, 2/24 in the center, and 1/24 on the left moved out for the attack. The 3d Battalion, commanded by Major Doyle A. Stout, advanced eastward along the division boundary northeast of Hill 382 and, while keeping contact with 3d Division elements on its left, advanced about 300 yards. As the battalion fought its way forward, enemy opposition stiffened until all further movement became impossible.

It was in the regiment's center and on its right that the most desperate fighting for the day was to occur. It fell to 2/24 to launch an assault against Hill 382 from the northeast, while 1/24 enveloped the hill from the south. At the time they jumped off, the men of 2/24 had spent an even more restless night than had other units in the division. The front lines on Hill 382 had been active throughout the night. Hand grenade duels and hand-to-hand fighting frequently erupted with small groups of the enemy that filtered out of recesses in the hill in front of the Marine positions, between them, and even to the rear. In fact, two Marines had received saber cuts during the nocturnal fighting. Nevertheless, the battalion attacked Hill 382 with vigor, even though it was immediately subjected to heavy machine gun, rifle, mortar, and artillery fire. Since Lieutenant Colonel Rothwell's men constituted the main effort, four Shermans and a section of the 1st Provisional Rocket Detachment furnished support, in addition to the division artillery. As the tanks and rocket launchers blasted the area ahead of 2/24 with shells and flame, they were spotted by the enemy and taken under such heavy fire that the armor had to pull back. The rocket launchers were able to fire three missions before they, too, had to be withdrawn. By 1100, the frontal assault on Hill 382 was beginning to bog down in the face of interlocking enemy machine gun fire, as well as heavy mortar fire. The importance that the Japanese attached to the defense of the hill was underscored not only by the severity of the mortar fire but also by the unusually large caliber of mortar shells employed. As elsewhere on Iwo Jima, the artillery and naval gunfire furnished in support of the attack was of little benefit to the infantrymen slowly inching their way up the reverse slope of Hill 382, exposed to everything the enemy was capable of throwing at them with little else but their own organic weapons to answer.

As the attack was on the verge of bogging down, Lieutenant Colonel Rothwell assembled his company commanders a short distance behind the lines and decided that one platoon of Company E, accompanied by two tanks, was to make an attempt to outflank the stubborn enemy defenders from the right. At this time, a platoon of Company E, commanded by 2d Lieutenant Richard Reich, had already reached the top of the hill and was locked in close combat with the enemy underneath the radar antenna at the same spot which already had seen vicious close fighting when the 23d Marines was attempting to seize the hill. As Major Roland Carey, commanding Company E, attempted to relay the orders for the flanking movement to his men, he was hit by machine gun fire and had to be evacuated. The executive officer, Captain Pat Donlan, took over and prepared to see that his predecessor's orders were carried out.

Just as Captain Donlan was in the process of orienting his platoon leaders and issuing orders for the flanking movement at the battalion command post, he was hit by a fragment of a mortar shell exploding nearby. As one of the platoon leaders, 1st Lieutenant Stanley Osborne, prepared to relieve him, another large mortar shell scored a square hit on the command post with devastating results: "Osborne was killed instantly, Donlan's right leg was blown off below the knee, and two other officers were wounded, one mortally. Reich, still holding under the radar screen, was in command. He was the only officer left in Company E." Despite the loss of five of its officers, Company E continued the assault on Hill 382. When elements of Company F, commanded by Captain Walter Ridlon, joined forces on the hill with Company E, the doom of the defenders was sealed. By 1530, 2/24 reported the objective secured. Colonel Jordan, the regimental commander, had by this time apparently grown somewhat leery of optimistic reports concerning the capture of this particular objective, and in consequence, in describing the action of 2 March, the 24th Marines reported only "that small gains were made throughout the day all along the line except in the vicinity of Hill 382 where the bitter opposition continued." The regiment did not officially record the capture of Hill 382 until the following day.

There was some truth to the comment that enemy opposition at Hill 382 continued, even though the Marines were now in possession of the crest. In the words of one account of the action on 2 March, "the hill was overrun, but it was not subdued." A clue to this seeming contradiction may be found in a 4th Division report for D plus 11, which introduces a new element in assessing the progress made by 2/24 on 2 March by pointing out: "It appears that there are underground passageways leading into the defenses on Hill 382 and when one occupant of a pillbox is killed another one comes up to take his place. This is rather a lengthy process." And that is precisely the way it turned out. For the remainder of D plus 11, 2/24 mopped up the objective and consolidated its positions atop the hill. Because of the underground tunnels linking various pillboxes and strongpoints on the slopes of Hill 382, "the mopup proved to be an almost interminable process." In fact, sealing the caves around Hill 382 and the elimination of isolated enemy holdouts would require several additional days. But for all practical purposes, one of the three strongpoints of the enemy defense system in the 4th Division zone of advance had been eliminated, which left the remaining two, Turkey Knob and the Amphitheater, somewhat more vulnerable to attack.

Operations on D plus 11 to the south of Hill 382 also differed from those of preceding days. While the enemy atop Hill 382 was treated to an exceptionally heavy preparation on that day, precisely the opposite was the case in the 25th Marines zone of advance. There, Colonel Lanigan decided to employ the element of surprise and launch an attack at 0630 without the benefit of any artillery preparation. During the early stages of the action, while the enemy was still off guard, 1/25 was to infiltrate and seize the high ground north of Turkey Knob. Elements of 1/25 and 3/23, the latter having been attached to the 25th Marines, were to execute an envelopment from the northwest and the south. The infiltration got under way at 0630 and proceeded on schedule for about 20 minutes. However, the Japanese soon recognized the multiple threat facing them, and at 0650 unleashed a devastating rocket and mortar barrage against the assault forces. As Marines hit the ground to escape the lethal shell fragments, enemy machine guns opened up at close range and raked the area in which the assault force was pinned down. All need for further secrecy having disappeared, Marine artillery and mortars retaliated, and eight Shermans moved forward in support of the attack. Once again, the large blockhouse atop Turkey Knob drew most of the supporting fire. A large number of 75mm shells and no less than 1,000 gallons of flamethrower fuel were hurled against this impressive obstacle, but no immediate effects of this fire became apparent. The blockhouse appeared to be unoccupied after the tank attack, but it was assumed that the enemy would feed replacements into it through tunnels as soon as the fury of the American assault diminished.

Under cover of the heavy supporting fire, the envelopment of Turkey Knob continued, though progress was slow. By 1430, the two pincers of the double envelopment were only 65 yards from each other, and for a while it appeared that the movement might still succeed. However, as soon as the enemy became aware of this latest development, he threw a tremendous barrage against Company B, 1/25, which had been inching its way north to the high ground from positions south of the Amphitheater. This murderous rocket and mortar fire, interlaced with a heavy volume of small arms fire, inflicted over 30 casualties on the company and forced its withdrawal.

In the center of the 25th Marines line, 2/25 was to extend its left flank to assist 1/25, and for this purpose one company of 3/23 was attached to the battalion. Since no appreciable gains were made by 1/25 during the day, the 2d Battalion remained in place and spent the day in mopping up enemy stragglers and reducing such fortifications in its zone as the enemy still occupied or had reoccupied. Similarly, 3/25, nearest the coast, remained in position during the early part of the day. Enemy mortar fire into these positions caused several casualties, leading Captain James C. Headley, the battalion commander, to make this comment: "Throughout this period of time we were suffering casualties from enemy mortar fire and our failure to advance while suffering casualties had a depressing effect upon the morale of the troops." During the late afternoon of 2 March, elements on the right of 2/25 and the 3d Battalion finally were given permission to advance to the high ground directly to their front. Surprisingly enough, the enemy did not contest this advance, and the 25th Marines gained 300 yards, enabling the regiment to consolidate on the freshly taken high ground. By evening of D plus 11, the 4th Division line protruded both in the north and in the south, hanging back only in the center where the Amphitheater and Turkey Knob remained to be taken. Overall, important progress had been made during the day with the seizure of Hill 382 and the unexpectedly easy advance near the coast during the latter part of the day. The fighting for Hill 382 had been costly for 2/24, in particular, which summed up the day's fighting as follows: "Today's fighting more intense than any other day up until now. Enemy resistance very heavy. Many pillboxes and strong emplacements to the direct front. Many officers, NCO'S and experienced personnel were casualties. Leadership now an acute problem. Enemy installations knocked out during the day's advance: 8 machine guns; 15 cave entrances, from which fire was being received, were sealed; one 47mm gun in bunker knocked out. No count of enemy dead, estimated to be over 100." Throughout 2 March, Marines on the ground had received excellent support from the sea as well as from the air. Two battleships and one cruiser furnished general support, while destroyers and gunboats deployed near the eastern bulge of the island to shell the rocky draws leading down to the sea. Carrier-based aircraft carried out six strikes against enemy positions in front of the 4th Division. The pilots and observers of VMO-4 flew five missions, including a rather unorthodox one in which a division public relations photographer took pictures from an altitude of 1,000 feet. This improvisation became necessary because "the sustained bombardment of Iwo Jima had so torn the face of the land that pre-D-Day maps were by now of little use in terrain appreciation."

The night from 2-3 March passed without major incidents. It almost appeared as if the Japanese were beginning to feel the results of the prolonged battle of attrition.

Along the 4th Marine Division lines, the only action occurred in front of 2/24, where the enemy attempted an infiltration. Once the presence of the intruders had been discovered, a lively fire fight ensued. It ended when the enemy withdrew, leaving behind 20 dead. Four Marines of 2/24 were killed in this action.

For the continuation of the assault on 3 March, General Cates made certain changes in the disposition of his forces. At 0500, the 23d Marines relieved the 25th and just before H-Hour, set for 0630, 1/23 passed through 1/25. The 2d and 3d Battalions, 25th Marines, were attached to the 23d and retained their positions in the center and on the right. There were no changes in the 24th Marines' sector, where Colonel Jordan's men were preparing to continue the attack, except that Company L, 3/24, suffered 22 casualties while relieving elements of the 9th Marines near the division boundary.

In an attempt to use the element of surprise, the 4th Marine Division attack was not preceded by any preparatory fire. On the division left, the 24th Marines jumped off against formidable new defenses in its zone of advance, the bulk of which appeared to be concentrated on the high ground to the northeast of Hill 382, and in the vicinity of Minami Village. Initial resistance was heavy, and mortar, artillery, machine gun, and rifle fire hit the assault companies as soon as they began to move out. Directly in front of 2/24 were pillboxes and reinforced concrete emplacements, including one emplacement containing a high velocity gun. Immediately following the jump-off, corps and division artillery began to pound these defenses with some effect. The regiment, with 3/24, 2/24, and 1/24 from left to right, slowly advanced against the enemy positions to its front. Some progress was made until the lines advanced to a point close enough to work on enemy emplacements with demolitions and flamethrowers. Once this close-in fighting got under way, fierce action ensued and the assault slowed to a crawl. The terrain consisted of numerous hillocks, mounds, and shallow cross-corridors with vertical sides. Covered reinforced concrete and sand-covered log machine gun and rifle emplacements with firing ports covering the front and both flanks blocked the advance. It soon became apparent that the line of defense to the north and east of Hill 382 had a depth of over 300 yards.

The difficulties accompanying an advance into prepared positions of this type were only too apparent. Due to the character of the terrain, these defenses were well protected from the supporting artillery fire. Tanks and flamethrower tanks, in particular, encountered major problems in getting into position. Once there, their fields of fire were limited so that they could effectively concentrate only on a few emplacements. As the infantry approached the enemy positions, the very close support needed could be furnished only by 60mm and 81mm mortars emplaced within 50 yards of the front lines. A shortage of ammunition limited the employment of the 81mm mortars, so that these weapons were fired only periodically and when dire necessity made their close supporting fires indispensable.

As usual, the infantry bore the brunt of the fighting. Marines, equipped with demolitions, portable flamethrowers, a variety of small arms, bazookas, and smoke and fragmentation grenades, maneuvered into position in small groups and attempted to neutralize the enemy positions one by one. It was a slow, tedious, and costly process calling for able leadership on the part of squad and fire team leaders, a number of whom were killed or wounded and had to be evacuated.

By late afternoon, the center of the 24th Marines had advanced 350 yards, with smaller gains along the northern and southern flanks. Throughout the day, the Shermans of Company B, 4th Tank Battalion, gave as much support to the regiment as the difficult terrain allowed. Rocket launchers employed their now customary hit and run tactics to escape counterbattery fire from the enemy mortars and artillery.

When Colonel Jordan's regiment consolidated on D plus 12, the 3d Battalion on the left had tied in with elements of the 9th Marines, while 1/24 on the right held a narrow front with only Company B in the line. After another day of fatiguing combat, the men were even more exhausted than on the previous day. Their condition was graphically outlined in a 2/24 report for the day: "Men very tired and listless, lack leaders. Close support by effective close support weapons, such as tanks and 37mm weapons, not possible except in rare instances, due to terrain limiting fields of fire. Tank support is seldom sufficient to warrant the casualties resulting from the countermortar fire." Bitter fighting also marked the day's operations to the south of the 24th Marines, where the enemy still retained a strong hold both on the Amphitheater and Turkey Knob. There, 1/23 was to make the main attack southeastward above the Amphitheater and link up with units on the left of 2/25. If completed, this envelopment would result in reduction of Turkey Knob and encirclement of the well-dug-in enemy troops in the Amphitheater. In order to support the attack, Company C, 4th Tank Battalion and a platoon of the 4th Engineer Battalion were attached to 1/23.

Following the artillery preparation which came after the jump-off, the enemy initially appeared stunned and, in the words of the regimental report, "the initial phase of the attack progressed favorably." However, progress on the regiment's right soon lagged when Marines drew fire from the concrete blockhouse atop Turkey Knob. In addition, the enemy had mined the routes of approach. Any attempt to remove these antipersonnel mines was frustrated by deadly accurate sniper fire, Nevertheless, by 1400 the attached engineer platoon had cleared a path over which flame tanks and infantry demolition teams were able to get within effective range of the blockhouse. As a result of the combined teamwork of these arms, the blockhouse atop Turkey Knob was partially reduced in a slow and costly assault that continued during the latter part of the afternoon. By evening of 3 March, however, when units consolidated for the night, the Japanese were still firmly in control of Turkey Knob.

While 1/23 was battling for possession of the Knob, the remaining two battalions of the 23d Marines remained in position, except for Company K, 3/23, which, supported by tanks and 75mm halftracks, assaulted stubborn enemy defenses along the southwestern portion of the Amphitheater. Towards the end of the day, Company I was moved into a gap south of the Amphitheater between 1/23 and 2/25. The 2d Battalion of the 23d Marines remained in corps reserve for the day; it occupied an assembly area between the Southern and Central Airfields and could be moved anywhere within the Corps zone of action as required. For the remainder of D plus 12, 2/25 and 3/25 remained in their respective positions on the division's right, while 1/25 in division reserve underwent reorganization and rehabilitation, and got some badly needed rest. Throughout the day, the slight but nevertheless important gains made by the 4th Marine Division had been achieved with the help of the supporting arms. Within the division, 2/14 had furnished direct support to the 23d Marines, while 1/14 had reinforced the fires of 2/14. The 24th Marines had been directly supported by 3/14, while 4/14 was in general support. The 4th Tank Battalion had furnished such assistance as the difficult terrain permitted. By the end of 3 March, 36 tanks were operational, 12 had been destroyed, and 8 had been damaged. Ships of TF 54 continued to provide supporting fire, but the use of such support was restricted because of safety factors dictated by the location of the front lines.

At the end of D plus 12, the combat efficiency of the 4th Marine Division was estimated to be 50 percent. All units were ordered to consolidate at 1700, prepared to continue the attack on the following day. With the capture of Hill 382, one of the main props of the enemy's defensive system in the 4th Division sector had been knocked out, and despite heavy losses, it could be assumed "that the Division was now fighting in the rear of the highly prepared defensive area in which the operations for the past three days had been conducted."

The night from 3-4 March passed without major incident in the 4th Marine Division zone of operations, except for the sector occupied by the 24th Marines. There, small groups of the enemy attempted unsuccessfully to infiltrate the lines of 3/24. The enemy placed heavy artillery and mortar fire into the 24th Marines area throughout the night, causing moderate casualties. Four destroyers provided illumination during the night.

At 0730, 4 March, the 4th Marine Division continued its attack with no change in its formation or direction of advance. Prior to the jumpoff, the corps and division artillery fired a half-hour preparation, which was further supplemented by naval gunfire. In contrast to the preceding days, the weather on D plus 13 was overcast and showers began to fall in the morning. Because of the leaden skies and the limited visibility, all air strikes had to be cancelled. It also was a very poor day for aerial observation.

On the ground, the battle of attrition continued. On the division left, the 24th Marines attacked in a generally southeasterly direction. The direction of advance was to be parallel to the corridors. Once again, the assault turned into a step-by-step affair, as usual combined with heavy casualties and little gain. Such progress as could be made was achieved with the assistance of the Shermans, which were employed with good effect against the numerous pillboxes and caves. Good results were also obtained from the flamethrower tank which scorched the enemy defenses. Even though the regiment advanced only about 100 yards, the steady destruction of the formidable enemy defenses sooner or later was bound to have a concrete effect. Indicative of the regiment's effort is the fact that 2,200 pounds of explosives were employed on D plus 13 to blow cave entrances and exits. On the division right, the 23d Marines, with 2,/25 and 3/25 still attached, 1/23 in line, and 2/23 in corps and 3/23 in division reserve, made small gains in the 1/23 zone of advance. The two attached battalions of the 25th Marines on the regiment's right had to sit it out in their positions, much against their will. As the division was to report the day's activities: "BLT's 2/25 and 3/25 could have advanced within their zones, but such an advance was not deemed advisable because it would have overextended the lines. The terrain in front of this RCT was the most difficult yet encountered; observation was limited to only a few feet, and it was impossible to support the attack with anything heavier than normal infantry weapons." By evening of 4 March, the combat efficiency of the 4th Marine Division had dropped to 45 percent, the lowest yet since the Marines had gone ashore on Iwo Jima. The enemy was still offering stubborn resistance from closely integrated positions, and General Cates' men were more exhausted than ever. This circumstance, combined with the murky skies, the discomfort created by the rain, and the ever present enemy snipers in front of, behind, and between the lines should, by all normal yardsticks, have reduced the morale of the wet and tired Marines to a new low.

Yet, strangely enough, this was not the case. There was no definite indication that the enemy's morale was sagging, and in his battered positions in the

Amphitheater, he was clinging to every foot of ground as resolutely as ever. Nevertheless, there was a quiet feeling of optimism that perhaps, after all, the enemy might be beginning to crack. Perhaps it was brought about by the decrease in the accuracy of the enemy artillery and mortar fire resulting from the accurate counterbattery fire furnished by the corps artillery. It was also possible that the loss of Hill 382 and the severe mauling that Turkey Knob had taken by this time had deprived the enemy's artillery observers of their choice observation sites.

The battle of attrition being waged all over northern Iwo Jima was beginning to affect the enemy's power to resist, even though his spirit was as high as ever. In recognition of the bitter struggle waged by General Kuribayashi against overwhelmingly superior American forces, his superiors in Tokyo sent a message addressed both to him and Admiral Ichimaru, expressing Japan's admiration for the battle they were waging. Ichimaru replied: "The enemy is hitting us hard, but we will hit back." For his part, General Kuribayashi had earlier stated defiantly, "I am not afraid of the fighting power of only three American divisions, if only there were no bombardments from aircraft and warships. This is the only reason why we have to see such miserable situations." Looking at the overall situation on Iwo and the decimated remnants of his garrison, consisting of only 3,500 effectives, General Kuribayashi saw clearly that his time was running short. In desperation, he signalled Tokyo for help on the evening of 4 March, calling for air and naval support. "Send me these things, and I will hold this island", he said. "Without them I cannot hold." But there was no response from the Japanese mainland, which itself was reeling underneath the intensified American bombing attacks. In view of total American air superiority in the Bonins and a mighty American fleet patrolling the surrounding waters, Iwo Jima was, indeed, isolated. The defenders of Iwo Jima had the full sympathy of almost the entire population of Japan, whose attention was riveted on the fierce battle in progress there. On its part "the Army High Command had meanwhile been conducting earnest investigations into the possibility of mounting an effective attack against the U. S. naval forces which were swarming around Iwo Jima. Air power on hand was small, however, while overwater flight training was inadequate; hence a massive effort could not be staged." As for the Japanese Navy contingent on Iwo Jima, Admiral Ichimaru did not even bother to radio for help. Admiral Toyoda, Commander in Chief of the Imperial Navy, had sent word that the Navy would be ready for the next expected American thrust by the end of April, but that all plans depended on the outcome at Iwo. The message ended with these words: "I regret that except for full submarine support and some air support, we cannot send reinforcements to Iwo. However, in view of overall requirements, I earnestly hope you will maintain calm and fight staunchly by any means."

The meaning of this was clear and Admiral Ichimaru, who had never expected reinforcements in the first place, accepted the inevitable. Clearly, the Iwo garrison was on its own, and its prolonged death throes would, in any case, be a lonely business.

Reorganization And Continuation Of The Attack
In accordance with General Schmidt's order that 5 March was to be a day of rest and rehabilitation for all VAC units, no offensive action was planned in the 4th Division sector on D plus 14. Instead, the division was to reorganize so that by noon it would have one regiment, less one battalion, available to continue the attack on a limited front on the following day. The general direction of the attack on 6 March was

to be eastward. The regiment which General Cates selected for the main effort was Colonel Wensinger's 23d Marines. In order to relieve this regiment from its other duties, the area on the division's right reverted to the 25th Marines. The 2d and 3d Battalions of the 25th Marines, hitherto attached to the 23d, reverted to the parent regiment. The 1st Battalion, 25th Marines, relieved 1/23 in almost identical positions held by 1/25 on 2 March. Since 3/23 was still heavily committed along the southern fringes of the Amphitheater, where it was mopping up previously bypassed enemy defenses and overcoming other stubborn pockets of resistance, Colonel Lanigan combined the division reconnaissance company, which had been attached to his regiment as of 0700 on 5 March, with Company L, 3/25, into a provisional battalion, commanded by Major Edward L. Asbill, executive officer of 1/25. In the northern portion of the division sector, three companies of the 24th Marines were pulled out of the line and stationed in the regimental rear area, where they were to form a strong regimental reserve. In order to further bolster the 25th Marines, Company B of the 2d Armored Amphibian Tractor Battalion was attached to the regiment. This company was to patrol the beach areas north of the 3/25 sector and fire on targets along the beach. The reorganization within the 4th Division area of responsibility was completed by noon of 5 March, as scheduled. During the entire period of reorganization, beginning on the evening of 4 March, the enemy did not initiate any offensive action, though his supporting arms remained active. During the night from 4-5 March, only sporadic fire hit the 4th Division zone, with the exception of the 24th Marines' area. There, heavy mortar and artillery fire was received almost incessantly during the hours of darkness. Throughout D plus 14, the 14th Marines continued to fire on targets of opportunity and executed harassing fires. A total of 17 missions employed air observation. VMO-4 flew 10 tactical observation missions. One pilot was wounded and evacuated. By late afternoon of 5 March, the squadron had four aircraft that were still operational. In addition to the artillery fire provided by the 14th Marines on D plus 14, elements of TF 54 fired call fire missions throughout the day.

It had, for all practical purposes, been a quiet day on Iwo Jima. There had been no gains since there had been no offensive action. Yet, as this day of rest ended, "there had been more than 400 casualties on the line where there was no fighting. The men got ready for the next big push."

Following the day of rest, the VAC offensive resumed on the morning of 6 March. In order to obtain the maximum results from extensive massed preparations, General Schmidt had ordered his divisions to attack in echelon. Each attack was to be preceded by an intensive artillery and naval gunfire preparation, in which the corps and division artillery, as well as the medium and heavy guns of the fire support ships, were to join. Altogether, not including the naval gunfire, 12 artillery battalions would unleash a devastating curtain of fire against the enemy garrison that still blocked the path of the VAC advance. They would first fire for approximately 30 minutes at the western portion of the front, then shift the preparation for a little over half an hour to the eastern half. Within the overall assault, the 4th Marine Division was to jump off at 0900, H plus 60 minutes, with the main effort on its left in conjunction with the adjacent 9th Marines of the 3d Marine Division. At 0845, the coordinated fire of the 132 guns and the naval gunfire shifted to support the second phase of the VAC attack along the eastern portion of the front. The shore-based artillery alone had expended 22,500 shells ranging from 75mm to 155mm in a little over an hour. In the zone of action of General Cates' division, the full force of the barrage was brought to bear on the left in the zone of action of the 23d Marines.

There, prior to 0600, the 23d Marines, less 1/23, had moved into position. In preparation for the assault, 2/23 had relieved 3/24 without enemy interference. The weather promised to be fair with good visibility; only a slight haze obscured observation in the early dawn.

Following the earth-shaking artillery preparation, which gave way to a rolling barrage, 2/23 jumped off at H-Hour, followed by the 3d Battalion at a 400-yard interval. As the assault battalion advanced eastward towards the high ground to its front, it became apparent that the heavy volume of artillery fire had not incapacitated the Japanese, who emerged from their dugouts little the worse for wear and, in the extremely rugged terrain, put up a spirited fight for every yard of the way and defended each cave, pillbox, and emplacement with the greatest tenacity.

As the advance gained momentum, in the face of accurate fire from rifles and automatic weapons to the front, the assault companies moved forward about 50 yards. On the left, where the terrain favored the employment of armor, Company G, 2/23, supported by four tanks, gained 300 yards. As the company prepared to move into a gap that had arisen between it and Company F, the enemy caught Company G in a murderous mortar barrage that caused numerous casualties and wounded the company commander. Fierce fighting continued throughout the day. At 1800, when 2/23 dug in for the night, Company G on the left still was 350 yards in front of the line of departure; the remainder of the 2d and 3d Battalions, 23d Marines, had gained approximately 100 yards during the day.

To the right of the 23d Marines, 2/24 and 1/24 jumped off abreast at H-Hour. Almost immediately, Colonel Jordan's Marines found themselves in the same type of terrain that had impeded the movements of the 23d Marines to the north. The ground was characterized by a series of jagged ridges and heavy undergrowth, both favoring the defending force. Despite support from gunfire ships and three heavy air strikes, enemy resistance continued undiminished. After a day of exhausting and costly fighting, the regiment gained 150 yards on the left and even less on the right.

Since the Amphitheater and Turkey Knob had, for all practical purposes, already been bypassed prior to D plus 15, no frontal assault was launched against these positions, which still formed a deep salient in the 4th Division lines. Because of these protruding enemy positions, the 23d and 24th Marines north of this salient attacked in an east-southeasterly direction, while the 25th Marines to the south were attacking generally to the northeast. As a result, it appeared that all the 4th Division thrusts on 6 March were directed generally towards the remnants of Higashi Village. For the three battalions of the 25th Marines, it was another day of waiting for the left wing of the division to move forward. Since no decisive gains were made by the 24th Marines, 2/25 and 3,/25 stayed in position and conducted mop-up operations within their respective areas. The only forward movement took place in the 1/25 sector, where Marines continued chipping away at enemy fortifications to the east of Turkey Knob near Minami Village, supported by flame and medium tanks and 75mm half-tracks. Once the armor had completed its mission, the tanks were pulled back in order to prevent their exposure to the expected enemy counterbattery fire.

By evening of 6 March, it was evident that the momentous artillery preparation which had so promisingly ushered in the resumed offensive had failed utterly in crushing the enemy's will or capacity to resist. At the time it consolidated for the night, the 4th Marine Division held a line extending for roughly 2,470 yards. A gap of 400 yards still separated the division's left flank from the right of the adjacent 3d Division.

Once again, despite meager gains, the division's losses on D plus 15 had been heavy. The division D-3 report for the day estimated combat efficiency at 40 percent and added that "the result of fatigue and lack of experienced leaders is very evident in the manner in which the units fight." Conversely, the enemy seemed to adapt himself readily to the changing conditions on Iwo Jima by making widespread use of American equipment. Thus it was discovered during the day that five enemy bodies in front of the 4th Division lines were fully dressed in Marine uniforms. One Japanese who decided to give American food a try was to record in his diary: "I tasted Roosevelt's rations for the first time, and they were very good." No doubt, the frequently maligned originator of the American combat rations would have been pleased with this compliment.

The night of 6-7 March turned into a veritable hell for many 4th Division Marines. The continuous and exhausting action in preceding days had been enough to wear down many of them, both physically and mentally. Instead of the rest which they so badly needed and desired, the men were kept in a state of upheaval all night by Japanese activity which, according to the official report, was "sporadic but costly".

At 2130, several enemy mortar shells fell in the lines of 2/23, wounding approximately 30 men. While confusion engulfed this hard-hit battalion, the action shifted to the right flank of the 4th Division. There, shortly after 2200, enemy were reported moving in front of 3/25. Immediate artillery fire was brought to bear on the enemy assembly, which was dispersed. Up to this time, all had remained quiet in front of 1/25, but as the night continued, an estimated 40-50 Japanese infiltrated the battalion sector and sneaked into the foxholes occupied by Major Mee's men. An occasional bursting hand grenade punctured the quietness of the night, a solitary rifle shot, a deep grunt or groan, and then stillness again. It was not until morning that an accurate tally of the 1st Battalion's losses was possible. Then it became evident that 1/25 had lost one officer and 12 men killed; the enemy had lost an estimated 50 men. Conversely, 1/24 reported that this had been the quietest night in its sector. Just as it appeared that this long night was nearing its end, disaster struck once more, this time in the 2/23 area. Shortly after 0500, one of the big, inaccurate enemy rockets wobbled its way into the 2/23 command post with devastating results. The battalion commander, Major Robert H. Davidson, was badly shaken up by the blast and suffered a severe concussion; the communications chief was killed, and the battalion executive officer, the operations officer, the adjutant, and two clerks were wounded. With practically all the headquarters staff officers out of action, a skeleton staff was quickly formed at regimental headquarters under Lieutenant Colonel Edward J. Dillon, the regimental executive officer, who proceeded to 2/23 around dawn and took over the battalion. H-Hour for D plus 16 had been set for 0730. The 4th Division was to continue the assault in the same direction and with the same lineup of units as on the preceding day. There was to be no preliminary artillery or naval gunfire preparation, though neutralization fire against known enemy mortar and artillery positions was scheduled between 0800 and 0830. Because of the disruption caused by the enemy rocket hit on the command post of 2/23, H-Hour was postponed for an additional half hour.

Promptly at 0800 the 4th Division attack resumed, with the battered 23d Marines, less 1/23, in the main effort. The supporting neutralization fire appeared to be having a salutary effect, since there was little response from the enemy supporting arms. As a result, 2/23, attacking along the 4th Division boundary, was able to make slow gains in the course of the morning, particularly along the regimental left. In the center and on the right, on the other hand, enemy resistance was as bitter as ever, and there the advance quickly ground to a halt. By shifting the focal point of the assault quickly between companies, comparable to a boxer who hits his opponent with a low blow and then follows with a haymaker to the uncovered chin, the 2d Battalion was able to catch the Japanese off balance long enough to make a gain of 150 yards within an hour after jumpoff. Following this limited success, strong enemy positions were encountered all along the battalion front and for the remainder of the day progress was minimal. Enemy resistance on 7 March consisted primarily of heavy machine gun fire and extremely accurate rifle fire from concealed positions in the rocky ridge formations and draws along the front. The virtual absence of enemy artillery fire at the 23d Marines' front was noticeable, though the regiment still drew intermittent fire from enemy mortars. The 24th Marines resumed the attack with 2/24 and 1/24 on the line and almost immediately encountered heavy opposition, particularly on the right where intense machine gun and mortar fire halted the advance of the 1st Battalion before it really got moving. For the remainder of the morning, the regimental advance could be measured in yards as small demolition teams blasted and burned the enemy out of his well concealed and strongly-held positions. At 1245, the 14th Marines fired a five-minute preparation which signalled a renewal of the attack. Employing the same tactics used during the morning, and with considerable air support, the regiment scored a gain of 50 yards before 1700, when the lines were consolidated for the day.

On the division right, Colonel Lanigan's 25th Marines continued mopping up the numerous stragglers in its rear area. On the regiment's left, the 1st Battalion, supported by regular and flame tanks, destroyed enemy emplacements to its front, while the Provisional Battalion continued the systematic reduction of stubborn enemy defenses in the bypassed Amphitheater and Turkey Knob. Even though the 25th Marines did not seize any new ground on D plus 16, its strategic location along the division right would shortly change its mission into a defensive one. As the 23d and 24th Marines very slowly and inexorably continued their east-southeastward advance towards Tachiiwa Point on the east coast, they threatened to envelop Captain Inouye's forces, which would be compressed in an area bounded by the sea in the east and the 25th Marines to the south. For all practical purposes, the northern wing of the 4th Division formed a hammer while the stationary 25th Marines would serve as the anvil. In all respects, this type of maneuver closely resembled the large-scale German antipartisan operations in Russia where precisely such tactics often led to success.

In anticipation of increased pressure once this pocket was compressed, Colonel Lanigan took preparatory measures to enable his regiment to cope with any threat posed by the Japanese whose encirclement was imminent. Engineers attached to the regiment laid antipersonnel mines across the front. Barbed wire was strung out along the line. The men sited machine guns, 37mm cannon, and 60mm mortars, waiting for the Japanese to be driven against the regimental line. For the time being, the mission of the 25th Marines would be a defensive one.

Activity during the night from 7-8 March was not comparable to that of the preceding night and along the 4th Division lines consisted mainly of mortar and small arms fire. Some of the enemy mortar shells fell into the positions of 1/24 and in front of the 25th Marines. At 0300, 3/24 returned to the parent regiment and two hours later relieved 2/24 in the line. On D plus 17, the division main effort changed from the left to the center, and the direction of the attack shifted to the southeast. Within the shrinking area left to the Japanese on Iwo Jima, the designation of phase or objective lines had become superfluous, and General Schmidt's operations order for 8 March was essentially "to capture the remainder of the island." No one familiar with the yard-by-yard struggle expected enemy resistance to cease on this day, or for a number of days to come, but the tenor of the order gave a vague assurance that there was to be an end to the bloodletting. Facing the Marines of all three divisions were only the jumbles of rock and the sea, and a dwindling number of highly motivated Japanese determined to sell their lives as dearly as possible.

H-Hour on 8 March had been set for 0750. However, in accordance with corps orders, the 4th Marine Division jumped off at 0620, 90 minutes ahead of the 3d and 5th Divisions. The jump-off was carried out without any artillery preparation, though for half an hour following it the 14th Marines and the corps artillery fired successive concentrations in support of the attack. In the zone of advance of the 23d Marines, there was initially only light resistance, the enemy apparently being confused by the early morning attack. Even though opposition stiffened in time, gains were made in the center of the regimental zone of advance, as 2/23 drove southeastward in the general direction of Tachiiwa Point.

The 24th Marines, with 3/24 on the left and 1/24 on the right, jumped off on schedule, but encountered far stronger resistance than the 23d Marines to the north, mostly from enemy units concealed in perfectly fortified positions. Enemy opposition was characterized by extremely heavy fire from small arms, knee mortars, and mortars of larger calibers. Gains made during the day were negligible, though at the end of the day the regiment was tied in with the 23d Marines on the left and the 25th Marines on the right. Throughout the day, 2/24 remained in division reserve.

On the right flank of the division, the three battalions of the 25th Marines remained in position and continued to strengthen the regimental lines in the event that the enemy decided to counterattack as he was driven into a corner. Behind the lines, various elements of the regiment and the division reconnaissance company continued to mop up; enemy stragglers were also rounded up in the vicinity of Minami Village.

In the course of D plus 17, Shermans of the 4th Tank Battalion gave such support as was feasible to the regiments of the 4th Division, though the movement of armor was restricted largely to the few existing trails, most of them in the 23d Marines' area. There, several tanks ran into a minefield and three were destroyed. During the time required to clear the minefield, the remaining tanks remained in place. In the course of an air strike, an auxiliary gas tank filled with napalm was dropped erroneously into the friendly lines. It landed directly behind one of the Shermans, and napalm splashed all over the tank. Even though the outer surfaces of the Sherman caught fire, the crew was able to evacuate the vehicle and put out the blaze with a portable fire extinguisher. There were no casualties and the mishap failed to put the Sherman, at this point somewhat the worse for wear, out of action. When the regiments of the 4th Division secured for the night around dusk of 8 March, the combat efficiency of the division was still clinging to a precarious 40 percent, but even this figure fails to convey the excessive number of key personnel, the driving force of any unit, that had been sent out of the lines suffering from wounds or battle fatigue. The weather had turned cloudy and cold, and the men of General Gates' division shivered in their foxholes while attempting to rest their weary bodies for the continuation of the struggle that would await them in the morning.

The Enemy Strikes Back

In the gathering dusk and during the early evening of 8 March, something was beginning to stir in front of the 23d and 24th Marines. At first, there was only the blur of muted voices and movement, nothing definite that would indicate anything out of the ordinary was brewing. But then the intensity of the enemy mortar, artillery, and roc~et fire against the two Marine regiments increased, followed at 2300 by large-scale infiltration of the 2/23 and 3/24 sectors. Had the Marines compressing the Japanese naval force into the pocket near Tachiiwa Point been able to look into the enemy lines, and had they been able to gauge the background and volatile temperament of the Japanese Navy captain commanding the 1,000-odd men about to be trapped, certain inevitable conclusions would have become apparent almost at once. Captain Samaji Inouye, commanding the Naval Guard Force on Iwo Jima, was a Samurai, a noisy, swashbuckling extrovert, a champion swordsman, who was prone to boast of his prowess as a fighter, lover, and drinker in front of his subordinates.

It was totally incompatible with Inouye's character that he would sit back in his dugout and idly watch his force being encircled. Also, he had felt deeply emotional about the loss of Mount Suribachi and, in his grief at the American capture of this landmark, he had nearly decapitated the hapless survivors of the force that had straggled into his lines following the fall of the mountain. For the Japanese, ever since the attack on Pearl Harbor, the eighth day of each month had a special significance, and Inouye was only too well aware that 8 March would be his last. He planned to make it a memorable one for all concerned.

Late in the evening, at 2200, he gathered the remainder of his troops, a mixture of survivors from many Navy units on Iwo Jima. It was anything but a uniformly equipped force: "many men had only bamboo spears, but some had hand grenades and rifles. There were a few machine guns, and some men strapped land mines across their chests, determined to blow up some Marines with themselves." What Captain Inouye had in mind was, of course, an all-out charge against the American lines. But, short of killing Americans, there had to be a definite purpose to the assault. Still preoccupied with the loss of Mount Suribachi, where the Stars and Stripes fluttering on the summit had kindled his anger anew every day, the Captain announced to his assembled force the objective of the imminent assault was Suribachi itself. En route, after breaking through the American lines, the men were to blow up as many American planes as they could on the airfields.

Judged by the standards employed earlier in the war on islands like Guadalcanal, and particularly when compared to the desperate Japanese all-out charge on the Garapan Plain at Saipan, what Inouye had planned could best be described as a mini-*banzai*. His objective was unrealistic, the Marines to his front were too alert, and above all, he lacked the approval of his superiors for the action he was about to take. As the attack got under way, the following situation developed:

The band started south, not in a wild charge, but crawling slowly and quietly. One group got within 10 yards of 2/23's command post, where Lieutenant Colonel Dillon was still in command, before the alarm was given. Then the sailors lobbed grenades and charged, shrieking "*Banzai!*" In a moment there was chaos. The Marines threw up flares and star shells lighted the sky. Machinegun fire, rifles, and mortars began to cut into them, but still the Japanese came on. Some of them carried stretchers and shouted "Corpsman, corpsman" in fair English. Finally the hordes faltered and broke, and no one knew where Captain Inouye was. He had last been seen running and shouting, his sword waving in the air. According to an account of Inouye's orderly, who became separated from the captain in the melee, Inouye charged ahead with loud shouts, followed by his men. As accurate Marine fire raked the ranks of the charging Japanese, Inouye shouted *"Banzai, Banzai,"* at the top of his voice, and that was the last heard of him. As one of the Japanese was to comment regretfully later: "It's a pity he could not reach the American position for a full display of his final swordsmanship. "

As the Japanese charged the boundary between the 23d and 24th Marines, it was inevitable that some of them would get through the Marine lines. There was vicious fighting throughout the hours of darkness. Some of the action eventually extended to the 24th Marines and, on a smaller scale, to the 25th. Company E, 2/23, continued to bear the brunt of the counterattack, expending 20 cases of hand grenades, 200 rounds of 60mm illumination shells, and an unknown quantity of machine gun, BAR, and rifle ammunition. Company E faced a critical situation around 0100, when ammunition began to run out. Finally, additional loads were sent forward in a jeep and trailer, which brought the badly needed supplies forward over an enemy infested road, with the aid of 60mm illumination. The jeep drew several rounds of enemy small arms fire but was able to deliver its badly needed cargo. Fire support ships expended 193 star shells during the night, thus lessening some of the confusion that accompanied the action. In the flickering light the chewed-up volcanic ground became visible, filled with wriggling forms. Artillery fire soon blanketed the area and many of the would-be infiltrators halted in their tracks. But many of the attackers did get into the Marine lines and, in the words of one account: "The night became alive with the noise and lights of a determined fire fight. Red tracer bullets shot across the flats. Jap rockets hurtled through the air, leaving a quarter-mile trail of golden sparks. Star shells of yellow and green hung in the sky. The battle kept up all night. Individual men in foxholes didn't know what was happening. They waited for Japs to appear and killed them as fast as they came. Men with telephones whispered into their instruments and tried to discover how strong the enemy attack actually was. Machine guns chattered incessantly. Grenades popped." As day dawned over Iwo Jima on 9 March, the area in and around the 2/23 positions, and to a lesser extent in front of the 24th Marines, showed the signs of horrible carnage. Mopping up continued until noon. A body count of enemy dead revealed approximately 650 at the focal point of the attack, while another 150 were discovered in the adjacent sectors. Among those who perished in the counterattack was Captain Inouye, who died as he had wished to die. The counterattack cost the Marines 90 men killed and 257 wounded, a large number of men to lose in one night's bitter fighting; yet beyond any doubt the cost would have been higher had it been necessary to ferret the enemy out of his dugouts one by one.

To the Japanese survivors of the slaughter, the arrival of daylight brought little comfort. Stripped both of the protective cover of darkness and leadership on which all of them so much depended, the 200 sailors that had survived the abortive *banzai* huddled in small groups, wondering what to do next. It was apparent to all that getting to Mount Suribachi or any of the airfields was far beyond their capabilities. A lieutenant finally gathered them together and those who could crawled away from the place of carnage, constantly harassed by the Marines hunting for them. As to their further operations: "Their fighting was over. Each night the lieutenant sent out patrols of three to five men. They never returned. Others went into caves, and some died of wounds, of sickness, or of thirst. Some drank urine and died." The lieutenant lasted until April 29, the Emperor's birthday, when he told the others, "We will steal a B-29 and fly to the homeland. You others do as you please after we're gone." He left, accompanied by the chief Navy medical officer, an ensign, and a petty officer.

There was to be one more sequel to Captain Inouye's counterattack: Obviously aware of General Kuribayashi's orders to stay in place and fight as long as possible, he had neglected to inform his superior, Admiral Ichimaru, of his intentions. As a result: "on the night of Inouye's last charge, Admiral Toyoda again messaged Admiral Ichimaru, praising the brave acts of the Navy men and again begging them to hold out as long as possible. Ichimaru did not know that Inouye had already sacrificed the last of the Japanese heavy force on Iwo Jima." For the men of the 4th Marine Division, Captain Inouye's abortive counterattack at one stroke eliminated a large segment of the enemy force holding the eastern part of the island. With just about all of this force out of the way, there no longer was any central direction of Japanese forces in the east. Major General Senda, with a force of undetermined strength, was still assumed to be blocking the 4th Division's path between Higashi Village and the coast. Enemy remnants were still in control of Turkey Knob, and a few other pockets of resistance still existed, but by this time the enemy's capability to resist was drastically reduced.

Even though the mop-up of survivors of the counterattack continued throughout the morning of 9 March, the 4th Division continued its attack in accordance with previously laid plans. At 0700, following a 10-minute preparation, the 4th Division jumped off. Once again, the division employed the same scheme of maneuver it had used in previous days, with the 23d Marines on the left, the 24th Marines in the center, and the 25th Marines on the right. The 23d Marines, with 2/23 in the assault, was able to advance in the center and to its right against resistance that lacked the bite of the preceding days. However, the left of the regiment drew heavy fire from a ridge near the division boundary about 500 yards north of Higashi. By 0900, the ridge had been seized in direct assault, and the battalion slowly but persistently forced its way forward. At 1500, 1/23 reverted to the regiment. Ordered to consolidate at 1700, Colonel Wensinger's men continued the attack to improve their positions and did not halt until half an hour later. Gains for the day were a respectable 300 yards. As the regiment dug in, it maintained contact with the 3d Marine Division on the left and the 24th Marines on the right.

In the remaining division sectors, enemy opposition was as strong as ever, and, in consequence, no additional ground was seized in the center and on the right of the division. To some extent, lack of progress in the center was due to depletion of manpower, which made it necessary to shuffle companies from one battalion to another in order to bring the assault battalion up to effective strength. As part of the reorganization of 1/24, Lieutenant Colonel Austin R. Brunelli, the regimental executive officer, assumed command of 1/24, relieving Major Treitel. Because of the heavy resistance on its left flank, the 25th Marines, less 3/25 but with 2/24 attached, remained in position.

During the night from 9-10 March, there was a relative lack of enemy activity. A small amount of light and medium mortar fire at infrequent intervals harassed the 4th Division lines during the night, and infiltration attempts remained on a large scale. In order to counter the threat still posed by groups of the enemy operating in the division rear, the Provisional Battalion, which had been mopping up in the Amphitheater and around Turkey Knob, was disbanded and its mission taken over by 2/25. At the same time, a 4th Provisional Battalion, consisting of 37 officers and 498 enlisted men, was organized from units of the Division Support Group. This unit, under the command of Lieutenant Colonel Melvin L. Krulewitch, had special responsibility for mopping up behind the division lines and retained this mission until 12 March, when it was disbanded. At 0800 on D plus 19, the 4th Marine Division continued its attack after a coordinated corps and division artillery preparation, which changed into a rolling barrage as the men moved out. On this day, which was to be full of significant developments for General Cates' men, the assault was made essentially by the 23d and 25th Marines. The 24th Marines reverted to division reserve. The 1st Battalion, 24th Marines, was pulled out of the line and replaced by 3/25. The 3d Battalion, 24th Marines, remained in its previous zone of action but was attached to the 23d Marines, while 2/24 remained attached to the 25th Marines.

The 23d Marines, with 2/23 on the left and 3/24 on the right launched a vigorous attack that encountered only light opposition on the right. The enemy, entrenched in the rocky ridges along the left boundary of the division, replied with accurate and effective mortar and small arms fire which reduced gains of 2/23 in this sector. Throughout the regimental zone of advance, small but determined groups of the enemy tried to impede the advance. Since the Japanese no longer held a solid line on commanding ground, the Marine assault elements were able to bypass such nests of resistance, leaving their annihilation to teams of engineers, tanks, and infantry, which blasted and scorched such obstacles with demolitions and flamethrowers.

As the regimental attack gained momentum, an enormous amount of ground was taken by Iwo standards. By 1500, Colonel Wensinger's men had advanced no less than 700 yards and were within 500 yards of the east coast. Having reached commanding ground in this area, the regiment halted in midafternoon. Patrols from 2/23, dispatched during the remainder of the afternoon, reached the coast near Tachiiwa Point without encountering any enemy opposition. A short distance to the south, elements of 3/24 reconnoitered to within 100 yards of the coast without making contact with the enemy.

On the division right, the 25th Marines, with 2/24 and the Reconnaissance Company attached, completed the relief of 1/24 by 0600. Following this relief, 3/25 took over the sector of 1/24. In order to complete the encirclement of those enemy remnants still holding out in the Amphitheater and on Turkey Knob, 3/25 was shifted to the north of the enemy salient, where, together with 1/25, it would attack to the southeast parallel to the axis of advance of the 23d Marines. Along the southern perimeter of the salient, 2/25 and 2/24 were to advance generally to the northeast or east respectively, which would enable 2/25 to effect a linkup with those units of the regiment attacking towards the coast from the northwest. Jumping off at H-Hour on 10 March, 3/25 and 1/25 attacked towards the high ground to their front from where the enemy still offered moderate to heavy opposition. It soon became apparent that the 3d Battalion would be able to move faster than 1/25 and, in consequence, 3/25 was ordered to continue regardless of its flanks. As the attacks of 3/25 and 2/25 converged, the distance separating the two units dwindled until, shortly after noon, the two battalions linked up. Overall gains for the 25th Marines on D plus 19 were 600 yards. More important than the yardage gained was the fact that Turkey Knob was at last completely surrounded and all resistance remaining could now be eliminated. As the 25th Marines consolidated for the night, its left flank was tied to the 23d Marines about 800 yards from the coast while the stationary right flank was still anchored on the beach to the south.

The significance of the 4th Division's movements and gains on 10 March was summed up in one historical narrative in these words: "It was now evident that the

Japanese counterattack had marked the turning point in the battle." Although bitter and costly fighting continued for six more days, particularly in the 25th Regiment's zone, organized resistance was now dying out in the 4th Division area. During the 14-day period covered in this chapter, the 4th Division, in constant head-on assault, fought its bloody way from Charlie-Dog Ridge past Hill 382, the Amphitheater, Turkey Knob, through Minami and formidable defenses northeast of 382, almost to the coast. The slow but relentless movement of this division front can be compared to the closing of a giant door. The right flank, which advanced less than 1,000 yards, acted as a hinge while the rest of the division (the door) turned upon it and attacked northeast, east, and southeast to close and sweep trapped enemy toward the sea.

The 4th Division assault on eastern Iwo Jima thus had broken the back of enemy resistance by 10 March. In the wake of the division's advance, there remained a staggering number of casualties, whose bodies and minds bore ample witness to the ferocity of the fighting. Between 25 February, when General Cates' men first attacked the Meat Grinder and 10 March, when they were within a stone's throw of the coast, the division had sustained 4,075 casualties. A total of 847 Marines had been killed or were dead of wounds; 2,836 had been wounded; 1 was missing, and 391 were suffering from combat fatigue.

As the three Marine divisions slowly approached the coastline in their respective zones of advance, it became apparent to all on the island that time for General Kuribayashi and his garrison was running out. In Japan, anxious eyes were watching the contest of wills being waged for possession of Iwo Jima. To the military observers, the outcome was a foregone conclusion. But the nation's morale was precariously perched on the faint hope that General Kuribayashi's masterful defense of the island would give the business-minded Americans food for thought about the cost of a full-scale invasion of the home islands. Thus, in Japanese eyes, the prolonged defense of Iwo Jima pursued not only the immediate tactical objective, but a vastly more far-reaching strategic one. Few of the surviving members of that garrison had any illusions left about the outcome of the war. One Japanese captured in the 4th Division area late on 9 March was better qualified than most others to comment on the overall situation. A peacetime editor and publisher of one of the large metropolitan newspapers of Japan, he remarked that "this is not a winning war for Japan—she cannot win, but she is trying her darndest to lessen her defeat."

That time was running out on the mainland as well was strongly reemphasized on the evening of 9 March, when more than 300 B-29s mounted one of the biggest air raids of the war against Tokyo. This attack severely devastated the enemy capital, serving notice to all Japanese that they were now open to American attack both from sea and air; that henceforth the citizens of Tokyo were as exposed to American explosives as General Kuribayashi's diminishing garrison on Iwo Jima.

Chapter 11. Final Operations on Iwo Jima

Elimination of the Pockets--3d Marine Division Area

On 11 March 1945, operations on Iwo Jima entered their final phase. No longer under any central direction, three more or less clearly defined enemy pockets fought a battle to the death in the zone of advance of each of the three Marine divisions. As the pockets became more constricted, the nature of the fighting changed, mostly because the terrain no longer permitted the employment of naval gunfire, air support, and in the end even artillery. Eventually, as Japanese resistance neared the end, tanks and half-tracks furnished the heavy supporting fire needed to root out the last of the obstinate enemy defenders. On D plus 20, the only major opposition in the zone of advance of the 3d Marine Division extended along the division's rough boundary, where enemy remnants still occupied a ridgeline paralleling the coast to the east of Kitano Point. A second center of resistance farther south, to the east of Motoyama Village, southeast of the Northern Airfield, and southwest of Hill 362C was a pocket which had already been under attack for several days prior to 11 March. Named after the commander of 2/9, Lieutenant Colonel Cushman, this pocket was honeycombed with caves and emplacements cut into sandstone. The pocket itself was ringed by antitank guns and Colonel Nishi's dug-in light and medium tanks, equipped with 37mm and 47mm guns. The most prominent occupant of the pocket was Colonel Nishi, who had thus far survived the ferocious fighting on the island.

On 11 March, 1/9 and 3/9 were to execute a converging attack from the high ground near the east coast into the northeastern fringes of the pocket. Once the two battalions had linked up, they were to launch a concerted drive into the pocket from the east. In the course of the morning, the 1st Battalion assaulted a ridge overlooking the pocket and blasted its way to the top, demolishing caves and other positions as it went along. The advance was supported by Shermans from the 3d Tank Battalion, whose fire either destroyed such enemy defenses as could be spotted or at least kept the occupants of strongpoints underground to permit the approach of demolition teams. The 3d Battalion was forced to assault similar terrain during the morning without tank support, which did not arrive until an armored bulldozer had carved out a road for the Shermans during the early afternoon. In mid-afternoon, shortly after 1500, the two battalions linked up. For the remainder of the day, elements of both battalions mopped up along the east coast, outposted the beach, and established defensive positions on the high ground east of Hill 362C. Even though no solid line of containment surrounded the pocket from the west or southwest, there was no activity on the part of the Japanese trapped within, aimed at either evading the encirclement or launching a direct assault against the Marines approaching them. Instead, the enemy followed the orders issued by General Kuribayashi to the letter. Remaining within their relatively secure pillboxes, dugouts, caves, and stationary tanks, the Japanese contested every foot of ground, continuing to make the Marines pay an exorbitant price for every yard gained.

In order to support the advance of 3/21, a 7.2-inch rocket launcher, mounted on a sled, was attached to the battalion. This improvisation was the idea of the VAC ordnance officer, who had four of the rocket launchers mounted on sleds when it was found that these weapons did not fit the M4A3 tank with which VAC was then equipped. The sled mount appeared to be the answer to the problem of getting this powerful supporting weapon into terrain which was impassable for tanks. Each rocket launcher, equipped with 20 tubes, was capable of delivering 640 pounds of TNT in a salvo. Effective range of the launcher was 250 yards. A volley of rockets, exploding within a narrow area, could be expected to have a gruesome and highly demoralizing effect upon the enemy.

As 3/21 approached the confines of the pocket, meeting very heavy resistance all the way, a rocket launcher was towed into action by a tank of Company C, 3d Tank Battalion. Altogether, 10 volleys were fired into the pocket with undetermined results. Only too soon did it become apparent that the efficiency of the launchers did not match the visual effect created by the exploding rockets. When the dust settled, the enemy still sat securely in his defenses, little the worse for wear. An official report of this action was to note with discouragement: "Nearly 200 of the 7.2-inch rockets were thrown into this pocket and still our infantry was unable to go in and occupy the ground." Elsewhere in the 3d Division zone of advance, General Erskine was able to pull 2/21 out of the line for a much needed rest after elements of the 27th Marines of the 5th Division had moved behind the left flank of that battalion. To fill the gap thus created, 1/21 extended its lines northward and tied in with the adjacent 5th Division. At the same time that 1/9 and 3/9 were converging on Cushman's Pocket from the northeast, 3/21, then attached to the 9th Marines, was approaching the pocket from the southwest.

For the remainder of 11 March, 3d Division engineers and riflemen blasted caves and dugouts. Because of the proximity of the battle lines, General Erskine's division did not receive any artillery support that day, though 1/12 stood by for call fires if needed. Similarly, there was no air support for the same reasons, except that aerial observation was used to report the movements of 3d Division units. After nightfall the Japanese, employing hit-and-run tactics, emerged from their hideouts and stealthily approaching the Marine positions, hurled a few hand grenades, and then attempted to disappear as quietly as they had come. Such tactics succeeded only infrequently, and many of the infiltrators did not survive to tell of their exploits.

On the evening of 11 March, 3/21 was facing eastward with a frontage of 200-300 yards, while 1/9 and 3/9 were facing westward with a frontage of about 600 yards. A distance of 500-600 yards separated 3/21 from the two battalions of the 9th Marines. The 2d Battalion, 9th Marines, was in division reserve just east of Motoyama Village, where it was engaged in mopping up the enemy units on the southern fringe of the pocket. At the same time, the battalion formed a line some 400 yards long which acted as a stop-gap for any enemy troops seeking to escape westward from the encirclement.

Early on 12 March, compression of Cushman's Pocket continued, with 1/9 and 3/9 again hammering from the east while 3/21 formed the anvil along the western fringes. Lieutenant Colonel Boehm's 3d Battalion, advancing westward, apparently hit one of the developing weak spots in the enemy lines and made fair progress. The 1st Battalion to the south, on the other hand, ran into heavy resistance and was unable to keep pace with 3/9. Finally, an armored bulldozer carved out a path over which the Shermans could move to the front lines. Once the tanks had arrived there, eager infantrymen accurately pinpointed the enemy position for the tankers, and, in the words of the official report, "successful work in eliminating these positions was done by the tanks."

In the zone of advance of the 1st and 3d Battalions, 9th Marines, extreme difficulty was encountered with the terrain which alternately featured steep banks and gulches filled with soft volcanic ash. The tankers constantly had to be on the alert for Japanese in the vicinity who were only too eager to seek death if there was a chance of blowing up an American tank along with themselves. Tanks bogged down in the difficult terrain proved irresistible objectives for suicidal Japanese, not to mention their attractiveness as stationary targets of opportunity for the remaining enemy antitank guns. In addition to the above, the tankers found it very difficult to maintain direction since their movements were directed over the radio through remote control. Many of the enemy positions were so carefully camouflaged that as often as not Marines were almost on top of them before they were spotted. Once again, flamethrowers and demolitions proved their worth in this type of fighting. Progress was made on D plus 21, but in the rear of Cushman's Pocket, specifically along the crest of the ridge overlooking the east coast of Iwo Jima, resistance remained stubborn. On the following day, 13 March, the pocket was further compressed when 1/9 and 3/9 continued their drive. Once again, the progress of the attack was impeded by caves, pillboxes, emplaced tanks, stone walls, and trenches. So masterfully had these defenses been camouflaged that "only those immediately in front of the troops could be located. . . . Out of about 150 of these positions (by later count), we knew roughly twenty or thirty of them." Nevertheless, despite the initial advantage accruing to the defenders, the Marine incursion into the pocket could not be stopped. Sherman tanks, particularly those equipped with flamethrowers, lent the necessary emphasis to the advance of the two battalions. The flame tanks proved most effective in reducing a number of troublesome concrete emplacements. Still operating in very rough terrain, the Shermans moved only short distances at a time, and then only with the aid of an armored bulldozer.

As far as the 9th Marines was concerned, the performance of the Shermans was of crucial importance. The regimental commander, Colonel Kenyon, considered them "to be the most formidable supporting weapon at our disposal . . . tank support was the deciding factor in this action."

By the end of D plus 22, Cushman's Pocket had shrunk to a mere 250 yards. The diminishing size of the pocket enabled the withdrawal of two units from the encircling force. On the morning of 13 March, 1/21 relieved those elements of 3/21 that were engaged on the line, and the latter battalion reverted to its parent regiment. Having cleared its zone of action by evening of the same day, 3/9 was pulled out of this area early on 14 March and shifted to the vicinity of Hill 362, where it commenced a systematic mop-up.

The morning of 14 March marked the beginning of the final drive aimed at eliminating Cushman's Pocket. The main burden of the attack now rested on 1/9, which pressed forward throughout the morning and by midafternoon had gained about 100 yards. Once again, the use of armor proved decisive in eliminating the stubborn enemy defenses. A flame tank belonging to Company B, 3d Tank Battalion, was hit by a rifle grenade which caused a small explosion inside the vehicle, wounding the driver and assistant driver. At 1530, 2/9 reverted from division reserve to regimental control. Shortly before 1800, the battalion passed through 1/9 and launched an attack into the enemy position which by this time had already shrunk to about 150 square yards. Shermans of the 3d Tank Battalion played a dominant role in reducing whatever stubborn resistance remained, but a flame tank borrowed from the 5th Marine Division outdid all others. This tank was able to shoot a flame about 125 yards and, according to the official report, it "proved to be the weapon that worked when all others failed. Its long flame range and the area covered by one burst were the contributing factors to its remarkable success." By the time the Shermans and flame tanks had roamed through the pocket, blasting and burning everything in their path, enemy resistance became sporadic and gradually began to flicker out. The stage was now set for the infantry to move in and finish the job.

What might have turned into a routine chore of mopping up turned instead into a rather protracted operation requiring all the skill the attacking force could muster. The action that 2/9 saw for the remainder of 14 March was subsequently described with the statement: "Inconclusive hand to hand fighting ensued until dark." Hidden within this sentence, however, was a factor which was to be brought out elsewhere, namely the combination of physical and mental exhaustion that was taking its toll among Marines on Iwo Jima at this phase of operations as surely as had shells and bullets of the enemy. Few Marines who had made the initial landing were left during the final phase of the fighting. Their places had been taken by willing though inexperienced replacements, whose performance in combat left much to be desired. As one Marine historian was to put it: "By this stage in the operation a large percentage of infantry troops were replacements who lacked the combat training and experience that prepared and conditioned men for closing with the enemy. Therefore, the skill and efficiency of assault Marines showed marked deterioration after three weeks of personnel attrition of original D-Day troop strength." During the final days of 3d Division efforts to smash remaining pockets, armor support made success possible. Gun tanks, armored bulldozers, and flame-throwing Shermans combined their operations to give the exhausted infantry a very effective and much needed assist. In dealing with the same subject matter, the battalion report was to state succinctly: "Almost all of the infantry were replacements. They lacked entirely the will to close with the enemy." Needless to say, this statement was not intended as an indictment of the men involved, but of the replacement system which forced men to join strange squads and platoons whose teamwork was dissipated by heavy casualties. For the individual Japanese, who fought to the end among friends, death was an infinitely less lonely and impersonal affair than for the average Marine replacement.

While bitter fighting continued in Cushman's Pocket, where one enemy position after the other was eliminated, a different type of action took place just to the east of the pocket on one of the ridges overlooking the east coast. Initially, this ridge had been seized on D plus 16 in the conventional manner—direct attack with flamethrowers, small arms, and demolitions—by 3d Division Marines, who blasted this objective like hundreds of others and then moved on, leaving behind blackened and battle-scarred cave entrances that looked sinister even in broad daylight. Several days passed and the front lines had moved on to the north when this desolate ridge came to life again.

The first indication that something was going awry in this so-called rear area came when a heavy Japanese machine gun, hidden somewhere in the previously cleared ridge, opened up on an unsuspecting Marine carrying ammunition and killed him. Other Marines near the ridge soon became startled victims of the enemy fire from the ridge which grew in intensity as small arms joined the machine gun. The next victims were stretcher bearers and their wounded burden. Eventually, tanks and demolitions men arrived and the dangerous, time-consuming job of clearing the ridge had to be repeated. To quote one report: "Despite their preponderance of weapons the Marines found that there were too many holes. They would attack one only to be shot at from another one half a dozen feet away. Moreover, the ridge was curved like an S. Entranceways protected each other, so that Marines would be hit in the back from holes guarding the one they were assaulting. The inter-connecting tunnels inside the ridge also allowed the Japs to play deadly tag with the Marines. They would shoot out of one hole. By the time Marines got close enough to that hole, the Japs had left it and were shooting from another one twenty yards away and higher up in the wall. The Marines had to post guards at every hole they could see in order to attack any one of them. The tunnels also curved and twisted inside the ridge. The Japs could escape the straight trajectory weapons and grenades thrown into the cave entrances, merely by running back into the interior. Finally, flamethrowers squirted their lethal liquid into the caves, which became boiling infernos." A number of the Japanese who had reoccupied the ridge were incinerated. Others, their clothing and bodies aflame, tried to escape, only to fall prey to accurate Marine bullets. In desperation, some of the enemy trapped inside the ridge blew themselves up with hand grenades. Before long: "the scene became wild and terrible. More Japs rushed screaming from the caves. They tumbled over the rocks, their clothes and bodies burning fiercely. Soon the flamethrowers paused. A Marine lifted himself cautiously into view. There were no shots from the caves. A Jap with his clothes in rags hunched himself out of one hole, his arms upraised. The Marines stood up behind the rocks and waved to him to come out. The Jap indicated that there were more who would like to surrender. The Marines motioned him to tell them to come out. In all, 40 men emerged from the ridge, many of them Koreans. Marines shouldered their weapons as the prisoners were marched to the rear. The tanks left the erstwhile battlefield and quiet descended over the area." Yet this peaceful interlude was soon to be shattered again a few hours later when the Japanese, moving through underground tunnels, reoccupied the ridge. One of the first victims proved to be Sergeant Reid Chamberlain, a Marine with an unusual background. As a member of the U.S. Army, he had witnessed the fall of Bataan and Corregidor, but instead of surrendering to the enemy, he had turned his activities towards the organization and training of Filipino guerrillas. He received a commission in the U.S. Army and returned to the United States, where he promptly resigned his commission and enlisted in the U.S. Marine Corps. En route to the forward positions of the 21st Marines, Sergeant Chamberlain was walking past the long, rocky ridge, unaware that there were any enemy in the vicinity. Suddenly, there were several shots, one of which hit the sergeant in the head. This incident took place in front of several Marine news correspondents, some of whom also drew enemy fire. When help arrived for the sergeant, it was too late. As one of the correspondents present was to put it later, speaking of the enemy: "In an instant they had claimed one of our best men. Chamberlain's wonderful war record had ended abruptly. After so many heroic deeds, it seemed an added tragedy that he was killed while doing nothing but walking. There was nothing anybody could do about it." Efforts to employ flamethrowers against the ridge during the fading hours of daylight proved unavailing, since all of these weapons were committed in the front lines. At dusk, elements of the 9th Marines bivouacked on the ridge, which had become dormant again. Apprised of the situation, the commanding officer posted sentries behind the rocks facing the ridge, ready to fire on anything that moved.

Hardly had dusk settled over the area, when there was stealthy movement on the slopes of the ridge as individual Japanese emerged from previously undetected cracks and holes. Marines opened fire on these blurred silhouettes. The results of this fire became quickly evident as some of the Japanese who had been hit groaned with pain, others jerked spasmodically and then lay silent while the remainder, realizing that they were trapped, attempted to burrow their way back into the ground. A few who managed to get back under cover committed suicide.

Shortly before midnight there was a tremendous blast which hurled huge pieces of rock through the air and shook the entire area. Some of the Marines were buried in volcanic ash and debris up to their necks and had to be dug out. Others were hit by chunks of concrete that rained down throughout the area. The ridge itself became a mass of fire and disintegrating matter. While the Marines were still engaged in assessing what had happened and trying to aid each other as best they could,

Japanese began to emerge from their holes on the ridge, some of them dazed, others carrying antipersonnel mines tied around their waists. A group of five Japanese, running along the wall of the ridge, was spotted by the light of the flames and all were instantly killed. At dawn it became apparent that, despite the explosion and subsequent bitter fighting, the Marines had suffered only one serious casualty. There might have been more if men, who found themselves buried in debris and volcanic ash, had not been rescued by fellow Marines before they were smothered. It was subsequently discovered that the enemy had used land mines and aerial bombs to blow up the ridge.

On 15 March organized resistance in the 3d Division sector had just about ended. General Erskine's division was ordered to relieve elements of the 5th Marine Division on the right of that division and attack to the northwest. Early on 16 March, D plus 25, the 21st Marines took over an 800-yard sector on the right of General Rockey's division. The boundary between the two divisions now extended from a point 400 yards east of Hill 362B to the northern tip of Iwo Jima near Kitano Point.

Following the relief of 3/27 and 2/26 by the 1st and 2d Battalions of the 21st Marines, that regiment prepared to attack to the north in conjunction with elements of the 5th Marine Division. A 20-minute preparation by the 3d and 5th Division artillery, as well as the 155s of the corps artillery, preceded the jumpoff, which was scheduled for 0815, and continued for 10 minutes following H-Hour. The rolling barrage, which marked the final phase of the preparatory fire moved only 50 yards ahead of the assault units and then moved forward at 100-yard intervals in conjunction with the advance. In addition to the shore-based artillery, a destroyer offshore shelled northern Iwo for nearly an hour and then stood by to deliver call fires. Fighters stationed on the Southern Airfield were available for air support, but the restricted area in which the final operations on Iwo Jima took place precluded their employment.

The attack of 1/21 made good headway against only light resistance. On the other hand, 2/21 encountered heavy small arms fire and extremely difficult terrain, both of which combined to retard its advance. Japanese, fighting from caves and spider trap positions, offered their customary obstinate resistance. Some of them, obviously bent on suicide, charged tanks or groups of Marines with grenades and demolition charges. For the most part, such sorties were marked more by fierce fanaticism than cool logic, and most of them failed before the human bomb could inflict much damage on the Marines or their armor. During the early afternoon both battalions reached the coast near Kitano Point. From that point, it became a matter of mopping up such enemy as remained in caves and other shelters. By the end of 16 March, General Erskine's men had completed the elimination of Cushman's Pocket and, at the same time, had completed their mission in helping out the 5th Marine Division. This action, for all practical purposes, ended combat operations of the 3d Marine Division on Iwo Jima. Late on D plus 25, General Erskine announced that all enemy resistance in the zone of action of his division had ceased. In fact, even though Cushman's Pocket had been overrun, Colonel Nishi, commanding the 26th Tank Regiment was still inside with about 450 men, all that had remained of his command. of these, 300 were wounded and few of them were able to move on their own. From their underground hideout, the Japanese could hear their erstwhile comrades, now prisoners of war and working for the Americans, calling on Colonel Nishi to surrender. But such appeals fell on deaf ears. Early on 19 March, with only two days' food supply remaining, Colonel Nishi ordered his men to make a final charge against the Americans. Only 60 were able to heed his call. Sometime between 19 and 22 March, Colonel Nishi died. Whether he was felled by an American bullet or by his own hand has never been clearly determined, though his widow finds solace in the thought "that he died at the foot of the northern cliffs, and that ocean waves have scattered his remains."

4th Marine Division Mopup

Following its impressive gains on 10 March, which had taken some of its assault units to the vicinity of the east coast, the 4th Marine Division continued the attack on the following morning. Jumping off with the 23d and 25th Marines at 0730, the division continued its advance to the coast. On the left the 23d Marines reached its objective rapidly, overrunning such enemy resistance as flared up in its path. In the wake of the regiment's advance, engineers sealed caves and constructed a road. In late afternoon, 1/23 relieved 2/23 and pulled back to the same positions held during the preceding night. Combat patrols were dispatched into the beach areas to search out enemy stragglers or holdouts. The advance of the 25th Marines did not progress as smoothly as that of the 23d. Almost immediately after the jumpoff, Colonel Lanigan's regiment ran into heavy fire from rockets, mortars, and small arms. As a result, little ground was gained. An explanation of the stubborn resistance came during the afternoon when the interrogation of a captured Japanese revealed that about 300 of the enemy were holed up in caves and tunnels directly in front of the regiment. The prisoner further volunteered that a Japanese brigadier general was trapped inside the pocket.

In describing the area of the pocket, 4th Division records had this to say: "It was at once apparent that this area was the final defensive position of the enemy in this zone." The terrain in this area was not normal in any respect; it could be classified only as a terrain freak of nature. However, it was well suited for the construction of cave positions, and the Japanese had utilized this advantage to the fullest extent. Their scheme of maneuver was to hold up the advance as long as it was possible, and to inflict as many casualties as they could before they were forced to adopt their usual suicidal tactics. The terrain itself consisted of a series of deep crevices and steep ridges that extended generally to the east towards the coast. Smaller gullies cutting through the area created a maze of compartments and cross compartments. The rough rocky outcropping and scrubby vegetation that had survived the extensive shelling provided the Japanese with excellent cover and concealment.

That the elimination of this small but tough pocket of resistance would be a difficult and time-consuming operation had already become apparent to 4th Division Marines by the end of 11 March. The presence of one of the big fish in the pocket, General Senda, commander of the 2d Mixed Brigade, made it virtually certain that the remnants of that unit would fight to the bitter end with undiminished fanaticism.

Even though there was only a marginal possibility that General Senda might be persuaded to surrender, intelligence personnel of the 4th Marine Division decided on 12 March that such an attempt was worth the effort. A prisoner of war volunteered to lead a detail of Marines to the vicinity of General Senda's presumed hideout during the early morning of D plus 21. Under sniper fire, which eventually caused a casualty, Marines set up an amplifier speaker system over which an appeal to surrender was to be broadcast. For more than two hours the psychological warfare team failed in its efforts to start a power generator which would have provided the electricity needed to drive the amplifier. A second motor-driven power plant failed to start and due to this technical breakdown the entire operation had to be called off. Whether General Senda might have heeded the appeal promising and guaranteeing him and his men the best of treatment, remains doubtful. Certainly none of the other Japanese commanders approached in this fashion on Iwo Jima proved responsive.

Following the two-hour delay engendered by the abortive surrender appeal, Marines of the 4th Division launched their attack into the pocket at 0900 with 2/25, 3/25, and 2/24. The scheme of maneuver called for 2/25 to attack down the draws toward the coast while 3/25 and 2/24 were to support the attack with heavy weapons fire. This fire, furnished by bazookas, antitank grenades, and 60mm mortars, had to substitute for artillery support. As of 12 March, the limited area occupied by the enemy in the 4th Division zone no longer constituted a practicable target area, and orders had been issued to secure all 4th Division artillery.

The Japanese, firmly entrenched in ravines, caves, and pillboxes, resisted in their customary tenacious fashion, with the result that only minimal progress was made. The character of the terrain precluded the employment of tanks, forcing Marines to flush the enemy out of his emplacements one or two at a time. In addition to the slow progress, this type of fighting was, as usual, expensive for the attacking force. By evening of 12 March, the combat efficiency of General Cates' division had dropped to a new low of 36 percent. The drive to eliminate General Senda's pocket continued on 13 and 14 March along the same lines as on the 12th. Progress throughout remained agonizingly slow, due to the depletion of personnel as much as enemy resistance. While the pocket was being reduced, the 23d Marines began a systematic mopping up of its area from the beach towards the regimental rear. At the same time, the regiment took care of other urgent business, notably the evacuation of the friendly dead, the burial of enemy dead, and the general policing of the area.

By 15 March, the slow and deliberate advance of the 25th Marines was beginning to bear dividends. Even though the enemy continued to offer desperate resistance, there were signs that his power to resist had been considerably reduced. Since 2/25 had become so depleted in strength that it required relief, 2/24 was ordered into the line. A provisional company composed of headquarters personnel and members of the 81mm mortar platoon of 1/25 was organized to take over the area previously held by 2/24. Colonel Lanigan ordered his men to press the attack into the pocket regardless of contact. At the same time, flame tanks stationed on the road paralleling the east coast of Iwo fired northwestward into the inaccessible draws with good effect.

This drive on D plus 24 resulted in a net gain of 200 yards. More important, it scored a deep penetration of the left flank of the pocket, where General Senda had established his strongest positions. In the midst of this bitter fighting, repeated attempts were made to induce the surrender of the Japanese, but none of them fell on fertile soil. The destruction of one cave after another, together with their occupants, continued.

Increased evidence that the pocket could not hold out much longer was received during the night of 15-16 March, when a group of 50-60 Japanese attempted to break out of the encirclement. Six of the enemy were killed and the remainder were driven back into the caves from which they had emerged. When the 25th Marines resumed the attack at 0630 on 16 March, the Marines drew rifle and machine gun fire, and hand grenades exploded all around them. Nevertheless, the Japanese now fought without any real organization and such resistance as was offered came from small, isolated groups. By midmorning, the assault battalions had fought their way through to the beach road and Colonel Lanigan declared all organized resistance in his zone of action ended as of 1030.

General Senda's body was never found; prisoners volunteered that he had committed suicide on 15 March. As the din of battle receded, all that remained in the hotly contested area were the torn and battered terrain, large numbers of enemy dead, and the scarred and blackened cave entrances. In six days of bitter fighting, General Senda's pocket had finally been reduced. The Japanese had fought practically to extinction. The 4th Marine Division had paid for the ground with 833 casualties.

5th Marine Division Drive To Kitano Point

Elimination of the enemy centers of resistance in eastern Iwo Jima left only one area in the hands of the Japanese. This was to be the final enemy pocket of resistance in the very northern part of the island, where General Kuribayashi with about 1,500 men was preparing to make his final stand. The Japanese pocket, squarely in the path of the 5th Marine Division's advance, occupied approximately one square mile between Kita Village and Kitano Point on the northwest coast. Not by coincidence, it also comprised the worst ground on the island. The badlands of northern Iwo, as this area may well be called, consisted of thousands of soft sandstone outcroppings. Here, the Japanese had dug in with their customary efficiency. Each underground position had been provided with multiple entrances and exits to protect the defenders against fire and to permit their escape if one or more of the entrances were sealed. These defenses had been dug to such a depth that flamethrowers could neither burn out their occupants nor exhaust the supply of oxygen available within this defensive system.

In addition to the excellent cover, the Japanese also had the advantage of effective concealment. Their uniforms blended closely with the color of the sandstone. They were familiar with the maze of tunnels that criss-crossed the entire area and could find their way around in the darkness as well as in the daytime. Fighting this type of defensive action, General Kuribayashi could continue to hang on with the austere means at hand. He had no logistics problem, for anything that had to be moved, be it men or supplies, travelled underground. Such vital supplies as ammunition, food, water and medicine all had been stockpiled underground long before the first Marines began to approach the northern portion of the island. In addition to his extensive preparations for combat, General Kuribayashi had seen to it that the knowledge of the entire defense layout was limited to very few of his men, most of whom were told only enough to be familiar with the immediate defenses in their vicinity. As a result, few of the enemy knew anything about the command setup of their own forces and most of them did not know the precise location of Kuribayashi's command post.

For General Rockey's men, the battle for northwestern Iwo meant a continuation of previous difficulties aggravated by worsening terrain. Once again, they would have to seize the forward face of a ridge, fight their way across the crest, then continue to fight their way down the reverse slope, all the while drawing fire from the front, the flanks, from the rear, and, in some instances, even from below. The latter circumstance was perhaps the most demoralizing, as pointed out by one participant in the fighting: "Perhaps worst of all, every Marine commander fighting through this sandstone jungle knew that underneath him were healthy Japanese who would be out that night to harass his rear, steal his supplies, either recover or booby-trap their own dead, and booby-trap his dead if he couldn't get them out first." And so the battle for Iwo Jima was ending as it had begun, at close quarters with Marine forces stripped of the advantages of their firepower, fighting an enemy who had been indoctrinated since childhood that the greatest honor he would ever know was to die for his Emperor. He could not be threatened out of his position by encirclement or by superior force; he could not be induced to surrender because of his hopeless position, tactically or strategically, he had to be killed.

The 5th Marine Division drive into the biggest enemy pocket remaining on the island got under way on 11 March. The attack was preceded by a 10-minute preparation, which continued until 20 minutes after the jumpoff. The half-hour barrage, fired by the 12th, 13th, and 14th Marines, as well as the corps artillery, provided an impressive spectacle but once again, in accordance with previous experience, was generally ineffective against enemy personnel who huddled in well-protected cave positions.

As the division attacked, with the 27th Marines on the right and the 28th on the left, the men faced a double foe: the Japanese and the terrain, each being equally formidable. The 27th Marines, with 1/26 attached, was able to carve out limited gains of 200 yards and to continue the systematic destruction of enemy cave positions. This was the job of small infantry-demolition teams, which operated more or less on their own, blasting their way forward as they went along. Operating on the division left, the 28th Marines encountered similar difficulties as Marines assaulted individual strongpoints guarding a rocky gorge to the front. The significance of this gorge, which was approximately 200 yards wide and 700 yards long, was not yet apparent to Colonel Liversedge's Marines. However, it was clear that the Japanese had taken great precautions to effectively cover all approaches leading into the gorge with rifle and machine gun fire.

While the enemy generally remained underground and invisible throughout the day, the entire division front erupted into action shortly after nightfall and remained that way throughout the night. Small groups of Japanese continuously attempted to infiltrate the Marine lines. A few were successful in reaching the 81mm mortar positions of 3/27. Seven of the infiltrators were killed in this attempt, one of them wearing a Marine uniform and equipped with an M-1 rifle. Around 2100, an enemy concentration opposite the 28th Marines was broken up by an artillery and mortar barrage which killed 26 of the enemy. Sporadic rifle fire and grenade duels continued for the remainder of the night.

The arrival of daylight on D plus 21 returned the initiative to the Marines, who, once again, carried the battle to the enemy. On this occasion, the day started off with several air strikes against enemy positions just south of Kitano Point. One of the 500-pound bombs aimed at a blockhouse missed its target, only to fall into the mouth of a cave, where a tremendous explosion caused not only this entrance, but various others connected to this cave system, to belch fire and smoke. A similar incident occurred during the early afternoon, when a 500-pound bomb hit a cave entrance and created a violent explosion with smoke observed coming out of caves 200-300 yards away. For the remainder of the day, the course of the fighting mirrored that of D plus 20. The enemy continued to resist from caves, emplacements, and spider foxholes, frequently holding his fire until Marines had approached to within a few feet of his positions. With the support tanks, the 27th Marines made slow progress against a network of pillboxes and prepared positions. In the course of this advance, between 15 and 18 pillboxes were destroyed, but overall progress still had to be measured in a few yards. The Japanese also had learned a few tricks in recent operations and, in order to escape American air strikes and artillery fire, attempted to hug the Marine lines. Backbone of the Japanese defense were his machine guns, rifles, and knee mortars, all of which continued to exact a continuous toll in Marine lives for each foot of the advance.

During the afternoon of 12 March, Company B of the Amphibious Reconnaissance Battalion scouted Kama and Kangoku Rocks, situated close to the northwestern shore of Iwo Jima. Intermittently throughout the campaign, Marines advancing up the west coast had been harassed from suspected Japanese positions on these two islands. There was no doubt that even if the enemy had not permanently stationed artillery there, they harbored keen-eyed observers who had helped to harass shipping approaching the western beaches during the early phase of the operation. As the Marines neared the two islands on 12 vehicles furnished by the 2d Armored Amphibian Battalion, they were greeted by silence. It was decided that a landing on the island would be made at 0900 on the following morning.

These landings, carried out by 6 officers and 94 men, proceeded without incident. The Marines went ashore first on Kama Rock and subsequently on Kangoku, the larger island. On the latter, there was evidence of previous enemy occupancy in the form of several caves and stone emplacements, but no Japanese were present to offer any resistance. Having completed its mission, the reconnaissance company withdrew from the islands.

In a report issued on 12 March, the 5th Marine Division intelligence officer estimated that at least 1,000 Japanese were still defending the northern end of Iwo Jima and concluded: "there is no shortage of manpower, weapons, or ammunition in the area the Japanese have left to defend." Actually, the battle was beginning to reach General Kuribayashi's very doorstep. As one account was to relate it: "On March 13, a patrol from the 26th Regiment came very near to Kuribayashi, peering into the cave in which he sat, near the eastern end of the Gorge. The General's orderly quickly blew out the candles and wrapped the General in a blanket. 'Thank you,' Kuribayashi said, and walked deeper into the cave. The Marines, one carrying a flamethrower, walked a little way into the cave then turned and went out. The orderly sighed."

While the Japanese on northern Iwo Jima had been suffering badly in the battle of attrition that was now reaching its climax, the Marines of all three divisions had hardly fared any better. As assault troops of General Rockey's division were beginning to close in on the final enemy pocket, the men wearily attacking the ridges above the gorge were tired to the point of exhaustion and many of them found it difficult to remain on their feet. Few veterans of the early battles were left, and death had reaped a grim harvest among the men who had gone ashore on the island 22 days before. Companies were now reduced to platoon size. Most of the aggressive and experienced small unit leaders had long since become casualties. Gaps in the decimated ranks had been filled with replacements who lacked combat experience that would enable them to fight and survive.

On 14 March it became apparent that the slow, step-by-step advance of the 27th Marines finally had cracked the strong enemy positions along the northeastern coast of Iwo Jima. Since the main ridge lines in this area ran from the center of the island to the sea on the west coast, General Rockey decided that the most practical direction of attack henceforth would be from east to west. As a result, the 28th Marines was ordered to hold its present line while the 27th Marines was to shift its direction of attack westward. In the center of the division line the 26th Marines took over a two-battalion front and was ordered to attack northward with 3/26 on the left and 2/26 on the right.

Enemy resistance was less obstinate on D plus 23 than it had been during the preceding days and the 27th Marines, with 2/26 attached, gained up to 600 yards. The attack was supported by tanks which were able to assist the infantry after armored tankdozers had carved routes of approach to the front lines for them. The official report, speaking of the flame tanks, pointed out: "this was the one weapon that caused the Japs to leave their caves and rock crevices and run. On many occasions the Japs attempted to charge our flame tanks with shaped charges and other explosives. Few of these attempts were successful."

Other developments on Iwo Jima on 14 March gave clear evidence that the end of the long battle was approaching. In mid-morning, five Army Air Forces planes bombed and strafed Japanese positions in front of 3/27 for what proved to be the last air support mission over Iwo Jima. The diminishing size of General Kuribayashi's pocket rendered all further air support impractical. Limited support until the end of the operation would continue to be furnished by artillery and destroyers, and even these supporting arms soon found it difficult to furnish fire in the small area still remaining under enemy control.

While compression of the northern pocket was under way, a ceremony was taking place at 0930 on 14 March at General Schmidt's headquarters. It was not an elaborate proceeding; in fact, its stark simplicity underscored the significance of the long awaited event. In the presence of flag and general officers of the fleet and landing force, assembled around a flagpole erected in these stark surroundings, the official flag raising on Iwo Jima was held. Among those present were General Holland Smith, Admirals Turner and Hill, and Generals Schmidt, Erskine, Cates, Rockey, and Major General Chancy, representing the Army Garrison Force. After the reading of an official proclamation in which the United States officially suspended the powers of government of the Japanese Empire and took over the occupation of the island, the flag was raised at the same time that the one on top of Mount Suribachi was taken down. Upon completion of the ceremony, General Holland Smith and his staff departed from the island by air. The night from 14-15 March was marked by continuous enemy activity directed against the 5th Division lines. Around 0200, close to 100 Japanese attempted to infiltrate the positions of 3/27. In the ensuing firefight, 15 of the enemy were killed, most of them by mortar fire. Around the same time, a small number of Japanese approached the lines of 2/26 and started tossing hand grenades. At dawn, the action shifted to 3/26, where 30 of the enemy were discovered attempting to enter caves southwest of Kitano Point. Half of this group were killed, the remainder committed suicide.

The 5th Division attack continued on 15 March. On the right, the 27th Marines advanced 400 yards and reduced enemy resistance in this sector to sporadic small arms fire. In the center, the 26th Marines made smaller but equally significant gains, carving out an advance of 200 yards. On the division left, in front of the 28th Marines, enemy reaction remained determined and formidable. At this time, enemy resistance was still centered in two areas: the steep draw that extended northwest to the sea across the front of the 28th Marines and the strong core of resistance in front of the 26th Marines, just east of the draw.

Within the diminishing pocket, General Kuribayashi and the surviving members of his staff were still in radio contact with the Japanese on Chichi Jima. They were also able to listen to the "Song of Iwo Jima," especially broadcast from Tokyo for the

Iwo Jima garrison. Already on the morning of 15 March, General Kuribayashi had announced that the situation was very dangerous and that his strength was down to 900 men. By the evening of the following day, his strength had been reduced to 500. Clearly, the end was drawing near. General Kuribayashi summoned the commander of the 145th Infantry Regiment, Colonel Ikeda, to see how much longer resistance could continue. When the regimental commander informed him that it would all be over in another day or so, General Kuribayashi admonished him to be certain that the regimental colors were burned lest they fall into American hands. Behind the Marine lines, additional signs of progress were becoming evident as the naval construction engineers put the final touches on the restoration of the Central Airfield. Even though the runways remained unpaved, they were usable and the field was about to become operational. Additional gasoline storage facilities had been completed, and the carpenters of the 5th Division were already busily engaged in building crates in which the division's equipment would be shipped. At the southern end of Iwo Jima, a dirt road leading to the top of Mount Suribachi had been completed and it was now possible to make the trip up by jeep or bulldozer.

Reduction of the northern pocket continued on 16 March. During this final phase of the operation, General Rockey's division was supported by elements of the 3d Marine Division, which passed through the 27th Marines and took over a sector on the right of the 5th Division. Attacking to the north, General Erskine's men reached the north coast shortly before 1400.

The 26th Marines, with 3/28 attached, attacked with three battalions abreast. The advance progressed slowly against heavy rifle fire, as it proceeded over rugged and rocky ground, where all movement was extremely difficult. However, it was a sign of the progress that had already been made that the volume of enemy machine gun fire had greatly diminished, as had the number of caves that were encountered. Nevertheless, there was still an abundance of spider foxholes and positions in the rocky outcrops which permitted the enemy to inflict a deadly fire from close range. In the course of the day, the 26th Marines advanced 200 yards. The 28th Marines remained in position along the southern rim of the rocky gorge and continued the reduction of enemy defenses to its immediate front and flanks. Losses of the 5th Marine Division at this time consisted of 89 officers and 1,993 men killed, 249 officers and 5,710 enlisted men wounded, and 3 officers and 128 men missing. Combat efficiency was estimated at 30 percent. The division had sustained a total of 8,162 casualties in 25 days of fighting.

At 1800 on 16 March, Iwo Jima was officially declared secured. Three hours earlier, the 13th Marines had fired its last rounds, since the regiment's guns could no longer furnish supporting fires in the limited area comprising the remaining pockets of resistance. It now became incumbent on the mixed 3d and 5th Division assault forces to complete the occupation of the island with all possible dispatch, a task easier contemplated than accomplished.

Following its relief by the 21st Marines on 16 March, the 27th Marines reorganized its badly depleted units into three battalions, each consisting of two rifle companies and a headquarters company. A composite battalion, consisting of a headquarters company and four rifle companies, was formed under the command of Lieutenant Colonel Dorm J. Robertson. A small remainder of the 27th Marines stayed in division reserve until the end of the operation. The unit mopped up in the rear area and prepared to leave the island. The composite battalion, numbering 460 men, subsequently was to be attached to the 26th Marines, where it would participate in eliminating the final enemy positions on northern Iwo Jima. All of the records dealing with this final phase of the operation emphasize the state of exhaustion in which the men found themselves. According to one account: "That the Division still moved forward at all was a credit to the men and their leaders, but the fearful strain of days in the line was showing up in every unit. Men were getting careless, exposing themselves to fire when they were tired. Too, many of the men now were replacements, men who fought gallantly and brought credit to themselves and the Division, but who were not, nevertheless, as highly trained as the Division's original men had been and for that reason probably took slightly heavier losses." A sustained effort was made on the part of General Rockey's division to keep up morale. Baked goods and fruit juice were sent to the units in the line; the wounded were evacuated and the dead buried with all possible dispatch. A division newspaper was circulated among the frontline units, and such articles of clothing and toilet articles as were available were sent up to the lines. Some of the more lucky Marines even enjoyed the luxury of hot showers. But, despite such amenities, the report concludes "Iwo Jima remained an unclean, evil little island, an island that these men would never forget, however much they would have liked to."

Despite their ebbing strength and often only through the application of sheer will power, those men of the 3d and 5th Marine Divisions still able to move on their feet and carry a weapon now entered the final phase of the battle for Iwo Jima. Fought in a narrow corner of the island, the final struggle would prove every bit as difficult as the early phase of the operation: death came no easier now than in the beginning.

With the end clearly approaching and under steadily increasing pressure from the advancing Marines, General Kuribayashi on 16 or 17 March left his headquarters, housed in a large dome shaped concrete structure, and moved to a cave occupied by Colonel Ikeda and Admiral Ichimaru, the remaining senior officers of the Iwo Jima garrison following the death of Major General Senda and Captain Inouye in the 4th Division sector. From this cave, situated near the southeastern end of the gorge, the Japanese officers could do little but exhort their men to continue resistance to the last. This cave was still linked to Chichi Jima by radio, and thus the final days of Japanese resistance on Iwo Jima have become a matter of record.

Battle for the Gorge and Final Operations

The final battle for Iwo Jima began on 17 March, D plus 26, when 1/26 reached the north coast and pivoted to the southwest towards the gorge which had already been blocked by the 28th Marines for the past few days. It was here that General Kuribayashi had determined to make his final stand, and he had chosen his final position with great care. The gorge, 700 yards long and 200-500 yards wide, would have been difficult to approach even under normal conditions. Outcrops of rocks subdivided the ravine into minor draws that greatly impeded all movement. The Japanese commander had taken care to insure that all routes of approach leading into the gorge were covered by machine gun and rifle fire from positions that were all but invisible to the approaching Marines. Units of the 5th Marine Division preparing to offer the coup de grace to the final enemy position on the island would have to use their last strength in attaining this objective. A brief breakdown of casualties in this connection speaks for itself: "Our own losses at this time had been extremely heavy. The average battalion which landed with 36 officers and 885 enlisted, now had about 16 officers and 300 enlisted from the original battalion. Most of the company commanders, platoon leaders, and squad leaders had become casualties and many platoons were commanded by Corporals or PFC'S. Assault squads were depleted." Plans for reducing the final pocket called for the 28th Marines, with elements of the 5th Pioneer Battalion and the division reconnaissance company attached, to occupy a blocking position along the southern rim of the pocket while the 26th Marines, in conjunction with 3/28 and 3/27, was to advance into the gorge from the north and east. Because of the depleted strength of the units and the condition of the men, assigned zones of action were relatively narrow. In their drive against the pocket on 17 March, 3/26 and 3/28 made slight gains in the northeastern perimeter of the pocket, but once again their progress could be measured in yards.

A drama of a different sort was enacted on the island on D plus 26. On the preceding day, prisoners captured by General Erskine's men had conveyed to their captors the whereabouts of General Kuribayashi and his staff, and, acting upon this information, General Erskine decided to make an attempt to induce these officers to surrender. Realizing that a direct appeal to General Kuribayashi would be fruitless, General Erskine instead dispatched a message to Colonel Ikeda, commanding the 145th Infantry Regiment. The message was handed to two prisoners of war who, carrying cigarettes and rations, proceeded into the gorge, fully aware of the importance of their mission. As they trudged off on this unusual errand, the pair was handed a walkie-talkie over which they were to maintain contact with the 3d Division Language Section. As they slowly continued on their journey, the two emissaries crossed lines and soon made contact with groups of Japanese, apparently without arousing anyone's suspicion. Several radio messages were received by 3d Division personnel indicating that the prisoners were getting close to their objective. At this point, the couriers stopped all further transmissions. One of them, who had incurred a leg wound, dropped out, but the other continued and six hours after embarking on his bizarre mission, reached the headquarters cave. There, he turned the message over to one of the sentries who passed it on to the regimental commander. Upon learning that Ikeda had taken the message in to General Kuribayashi, the prisoner lost his nerve and beat a hasty retreat.

As soon as he had rejoined his fellow courier, the radio transmissions to the 3d Division resumed and the Marines were informed that the two were on their way back. Upon reaching the Marine lines at the rim of the gorge, the prisoners thought themselves safe and were more than slightly disturbed at the rude reception accorded to them by 5th Division Marines, who were unaware of General Erskine's psychological warfare effort. The situation was finally straightened out before the two messengers came to any harm, though it took some convincing of the skeptical 5th Division Marines that the two Japanese were indeed working for General Erskine.

The practical results of this surrender attempt, as in previous instances, were nil. None of the high-ranking Japanese officers on Iwo Jima surrendered, and the battle of attrition continued to take its slow and agonizing course. Even though nearly all of the Japanese on Iwo Jima, under General Kuribayashi's dynamic leadership, would fight to the end, there were some who heeded the repeated appeals to surrender. American planes dropped propaganda leaflets, and the artillery fired shells filled with surrender leaflets and passes. For the Japanese soldier on Iwo Jima, surrender was not an easy matter. He could count on being executed by his own people if caught with American propaganda on his person. Surrender might mean that he could never again return to his homeland and face his compatriots. And, last but not least, he had no guarantee that the Marines would honor their promise of fair treatment once he turned himself in to them. No wonder that the Japanese were hesitant to take the final and irreversible step in view of the uncertainty surrounding it. A sampling of 65 prisoners of war showed that 53 had been influenced in their decision to give up by some contact with American propaganda. The remaining 12 had been deterred by fear of their officers and distrust of the Marines and were captured under different circumstances.

Meanwhile, the Marines continued to close in on General Kuribayashi's pocket. With the end in sight, the Japanese garrison commander addressed this order to his men on 17 March: "The battle situation comes to the last moment. I want my surviving officers and men to go out and attack the enemy tonight. Each troop! Go out simultaneously at midnight and attack the enemy until the last. You all have devoted yourself to His Majesty, the Emperor. Don't think of yourself. I am always at the head of you all." Strangely enough, there was no unusual activity during the night from 17-18 March, and nothing even resembling a *banzai* charge occurred.

From this point onward, the information concerning the last days of the enemy's battle for Iwo Jima becomes increasingly hazy. Most of what has remained passed through the hands of the Chichi Jima garrison, which continued to receive radio messages from Iwo that were filed and subsequently turned over to the Americans. Thus, early on 17 March, Chichi Jima was notified that "the 145th Infantry Regiment fought bravely near 'Hyoriuboku' holding their regimental flag in the center." Later in the day, Colonel Ikeda sent this cryptic message: "Here we burnt our brilliant Regimental Flag completely. Good bye."

Iwo Jima became the scene of a wild celebration on the evening of 18 March. It had nothing to do with the fact that the enemy was finally cornered in the northwestern portion of the island and his elimination now was but a matter of days. Instead, someone had leaked word that Germany had surrendered, and this item of news, entirely unfounded and nearly two months premature, spread all over Iwo Jima like wildfire. As a result: "for about an hour the island was the happiest spot on earth. Antiaircraft and other units in rear areas opened up a jubilant barrage with machine guns, antiaircraft guns, carbines, rifles, and pistols. Before it was over, units all over the island and the ships offshore had the news." An end to the celebration came only when Condition Red was declared, a warning that enemy planes were in the area. As one account has it, "The Fifth Division hospital treated three casualties from 'the German war' and there were certainly others." Following the excitement, Marines on Iwo Jima returned to the more normal routine of routing individual Japanese and thwarting the enemy's infiltration attempts.

As the advance continued on 19 March, enemy resistance became centered around General Kuribayashi's erstwhile headquarters. The structure proved completely impervious to the 75mm tank shells and likewise defied all attempts to demolish it with 40-pound shaped charges. It would take the assaulting Marines two days to destroy the surrounding positions and then commence a direct assault on the command center. Engineers with bulldozers sealed an entrance on the north side of the structure and several air vents. Finally, four tons of explosives, divided into five charges, proved sufficient to destroy this stubborn center of resistance. Just who and how many among the Japanese perished within has never become known. However, the garrison commander and the high-ranking officers were safely tucked away in Colonel Ikeda's cave, and reports continued to reach Chichi Jima, though communications daily became more sporadic. Around 17-18 March, General Kuribayashi sent his final message to Imperial General Headquarters, in which he apologized to the Emperor for his failure to hold the island. The message was accompanied by a poem in which the garrison commander promised:

"My body shall not decay in the field
Unless we are avenged;
I will be born seven more times again
To take up arms against the foe.
My only concern is
Our country in the future
When weeds cover here."

About the same time, but in a less poetic and more down-to-earth fashion, Admiral Ichimaru penned a rather vituperative letter to none other than President Roosevelt, charging the latter with a lack of understanding for Japan's problems and accusing the white race, and the Anglo-Saxons in particular, "of monopolizing the fruits of the world, at the sacrifice of the colored races."

Meanwhile, reduction of the pocket continued unabated. Tanks moved up to the front lines over paths cleared by the tank dozers which themselves frequently came under attack by individuals or small groups of Japanese bent on suicide. The slow but steady Marine advance into the gorge was carried out under the command of the assistant division commander, General Hermle, whom General Rockey had entrusted with operational control of all units engaged in the final mop-up at the gorge. From an observation post affording a clear view of the gorge, General Hermle directed the operation that would bring organized enemy resistance in this sector to an end.

On Chichi Jima, Major Horie learned with astonishment on 21 March that General Kuribayashi and his men were still fighting. The durable garrison commander reported that his cave was under direct attack by tanks and demolition teams. Of American attempts to induce his surrender he mentioned disdainfully that "they advised us to surrender by a loud-speaker, but we only laughed at this childish trick and did not set ourselves against them." Major Horie radioed to Iwo Jima the information that, effective 17 March, the Imperial government had promoted Kuribayashi to the rank of full general, Ichimaru to vice admiral, Inouye to rear admiral, and Nishi to full colonel. The two latter promotions were made posthumously, though most likely all of them were intended that way.

On D plus 30, 21 March, the 26th Marines, with 3/27 and 3/28 attached, continued the assault as 1/26 and 3/27 advanced into the gorge. At the rim, 3/28 held its positions. Fighting on this day, as on the preceding ones, was exceedingly bitter. The Japanese refused to yield; in fact, there no longer was any place for them to go but stand their ground and die. Thus, the Marines had to eliminate them one by one. As on an earlier occasion, it was noticed that many of the enemy were wearing Marine uniforms and firing M-1 rifles. In the course of the day's advance, elements of 1/26 made gains of 200 yards down the gorge, but beyond that point required the support of flame tanks. It developed that the terrain did not permit their employment, so that portable flamethrowers were used until the Japanese shot the liquid out of the tanks. When his equipment was hit, one of the operators became a human torch and burned to death; another was just barely saved from suffering the same fate. As D plus 30 ended, 1/28 had gained 400 yards at the edge of the cliff, while 2/28, after one of its patrols had eliminated 20 of the enemy, moved forward 100 yards to the very edge of the cliff. On this day, Major Horie received a message from Iwo Jima, informing him: "We have not eaten nor drunk for five days. But our fighting spirit is still running high."

The end was now very near, yet the battle for Death Valley, a name Marines had given to the gorge, continued. In a situation where the orthodox arms and tactics of warfare proved unavailing, other means had to be improvised. In the words of one account: "The Marines tried everything in the book, and a good many things that weren't, to clean the Japs out of the gorge. Explosives were lowered over cliffs by rope to blast the Japs from their caves. Drums of gasoline were emptied into canyons and set afire. Over-sized rockets were hauled up to the front on bulldozers and used to blow the Japs off hillsides. Aerial observers dropped grenades on enemy positions from their low-flying grasshoppers. For four days men of the 5th Division tried to take Death Valley by direct assault. They failed, because any man who set foot in the gorge was dead."

Still, some progress was apparent as one enemy defensive position after another was whittled away. On 22 March, 3/27, supported by tanks, tank dozers, and flame tanks, gained another 300 yards. On the following day, D plus 32, Major Horie received one final message from Iwo Jima which said: "All officers and men of Chichi Jima, good-bye." For three more days, Horie tried to communicate with Iwo Jima, but there was no answer and it was assumed that all resistance on the island had ended. This fact had already been mournfully announced over Tokyo Radio by the Japanese Prime Minister, who bemoaned the fall of the island as "the most unfortunate thing in the whole war situation."

By 24 March, the backbone of enemy resistance in Death Valley had been broken, and the size of the pocket was down to a square of 50 by 50 yards. On the following day, D plus 32, exhausted Marines of 3/26 and 3/28 moved down into Death Valley and completed the task of mopping up, sealing caves and squeezing the enemy into an area that was no longer defensible. Still, individual Japanese held out until 25 March, when death-tired remnants of the 26th, 27th, and 28th Marines staggered into the gorge and silenced what remained of enemy resistance. At 1045 on D plus 34, the gorge was declared secured and fighting on northern Iwo officially came to an end.

Withdrawal of Marine units from Iwo Jima got under way on 17 March, when the VAC artillery completed embarkation. Artillery of the three divisions reembarked on subsequent days, except for 4/12, which stood by for several days, prepared to deliver fire on request. On 18 March, the 3d Marine Division relieved the 4th and General Cates closed his CP on Iwo Jima. On the same day, men of this division embarked. Two days later, the ships carrying the division departed from the island en route to their rehabilitation area in Hawaii. The arrival of the 147th Infantry Regiment on 20 March brought Army troops into the picture. The regiment was attached to General Erskine's division for operational control. As early as 7 March, General Chancy had assumed responsibility for base development and antiaircraft defense of all Iwo ground installations. He had delegated the air defense of Iwo Jima to General Moore effective that date. At 0800 on 26 March, General Chancy took over as Iwo Jima garrison commander, in effect assuming operational control of all units stationed on the island. General Moore continued as Air Defense Commander.

Just as it appeared that Iwo Jima was about to become a garrison, rather than a fiercely contested battlefield, the Japanese decided to strike a last blow against the invaders who by this time had victory all but within their grasp. Mopping up operations up to this time had continued daily in northern and central Iwo, and day and night individual Japanese had either been killed or captured. As a precautionary measure, a LCI patrolled off the northwest beaches to prevent the escape of any of the enemy by water during the hours of darkness.

Early on 26 March, a force of between 200 and 300 Japanese moved down from the area near the Northern Airfield over a trail skirting the western coast of the island and launched a full-scale attack against Marine and Army units encamped near the western beaches. Far from executing a howling *banzai* charge, the Japanese launched a well-organized attack which was carried out in echelon from three directions. Carefully calculated to achieve the maximum confusion and destruction, the Japanese set about to do their deadly work in silence. Beginning at 0515, and for more than three hours, the enemy ranged through the Marine and Army bivouacs, slashing tents, knifing sleeping airmen, and throwing grenades at random.

The units engaged and partly overrun were the 5th Pioneer Battalion, elements of the 5th Field Depot, comprising the VAC Shore Party, the 98th Naval Construction Battalion, elements of the 21st Fighter Group, the 465th Aviation Squadron, and the 506th Antiaircraft Artillery Gun Battalion. In the darkness, the fighting was confused and terrible. The chief difficulty, that of distinguishing between friend and enemy, was compounded by the fact that many of the attackers were armed with BARs, M-1 rifles, .45 caliber pistols, and one even with a bazooka. Other Japanese charged with their swords, a sure indication that a sizable part of the assault force consisted of officers.

At the height of the attack, the Japanese penetrated to the Army 38th Field Hospital, where they tore out the telephone lines, slashed tents, and machine-gunned ambulances. In the midst of the prevailing turmoil, officers of the 5th Pioneer Battalion organized the first resistance, and there were instances of great personal heroism and sacrifice. Initially, a firing line was established in some foxholes. Subsequently, as the din of battle increased, other Marines arrived on the scene and Army flame tanks began to go into action. The 5th Pioneers organized a skirmish line and, for the first time, the enemy was forced to give ground. Joining in the action was anyone who had a weapon, including airmen, Seabees, Army medical personnel, and members of the Corps Shore Party. In fact, the performance of the latter Marines earned them a special commendation from their commanding officer who stated: "The Corps shore Party Commander is highly gratified with the performance of these colored troops, whose normal function is that of labor troops, while in direct action against the enemy for the first time. Proper security prevented their being taken unawares, and they conducted themselves with marked coolness and courage." Careful investigation shows that they displayed modesty in reporting their own part in the action. When it was all over, 196 Japanese littered the area of the 5th Pioneer Battalion alone; 66 of the raiders were killed in the adjacent areas and a total of 18 were captured. Rumor had it that General Kuribayashi had led the attack, and the efficiency with which it was carried out would lend some substance to the report. The 40 swords gathered up on the field of battle after the action gave evidence of the high percentage of officers and senior noncommissioned officers that participated. Years after the war, a Japanese who had been taken prisoner during this final attack and who had been subsequently repatriated, was to claim that one-legged Admiral Ichimaru had taken part in the charge. But a body count following the battle and examination of the bodies failed to identify either Kuribayashi, Ichimaru, or Ikeda, and their exact fate has never been determined.

The final Japanese attack also proved costly to the Americans in terms of casualties. The 5th Pioneers lost 9 killed and 31 wounded in this action; units of the VII Fighter Command had 44 killed and 88 wounded. At just about the time that the last of the enemy raiders were being killed off on western Iwo, the capture and occupation phase of the Iwo Jima operation was announced completed. As of 0800, 26 March, the Commander Forward Area, Central Pacific, Vice Admiral John H. Hoover, assumed responsibility for the defense and development of the island. General Schmidt closed his CP and departed from Iwo Jima by air shortly after noon. The remainder of his headquarters embarked on the USS *President Monroe*.

Embarkation of the remaining Marine units followed a schedule long worked out in advance. Thus, elements of the 3d Marine Division began to embark on 27 March, when the 21st Marines and the division CP went aboard ship. The remainder of General Erskine's men departed on the return run of ships carrying garrison forces to Iwo. On 4 April, the Army's 147th Infantry Regiment, commanded by Colonel Robert F. Johnson, assumed full responsibility for the ground defense of the island and the 9th Marines prepared to embark. The last unit of General Erskine's division left Iwo on 12 April and arrived on Guam six days later. During the final phase of the operation between 11 and 26 March, the Marines had sustained a total of 3,8S5 casualties. Total Marine casualties for the Iwo Jima operation came to 25,851. The total number of Japanese who died in the defense of Iwo Jima has never been definitely established, but nearly the entire garrison went down fighting. As of 26 March, the Marines had taken only 216 prisoners, a large number of whom were Korean laborers. Nor did the fighting and dying on the island end with the departure of the VAC Landing Force. Aggressive patrols and ambuscades by the 147th Infantry Regiment continued throughout April and into May, resulting in additional Japanese killed and captured. Isolated enemy strongpoints continued to hold out and had to be reduced, some of them more than once.

During the first week of April, in an incident reminiscent of the unexpected enemy attack of 26 March, about 200 Japanese materialized just above the East Boat Basin, where they attempted to rush an infantry command post. This battle continued all night and all of the attackers were killed, but not before they had succeeded in exploding 6,000 cases of dynamite, which rocked the island and caused a number of casualties. Nor was this the end. Also during the month of April, Army troops stumbled upon the field hospital of the 2d Mixed Brigade, located 100 feet underground on eastern Iwo Jima. The surrender of the hospital proved to be somewhat complex, as outlined by this account: "A language officer appealed to the Japanese to come out. After a long discussion, the senior medical officer, Major Masaru Inoaka, called for a vote. The ballot turned out sixty-nine for surrender, 3 opposed. Of the three nays, Corporal Kyutaro Kojima immediately committed suicide. The others came out, including two more medical officers, Captain Iwao Noguchi and Lieutenant Hideo Ota." Captain Noguchi, beset by remorse that he had lived while so many died, later emigrated to Brazil, unable to accept life in Japan.

For the remainder of April and May, members of the 147th Infantry Regiment accounted for 1,602 Japanese killed and 867 captured. As the fighting and dying gradually subsided, the utilization of the island as a forward base went into high gear. But even as bulldozers tore across ground that had previously been so bitterly contested and aviation gas was beginning to reach Iwo in large quantities, three large Marine Corps cemeteries remained to offer a mute eulogy to the men who had fought and died there. Arriving on Iwo Jima on 20 April 1945, one eminent Navy historian counted 5,330 graves in the Marine Corps cemeteries, but, in his own words: "there were about 31,000 soldiers, Air Force ground crews and Seabees on the island, very much alive, healthy and in high spirits. Army officers said they wouldn't trade Iwo for any South Pacific island. There were many who would pay tribute to the heroism of the Marines who captured this key bastion of the Japanese inner defense ring, bristling with the most powerful defenses a clever and crafty enemy could devise." None of them put it better than Admiral Nimitz, Commander in Chief of the Pacific Fleet and Pacific Ocean Areas, who made this comment:

"The battle of Iwo Island has been won. The United States Marines by their individual and collective courage have conquered a base which is as necessary to us in our continuing forward movement toward final victory as it was vital to the enemy in staving off ultimate defeat. By their victory the Third, Fourth and Fifth Marine Divisions and other units of the Fifth Amphibious Corps have made an accounting to their country which only history will be able to value fully. Among the Americans who served on Iwo Island, uncommon valor was a common virtue."

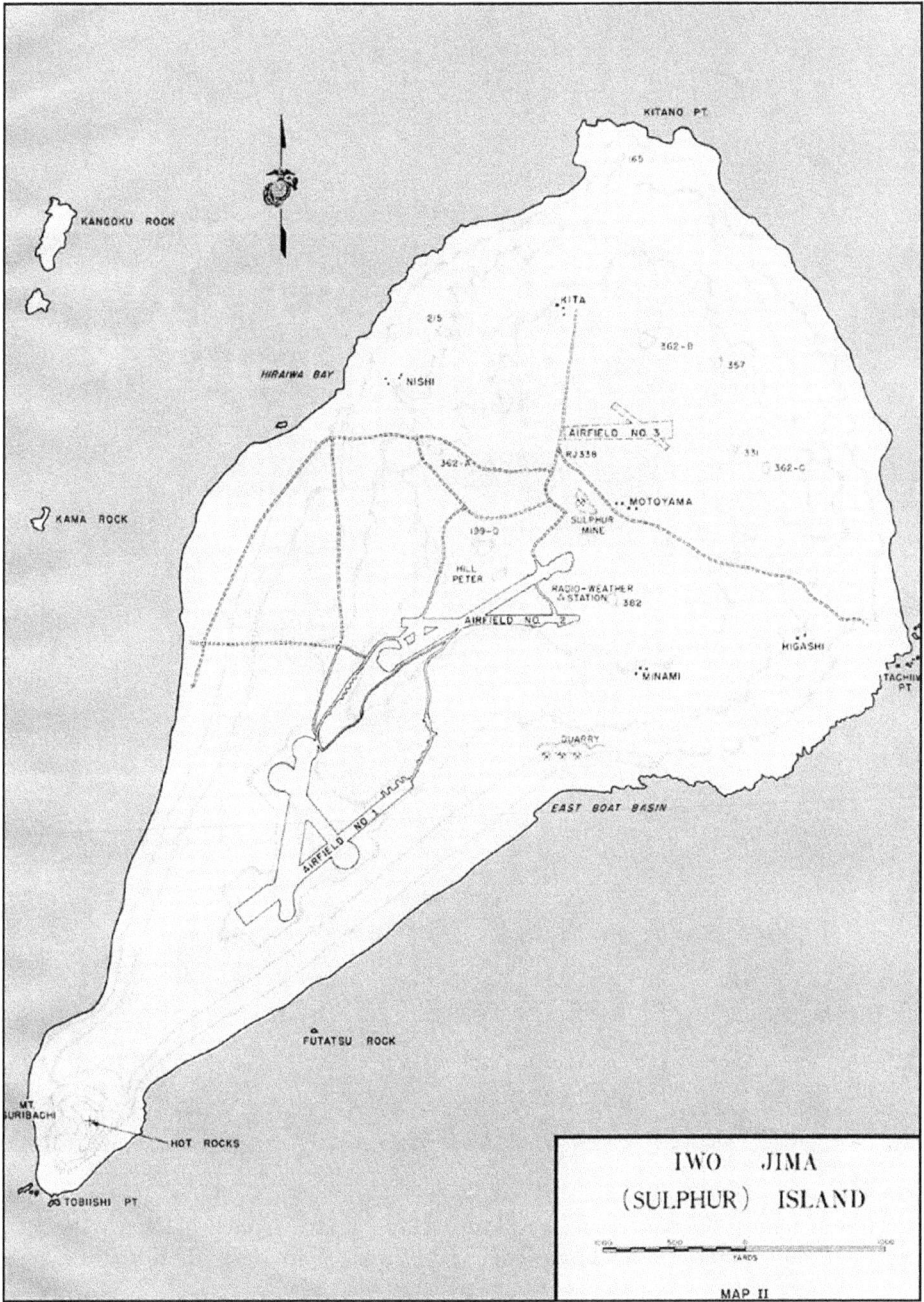

Iwo Jima

General Tadamishi Kuribayashi. He knew that he did not have the strength to hold the island against the Americans, and instead drew up his defense plans to make its capture as long and difficult as possible to give the Japanese home islands additional time to prepare their defenses.

An aerial view of Iwo Jima during the pre-invasion bombardment. Mt Suribachi is at the bottom, the landing beaches are at the right.

Amphibious landing vehicles approach Iwo Jima.

The Japanese allowed the Marines to land unopposed, opening fire only after the beach was crowded with men and equipment.

Wrecked vehicles and dead Marines litter the landing beach.

Mt Suribachi dominated the beaches where the Marines came ashore. Gunners on Suribachi could rake the entire landing with fire.

Exposed Marines dig into the volcanic sand for cover.

Captured 120mm gun emplacement.

A Japanese gun emplacement. The defender had honeycombed the island with a network of bunkers, connected by underground tunnels.

An American 37mm gun fires on Suribachi from the beach.

Taking Mt Suribachi was the first priority.

The first flag raised on the top of Mt Suribachi. A short time later, a second larger flag was raised—an event captured in the famous photo by war correspondent Joe Rosenthal.

After Suribachi was captured, Marines fanned out to take the rest of the island. Here, a 60mm mortar crew fires on entrenched Japanese positions.

Armored tank flamethrower in action. Every Japanese gun position was defended to the last and had to be blasted out, one at a time.

Marines display a captured Japanese battle flag

Dead Marines. The Americans paid a heavy price for capturing Iwo Jima.

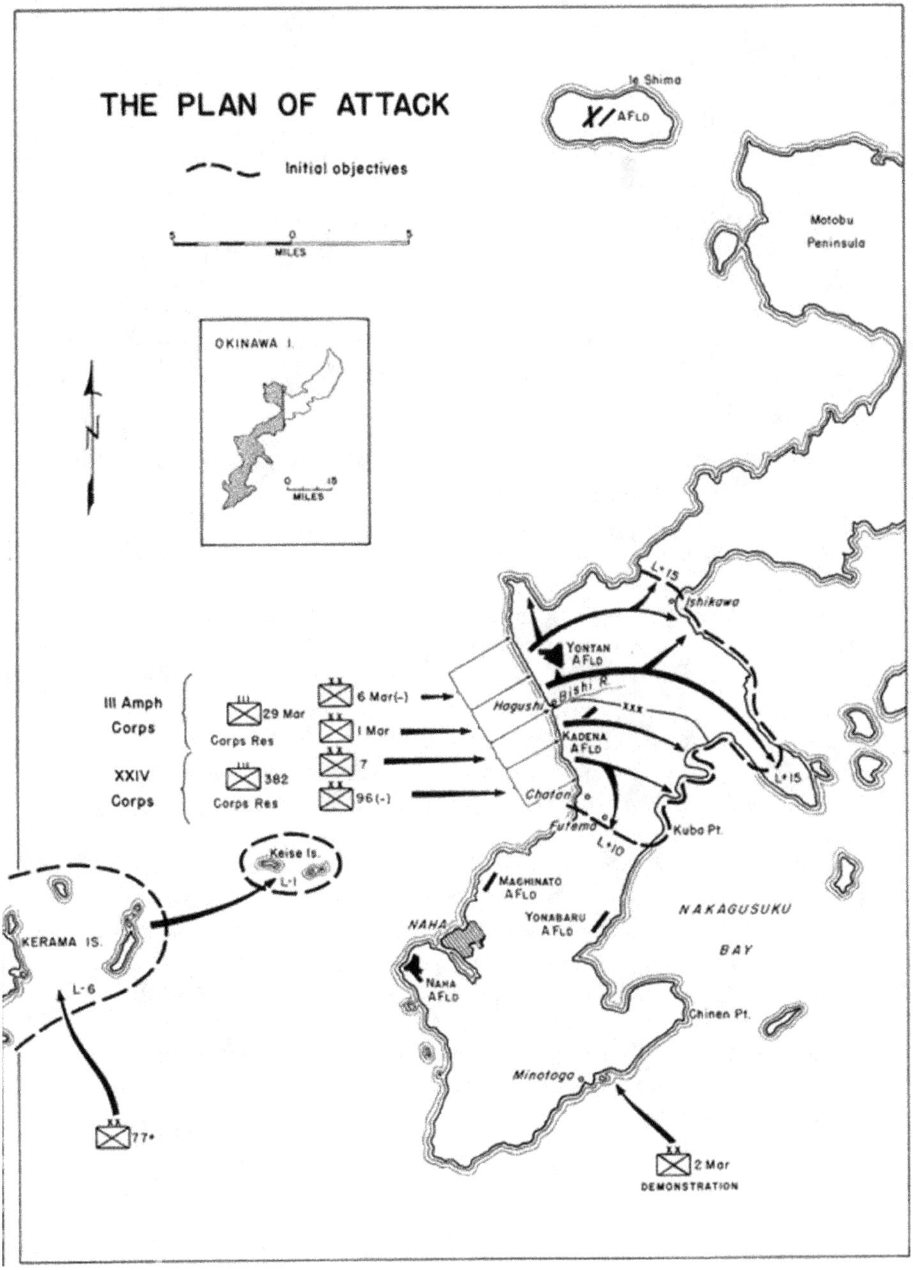

THE PLAN OF ATTACK

Ie Shima

X / AFLD

~~~ Initial objectives

5   0   5
MILES

OKINAWA I.

N

0   15
MILES

Motobu Peninsula

L+15

Ishikawa

YONTAN AFLD

Bishi R.

III Amph Corps

29 Mar — Corps Res

6 Mar(-) →

I Mar →

Hagushi

xxx

KADENA AFLD

XXIV Corps

382 — Corps Res

7 →

96(-) →

Chatan

Futema

L+10

Kuba Pt.

L+15

Keise Is.

L-1

MACHINATO AFLD

NAHA

YONABARU AFLD

NAKAGUSUKU

BAY

KERAMA IS.

L-6

NAHA AFLD

Chinen Pt.

Minotoga

77*

2 Mar

DEMONSTRATION

Okinawa, showing the planned landings.

General Mitsuru Ushijima. Like Kuribayashi, Ushijima knew he could not hold the island, but aimed to hold out for as long as possible to give Japan time to build her defenses against the inevitable invasion of the homeland.

Aerial view of Okinawa.

The Marine landing on Okinawa was completely unopposed.

(Above) Japanese 120mm gun position. (Below) Concrete pillbox machine gun bunker. Learning the lessons of Iwo Jima, Ushijima allowed the Marines to move inland on Okinawa, where they ran into concentric rings of interlocking positions that swept the landscape, catching the Americans in a lethal trap.

Hand-held flamethrower in action. Each individual Japanese position had to be blasted or burned out, one at a time.

US Marine running for safety. Hidden Japanese snipers and machine guns were everywhere, and getting caught in the open was a fatal mistake.

American Marines file past a dead Japanese soldier.

Carrier-based Corsair fighter fires rockets against dug-in Japanese positions. The Americans had complete air and sea superiority over the Japanese.

The Japanese Zero fighter. At the beginning of the war, it was the best fighter plane in the world. By Okinawa, it was obsolete and outclassed, and the Japanese decided to use it as a last-ditch weapon to try to neutralize the American's overwhelming superiority by deliberately crash-diving their few remaining planes into US carriers.

Kamikaze pilot prepares for his last mission. Perplexed Americans spread stories that the suicide pilots were drafted flight students who were chained into their cockpits. In reality, the kamikaze were all volunteers.

Japanese civilians cheer and wave cherry blossoms as a kamikaze pilot takes off. The plane is a Japanese Army "Oscar" fighter.

A kamikaze streaks in to strike the battleship USS *Missouri*.

The American carrier *Bunker Hill* burns out of control after being struck by kamikaze planes. Although suicide attacks had been carried out in the Philippines and Iwo Jima, Okinawa was the first time that large numbers of "special attack" forces were sent into action. The kamikaze sunk or damaged 304 ships at Okinawa.

Demolition team blows up a Japanese bunker.

Prisoners. Most of those captured were Korean laborers. Nearly the entire Japanese garrison was killed or committed suicide.

Near the end of the battle for Okinawa, a US Marine plants a flag on the ruins of Shuri Castle.

Okinawa

Chapter 1. The Target and the Enemy

Background
Once the Joint Chiefs of Staff decided on Okinawa as a future target, intensive planning and preparations were begun for the assault on this once obscure island. Large amounts of information of varying importance poured into the intelligence centers concerned with the impending operation, and were added to files already bulging with a store of knowledge of the Ryukyus group. Okinawa soon became the focus of attention of the CinCPac-CinCPOA headquarters and staff members who, in compliance with the JCS directive to Admiral Nimitz ". . . to occupy one or more positions in the Nansei Shoto," filled in the details of an outline plan. A flurry of disciplined activity immediately engulfed the commands and staffs of the expeditionary forces assigned to the assault as they began their operational studies for ICEBERG, the code-name given to the approaching invasion. The strategic importance of Okinawa was its location, and all other considerations stemmed from this. The Japanese viewed it as an integral link in a chain of islands, the Ryukyus or the Nansei Shoto, which formed an effective barrier to an Allied advance from the east or southeast towards the Chinese mainland, Korea, or the western coast of Japan. This group of islands was ideally situated to aid in the protection of the Japanese maritime lines of supply and communication to imperial conquests in southeast Asia. The island chain also provided the Japanese Navy with the only two substantial fleet anchorages south of the Home Islands between Kyushu and Formosa, and numerous operating bases for aircraft of all types as well. From the Allied point of view, the conquest of Okinawa would be most lucrative. As the largest island in the Ryukyus, it offered excellent locations for military and naval facilities. There was sufficient land area on the island on which to train and stage assault troops for subsequent

operations against the heart of the Empire. Kyushu was only 350 nautical miles away, Formosa 330 miles distant, and Shanghai, 450. Two other major purposes of the impending invasion were to secure and develop airbase sites from which Allied aircraft could operate to gain air superiority over Japan. It was expected that by taking Okinawa, while at the same time subjecting the Home Islands to blockade and bombardment, Japanese military forces and their will to resist would be severely weakened.

Okinawa : History, Land, And People

Before Commodore Matthew C. Perry., USN, visited Okinawa in 1853-54, few Americans had ever heard of the island. This state of ignorance did not change much in nearly a century, but American preinvasion studies in 1944 soon shed some light on this all-but-unknown area. The course of Okinawa history—from the Chinese invasions about 600 A. D. until Japanese annexation in 1879—was dominated by an amalgamation of Chinese and Japanese cultural and political determinants. For many years, the Chinese influence reigned supreme. After the first Chinese-Okinawan contacts had been made, they warred against each other until the island peoples were subdued. Shortly after 1368, when the Ming Dynasty came to power, China demanded payment of tribute from Satsudo, the King of Okinawa. The payment was given along with his pledge of fealty as a Chinese subject.

In the midst of incessant Okinawan dynastic squabbles, Chinese control remained loose and intermittent until 1609, when the Japanese overran the island, devastating all that stood in their way. The king of Okinawa then reigning was taken prisoner, and a Japanese local government was established temporarily.

For the next 250 years, the Okinawan Kingdom, as such, was in the unenviable position of having to acknowledge both Chinese and Japanese suzerainty at the same time. Finally, in May 1875, Japan forbade the islanders to send any more tribute to China, whose right to invest the Okinawan kings was now ended. In the face of mounting Okinawan protests against this arbitrary action, Japan followed its decree by dethroning the king in March 1879; he was reduced in rank, becoming a marquis of Japan. Okinawa and its neighboring islands were then incorporated within the Japanese political structure as the Okinawan Prefecture. Over the years, China remained restive at this obvious encroachment, until the question was one of many settled in Japan's favor by its victory in the Sino-Japanese War of 1894. The islands to which the Japanese successfully gained title, the Ryukyu Retto, were in the southernmost of two groups which make up the Nansei Shoto. The shoto is a chain of islands which stretch in a 790-mile-long arc between Kyushu and Formosa, separating the Pacific Ocean from the East China Sea. One of the groups which make up the Ryukyu Retto is the Okinawa Gunto. The other four major island groups in the retto are Osumi, Tokara, Amami, and Sakishima. Okinawa Gunto is located at the half-way point in the arc and consists of Okinawa and numerous smaller islands. These include Kumi Shima, Aguni Shima, Ie Shima, and the Kerama Retto in the west; Iheya Retto and Yoron Shima in the north; and a group of small islands, named the Eastern Islands by the Americans, roughly paralleling the east central coast of Okinawa.

The island of Okinawa is narrow and irregularly shaped throughout its 60-mile length. In the north, the Motobu Peninsula juts out into the East China Sea and extends the island to its maximum breadth, 18 miles; immediately to the south is the narrowest part, the two-mile-wide Ishikawa Isthmus. The coastline of the island ranges in nature from a precipitous and rocky shore in the north, through a generally reef-bound lowland belt just below the isthmus, to an area of sea cliffs and raised beaches in the south. Landing beaches suitable for large-scale amphibious operations were neither numerous nor good. The most extensive flat areas and largest beaches on the east coast were found along the shores of Nakagusuku Wan (or bay) and, on the west coast, in the area between Zampa Misaki (or point) and Oroku Peninsula. Two major fleet anchorages existed, both on the eastern side of the island: Nakagusuku Wan (later named Buckner Bay by the Americans in honor of the Tenth Army Commander) and Chimu Wan. The leading port of the Okinawa Gunto was on the west coast at Naha, the major city of the island group. Port facilities elsewhere were limited to small vessels.

Okinawa is easily divisible into three geographical parts, each one physically different from the other. The territory north of the Ishikawa Isthmus, constituting about two-thirds of the island area, is largely mountainous, heavily wooded, and rimmed with dissected terraces — or one-time flatlands which became deeply ravined by the ravages of erosion. About 80 percent of the north is covered with a dense growth of live oak and conifers, climbing vines, and brush. The highlands, rising to rugged peaks, 1,000 to 1,500 feet in height, dominate the area. Small, swift streams drain the clay or sandy-loam topsoil of the interior which is trafficable under most conditions. Cross-country movement is limited mainly by the steepness of the hills and the lush vegetation. The few roads that existed in 1945 were mostly along the coast. The middle division, consisting of that area lying between Ishikawa Isthmus and an east-west valley running between the cities of Naha and Yonabaru, is broadest in its northernmost part. Just south of the isthmus is an area resembling northern Okinawa, but the rest of the sector is, for the most part, rolling, lightly wooded country interrupted by steep cliffs and ravines. The few streams, flowing through hills which rarely exceeded a height of 500 feet, are generally narrow and shallow, so they could be easily bridged or forded.

The southernmost tip of the island, triangular in shape, is extremely hilly and was dominated by extensive limestone plateaus, some reaching over 500 feet in height. At each angle of the base of the triangle is a peninsula, Oroku on the west, and Chinen on the east.

The primary roads built by the Japanese were little more than coral- or limestone-surfaced trails, varying in width from 12 to 16 feet, on a sand and clay base. Use of these roads depended largely upon the weather, since rain reduced them to sticky and slow-drying morasses. In the dry season, the slightest movement on the roads threw up dense clouds of dust. The major arteries threaded along the coastlines, branching off into a few cross-island roads which then broke down into a capillary system of trails connecting the small villages, settlements, and individual farms. The central sector, the densely populated part of the island, contains an intricate network of roads. Only one, the broad stone-paved highway connecting the cities of Shuri and Naha, could support two lanes of traffic. In this area, the road net was augmented by a narrow gauge railway, with approximately 30 miles of track. This system provided the major trans-island communications net, running from Naha to Yonabaru on the east coast, via the towns of Kobakura and Kokuba, while trunk lines linked Kobakura and Kokuba with the west coast towns of Kadena and Itoman, respectively.

Okinawa's climate is tropical, with moderate winters, hot summers, and high humidity throughout the year. The annual temperature range is from a minimum of

40 degrees to a mean maximum of 95 degrees in July. The months of May through September are marked by a heavy and erratic rainfall. During the typhoon season (July-November), torrential rains and winds of over 75 miles-per-hour have been recorded. During the rest of the year, except for brief downpours, good climatic conditions generally prevail.

The inhabitants of Okinawa in 1945 were heirs to a complex racial mixture. The original population is believed to have been a branch of the hairy Ainu and Kumaso stock which formerly inhabited Kyushu and other Japanese islands. A Mongoloid strain was introduced when Japanese pirates, who made Okinawa their headquarters, engaged in their time-honored habit of kidnapping women from the Chinese mainland.

Malayan blood was infused into this melting pot through intermarriage, immigration, and invasion. This evolution produced a people with the same basic characteristics as those of the Japanese, but with slight physical differences. The Okinawans are shorter, darker, and are inclined to have more body hair. The 1940 census gave an estimate of slightly over 800,000 people in the Nansei Shoto as a whole, with nearly a half-million of these on Okinawa proper. Farmers constituted the largest single population class, with fishermen forming a smaller, but important, group. Approximately 15 percent of the Okinawa populace lived in Naha, and within this community were most of the higher officials, businessmen, and white collar workers—most of them Japanese who either had emigrated or been assigned from the Home Islands.

During the period of the Okinawan monarchy, there was an elaborate social hierarchy dominated by nobles and court officials. After Japanese annexation, the major social distinctions became those that existed between governing officials and natives, between urban and rural inhabitants, and between the rich and the poor— with the latter in the majority. Assimilation of the Japanese and Okinawan societies was minimal, a situation that was further irritated by the preferential treatment tendered by the Japanese to their fellow-countrymen when the more important administrative and political posts were assigned.

Another chasm separating the Japanese and Okinawan was the difference in languages. Despite a common archaic tongue which had branched into the language families of both Okinawa and Japan, there were at least five Ryukyuan dialects which rendered the two languages mutually unintelligible. The Japanese attempted to reduce the language barrier somewhat by directing that standard (Tokyo) Japanese was to be part of the Okinawan school curriculum. Several decades of formal education, however, failed to remove the influence of many generations of Chinese ethnic features which shaped the Okinawan national characteristics. The Chinese imprint on the island was such that one Japanese soldier noted that "the houses and customs here resemble those of China, and remind one of a Chinese town." The natives retained their own culture, religion, and form of ancestor worship. One outward manifestation of these cultural considerations were the thousands of horseshoe-shaped burial vaults, many of impressive size and peculiar beauty, which were set into the sides of numerous cliffs and hills throughout the island.

The basic Okinawan farm settlement consisted of a group of farmsteads, each having the main and other buildings situated on a small plot of land. The farmhouses were small, thatch-roofed, and set off from the invariably winding trailside by either clay or reed walls. The agricultural communities generally clustered around their own individual marketplaces. Towns, such as Nago and Itoman, were outgrowths of the villages, differing only in the fact that these larger settlements had several modern business and government structures.

The island's cities, Naha and Shuri, were conspicuous by their many large stone and concrete public structures and the bustle that accompanies an urban setting. Shuri was the ancient capital of the Ryukyuan kingdom and its citadel stood on a high hill in the midst of a natural fortress area of the island. The fundamentally agrarian Okinawan economy was dependent upon three staple crops. About four-fifths of southern Okinawa was arable, and half of the land here was used for the cultivation of sweet potatoes, the predominant foodstuff of both men and animals. Sugar cane was the principal commercial crop and its cultivation utilized the second largest number of acres. Some rice was also grown, but this crop consistently produced a yield far below local requirements. Since rice production was sufficient to satisfy only two-thirds of the population's annual consumption needs, more than 10 million bushels had to be imported annually from Formosa.

Industrial development on the island was rudimentary. The Naha-Shuri area was the leading manufacturing center where such items as alcoholic beverages, lacquerware, and silk pongee were produced. Manufacturing was carried out chiefly in small factories or by workers in their homes. The only relatively important industry carried on outside of the Naha-Shuri complex was sugar refining, in which cattle supplied the power in very primitive mills. The fishing trade, of some importance, centered around Naha and Itoman. There were also small numbers of fishing craft based at all of the other usable harbors on the island; however, lack of refrigeration, distance to the fishing grounds, and seasonal typhoons all hindered the development of this industry and prevented its becoming a large source of income for the Okinawans.

From the very beginnings of the 1879 annexation, the Japanese government made intensive efforts to bring the Ryukyuan people under complete domination through the means of a closely controlled educational system, military conscription, and a carefully supervised system of local government. The prefectural governor was answerable only to the Home Minister in Tokyo. Although the elected prefectural assembly acted as the gubernatorial advisory body, the governor accepted, rejected, or ignored their suggestions as he saw fit. On a local level, assemblies elected in the cities, towns, and townships in turn elected a mayor. All local administrative units were, in effect, directly under the governor's control, and their acts or very existence were subject to his pleasure.

In every aspect—social, political, and economic—the Okinawan was kept in a position inferior to that of any other Japanese citizen residing either on Okinawa or elsewhere in the Empire. This did not prevent the government from imposing on the Okinawan a period of obligated military service. The periodic call-ups of age groups was enforced equally upon the natives of Okinawa and the Ryukyus as on the male inhabitants of Japan proper. This provided Japan with a reservoir of trained reservists from which it could draw whenever necessary. With the exception of those drafts of reservists leaving for active duty elsewhere, Okinawa, for all practical purposes, was in the backwash of the early stages of World War II. The island remained in this state until April 1944, when Japan activated the Thirty-second Army, set up its headquarters on Okinawa, and assigned it responsibility for the defense of the island chain.

The Japanese Forces

Following the massive and devastating United States naval air and surface bombardment of Truk, 17-18 February 1944, and the breaching of the Marianas line shortly thereafter, the Japanese Imperial General Headquarter awakened to the obviously weak condition of the Ryukyus' defenses. Prior to 1944, little attention had been paid to the arming of the Nansei Shoto. The island group boasted two minor naval bases only, one at Amami O-Shima and the other at Naha, and a few small Army garrisons such as the Nakagusuku Wan Fortress Artillery Unit on Okinawa. Acting with an alacrity born of distinct necessity, IGHQ took steps to correct this weakness in the Empire's inner defensive positions by expediting and intensifying "operational preparations in the area extending from Formosa to the Nansei Islands with the view of defending our territory in the Nansei area and securing our lines of communication with our southern sector of operations, and thereby build a structure capable first, of resisting the enemy's surprise attacks' and, second, of crushing their attempts to seize the area when conditions [change] in our favor."

In order to improve Japanese defenses in the Ryukyus, IGHQ assigned this mission on 22 March 1944, to the Thirty-second Army, the command of which was assumed formally on 1 April by Lieutenant General Masao Watanabe. At Naha, headquarters of the new army, staff officers hoped that enough time would be available for adequate fortification of the island. All planning was tempered by memories of the immediate past which indicated that "an army trained to attack on any and every occasion, irrespective of conditions, and with no calculation as to the real chances of success, could be beaten soundly." Added stimuli to Japanese preparations were the American invasions of Peleliu and Morotai on 15 September 1944. By this time, the Japanese high command became quite certain that either Formosa, the Ryukyus, or the Bonins, or all three, were to be invaded by the spring of 1945 at the latest. Initially, Japanese Army and Navy air forces were to blunt the assaults in a major air counteroffensive. The establishment of Allied air superiority and demonstrated weaknesses of Japanese air forces, however, caused the military leaders in Tokyo to downgrade the aviation role in the coming struggle for the defense of the Home Islands. The ground forces, then, would carry the major burden. The Thirty-second Army staff planners wasted no time in organizing the ground defenses of Okinawa. They had learned by the cruel experiences of Japanese forces on islands which had been invaded by the Americans that a stand at the shoreline would only result in complete annihilation and that their beach positions would be torn to pieces in a naval bombardment. It became apparent, therefore, that the primary defensive positions had to be set up inland. Then, should the invaders escape destruction at sea under the guns and torpedoes of Japanese naval forces, or at the beachhead under the downpour of artillery shells, the death blow would be administered by the ground forces' assumption "of the offensive in due course." To steel the troops' determination to fight and to keep their morale at a high peak, army headquarters devised the following battle slogans:

One Plane for One Warship
One Boat for One Ship
One Man for Ten of the Enemy or One Tank.

The command of the Thirty-second Army was assumed by Lieutenant General Mitsuru Ushijima in August 1944, when General Watanabe was forced to retire because of a continuing illness. Because of the importance of the impending Okinawa battle, IGHQ assigned General Ushijima one of the most competent officers of the

Japanese Army, Major General Isamu Cho, as his chief of staff. On 21 January, army headquarters was split into two groups. Ushijima's operations staff moved to Shuri where the general was to direct his army for the major portion of the campaign. A "rear headquarters" composed of the ordnance, veterinary, judicial, intendance, and the greater part of the medical staff set up near Tsukasan, south of Shuri.

Lieutenant Generals Ushijima and Cho complemented each other's military qualities and personality, and formed a command team that reflected mutual trust and respect. They were ably abetted by the only holdover from the old staff, Colonel Hiromichi Yahara, who retained his billet as Senior Officer in Charge of Operations, and Major Tadao Miyake as the logistics officer. Ushijima, a senior officer slated for promotion to general in August 1945, was reputedly a man of great integrity and character who demonstrated a quiet competence which., in turn, inspired great confidence, loyalty, and respect from his subordinates. Cho, in comparison, was a fiery, ebullient, and hard-driving individual with a brilliant, inquiring mind. He spared neither himself nor his staff. His abounding energy was effectively counterbalanced by his senior's calm outward appearance. This combination of personalities was served by comparatively young and alert staff members who were allowed a great latitude of action and independence of thought. The new commander of the Thirty-second Army inherited a combat organization which had been specially established for the expected invasion of Okinawa. Many independent artillery, mortar, antiaircraft artillery (AAA), antitank (AT), and machine gun groups supplemented the fire power of the basic infantry units assigned to the army. As a result of the IGHQ decision in June 1944 to reinforce the Okinawa garrison, nine infantry and three artillery battalions were to be sent to augment the force already on the island. The majority of the reinforcements arrived from their previous stations in China, Manchuria, and Japan between June and August 1944.

The veteran 9th Infantry Division, first to arrive, possessed battle honors dating from the Russo-Japanese War of 1904-5. Coming directly from Manchuria, and scheduled by the high command as the backbone of the defense force, the 9th's stay on Okinawa was short-lived. The critical situation on Leyte required the assignment of the 9th there, and Ushijima, ". . . in accordance with orders of Imperial General Headquarters, decided on 17 November to redeploy the 9th Division in order to send an elite unit with a proud and glorious war record to a battlefield where the Imperial Army would engage in a decisive battle."

Probably, the most important of all of the factors which may have influenced the course of the coming battle for the Japanese, and favored an Allied victory, was the loss of this division and the fact that it was never replaced. It left in late December for the Philippines by way of Formosa where it sat out the rest of the war, prevented by Allied submarines and airplanes—and MacArthur's landing on Luzon in January—from either continuing on to its destination or returning to Okinawa.

Since the 9th Infantry Division was no longer available to the Thirty-second Army, and in order to carry out his defensive plans, Ushijima asked for replacements. He was notified by IGHQ on 23 January 1945 that the 84th Division in Himeji would be sent to Okinawa. This notification was cancelled that same day with the explanation that the greatest possible supply of munitions would be sent, but replacements neither could nor would be sent to the army. This, in effect, put Ushijima on notice that the means to improve his situation had to be found locally. In June 1944, the Thirty-second Army was to have been reinforced by Major General Shigeji Suzuki's 44th Independent Mixed Brigade (IMB), a unit of approximately 6,000 men organized that very month on Kyushu. It was originally composed of the 1st and 2d Infantry Units (each essentially of regimental size) and attached artillery, engineer, and signal units. While en route to Okinawa, the *Toyama Maru*, the ship carrying the brigade, was torpedoed by an American submarine off Amami O-Shima on 29 June. More than 5,000 men were lost and only about 600 survivors of the ill-fated brigade landed on Okinawa; these were used as the nucleus of a reconstituted 2d Infantry Unit. Other replacements were obtained from Kyushu as well as from the ranks of conscripted Okinawans, but the reorganized unit was never fully re-equipped. As a result, this lack of basic infantry equipment caused the 2d Infantry Unit to be known among other soldiers on the island as the Bimbo Tai or "have-nothing-unit." The 1st Infantry Unit was never rebuilt and existed merely as a headquarters organization. Instead, the 15th Independent Mixed Regiment (IMR), a unit newly raised in Narashino, Chiba-ken, was flown directly to Okinawa during the period 6-11 July and added to the 44th IMB in September, bringing its strength up to about 5,000 men.

The next unit of importance to arrive was the 24th Infantry Division which landed in August. Since its initial organization as part of the Kwantung Army in October 1939, the 24th had been responsible for the security of the eastern boundaries of Manchuria. The division, commanded by Lieutenant General Tatsumi Amamiya, was well-equipped and well-trained, but not battle-proven, before it joined the Thirty-second Army. The 24th was a triangular division which had been stripped of its infantry group headquarters, one battalion from each infantry regiment, an artillery battalion, and an engineer company, all of which had been added to expeditionary units sent from Manchuria to the Central Pacific in early 1944. Until a general Thirty-second Army reorganization in February 1945, the 24th's infantry regiments (22d, 32d, and 89th Infantry) functioned with only two battalions each. The division set up its headquarters at Kadena, and in October, it assigned 300 Okinawan conscripts, received from the Thirty-second Army, to each of its infantry regiments for training and retention later by the training unit. The February reorganization brought the 24th nearly up to its original strength and made it the largest tactical unit in the Thirty-second Army, with more than 14,000 Japanese troops and Okinawan draftees assigned to infantry, artillery, reconnaissance, engineer, and transport regiments, and divisional troops. The final major unit assigned to General Ushijima's command was the 62d Infantry Division, commanded by Lieutenant General Takeo Fujioka. This was a brigaded organization which had seen action in China following its activation there in June 1943. Its table of organization, considerably different from the 24th Division's, was similar to that of like units in the Chinese Expeditionary Army. Both of the 62d's brigades had served as independent commands in China since 1938, while the division as a whole fought in the April-June 1944 campaigns in northern Honan Province. Each brigade had four independent infantry battalions (IIBs); the 63d Brigade had the 11th, 12th, 13th, and 14th IIBs, while the 15th, 21st, 22d, and 23d IIBs were assigned to the 64th Brigade. In 1944, two additional IIBs were sent to Okinawa as reinforcements and attached on 15 December to the division which, in turn, assigned them to the brigades. The 272d IIB went to the 64th Brigade, while the 273 IIB went to the 63d.

The 62d Division lacked organic artillery and had few other supporting arms. It never attained a strength greater than 12,000 troops, the largest proportion of whom were infantrymen. The infantry battalions of the 62d were the strongest units of their type on Okinawa, as each battalion mustered a total of 1,200 men organized into five rifle companies, a machine gun company, and an infantry gun company armed with two 75mm guns and two 70mm howitzers. The 272d and 273d IIBs were reported later as having a strength of 700 men each, but with one or two less rifle companies per battalion.

Some variance in strength was found in the infantry components of the other two major fighting organizations of the Thirty-second Army. The 2d Infantry Unit and 15th IMR of the 44th IMB had in common three rifle battalions, an antitank company (four 37mm or 47mm AT guns), and a regimental gun company (four 75mm guns). Each of the battalions listed a total strength of 700 men who were assigned to three rifle companies, a machine gun company, and an infantry gun unit (two 70mm howitzers). The 24th Division regimental organization was similar except for the replacement, in one battalion of each regiment, of the 70mm howitzers by a mortar platoon manning four 81mm mortars.

Since the Japanese high command envisioned the coming battle for Okinawa as developing into one of fixed position defense, the defenders were not assigned any appreciably strong armored force. The entire Japanese tank strength, given to the Thirty-second Army in July, consisted of the 27th Tank Regiment, organized originally in Manchuria in April 1944, from elements of the 2d Armored Division. It was a regiment in name only, as one of its medium tank companies was sent to the garrison at Miyako Jima. What remained was an armored task force with a strength of 750 men who filled the ranks of one light and one medium tank company, a tractor-drawn artillery battery, an infantry company, a maintenance company, and an engineer platoon. The regiment's heavy weapons included 14 medium and 13 light tanks, 4 75mm guns, 2 47mm AT guns, and 10 machine guns. The heaviest tank-mounted weapon was the 57mm gun on the medium tanks. As the Japanese position in the Philippines became hopeless, shipments of weapons to be sent there were diverted by IGHQ to Okinawa. The result was that the Thirty-second Army possessed a heavier concentration of artillery power, grouped under a single command, than had been available to any Japanese force in previous Pacific campaigns. The total artillery strength on Okinawa, with the exception of the 24th Division's organic 42d Field Artillery Regiment, was grouped within Major General Kosuke Wada's 5th Artillery Command. Besides the comparatively weak 7th Heavy Artillery Regiment (formerly the Nakagusuku Wan Fortress Artillery Unit), General Wada's command included two medium regiments, a heavy battalion, and the artillery units of the 44th IMB and 27th Tank Regiment. Combat-tested at Bataan in the Philippines, the 1st Medium Artillery Regiment had one of its two battalions assigned to Miyako Jima upon arrival from Manchuria in July. The other medium regiment was the 23d which, until its departure for Okinawa in October, had been stationed in eastern Manchuria from the time of its activation in 1942. The two medium artillery regiments together mustered a total of 2,000 troops who manned 36 150mm howitzers. The artillery command also contained the 100th Independent Heavy Artillery Battalion. This unit was formed in June of 1944 in Yokosuka and sent to Okinawa in July with 500 men and 8 150mm guns.

Besides artillery units, General Wada's troop list included a mortar regiment and two light mortar battalions. The 1st Independent Heavy Mortar Regiment's 320mm spigot mortars were an unusual type of weapons which Marines had first encountered on Iwo Jima. These awesome weapons, firing a 675-pound shell dubbed a "flying ashcan" by Americans, were the basic armament of this unit. Only half of its six batteries were on Okinawa, as the other three had been sent to Burma in mid-1942. Although the 96 81mm mortars of the 1st and 2d Light Mortar Battalions were nominally under the command of General Wada, actually they were assigned in close support of the various infantry units and usually operated under the direction of their respective sector defense commanders.

The infantry was strengthened with other types of artillery weapons from antiaircraft artillery, antitank, and automatic weapons units which were attached to them during most of the campaign. A dual air-ground defense role was performed by the 72 75mm guns and 54 20mm machine cannon in 4 independent antiaircraft artillery, 3 field antiaircraft artillery, and 3 machine-cannon battalions. In addition, 48 lethal, high-velocity, flat trajectory 47mm guns (located in 3 independent antitank battalions and 2 independent companies) were added to the defense. Completing the infantry fire support of the Thirty-second Army were 4 independent machine gun battalions which had a total of 96 heavy machine guns. The rest of General Ushijima's army consisted of many diverse units and supporting elements. The departure of the 9th Division created a shortage of infantry troops which had to be made up in as expeditious a manner as possible. The reserve of potential infantry replacements on the island varied in quality from good, in the two shipping engineer regiments, to poor, at best, in the various rear area service organizations. The 19th Air Sector Command, whose airfield maintenance and construction troops were stationed at the Yontan, Kadena, and Ie Shima airstrips, provided the largest number of replacements, 7,000 men.

Another source of troops to fill infantry ranks was found in the sea-raiding units. These organizations, first encountered by American forces in the Philippines, were designed for the destruction of amphibious invasion shipping by means of explosive-laden suicide boats. There were a total of seven sea-raiding squadrons in the Okinawa Gunto, three of which were based at Kerama Retto. Each of the squadrons had assigned to it 100 hand-picked candidates for suicide and martyrdom, whose caliber was uniformly high since each man was considered officer material. When one of these men failed to return, it was presumed that his had been a successful mission and, reportedly, he was therefore given a posthumous promotion to second lieutenant.

Japanese naval base activities on Okinawa were under the command of Rear Admiral Minoru Ota. Admiral Ota was commander of the Naval Base Force for the Okinawa area, commander of the 4th Surface Escort Unit, and also was in charge of naval aviation activities in the Nansei Islands. Army-Navy relations and the chain of command on Okinawa were based locally on mutual agreements between the Thirty-second Army and the Naval Base Force.

Admiral Ota directed the activities of approximately 10,000 men, of whom 3,500 were Japanese naval personnel and the other 6,000-7,000 were civilian employees belonging to sub-units of the Naval Base Force. Of the total number of uniformed naval troops, only about 200 were considered to have received any kind of infantry training. Upon the activation of the base force on 15 April 1944, a small number of naval officers and enlisted men, and most of the civilians, were formed into maintenance, supply, and construction units for the large airfield on Oroku Peninsula and the harbor installations at Naha. At Unten-Ko, on Motobu Peninsula in the north, were stationed a torpedo boat squadron and a midget submarine unit. In organizing for the defense of the island, the greater portion of regular naval troops were formed into antiaircraft artillery and coastal defense batteries.

These were broken down into four battery groups which were emplaced mainly in the Naha-Oroku-Tomigusuku area. The antiaircraft units manned 20 120mm guns,

77 machine cannon, and 60 13mm machine guns, while the 15 coast defense batteries, placed in strategic positions on the coastline under the control of Army local sector commanders, stood ready by their 14cm and 12cm naval guns. Although the total strength in numbers was impressive, the Okinawa Naval Base Force did not have a combat potential commensurate with its size. Continually seeking means to bolster his defenses, General Ushijima received permission to mobilize a home guard on the island. In July 1944, the Okinawa Branch of the Imperial Reservists Association formed a home guard, whose members were called Boeitai. They were organized on a company-sized basis by town or village and were mainly comprised of reservists. Since the Boeitai represented a voluntarily organized group, it did not come under the Japanese Military Service Act, although their training and equipment came from the regular forces into whose ranks they were to be integrated when the battle was joined. The total number of Boeitai thus absorbed by the Thirty-second Army has been estimated between 17,000 and 20,000 men.

On Okinawa there were certain units which have often been confused with the Boeitai. These were the three Special Guard Companies (223d, 224th, and 225th) and three Special Guard Engineer Units (502d, 503d, and 504th) which were special components of the Thirty-second Army. During peacetime, each unit had a cadre of several commissioned and noncommissioned officers, When war broke out, certain designated reservists reported to the above units to which they had been previously assigned.

Even the youth of the island were not exempt from the mobilization. About 1,700 male students, 14 years of age and older, from Okinawa's middle schools, were organized into volunteer youth groups called the Tekketsu (Blood and Iron for the Emperor Duty Units). These young boys were eventually assigned to front-line duties and to guerrilla-type functions for which they had been trained. Most, however, were assigned to communication units.

It has not been conclusively determined how many native Okinawans were actually added to the forces of the Thirty-second Army, or to what extent they influenced the final course of battle. What is known, however, is that their greatest contribution was the labor they performed which, in a period of nine months, transformed the island landscape into hornets' nests of death and destruction.

The Japanese Defenses

Continuing American successes in the conduct of amphibious operations forced the Japanese to recognize the increasing difficulties of defending against assaults from the sea. The loss of some islands in 1944 reportedly caused Japanese garrison units at other Imperial bases in the Pacific to lose confidence in themselves and their ability to withstand an American seaborne invasion. The Japanese high command hastily published the "Essentials of Island Defense," a document which credited Americans with overwhelming naval and air power, and emphasized that the garrisons should "lay out and equip positions which can withstand heavy naval and aerial bombardment, and which are suitable for protracted delaying action . . . . diminish the fighting effectiveness of landing units . . . seize opportunities to try to annihilate the force in one fell swoop." This document may have influenced General Ushijima's decisions when he settled on a final defense plan, although his particular situation was governed primarily by the strength of the Thirty-second Army and the nature of the area it was to defend. Captured on Okinawa were a set of instructions for the defense of Iwo Jima, which were apparently a blueprint also for the defense of critical areas on the coasts of the islands of Japan. It is assumed that Ushijima may have seen these instructions, for they bore directly on his problem: "In situations where island garrisons cannot expect reinforcements of troops from rear echelons, but must carry on the battle themselves from start to finish, they should exhaust every means for securing a favorable outcome, disrupting the enemy's plans by inflicting maximum losses on him, and, even when the situation is hopeless, holding out in strong positions for as long as possible."

In order to deceive the assaulting forces as to Japanese intentions a Thirty-second Army battle instruction warned the troops to "guard against opening fire prematurely." A later battle instruction explained that "the most effective and certain way of [the Americans'] ascertaining the existence and organization of our firepower system is to have us open fire prematurely on a powerful force where it can maneuver."

These instructions were a forewarning that, rather than forcing the issue on the beaches, "the Japanese soldier would dig and construct in a way and to an extent that an American soldier has never been known to do." Japanese organization of the ground paralleled that which assault troops had discovered on Biak, Saipan, and Peleliu in 1944 and Iwo Jima in 1945. General Cho, a strong advocate of underground and cave fortifications, took an active part in designating where defensive positions were to be placed. The most favorable terrain for the defense was occupied and honeycombed with mutually supporting gun positions and protected connecting tunnels. Natural and man-made barriers were effectively incorporated to channel attackers into prepared fire lanes and pre-registered impact areas, The reverse as well as the forward slopes of hills were fortified, while artillery, mortars, and automatic weapons were emplaced in cave mouths, with their employment completely integrated within the final protective fire plan. Each unit commander, from brigade down to company level, was made responsible for the organization of the ground and fortification of the sector assigned to him. The need for heavy construction was lessened, in some cases, by the abundance of large caves on Okinawa which required but slight reinforcement to enable them to withstand even the heaviest bombardment. Once improvements were made, these natural fortresses served either as hospitals, barracks, command posts, or all of these combined when the size of the cave permitted. There were generally two or more entrances to the caves, which sometimes had more than one level if time and manpower was available for the extensive digging necessary. Tunnels led from the caves to automatic weapons and light artillery positions which, in conjunction with the pillboxes and rifle pits in the area, dominated each defense zone. The approaches and entryway to each cave were invariably guarded by machine guns and, in addition, by covering fire from positions outside the cave.

Integrated within the whole Japanese defensive system, these cave strongholds were, in turn, centers of small unit positions. Item Pocket, one of the most vigorously defended sectors on Okinawa, was typical of the ones American forces ran into. The area encompassed by this position, roughly 2,500 by 4,500 yards in size, was in the vicinity of Machinato Airfield. Both the 1st Marine and 27th Infantry Divisions fought bitterly to gain it. Disposed within the caves and bunkers of the pocket was a reinforced infantry battalion which manned approximately 16 grenade launchers, 83 light machine guns, 41 heavy machine guns, 7 47mm antitank guns, 2 81mm mortars, 2 70mm howitzers, and 6 75mm guns. A minefield and an antitank trench system completed the defenses. This sector was so organized that there were no weak points visible to the attacker. Any area not swept by automatic weapons fire could be reached by either artillery or mortars. These defensive positions formed a vital link in the chain of the tough outer defenses guarding Shuri.

Based on the dictum that "the island must be divided into sectors according to the defense plan so that command will be simplified," each combat element of the Thirty-second Army was assigned a sector to develop and defend as it arrived on Okinawa. By August 1944, the 44th IMB's 2d Infantry Unit (400 troops) under Colonel Takehiko Udo had occupied its assigned area, Kunigami Gun (County), and had assumed responsibility for all of the island north of the Ishikawa Isthmus, and also for Ie Shima and its airfields. Upon its arrival on Okinawa, the 24th Division had begun to construct field fortifications around Yontan and Kadena airfields in an area bounded by Ishikawa Isthmus in the north and a line from Sunabe to Ozato in the south. Below the 24th's zone of defense, the 62d Division was unflagging in its efforts to alter the ridges, ravines, and hillsides north of Shuri. Responsibility for the entire southern portion of Okinawa below Shuri had been assumed by the 9th Division commander. The receipt of orders in November for the transfer of the 9th Division forced a redeployment of Thirty-second Army troops and strained a defense that was already dangerously weak. The 24th Division began moving south to take over some 9th Division positions while the 44th IMB, leaving two reinforced battalions of the 2d Infantry Unit behind on Ie Shima and Motobu Peninsula, occupied an area which reached from Kadena airfield southward to Chatan. The 62d Division positions were likewise affected by the withdrawal of the 9th's 14,000 combat troops, as the northern divisional boundary of the 62d dropped to the Chatan-Futema line. In the south, the 62d zone of responsibility was increased tremendously to include all of Naha, Shuri, Yonabaru, and the entire Chinen Peninsula.

Although the construction of fortifications, underground positions, and cave sites had been going on since the spring of 1944, the urgency of the war situation and the expectance of an imminent invasion compelled the defenders to reevaluate their plans of deployment for blunting the assault. The exact date of the new Thirty-second Army plan is not known, but a reasonable assumption is that the loss of the 9th Division in November which triggered the shuffling of units also forced a decision on a final defense plan. At the end of the month, General Ushijima and his staff pondered the following alternatives before settling on the one which they believed would guarantee the success of their mission:

"Plan I: To defend, from extensive underground positions, the Shimajiri sector, the main zone of defenses being north of Naha, Shuri, and Yonabaru. Landings north of these defenses were not to be opposed; landings south of the line would be met at the beaches. Since it was impossible to defend Kadena airfield [with available troops], 15cm guns were to be emplaced so as to bring fire on the airfield and deny the invaders its use.

"Plan II: To defend from prepared positions the central portion of the island, including the Kadena and Yontan airfields.

"Plan III: To dispose one division around the Kadena area, one division in the southern end of the island, and one brigade between the two divisions. To meet the enemy wherever he lands and attempt to annihilate him on the beaches.

"Plan IV: To defend the northern part of the island, with Army Headquarters at Nago, and the main line of defense based on Hill 220, northeast of Yontan airfield."

Realistically appraising the many factors which might effect each one of the alternate plans, the Japanese settled on Plan I. Plan III was abandoned simply because the Thirty-second Army did not have the strength adequate to realize all that the plan encompassed. Plan IV was rejected because it conceded the loss of the militarily important south even before the battle had been joined. Plan II, the one which American staff planners feared as offering the greatest threat to a successful invasion, was regretfully relinquished by the Japanese. Ushijima, recognizing his troops' capabilities and limitations, realized that his forces, in the main, had not been trained to fight this type of delaying action which would prolong the battle, bloody the invaders, and permit the bulk of this army to withdraw to the more heavily fortified southern portion of Okinawa. Yet, in effect, this is exactly the strategy he was forced to employ after the initial American landings. Placing Plan I into effect, the Japanese centered the main battle position in the Shuri area, where the rugged terrain surrounding the ancient capital was developed with the strongest installations oriented north toward the Hagushi beaches. The Hagushi region, coincidentally, evolved as a secondary target to the Japanese and a primary target to American staff planners. In addition, "handicapped by their lack of ability to make a logistics estimate for a landing operation," the Japanese believed that the major effort would be made in the southeast with an assault across the Minatogawa beaches. overlooking both the Minatogawa and Nakagusuku Wan beaches, Chinen Peninsula heights presented the defenders with the most favorable terrain of its type on Okinawa and, as such, it was hoped that the invaders could be met and defeated here. Since, from the standpoint of actual manpower, the Chinen sector was the weakest area in the final defense plan, a goodly portion of the artillery and infantry strength of the Thirty-second Army — which could have been better employed in reinforcing Shuri positions — was diverted to the peninsula, remaining there out of action during the first weeks of the campaign.

Among Ushijima's most pressing needs were additional troops and time in which to train them. Extra time was needed also to provide for expanding and strengthening existing fortifications as well as the communications net. With the exception of a drastic fuel shortage, the army was in good logistical shape. Although the Thirty-second Army itself had no provisions in reserve, enough had been distributed to subordinate units, and stored by them in caves near troop dispositions, to last until September 1945. This system was satisfactory in that the strain on the overworked transportation facilities was removed, but when an area was overrun by Americans and the Japanese were forced to withdraw, the supplies were lost. Unable to halt the inexorable press of time, General Ushijima now found it imperative to beef-up his infantry component from sources on the island, for he knew that he could expect no outside help. In addition to the mobilized Boeitai and a continuing stream of Okinawan conscriptees, the Japanese commander attempted to free his uniformed labor and service personnel for frontline duty by replacing them with able-bodied males from the large population of the island. In February 1945, more than 39,000 Okinawans were assigned to Japanese Army units on the island. The natives were placed into such categories as Main Labor (22,383), Auxiliary Labor (14,415), and Student Labor (2,944). The Japanese attempted to evacuate to the northern part of the island all of the rest of the population who were incapable of aiding the war effort or who were potential obstacles in the battle zone.

General Ushijima found the additional infantry troops he required in the ranks of Thirty-second Army special and service units. The first elements affected by an army-wide reorganization at this time were seven sea-raiding base battalions. Each suicide squadron was supported by a base battalion of 900 men, and since they had completed their basic assignment of cave and suicide boat site construction, the army decided to utilize these men in an area where they were critically needed. Beginning 13 February 1945, these battalions, although retaining their original numerical designations, were reassigned as the 1st, 2d, 3d, 26th, 27th, 28th, and 29th Independent Battalions (each averaging about 600 men) to the 24th and 44th IMB for thorough training and subsequent absorption. Only the maintenance company of each battalion was to remain with its respective sea-raiding suicide unit. In comparison with the regular infantry of the Japanese Army, the new battalions were poorly trained and equipped, but these 4,500-5,000 men invested enemy forces with an additional source of strength.

During the next month, March, a final army reorganization took place, at which time the Thirty-second Army directed "the various shipping, air, and rear echelon forces [to] set up organizations and dispositions for land combat." Besides their basic missions, these units now had to give infantry training and field fortification construction priority in their schedules. The March reorganization supplied the army with two brigades and a regiment which appeared more significant on paper than actually was the case. These lightly equipped and untrained service troops could serve only as combat replacements with slight tactical value.

Units from the 19th Air Sector Headquarters were funneled into the 1st Specially Established Regiment which, under 62d Division control, was responsible for the defense of the areas in the vicinity of Kadena and Yontan airfields. Support positions in the Naha-Yonabaru valley were assumed by the 1st Specially Established Brigade, composed of three regiments and formed from Thirty-second Army transport, ordnance, construction, and supply troops formerly within the 49th Line of Communications Headquarters command. A 2d Specially Established Brigade of three regiments, culled from the 11th Shipping Group Headquarter's shipping, sea transport, and engineer rosters, was deployed in support of the 24th Division mission—the defense of southernmost Okinawa. "Army rear echelon agencies not included in this order and their personnel will be under command of the front line unit in the vicinity where their duties are carried on, and will reinforce it in combat," stated the all-inclusive 21 March order which put the entire Thirty-second Army in a status of general mobilization for combat. By 26 March, Okinawa Base Force naval and civilian personnel had been formed into the same type of jerry-built, poorly equipped, and undertrained defense units as had been the service troops of the Thirty-second Army. On Oroku Peninsula, naval lieutenants commanded those units designated as battalions while lieutenants (junior grade) became company commanders. Admiral Ota's 13mm and 25mm antiaircraft batteries were re-equipped and transformed into an 81mm mortar battery and two independent machine gun battalions and, thus armed, were the only adequately weaponed units in the naval garrison.

In less than two months after the first reorganization order had been published, General Ushijima had nearly doubled the potential combat strength of his army by the addition of approximately 20,000 Boeitai, naval, and service troops. Hurriedly, the concerted efforts of this determined Japanese force converted the Shuri area into what was to be an almost impregnable bastion, for the final defensive plan was strengthened by the defenders' determination to hold Shuri to the last man.

Concurrent with the February army reorganization, the troops were deployed in their final positions. General Ushijima's main battle force was withdrawn to an outpost zone just north of Futema, while elements of the 1st Specially Established Regiment were loosely disposed in the area immediately behind the Hagushi beaches. Although this was the least likely place where the Americans were expected to land, the Japanese troops defending this area were to fight a delaying action in any such eventuality, and then, after destroying the Yontan and Kadena airfields, were to beat a hasty retreat to the Shuri lines.

In the suspected invasion area, the Minatogawa beaches, the bulk of the Japanese infantry and artillery forces were positioned to oppose the landings. The 5th Artillery Command observation post was established near Itokazu in control of all of its major components, which had been emplaced in defense of the Minatogawa sector. Since landings further north on Chinen Peninsula would give the invaders a relatively unopposed, direct route into the heart of the major Japanese defense system, the 44th IMB was assigned control of the rugged heights of the peninsula. The 24th Division, taking over the defense works begun by the 9th Division, occupied the southern portion of Okinawa from Kiyan Point to an area just north of Tsukasan. The whole of Oroku Peninsula was assigned to Admiral Ota's forces, who were prepared to fight the "Navy Way," contesting the invasion at the beaches in a manner reminiscent of the Japanese defense of Tarawa. Since the heart and soul of the Japanese defenses were located at Shuri, the most valuable and only battle-tested organization on the island, the 62d Division, was charged with the protection of this vital area. The Japanese had shrewdly and industriously constructed a stronghold centered in a series of concentric rings, each of which bristled with well dug-in, expertly sited weapons. Regardless of where the Americans landed, either at Hagushi or Minatogawa or both, the plans called for delaying actions and, finally, a withdrawal into the hard shell of these well-disguised positions.

The isolated north was defended by the Udo Force, so-called after its leader and commanding officer of the 2d Infantry Unit—Colonel Takehiko Udo. Its mission was twofold, defense of both Motobu Peninsula and Ie Shima. The reinforced battalion on Ie Shima was assigned secondary missions of destroying the island's airfield and assisting in the transfer of aviation matériel to the main island. Upon completion of these duties, the unit was then to return to Okinawa where it would be assigned to the control of the 62d Division. Udo's battalion on Motobu Peninsula, in expectation of an invasion of Ie Shima followed by a landing on the peninsula, was disposed with its few artillery pieces so placed as to make its positions and positions on Ie Shima mutually supporting. As a result of its detachment earlier from the larger portion of the Thirty-second Army, Udo's command was destined to fulfill a hopeless undertaking to the very end.

Air defense was not included in the Thirty-second Army plan, nor was any great aviation force available to Ushijima. He had expected that approximately 300 airplanes would be sent to Okinawa, but feared that their projected time of arrival, April, would be too late to influence the local situation. The American preinvasion air and naval bombardments in March, combined with planned Japanese destruction efforts, had rendered the Ie Shima, Yontan, Kadena, and Oroku airfields unusable.

The army did expect, however, that its exertions would be complemented by the combat activity of its organic suicide sea units. The sea-raiding squadrons located at positions in Kerama Retto and along the Okinawa coast, would "blast to pieces the enemy transport groups with a whirlwind attack in the vicinity of their anchorages."

Unfortunately for the Japanese, their midget submarines and motor torpedo boats at Unten-Ko could not join this offensive endeavor, for, by the day of the American invasion, they had all been destroyed by American carrier strikes or scattered in the aftermath of an unsuccessful attack on the destroyer *Tolman* of Task Force 52. The significance of Thirty-second Army deployments and redeployments, the frenzied last-minute preparations, and the general air of expectancy were not lost upon even the lowest ranks. One private wrote as early as February, "it appears that the army has finally decided to wage a decisive battle on Okinawa." Another soldier noted that "it's like a frog meeting a snake, just waiting for the snake to eat him."

Between 20 and 23 March 1945, the Japanese command on Okinawa made an even more realistic estimate than had the troops of what the future held for the garrison. The Japanese reacted to news of a conference held in Washington between Admirals King and Nimitz in early March by placing a general alert into effect "for the end of March and early April," since statistics demonstrated "that new operations occur from 20 days to one month after [American] conferences on strategy are held." This estimate of when the Americans were expected was reduced three days after its publication following receipt of reports of increased shipping in the Marianas, and when repeated submarine sightings and contacts were made. All of this enabled the Japanese intelligence officers to predict without hesitation that the target was to be "Formosa or the Nansei Shoto, especially Okinawa."

Chapter 2. Project ICEBERG

The Task Defined
Three weeks after receipt of the Joint Chiefs of Staff directive ordering the Okinawa invasion, Admiral Nimitz' headquarters published and distributed the ICEBERG Joint Staff Study. This study served as a planning guideline for the units assigned to the campaign and defined for them the objectives, the allotment of forces, and roughly outlined the scheme of maneuver ashore. Although Operation CAUSEWAY, the invasion of Formosa, had been cancelled in favor of ICEBERG, the principal commanders for CAUSEWAY were retained for the Okinawa landing and redirected their staffs' efforts towards planning for the assault on the newly assigned target. Admiral Raymond A. Spruance, whose Task Force 50 (TF 50) contained the Fifth Fleet and the Central Pacific Task Forces, was made responsible for the Ryukyus operation. His staff, previously charged with preparing plans for the Iwo Jima invasion scheduled for 20 January 1945, was now given the concurrent assignment of planning for Okinawa.

Certain assumptions governed task planning and the assignment of assault and garrison forces for ICEBERG. Adherence to the scheduled 1 March 1945 invasion date (L-Day) for Okinawa was based on the presupposed seizure of Iwo Jima at a date early enough to permit release of naval gunfire and air support units for the second operation. It was further assumed that ICEBERG commanders would be able to secure the prompt release from General MacArthur of assault shipping, support shipping, supporting naval forces, and Army troops assigned to the Philippines operation which had been earmarked for use later at Okinawa. Finally, before Okinawa was invaded, Allied air and surface superiority had to be gained in the target area.

This last point was one of the most important in the overall concept of the operation, for it was believed that air attacks on Japan, together with the conquest of Iwo Jima, would force a concentration of Japanese air strength on the bases which ringed the Home Islands. It would be necessary, therefore, to destroy enemy air installations at Japanese staging areas in Kyushu and Formosa, and neutralize those at Okinawa, since it was a basic assumption that enemy aircraft. would vigorously oppose any invasion attempt. For this reason, the scheme of maneuver ashore included plans for the early securing of airfields on Okinawa and their equally early use by Allied land-based aircraft. Japanese sea communications in the Ryukyus area were to be severed before the operation by surface and air attacks on enemy shipping and by a maximum effort mounted by American submarines. According to the ICEBERG staff study, operations ashore were to be conducted in three phases. To be accomplished in the first phase were the capture of the southern portion of Okinawa and small adjacent islands and the initial development of base facilities. In Phase II, Ie Shima and the remainder of Okinawa were to be seized and the base build-up continued with the construction of installations in favorable locations designated in the development plan. Phase 111 required the exploitation of Allied positions in the Nansei Shoto and, when Admiral Nimitz directed, the seizure and development of additional positions with forces then locally available.

It was envisioned that an army of two corps, each composed of three reinforced infantry divisions, would be required in the initial assault. In addition, two divisions were to be assigned as area reserve. Okinawa's proximity to the heart of the Empire as well as to other major Japanese bases, and the expectation of fanatic resistance by enemy troops on a battleground of such large dimensions, presaged a prolonged period of fierce combat. For these reasons, a new command relationship was established for the Okinawa operation differing, in some respects, from that which had been effective in previous Pacific campaigns.

As strategic commander of the invasion forces, Admiral Nimitz directed that the chain of command would descend to Admiral Spruance, thence to Vice Admiral Richmond K. Turner who would command Task Force 51 (Joint Expeditionary Force), and then to Lieutenant General Simon B. Buckner, Jr., USA, who would command the Army, Navy, and Marine units comprising the Expeditionary Troops. When Spruance had determined that the amphibious phase of the invasion had ended, he would pass the command of all forces ashore to Buckner. As Commanding General of the Tenth Army, Buckner would assume responsibility for the defense and development of positions captured on the island. When the situation permitted, he would also relieve Admiral Spruance of the responsibility for the defense and development of the Ryukyus as a whole and, at that time, he would be directly responsible to CinCPOA for the captured island positions and for the waters within a 25-mile radius. Concurrently, responsibility for the establishment of an Island Command and a military government on Okinawa would be General Buckner's also.

Allied Commanders And Forces

Many units of Admiral Nimitz' command not directly assigned Task Force 50 were to support the Okinawa landing from bases widespread in the Pacific Ocean Areas. Additionally, from their airdromes in China and the Southwest Pacific, Army Air Forces elements were to assist the ICEBERG effort, both prior to and during the course of the campaign. In all, about 548,000 men of the Marine Corps, Army, and Navy, together with 318 combatant and 1,139 auxiliary vessels — exclusive of numerous small personnel craft of all types—and a profusion of strategic and tactical aircraft were to strike some of the last blows dooming the Japanese attempts to gain supremacy in Asia and the Pacific. In the Fifth Fleet were the Covering Forces and Special Groups which included the Fast Carrier Force (TF 58, Vice Admiral Marc A. Mitscher) and the British Carrier Force (TF 57, Vice Admiral Sir H. Bernard Rawlings, RN). These two forces were to conduct air strikes and neutralize Japanese air power prior to the landing, and prevent enemy air and surface interference with the Allied landing and subsequent occupation of Okinawa.

The units more directly concerned with the landing were components of Turner's Task Force 51. Its complex composition reflected its many assignments incident to the capture, occupation, and defense of Okinawa. Any enemy attempt to disrupt the movement to the target or landing on the beach would be handled by the force's support elements. These naval units would also undertake air support and minesweeping operations once the beachhead had been gained. Assignments for these tasks were allocated, in turn, to the Amphibious Support Force (TF 52, Rear Admiral William H. P. Blandy) which provided direct air and naval support, and to the Gunfire and Covering Force (TF 54, Rear Admiral Morton L. Deyo). The Northern Attack Force (TF 53, Rear Admiral Lawrence F. Reifsnider) and the Southern Attack Force (TF 55, Rear Admiral John L. Hall, Jr.,) contained the transports which were to lift the assault troops to the objective and the tractor units which were to land them on L-Day.

The assault of Okinawa and its surrounding islands was to be accomplished by the landing forces of Buckner's Expeditionary Troops (TF 56). The assault force of the Northern Attack Force was Major General Roy S. Geiger's III Amphibious Corps (IIIAC), composed of the 1st Marine Division (Major General Pedro A. del Vane) and the 6th Marine Division (Major General Lemuel C. Shepherd, Jr.). The Army XXIV Corps (Major General John R. Hedge) would be lifted by the Southern Attack Force and would consist of the 7th Infantry Division (Major General Archibald V. Arnold) and the 96th Infantry Division (Major General James L. Bradley).

One other major Marine echelon in the Tenth Army was Major General Francis P. Mulcahy's joint air task command, Tactical Air Force (TAF), which was to provide land-based air support for the operation once its squadrons were ashore. The elements initially assigned to TAF were to come primarily from the 2d Marine Aircraft Wing (2d MAW). Although TAF was established under the Tenth Army on 21 November 1944, its staff was not really organized until late in December. By that time, much of the earlier, basic, and important preinvasion planning had been completed without TAF participation. As a matter of fact, the last of the personnel assigned to TAF staff did not even report until after the assault echelon had already left for the target. Although he had not taken part in ICEBERG planning, General Mulcahy was kept fully abreast of Tenth Army activities and decisions by his chief of staff, Colonel Perry O. Parmelee, who daily visited Buckner's headquarters and attended briefings and conferences there. A most important element of TAF was its fighter arm, the Air Defense Command (ADC), headed by Brigadier General William J. Wallace who had formerly been AirFMFPac Chief of Staff. Wallace's squadrons were to begin operations from previously designated airfields on Okinawa as soon as they had been captured by the ground troops. Initially, General Wallace's command consisted of a headquarters squadron and a service squadron, and three MAGs with a total complement of nine fighter, two night fighter, and four air warning squadrons, The radar installations of the units last named would give early warning of enemy air attacks. An Army Air Forces fighter wing was also part of ADC, but only one group was to join TAF before the campaign was brought to a close.

General Mulcahy's Bomber Command was made up wholly of AAF flight and support elements, none of which arrived on Okinawa before the beginning of June. Photographic coverage of enemy installations, interpretation of the pictures thus obtained, and an aerial photographic survey of the island for mapping purposes were to be the missions of an AAF photo-reconnaissance squadron which was also part of the TAF organization.

Rounding out the Tenth Army air force were two Marine torpedo-bomber squadrons which were to conduct antisubmarine warfare operations together with the carrier-based naval aircraft at the target. The Marine squadrons were also prepared to conduct bombing attacks on ground targets and any other missions when the need for them arose.

Marine aviation, other than that which was organic to TAF, was to play an important part in the invasion. Artillery spotting was the assigned mission of Marine observation squadrons attached to the Marine divisions and corps. Scheduled to control all aircraft in support of the ground forces were Colonel Vernon E. Megee's Landing Force Air Support Control Units (LFASCUS) . When directed by Admiral Turner, LFASCUS, set up ashore at the headquarters of Tenth Army and its two corps, would take over control from their shipboard naval counterparts. In addition to the tactical units assigned to the Tenth Army for the assault and consolidation phases of the operation, General Buckner was to have direct command of the defense and service troops assigned for the garrison phase, Major General Fred C. Wallace, USA, was designated Island Commander, Okinawa, while the Naval Forces, Ryukyus, were to be commanded by Rear Admiral Calvin H. Cobb, who would assume his command upon completion of the amphibious phase of the operation, Although strategic air force and naval search squadrons were to be based on Okinawa, they would remain under the operational control of the Commanding General, Army Air Forces, Pacific Ocean Area, and Commander, Fifth Fleet, respectively.

Infantry units were assigned also to the Western Islands Attack Group (TG 51.1, Rear Admiral Ingolf N. Kiland) which had the 77th Infantry Division (Major General Andrew D. Bruce) as its landing force; the Demonstration Group (TG 51.2, Rear Admiral Jerauld Wright) whose landing force was the 2d Marine Division (Major General Thomas E. Watson) ; and the Floating Reserve Group (TG 51.3, Commodore John B. McGovern) which carried 27th Infantry Division (Major General George W. Griner, Jr.).

Joint Preparations And Planning

Intensive joint planning attested to the immensity of the future operation. Smooth Army, Navy, and Marine Corps coordination of operational, logistical, and administrative matters was imperative. Since the Tenth Army, under CinCPOA, would consist of an Army corps and a Marine amphibious corps, and a large naval contingent, General Buckner believed that it was important for him to have a joint staff. He therefore requested Admiral Nimitz to authorize a Marine and naval augmentation of his staff. When this request was granted, approximately 30 Marine and 30 Navy officers, and enlisted assistants from each of these services, were assigned and integrated within the Tenth Army staff. "There was no Marine or naval section of the staff." One of the Marine officers was Brigadier General Oliver P. Smith, who became the Marine Deputy Chief of Staff; he had been the Assistant Division Commander of the 1st Marine Division in the Peleliu campaign. His counterpart on the Tenth Army staff was Brigadier General Lawrence E. Schick, who filled the billet of Army Deputy Chief of Staff. When General Smith arrived at Tenth Army headquarters, he found that CinCPOA had already approved the Marine augmentation for the Army staff. The Marine general believed that this augmentation was overly large, for: "This padding would result in Marine officers doing clerical duty at Army Headquarters as there were manifestly not enough bona fide billets to take care of all the Army officers on the staff as well as the Marine and naval officers."

After considerable discussion with the Army officer responsible for the assignment of staff billets, General Smith managed to have the number of Marine officers on the Tenth Army staff reduced by nearly 30 percent.

A tactical concept based upon the directive stated in the ICEBERG joint staff study, and later incorporated in the TF 50 operation plan, required "early use of sufficient airdrome capacity in Okinawa, together with unloading facilities adequate to support its development and to maintain positive control of the air in the area." In a study of all landing beach areas in southern Okinawa, those beaches on the west coast which lay north and south of Hagushi were deemed to be best suited to support the ICEBERG landing. Admiral Turner's operation plan assumed that there would be bitter Japanese air reaction to the Okinawa invasion; that enemy submarines would be very active in the target area; that the Japanese surface fleet might possibly sortie out from its bases in Japan; and, that attempts might be made to reinforce the garrison on Okinawa. The first three assumptions proved correct; the fourth was not tested because, in accordance with the JCS directive ordering the invasion of Okinawa, Allied air and surface superiority had been gained prior to L-Day.

Based on Admiral Turner's plan, the Tenth Army staff drew up Plan Fox, which committed the assault forces to a landing on the west coast. Plan Fox also included the pre-L-Day capture of Keise Shima, since a study of this small island indicated the feasibility of its use as a fixed emplacement for artillery which would first augment the naval and air bombardment of the main objective before the landing, and afterwards provide support during the land campaign. This plan, approved by Buckner, was presented to Turner at the initial joint conference held at Pearl Harbor on 1 November 1944.

Following this presentation, Turner stated his views of the operation and outlined what would be the requirements of the Navy during the course of ICEBERG. He believed that, prior to the landings on Okinawa, the adjacent islands had to be neutralized. Once this had been done, the major landings on Okinawa would be more secure and the fleet could be replenished in a safe anchorage without danger from enemy surface vessels or submarines. Two provisions of Plan Fox particularly concerned the Fifth Fleet commander. Because of the suspected presence of Japanese mines and submarines immediately west of Okinawa, should the Hagushi beaches be used for the invasion, the landings here would perforce require the fleet to steam into a hazardous area. The second apprehension arose because 1 March had been scheduled as L-Day. He feared that unfavorable weather conditions, which generally prevailed in March, might possibly affect the conduct of the landings and unduly prolong the unloading of supplies on exposed beaches. Available meteorological data justified this concern, for from October to March the Ryukyus experienced strong northerly winds with a mean velocity of 17-19 miles-per-hour as well as frequent gales. A generally moderate wind, averaging 11 miles-per-hour, marked the beginning of the summer monsoon period and characterized the weather of Okinawa in April, which was a more suitable time for the invasion. In any case, Turner requested that the possibility of landings along the east coast be restudied. At the same time, he suggested that the value of a feint landing be determined and, if valid, should be incorporated in the plan finally adopted for ICEBERG.

After a lengthy discussion of the problems inherent in the proposed plan, the conferees concluded that a landing on the western beaches on 1 March was fraught with considerable risk. The alternatives were either a 30-day delay of the operation or a landing on the southeast coast on the date originally scheduled for the assault. All other possible courses of action were re-examined, with the result that the Hagushi beaches were recommended again as the site for the landings. Final approval was withheld by Turner because he retained doubts as to the practicality of landing and supporting the proposed assault force of four divisions over the Hagushi beachhead. In spite of the objections of Admiral Turner, the Plan Fox estimate was distributed on 5 November. When completed on 9 November, another detailed study upheld the original contention that Hagushi held the only beaches in southern Okinawa adequate to receive four divisions abreast and, subsequently, to handle sufficient logistical support for the operation.

In the face of these convincing arguments, Admiral Turner accepted the plan with the proviso that both Kerama Retto and Keise Shima were to be captured prior to the main landing. With minor exceptions, General Buckner concurred with these modifications, and the revised plan was forwarded to Turner on 11 November. The original target date of 1 March was changed twice within the next month, first to 15 March and finally to 1 April. The first change was made on 19 November in anticipation of bad weather at the target at the beginning of March. On 7 December, Admiral Nimitz advanced L-Day two more weeks when doubts arose as to whether the shipping assigned to General MacArthur's Lingayen Gulf operations could be returned in time to permit its reemployment at Okinawa. Since the naval planning staff recommended a sustained seven- or eight-day bombardment of the assault beaches, the resulting expenditure of Navy supplies and ammunition would force the bombardment group to either withdraw from the area for resupply and refueling or to conduct these operations under dangerous conditions in the open sea offshore of the objective. Basically, it was this consideration that prompted Turner's insistence on the pre-L-Day capture of the entire Kerama group. At first, these islands appeared to be only worthy as targets for amphibious raids in which the raiding parties would retire after destroying enemy coastal artillery. Later plans for their capture grew out of Admiral Turner's proposal that, once taken, the Keramas provide a protected anchorage for the establishment of a small-boat pool and a seaplane base.

Because the Kerama assault was now to be a full-scale invasion instead of a raid, the assignment of a larger force was indicated and Major General Thomas E. Watson's 2d Marine Division was chosen initially. This unit, designated IIIAC Reserve, had been slated for early commitment in support of operations on Okinawa, and so the task of capturing the Keramas was given instead to the 77th Infantry Division while the Marine division was assigned tentatively to a feint landing off southeastern Okinawa.

As the scope and importance of preliminary operations grew, the reserves which had been made available to General Buckner originally decreased in number, and it was found necessary to secure from CinCPOA release of the area reserve division

(27th Infantry Division). This unit was then designated as the Tenth Army floating reserve and was replaced by the 81st Infantry Division which remained in New Caledonia under Admiral Nimitz' control.

The alternate plan for the operation, Plan BAKER, was approved on 3 January 1945. It envisioned first the capture of Kerama Retto, followed by a sweep of the Eastern Islands by General Watson's Marines. Both of these actions were to be conducted prior to the assault of Okinawa itself. A mixed Marine and Army corps artillery group was to support both the XXIV and III Amphibious Corps assault of the east coast. On L-Day, General Geiger's Marines would land between Chinen Point and Minatoga, secure the high ground behind the beaches, and, following the Army landing two days later, tie-in with XXIV Corps at Yonabaru. After effecting this juncture, both corps were to make a rapid advance across the island during which time the Marines were to take the airfield on Oroku Peninsula and the Army was to capture the unfinished field at Yonabaru. Included in the alternate plan were provisions for the capture of Ie Shima, feints against Chimu Wan on L plus 3 or 4, and, overall, the maintenance of flexibility of action in the commitment of Army reserves to either of the corps zones or for the protection of XXIV Corps' northern flank.

Although the principal advantages of Plan Baker were that the approach to the east coast of Okinawa was more direct and the weather here was vastly superior to that of the west coast, they were outweighed by the disadvantages. These included: (1) the difficulty of providing optimum naval gunfire support because of the interposition of the Eastern Islands and off-shore islets, (2) the paucity of good beaches, (3) the length of time it would take to uncover airfields, located, for the most part, on the west coast, and, (4) because of Plan Baker landing zone assignments, the possibility that Japanese forces might be able to concentrate considerable strength against IIIAC troops before they could even contact the XXIV Corps. General Smith was convinced at this time that "in the advent of bad weather on the west coast, landings would have been delayed rather than resort to the east coast landing as provided in the alternate plan."

General Geiger became involved in the planning for ICEBERG in November 1944, when he was directed to report to General Buckner for planning purposes. Upon receipt of this order, the IIIAC commander immediately reported by dispatch. Shortly thereafter, IIIAC headquarters received a copy of the tentative Plan Fox together with all available intelligence on the prospective target, and a request that Geiger prepare a tentative corps operation plan.

When the IIIAC plan was completed, and at the request of Buckner, Geiger, accompanied by his chief of staff, Colonel Merwin H. Silverthorn, his G-2, Lieutenant Colonel Sidney S. Wade, his G-3, Colonel Walter A. Wachtler, his G-4, Colonel Francis B. Loomis, Jr., and other members of his staff, departed Guadalcanal for Pearl Harbor, arriving at Schofield Barracks on 9 December. After personally contacting their opposite numbers on the Tenth Army staff, the IIIAC staff officers prepared to present their plan to General Buckner.

Geiger planned to employ the 1st and 6th Marine Divisions in the assault, with General del Vane's division on the right or south flank. The choice of these divisions was logical since they were both located in the Solomons and there would be no problem in establishing liaison. The 2d Division, based on Saipan, would be the floating reserve of the army, according to the IIIAC plan. The question then arose regarding what steps would be taken if the Japanese were encountered in strength as

IIIAC advanced eastward across Okinawa, for there was no doubt that an additional division would have to be inserted in the line before the east coast was reached. General Smith took this question up with the Tenth Army commander, who agreed that IIIAC would have first call on the 2d Marine Division. General Watson's division was scheduled to make the feint landings on the southeast coast of Okinawa on L-Day and L plus 1, and it was not contemplated that Geiger would need it before the third day of the operation. The IIIAC staff presented their plan orally to General Buckner on 19 December, when it was approved. According to General Smith, who was present on this occasion, Geiger's staff members "did a very creditable job."

Scheme Of Maneuver

Basically, the scheme of maneuver ashore was designed to attain early use of the airfields so that land-based air supremacy over the target could be gained and held. An additional dividend derived from the capture of the airfields would be their use as staging bases for continuing mass air raids on both Japan and those areas within flying range of Okinawa under enemy control. As in the case of earlier amphibious landings in the Pacific, certain preliminary softening-up steps had to be taken before the main assault was launched. Kerama Retto was to be seized by the 77th Infantry Division (Reinforced) on 26 March 1945, or six days before L-Day. Following the first day of operations in the Kerama Retto and beginning the night of the 26th, Marines of the FMF Amphibious Reconnaissance Battalion were to reconnoiter the reef islets of the island group. First they were to investigate Keise Shima for the presence of enemy troops, and in the following days and nights prior to L-Day, they were to land on Aware Shima, Mae Shima, and Kuro Shima. To support the landing on Okinawa, a field artillery group of XXIV Corps Artillery was to land and be emplaced on Keise Shima prior to L-Day. While these operations were underway, Okinawa would receive increased air and naval gunfire bombardment which would mount in intensity until the first assault waves neared the beaches. At this time, the fire would lift from the beach area and continue inland.

The Army and Marine divisions were to land on the Hagushi beaches, General Geiger's corps on the left. The mouth of the Bishi Gawa marked the beginning of the corps boundary, which roughly followed the course of the river to a point just north of Kadena; here, the line headed almost due east to bisect the island. Once landed north of Hagushi town, the Marine assault divisions were to move rapidly inland, coordinating their advance with that of XXIV Corps. On the Marine left flank was the 6th Division; the 22d Marines on the left and the 4th Marines, less its 2d Battalion in division reserve, on the right. The 29th Marines, the third infantry regiment of the 6th Division, was corps reserve and was to be ready to land on any of the beaches. It was also to be prepared to revert one battalion landing team to the 6th Division on order. General Shepherd's initial mission was the capture of Yontan airfield while protecting the northern flank of the Tenth Army.

General del Vane's division, landing to the right of the 6th, was to assist in the capture of Yontan by quickly seizing the high ground northeast of China. The attack was then to continue, with major emphasis placed on maintaining contact with General Hodge's corps and assisting his advance. The 1st Marine Division scheme of maneuver placed the 5th and 7th Marines in the assault, 7th on the left, and the 1st Marines in division reserve.

Adjoining the 1st Marine Division was to be the 7th Infantry Division, with one regiment in division reserve but under the operational control of XXIV Corps. The other Army assault division was to be 96th, which was to land with two regiments abreast and a third in corps reserve.

Artillery support for the Marines was to come from IIIAC Corps Artillery and those artillery units organic to the divisions. General Geiger's guns were to land on his order to support the attack and, once ashore, corps artillery would coordinate all supporting arms in the Marine sector. XXIV Corps Artillery, less the group on Keise Shima, would land on General Hedge's order and support the attack with long-range interdiction, counterbattery, and harassing fires.

Following the initial landing, operations were designed to isolate the Phase I objective, which consisted of that part of the island lying south of a general line drawn across the Ishikawa Isthmus, through Chimu, and including the Eastern Islands. In order to prevent enemy reinforcement from the north and to fulfill its assignment in Phase I, IIIAC was to gain control of the isthmus as swiftly as possible. To seal off the Japanese in the south, General Hodge's troops were to drive across the island, his right flank units holding a line that ran through Futema to Kuba Saki. Once the central portion of the island had been captured and secured, the direction of attack would be faced to the south and continued until all of the objectives of the first phase had been achieved.

Phase II, the seizure of northern Okinawa and the capture of Ie Shima, was to be executed with Tenth Army troops locally available when Buckner was satisfied that Phase I had been accomplished. The first major military objective in the north was Motobu Peninsula, which was to be taken by means of simultaneously launched attacks from sea and land. Once the peninsula had been gained, a shore-to-shore assault would be made against Ie Shima. The end of Phase II would be signalled when the rest of northern Okinawa had been captured. While higher echelon air planning for ICEBERG detailed both strategic and tactical missions, the Tenth Army was more immediately concerned with the latter. Carrier-based tactical aviation, aboard the TF 52 escort carrier group (TG 52.1, Rear Admiral Calvin T. Durgin), was to provide the invasion force with air support until General Mulcahy's squadrons were established ashore and could take over. At this time, TAF would also be responsible for overall air defense.

When this responsibility was assumed, TAF operations would be based on the following order of priority: (1) attainment of air superiority by annihilation of enemy aircraft in the air and on the ground, and destruction of enemy air installations; (2) interdiction and destruction of enemy troop and supply movements immediately within or heading towards the target area; and (3) execution of combined air-ground attacks on specific frontline objectives. The importance of the first priority lay in Tenth Army recognition of the yet-existing Japanese air strength and the threat it posed to the invasion force.

As soon as Air Defense Command fighter squadrons were established ashore on captured airfields, they were to begin fulfilling their assigned missions. From these fields, ADC was to provide air defense to ground units on the island and naval forces in its environs. Combat air patrols, close air support, and other related flight missions were considered the means by which the defense was to be maintained. Although it was a function of ADC, close air support is not normally a part of air defense; it is more closely associated with a ground offensive concept. Despite this fact, however, Okinawa's terrain and the nature of the Japanese defenses were to provide Marine aviators of the Air Defense Command with ample opportunities to display close air support techniques born of experience accumulated in earlier Pacific campaigns.

Logistic Support Planning

Fortunately for those preparing ICEBERG, much in the logistical plans for the cancelled Formosa operation could be salvaged and adapted for the invasion of Okinawa with but few changes. Without competent logistics planning of the highest order, and utilization of a resupply and shipping support schedule designed to function with clockwork precision, the target date for the Okinawa operation could not have been met. This would have caused all related planned strategy to have been either nullified or advanced to a later date. The logistics plan for Okinawa "was the most elaborate one of its kind developed during World War II, involving prearranged movement of both assault and cargo shipping over vast ocean distances." The plan required establishment of a 6,000-mile-long supply line, stretching across the Pacific, with 11 different ports-of-call, to support the mounting of 182,821 troops encumbered with some 746,850 measurement tons of cargo loaded into 434 assault transports and landing ships.

A great limitation imposed upon preinvasion logistical planning was the shortage of shipping and the delay in the return from the Philippines of the vessels which were to be used for Okinawa. Seeking a solution to lift and timetable problems was not the only concern of the Tenth Army logistics staff, "for the mere loading of more ships led only to congestion at the receiving end unless the development of unloading facilities kept pace."

It had been decided that the Hagushi beaches were sufficiently large to handle the supply tonnage required by the assault echelon of two corps and their support troops; however, it was impossible to prophesy exactly how soon after the landings the beachhead would be secured and the advance continued inland, or how soon thereafter base development could begin and the supplies for this aspect of Phase I would be required and available. Nor was it possible to forecast the possibility that Phase II would be completed before the accomplishment of Phase I. Nonetheless, estimates of troop progress had to be made in order to prepare a logistics plan at all.

The main features of the ICEBERG logistics plan required an initial supply level to be taken to Okinawa by the assault troops who were mounted at such distantly scattered points as Leyte, Guadalcanal, Espiritu Santo, Banika, Pavuvu, Saipan, Eniwetok, Oahu, and the west coast of the United States. Upon completion of the assault phase of the landing, a staggered series of supply shipments would replenish the Tenth Army in accordance with a schedule established earlier. This timetable had been based on the estimated time required to conduct combat operations ashore and, in turn, on how quickly the beach and port capacity could be expanded.

Beginning on 20 February 1945, ICEBERG replenishments were to leave the west coast every 10 days for regulating points at Ulithi, Eniwetok, and Saipan, the first shipments to arrive at each place on L minus 5 (27 March). The supplies would remain at these points until they were called-up by General Buckner. It was planned to continue these automatic resupply shipments for a period of 210 days beyond L-Day. The Tenth Army was also to have emergency reserves located at Saipan, Tinian, and Guam. The prediction of supply requirements depended upon completed tactical plans, a firm troop basis, and other necessary items of information which either were nonexistent or had not yet been made available to the logistics planners. Adding to the logistics dilemma was the factor of time, for it took 120 days for supplies to be requisitioned, procured, and shipped from the Pacific Coast of the United States to the objective.

To facilitate the preparation and shipment of resupply items in accordance with the scheduling of the various invasion echelons, Army commanders established a standard unit of supply, or "block requisitions," tailored specifically to the organization of each of the support and assault elements. The composition of the individual block requisition was determined by estimating the logistic support required by a particular unit for a given number of days regardless of the combat situation.

In contrast to this approach, Marine supply agencies, drawing on their experience, felt that the combat situation as envisioned in the planning stages should govern the nature of the supplies requisitioned, and the number, types, and frequency of shipments. Tenth Army considered the Marine system to be more flexible than the Army's because the requisitioning agencies were better able to make the several automatic resupply shipments conform to their view of how the campaign would progress.

Each service was responsible for initial support of its own elements in the Okinawa task force, with the exception of troops mounting in the South and Southwest Pacific. Area commanders there would be charged with logistical support of units assigned to ICEBERG. After the landing had been accomplished, and when directed by Admiral Turner, Island Command would take over as the Tenth Army central support agency charged with funneling supplies to all of the assault forces.

Early in January it became obvious that ICEBERG had been allocated insufficient shipping to accomplish the tactical mission, to support base development, and to lift to the target those air units which were to be committed early in the campaign. An inadequate transport quota for engineer units, whose services would be needed in the early development of airfields, roads, and waterfront facilities, was improved slightly by scheduling the immediate return of assault LSTS to Saipan after the initial landings to shuttle eight naval construction battalions (Seabees) to the target. In the same manner, other LSTs would be sent to Leyte to pick up any XXIV Corps equipment not carried in assault shipping. Of the overall inadequate shipping situation and its effect on the combat divisions, the former G-4 of the Tenth Army recalled that, if needed, ICEBERG was to get all shipping available in the Pacific, because "the amount of assault shipping assigned for the operation was far below that required to properly lift the assault elements of the Tenth Army. This resulted in [the Tenth Army being given] authority to modify Combat Loading Doctrine so that the most essential equipment and supplies could accompany the assault echelon. Additional items that should have been in the assault echelon were loaded in a subsequent shipping echelon."

The overall assault lift was augmented by other means also. Vessels to be used for the Luzon and Iwo Jima landings were made available later for Okinawa through adherence to a stringently monitored and thoroughly regulated shipping schedule. Additional space for Tenth Army troops was gained by reducing the tonnage requirements of IIIAC, substantially at the expense of the 2d Marine Division. It was reasoned that since the division was not going to be committed immediately, it could acquire whatever additional shipping it needed within a short time following the initial assault. Further lift capacity was gained by loading landing ships to their rated limits, by the addition to the invasion flotilla of newly constructed attack transports

(APAs) with greater cargo-carrying characteristics, and by an increased allocation of landing ships, tank, (LSTs) and landing ships, medium (LSMs).

The shipping allocation for the garrison forces was governed by the estimated capacity of Okinawan beach and port unloading facilities. Past experience, however, resolved the size of the lift necessary to transport an assault echelon of three reinforced Marine divisions, three reinforced Army divisions, a Marine amphibious corps headquarters and corps troops, and an Army corps headquarters and corps troops. Thus, the required assault tonnage was a firm figure from the beginning and was deducted from that allotted to the ICEBERG forces overall. The remainder was assigned as the lift for Tenth Army support troops, which included air, naval, and airfield construction units.

After the Marianas and Palau operations, it was found that one transport group (12 APAs and 3 cargo ships, attack (AKAs)), made up of three transport divisions, had sufficient lift capacity for a combat-loaded reinforced infantry division. For the ICEBERG lift, however, a new shipping echelon, the transport squadron (TransRon) was formed to carry a proportionate share of assault forces, corps troops, and elements from corps and army headquarters. The TransRon was nothing but the old transport group augmented by three APAs and three AKAs. Each transron was to be accompanied by one APH, which was a troop transport specially rigged as a hospital and equipped to treat casualties and then evacuate them from the battle zone. There were to be six hospital ships (AHs) assigned to ICEBERG; one was to be on station L minus 5 with the Kerama Retto invasion group, three were assigned to the main attack forces and were to arrive off Hagushi on L plus 1, while the other two were scheduled to reach Okinawa three days later.

Improved casualty evacuation was planned for this invasion by assigning four hospital landing ships (LST(H)s) to each of the two naval attack forces in the major assault. Assigned to each vessel was a naval medical officer who functioned as an evacuation control officer and, as such, was responsible for screening the wounded as they arrived, giving treatment and classifying them with reference to their estimated recovery time, and transferring the casualties in accordance with the provisions of a system related to their recovery classification. Accordingly, hospital ships would evacuate those men wounded seriously enough to require hospitalization for two months or more. Casualties requiring treatment for a minimum of two and a maximum of eight weeks would be evacuated in APHs during the initial assault phase and, after that, would receive further treatment in hospitals established on Okinawa. Those men who could be returned to duty within two weeks after being wounded would be treated and held in the hospital transports or landing ships until they had fully recovered or until the land-based hospitals had been established.

The LST(H)s were to remain on station until released by Admiral Turner, at which time the medical officers aboard would land and assign casualties directly to the ships from aid stations set up on the beaches. When General Buckner assumed command ashore, he would become responsible for the establishment and administration of medical services on the island, and for air evacuation of casualties, when airfields became operational.

The equipment and supplies to be taken to Okinawa by the corps and the divisions had been specifically designated by Tenth Army order. After cargo space in assigned shipping had been allocated to this material, any other available space would be filled by additional items which the corps and division commanders had decided the troops could carry. Logistical planning on the division level was influenced by the supposition that the beaches would be heavily defended and that the inland advance stubbornly resisted. As a result, only "hot cargo," predetermined blocks of high-priority supplies, was to be landed on L-Day. Included in a block of cargo were one CinCPOA unit of fire for all weapons and rations and water for one day. Moreover, all organic division motor transport would be taken to the target in available shipping space because the prospect of prolonged operations over a relatively large land mass envisioned wide-spread use of vehicles. To assist in Marine logistical planning and preparations, Fleet Marine Force, Pacific, established the 2d Field Service Command on Guadalcanal. Here relatively close liaison could be maintained with Marine ICEBERG elements mounting from the Solomons. This service command was empowered to coordinate the efforts of the supply agencies of both the 1st and 6th Marine Divisions and to deal with Army and Navy sources of supply directly. In the same manner, the Marianas-based 1st Field Service Command assisted the 2d Marine Division. Re-equipment of General del Vane's division on Pavuvu was relatively simple since its primary supply source, the 4th Base Depot, under the 2d Field Service Command, was on the other major island in the Russells, Banika. General Shepherd's division experienced some difficulties, however, because its supply source was a transfer rather than a stocking agency and had to obtain its requisitioned items from the 4th Base Depot. As a result of the cumbersome and time-consuming administrative procedures involved in processing requisitions through the several service echelons in the area, the 6th Division experienced many delays in the delivery of much of its needed equipment and supplies. Both assault divisions, however, embarked for the target with but few shortages, none of which affected combat readiness and efficiency.

By the time that the TAF logistics section had been activated, AirFMFPac had already issued warning orders and was in the process of preparing subordinate units for the impending campaign. The basis for logistic support of Marine aviation units was different, in certain ways, from that of Marine ground elements. While items peculiar to the Marine Corps were drawn by both ground and air units from the same sources, all technical aviation materiel was received through Navy supply channels or, in some cases, from the Army. Since this was the case, the TAF logistics staff established liaison with representatives of Commander, Aircraft, Pacific Fleet (ComAirPac), the agency responsible for fulfilling the fuel and installation requirements at the Okinawa air fields the TAF units were to occupy. The supply section of Commander, Naval Air Bases, Okinawa (ComNABS) was made the ComAirPac type command logistics representative for these matters. All other supply requirements were to be handled by the supply section of the Navy's Pacific service command. Liaison was also established with Army Air Forces logistics representatives to determine the nature and extent of support required by Army elements in General Mulcahy's command. Arrangements were then made to obtain special combat clothing and equipment for the AAF personnel to be assigned to TAF. Based upon the latter's recommendations, automatic resupply shipments for the Army squadrons were adjusted to coincide with the schedule established for the Marines.

The organization and general administration of the supply system on Okinawa was to be an Island Command function, in which it would receive and distribute Tenth Army supplies. The Marine groups in TAF, however, would support their own squadrons and would draw Marine Corps supplies from the 2d Wing or other designated Marine sources. Air base commanders would provide aviation fuel and lubricants to squadrons operating from their strips; all technical aviation supplies were to be requisitioned through ComNABS, Okinawa.

Service units organic to the AAF fighter and bombardment groups would support the flying squadrons of each. All supplies other than the technical items peculiar to AAF planes would be requisitioned from sources designated by the Island Commander. Until an Air Service Command Depot was established on Okinawa, the one at Guam would supply the remainder.

Base Development And Military Government Planning

A second logistic mission given to ICEBERG, separate yet related to the assault effort, was the immediate development of Okinawa as an advanced air and fleet base. In order to support all of the aircraft assigned to the invasion, eight airfields and one seaplane base were to be built almost immediately and during the later phases of the operation this number would be increased. Also, two ports were to be developed — one, Nakagusuku Wan, by the Navy and the other, Naha harbor, by the Army. Since Okinawa was to serve merely as a staging base for final operations against Japan, it was not contemplated that the installations on the island were to be of permanent construction. Ie Shima was included in the base development program as the island was to hold four airfields and to garrison ground and antiaircraft artillery defense troops. Base development would proceed right on the heels of the assault troops as two of Okinawa's airfields were to be seized, improved, and made operational by L plus 5, while two more fields were to be available by L plus 20. The preparation of Okinawa as a mounting and staging point was to be undertaken concurrently. First priority was given the early development and activation of airfields; next in order of importance was the construction of bulk fuel storage facilities; and the third most important matter was the development of waterfront installations. Reflecting the urgency of these tasks, every effort was made to schedule the shipments of supplies required to support base improvement so that they would arrive at the island when they were needed. Accordingly, garrison troops and the materials which they were to employ were to arrive in 17 successive echelons. The timing of their arrival was governed not only by the preplanned work schedule but also by the projected unloading capacity of the captured beaches. To establish this schedule, a series of echelonment conferences were held between the staffs of the Tenth Army and the different type commanders who were furnishing troops for the operation. In any large amphibious operation, it is neither possible nor feasible, because of shipping limitations, to transport to the target in the assault convoy both those troops required to undertake the campaign to its end and the troops, equipment, and supplies required to develop the captured base. Even if all required shipping had been made available for an operation of the size of Okinawa, it would have been patently undesirable to schedule the simultaneous arrival at the target of both assault and garrison troops. Until the assault forces had landed, unloaded their shipping, and gained enough room on the beaches for the landing of the garrison elements and equipment, the shipping in which garrison troops were embarked would have had to lie off Okinawa, where it would have been vulnerable to enemy submarines and aircraft. For these reasons, it was imperative that echelonment plans covering the movement of thousands of assault, service, and construction troops had to be precise.

In addition to its other functions, Island Command was also to establish a military government on Okinawa. Since this was to be the first Pacific operation in which large numbers of enemy civilians would be encountered by combat troops, it was expected that the island would serve as a valuable testing ground of civil affairs and military government procedures which would be applied later when Japan itself was occupied.

In 1943, the JCS gave the Navy basic responsibility for establishing military government on certain outlying islands of the Japanese Empire, once they had been captured. Included in this group were the Ryukyus. Because the Tenth Army would be in overall control of the Okinawa land campaign, Admiral Nimitz believed that General Buckner should be responsible for military government on the island. Accordingly, once the War Department concurred in this transfer of authority, CinCPOA was able to get the 1943 JCS order reversed.

Because of its European commitments, the Army was unable to furnish all of the civil affairs personnel needed to round out the entire Tenth Army military government component. Therefore, the Navy supplied Brigadier General William E. Crist's command with naval officer and enlisted personnel so that Military Government would have well-balanced teams.

Direct naval participation in military government planning for Okinawa began in July 1944, when work was begun in New York City by the research staff of the Chief of Naval Operations' military government section. The pooled efforts of the staff resulted in the Civil Affairs Handbook for the Ryukyu Islands, a publication which proved to be of inestimable value to Tenth Army civil affairs administrators during both the ICEBERG planning phase and the rehabilitation period after Okinawa had been secured. The ICEBERG joint staff study originally anticipated that, within the Okinawan population to come under Tenth Army control, a small element would be "antipathetic" and would have to be "placed under detainment pending screening and probable internment." No figures were available to determine how many mainland Japanese civilians on Okinawa might possibly be captured, but preparations had to be made for the construction of an internment camp whose facilities were flexible enough to provide for upwards of 10,000 island natives and Japanese civilian internees. It was expected that by L plus 40 this number would skyrocket to an approximate total of 306,000 captured civilians, whose food, clothing, and housing would have to come from captured stocks of salvageable material, since there was no room aboard assault ships for supplies of this nature. By the time ICEBERG had reached the garrison phase, 12 military government camps were to be in operation, each unit staffed and equipped to handle 2,500-10,000 civilians.

Assigned to General Crist's jointly staffed military government section were such varied Army and Navy units as a military police battalion, a truck company, 20 Navy dispensaries, and 6 Navy hospital units. In addition to these and some purely administrative elements, 350 officer and 890 enlisted civil affairs personnel were organized into four types of teams, each of which had been tailored for specific functions. One of the teams was assigned to each of the assault divisions and, after landing, was to conduct preliminary reconnaissance missions relating to military government as the attack advanced. Teams in another group, attached to the two corps and all divisions also, were to take charge of civil affairs behind the front lines as civilians were encountered by the combat forces. A third type of team was made up of refugee camp administrators, while in the fourth category there were six teams, each of which was to take charge of one of the six military government districts into which Okinawa was to be divided.

The Chief Military Government Officer was to be directly subordinate to the Island Commander and would function as his deputy. The importance of this close relationship and the emphasis placed on intensive civil affairs planning was justified later during the campaign, when, by 30 April, there were approximately 125,000 civilians under military government jurisdiction on Okinawa. This figure climbed steadily following this date, reached 147,829 by 31 May, 172,670 by 15 June, and totaled 261,115 on 30 June.

Intelligence Planning

In October 1944, the statement that "information as to enemy defensive installations on Okinawa Jima is meager," was indisputable. Despite the early lack of information concerning the island, the various intelligence gathering and processing agencies in the Pacific, as well as those in the United States, began to sift through available material and soon were able to clarify the enemy situation for ICEBERG forces. In keeping with the established principle of coordinated planning, the corporate activities of all intelligence agencies in the various Pacific commands quickly resulted in the production of urgently needed basic intelligence. Currently valid military information of the Japanese situation was difficult to obtain because of the location of Okinawa within the Empire's well-protected, strategic, inner defense line. For the most part, captured documents, interrogations of prisoners as well as of former island inhabitants, and old Japanese publications provided the basis for the intelligence estimates initially issued. In addition, the Navy was able to make use of both captured and previously available hydrographic charts for navigational studies of the waters surrounding Okinawa.

For a terrain study, a determination of the location and nature of enemy defenses, and an estimate of enemy strength, most of the data at hand was inadequate and an aerial photographic mission over the target had to be laid on. In conjunction with other information of the enemy received right up to L-Day, the thorough interpretation and evaluation of these photographs enabled Tenth Army to issue detailed intelligence studies which contained an accurate estimate of the Japanese situation.

Aerial photos were required also for use in the production of a map of the target. It was difficult to obtain adequate photographic coverage at first because of the distance of Okinawa from the closest Allied air base, some 1,200 nautical miles. This factor limited the conduct of such missions to either carrier aircraft, whose ships could carry them close to the target, or B-29s. Other obstacles to the amassing of a complete intelligence picture of Okinawa were the notoriously poor weather over the target, the vastness of the land mass to be photographed, and the schedule of carrier strikes against the target—few of which were timed to coincide with immediate Tenth Army intelligence requirements.

On 29 September 1944, the first ICEBERG photographic mission was flown by B-29s. While they covered all of Okinawa, and the outlying islands to a degree, the results of this flight were limited by clouds which obscured about half of the area photographed, mainly the northern portion of the major island. Because of this inadequate photo coverage, the first map produced and distributed had many blank portions in which there was little or no topographic detailing. Modifications of this first map were made later in the campaign, when captured Japanese maps provided more thorough contouring information. During the first fast-carrier strikes on Okinawa Gunto of 10 October 1944, large scale vertical and oblique aerial photographs were acquired, giving 90 percent coverage of the area. From 29 September 1944 to 28 March 1945, a total of 224 photo-reconnaissance sorties were flown over the target. Information gained from these photographs was collated and analyzed, and the resultant intelligence summaries were distributed to Tenth Army units.

In the week preceding L-Day, escort carrier-based photographic aircraft flew daily missions over the island. Careful interpretation of the photos thus obtained permitted bomb damage assessments and, at the same time, comparison of these photos with ones taken earlier enabled the interpreters to locate many enemy installations previously concealed by effective camouflage. From a close study of successive sorties, it was possible to determine each displacement of the enemy's defensive positions, to hazard guesses of his relative strength, and to compile a preliminary target information list for distribution to artillery units.

After L-Day and while the fighting was still in progress, the island was completely rephotographed, the results of which enabled a more accurate map to be printed and distributed. A scale of 1:25,000 was used for the basic map originally issued, from which maps of the initial zones of action, scaled at 1:10,000, were produced for the use of the lower echelon assault units. At the same time, smaller scale maps were reproduced for use as road maps in traffic control planning.

The Tenth Army made rubber relief maps on a scale of 1:10,000, which were issued to General Geiger's troops in sufficient quantity to permit distribution down to and including assault battalions. The mapping sections of IIIAC, and the 1st and 6th Marine Divisions worked together to produce plastic terrain models of the corps zone of action. Made to a scale of 1:5,000 and constructed with a 2:1 vertical exaggeration, these models facilitated the briefing of commanders and their troops for the prospective operation. Wholesale distribution of these relief models was made soon after the troops embarked for the target, at which time some 600 copies of a 1:5,000 map of the landing beaches, specially prepared by the 1st Marine Division, were issued to its assault units. To supplement aerial photographs, the USS *Swordfish*, a specially equipped submarine, was dispatched to Okinawa from Pearl Harbor on 22 December 1944 with the mission of photographing Okinawa's beaches and Japanese defensive installations on the island coasts. After making her last known radio transmission on 3 January 1945, the submarine was never heard from again and was reported missing. As a result, no beach photographs were taken before L-Day for, as succinctly stated in the TF 51 AR, "no information from submarine reconnaissance was available."

In October 1944, enemy strength on Okinawa was set at 48,600. It was estimated that two well-trained and experienced infantry divisions, and a tank regiment, comprised the major defense force on the island. At this time, it was recognized that an additional threat to the landings was posed by the size of the civilian population located in southern Okinawa. This manpower potential of more than 300,000 individuals would swell the enemy strength figure if they were used to form a home guard or militia, or to conduct guerrilla activities. In January 1945, the Tenth Army estimate assumed that the Japanese reinforcement capability could increase the regular force figure to 66,000 by L-Day, at which time enemy defense forces on Okinawa would be two and a half infantry divisions. If the enemy exerted his maximum reinforcement capability, he could then oppose the landing with four infantry divisions constituting the principal combat elements of the defense. Total Japanese strength would then be 87,000 men.

All possible Japanese courses of action were considered, and troop dispositions for each course were analyzed in light of what was known of current Japanese tactical doctrine and its evolution to date. All indications pointed to the fact that the enemy would most likely organize the southern third of Okinawa for a defense in depth while the bulk of his troops were withheld as a mobile reserve. This course of action would present a potentially more dangerous situation to the landing force than would the more commonly experienced alternative of a determined defense of the beaches.

An interpretation of aerial photographs in February revealed that the enemy force on Okinawa comprised two infantry divisions and an independent mixed brigade, service and support troop reinforcements for the infantry, all totaling an estimated 56,000-58,000 men. It also appeared that, while the far northern sector was defended by a single battalion only, the main force was disposed in the south in the projected XXIV Corps area. In the III Amphibious Corps zone of action, it was estimated that two infantry regiments defended. Conceivably, these six or seven thousand men could be reinforced by local auxiliaries.

While the small garrison in the north was given the capability of mounting counterattacks against the invader left flank, it was expected that the most violent enemy reaction would come from the heavily defended south, on the XXIV Corps' right flank, where the Japanese mobile reserve would be maintained in considerable strength. It was anticipated that, as soon as the Japanese had appraised the landing force's dispositions, a counteroffensive in force would be mounted by the enemy reserve. The estimate of Japanese strength was again revised in mid-February, this time downwards to 37,500-39,500, when information was received that a full division had been withdrawn from Okinawa. In view of this reduction, and supplemented by indications that the enemy was concentrating in the Nakagusuku Bay area, it was presumed that the two Marine divisions would be opposed in their zones by no more than one infantry regiment deployed in position, and that the total number of Japanese troops in the overall sector would be more than 10,000.

This numbers guessing game continued when, a month later, the estimate of Japanese defense forces was revised upwards to 64,000. It appeared that the enemy had been able to reinforce the garrison with an understrength infantry division as well as with some miscellaneous units of unknown origin, in all about 20,000 men. It was believed that an additional force of 4,000-6,000 men had arrived in March, having been lifted by shipping which successfully evaded the Allied blockade. The Tenth Army assumed that, if the March enemy reinforcements were the advance elements of another division, it was reasonable to assume further that by 1 April the landing force would be opposed by at least 75,000 men. In the week preceding L-Day, while the assault elements sortied for the target, still another estimate of enemy strength in the IIIAC zone was issued. In this supplementary revision., it was stated that the principal Japanese opposition now would come from two reinforced infantry regiments with a strength of 16,000 men.

Air and naval capabilities assigned to the Japanese remained relatively unchanged all during the planning phases of ICEBERG, At all times it was expected that the enemy would be capable of mounting heavy and repeated air attacks against invasion shipping. It was expected that this vigorous air effort would include continued employment and intensification of the suicide bombing tactics which first had appeared during the invasion of Leyte in October 1944. The Japanese were credited with an air strength of approximately 3,000 planes which were based within range and capable of blunting the Okinawa landing. Along with this air capability, the enemy was believed able to mount an airborne counterattack, for "as air action is practically the only assistance he can give the Okinawa garrison from outside [the island], he may expend considerable aircraft and endeavor to land several thousand troops within our beachhead."

It was known that the Japanese had suicide motor torpedo boat units at Okinawa and it was assumed that midget submarines were based there also. Added to the possible tactical employment of these suicide organizations was the potential use of suicide swimmers whose mission was also disruption of the invasion fleet at anchor off the objective. Although the Japanese Navy was a mere shadow of its former self, it still retained operational forces strong enough to pose a threat to the landing's success. For that reason, it was deemed necessary to maintain a strong surface cover at the objective. While the southern part of Okinawa was ideally suited for the tactical use of tanks, the enemy was not given an armored capability. This was because the relation of estimated tank strength to the total estimated garrison strength was too low, and it was not felt that this support arm would offer any great opposition. Three months after Admiral Nimitz had received the JCS directive for Okinawa's invasion, General Buckner issued the initial operation order setting the ICEBERG juggernaut's wheels into motion. During the course of this planning period, each Tenth Army general and special staff section prepared that portion of the operation order for which it was responsible while maintaining liaison with the subordinate units which were preparing to put words into action. Although most of the ICEBERG assault, support, and garrison forces did not issue their own operation orders until January 1945, warning orders had already alerted them to the impending invasion.

Chapter 3. Assault Preparations

Training And Rehearsals
The Pacific-wide dispersion of troops and shipping assigned to ICEBERG prevented the Tenth Army from conducting either training or rehearsals as a cohesive unit. Because of the vast distances separating General Buckner and his corps and division commanders, the latter were invested with the responsibility for training their respective organizations along the lines of Tenth Army directives. With these orders as a guide, all Marine units committed to the operation were trained under the supervision of FMFPac. Assault preparations of ICEBERG Army divisions were hindered by the limited time available for their rehabilitation, reorganization, and training. This was especially true in the case of XXIV Corps units already in combat in the Philippines. Many of the garrison and service units which were to be attached to the various assault forces were also handicapped by the time factor because they, too, were either fighting or heavily committed in support of operations in the Philippines. In order that Tenth Army staff planners could better evaluate the combat readiness of all organizations within the command, each of General Buckner's commanders submitted a monthly training status report to ICEBERG headquarters on Oahu. Since the reports lacked what an inspection at first-hand could provide, Buckner and some of his principal staff officers made a series of flying trips to each of the corps and divisions. These personal visits at the end of January 1945 "did much to weld the far-flung units of the Tenth Army into a unified whole." One determinant forcing the postponement of the Formosa-South China invasion in favor of the Okinawa assault had been the shortage of service and support troops, a shortage that still existed when

the Tenth Army began its final training and rehearsal phases. Many of these specialist units were slated to reinforce corps and divisions for the assault and then to augment Island Command during the initial base development. Because they were too deeply involved otherwise, often with primary missions related to the build-up for the operation, the support troops could not train with the assault units they were to reinforce. The time borrowed for training would seriously disrupt the mounting and staging efforts for ICEBERG. Nevertheless, support unit commanders carried out adequate individual weapons' qualification and physical conditioning programs which met Tenth Army training requirements. Although they were released to General Buckner's control only a few days before mounting for the target, a number of garrison organizations were able to conduct limited training with the combat outfit to which they were attached.

The major assault components of the Tenth Army were battle-experienced for the most part, but they needed to undertake an intensive training schedule in order to bring veterans and newly absorbed replacements alike to peak combat efficiency. To accomplish this task, Army and Marine Corps units in the South Pacific, and the 2d Marine Division on Saipan, conducted extensive programs which fulfilled the training requirements stipulated by General Buckner's directives. General Hedge's XXIV Corps, however, was engaged in operations on Leyte, and his divisions were not released to Tenth Army by General MacArthur until 10 February 1945, just two months before L-Day.

After the extended period of bitter fighting in the Philippines, however, the combat units slated for ICEBERG were understrength. General Hodge's problems were further aggravated when his infantry divisions were required to furnish the Leyte Base Command6 with large working parties as soon as the troops returned from mopping-up operations at the front. The servicing, crating, and loading of organic division equipment siphoned off the services of other infantrymen as well as making it impossible to impose a major training program on any of the divisions. Finally, as one command reported, the "deterioration of the physical and mental condition of combat personnel after 110 days of continuous contact with the enemy made it plain that rigorous field training in the wet and muddy terrain would prove more detrimental than beneficial." Besides undertaking the many other incidental duties preparatory to mounting for Okinawa from Leyte, some Army units had to construct their own camps and make their own billeting arrangements as soon as they arrived in the rear area from the front lines. What little time was available to the Southern Landing Force before L-Day was divided between training in small-unit tactics and practice for breaching and scaling operations, in anticipation of the conditions to be found at Okinawa beaches. Because of the large influx of raw replacements into the divisions, great emphasis was placed on developing the teamwork of riflemen and their supporting weapons.

Of the three divisions in XXIV Corps, the 96th was the most fortunate in that some of its new troops arrived during mopping-up stages on Leyte. At that time, the replacements were given an opportunity to take an "active part in combat and reconnaissance patrols, gaining valuable battle indoctrination through physical contact and skirmishes with small isolated groups of Japanese."

According to the Tenth Army Marine Deputy Chief of Staff, General Smith: "The conditions of the Army divisions on Leyte gave General Buckner considerable concern. This was not the fault of the divisions; they were excellent divisions. However, they had been in action on Leyte for three months and two of the divisions were still engaged in active operations. The divisions were understrength and adequate replacements were not in sight. There were [numerous men suffering from] dysentery and skin infections. Living conditions were very bad. A considerable number of combat troops had been diverted to Luzon and converted into service troops. There was some doubt as to whether reequipment could be effected in time."

The fighting record of the XXIV Corps on Okinawa indicates how well it overcame great obstacles in preparing for its ordeal. Once they had reconstituted their combat organizations, trained their fresh replacements, and attended to the many details incident to mounting for the target, the veteran units of this corps were able to give good accounts of themselves against the enemy.

In the South Pacific and the Marianas, Tenth Army units were not as heavily committed as the units of the Southern Landing Force, and completed a more comprehensive training program.

The 27th Infantry Division, ICEBERG floating reserve, arrived at Espiritu Santo in the New Hebrides from Saipan during September and October 1944. The division was undivided in its opinion that this base was a "hellhole" unfitted for the division's rehabilitation and training because of the island's torrid climate, its topography, and lush, tropical vegetation. Upon receipt of advance information that it was to take part in the Okinawa assault, the 27th instituted an accelerated combat training program which was calculated to qualify it, by 30 January 1945, for a period of prolonged operations against the enemy. Launched on 23 October, the level of the program advanced progressively from individual schooling to combined company and battalion exercises and, finally, to a two-week stretch of regimental combat team (RCT)11 maneuvers. During this staging period, in which 2,700 replacements arrived and were assigned, the division stressed training for offensive and defensive night operations.

Most Marines in IIIAC assault divisions had recently been in combat, yet their training programs were stringent and comprehensive. Like all other veteran ICEBERG forces, the Marine divisions were confronted with the need to obtain, integrate, and train replacements. Marine training overall emphasized the development of a tank-infantry-artillery team and focused attention on tactical innovations such as the use of the armored amphibian's 75mm howitzer for supplementary artillery support. While other Tenth Army units were required to undertake amphibious training, General Geiger's troops did not have to, since General Buckner considered his Marine divisions eminently qualified in this aspect of warfare.

Following the Peleliu campaign, General del Vane's 1st Marine Division had returned to Pavuvu for rest and rehabilitation. The division was first based on the island in April 1944, arriving there after completion of the New Britain operation. At that time, and with some difficulty, the Guadalcanal and Cape Gloucester veterans converted the overrun coconut groves into some semblance of a habitable cantonment. Because of its small size, Pavuvu was not particularly suited for training as large a unit as a division; its terrain limited the widespread construction of machine gun and mortar firing ranges. All artillery firing had to be conducted on Guadalcanal.

The ranks of the 1st held some 246 officers and 5,600 enlisted Marines who had already served overseas nearly 30 months. Within that time, the division had made three assault landings and it was now to make a fourth. If the division was to go ashore at full strength, it appeared, at first, that it would be necessary for the veterans of Guadalcanal, Cape Gloucester, and Peleliu to fight at Okinawa too. A potentially serious morale problem was alleviated when the division received four replacement drafts by 1 January. These drafts, plus a steady flow of individual replacements, brought officer strength to slightly above the authorized figure and exceeded the authorized enlisted strength figure by more than 10 percent. As a consequence, all eligible enlisted Marines were able to return to the States. At the same time, an extensive leave program was established for officers who, though eligible, could not be spared for rotation. Fifty-three of them were permitted to take 30 days leave in the United States, after which they were to return to Pavuvu. "In addition, six went to Australia and one to New Zealand. Some fifty key enlisted men [eligible for rotation] also elected to take leave in Australia in order that they could continue to serve in the First Marine Division." By the time the division embarked for Okinawa, approximately one-third of its Marines had been in two invasions, one-third had faced the enemy once, and the remainder were men who had seen no combat whatsoever. The majority of the latter were replacements who had arrived at Pavuvu while the 1st was at Peleliu.

As soon as the training cycle of General del Valle's infantry units reached the regimental level and outgrew Pavuvu's facilities, each RCT was rotated to Guadalcanal, about 65 miles to the southeast, for two weeks of more intensive combined-arms training. Special emphasis was given to preparing the division for warfare of a type and on a scale differing in almost every respect from that which it experienced in the tropical jungles of Guadalcanal and New Britain, and on the coral ridges of equatorial Peleliu. As an integral part of a much larger force, this division was to invade, for the first time, a land mass "which contained extensive road nets, large inhabited areas, cities and villages, large numbers of enemy civilians, and types of terrain" not found in the South Pacific. Besides being schooled to fight under the conditions anticipated at Okinawa, the troops were trained to defend against paratroop attack and indoctrinated in the techniques of dealing with hostile civilians.

In commenting on the personnel situation of his regiment during its training period, the former commanding officer of the 11th Marines stated: "The heavy casualties suffered at Peleliu, plus the rotation without immediate replacement of all officers and men with 30 months' service in the Pacific after that battle, posed a severe problem. Only one battalion commander remained of the four who went to Peleliu. There were only eight field officers in the regiment including myself and the [naval gunfire] officer. Fourteen captains with 24 months' Pacific service were allowed a month's leave plus travel time in the United States, and they left Pavuvu at the end of November and were not available for the training maneuver at first. I recall that the 4th Battalion (LtCol L.F. Chapman, Jr.) had only 18 officers present including himself. He had no captains whatever. The other battalions and [regimental headquarters] were in very similar shape. The 3d Battalion had to be completely reorganized due to heavy casualties on Peleliu and was the only one with two field [grade] officers. But it had only about 20 officers of all ranks present." General Shepherd's 6th Marine Division was activated on Guadalcanal in September 1944, and was formed essentially around the 1st Provisional Marine Brigade. This unit had taken part in the Guam invasion and had been withdrawn from that island late in August. The infantry components of this new division were, with a few exceptions, veterans of the Pacific fighting. The 4th Marines was made up of the disbanded Marine raider battalions, whose troops had fought on Guadalcanal, New Georgia, and Bougainvillea; the infantry regiment as a whole had landed on Emirau and

Guam. The 22d Marines had participated in the Eniwetok and Guam campaigns, and the 1st Battalion, 29th Marines had augmented the 2d Marine Division for the Saipan assault. After its relief on Saipan, 1/29 was sent to Guadalcanal to await the arrival from the United States of its two sister battalions, and eventual assignment to the 6th Division.

At the time of the 6th Marine Division activation, the division was some 1,800 men understrength and, as was the case with other IIIAC units, in very few instances did the classification of the replacements received by General Shepherd, correspond to his actual needs. Paralleling other instances, where the composition of stateside-formed replacement drafts did not satisfy critical shortages in specific specialist fields, the 15th Marines was assigned and forced to retrain antiaircraft artillerymen from disbanded defense battalions whose previous experience and training was not considered the same as that needed by field artillerymen.

Most of the men in the 6th Division had fought in at least one campaign, while others were Pacific combat veterans who were now beginning a second tour of overseas duty. The division was based on Guadalcanal, where kunai grass and steaming tropical jungle provided an excellent environment in which General Shepherd's men could fulfill a rugged training schedule. The program began on 1 October and proceeded from small-unit exercises through large-scale combined-arms problems employing battalion landing teams (BLTs) and RCTs; all training culminated in an eight-day division exercise in January 1945. Anticipating how the division was to be employed on Okinawa, General Shepherd emphasized the execution of large-unit maneuvers, swift movement, and rapid troop deployment.

The IIIAC Artillery faced the same replacement retraining problems that plagued the 15th Marines. When the 6th 155mm Howitzer Battalion and the Headquarters Battery, 2d Provisional Field Artillery Group, were formed in October and November 1944, their cadres were withdrawn from existing units of corps artillery. The latter was further drained when 500 combat veterans, mostly valuable noncommissioned officers, were rotated home in November. There were few experienced artillerymen in the group replacing them. At the same time that rehearsals were being conducted for the coming operations, Brigadier General David I. Nimmer's Corps Artillery battalions were forced to conduct training sessions (retraining classes in the case of radar technicians and antiaircraft artillerymen coming from disbanded defense battalions) in order to ensure that all firing battery personnel would be completely familiar with the weapons to which they were newly assigned. Another matter adversely affecting the artillery training program was the delay, until 15 November and 10 December respectively, in the return of the 3d 155mm Howitzer and the 8th 155mm Gun Battalions from the Palaus operation. General Nimmer's organizational and personnel problems were complicated further by the fact that approximately 10 percent of his unit strength joined after active training ended in February, while 78 communicators and 92 field artillerymen did not join until after Corps Artillery had embarked for Okinawa.

VMO-7, the Marine observation squadron assigned to Corps Artillery, did not arrive before General Nimmer's units mounted out, but joined them later at the target. Three days before embarkation, the commanding officer of the 2d Provisional Field Artillery Group joined. Despite these hitches to IIIAC Corps Artillery pre-combat preparations, General Nimmer considered all of his embarked artillery units ready, although "both individual and unit proficiency were not up to the standards that could have been obtained under more favorable circumstances."

As soon as General Geiger's staff began planning for the Marine Corps role in ICEBERG, the commanders of the IIIAC Corps Artillery and the 11th and 15th Marines established liaison with one another in order to coordinate their unit training programs. These senior Marine artillery officers "resolved that in this operation we would take advantage of all previous experience, good and bad, and give a superior performance. Accordingly, great care was given to . . . the ability to rapidly mass fires of all available guns at any critical point."

Artillery training was directed toward attaining this capability. General Nimmer's staff devised and wrote the standard operating procedures to be used by all Marine artillery units assigned to ICEBERG. These procedures established the techniques to be used for requesting and the subsequent delivery of reinforcing fires. During the training period, firing batteries constantly put the new doctrine into practice.

With the exception of the 12th Marines, the 2d Marine Division artillery regiment, all other Marine artillery units in the Tenth Army conducted a combined problem on Guadalcanal, 11-13 January. A majority of the firing missions were spotted by aerial observers. Conditions anticipated on Okinawa were simulated as closely as possible, although the large military population and the consequent profusion of various installations on Guadalcanal necessarily limited the size of the artillery ranges available for the big guns. By the end of the combined problem, when a firing mission was called in, the Marines "were able to have all artillery present, laid and ready to fire in an average of five minutes from the time it was reported." General Watson's 2d Marine Division, reserve for IIIAC and its third major element, was in garrison on Saipan where a division-wide training program was effectively integrated with mopping-up operations against enemy forces remaining at large on the island. More than 8,000 Marine replacements received valuable on-the-job experience routing Japanese holdouts during the first months of the division training program which began 15 September. Saipan's rapid build-up as a supply center and an air base restricted the training efforts of the division, however, and maneuver room and impact areas were soon at a premium.

In the course of his inspection trip to Tenth Army units, General Buckner visited the 2d Marine Division. On the morning of 3 February, he trooped the line of the 8th Marines and then inspected the regimental quarters and galleys. It seemed to General Smith that the men of the 2d Division looked very fit, and that they had made a tremendous impression on the Tenth Army commander. Buckner was particularly impressed with the battalion commanders, and told his deputy chief of staff that "he had never before had the privilege of meeting such an alert group."

A lack of suitable beaches on Saipan confined final division rehearsals to simulated landings only. Because of the indefinite nature of its employment once it had made the feint landings on L-Day and L plus 1, the 2d Division had to select an arbitrary landing scheme of two RCTs abreast for the rehearsal pattern. Bad weather prevented LVT launchings on two days, neither air nor naval gunfire support was available, and, finally, on 19 March—the last day of the exercises—only the naval portion of TG 51.2 (Demonstration Group) was able to participate in the demonstration rehearsal.

On Espiritu Santo, the Tenth Army's other relatively isolated unit—the 27th Infantry Division—conducted rehearsals from 20 to 25 March while its transport squadron was being loaded. This division was in the same position as General

Watson's in that it faced a profusion of potential missions. The rehearsals of both reserve divisions were based, therefore, on a number of hypothetical landing assignments. Satisfactory practice landings were made by all of the other Tenth Army assault divisions. IIIAC rehearsals took place off the Cape Esperance-Doma Cove beaches on Guadalcanal from 2 through 7 March. Although reefs do not exist here, a transfer line was simulated 200 yards from the shore in an attempt to duplicate actual landing conditions in the corps zone on Okinawa. During the six days of rehearsals, Rear Admiral Reifsnider's staff officers made certain that assault wave control was emphasized and that the training of communications elements was intensified at all command levels.

Because naval gunfire and air-support units assigned to ICEBERG were committed elsewhere at this time, the token prelanding bombardment furnished by vessels in the area, and the air support supplied by F6Fs (Hellcats) and TBMs (Avengers), flying in from Henderson Field and nearby carriers, only approximated the tremendous volume of fire to be laid on the Hagushi beaches. Practice landings were made by IIIAC units on 3 March, followed the next day by a critique aboard the TF 53 flagship, USS *Panamint*. Other preliminary landings on the 5th preceded the landing of the entire IIIAC assault echelon on 6 March. Corps and division command posts were set up ashore, a primary communications net was established, and some equipment was unloaded. On 7 March, the reserve regiments—the 1st Marines for the 1st Division and the 29th Marines for the IIIAC—climbed down the nets into invasion craft, which were formed into boat waves, and then landed on the beaches.

General Geiger's corps artillery units did not participate in these final rehearsal exercises except to land battalion, corps, and group headquarters reconnaissance parties. The shortage of time prevented the landing of any of the artillery pieces which were to go ashore at the target.

Nearly 3,000 miles away from Guadalcanal, in the Philippines, assault elements of XXIV Corps conducted rehearsals in Leyte Gulf from the 15th to the 19th of March under the watchful eyes of Admiral Hall and his attack force staff officers. Because the missions assigned XXIV Corps divisions varied so widely, the nature and conduct of their rehearsals tended to reflect this variance.

The 77th Infantry Division was to make the initial ICEBERG assault, the landing on Kerama Retto. In order to familiarize the troops with conditions at their impending target, practice landings were made in southeastern Leyte's Hinunangan Bay on islands that closely resembled some of those in the Keramas. For two days, 14 and 15 March, adverse weather conditions and heavy swells prevented any landings at all, but adherence to any firm rehearsal schedule was not considered necessary since the mission of the 77th involved several landings independent of each other.

Poor weather on the 15th forced the cancellation of a planned rehearsal for the Ie Shima invasion, while only the division reserve (307th Infantry) made any practice landings on the 16th. Although General Bruce was satisfied with the rehearsals since "all elements scheduled for a specific mission satisfactorily executed a close approximation of their mission, Admiral Kiland was not so confident. The Western Islands Attack Group Commander felt that "considering the complexity of the operation and the relative inexperience of naval personnel involved, the curtailment of these exercises by weather conditions made the training provided entirely inadequate." On 16 March, the 7th and 96th Divisions landed under perfect weather conditions and on the 18th held unit critiques, in which certain basic discrepancies and difficulties discovered in the first exercise were ironed out. The following day, the two divisions landed again. A high-level critique was held on the 21st for the major Army and Navy commanders on Admiral Hall's flagship, USS *Teton*. Also present were Admiral Turner and General Buckner. At this time, all of the XXIV Corps rehearsals were evaluated, and efforts were made to ensure that the actual landing would be better coordinated.

As the normal duties of most of the flying squadrons assigned to TAF constituted their combat training, and since they would not begin operations at Okinawa until after the landing, when the airfields were ready, they were not required to conduct rehearsals for ICEBERG. TAF ground personnel scheduled to travel to the target with the assault echelon participated in the landing rehearsals that were held at Guadalcanal and Leyte. Their troop training, for the most part, was conducted aboard ship en route to the staging areas, and consisted of familiarization lectures about the enemy, his tactics, and his equipment.

Like the other Okinawa-bound Tenth Army units mounting from Pearl Harbor, Island Command troops conducted individual and unit training programs which consisted of specialist as well as combat subjects. The Island Command assault echelon was composed chiefly of headquarters personnel who were to initiate the base development plan as soon as practicable after the landing. Within this echelon also were shore party, ordnance, ammunition, supply, signal, quartermaster, truck, and water transportation units, whose support services would be required immediately after the initial assault.

At Fort Oral, California, officers to staff military government teams began assembling in late December 1944. A number of these officers had already received approximately three months of military government training at either Princeton or Columbia Universities. In California and at the staging areas where they joined the assault forces., these Army and Navy officers received instructions pertinent to the ICEBERG military government plan. Many in the Navy enlisted component in the military government section had never received any specialized civil affairs training before they arrived at Fort Oral, where they were assembled just in time to embark with the teams to which they were assigned.

By 1945, the roll-up of enemy positions in the Pacific had progressed to the point where some Tenth Army units were able to mount and stage on the threshold of Japan. XXIV Corps prepared for Okinawa in the Leyte Gulf area, only 1,000 miles from the Ryukyus, while in the Marianas, just slightly farther away from the target, other ICEBERG forces made ready for the attack. Northern Attack Force units, however, had a considerably longer journey to the Ryukyus as they prepared in the Solomons.

Mounting And Staging The Assault

Each attack force of the Joint Expeditionary Force was organized differently for loading, movement, and unloading at the target. The nine transport divisions in the three transrons of Admiral Hall's Southern Attack Force were reorganized and expanded to number 11 transport divisions (transdivs). Assigned to these two additional transdivs were those ships slated to lift XXIV Corps troops at Leyte and those which were to load Tenth Army and Island Command forces waiting on Oahu. The Northern Attack Force, which was to carry IIIAC troops, was not so augmented. General Geiger was so impressed with how well the reorganization of Admiral Hall's transport force had eased movement control and increased the efficiency of loading and unloading operations, that he requested the formation of a similar corps shipping group for future IIIAC operations. The commanding generals of the 1st and 6th Marine Divisions were made responsible for the loading and embarkation of their respective organic and attached units, while IIIAC itself supervised the loading of corps troops. In addition, General Geiger was responsible for embarking Marine Air Group 33 (MAG-33) of TAF, which was based on Espiritu Santo, 555 miles southeast of Guadalcanal.

Although some Northern Attack Force vessels were partially combat-loaded before the rehearsal period, all required additional time off the Guadalcanal, Banika, and Pavuvu beaches to take on vital cargo and to top-off water and fuel tanks. The Northern Tractor Flotilla was the first increment of TF 53 to leave the Solomons for the staging area at Ulithi. Departing on 12 March, the holds and above decks of the landing ships in the convoy were solidly packed with amphibious vehicles, tanks, artillery, and various other combat gear. For this invasion, IIIAC wanted to avoid subjecting assault troops to the crowded conditions and debilitating effects of prolonged confinement aboard LSTs and LSMs.

While APAs were hardly luxurious, their accommodations were far better than those of the landing ships. To ease the first leg of the journey to Okinawa, many assault wave Marines were embarked on the faster attack transports which, together with the rest of the Northern Attack Force transport groups, left from the mounting area on 15 March to join the ICEBERG force gathering at Ulithi. The immense lagoon at Ulithi Atoll was the westernmost American fleet anchorage, staging base, and repair depot in the Pacific. Midway between the Marianas and the Palaus, Ulithi was captured without opposition in September 1944, and was developed immediately to support naval operations in the western Pacific as well as to serve as an advance base for the Philippines invasion. Once occupied and built up, the islets of the atoll served also as limited recreation areas where personnel of all services could regain their landlegs and participate in a somewhat restricted physical conditioning program.

On 21 March, both the transport group and the tractor flotilla of TF 53 arrived at Ulithi, anchored, and on the following day, APA-borne assault troops were transferred to the landing ships which were to carry them the remaining 1,400 miles to Okinawa. Once the transfer was completed, small boats began ferrying recreation parties ashore. Here the rigors of shipboard confinement were forgotten by a combination of organized athletics and an issue of not-too-cool cokes and beer.

For many of the troops, this stopover on the long voyage towards the unknown was made exciting by the fascinating sight of the constantly shifting fleet groupment whose makeup changed from day-to-day and hour-to-hour as carriers, battleships, cruisers, and smaller combat vessels departed for strikes against the enemy or returned from completed missions. In the midst of this activity, the scattered elements of the Expeditionary Troops filtered in to join those forces which had arrived earlier.

Despite the relaxing effect of sun, sand, and surf at Ulithi, the nightly alerts to the presence of Japanese snooper planes was a continual reminder that a war still existed. This grim fact was brought home to many men in the invasion force on the gloomy, fog-bound Saturday afternoon of 24 March when the battered carrier *Franklin* limped into the anchorage shepherded by the USS *Santa Fe*.

On the next day, a brilliantly sunlit Sunday, the bruised and battered *Franklin* could be seen more clearly as she lay at anchor. Her top rigging, aerials, and radar towers were gone or twisted completely out of shape. Her flight deck was buckled and undulating. These were the external damages wrought by the internal explosions of bombs that had penetrated to lower decks when Japanese suicide planes furiously attacked the carrier on 19 March, during TF 38 strikes against enemy shipping at Kure and Kobe. As the most heavily damaged carrier to be saved in the war, the *Franklin* was able to make the 12,000-mile trip to New York for repairs under her own power, stopping only at Pearl Harbor on the way.

The Northern Tractor Flotilla sortied from the Ulithi anchorage for Okinawa on 25 March and, two days later, the remainder of the assault echelon set forth in its wake. Saipan was the scene, on the same dates, of the Demonstration Group departure. Loading operations of the 2d Marine Division were eased by the fact that its lift, Transron 15, had laid over briefly at Saipan in February while en route to Iwo Jima. At that time, division transport quartermasters (TQMs) obtained ships' characteristics data which proved more accurate than the information provided earlier by FMFPac. As a result, the TQMs were better able to plan for a more efficient use of cargo and personnel space.

In addition to the responsibility for loading his reinforced division, General Watson was given the duty of coordinating the loading of all ICEBERG Marine assault and first echelon forces elsewhere in the Marianas and at Roi in the Marshalls.

In preparing for Okinawa, the only real problem confronting General Mulcahy's Marine air units was the coordinated loading of ground and flight elements. According to the logistical planning, planes and pilots were to be lifted to the target on board escort carriers, while ground crews and non-flying units were to make the trip in assault and first echelon shipping. As the organizations comprising the Tactical Air Force were widely dispersed, their loading and embarkation was supervised, of necessity, by local commanders of the areas where the air groups and squadrons were based.

Mounting from Oahu in the TAF assault echelon were the headquarters squadrons of the 2d Marine Aircraft Wing and MAG-43, and Air Warning Squadrons (AWSs) 7 and 8. Headquarters Squadrons 2 and 43 became the headquarters commands of TAF and General Wallace's Air Defense Command, respectively, The TAF transport quartermaster coordinated the mounting out of the Oahu-based units with his opposite numbers on the staffs of the Tenth Army and the 2d MAW. The Marines from AWS-8 and the forward echelons of Mulcahy's and Wallace's headquarters commands left Pearl Harbor on 22 February, while AWS-7 departed Pearl the same month in two increments, one on the 10th and the second on the 21st.

Colonel John C. Munn's MAG-31 embarked from Roi and Namur in the Marshall Islands. The group service squadron and ground personnel of Marine Fighter Squadrons 224, 311, and 441 boarded transport and cargo vessels which, in turn, joined the ICEBERG convoy forming at Saipan. Flight personnel and their planes went aboard the escort carriers *Breton* on the night of 22-23 March, *Sitkoh Bay* on 24 March, and were staged through Ulithi where they were joined by Marine Night Fighter Squadron 542.

MAG-33 (Colonel Ward E. Dickey) mounted from Espiritu Santo in the New Hebrides. While IIIAC was responsible for the embarkation of the MAG, the group itself supervised the loading of its ground and service elements which joined the Northern Attack Force off Guadalcanal. The pilots of VMF-312, -322, and -323 flew their F4Us (Corsairs) to Manus via Guadalcanal and Green Island. There they boarded the escort carriers *White Plains* and *Hollandia*. Already on board the latter was VMF(N)-543 which had boarded the vessel at Pearl Harbor on 11 March. Its ground personnel had departed from the same port three weeks earlier. Outside of the TAF chain of command, but closely related to its combat functions, were Landing Force Air Support Control Units 1, 2, and 3. Two weeks after returning to its Saipan base from the Iwo Jima operation, LFASCU-1 loaded aboard ship for an immediate return engagement with the enemy at Okinawa. The other two LFASCUs were based at Ewa, T.H., where they trained for ICEBERG, and mounted for the invasion in February 1945, later staging for the target through Leyte.

As it had no need for an intermediate staging area, the XXIV Corps departed for Okinawa directly from Leyte. General Bruce's 77th Infantry Division, which was to open the Ryukyus operation with the assault on Kerama Retto, finished loading its landing ships on 18 March and its transports on the 20th, each echelon leaving for the target on the day following. The 7th and 96th Divisions conducted their own loading under the supervision of XXIV Corps TQMs, who spotted Southern Landing Force shipping at the most satisfactory point on the landing beaches. The Southern Tractor Flotilla departed Leyte during the morning hours of 24 March; the transport groups followed three days later.

By the evening of 27 March, all ICEBERG assault elements were at sea, converging on Okinawa. Soldiers and Marines aboard the transports and landing vessels had already made themselves as comfortable as possible under the crowded conditions and had settled down to shipboard routine. Officers and key NCOs reviewed their unit operation plans, examined maps and terrain models of the landing area, and held daily briefing sessions with their men. At the same time they squared away their combat gear for the invasion, most of the men of Hebrew and Christian faiths also prepared themselves for religious observances of Passover or Good Friday and Easter, all three holidays falling within a few days of each other in 1945.

Neutralizing The Enemy

After the first carrier strike of 10 October 1944, Naha's fire- and explosion-gutted ruins furnished the Japanese defenders with visual evidence of the effectiveness of American naval air power and served as an ominous portent of the future. One observer, a Japanese soldier, complained in his diary that, "the enemy is brazenly planning to completely destroy every last ship, cut our supply lines, and attack us." Okinawa was not visited again by Vice Admiral John S. McCain's Fast Carrier Force (TF 38) until 3 and 4 January 1945, when, in conjunction with a heavy attack on Formosa, the Ryukyu and Sakashima Islands were also struck. Commenting on this raid, a Japanese replacement confided in his diary that "seeing enemy planes for the first time since coming to Okinawa somehow or other gave me the feeling of being in a combat zone." The return of the Navy planes on 22 January reinforced his first impression and further shook his seeming complacency, as that day's diary entry implied resentment. "While some fly around overhead and strafe, the big bastards fly over the airfield and drop bombs. The ferocity of the bombing is terrific. It really makes me furious. It is past 1500 and the raid is still on. At 1800 the last two planes brought the raid to a close. What the hell kind of bastards are they? Bomb from 0600 to 1800!" During January, TF 38 struck Formosa and the Ryukyus twice, and made some uninvited calls on South China coastal ports, all while covering the Luzon landings. After its last attack, the force retired to Ulithi where reinforcing carriers were waiting to join. On 27 January, the same day that Admiral Nimitz arrived at his new advance headquarters on Guam, the command of the Pacific fleet's striking force was changed and Admirals Spruance and Mitscher relieved Halsey and McCain.

When Mitscher's carriers departed Ulithi on 10 February, it was in the guise of Task Force 58, which was destined to continue the work that TF 38 had begun.

As a diversion for the 19 February Marine landing on Iwo Jima, and to reduce the Japanese capability for launching air attacks against the expeditionary force, Mitscher's Fast Carrier Force struck at the Tokyo area on 16-17 February and again on the 25th. In between these attacks, Mitscher's planes and ships supported the Iwo assault from D-Day until the 23d, at which time they sortied for the 25 February Tokyo strike. As TF 58 retired to Ulithi on 1 March, planes of Task Units 58.1, 58.2, and 58.3 photographed Okinawa, Kerama Retto, Minami Daito, and Amami O Shima, and bombed and strafed targets of opportunity. These three units returned to Ulithi on the 5th.

At the same time that the fast carriers were making their forays, American submarines and naval patrol bombers ranged the western Pacific taking a steadily increasing toll of Japanese shipping. The bottom of the China Sea was littered with the broken hulls and loads of enemy transports and cargo ships which never reached their destinations. Almost complete isolation of the Okinawa garrison was accomplished by mid-February 1945 through the combined efforts of Navy air and submarine forces. It soon became apparent to General Ushijima that his Ryukyus command stood alone since "communications between the mainland of Japan and Formosa had been practically severed." The neutralization and isolation of Okinawa was furthered by the continuous series of strategic air strikes on the Japanese industrial network by Army Air Forces bombers, which mounted attacks from bases in China, India, the Philippines, the Marianas, and the Palaus. Massive raids on the factories of the main islands as well as on outlying sources of raw materials hindered Japan's ability and will to continue the war. Giant super-fortresses also rose from airfields in the southern Marianas in steadily increasing numbers to hit Tokyo, Osaka, Nagoya, and Kobe, widening the fire-swept circle around the expanse of previously devastated areas. During the interludes between carrier-plane attacks on the Ryukyus, B-29 appearances over Okinawa became so commonplace that the Japanese defenders referred to their visits as "regular runs."

With the approach of L-Day, the tempo of covering operations was accelerated throughout the Pacific. For its final strike on Japan prior to the Okinawa landing. TF 58 steamed out of the Ulithi anchorage on 14 March. Four days later, carrier-launched planes interdicted Kyushu's heavily-laden airfields, and attacked installations on Shikoku and Honshu islands on the 19th. The task force did not escape unscathed this time, however, for the enemy was ready, and retaliated with heavy counterstrikes during which the Japanese pilots displayed reckless abandon and a wanton disregard for their lives. Five carriers and other ships in the task force were hit hard. A temporary task group composed of the damaged carriers *Wasp*, *Franklin*, and *Enterprise*, the cruiser *Santa Fe*, and Destroyer Squadron 52 returned to Ulithi for necessary repairs. The ships remaining in TF 58, the carriers, the battleship force, and the protective screen, were reorganized into three task groups of relatively equal strength on 22 March. With this force, Admiral Mitscher then began the final run on Okinawa for the beginning of the preinvasion bombardments.

Preinvasion Preparations And The Kerama Retto Landing

The first elements of the ICEBERG force to appear at the target were the doughty sweepers of Mine Group One, which began operations off Kerama Retto and the southeastern coast of Okinawa on 24 March, just two days before the 77th Infantry

Division was to land in the Keramas. After the minecraft cleared a channel outside the 100-fathom curve off the Minatoga beaches, part of Admiral Mitscher's battleship force, temporarily organized as TF 59, steamed through the swept area and bombarded Okinawa while TF 58 planes covered and neutralized enemy shore installations. By late afternoon, as TF 59 withdrew to rejoin the carrier force, the mine vessels finished that day's planned program of preliminary sweeps. During these operations, the Amphibious Support Force, with elements of the Gunfire and Covering Force (Admiral Deyo serving as Officer in Tactical Command), had completed the run from Ulithi and deployed into approach formation. Two fire support units left TF 54 to begin their respective assignments — one unit to cover the sweep conducted between Tonachi Shima and Kerama Retto, and the other to cover the mine sweepers off Okinawa and to begin bombarding the demonstration beaches. An important TF 52 element was the Underwater Demolition Flotilla, consisting of 10 underwater demolition teams (UDTs) organized into two groups, Able and Baker. On the afternoon of 24 March, the high speed destroyer transports (APDs) of Group Able and destroyers of TF 54 formed for the next day's UDT and NGF operations at Kerama. The remainder of Admiral Deyo's force was concentrated and ready to repulse all Japanese surface or air attacks.

A carefully planned feature of the ICEBERG operation was this concentration of naval strength. With ample sea room and sufficient fighting power to eliminate any or all of the remnants of the Japanese Navy, TF 58 lay to the east of the Ryukyus in the Pacific Ocean. In the East China Sea, to the west of Okinawa, the majority of the combat ships of the Amphibious Support Force was concentrated, ready to stop any attempt to reinforce or evacuate the garrison. At night, the ships assigned to the bombardment of Okinawa's southeastern coast retired together so that their mission could be resumed without delay the following morning. In the event of any surface action, each of these task groups was able to operate and support itself independently.

As vaster areas surrounding Okinawa were swept clear of mines, destroyers and gunboats began patrol operations and made the beleaguered enemy's isolation a certainty. Shipborne radar picket stations, disposed from 15 to 100 miles offshore, encircled the island to protect the invasion force from the constant threat of surprise enemy air attacks. Aboard the destroyers and destroyer minesweepers serving as picket vessels were fighter-director teams which controlled the combat air patrols (CAPs) of carrier planes which orbited overhead during the hours of daylight. When Japanese flights were detected on picket radar screens, the CAP was vectored out to intercept and destroy the enemy. The bulk of the heavy losses incurred by the Navy during the battle for Okinawa was borne by the vessels comprising the radar picket fleet. The value of their services in protecting the vulnerable transport and service areas is measured by the large number of Japanese planes shot down before they had reached their objectives. Although the destructive TF 58 raids on Kyushu had temporarily disrupted enemy plans for air attacks from the home islands, the Japanese managed to mount an increasing number of raids from fields in the Formosa area. Once it became apparent that Okinawa was to be invaded and that Okinawa waters held lucrative targets, forward elements of the 8th Air Division rose from their fields in the Sakashimas to make their first Kamikaze attack on ships standing off Kerama Retto at dawn on 26 March.

Beginning with this first hour-long enemy air raid, the loss of lives and damage to ships mounted as Japanese bombers and suiciders made sneak attacks on the amphibious force in the dawn and dusk twilight hours. As part of its planned schedule of preliminary operations supporting ICEBERG, Vice Admiral Sir H. Bernard Rawling's British Carrier Force (TF 57) struck Sakashima Gunto on the 26th and 27th. Since the carriers had blocked the use of Sakashima and Kyushu, the Japanese had to use Okinawa-based planes to attack the American invasion forces. The employment in three suicidal forays of all available aircraft, including trainers, liaison craft, and planes of a Special Attack Unit which managed to fly in from Kyushu, led to the complete elimination of the air strength of the Okinawa garrison by 29 March.

Claims of enemy airmen who survived to return to home bases were grossly exaggerated, but their destructiveness was extensive. A summary of damages to American forces for the period 26 to 31 March reveals that six ships, including Admiral Spruance's flagship *Indianapolis*, were crashed by suicide-bent enemy pilots. Near misses accounted for damage to 10 other vessels, while floating mines sank 2 ships and an encounter with a Japanese torpedo boat gave another American ship minor damage.

Despite costly harassment from Japanese air attacks, Admiral Blandy's force proceeded with its primary task of preparing the target for the assault. Four Group Able UDTs cleared beach approaches in Kerama Retto on 26 March and began blowing Keise Shima reefs the next day. Because Okinawa's offshore waters had not been completely cleared of mines, the reconnaissance and demolition work scheduled for the 28th was delayed a day. Elements of Group Able scouted the demonstration beaches on the 29th, while Group Baker teams reconnoitered the Hagushi beaches.

During this reconnaissance of the west coast landing area, Group Baker swimmers discovered approximately 2,900 wooden posts embedded in the reef near its seaward edge and stretching for some distance on either side of the Bishi Gawa. These posts, which were on the average six inches in diameter and from four to eight feet in height, were generally aligned five feet apart in rows of three or four. Although some of these obstacles were loose, a few were set in concrete and the rest wedged into the coral. On 30 March they were blown up with hand-placed charges. All but 200 posts were destroyed by L-Day and it was believed that the landing would not be hindered by those that remained. Accompanying the UDTs during the beach reconnaissance and initial demolitions operations were assault troop observers, who acted as liaison and reconnaissance personnel. Their primary function was to brief the UDTs on the schemes of maneuver and location of the landing areas of their respective assault units, to make certain that specific beaches were cleared, and to obtain current intelligence concerning the beaches and surrounding terrain. As soon as these preinvasion operations had been completed (29 and 30 March), the observers were returned by ship to join their parent organizations in the approaching attack groups. In general, the intelligence reports submitted by the observers favored a successful landing across the entire Tenth Army front.

Because the waters surrounding Okinawa had been heavily mined, the scheduled NGF bombardment did not begin until 25 March (L minus 7) when TF 54 fire support vessels were able to close to ranges of maximum effectiveness. Carrier air was able to pound Okinawa repeatedly, however, and was met by only ineffectual and desultory fire from enemy antiaircraft defenses. In the course of the 3,095 sorties that the TF 52 Combat Air Support Control Unit (CASCU) directed against Okinawa prior to L-Day, special attention was given to the destruction of submarine pens, airfields, suicide boat installations, bridges over the roads leading into the landing area, and gun positions. After the pilots were debriefed, each day's strike results were evaluated by the CASCU on board Admiral Blandy's flagship, USS *Estes*, and considered together with damage estimates of ships' guns. The schedule of air missions and the NGF plans were revised and coordinated, and plans for the next day's sorties and shoots were then issued.

Initial target lists compiled by the Tenth Army artillery section and TF 54 intelligence section were constantly revised as analyses, based on aerial observation and photo reconnaissance, were received. As new evaluations were made of the destruction of enemy positions and installations, and new targets tabulated, cards listing the corrected data were delivered to the target information centers (TICs) of IIIAC and XXIV Corps. From the time that the bombardment of Okinawa began until L-Day, General Nimmer's TIC received copies of all dispatches sent from the objective by CTF 54. From these reports, all information relative to the discovery, attack, damage, and destruction of targets in the IIIAC landing zone was excerpted and used to bring the target map and target file up-to-date. Although Admiral Blandy's bombardment force expended 27,226 rounds of 5-inch or larger-caliber ammunition on Okinawa, extensive damage was done only to surface installations, especially those in the vicinity of the airfields. As the ground forces were to discover later, the Japanese sustained little destruction of well dug-in defenses, and few losses among the men who manned them. On the day before the landing, as a result of his evaluation of the effect of air and NGF bombardment, CTF 52 could report that "the preparation was sufficient for a successful landing." Admiral Blandy also stated that "we did not conclude from [the enemy's silence] that all defense installations had been destroyed. . . ."

A prerequisite which Admiral Turner felt would guarantee the success of ICEBERG was the seizure of Kerama Retto and Keise Shima prior to L-Day. Because of the advantages to be gained by all ICEBERG assault and support elements, the taking of these islands was made an essential feature of the Tenth Army operation plan. Naval units, particularly, would benefit since the Keramas provided a sheltered fleet anchorage in the objective area where emergency repairs, refueling, and rearming operations could be accomplished. Once the envisioned seaplane base was established, Navy patrol bombers could range from Korea to Indochina in search and rescue missions and antisubmarine warfare operations. With the emplacement of XXIV Corps Artillery guns on Keise Shima and their registry on Okinawa, preliminaries for the main assault would be complete.

Even if the Keramas had had no value as an advanced logistics base, they would have been taken. The suspected presence of suicide sea raiding squadrons in the island chain was confirmed when the 77th Infantry Division landed, and captured and destroyed 350 of the squadrons' suicide boats. Their threat to the Okinawa landing was undeniable, for these small craft were to speed from their hideouts in the Keramas' small islands to the American anchorages. Here, "The objective of the attack will be transports, loaded with essential supplies and material and personnel . . ." ordered General Ushijima. "The attack will be carried out by concentrating maximum strength immediately upon the enemy's landing." The surprise thrust into the Keramas frustrated the Japanese plan and undoubtedly eased initial ICEBERG operations at the Hagushi beaches. At the time that the 77th was poised to strike the Keramas, the islands were defended by approximately 975 Japanese troops, of whom only the some 300 boat operators of the sea raiding squadrons had any combat value. The rest of the defense was comprised of about 600 Korean laborers and nearly 100 base troops. On 26 March, the day following the sweep of Kerama waters by the minecraft and reconnaissance of its beaches by UDT personnel, Admiral Kiland's Western Islands Attack Group moved into position for the assault. A battleship, two large cruisers, and four destroyers had been assigned to provide NGF support for the landing, but only the 5-inch guns of the destroyers were used extensively. The capital ships were not called on to fire but remained on standby. As LSTs disgorged their cargo of armored amphibians and troop-laden assault tractors for the run to the beaches, carrier planes orbited the transport area to ward off Japanese suicide planes which were beginning to filter through the outer fighter screen. Aircraft bombed the beaches as the assault waves were guided toward the target by LCIs assigned to give close-in support.

At 0801, the first of the four assault battalions of the 77th hit its target and in a little over an hour's time the other three had attacked their own objectives. Before noon, General Bruce saw that the rapid progress of his landing teams ashore would permit yet another landing that day, so he directed the 2d Battalion, 307th Infantry, a reserve unit, to take Yakabi Shima. Since this island's defenders offered little resistance, it was secured by 1341. By the end of the day the 77th had done quite well, having seized three Kerama islands outright and established a firm foothold on two others.

Within a six-day period, 26-31 March, at a cost of 31 killed and 81 wounded, the 77th Infantry Division completely fulfilled its mission as the vanguard of ICEBERG Expeditionary Troops. In the process of removing the threat posed by the Japanese to operations in the Kerama anchorage, General Bruce's troops killed 530 of the enemy, captured 121 more, and rounded up some 1,195 civilians. All of the enemy were not disposed of, however, for scattered Japanese soldiers remained hidden in the hills of the various Kerama islands and even occasionally communicated with units on Okinawa.

Marine participation in pre-L-Day activities was confined to the operations of Major James L. Jones' FMF Amphibious Reconnaissance Battalion. For the Keramas invasion, it was split into two tactical groups, one under the battalion commander and the other under his executive officer. Only two companies of the battalion were available for anticipated missions, since Company B had been assigned to the V Amphibious Corps for the Iwo Jima landing and did not return to its parent organization until after L-Day.

On the night of 26-27 March, while the 77th consolidated its conquests and prepared for the next day's battles, Major Jones' men landed on and reconnoitered the reef islets comprising Keise Shima. When reconnaissance of the small group revealed no trace of the enemy, the Marines reboarded their APDs with information of reef, beach, and terrain conditions. Their findings were then forwarded to the 77th Division intelligence officer for evaluation and distribution to the units which were to land on Keise Shima. During the night of 27-28 March, scouts from Company A landed on Aware Saki, a small island off the southern tip of Tokashiki Shima. Again there was no evidence of the enemy. The only encounter with the Japanese occurred on 29 March, during early morning landings on Mae and Kuro Shima, two small islands which lie between the Kerama Retto and Keise Shima. At 0630, a suicide boat, apparently manned by only one soldier, was observed heading at high speed for Mae Shima's beach from Tokashiki Shima. The one-man regatta was brought to a speedy and spectacular end as the explosive-laden craft disintegrated under a hail of machine gun fire. A reconnaissance of Kure Shima shortly thereafter indicated no troops or civilians, nor any installations.

In order to remove some of the obstacles to the landing of XXIV Corps Artillery units on Keise Shima on 31 March, UDTs blasted a path through the off-shore coral reefs early that morning, and this completed the work they had begun on the 27th. Then, after 2/306 landed unopposed and determined that no enemy had slipped back to Keise after the Marine reconnaissance, men and equipment of the 420th Field Artillery Group went ashore and immediately set up to fire. By 1935, the group's 155mm guns ("Long Toms") began registering on preselected targets in southern Okinawa. There, the Japanese later reported, they "incessantly obstructed our movements by laying an abundant quantity of fire inside our positions, the fire being directed mainly to cut off our communications." Also landing on Keise were part of a team from an Army air warning squadron and an AAA (automatic weapons) platoon which, when ashore and set up, became part of the area antiaircraft defense system.

Already beset by American carrier-based strikes and by ships' gunfire which blasted Okinawa in a precise and businesslike manner, the Japanese felt that the artillery fire from Keise was overdoing it a bit. A special attack unit was formed to raid the island artillery emplacements, and the 5th Artillery Command's 15cm guns were ordered to conduct counterbattery fire in an attempt to destroy the American Long Toms. Neither measure attained success, and the Thirty-second Army was never able to enforce its order to "stop the use of enemy artillery on Keise Shima." Before L-Day, the floating naval base in the Kerama Retto was functioning at a high pitch. From watery take-off lanes, seaplanes rose to harass enemy submarines and shipping in the China Sea. Kamikaze-damaged vessels were salvaged and repaired on an around-the-clock schedule, while the rearming, refueling, and revictualling of healthy ships kept pace. Without this frontline logistical facility, "many more ships and personnel of the service force than were available in the Okinawa area would have been required at sea to make replenishment an accomplished fact for all fleet forces."

In contrast to the conspicuous prelanding operations of ICEBERG forces in the target area, the Thirty-second Army was able to surround its tactical dispositions with a greater degree of secrecy. Not until after the landing on Okinawa and relentless probing by the assault forces did the Tenth Army learn what the strength of the enemy was and where his positions were. Before L-Day, American knowledge of enemy dispositions was sketchy, and as late as L minus 1 (31 March), the G-3 of the 6th Marine Division was told that "the Hagushi beaches were held in great strength."

The factor which tipped the scales in favor of an unopposed Allied landing on the Hagushi beaches was General Ushijima's decision to defend the southeast coast of Okinawa in strength. When the 2d Marine Division made its feint landings on D-Day and D plus 1, the Japanese commander's staff believed its earlier estimate that "powerful elements might attempt a landing [on the Minatoga beaches]" was fully justified. Consequently, a substantial portion of the artillery and infantry strength of the Thirty-second Army was immobilized in face of a threat in the southeast that never materialized.

Although Ushijima's command had prepared for an American landing elsewhere, from the Japanese point of view the Hagushi beaches remained the most obvious target. Even while propaganda reports—mostly untrue—of successful Kamikaze attacks against the invasion fleet bolstered Japanese morale, the commander of a scratch force formed from airfield personnel on the island warned his men not "to draw the hasty conclusion that we had been able to destroy the enemy's plan of landing on Okinawa Jima." The commander of the 1st Specially Established Regiment, Lieutenant Colonel Tokio Aoyangai, proved himself clairvoyant, for in less than 24 hours after his message had been distributed, the Northern and Southern Attack Forces were moving into their transport areas ready to launch the assault.

Chapter 4. The First Days Ashore

Seizure Of The Beachhead

Optimum weather conditions for an amphibious landing prevailed at the target on L-Day when the Central Pacific Task Forces launched the attack against Okinawa on 1 April 1945, Easter Sunday. The coming of dawn revealed cloudy to clear skies and a calm sea with but a negligible surf at the shore. Moderate easterly to northeasterly winds were blowing offshore, just enough to carry the smoke away from the beaches. To the many veteran jungle fighters among the invading troops, the 75-degree temperature seemed comfortably cool. At the target, the major naval lift and support elements moved into their assigned areas off the Hagushi beaches. Once in position, the ships prepared to debark troops. Off the Minatoga beaches on the other side of the island, the same preparations were conducted concurrently by the shipping that carried the 2d Marine Division.

Admiral Turner unleashed his forces at 0406 with the traditional order, "Land the Landing Force," and Okinawa's ordeal began with a percussive overture of naval gunfire. The enemy reacted to the landing shortly after dawn as he mounted scattered air attacks on the convoys. In the continuing belief that the main effort was directed at the Minatoga area, the few Japanese aircraft not destroyed by American carrier air or ships' antiaircraft guns disregarded the more lucrative targets off Hagushi and concentrated on Demonstration Group shipping. Kamikazes struck the transport *Hinsdale* and LST 884 as troops, mostly from the 3d Battalion, 2d Marines and its reinforcing elements, were disembarking for the feint run into the beaches. Reported killed were 8 Marines; 37 were wounded, and 8 were listed as missing in action. It is somewhat ironic that units not even scheduled to land on Okinawa on L-Day sustained the first troop casualties. Air support arrived over the target in force at 0505 and the assault forces began to debark ten minutes later. The transport areas became the scenes of purposeful activity as troops climbed down landing nets into waiting landing craft, while armored amphibians, and amphibian tractors preloaded with troops and equipment, spewed forth from the open jaws of LSTs. At the same time, tank-carrying LCMs (landing craft, mechanized) floated from the flooded well decks of LSDs (landing ships, dock). Other tanks, rigged with T-6 flotation equipment, debarked from LSTs to form up into waves and make their own way onto the beaches.

In reply to the murderous pounding of the Hagushi beaches by 10 battleships, 9 cruisers, 23 destroyers, and 177 gunboats, the Japanese returned only desultory and light artillery and mortar fire. Even though the assault waves formed up in assembly areas within range of this fire, neither troops nor invasion craft were hit. During the early morning hours, the two battalions of the 420th Field Artillery Group on Keise

Shima received heavy enemy counterbattery fire, which stopped American unloading operations on the reef for four hours but caused no damage.

Lying off each Okinawa invasion beach were control vessels marking the lines of departure (LD). Landing vehicles quickly formed into waves behind the LD and at 0800, when the signal pennants fluttering from the masts of the control vessels were hauled down, the first wave, composed of LVT(A)s (landing vehicle, tracked (armored)), moved forward to the beaches in an orderly manner behind a line of support craft. Following on schedule, hundreds of troop-carrying LVTs, disposed in five to seven waves, crossed the lines of departure at regular intervals and moved determinedly towards the shore.

Despite the ferocity of the prelanding bombardment, enemy artillery and mortars continued scattered but ineffectual fire on the invasion waves as they made the 4,000-yard run to the beach. On approaching the shoreline, the LVT(A)s fired upon suspected targets, while naval gunfire lifted from the beach area to hit inland targets. Carrier fighters that had been orbiting lazily over the two flanks of the beachhead began diving over the landing area and neutralized it with repeated strafing, bombing, and napalming runs.

As the assault waves hit the beaches, smoke was laid down on the hills east of Yontan to prevent enemy observation of the landing zone. On the other side of the island, Demonstration Group landing craft raced toward the Minatoga beaches only to reverse their course and retire to the transport area behind a smoke screen as the fourth wave crossed the line of departure. Neither the reef fringing the beaches nor enemy mortar fire on the beaches themselves interfered with the successful XXIV Corps landing south of the Bishi Gawa. The eight Army assault battalions were landed by six successive waves of LVTs and moved forward without opposition.

The sea wall, which had caused some concern to XXIV Corps planners, had been breached by naval gunfire. In anticipation of the early build-up ashore, engineers, landing in the first waves, blasted additional beach exits in those portions of the wall which remained standing. Upon landing, the LVT(A)s poured through these breaches, hard on the heels of the infantry, and moved to protect the flanks, while amphibious trucks (DUKWs), preloaded with 4.2-inch mortars, and tanks rolled inland.

Off the Marine landing zone, north of the Bishi Gawa, the reef was raggedly fissured and became smoother only as it neared the beach. A rising tide floated the landing vehicles over a large portion of the reef and the boulders which fringed it. On the northern flank of the 1st Marine Division, however, the large circular section of the reef off the Blue Beaches presented difficulties to the tractors attempting to cross at that point, and delayed their arrival at the beach.

During the approach of IIIAC assault waves to assigned beaches, several instances occurred when inexperienced wave guide officers failed to follow correct compass courses or when they did not guide by clearly recognizable terrain features on the shore. Some troops were thus landed out of position. For example, Lieutenant Colonel Bruno A. Hochmuth's 3d Battalion, 4th Marines—assigned to RED Beach 1-- was landed on the right half of GREEN 2 in the zone of the 22d Marines (Colonel Merlin F. Schneider), and on the rocky coast line between GREEN 2 and RED 1.

Elements of Colonel Edward W. Snedeker's 7th Marines were landed in relatively insignificant numbers on the beach of the 4th Marines (Colonel Alan Shapley). On the extreme right flank of the 1st Marine Division, however, the fourth wave of RCT-5 was diverted across the corps boundary and landed on the right flank of the 7th

Infantry Division. The Marine wave consisted principally of Lieutenant Colonel Charles W. Shelburne's 1/5 reserve—Company B—and part of the battalion command post group. By 0930, a sufficient number of LVTs had been sent to pick up all but one lieutenant and two squads, who did not rejoin their parent unit until L plus 3. The fifth and sixth waves of the 5th Marines landed on their assigned beaches after the guide officers of these waves corrected the faulty course heading followed by the fourth wave. Despite these unexpected deviations from the landing plan, all the LVT(A)s spearheading the IIIAC attack reached the beach by 0830 and all eight assault battalions were ashore by 0900. The beaches had not been mined and opposition to the landing consisted only of sporadic mortar and small arms fire. This resulted in but few casualties and caused no damage to the LVTs. "With utter consternation and bewilderment and with a great deal of relief the assault wave landed against practically no opposition."

As the assault troops surged up the terraced slopes behind the beaches and sped inland, the center of invasion activity shifted from the line of departure to the transfer line at the edge of the reef. There, small boat, LVT, and DUKW control was established to unload support troops and artillery units on call. Supporting units continued to pour ashore during the morning as the attack progressed against only slight resistance. At the transfer line, reserve infantry elements shifted from ships' boats into the LVTs which had landed assault troops earlier. Flotation-equipped tanks made the beaches under their own power, others were landed at high tide from LCMs, and the remainder were discharged directly onto the reef from LSMs and LSTs. DUKWs brought the 75mm and 105mm howitzers of the light field artillery battalions directly ashore.

All tanks in the 1st Division assault wave, landing from LCMs and LCTs, were on the beach by noon. One exception was a tank that foundered in a reef pothole. The captain of LST 628, carrying the six T-6 flotation-equipped tanks of the 1st Tank Battalion (Lieutenant Colonel Arthur J. Stuart), disregarded the operation plan and refused to allow them to launch until H plus 60 minutes. At that time, he set them in the water 10 miles off the landing beaches. These tanks finally reached shore after being afloat for more than five hours, but two of them were hung up on the reef because of the ebbing tide. Because the LSMs carrying Lieutenant Colonel Stuart's reserve tanks had great difficulty in grounding on the reef on L-Day, the first tracked vehicle off the ramp of one was lost in an unseen pothole. Of the four LSMs employed, two finally landed their cargo late on L-Day, another at noon on L plus 1, and the last on 3 April.

Tanks were landed early in the 6th Division zone, where each of the three companies of the 6th Tank Battalion (Lieutenant Colonel Robert L. Denig, Jr.) employed a different landing procedure. Tanks equipped with flotation gear swam to the reef, easily negotiated the rugged coral, continued on to the beaches, where they jettisoned their pontoons and became operational by H plus 29 minutes. The company in LCMs came in at high tide (0930) and landed without incident. The third company successfully landed directly from the LSMs grounded on the reef but forded the deep water between the grounding point and the shore with difficulty. Soon after landing, the accelerated pace of the 6th Division assault to the north overextended Colonel Schneider's 22d Marines. Troops were taken from his left battalion, 2/22 (Lieutenant Colonel Horatio W. Woodhouse, Jr.), to guard the exposed flank. This, in turn, weakened the 22d attack echelon and gave it a larger front than it could adequately cover. Consequently, a considerable gap developed between the 2d

Battalion and the 3d Battalion (Lieutenant Colonel Malcolm "O" Donohoo), advancing on the right. In less than 20 minutes after the landing, Colonel Schneider ordered his reserve, 1/22 (Major Thomas J. Myers), ashore. Upon landing, the 1st Battalion (less Company C, remaining afloat as regimental reserve) was committed in the center of the regimental zone.

Still meeting no opposition while it continued the rapid move inland, by 1000 the 22d Marines found its left flank unit stretched dangerously thin. As he pressed the division attack to exploit initial success, General Shepherd anticipated Schneider's request for reinforcements to cover the exposed flank, and asked corps to release one BLT of the 29th Marines.

During the unopposed 22d Marines advance on Hanza, the 4th Marines moved on Yontan airfield against light to moderate resistance. Isolated enemy pockets, built around light machine guns, slowed the regiment only slightly as it penetrated several hundred yards inland and made contact on its right with the 7th Marines at the division boundary. By midmorning, the 4th reached the airfield and found it unguarded.

Only intermittent sniper fire coming from beyond the field opposed the 4th Marines as it swept across the air facility and secured its objective by 1300. The airfield was found to be essentially intact, but all buildings had been stripped and the antiaircraft emplacements contained only dummy guns.

As this rush carried Colonel Shapley's regiment beyond adjacent units, a wide gap developed between its left flank and the right of the 22d Marines, then in the vicinity of Hanza. Shapley's regiment jumped off again at 1330 against only light resistance on its left. Tanks were called in to reduce several cave positions in this area. After these positions were neutralized, the attack continued slowly through rugged, wooded terrain. In order to maintain contact with the 7th Marines and to rectify the overextended condition of the 4th, 2/4 was released from division reserve at 1500 and immediately committed on the regiment's left to establish contact with the 22d Marines.

Because the division left flank was still dangerously exposed, General Shepherd regained 1/29 (Lieutenant Colonel Jean W. Moreau) from corps. Released by IIIAC at 1300, the battalion landed at 1500 and, with its left flank anchored on GREEN Beach 1, completed tying in with 22d Marines at 1700.

The 1st Marine Division, to the south of the 6th, met with the same surprising lack of resistance. By 0945 on the division left, Colonel Snedeker's 7th Marines had advanced through the village of Sobe, a first priority objective, and the 5th Marines (Colonel John H. Griebel) was 1,000 yards inland standing up. With the beaches clear, and in order to avoid losing any troops as a result of anticipated enemy air attacks against the congested transport area, the division reserve was then ordered ashore. Colonel Kenneth B. Chappell's 1st Marines embarked two BLTs, and the third was to land as soon as transportation became available. Reserve battalions of both assault regiments were picked up by LVTs at the transfer line and shuttled to the beach before noon. The 3d Battalion, 7th Marines (Lieutenant Colonel Edward H. Hurst), landed in the center of the regimental zone of action and then moved to the rear of Lieutenant Colonel Spencer S. Berger's 2/7, the left flank unit. At 1400, 3/5 was positioned 400 yards behind 1/5 on the division right boundary. When the 5th Marines reserve was moved up behind the assault battalions, the commanding officer of 3/5, Major John A. Gustafson, went forward to reconnoiter. An hour later, at 1500, his group was fired on by a small bypassed enemy pocket and Gustafson was wounded and evacuated. His executive officer, Major Martin C, Roth, took over temporarily until 4 April, when Lieutenant Colonel John C. Miller, Jr., assumed command.

Thus disposed in depth with its reserve elements echeloned to guard the flanks, the 1st Division continued its steady advance over the rolling checkerboard terrain. In addition to having developed the numerous caves that honeycombed the many hillsides in the zone, the Japanese had begun to organize other positions throughout the area and the Marines encountered innumerable field fortifications in varying stages of development. These defenses, however, were only held by small, scattered groups of service troops and home guards. According to a postwar Japanese source, these troops comprised ". . . a hastily organized motley unit . . . facing extreme hardship in trying to achieve an orderly formation."

The principal bridge over the Bishi Gawa below Hiza was undamaged and standing, and local defense forces had made little or no effort to destroy the narrow bridges that spanned lesser streams. What proved a greater hindrance to the advance than the desultory enemy attempts at halting it was what one observer described as "an excellent network of very poor roads."

By 1530, the majority of IIIAC supporting troops and artillery was ashore. One howitzer of Colonel Robert B. Luckey's 15th Marines and three of the 11th Marines (Colonel Wilburt S. Brown) were lost when the DUKWs carrying them foundered on the reef, but the remaining divisional artillery of IIIAC was landed successfully. Even though the artillery arrived early, a combination of the rapid infantry advance and the resulting strain on communications made it difficult for forward observers to register their battalions. Corps artillery reconnaissance parties began landing at 1300, and found that "selection of position areas from map and photo study proved suitable in every case." The advance was halted between 1600 and 1700, and the attacking infantry dug in, established contact all along the IIIAC line, and carried out extensive patrolling to the front. To maintain the impetus of the attack of his division on L-Day, General Shepherd had committed his entire reserve early. The 6th Marine Division remained in good shape and was well disposed to resume the advance on the 2d. Both the 4th and 22d Marines still maintained a company in reserve, while the corps reserve (29th Marines, less 1/29) was located northwest of Yontan airfield, in the vicinity of Hanza, after its landing at 1535.

General del Valle's division was unable to close the gap on the corps boundary before dark and halted some 600 yards to the rear of the 7th Infantry Division on the right. A company was taken from the reserve battalion of the 5th Marines and put into a blocking position to close the open flank. Two 1st Marines battalions, 1/1 and 2/1 (commanded by Lieutenant Colonels James C. Murray, Jr., and James C, Magee, Jr., respectively), landed at 1757. Lieutenant Colonel Stephen V. Sabol's 3d Battalion was on the transfer line at 1800 but, unable to obtain LVTs, remained in the boats all night. The 1st Battalion was attached to the 5th Marines for administrative control and moved inland to Furugen, while 2/1, similarly attached to the 7th Marines, dug in east of Sobe by 1845.

Artillery support for the Marine infantry was readily available by nightfall. The 15th Marines had established its fire direction center (FDC) by 1700, and its batteries were registered by 1830. All of Colonel Brown's artillery battalions were prepared to fire night defensive missions, though two of the 11th Marines battalions did not complete their registration because of the late arrival of spotter planes. Since enemy action was confined to unsuccessful attempts at infiltration of the lines and to intermittent mortar and machine gun fire in the 4th Marines sector, there were relatively few requirements for artillery support that first night on Okinawa.

ICEBERG's L-Day had been successful beyond all expectations. In conjunction with the extended initial advance of IIIAC, XXIV Corps had captured Kadena airfield by 1000, driven inland to an average depth of 3,500 yards, and advanced south along the east coast to the vicinity of Chatan. On 1 April, the Tenth Army had landed an estimated 50,000 troops in less than eight hours and established a beachhead that was 15,000 yards wide and varied from 4,000-5,000 yards in depth. For the entire day's operations by four assault divisions, casualties were reported to Admiral Turner as 28 killed, 104 wounded, and 27 missing.

Progress Inland

Following a relatively quiet night, which was punctuated only by sporadic sniper, machine gun, and mortar fire, Tenth Army units resumed the attack on L plus 1 at 0730. Perfect weather again prevailed, as the early morning was cool and a bright sun soon dispelled the ground fog and haze to provide unlimited visibility. While no artillery preparation preceded the jump off on the second day, all guns were available on call for support fires, and registration of all battalions, including those of the 11th Marines, had been completed. Carrier planes were on station at 0600 before the attack began. With the resumption of the advance, the 6th Marine Division continued to the east, while its left flank unit, 1/29, began clearing operations to Zampa Misaki. Admiral Turner wanted the point captured as a site for a radar station. He also wanted the BLACK Beaches uncovered so that unloading operations could begin. Throughout the day, the 22d Marines and 1/29 advanced rapidly against light resistance. By 1025, the latter unit had seized Zampa Misaki and found that the beaches there were unsuitable for use by IIIAC.

Major Anthony Walker's 6th Reconnaissance Company was then ordered to reconnoiter the beaches on the north coast of Zampa and the villages of Nagahama and Maeta Saki. Walker's scouts accomplished this mission before noon without opposition, and while doing so, encountered 50 civilians, who were taken into custody and transferred to stockades. The Nagahama beach was reported satisfactory for landing supplies.

On the 6th Division right, the 4th Marines advanced through rugged terrain, meeting intermittent enemy reaction. As the day wore on, however, pockets of stiff resistance were increasingly encountered, and at 1100, 3/4 came up against strong enemy positions, consisting of mutually supporting caves on both sides of a steep ravine. When the leading platoon entered the draw, it was met by a hail of small arms fire so heavy that the Marines could not bring out their 12 wounded until four hours later. "Every means of painlessly destroying the strongpoint was unsuccessfully tried and it was finally taken by a typical '*Banzai*' charge with one platoon entering the mouth of the draw and one platoon coming down one side of the two noses that formed the pocket."

The speed of the second day's advance again caused the assault units to become overextended. About midmorning, Colonel Shapley reported that there was a gap between his regiment and the 7th Marines, which he believed to be some 1,000 yards south of the division boundary, and an adjustment was requested by Shepherd. The 7th was ordered to cover the gap, a movement that placed it ahead of 1/4. In sideslipping back to its own zone, 1/4 met with stiff opposition from strongly entrenched enemy forces similar to those that had held up 3/4. With the aid of a platoon of tanks, this position was finally reduced. The two battalions killed some 250 Japanese in the course of the day's operations before the 4th Marines attack ceased at 1830, some 1,000 yards ahead of the L plus 3 line. During the day, Major Paul F. Sackett's 6th Engineer Battalion repaired the strips on Yontan and placed one taxiway in good enough condition to permit a VMO-6 spotter plane to land at 1500. By 4 April, all three Yontan runways were ready for emergency landings.

Spearheaded by extensive advance patrolling, the 1st Marine Division moved out on L plus 1 unopposed except for the slight interference presented by local defense units, which were part of a force officially designated the 1st Specially Established Regiment. Activated by the Thirty-second Army on L minus 4, it was composed of 3,473 airfield service troops and Boeitai, less than half of whom were armed with rifles. In addition, the equipment of this regiment consisted of 55 light machine guns, and 18 grenade launchers. The heaviest weapons of this unit were 10 heavy machine guns and 5 20mm dual-purpose machine cannon, For the most part, the troops were completely untrained, and even the regular Army service troops had not been given such basic infantry training as firing a machine gun.

When Ushijima pulled his combat troops south, the 1st Specially Established Regiment had been assigned the mission of servicing final air traffic on the Yontan and Kadena fields. The regiment was to destroy those fields on order after the Americans had landed and then to retire to positions from which it could deny their use to the invaders. The 1st Battalion was located in the 6th Division zone; the 2d and part of the 3d Battalion in the 1st Marine Division area; the remainder of the 3d Battalion faced the 7th Infantry Division; and the 5th Company of the 12th Independent Infantry Battalion was assembled in regimental reserve at Hanza. Uniquely enough, upon interrogation of some troops captured from these organizations, it was found that not one knew that he was in this paper organization, and only one had ever heard of it. Without exception, the prisoners gave as their unit the service or home guard element with which they had served at the airfields. Despite their motley makeup, their commanding officer., Lieutenant Colonel Tokio Aoyanagi, determined to employ them in slowing the advance of the invaders. At 1400 on L-Day, he issued an order directing all of his battalions to hold every strongpoint, to carry out night raids, to destroy all bridges, and to construct tank obstacles. The colonel pleaded for "each and every one [to] carry out his duty with the conviction of certain victory."

His men were poorly armed and mostly leaderless. Moreover, they lacked communications. When the escape routes to the organized forces in the south were cut off, therefore, this haphazardly organized group collapsed. The greater portion of these troops apparently fled to the northern hills, while a few, undoubtedly, escaped to the south; 26 were captured and 663 killed by the 1st Marine Division alone. Most of those who remained in the combat area quickly divorced themselves from the military, but others operated as snipers or guerrillas dressed in civilian attire.

Reliable intelligence was meager and hard to come by owing to the lack of contact with the enemy regular forces. As tactical operations developed rapidly against light opposition, hundreds of dazed civilians filtered through the lines and into the paths of the assault forces, When the Marines met these Okinawans, they interrogated, screened, and sent natives back to division stockades. Attempts to obtain information of the enemy from the older inhabitants were stymied because of the difficulties imposed in translating the Okinawan dialect. Younger natives of high school age, who had been forced to learn Japanese by the Nipponese overlords, proved to be a lucrative source of information, however.

Even though most civilians were cooperative with the Americans, they could provide very little information of immediate tactical importance. Nonetheless, the Okinawans confirmed the picture of the Japanese withdrawal to the south, clarified the presence or absence of units suspected of being in the area, aided in establishing an order of battle, and revealed the general and specific areas to which the rest of the civilian population had fled.

Military government personnel soon discovered that local inhabitants had moved with all their belongings to caves dug near their homes to escape from the path of war. Although interpreters roving the area in trucks mounted with loudspeakers assured the natives that they would be saved and induced them to leave their refuges voluntarily, other Okinawans continued to believe Japanese propaganda and viewed the American "devils" as barbarians and cutthroats. In many cases, particularly in isolated regions, it was necessary for language and civil affairs personnel "to enter the caves and verbally pry the dwellers loose." Sometimes this resulted in troops coming upon a tragic scene of self-destruction, where a father, fearing for the lives of his family and himself at the hands of the invaders, had killed his wife and children and then had committed suicide. Fortunately, there were no instances of mass suicide as there had been on Saipan or in the Keramas. Specifically organized patrols were dispatched to round up civilians and transfer them to stockades in areas predesignated in military government plans. These patrols were often accompanied by language officers searching for documents, but most of the material found was of no military value. When a rewarding find was made pertinent information was orally translated to the regimental S-2, who took down matters of local significance. The paper was then sent to the division G-2 language section.

The 1st Division learned from documents captured in its zone that the Japanese authorities had actively conscripted Okinawan males between the ages of 17 and 45 since the bombings of 10 October 1944. After their induction, these men were placed into three types of organizations; regular Thirty-Second Army units, specially organized engineer units, and labor forces. In order to neutralize the effects that might result from the presence of such a large hostile group in its midst, the Tenth Army decreed that all able-bodied males between the ages of 15 and 45 years were to be detained for further screening together with bona fide prisoners of war.

Special agents from Army Counterintelligence Corps detachments assigned the division assisted the Marines in interrogating and screening each male Okinawan detainee. Eventually, after their clearance by the American agents, cooperative and intelligent natives were enlisted to aid in the interrogations. Specially qualified Okinawans were moved to liberated villages and districts to serve as informants for the Island Command.

Even more of a problem than the inability of the Marines to come to grips with the enemy or their difficulty in obtaining usable intelligence was the dislocation of the logistical plan and the subsequent strain on supporting units that resulted from the unopposed and rapid troop advance. The logistics annex of the operation plan had been based on the premise that the landings would be stubbornly contested, and unloading priorities were assigned accordingly. When the uncontested landing permitted the immediate debarkation of troops who had not been scheduled ashore until 2 or 3 April, landing craft originally allocated to move cargo were diverted for this troop movement. As a result, the unloading of supplies was delayed on L-Day.

Because the road net ranged in degree from primitive to nonexistent and in order to prevent traffic congestion, LVTs were not sent too far inland. The front lines were supplied, therefore, by individual jeeps, jeep trailers, Weasels, and carrying parties, or a combination of all four. As forward assault elements moved farther inland, the motor transport requirement became critical and a realignment of unloading priorities was necessary. As a consequence, the unloading of trucks from AKAs and APAs was given the highest priority. By the night of L plus 1, all of the units supported by the 11th Marines had moved beyond artillery range, and Colonel Brown's regiment had to displace forward. The movement of 1/11 (Lieutenant Colonel Richard W. Wallace), in particular, was long overdue. Artillery displacements were not yet possible, however, since organic regimental transportation had not landed and no other prime movers were available. Two battalions were moved forward on L plus 2 by shuttle movements and an increased transportation capability, which resulted when more trucks came ashore and were made available. The other two battalions moved up on the 4th. Although it had been planned to have the bulk of Corps Artillery on the island by the end of L plus 1, and all by the end of L plus 2, it was not until 10 April that General Nimmer's force was completely unloaded. "This melee resulted from the drastic change in unloading priorities." Fortunately, unloading operations were improved by L plus 2.

Engineer battalions organic to the Marine divisions were generally relieved of mine removal tasks by the unfinished state of Japanese defenses, but there was no letup in their workload. Owing to the accelerated movement forward, the "narrow and impassable stretches of roads [and] lack of roads leading into areas in which operations against the enemy were being conducted, the engineers were called upon more than any other supporting unit." A priority mission assigned to the engineers was the rehabilitation of the airfields after they had been captured. Their early seizure permitted work to begin almost immediately, and after the engineers had reconditioned Yontan airfield beyond merely emergency requirements, the first four-engine transports arrived from Guam on 8 April to begin evacuating the wounded.

The only real problem facing General del Valle's units during the second day ashore, and one that tended to check a more rapid advance, was "the difficulty of supply created by the speed with which our units were moving and by lack of good roads into the increasing rough terrain." In viewing the lack of any formidable resistance to either one of his assault divisions, General Geiger gave both of them permission to advance beyond the L plus 5 line without further orders from him.

By 1500 of L plus 1, the progress of the 5th Marines had caused its zone of action to become wider, and in order to secure the division right flank and maintain contact with the 7th Infantry Division, the 1st and 2d Battalions of the 1st Marines were echeloned one behind the other on the corps boundary. Upon landing that morning, 3/1 moved inland to a point east of Sobe and remained there in division reserve. As the 1st Marine Division had not yet located the center of the enemy defenses or determined his strength, "the weakness of the resistance . . . [remained] a source of astonishment" to General del Valle. During the day, attempts at infiltration and the occasional ambushing of patrols by small hostile groups had little effect on the tactical situation. When the troops dug in at 1600, the division position was stabilized for the night on a line generally conforming to the L plus 5 line in the 7th Marines zone, while the 5th was slightly short of it.

To search out enemy positions, the 1st Reconnaissance Company (1st Lieutenant Robert J. Powell) was ordered to scout the division zone on 3 April, taking a route that followed along the corps boundary to the base of the Katchin Peninsula on the east coast. On this same day, the assault regiments were to continue the attack with an advance to the L plus 10 line. Because there had been only slight activity on the 1st Division front during L plus 1, the 11th Marines fired only five missions. While night defensive fires were planned for the second night ashore, they were not called for.

On this day in the XXIV Corps zone, the Army divisions also were able to exploit unexpectedly light resistance. The 7th Infantry Division had reached the east coast at Tobaru overlooking Katsuren Wan (Bay), effectively cutting the island in half and severing the enemy line of communications. Units of the 96th Division had advanced to the east and south, and succeeded in penetrating irregularly defended positions, some of which consisted merely of road mines and booby-trapped obstacles. At the end of L plus 1, General Bradley's front lines extended from the vicinity of Futema on the west coast to approximately one mile west of Unjo in the east.

By the close of 2 April, all assault division command posts had been established ashore, and the beachhead and the bulk of the high ground behind the landing beaches firmly secured. Enemy observation of Tenth Army movement and dispositions was thus limited, and any land-based threat to unloading operations removed.

Commenting on the conduct of Marine operations for the two days, General Buckner signalled General Geiger: "I congratulate you and your command on a splendidly executed landing and substantial gains in enemy territory. I have full confidence that your fighting Marines will meet every requirement of this campaign with characteristic courage, spirit, and efficiency."

During the night of 2-3 April, enemy activity was confined to sporadic sniper, machine gun, mortar, and artillery fire, and intermittent infiltration attempts by individuals and small groups. Undeterred by this harassment, General Geiger's corps jumped off at 0730 on the 3d and again found slight opposition to the attack. The 6th Marine Division resumed the offense in the same lineup with which it had ended the previous day. Both the 4th and 22d Marines advanced an average of more than 7,000 yards through difficult and heavily broken terrain to seize the dominating Yontan hill mass and the division objective beyond. While the 22d Marines moved forward, 1/29 patrols covered the entire Zampa Misaki without discovering any enemy troops on the peninsula. There was no repetition of the fierce clashes experienced by the 4th Marines the preceding two days. Throughout the day, the division was supported by tanks, which operated along the hazardous narrow trails existing on the precipitous ridge tops to the front.

By midmorning, the axis of advance of the 6th Division began to swing to the north as the towns of Kurawa and Terabaru were gained. Scattered rearguard action from withdrawing enemy troops was the only resistance encountered by the 22d Marines advancing on Nakadomori. In order to develop the situation on the division front and to determine the nature of Japanese defenses in the Ishikawa Isthmus, General Shepherd ordered his reconnaissance company to scout the coastal road from Kurawa to Nakadomori, and, at that point, to cross the isthmus to Ishikawa. Supported and transported by a reinforced platoon from the 6th Tank Battalion, the tank-infantry reconnaissance force completed the assignment and returned to its lines before nightfall. In the course of the patrol, the Marines made no enemy contacts and were fired upon only once from the vicinity of Ishikawa.

While 1/4, the right battalion, had relatively easy going most of the day, 3/4 on the left lagged behind because of the increasingly difficult terrain. When the division attack ceased at 1700, General Shepherd's troops were tied in with the 1st Division nearly a mile northeast of Kubo.

Following its sweep of Zampa Misaki, Lieutenant Colonel Moreau's 1/29 occupied new reserve positions east of Yontan airfield from which it could support either division assault regiment. At 2000, when IIIAC warned of an imminent enemy airborne attack, Moreau was reinforced with a tank company, which was deployed to defend the airfield by 2300; no Japanese paratroops or airborne infantry landed that night.

The only notable enemy activity experienced by the 1st Division during the hours of darkness, 2-3 April, occurred in the 7th Marines sector where the Japanese attempted extensive infiltration. In the firefight that ensued, 7 Marines were killed and 7 wounded, while approximately 20-25 of the would-be infiltrators perished.

This brief flurry was not an indication of an imminent major engagement, for when del Valle's three combat teams pushed forward on 3 April they met only light opposition on the left and virtually none on the right. "Our ever-widening zone of action prohibited the 'hand-in-hand' advance of some small island operations and our units were able to maintain contact and clear their areas only by patrolling to the flanks and front." With the resumption of the advance, motorized units of the 1st Reconnaissance Company began a series of patrols which were to encompass almost all of the division zone of action. In the morning, the Ikebaru-Napunja area was reconnoitered, after which the company was ordered to proceed down the Katchin Peninsula. Completing this mission by 1300, Lieutenant Powell's scouts were ordered up the east coast to Hizaonna and to return to division lines before dark. During the entire trip the only sign of enemy activity was a lightly held tank trap. All units of the division were ordered to halt at 1700 on ground most favorable for defense. On the left, the 7th Marines had pushed forward against moderate opposition over increasingly difficult terrain. As the regimental commander later stated: "The movement from the west coast landing beaches of Okinawa across the island to the east coast was most difficult because of the rugged terrain crossed. It was physically exhausting for personnel who had been on transports for a long time. It also presented initially an almost impossible supply problem in the Seventh's zone of action because of the lack of roads."

Despite these hardships, Snedeker's troops gained 2,700 yards of enemy territory and dug in for the night after overrunning a strongpoint from which heavy mortar, 20mm, and small arms fire had been received. Shortly thereafter, Colonel Snedeker received permission to exploit what appeared to be an apparent enemy weakness and to continue the attack after the rest of the division had ended it for the day. He then ordered his reserve battalion to pass between 1/7 and 2/7 and advance towards the village of Hizaonna on the high ground overlooking the east coast.

The major fighting in this advance occurred when the 81mm mortar platoon was unable to keep up with the rest of 3/7. Company K, following the mortars, became separated from the main body upon reaching a road fork near Inubi after night had fallen. When he became aware of the situation, Lieutenant Colonel Hurst radioed the company to remain where it was and to dig in after its repeated attempts to rejoin the battalion were defeated by darkness and unfamiliar terrain. An estimated platoon-sized enemy group then engaged the Marines in a heavy fire fight, which continued through the night as the Japanese effectively employed mortars, machine guns, and grenades against the isolated unit. By noon on 4 April, a rescue team from 3/7 was able to bring the situation under control and the company was withdrawn after having sustained 3 killed and 24 wounded. With its right flank anchored on Nakagusuku Wan, 1/1 held a line sealing off two-thirds of the Katchin Peninsula.

The 2d Battalion, 1st Marines, meeting negligible resistance from armed civilians, occupied the high ground immediately west of Gushikawa, where the eastern shore could be covered by fire. During the day's gains, "supply had been almost nonexistent and the troops were without water and still depending on the food they landed with."

The advance of the 5th Marines gained momentum throughout the day, the troops having met only a four-man enemy patrol. The 1st Battalion reached Agina, where 3/5 was committed on the right to contact 2/1. One thousand yards away, on the left of the regiment 2/5 occupied the village of Tengan and then advanced to the east coast of Okinawa.

By the end of L plus 2, the 1st Marine Division had driven to the coast, advancing 3,000-5,000 yards, and thus placed its lines 8-13 days ahead of the ICEBERG schedule. The 6th Division meanwhile, had moved through difficult and heavily broken terrain honeycombed with numerous caves to gain 3,500-7,000 yards of enemy ground in its zone.

At dark on 3 April, the 6th Division left flank was anchored at the base of the Ishikawa Isthmus, thereby placing the Tenth Army 12 days ahead of schedule in this area. During this same day, the XXIV Corps had reached the eastern coast in force and its units had begun reorganizing and regrouping for the attack to the south. The 7th Infantry Division had secured the Awashi Peninsula, and pivoting southward in a coordinated move with the 96th Division, secured an additional 3,000 yards before the end of the day. In the vicinity of Kuba-saki, the 32d Infantry came up against its first real opposition on Okinawa, when it made contact with an enemy force estimated at 385 men. The regiment overran the enemy position and finally took Kuba-saki. After completing the wheel to the right, the 96th Division reorganized its front lines, putting its units in position for the southerly drive.

While observation planes, OYs (Consolidated-Vultee Sentinels), operated from Yontan airfield during the day, the 6th Engineer Battalion and the 58th Seabees continued working on the field. An F6F (Grumman Hellcat) from the carrier *Hancock* made an emergency landing at 1110, and the pilot reported that, in his opinion, the runway could satisfactorily accommodate all types of carrier planes. The other runways were expected to be operational for fighter-type aircraft by noon on the 4th. Because of the very favorable situation that had developed during the day, General Buckner removed all restrictions he had placed on movement past the L plus 10 line and ordered IIIAC to seize the L plus 25 line at the earliest possible time. Geiger then ordered the 6th Marine Division to continue the attack on 4 April and to take the L plus 15 line, prepared to continue the advance to the L plus 20 line. General del Valle's division was ordered to advance to the L plus 20 line.

The continuing cool and clear weather on 4 April again served as a welcome change from the torrid humidity of the Philippines and the Solomons. Following a quiet night, broken only by the fighting in the Inubi area, the IIIAC jumped off on schedule at 0730 on L plus 3.

As the 6th Division pushed forward, no enemy hindered the 4th and 22d Marines advance to the L plus 15 line. General Geiger's reserve, the 29th Marines (Colonel Victor F. Bleasdale), less its 1st Battalion, had reverted to division control earlier, and Shepherd assigned it as his reserve. When it became apparent that the day's objectives would be reached by noon, the assault regiments were ordered to continue beyond the L plus 15 line to additionally assigned division objectives.

With all three battalions in the assault, the 22d Marines reached their Phase 1 objective at 1250. Organized as a fast tank-infantry column, Lieutenant Colonel Woodhouse's 2/22 sped up the west coastal road. All the while, he sent patrols inland along the route to maintain contact with 1/22 patrol columns in the interior of the regimental attack zone. On the right, the 3d Battalion reached Ishikawa before noon, having gradually pinched out the 4th Marines when that regiment reached the coast at about the same time. Colonel Shapley was then ordered to reconsolidate his unit in the Ishikawa area, and to prepare to support either division flank unit in the attack northward. In the course of the morning operations, exceedingly rough terrain, and the logistical support problems it posed, created greater obstacles to the advance than did the enemy.

At 1300, the attack up the Ishikawa isthmus was resumed, with RCT-22 and 1/29 attached, taking over the entire division front from the west to the east coast. Advance was rapid in the afternoon as patrols met only scattered resistance until 1730, when a Japanese strongpoint, built around several heavy machine guns, fired upon a 3/22 patrol north of Yaka. Night defenses were not taken up until after this obstacle was reduced by units of Donohoo's 3/22 and Moreau's 1/29, the latter having assumed the 1/22 sector when Major Myers' unit was placed in regimental reserve.

When the 6th halted for the day, its Marines had advanced over 7,500 yards and held a line that stretched across the isthmus from a point just south of Yakada on the west coast to Yaka on the east. In this day's fighting, the increasingly rugged terrain forecast the difficulties to be faced during the march northward. Supply lines were strained almost to their limit as they were extended across numerous ravines and steep valleys in the mountainous interior. Despite this, the troops were fed and logistical replenishment continued as the division prepared to continue the advance the next day. With the exception of the few enemy positions encountered in its push to the east coast, the 1st Marine Division still did not have a clear picture of what Japanese defenses lay ahead on 4 April. As on the day before, the attack jumped off without artillery preparation. Rapid progress with little resistance was the general order, except on the left where the 7th Marines was still busy with the enemy in the vicinity of Inubi. The 2d Battalion reached the east coast by 1130 and, shortly thereafter, made firm contact with the 4th Marines. On the extreme right of the regiment, light but stubborn enemy fire enfiladed the 1/7 right flank, and delayed its arrival at the coast until 1700. Because of the rapid advance of the regiment over a roadless terrain, Colonel Snedeker requested supply airdrops during the day. The first drop was made at Hizaonna at 1400, about the same time that General del Valle's new CP was opening at a point between Ikebaru and Napunja.

After dark, when the 7th Marines was consolidating its positions on the L plus 15 line, the enemy began numerous attempts at infiltrating American lines. Although 45 Japanese were killed as they probed the regimental positions, it was difficult to obtain any information regarding the units represented by these men, who employed rifles, grenades, bayonets, and sharply pointed bamboo spears, which the Marines promptly dubbed "idiot sticks."

In the center of the division line the 5th Marines reached the shores of Kimmu Wan by early afternoon, when the battalions consolidated their positions and established firm contact with all flanking units. The same day, the 1st Marines occupied Katchin Peninsula in orderly fashion by noon and set up its defenses. Once these two regiments were in position on the L plus 15 line, they initiated patrolling to the rear to eliminate bypassed positions, a task in which the reconnaissance company and the division reserve (3/1) also participated.

That evening, 3/1 was ordered to take over the defense of Yontan airfield from the 29th Marines on 5 April. Tentative plans were formulated to release the 7th Marines to IIIAC in order to assist the 6th Division in its drive north. The next day, the 7th Marines (less Hurst's 3/7, which was attached to the 5th Marines) went into IIIAC reserve with orders to occupy and defend the village of Ishikawa, pending further tactical developments.

In the course of its four-day drive across Okinawa, the 1st Marine Division found only negligible resistance, and this from Japanese units of undetermined strength employing delaying or rearguard tactics. The question remained: Where was the enemy? The division had killed 79 Japanese, captured 2 prisoners of war (POWs), and encountered 500-600 civilians, who were quickly interned. To the south of the 1st Division, the tactical situation in the XXIV Corps zone had been undergoing radical change. Army assault divisions had aggressively exploited the initial lack of enemy resistance. During the same time, they were hampered less by supply difficulties than the Marine divisions had been. Once General Hedge's divisions had wheeled to the right on 3 April for the drive southward, the lines were reorganized and preparations made for fresh assault units to effect passage of the lines the next day. The corps was now ready for the Phase I southern drive.

The 7th Division pushed forward on 4 April only to meet stiffening resistance from hostile artillery-supported infantry at Hill 165. After a day's fighting, the division drove the Japanese from this dominant piece of terrain and continued forward to net approximately 1,000 yards for the day. Meanwhile, in the 96th Division zone, Army infantry battalions were held up by reinforced enemy company strongpoints several times during the day. Heavy Japanese machine gun, mortar, and artillery fire impeded the advance, but by the night of 4 April, the XXIV Corps had seized the L plus 10 line, which had been originally designated the southernmost limit of the Tenth Army beachhead.

An increasing volume of enemy defensive fires was placed on the Army divisions as they moved out for their fifth day of ground action. On the XXIV Corps left flank, resistance came mainly from small, scattered enemy groups in the hills and ridges bordering the east coast. In the 96th Division zone to the right, both assault regiments became heavily engaged with Japanese outpost strongpoints during L plus 4. About noon, an enemy counterattack was broken up by tank-artillery supported infantry action just when the right flank regiment of the 96th, the 383d Infantry, drove unsuccessfully against the first of a series of prepared ridge positions guarding the approaches to Kakazu. Four tanks were lost during the day's fighting, one to a mine and the others to enemy antitank fire. Compared to the long advances of the previous four days of ground action, the 96th Division was able to take only 400 yards on L plus 4.

The Swing North

Although the Japanese forces in the south offered an increasingly stiff defense as their positions were uncovered, the exact whereabouts of the main enemy strength in the northern part of the island remained as clouded as was his order of battle. Even though Phase I of the ICEBERG plan did not specify any action beyond isolation of the area above the Ishikawa Isthmus for the IIIAC, General Buckner believed that it would be profitable to exploit initial Marine successes. As a result, on 5 April he ordered IIIAC to reconnoiter Yabuchi Shima, to conduct a vigorous reconnaissance northwards to the Motobu Peninsula, and to initiate preparations for the early completion of Phase II. At the same time that the 6th Division conducted its reconnaissance up the isthmus, the 1st Division entered a period devoted primarily to defensive activity. Supplies were brought up from the rear, positions were improved and camouflaged, and all units began heavy patrolling to the rear. At noon on L plus 4, a 1st Marines patrol waded across the reef to Yabuchi Shima from the Katchin Peninsula, captured five Boeitai, and reported the presence of some 350 civilians.

The nearly perfect weather which had prevailed since L-Day, deteriorated with light rain over scattered areas in the early evening of the 5th. Although there was no evidence that it was organized, enemy activity behind the lines increased during the day but only from small separated groups apparently operating independently of each other. Of this period, a regimental commander noted: "There [were] almost daily patrol contacts with well-armed enemy groups. . . . Some of these groups were wandering aimlessly about while others occupied well defended, organized, and concealed positions. These patrol operations were extremely valuable in giving to the officers and men of the regiment added confidence in each other and helped all to reach a peak of physical perfection . . . independent patrols . . . often under fire, added greatly to the ability of the leaders of small units."

Because it was necessary to move supplies forward to support the advance, the 6th Division delayed H-Hour on the 5th until 0900. At that time, armor-supported infantry columns were dispatched on deep reconnaissances up both sides of the isthmus, the 6th Reconnaissance Company on the left (west) flank and Company F, 4th Marines on the right. The latter advanced 14 miles before turning back in the late afternoon. During the day, the patrol had been delayed three times by undefended roadblocks but met no opposition until the tanks entered Chimu, where two of the enemy encountered were killed and a Japanese fuel truck was destroyed. The drive up the other side of the island was unopposed, but the tanks could not bypass a destroyed bridge at Onna. The reconnaissance company, forced to continue on to Nakama by foot, returned to the lines that evening.

While 6th Division mobile covering forces searched out routes of advance, the assault battalions rapidly moved forward, detaching companies as necessary to reduce bypassed enemy pockets of resistance inland. Although the terrain had become more difficult to negotiate and the enemy increasingly active, the division gained another 7,000 yards. The 22d Marines held the general line Atsutabaru-Chimu, with the 4th Marines (less 1/4 bivouacked at Ishikawa) located in assembly areas just behind the front line, prepared to pass through early the next day. At 1000 on the 5th, the 29th Marines were released to parent control by IIIAC and moved to an assembly area in the vicinity of Onna. As the 6th Division began its dash up the isthmus on 6 April, the 7th Marines in corps reserve patrolled the division zone south of the Nakadomari-Ishikawa line while the 6th Reconnaissance Company mopped up enemy remnants from this boundary north to the Yakada-Yaka line. After its lines had been passed by the 29th Marines on the left and the 4th Marines on the right, the 22d reverted to division reserve and began patrolling back to the area of responsibility of the reconnaissance company.

Because there were only a few roads inland, Colonel Shapley planned to move rapidly up the main road along the shore, detaching patrols from the advance guard to reconnoiter to their source all roads and trails into the mountainous and generally uninhabited interior. In order to maintain control during the anticipated rapid advance, the regimental march CP moved out in a jeep convoy at the head of the main body. By 1300, 2/4 had been used up by the detachment of small patrols, and the 3d Battalion then passed through in accordance with the prearranged plan of leapfrogging the battalions. When the regiment halted for the day at 1600, it had advanced seven miles, encountering only scattered enemy stragglers. The supply operations of the 4th Marines on L plus 5 were hampered more than usual by the fact that three bridges along the route had been bombed out earlier by friendly air.

The 4th Marines resumed operations the next morning deployed in the same manner in which it had halted the night before—3/4, 1/4, and 2/4 in that order. The advance on L plus 6 was virtually a repeat of the previous day as the regiment continued the push up the east coast, the lead battalion dissipating its strength with the dispatch of patrols into the interior. As a result, the 1st Battalion (Major Bernard W. Green) passed the 3d at noon and led the way to the regimental objective, opposed only by the difficult terrain, poor roads, and fumbling enemy defense measures.

Nearly all such efforts failed, however, for in very few instances was the 6th Division drive slowed. Enemy defensive engineering efforts were almost amateurish, for abatis, with neither mines nor booby traps attached or wired in place, were pushed aside easily by tank-dozers or bulldozers. Even basic defensive combat engineering principles were violated by the Japanese, who did not distribute their mines in roads and defiles in depth. They even failed to cover with either infantry fire or wire what they had placed. On the whole, the mines were little more than a nuisance and caused but few casualties. Bridges were often incompletely destroyed by Japanese demolitions, and Marine engineers were able to save valuable time by utilizing the remaining structural members as foundations for new spans in hasty bridge construction.

When the 6th Division drive towards the north began, each assault regiment was assigned one company of the 6th Engineer Battalion in direct support. A platoon from each of these companies was attached to advance guards to clear roadblocks, remove mines, and build bypasses for combat vehicles around demolished bridges. The remainder of each company followed up the advance, repairing and replacing bridges and widening narrow thoroughfares wherever possible to accommodate two-way traffic. Following closely in the wake of the assault regiments, the third company of the engineer battalion further improved roads and bridges. At the end of the Ishikawa Isthmus, where the mountains came down to the sea, engineer services were in even greater demand as they were required to widen roads that were little more than trails. The infantry advance was slowed by the terrain as well as by the near-physical exhaustion of the patrolling Marines, who had been going up and down the thickly covered broken ground. Despite this tortuous journey, the 4th Marines had made another seven miles by the late afternoon of 7 April. Then, just north of Ora, the 1st Battalion set up a perimeter defense with its flanks secured on the coast. Colonel Shapley's CP and weapons company were located in the village itself, while 3/4 and 2/4 were deployed in defensive perimeters at 1,000-yard intervals down the road.

On the west coast, the 29th Marines had seized its next objective on 7 April, again with little difficulty. Advance armored reconnaissance elements reached Nago at noon to find the town leveled by naval gunfire, air, and artillery. Before dark, the regiment had cleared the ruins and organized positions on its outskirts.

As the advance northwards continued, the difficult road situation had made it imperative to locate forward unloading beaches from which the 6th Division could be supplied. When Nago was uncovered, it was found suitable for this purpose, and IIIAC requested the dispatch to this point of Marine maintenance shipping from the Hagushi anchorage. On 9 April, cargo was discharged for the first time at Nago, relieving the traffic congestion on the supply route up the coast from Hagushi.

When planning for ICEBERG, General Shepherd had determined that Major Walker's company would be employed only in the reconnaissance mission for which it was best fitted and trained. In effect, the unit was intended to serve as the commanding general's mobile information agency. Pursuant to this decision, the reconnaissance company, supported and transported by tanks, was dispatched up the west coast road ahead of the 29th Marines in an effort to ascertain the character of Japanese strength on Motobu. After the company scouted Nago, it swung up the coastal road to Awa, and then, after retracing its steps to Nago, crossed the base of the peninsula in a northeasterly direction to Nakaoshi. Before returning to Nago for the night, the patrol uncovered much more enemy activity than had been previously revealed in the division zone of action and had met several enemy groups that were either destroyed or scattered. From the very beginning of the drive to the base of the Motobu Peninsula, the 15th Marines was employed so that each assault regiment had one artillery battalion in direct support and one in general support. The rapidity of the 6th Division advance during this phase of the campaign forced the artillery regiment to displace frequently, averaging one move a day for each battalion and the regimental headquarters. To keep up with the fast moving infantry, the artillerymen were forced to strip their combat equipment to a bare minimum; they substituted radio for wire communications and, by leapfrogging units, managed to keep at least one artillery battalion in direct support of each assault infantry regiment throughout the advance up the isthmus.

Augmenting the 15th Marines, 6th Division artillery support was reinforced by the 2d Provisional Field Artillery Group (Lieutenant Colonel Custis Burton, Jr.) which displaced to positions north of Nakadomari on the eve of the drive up the Ishikawa Isthmus. Four days later, when resistance on Motobu Peninsula began to stiffen, the 15th Marines was reinforced further by the attachment of the 1st Armored Amphibian Battalion as artillery. The following day, the corps artillery supporting the advance was moved to Besena Misaki, a promontory at the southern extremity of Nago Wan, where it remained throughout the period of Marine operations in the north.

Motobu Uncovered

Owing to the lack of intelligence about the location of the enemy, and a Tenth Army order to avoid unwarranted destruction of civilian installations unless there was a clear indication or confirmation of enemy presence, naval gunfire support was not used extensively in the drive up the Ishikawa Isthmus. After 5 April, however, all IIIAC naval fire support was diverted to the 6th Division zone of action. As the Marines moved north, these ships kept pace, firing up the numerous ravines leading down to the beach. Each assault battalion was furnished a call-fire ship during the day, and each regiment was furnished a ship to fire illumination at night. The Tenth Army gained land-based air support when TAF squadrons from MAG-31 and -33 arrived ashore on 7 and 9 April. The 6th Division did not need them immediately during the first two weeks in the north, however, for the division advance had been rapid and suitable targets scarce. Daylight combat air patrols were flown almost as soon as the squadrons landed, but strikes in support of ground operations did not begin until L plus 12, and then they were directed at Japanese targets in the XXIV Corps zone in the south. As enemy resistance stiffened on Motobu Peninsula, Marine air was called upon to destroy emplacements, observation posts, and troop concentrations. After the division had gained the base of the Motobu Peninsula and had begun extending reconnaissance operations to the west on 8 April, aerial observation and photo studies confirmed the fact that the enemy had chosen to make his final stand in the rugged mountains of the peninsula. In order to reduce this Japanese bastion, and at the same time maintain flank security and continue the drive to the northernmost tip of Okinawa, General Shepherd needed to reorient the axis of operations and redeploy his forces. Consequently, the 22d Marines was taken out of division reserve and set up on a line across the island from Nakaoshi to Ora to cover the right and rear of the 29th Marines attacking to the west. Assembled near Ora, also, was the 4th Marines, which was positioned to support either the 29th Marines on Motobu or the 22d in the north.

During the next five days, the 4th and 22d Marines combed the interior and patrolled in the north, while the 29th probed westward to uncover the enemy defense. On L plus 7, 2/29 moved northeast from Nago to occupy the small village of Gagusuku. The 1st Battalion, initially in reserve, was ordered to send one company to secure the village of Yamadadobaru, a mission accomplished by Company C at 0900. An hour later, the battalion as a whole was ordered to the aid of Company H, 3/29, which had encountered heavy resistance in the vicinity of Narashido. By 1500, 1/29 had converged on this point and, despite heavy enemy machine gun and rifle fire, had reduced two strongpoints, after which Lieutenant Colonel Moreau's men dug in for the night. Intending to locate the main enemy force on Motobu, the 29th Marines moved out on 9 April in three columns; the 3d Battalion (Lieutenant Colonel Erma A. Wright) on the left flank, the 2d Battalion (Lieutenant Colonel William G. Robb) on the right flank, and Moreau's 1st Battalion up the mountainous center of the peninsula. All three columns encountered opposition almost immediately. This was an indication that the division may have at last hit the major enemy resistance in the north, and it was located in the area from Itomi west to Toguchi.

In the 3/29 zone on the left, roads were found to be virtually impassable as a result of effective enemy use of roadblocks, mines, and demolitions. The 6th Engineer Battalion reported that from Nago westward on the Motobu Peninsula the enemy had been even more destructive. They had demolished every bridge and blasted numerous tank traps in the roads. The Japanese had been careful to place these obstacles at points where no tank bypass could be constructed. Traps that had been made in the narrow coastal roads were put at the foot of cliffs where back fill was unavailable. Those in the valleys were always located where the road passed through rice paddies, When the crater was in a cliff road, trucks had to travel long distances to obtain fill for the hole.

In the center, 1/29 was to occupy and defend Itomi before nightfall; about 600 yards short of the objective, however, the battalion was met by a strong enemy force and compelled to dig in for the night in place. The north coast was patrolled as far as Nakasoni by Robb's 2d Battalion, which destroyed supply dumps and vehicles and dispersed small enemy groups. The battalion also scouted Yagachi Shima with negative results.

The next day, L plus 9, Robb's men seized Unten and its harbor, where the Japanese had established a midget submarine and torpedo boat base. The base had been abandoned and large amounts of equipment and supplies were left behind by approximately 150 Japanese naval personnel, who were reported to have fled inland to the mountains. Toguchi, on the other side of the peninsula, was captured by 3/29, which sent patrols inland to Manna. On 10 April, 1/29 pushed forward through Itomi, and on the high ground north of the town it uncovered numerous well-prepared positions from which the enemy had fled.

During the first two days of the drive to clear Motobu Peninsula, frequent enemy contacts were made in the difficult terrain northwest and southwest of Itomi. Night counterattacks increased in intensity; one particularly strong attack, supported by artillery, mortars, machine guns, and 20mm dual-purpose cannon, struck the 1/29 defense perimeter on the night of 10-11 April and was not broken up until dawn.

Patrols from 2/29 were sent out on 11 April to make contact with 1/29 near Itomi. They met little opposition but substantiated previous intelligence estimates locating the main Japanese battle position in an area between Itomi and Toguchi. As a result of this verification, 2/29 (less Company F) was recalled from the north coast and ordered to set up defensive installations and tie them in with 1/29 on the high ground near Itomi. Company F continued patrolling. During the day, 1/29 patrols scouted just to the north and northeast of Itomi and met only light resistance. On the other hand, 3/29, moving inland to contact the 1st Battalion, ran into heavily defended enemy positions at Manna and was forced to withdraw under fire to Toguchi. In compliance with Admiral Turner's expressed desire that Bise Saki was to be captured early for use as a radar site, the 6th Reconnaissance Company was ordered to explore the cape area on 12 April, and to seize and hold the point unless opposed by overwhelming force. As anticipated, resistance was light, and the area was captured and held. That evening, Company F, 29th Marines, reinforced the division scouts. Overall command of this provisional force was then assumed by the reconnaissance company commander.

In order to fix more definitely the hostile battle position, the 29th Marines continued probing operations. On the 12th, the 1st and 2d Battalions were disposed in positions near Itomi, and 3/29 was located in the vicinity of Toguchi. Company G was sent north to contact the reinforced division reconnaissance company and to meet 2/29 at Imadomari. Company H was ordered east to meet 1/29 at Manna, and Company I was ordered to patrol to the high ground south and east of Toguchi and to remain there overnight. As these last two companies proceeded on their missions, they came under intense fire that prevented the completion of their assignments unless they were to risk sustaining unacceptable casualties. Under cover of prompt call fires from the destroyer *Preston*, LVT(A) fire, and an 81mm mortar barrage, Company I was withdrawn while Company H served as rear guard. Both companies had organized a perimeter defense at Toguchi by midafternoon when the battalion CP received considerable artillery and mortar fire. The day's action cost the battalion 9 killed and 34 wounded.

Because of this significant enemy reaction in the Toguchi area, Company G, upon its arrival at Imadomari at 1415, was recalled by the battalion. When Company H had been hit in the morning, 3/22 was alerted for possible commitment, and in the afternoon it was ordered to assemble in division reserve at Awa. Battalion headquarters and Companies I and K completed the motorized move after 1700, and L arrived at 0900 the following morning.

By the night of 12 April, General Shepherd's division was confronted with a fourfold task: to continue occupation and defense of the Bise area; to secure the line

Kawada Wan-Shana Wan and prevent enemy movement through that area; to seize, occupy, and defend Hedo Misaki, the northernmost tip of Okinawa; and to destroy the Japanese forces on Motobu Peninsula. On 10 April, 1/22 had established a perimeter defense at Shana Wan from which it conducted vigorous patrolling eastward to the coast and north towards Hedo Misaki. By the 12th, battalion patrols had contacted the 4th Marines on the east coast; 3/4 was ordered to move to Kawada the next day. During the period 8-12 April, the 4th Marines, located near Ora, patrolled all areas within a 3,000-yard radius of the regimental bivouac. On the 10th, Company K was sent north along the east coast on extended patrol after which it was to rejoin its battalion at Kawada. While in the field, the company relied on LVTS for daily support and evacuation. In a week's time, the patrol had travelled 28 miles up the coast.

Assigned the capture and defense of Hedo Misaki, Woodhouse's 2/22 moved rapidly up the west coast on 13 April in a tank- and truck-mounted infantry column, "beating down scattered and ineffective resistance." At 2110, the 2/22 commander reported that a patrol had entered Hedo by way of the coastal road and that the entry had been opposed only by 10 Boeitai. As soon as the rest of the battalion arrived, a base was set up and patrols were sent out to make contact with the 4th Marines advancing up the east coast.

At the end of the second week on Okinawa, on Friday, 13 April (12 April in the States), ICEBERG forces learned of the death that day of President Franklin D. Roosevelt. Memorial services were held on board American vessels and behind Tenth Army lines; those who could attend these services did so if the fighting permitted. One senior officer of the 1st Marine Division said later: "It was amazing and very striking how the men reacted. We held services, but services did not seem enough. The men were peculiarly sober and quiet all that day and the next. Plainly each of them was carrying an intimate sorrow of the deepest kind, for they paid it their highest tribute, the tribute of being unwilling to talk about it, of leaving how they felt unsaid."

The Battle For Yae Take

While three of its four assigned missions in the north were being accomplished by extensive patrolling against little or no opposition, the 6th Marine Division found that destroying the firmly entrenched bulk of the enemy was becoming an increasingly difficult problem. Company I had apparently touched a sensitive nerve during its probings near Toguchi, judging by the immediate enemy reaction. This assumption was confirmed on the night of 12-13 April, when the 29th Marines encountered some English-speaking Okinawans, who had at one time lived in Hawaii. The Marines were told that there was a concentration of 1,000 Japanese on the high ground overlooking the Manna-Toguchi road south of the Manna River. The civilians said further that the enemy force was commanded by a Colonel Udo, and that it contained an artillery unit under a Captain Kiruyama. Previous reports of enemy order of battle were corroborated by the operations of strong combat patrols; the 6th Division now firmly fixed the Japanese defenses in an area some six by eight miles surrounding the rugged and dominating Mount Yae Take. The ground around this towering 1,200-foot-high peak prohibited extensive maneuvering and completely favored the defense. Yae Take was the peninsula's key terrain feature and its heights commanded the nearby landscape, the outlying islands, and all of Nago Wan. The steep and broken approaches to the mountain would deny an attacker any armor support. Infantry was sure to find the going difficult over the nearly impassable terrain. The Japanese defenses had been intelligently selected and thoroughly organized over an obviously long period. All natural or likely avenues of approach were heavily mined and covered by fire.

It was soon concluded that approximately 1,500 men were defending the area and that the garrison, named the Udo Force after its commander, was built around elements of the 44th Independent Mixed Brigade. Included in this group were infantry, machine gun units, light and medium artillery, Okinawan conscripts, and naval personnel from Unten Ko. In addition to 75mm and 150mm artillery pieces, there were two 6-inch naval guns capable of bearing on the coastal road for 10 miles south of Motobu, on Ie Shima, and all of Nago Wan.

General Shepherd's estimate of the situation indicated that reduction of the Yae Take redoubt was beyond the capabilities of a single reinforced infantry regiment. In face of this conclusion, the 4th Marines (less 3/4) was ordered to move from the east coast to Yofuke. The 29th Marines was ordered to continue developing the enemy positions by vigorous patrolling on 13 April and to deploy for an early morning attack on the next day.

Complying with General Shepherd's orders, Colonel Bleasdale again attempted to clear the Itomi-Toguchi road and join his 1st and 3d Battalions. As elements of 1/29 moved out of Itomi towards Manna, they were ambushed and hit hard again by the 20mm cannon fire coming from the commanding heights. Probing north from Awa, 3/22 patrols also came under fire. Before these patrols could withdraw under the cover of their battalion 81mm mortars, an hour-long firefight ensued. Adding to the general harassment from the enemy, artillery fire was placed on 3/22 positions in the afternoon.

At this same time, Japanese counterbattery fire was delivered against the emplaced artillery of 2/15 (Major Nat M. Pace). This heavy bombardment inflicted 32 casualties, including two battery commanders and the executive officer of a third battery, and destroyed the battalion ammunition dump and two 105mm howitzers. Air strikes were called in on the suspected sources of the fire and 3/22 dispatched patrols in an attempt to locate the enemy mortar batteries. Fires and exploding ammunition made the Marine artillery position untenable, so Pace's men withdrew to alternate positions. Earlier in the day, the 4th Marines (less 3/4) began its move to Yofuke with Hayden's 2d Battalion in the lead. The west coast was gained after a difficult hike over primitive roads, but Hayden was ordered to continue the march to a point on the southwest corner of the peninsula just below Toguchi, and the battalion arrived there at 1700. Green's 1st Battalion arrived at Yofuke at 1630 and, while digging in for the night, was ordered to move to a position just west of Awa. This displacement was accomplished just prior to darkness by shuttling the battalion by truck, a company at a time. When nightfall came, the 4th Marines was disposed with the 1st and 2d Battalions in perimeter defense, a little less than three miles apart on the southwest coast of Motobu; the 3d Battalion was 20 miles away on the east coast; and regimental headquarters was set up at Yofuke with the Weapons Company.

Based on his original estimate of the situation, General Shepherd planned a coordinated attack for 14 April when the 4th Marines, with 3/29 attached, would advance inland to the east. At the same time, the 29th Marines (less 3/29) would drive to the west and southwest from the center of the peninsula. In effect, this was a situation where two assault regiments attacked a target from directly opposing positions. The danger of overlapping supporting fires was lessened, in this case, by the intervention of the high Yae Take mass. Nevertheless, success of this rare maneuver required close and careful coordination of all supporting arms.

In the 4th Marines zone of action, Colonel Shapley's troops were ordered initially to seize a 700-foot-high ridge about 1,200 yards inland and dominating the west coast and its road. It was immediately behind this ridge that Company 1 of 3/29 had been mauled on the 12th. Intermittent machine gun fire had been received from this area since that time.

The attack jumped off at 0830 on the 14th with 3/29 on the left, 2/4 on the right, and 1/4 initially in regimental reserve. Preceded by an intense artillery, aerial, and naval bombardment, the Marines advanced against surprisingly light resistance. Disregarding scattered Japanese machine gun, mortar, and light artillery fire, the Marines gained the ridge before noon with the left flank of 3/29 anchored to a very steep slope.

In order to protect his open right flank, Colonel Shapley moved 1/4 up to an assembly area to the right rear of 2/4. Company C was ordered to take a dominating ridge 1,000 yards to the right front of the 2d Battalion. By noon the company made contact with small enemy groups and soon thereafter began receiving mortar and machine gun fire. Company A was then committed on the left of Company C and the advance was continued. At the same time, 2/4 and 3/29 resumed the attack to seize the next objective, another ridge 1,000 yards to the front. As the troops headed into the low ground approaching the height, enemy resistance began to stiffen appreciably even though the advance was again preceded by heavy naval gunfire and artillery barrages, and two air strikes. The ground, ideally suited for defense, consisted of broken terrain covered with scrub conifers and tangled underbrush, and the Japanese exploited this advantage to the utmost.

The enemy defense was comprised of small, concealed groups which formed covering screens to the main positions. The Japanese employed every possible stratagem to delay and disorganize the advance, and to mislead the attackers as to the location of the main battle position. Enemy soldiers would lie in a concealed position with their weapons zeroed in on a portion of the trail over which the Marines would have to pass. After allowing a sizable force to pass without interference, the enemy would open up on what they considered a choice target. When a company commander passed the ambush point with his headquarters section, the machine guns opened up, killing him and several other nearby Marines. There were many officer casualties. It was in this manner that the commander of 1/4 was killed in an area where there had been no firing for over half an hour. No one else was hurt, though Major Green's operations and intelligence officers were standing on either side of him. Lieutenant Colonel Fred D. Beans, regimental executive officer, assumed command of the battalion.

Although the hills and ravines were apparently swarming with Japanese, it was difficult to close with them. "It was like fighting a phantom enemy," stated one Marine officer. The small enemy groups, usually armed with a heavy Hotchkiss machine gun and several light Nambu machine guns, frequently changed positions in the dense undergrowth. When fired upon, furious Marines raked the area from where the volleys had come. After laboriously working their way to the suspected enemy position, the Marines came upon only an occasional bloodstain on the ground; they found neither live nor dead Japanese.

Company G of 2/4 made the first strong contact with the enemy at 1350 when it came under rifle, machine gun, mortar, and artillery fire. Less than five minutes later, Company E began receiving similar treatment. After being spotted, a Japanese artillery piece was silenced by naval gunfire and artillery brought to bear on it. Despite heavy casualties in Company G and stubborn enemy delaying tactics, Hayden's battalion drove the covering forces back and took the ridge with a frontal attack combined with an envelopment from the right. By 1630, the attack had halted with both 3/29 and 2/4 on the regimental objective and 1/4 on the high ground to the right. Contact was then established all along the line. East of Yae Take the 29th Marines jumped off from Itomi in a column of battalions to clear the Itomi-Toguchi road and to eliminate the strongpoints that patrols had discovered the previous four days. As the attack developed, it became apparent that an advance in a westerly direction would be both difficult and costly. The axis of the attack was reoriented, therefore, to the southwest in order to take advantage of the high ground. With Lieutenant Colonel Moreau's 1st Battalion leading, the 29th Marines advanced 800 yards up steep slopes against determined enemy resistance. By late afternoon, 1/29 had become pinned down by overwhelming fire from the high ground to its front. The 2d Battalion was committed on the left flank to strengthen the defense and the troops dug in for the night.

When it was relieved during the day by 1/22, 3/4 made a motor march from its east coast position to relieve 3/22 in division reserve. The latter then returned to its patrol base at Majiya.

The following day, L plus 14, Colonel William J. Whaling assumed command of the 29th Marines from Colonel Bleasdale, and the regimental CP displaced to Itomi. During the day, the regiment consolidated its position and organized defensive positions on the high ground. Constant pressure in the rear of Yae Take was maintained by vigorous patrolling which assisted the 4th Marines on the other side of the mountain. At 1600, heavy 20mm cannon fire began raining down on the battalion command posts and, about the same time, enemy forces unsuccessfully attempted to infiltrate 2/29 lines under the cover of grenade, rifle, and mortar fire. By 1700, 2/29 had tied in with the 1st Battalion, and shortly after was able to stem the forces of the attack, but not before 35 Marines had become casualties. Artillery and mortar fire, and naval gunfire from the main and secondary batteries of the Colorado were placed on the suspected 20mm cannon emplacements and silenced them for a time.

When the 4th Marines began its attack at 0700 on the 15th, it was in the same formation in which it had halted the previous night. The advance was resisted by small scattered groups such as those that opposed the Marines the day before. At noon, as the regiment approached the half-way mark to that day's objective, Japanese resistance became came markedly stiffer. From caves and pillboxes emplaced in dominating terrain, the enemy poured down effective fire as the assaulting units climbed the steep mountainside. As 3/29 pushed forward some 900 yards to the east and south, it engaged in numerous fire fights while it received intense machine gun, mortar, and artillery fire. An enemy strongpoint on Hill 210, 500 yards to the battalion right front, held up the advance. In addition to well-dug-in machine guns and mortars, the position also contained the mountain gun that had been pinpointed the day before, For the second day, attempts were made to destroy this devastating weapon with naval gunfire and artillery, as well as air strikes which employed 500-pound bombs and napalm. Despite these efforts, the piece continued functioning and causing considerable damage.

All along the line bitter fighting ensued as 2/4 again bore the brunt of the rugged going in attempting to capture the high ground dominating the right flank. Although it jumped off with three companies abreast (less one platoon in battalion reserve), 2/4 was able to make only small gains against intense small arms fire. After a day's fighting, the battalion managed to place two companies on Hill 200, while the third one, despite severe casualties (65, including 3 company commanders), eventually advanced three-fourths of the way up a hill to the right of 200. In order to establish a better position, Company G withdrew partway down the hill where it tied in with Company F. On the right of the regimental line, 1 200-yard gap between the 2d and 1st Battalions was covered by fire. In the late afternoon, in the area immediately southwest of Yae Take, 1/4 finally seized a key hill mass from which it had been driven back earlier in the day.

When the attack ceased at 1630, the center and right battalions were on their objectives and 3/29 was slightly behind them, organizing ground favorable for defense. During the day, resupply operations and the evacuation of the mounting number of casualties over the tortuous terrain became more and more difficult, and the troops had become very tired. Nonetheless, many caves had been sealed and there were 1,120 enemy dead counted. Colonel Udo apparently foresaw defeat; that night he decided to resort to guerrilla operations and also to move his command to the mountain strongholds of northern Okinawa by way of Itomi.

The 4th Marines knew by this time that it was attacking a force of at least two companies which had organized the terrain to their best possible advantage. Moreover, it became apparent that the Japanese had oriented their defenses to face the anticipated direction of the attack. Owing to these circumstances, and since the advance was still toward friendly troops and artillery, it was decided to contain Udo's mountain force and envelop his defenses by a flanking action from the south; this shifted the direction of the main Marine effort to the north. Implementing these decisions, 3/4 reverted to regimental control and was to be committed in the attack the next day, and 1/22 was ordered into division reserve at Awa. On 16 April, the 6th Marine Division was deployed to wage a full-scale attack on the enemy from three sides. As the 29th Marines continued pressuring in from the east, the 4th Marines with 3/29 would complete the squeeze play from the west and southwest. A juncture between the 4th and 29th Marines would be effected when 1/22 sent strong patrols north into the gap between the two regiments. Each of these three principal assault elements was assigned an artillery battalion in direct support. The artillery was so deployed that the fires of two battalions of the 15th Marines, one company of the 1st Armored Amphibian Battalion, and a battery of the 7th 155mm Gun Battalion could be placed in any of the three zones of action. In the 4th Marines zone, 3/29 was to seize the high ground 500 yards to its front, including the redoubtable Hill 210. To the right of this battalion, 2/4 was to remain in position and support the attacks of Wright's 3/29 and Beans' 1/4 by fire, while units on the right flank of 1/4 wheeled to the north. The 3d Battalion, 4th Marines, was to attack to seize the division objective establish contact with 1/4 on the left, and to protect the right flank until 1/22 drew abreast of the line. Weapons Company, 4th Marines, organized as an infantry company, was ordered to patrol thoroughly the right rear of Beans' and Wright's battalions, since 1/22 was not scheduled to start from Majiya until first light.

Because of resupply difficulties, the attack did not resume until 0900 on the 16th. By 1200, 3/29 had seized its objective with a perfectly executed basic maneuver, a single envelopment. As the attack began, Company H, on the 3/29 right flank faced Hill 210 frontally. Company G in the center was ordered to break contact with Company I on its left and to make an end-around play assaulting the enemy from the south. A Company H support platoon moved into the gap left by G and supported that company by fire, as did 2/4 from its commanding position on the right.

Supporting fires effectively neutralized the Japanese defenders and kept their heads down until Company G Marines had gained the top of 210 and swarmed over the forward slope. Grenades and demolitions blasted the shocked enemy from their caves and they retreated hastily, pursued all the while by effective fire from both the assault and support units. In capturing this objective, the Marines had silenced the troublesome mountain gun and killed 147 of the enemy. The positions of Companies H and G were now inverted, with Company H in the center of the line and G on the right flank firmly holding Hill 210. While 3/29 was securing its objective, 1/4 completed its pivot northwards and had established contact with 3/4. Well to the rear, Myers' 1/22 advanced to cover the open 4th Marines flank. With 3/29 and 2/4 solidly established as landlords of the high ground facing east, 1/4 and 3/4 looked north in positions at a right angle to the other two battalions. When the attack resumed a half-hour later, 3/29 and 2/4 remained in position providing fire support to the advancing 1/4 and 3/4. At this time, the formidable Mount Yae Take was in the 1/4 zone.

The 1st Battalion moved out with Company A on the left attacking frontally up one nose, and Company C working up a draw on the right. Progress up the steep slope was arduous and not helped by enemy small arms fire, light and scattered though it was. As Company A reached the crest, the Japanese met it with withering fire at very close range. In the face of the rifle, machine gun, grenade, and knee mortar drumfire, the Marines withdrew below the summit, and in turn, employed their own 60mm mortars and grenades against the enemy entrenched on the reverse (north) slope. The battle waged fiercely at close quarters, as neither side was able to hold the height for long. At last the tide turned in the Marines' favor, helped mainly by supporting fire of 2/4 coming from the high ground overlooking the enemy.

The victory was not bought cheaply; even though the two companies possessed Yae Take, the situation was critical. Over 50 Marine casualties had been sustained in the assault and the ammunition supply was nearly spent. It also appeared that the Japanese were regrouping for a counterattack. Fortunately, effective 15th Marines artillery fire and the excellent mortar and machine gun support of 2/4 held the enemy in check until ammunition could be brought up.

Recalling this phase of the battle for Mount Yae Take, the operations officer of the 4th Marines wrote: "If the supply problem was difficult before, it was a killer now. That 1,200-foot hill looked like Pike's Peak to the tired, sweaty men who started packing up ammunition and water on their backs. Practically everyone in the 1st Bn headquarters company grabbed as much ammunition as he could carry. A man would walk by carrying a five-gallon water can on his shoulder and the battalion commander would throw a couple of bandoleers of ammunition over the other! . . . The Battalion commander, on his way up to the front lines to get a closer look at the situation, packed a water can on his way up. Stretchers also had to be carried up, and all hands coming down the hill were employed as stretcher bearers."

Additional assistance in resupply and evacuation was afforded the 1st Battalion when Company K, coming up from the rear in late afternoon to revert to the control of 3/4, took out the 1/4 wounded and returned with water and ammunition. The resupply of the 1st Battalion occurred just in time, for at 1830, an hour after Yae Take had been seized, the enemy reacted with a fanatic *Banzai* charge across the battalion front. An estimated 75 Japanese made up the wildly attacking group, but again the supporting fires of artillery and 2/4 stemmed the rush and virtually annihilated the force. As the Marines dug in for the night, Mount Yae Take was held securely. Lieutenant Colonel Beans' battalion consolidated its holdings in the afternoon while receiving small arms and mortar fire. On the left, Company B was committed to tie in 3/4 with the 1st Battalion. Because its progress was slowed more by the terrain than the enemy, 1/22 on the right was unable to gain contact with either the 4th or the 29th and established a defense perimeter for the night.

While the 4th Marines was storming Yae Take, Colonel Whaling's regiment maintained unrelenting pressure against the enemy's rear positions. As the attack rolled forward, the Japanese resisted stubbornly from log-revetted bunkers and occasional concrete emplacements, and from machine gun, mortar, and artillery positions concealed in ravines and in caves on the heights.

In this phase of the 6th Division's northern campaign, the Japanese exhibited their well-known ability to exploit the terrain and gain maximum benefit from weapons emplaced in caves and pits and concealed by natural camouflage. Of all the weapons that the enemy employed effectively, his use of the 20mm dual-purpose cannon was most noteworthy. Marine battalion CPS received a daily ration of fire from these weapons, and all roads and natural avenues of approach were covered. Any Marine attempt to move over these easier routes often proved disastrous.

Since there was no alternative, "the method of reducing the enemy positions followed a pattern of 'ridge-hopping'," in which all supporting arms covered the attacking force as it enveloped hostile defenses and reduced them in detail. In some cases, the 29th discovered abandoned positions and weapons, suggesting that the Japanese determination to resist was considerably diminished when attacked on the flank. The action in the 29th Marines zone was characterized by simultaneous attacks which, in effect, consisted of a series of local patrol actions to seize critical positions, followed by mopping-up activity within the area.

A heavier-than-usual artillery preparation was laid down before the jump off on the morning of 17 April. At 0800, the 29th Marines began an advance to join up with the 4th Marines along the Itomi-Toguchi road. From here, the two regiments would then sweep northward abreast of each other. Moving out over difficult terrain against light resistance, 1/29 made slow progress, but by 1300 had secured its objective, the highest hill in its area.

The enemy positions which confronted 1/29 were on the crest and face of this hill and presented a problem in precision naval gunnery to the *Tennessee* whose line of supporting fire was almost parallel to the target. As troops rapidly advanced, the ship's main and secondary batteries delivered such an intense bombardment that the hill was taken without Marine casualties. On the way to the top, the infantry killed 8 Japanese and 32 more on the crest itself, but the huge craters produced by the *Tennessee's* guns contained in excess of 100 more enemy dead. Within an hour after 2/29 had resumed its attack, some 50 enemy troops had been flushed out and were observed fleeing to the northwest. Shortly after, the battalion was able to move forward against negligible opposition, stopping only to destroy large enemy stores of equipment, ammunition, and supplies. Before noon, physical contact had been established with 1/22, which had reduced the positions met in its zone and had captured a considerable amount of enemy clothing and ammunition. After having made contact with the 4th Marines on its left, 1/22 was pinched out of the line and withdrew to Awa, where it set up defenses for the night.

The first missions flown by TAF squadrons in support of Marine ground forces during the Motobu campaign struck enemy targets early in the morning of the 17th. At 1000, eight VMF-322 aircraft attacked and destroyed Manna. Upon completion of that mission, the flight was radioed by the ground commander that "the town was wiped out. One hundred percent of bombs and rockets hit target area." VMF-312, 322, and 323 flew a total of 47 sorties during the day. In the afternoon, one mission of eight planes was cancelled when the assigned target was overrun by Marine infantry.

As it still faced a critical supply shortage on the 17th, the 4th Marines did not launch its attack until 1200, after replenishment. Then the advance toward the Itomi-Toguchi road was resumed with the 1st and 3d Battalions on the right. In reverse of the previous day's situation, 2,/4 and 3/29 on the left faced east at a right angle to the front of the other two battalions in assault. They were, therefore, ordered to remain in place and to support the assault from present positions until the attacking units masked their fires.

The attacking element made rapid progress as their downhill path was blocked only by isolated enemy stragglers. Without too great an effort, the Marines overran elaborately fortified positions, intricate communications systems, and bivouac areas. The hastily departing enemy left behind a scene of an undisciplined retreat—for dead bodies and military paraphernalia were strewn all over the area. Large stores of equipment, food, weapons, and clothing were either captured or destroyed. As 1/4 swept across the 3/29 front, 2 8-inch naval guns, 5 artillery pieces, 8 caves full of ammunition, and over 300 dead Japanese were found before the Company G position on Hill 210. Although the 1st Battalion met but few of the enemy during the day, Hochmuth's 3d Battalion killed 56 without losing a Marine. After their attack axes had shifted northward, the 4th and 29th Marines made contact with each other in late afternoon on the high ground overlooking the Itomi-Toguchi road. At that time, 2/29 was withdrawn from the line to clear out any bypassed enemy pockets in the regimental zone. By the end of 17 April, a review of that day's operations indicated that the enemy was unable to maintain his position and was, in fact, attempting to retreat in order to escape annihilation, There was little doubt that the 6th Marine Division had broken the back of enemy resistance on the peninsula, an assumption that was confirmed when an enemy map captured by the 4th Marines showed that the Yae Take position was the only organized Japanese defense on Motobu.

After four days of vigorous fighting, activities on the 18th were confined to reorganizing, resupplying, and consolidating the gains of the previous day, and patrolling the Itomi-Toguchi road. In an attempt to prevent the further escape of any of the enemy and to destroy his trenches and camouflaged emplacements in front of the lines, at 0750, four VMF-312 planes attacked targets with general purpose (GP) and napalm bombs, rockets, and then strafed the smoking positions. The ground troops later reported that all of the hits were in the target area and the enemy trenches were completely destroyed. During the rest of the day, VMF-312 and -322 flew 12 additional sorties in support of General Shepherd's troops.

The now-bypassed 3/29 was detached from the 4th Marines and moved around the base of the peninsula by truck to rejoin its parent organization at Itomi. In the same way, 1/22 rejoined its regiment at Majiya. In the 4th Marines area, the 1st Battalion went into reserve, bivouacking near Manna. Upon its reversion to regimental control, 3/29 took up blocking positions on the right flank, north of Itomi, to prevent any enemy escaping to the east. The 29th Marines left flank was pushed northward to straighten out the division lines. As 3/4 conducted local patrols, the 2d Battalion patrolled the area through which the 1st and 3d Battalions had attacked the previous day. Resupplying the assault regiments continued to be difficult, for the enemy had thoroughly mined the area now held by the division and had denied the Marines use of the Itomi-Toguchi road by digging tank traps there. In addition, many trees had been felled across the road., which was pockmarked with numerous shell craters.

On L plus 18, the final drive to the northern coast of the peninsula began with the 4th and 29th Marines abreast. Preceding the 0800 jump off, four Corsairs from VMF-312 struck at a hillside containing gun emplacements and strongpoints that opposed the ground attack. Again napalm, GP bombs, rockets, and strafing attacks were employed to ease the infantry advance. When the Marines pushed forward against negligible resistance, they came across elaborate cave and trench systems filled with numerous enemy dead, undoubtedly the victims of the artillery, naval gunfire, and air bombardments. All organized resistance ended on Motobu Peninsula when the 4th and 29th Marines gained the north coast on 20 April. General Shepherd assigned garrison and patrol sectors to his units on Motobu; at the same time, mopping-up operations continued in the rest of the IIIAC zone. In the course of the fighting for the peninsula, the 6th Marine Division had sustained casualties amounting to 207 killed, 757 wounded, and 6 missing in action. The Marines counted over 2,000 Japanese dead, men who had forfeited their lives while defending their positions with a tenacity that was characteristic.

Of the 6th Division drive up the isthmus and into the peninsula, Brigadier General Oliver P. Smith noted: "The campaign in the north should dispel the belief held by some that Marines are beach-bound and are not capable of rapid movement. Troops moved rapidly over rugged terrain, repaired roads and blown bridges, successively opened new unloading points, and reached the northern tip of the island, some 55 miles from the original landing beaches, in 14 days. This was followed by a mountain campaign of 7 days' duration to clear the Motobu Peninsula."

Chapter 5. Phase I Continued

Progress Of Logistical Support
Shortly after the L-Day landings, Radio Tokyo predicted that the beachhead on Okinawa would be wiped out. From L-Day on, the impressive flow of troops and supplies ashore gave little support to this optimistic enemy forecast, however, as the Tenth Army hold on the island rapidly tightened. While the assault units fanned out to gain assigned initial objectives, battalion shore party commanders assumed control of their beach sectors. During L-Day, successively higher command echelons landed, and, by nightfall, divisions had assumed control of shore party operations. A coral reef extending the length of the beaches was the only real obstacle to early unloading operations. During flood-tide, a steady procession of DUKWs and LVTs shuttled cargo across the reef, and only within this 4-to-5 hour period of high tide could ships' landing craft make runs directly to a few scattered places on the beaches. Low tide, however, exposed the coral outcropping, and necessitated the establishment of

offshore transfer points to maintain the flow of supplies to the beach. Barge cranes required at the transfer points to transship cargo were not available in appreciable numbers until L plus 2.

Increasingly intense Kamikaze raids posed a threat to the transport groups and caused delays in the buildup of supplies ashore. Additionally, the unexpected rapid infantry advances disrupted the unloading schedule. Meanwhile, shore party officers faced such other problems as the lack of suitable beach exits and the scarcity of engineering equipment to prepare them. Another critical matter of note was the shortage of transportation to clear the beaches of supplies. As the volume of cargo being landed increased, the number of trucks available for hauling to inland dumps decreased. According to the operation plans, organic assault division motor transport was to have supported the efforts of the shore parties initially. When frontline troops began to outdistance their support elements, the divisions were forced to withdraw their trucks from the beaches to resupply forward assault units. The effort beginning on L-Day to bridge the reef barrier off the Hagushi beaches bore fruit by 4 April. In place opposite Yontan airfield on Red Beach 1 were ponton causeways that had been side-lifted to the target by LSTs. Earth fill ramps were constructed across the reef to Purple Beach 1 and the Orange Beaches near Kadena. Within the mouth of the Bishi Gawa, close to Yellow Beach 3, a small sand bar had been cleared of surface obstructions and enlarged. A loop access road was then cut through the beach cliff to the bar by engineers with Seabee assistance. As soon as these facilities were ready, cargo from landing craft as large as and including LCTs, could be unloaded directly over the two causeways and the improved sand bar.

A total of 80 self-propelled barges, also side-carried to Okinawa, was in use constantly from the beginning of unloading operations. The barges were employed in various ways, essentially at the discretion of the division commanders. One barge was assigned to each LST(H) as a landing float onto which the bow ramps of the landing ships were dropped to ease the transfer of casualties from small boats or amphibians. The majority of the barges served as floating supply dumps. These were particularly valuable for supplying critical items to the units ashore at night when cargo ships carrying needed supplies retired from the transport areas.

IIIAC mounted cranes on 12 of these self-propelled units and positioned them at the reef where netted cargo was transferred from boats to LVTs or DUKWs for the final run to inshore dumps. Referring to the demonstrated success of this method, one Marine shore party commander commented: "This was the [1st Marine Division's] innovation, first practiced successfully at Peleliu. Two of these barge-mounted cranes were loaned to [the] 6th MarDiv on [L plus 1] to facilitate their cargo handling, and XXIV Corps took up the method. That method accounted for the comparative lack of clutter on the 1st MarDiv beaches. That [the 1st Marine] Division had no beach dumps is a fact of prophetic import for future operations, for I believe establishment of such will invite their destruction in an assault landing."

Encouraged by the satisfactory tactical picture, Admiral Turner authorized the use of floodlights and night unloading on all beaches starting 2 April, and directed that ships' holds be cleared of all assault cargo immediately. On the same day, he ordered that the personnel and equipment of the aviation engineer battalions and the MAGs be expeditiously unloaded. On 3 April, General Geiger recommended to Turner that all priorities established for LSTs unloading over IIIAC beaches be suspended until every member of the airfield headquarters, service, construction, and maintenance units had arrived ashore. Planned unloading priorities were upset, however, by Tenth Army insistence on getting Yontan and Kadena airfields operational at the earliest possible time, and by General Buckner's authorization on L plus 2 for corps commanders to bring garrison troops ashore at their discretion. Those on board control vessels and shore party personnel soon viewed many situations wherein low priority units and equipment intermingled with the shoreward flow of essential assault matériel. This interruption of supposedly firm unloading schedules was due, in part, to the natural desires of ships' captains to unload their vessels and to clear the vulnerable Hagushi anchorage as quickly as possible. The inadequacy of the motor transport available to the shore parties and the radical change in the unloading priorities, however, forced many ships to stand off shore with half-empty holds while awaiting the return of boats which were, meanwhile, stacked up at the control vessels.

Further complicating the critical control problem were the efforts of individual landing boat coxswains who, disregarding their instructions, attempted to "get to the beaches at all costs." Commenting on this matter, one transport group commander said: "There seemed to exist on the part of most coxswains an almost fierce determination to be first ashore with their individual boats, regardless of the orderly assignment to unloading points, which it is the function of the control vessel to carry out. Coxswains simply would not follow orders to form and remain in cargo circles, but jockeyed for positions of advantage from which to come along side the control vessel. Many even attempted to ignore the control vessel and bypass it, proceeding directly to whatever beach they had a preference for."

Despite this, the control of ship-to-shore traffic was probably handled better at Okinawa than in previous Pacific operations, except those at Peleliu and Iwo Jima. After observing the assault landings in the Marianas, Admiral Turner was convinced that only "the most experienced personnel obtainable should be used in the Control Parties for assault landings." Consequently, the key members of the control groups which operated in the Palaus and Bonins served on board the control vessels at Okinawa, where their collective experience helped make ICEBERG a more efficient operation.

Although the ship-to-shore cargo transfer procedures were soon ironed out, problems at the beaches still existed. Organization of the northern landing beaches, for example, progressed slowly. In a critical but friendly evaluation of Marine shore party operations, experienced British observers stated that: "There seemed to be little or no traffic control, no sign posting of roads or dumps, and no orderly lay-out of the beach areas. It has been said already that the speed of advance inland outran the landing of vehicles. The rapid landing of [motor transport] therefore became an imperative need and there is no doubt . . . that the rate of landing could have been greatly accelerated by proper organization. For instance, although vehicles were able to wade ashore at low tide on Yellow 2, they were only using one exit. This had no beach roadway on it, although its gradient and surface were such that a tractor was frequently required to pull vehicles through it. This considerably retarded progress. (It was noted both here and at other beaches that where beach matting had been laid down, it had usually been cut up by tractors. Separate exits for wheels and tracks is not one of the Marine Shore Party rules!) It is easy to be critical, but the general impression remains that unloading organization in this sector was insufficiently flexible to cope with the unexpected military situation." However, the Shore Party work in this Corps [IIIAC] must be judged by results, and the fact is that after L-plus

1 day, no serious criticism of the unloading progress was made by the Corps Commander.

The planned and orderly transition of shore party control to progressively higher troop echelons continued as the beachhead expanded. On 3 April, the XXIV Corps commander took charge of the southern beaches, and, three days later, the commander of the III Amphibious Corps Service Group assumed control for the unloading of the Marine divisions. After a conference of responsible fleet and troop logistics officers on board Admiral Turner's flagship on 8 April, arrangements were made for Tenth Army to take over all shore party activities on the Hagushi beaches the following morning. Major General Fred C. Wallace, the Island Commander, was placed in charge and his 1st Engineer Special Brigade was directed to assume control of all beaches, with the exception of the one which had recently been opened at Nago. In order to operate a much-needed forward supply dump for the far-ranging infantry units of the 6th Marine Division, the IIIAC Service Group retained control of this northern landing point.

Many of the shore party troops in the IIIAC zone of action were from replacement drafts. They had trained with the divisions as infantrymen and accompanied the assault echelon to the target. Until needed to replace casualties in the combat units, these Marines fulfilled a vital function while assigned to shore party and ships' working parties. Although the weather remained perfect until the afternoon of L plus 3, heavy rain and winds during that night and most of the following day hampered unloading activities. With the abatement of high winds on 6 April, a stepped-up unloading pace resulted in the emptying of 13 APAs and AKAs, and 60 LSTs. The day before, in the midst of the storm, 32 empty cargo and transport vessels left the target area. Between L-Day and 11 April, when the first substantial increment of garrison shipping arrived, unloading over the Hagushi beaches was confined primarily to assault shipping. By noon of 11 April, 532,291 measurement tons of cargo had been unloaded, an amount greater than had been put ashore during the entire course of the Marianas campaign.

Securing The Eastern Islands And Ie Shima

Since the rapid sweep of the Tenth Army had cleared the shoreline of Chimu Wan and a large section of the upper portion of Nagagusuku Wan by 5 April, Admiral Turner was anxious to utilize the beaches and berths on the east coast as soon as possible. Although minesweepers were clearing the extensive reaches of both anchorages, before unloading operations could be safely started the Japanese strength on the six small islands guarding the mouths of the two bays had to be determined. To acquire this information, the FMFPac Amphibious Reconnaissance Battalion was attached to the Eastern Islands Attack and Fire Support Group and assigned the mission of scouting the islands. Tsugen Shima, the only island suspected of being heavily defended, was the first target of the battalion. Although Tsugen is relatively small, its position southeast of the Katchin Peninsula effectively controls the entrances to Nakagusuku Wan. Aerial observers reported that the village of Tsugen and the high ridge overlooking it contained extensively developed strongpoints. After midnight, early on 6 April, high-speed APDs carrying the battalion arrived off the objective, and Companies A and B embarked in rubber boats to land on the western coast of the island at 0200. Just a short way inland from the landing point, four civilians were encountered; two were made prisoner, but the other two escaped to alert the garrison.

Enemy reaction came almost immediately. Company A began receiving machine gun fire from the vicinity of Tsugen, while Company B was similarly taken under fire from a trench system in the northwest part of the island. Japanese mortars soon found the range of the landing party, whereupon the Marines withdrew to the beach under an unceasing shower of shells. Since the battalion assignment was to uncover enemy opposition and not engage it, Major Jones reembarked his unit at 0300. Although the Japanese claimed an easy victory over an "inferior" force, the scouts had accomplished their mission. Company A lost two Marines killed and eight wounded. On the evening of 6 April, Major Jones' men resumed their investigation of the rest of the islands in the offshore group. At 0015 on 7 April, the entire battalion landed on Ike Shima, the northernmost island. When no sign of enemy troops or installations and only one civilian was discovered there, Company B went on to Takabanare Shima. Landing at 0530, it discovered that 200 thoroughly frightened Okinawan civilians were the island's only inhabitants. At about the same time, two platoons of Company A went to Heanza Shima and, using their rubber boats, crossed over to Hamahika Shima. Daylight patrols confirmed the absence of enemy soldiers, but 1,500 more civilians were added to those already counted. These islands were occupied later in April by 3/5.

After nightfall on 7 April, Company B reboarded its APD, which then circled Tsugen Shima to land the Marines on Kutaka Shima, opposite enemy-held Chinen Peninsula. As the company paddled in to shore, the heavy surf capsized three of the boats and one man drowned. The island had neither enemy troops, installations, nor civilians, and the scouts withdrew shortly after midnight.

While the reconnaissance battalion was searching the rest of the Eastern Islands on 7 April, UDT swimmers checked the proposed landing beach on the east coast of Tsugen Shima preparatory to the assault there. The capture of the Eastern Islands had been assigned to the 27th Infantry Division as its part in Phase I of the Tenth Army preferred invasion plan. The information gained from the 6-7 April reconnaissance indicated that commitment of an entire division was not warranted, and only one regiment was assigned for the operation.

As the main body of the Army division was landing over the Orange beaches near Kadena on 9 April, the ships of the 105th RCT were rendezvousing at Kerama Retto with the command ship of the Eastern Islands Attack and Fire Support Group. The assault unit selected for the landing on Tsugen was 3/105, while the other two battalions of the RCT were designated floating reserve to be called up from Kerama if needed. Although Tsugen had been pounded intermittently by air and naval gunfire since L-Day, the ships' guns again blasted the island on 10 April, the day of the landing. Initial resistance was light when the soldiers landed at 0839, but the enemy, strongly entrenched in the stone and rubble of Tsugen, soon engaged the invaders in a day-long fire fight. The battle continued throughout the night, during which time the Army battalion sustained many casualties from the incessant enemy mortar fire coming from the heights above the village.

At daylight on the 11th, the rifle companies of 3/105 made a concerted attack against stubborn opposition which gradually died out. Organized resistance was eliminated by 1530, and the battalion was ordered to embark shortly thereafter to join the rest of the regiment at Kerama Retto. In a day and a half of fighting, the battalion lost 11 men, had 80 wounded, and 3 missing. An estimated 234 Japanese were killed and no prisoners were taken. The seizure of Tsugen Shima opened the approaches to Nakagusuku Wan, and ensured that XXIV Corps would receive supply shipments over the eastern as well as the western beaches. This operation also uncovered beaches in Chimu Wan which were developed by the Seabees and used for unloading the LSTs which brought construction supplies and equipment from the Marianas. This action relieved the load which had been placed on the Hagushi beaches, expedited base development, and hastened the building of additional unloading facilities. In its rapid advance leading to the capture of the Motobu Peninsula, the 6th Marine Division demonstrated that Okinawa north of the Ishikawa Isthmus could be taken by an attack overland. ICEBERG commanders were forced in turn to reappraise the original plans for Phases I and II. They found that naval requirements were now reduced to resupply and fire support operations, and that the ships which might have been needed for an amphibious assault of Motobu Peninsula—a possibility considered in all advance planning—were now available for the capture of Ie Shima. Losing no time, Admiral Turner issued the attack order directing the seizure of the island and its vital airfield, and designated the Northern Attack Force commander, Admiral Reifsnider, as Commander, Ie Shima Attack Group.

Ie Shima was important because its size and physical features permitted extensive airfield development. Three and a half miles northwest of Motobu Peninsula, the island plateau was mostly flat land, broken only by low hills and scattered clumps of trees. Located in the middle of the eastern part of the island was a rugged and extremely steep 600-foot-high limestone mountain, Iegusugu Yama. There were few obstacles to widespread construction of airdromes besides this prominent terrain feature. This factor escaped the attention of neither Japanese nor American planners. The enemy had already laid out three runways, each a mile in length, on the central plateau, and the ICEBERG plan called for the expansion of these existing strips as well as the addition of others which would eventually accommodate an entire wing of very-long-range fighter aircraft.

The landing force selected for the invasion was General Bruce's 77th Infantry Division. After the Keramas landing, this unit spent two weeks on board ship in a convoy which steamed in circles approximately 300 miles southeast of Okinawa. Without warning, on 2 April enemy aircraft dove out of clouds which had hidden their approach and crash-dived four ships (three of which were command ships), before antiaircraft fire could open up on the intruders. The entire regimental staff of the 305th Infantry was killed and wounded, and the total number of casualties listed in this one attack was 17 soldiers killed, 38 wounded, and 10 missing. Ten days after this disaster, the division was committed to land on 16 April, its second assault landing in less than a month. Major Jones' Amphibious Reconnaissance Battalion was assigned to execute the first mission of the operation. His unit was directed to seize and occupy Minna Shima, a small crescent-shaped island lying 6,500 yards southeast of the main target. Two 105mm and one 155mm howitzer battalions from 77th Division artillery were to be emplaced there to provide supporting fires during the Ie Shima battle.

The Marine scouts landed at 0445 on 13 April and within two hours had swept the island. They discovered 30 civilians but found no enemy soldiers. The battalion remained on the island the rest of the 13th and, on the morning of the 14th, occupied positions from which it covered UDT preparations of the reef and beach for the landing of artillery. By noon of 14 April, Major Jones had reembarked his men on board the APDs. Three days later, the battalion was released from attachment to the 77th Division and attached to IIIAC.

As scheduled, the preliminary bombardment of Ie Shima began at dawn on 16 April and was stepped up at 0725 when missions in direct support of the landing were fired. Five minutes before S-Hour (as the landing time was designated for this operation), 16 fighter planes made a strafing and napalm attack on the beaches while other fighters and bombers orbited over the island, ready to protect the attack group and support the ground assault.

Although there was little opposition to the landing, the troops experienced stiffening resistance by afternoon when enemy delaying groups, concealed in caves and fortified tombs, started to contest every yard of advance. For a period of six days, 77th Division ground forces struggled. Initially making only slight gains, in many cases, they fought hand-to-hand with defenders who contested every inch of ground. As the battle unfolded, it was found that Japanese defenses were centered about Iegusugu Yama and the small village of Ie, which lay at the foot of the southern slope of the mountain. A masterful camouflage job had been performed by the Ie Shima garrison, for nearly 7,000 people were concealed on the island. The mountain contained a maze of hidden firing positions; Ie itself had been converted into a veritable fortress. The ground approaching the mountain and the town was honeycombed with caves, tunnels, bunkers, and spider holes on which the Japanese had expended their great industry and defensive skills. The advance route to the core of enemy defenses was open land and uphill all the way, flanked by Japanese positions in the village and dominated by emplacements located in a reinforced concrete building on a steep rise facing the attacking troops. The infantry soon named this structure "Government House" and the terrain on which it stood "Bloody Ridge."

On 20 April, after a grim grenade and bayonet battle, the top of Bloody Ridge was finally gained and Government House taken. The island was declared secure on 21 April after the 77th Division had won a victory for which a heavy price was exacted; 239 Americans were killed, 879 wounded, and 19 missing. Japanese losses were 4,706 killed and 149 captured. For the next four days, scattered Japanese and Okinawan soldiers were hunted down and, on the 25th, LSTs began shuttling units of the division to Okinawa, where their extra strength was needed in helping the XXIV Corps maintain pressure on enemy defenses in front of Shuri. Remaining in garrison on Ie Shima were the regimental headquarters and the Mt Battalion of the 305th. This force was considered adequate to handle the rest of the cleanup operations in the island.

The Marines' "Guerrilla Wars"

The capture of Motobu Peninsula constituted the major portion of IIIAC offensive operations in April. A lesser but continuing Marine task during the period was ridding the area of the pesky and omnipresent guerrillas. Irregulars attempted to harass, delay, and wear down American units by partisan tactics classically employed against patrols, convoys, or isolated detachments. Once Yae Take fell and Marines advanced to the northernmost reaches of Okinawa, guerrilla activities increased in scope and intensity. Under the conditions offered by the rugged and primitive wilderness of the north, the lack of roads there, and a shortage of information, a modern force of superior strength and armament was unable to engage the guerrilla decisively in his own element.

In the southernmost area of the IIIAC zone, aside from picking off occasional stragglers, Marines were kept busy improving the road net, sealing burial vaults, and closing the honeycomb of caves. To the north, however, as advance elements of General Shepherd's fast-moving division approached Motobu Peninsula, and the lines of communication were extended progressively, guerrillas took advantage of the situation. During the night of 8-9 April, a group of marauders broke into the area of IIIAC Artillery, near Onna, and destroyed a trailer and a small power plant. Following this attack at dawn, other enemy groups attempted to disrupt north-south traffic passing through Onna by rolling crudely devised demolition charges down upon passing vehicles from the cliffs above.

In the south of the 6th Division zone, on 7 April the 7th Marines (less 3/7), in corps reserve at Ishikawa, was assigned to patrol tasks. The northern half of the regimental patrol sector was covered by Lieutenant Colonel John J. Gormley's 1/7, which had moved to Chimu, while Berger's 2d Battalion and certain designated regimental troops in a perimeter defense around the bombed-out ruins of Ishikawa, had a related mission of patrolling north and inland from the village. One 7th Marines task was warding off nightly infiltration attempts by individual or small groups of Japanese and Okinawan irregulars in search of food. Most of them were killed or wounded either entering the village or leaving it. The initial patrols in the region were without incident, but, as pressure was applied to Colonel Udo's force in the mountain fastnesses of Motobu Peninsula, the quiet that had prevailed in the supposed-rear zone was dispelled. On 12 April, a 2/7 patrol fell victim to a well-planned ambush on Ishikawa Take, the highest point on the isthmus. By the time that the entrapped Marines were able to pull out under cover of the fires of the regimental weapons company, 5 men had been killed and 30 wounded.

The next day, Lieutenant Colonel Berger sent two companies into the ambush zone and occupied it against only token resistance. In customary partisan fashion, the elusive guerrillas had departed the area, seemingly swallowed up by the heavy vegetation, deep gorges, and spiny ridges of the complex terrain.

After spending a quiet night on the twin peaks of the heights, the two companies, E and F, were withdrawn to approach the guerrilla lair from a different direction. While retiring, the Marines were fired upon from above by the reappearing enemy, and a number of men were hit. After circling to the far (west) side of the island and establishing a skirmish line, the two companies moved in on the commanding ground where the guerrillas were well dug-in and concealed. The irregulars were engaged, but "did not appear to be well organized." Those of the enemy who escaped were hunted down by patrols.

This task proved to be painstaking and time-consuming, for the vegetation on the western slopes of Ishikawa Isthmus seriously hampered effective patrolling despite the fact that this section was the least precipitous in the neck of the island. Visibility off the trails frequently was limited to five feet, at most, by dense stands of bamboo and scrub conifer. Since flank security was impractical in this terrain, the war dogs accompanying the Marines proved a valuable asset in alerting their masters to enemy hidden in the undergrowth. Lack of roads and the difficult terrain here raised resupply problems which were solved by the organization of supply pack trains to support 2/7 patrols. Enemy resistance continued here for nearly two weeks, during which time Berger's Marines killed about 110 of the guerrilla force. As the 6th Marine Division closed in on the main Japanese position in the Motobu heights, the tempo of guerrilla activity on the fringe of the battle increased proportionately. A daily occurrence at dusk was the harassing of artillery positions by irregulars, who caused the registration of night defensive fires to be delayed. When Major Pace's 1/15, in direct support of the 22d Marines, displaced to cover the infantry drive to the northernmost limit of the island, its perimeter was hit almost nightly by sporadic sniping and knee mortar fire. In addition, grenades, demolition charges, and even antipersonnel land mines were thrown into the defensive installations encircling the battalion area. The hills in the rear of the 1/15 position afforded the enemy excellent observation and apparently permitted him to coordinate his attacks on the Marines.

From 14 through 16 April, as the battle for Yae Take was coming to a climax, fires mysteriously broke out in various west coast villages from the southern extremity of Nago Wan to the northern tip of the island. On 17 April at dawn, Nakaoshi was struck by an enemy hit-and-run attack that simultaneously swept over the 6th Engineer Battalion command post (CP), water point, and supply installations nearby. Civilian collaboration with Japanese military forces appeared to be a factor in these incidents, when evidence of native sabotage was uncovered during an investigation of the series of fires on the west coast.

The security threat presented by Okinawan civilians appeared to be pervasive, for it arose within the 1st Marine Division zone also. As early as 9 April, Lieutenant Colonel Miller, the 3/5 commander, reported that many civilians were destroying their passes and appeared to be roaming about freely at night. It was reasonable to assume that they were contacting the Japanese at this time.

For better zonal security control, the 1st Marine Division began rounding up all civilians on 11 April and herding them into stockades built on Katchin Peninsula. The following day, all able-bodied Okinawan males were taken into custody in order to determine their military status. The prevailing tactical situation in the north at this time required that organized resistance be broken before Marine control over civilians could be established and combat troops spared for this duty.

From the beginning of the 6th Division drive north, an increasing number of Okinawans was encountered on the roads. Only a few men were of obvious military age and were detained. The others, stopped and questioned, were allowed to continue on with their affairs. At the height of operations in the north, 12-16 April, the division was unable to collect able-bodied males methodically in the manner of the 1st Division in central Okinawa. Civilians of doubtful character and background, however, were seized. When hostilities on Motobu ceased, the 6th Division organized a civilian control center at Taira where, beginning 16 April, from 500 to 1,500 natives were interned daily until operations in the north were ended. On 15 April, Hurst's 3/7 (attached earlier to the 5th Marines) reverted to parent control and began active patrolling from its base at Chuda on the west coast. General del Vane regained the 7th Marines the next day, and, as the 6th Division began meeting increased resistance, the boundary between the Marine divisions was readjusted along the Chuda-Madaira road.

From 17 to 19 April, it appeared that, parallel to the steady reduction of their positions on Yae Take, the Japanese were shifting from a tactical policy of defense to one based on partisan warfare. After the 6th Division took the mountain redoubt, and following a reorganization of Marine units, General Shepherd's command moved to assigned garrison areas. Here it began patrolling vigorously to fix and destroy remaining pockets of enemy resistance. To assist the division in securing northern Okinawa, the Amphibious Reconnaissance Battalion, part of IIIAC since 17 April, was attached with a mission of seizing and occupying the small islands lying off Motobu Peninsula.

In a period of two days, 21-22 April, the battalion reconnoitered the islands of Yagachi and Sesoko with negative results. Though no enemy forces were encountered, the Marines found a leper colony containing some 800 adults and 50 children on Yagachi Shima. Before they landed on Sesoko, the scouts met more than 100 natives moving by canoe from islands to the west in search of food, and "considerable difficulty was involved in corralling and controlling" them. On the 23d, Walker's 6th Reconnaissance Company scouted Kouri Shima and found no enemy.

While the battle for Yae Take raged, and even after it had ended, 6th Division rear area patrols began making contacts with enemy troops attempting to escape from the fighting on Motobu. On 22 April, near Nakaoshi, 1/22 patrols killed 35 enemy in a fire fight. On the next day, this battalion met a strong force, estimated at three rifle squads, three light machine gun squads, and one mortar squad, firmly entrenched in previously prepared positions, including caves and pillboxes, in the mountainous area east of Nago. Two Marine companies assaulted the Japanese killing 52, before an ammunition shortage forced the battalion to break off the action. It returned to the battle scene on 24 April, this time with 4/15 (Lieutenant Colonel Bruce T. Hemphill) in direct support, and the strongpoint was reduced. The engagement ended towards evening with the deaths of a Japanese officer and two NCOs and the remainder of the group fleeing. The battalion continued patrolling the region on the next day and cleaned out the enemy pocket. Intensified patrolling of the Ishikawa Isthmus began on 23 April after a small IIIAC military police group was extricated from an ambush by a 7th Marines detachment. The 2d Battalion, 1st Marines, reinforced the 7th, and all available 1st Division war dogs were attached to that regiment. At the same time, stricter travel regulations within the IIIAC area were enforced, and the movement of single vehicles in the corps zone during hours of darkness was forbidden.

In the 6th Division zone, while the 29th Marines remained on Motobu Peninsula, the 4th Marines moved to its assigned area in the northern part of the island. At Kawada, 3/1 was relieved by Hochmuth's 3/4 and returned to parent control on the 23d. During the next two days, the rest of Colonel Shapley's regiment was disposed with Hayden's 2/4 at Ora, and Beans' 1/4, regimental troops, and the headquarters complement bivouacked in the vicinity of Genka, a small west coast village located about five miles north of the juncture between Motobu Peninsula and the rest of the island. From this point, Colonel Shapley's mission was to seek and exterminate stragglers in the southern half of what had been the 22d Marines area. Upon being relieved, 1/22 prepared to move to the west coast to a point just south of Ichi, which had been the 3/22 patrol base since 16 April.

The mountainous interior of the north was combed continually by Marine patrols for Udo Force survivors and semi-independent guerrilla bands. The 6th Division learned from civilians in the area that small groups of Okinawan home guardsmen were in the hills of the northern part of the island and had been preparing to wage partisan warfare for nearly a year. As part of the preparations, they had reportedly established stockpiles of supplies in the interior. The civilians further stated that some of the guardsmen had returned to their homes and civilian pursuits. They also said that home defense units were being trained in the villages by Okinawan veterans who had served previously in China with Japanese forces.

Until the afternoon of 27 April, however, patrol results were negative with the exception of an occasional flushing out of individuals or small groups. At this time, a 3/4 reconnaissance patrol sighted a 200-man enemy column moving through the northeastern corner of the Marine regimental zone toward the east coast. It was believed that these Japanese had survived the Motobu Peninsula fighting by infiltrating in groups of 20 to 40 from the combat area by way of Taira and that they were going to try to join up with the main enemy force in the south.

Steps were taken immediately to destroy the group. Two battalions of the 22d Marines were ordered to the south to block the column, while 3/4 moved inland from Kawada. Further ringing the escape-minded enemy was Donohoo's 3/22, which proceeded toward the interior on a cross-island trail 1,000 yards north of, and parallel to, the 1/22 advance from Hentona. Since it was anticipated that the fugitives would be apprehended in the 22d Marines zone, 3/4 was attached to that regiment, Additionally, two artillery battalions were to support the pursuers. The first contact was made just prior to noon on 28 April, when one of 3/4's companies engaged the escaping Japanese in a firefight. At the end of the three-hour contest, 109 enemy soldiers were dead; 1 Marine was killed and 8 wounded. The other pursuing units were unable to reach the scene of the action because of the difficult terrain; 1/22 encountered small scattered groups as it advanced, while 3/22 was still underway when 3/4 radioed that it had destroyed the enemy. Thereupon, Colonel Schneider ordered his 3d Battalion to continue on to the east coast, and Colonel Shapley's 3/4 returned to Kawada and parent control.

Even though the guerrillas in the IIIAC area had forced the Marines to remain constantly on the alert, General Geiger was able to declare the end of organized resistance in the north on 20 April. Continuous patrolling remained the general order, however. As usual in counter-guerrilla operations, the number of combat troops employed was out of proportion to the size and number of guerrillas hunted. In most cases, it was a one-sided fight, for a substantial percentage of the partisan ranks were filled with the poorly trained and equipped Boeitai. The primary contribution of native Okinawans to the guerrilla effort was a knowledge of the land over which they fought; their offensive efforts were limited mainly to night forays against supply installations, disrupting communications systems and centrals, and attacking water points and hospitals. Although these destructive attempts usually ended in failure, they forced friendly units to maintain extensive security detachments, sometimes in platoon or company strength.

As of the 20th, when Motobu Peninsula was reportedly cleared of enemy troops, the Tenth Army began to pay greater attention to the native population in occupied sections of the island. All civilians, irrespective of age or sex, found in the areas of combat units were to be interned. Furthermore, Okinawans were prohibited from moving about freely unless accompanied by an armed guard. General Geiger established eight internment camps in the IIIAC zone, but the number of collection points in the Marine area was later reduced to three; Katchin Peninsula, Chimu, and Taira. Although tighter security controls prevailed in the corps zone, isolated incidents behind the battleline still occurred. In the last week of April, a 7th Marines patrol killed a Japanese corporal who was wearing a kimono over his uniform. Intelligence agencies found evidence of a Japanese-planned and -sponsored program of espionage and sabotage for the rear areas. In the XXIV Corps zone, the following document was recovered: "Permit Army line probational officer Inoye Kuchi and two others: The above mentioned are permitted to wear plain clothes for the purpose of penetrating and raiding enemy territory from April 25, 1945, until the accomplishment of their mission."

TAF Operations In April And The Kamikaze Threat

Owing to the early and unopposed capture of Yontan and Kadena airfields, Tactical Air Force, Tenth Army, began land-based operations sooner than expected. On 2 April, General Mulcahy and his staff went ashore and selected a CP site midway between the two fields. General Wallace's ADC headquarters was dug in nearby. While TAF personnel were kept busy constructing camp and repair facilities, Marine engineers and Seabees began repairing the runways on Yontan and Kadena. The airfields were found to be lightly surfaced and badly damaged by naval gunfire and bombings. Hurried grading permitted the use of Yontan by 7 April, but the problems at Kadena were more extensive. Damage here was greater, and the source of coral for surfacing was at some distance from the field. Nevertheless, the strips on Kadena were ready for dry-weather use two days after those on Yontan and, by 1 May, they were all-weather operational.

Three weeks earlier, the ADC Air Defense Control Center (ADCC) had come ashore and, on 7 April, begun operating from three LVTs specially rigged to serve as the defense command CP and to function as both an ADCC and the Air Defense/Fighter Command operations center. On 19 April the center moved to more spacious quarters in an abandoned farmhouse nearby.

When General Wallace opened his CP on Okinawa, the air defense commander became the land-based agent of CASCU, which continued operating on board Admiral Turner's flagship. Under ADC operational control were land-based aircraft, radar air warning and control installations, and antiaircraft artillery units. It was the air defense commander's primary mission to coordinate the combined efforts of these three disparate support activities so that they meshed with the operations of the overall air defense system of the expeditionary force. ICEBERG plans had stipulated that TAF would assume full responsibility for the air defense of Okinawa when the amphibious landings were completed, but, because of "the all-out efforts of Japanese aircraft and the success of their kamikaze suicide attacks directed against naval units, operational control of aircraft in the Ryukyus remained with the Navy until the area was secured." General Wallace believed that the major tactical task of ADC was to meet the Kamikaze threat. From 7 April, when VMF-311 pilots scored the first TAF kill of a suicider as they flew in to Yontan from their CVE lift, ADC efforts were directed toward confronting and stopping the destructive enemy air attacks. The fighter squadrons of MAG-31 and -33 mounted combat air patrols from Yontan and Kadena fields on the first days that they arrived at these bases.

As the battle was joined on Okinawa by the Tenth Army and General Ushijima's forces, the American fleet in surrounding waters was engaged in a desperate battle of its own. The Japanese air attacks on the Kerama Retto invasion group merely heralded even greater enemy attempts to destroy the radar pickets and support vessels safeguarding the troops on Okinawa. Many of these enemy aircraft were on either conventional bombing or reconnaissance missions; others in the aerial attacks were part of the Special Attack Force, the Kamikazes.

As the success of American operations in the Philippines became apparent and MacArthur's air strength reigned supreme, enemy naval air commanders saw that there was no prospect of any advantage to be gained in the sky while Japanese squadrons continued employing orthodox tactics. The Kamikaze effort evolved as a result of these considerations. Appearing first in the Philippines, this was an organized and desperate attempt by suicide-bent Japanese naval aviators to deprive American shipping at Leyte of aerial protection by crashing the flattops of the covering carrier force. The enemy anticipated that the success of their tactics would then guarantee a Japanese surface victory in the event of an all-out engagement with United States naval forces. Although Japanese commanders felt that suicide missions were a "temporary expedient" only, used "because we were incapable of combatting you by other means . . . ," initial success gave added impetus to their fuller employment. Correctly anticipating that the next invasion attempts would be at Iwo Jima and, after that, Okinawa, Imperial General Headquarters withdrew the remnants of some Army and Navy air units from the Philippines in early January 1945 to strengthen the defense of the Home Islands and the Ryukyus. Upon completion of this transfer, designed to "produce a more unified [defense] strategy," brigades and regiments of the Sixth Air Army and naval squadrons of the Fifth Air Fleet were combined into a single tactical command on 19 March under Admiral Soemu Toyoda, Commander in Chief, Combined Fleet. At the outset, it was determined that operations of this combined force of about 1,815 planes were to be well planned and organized—a definite contrast to the sporadic, albeit somewhat successful, Kamikaze attacks at Leyte.

One of the first opportunities for the Japanese to mount coordinated suicide and conventional air attacks occurred during the TF 58 raids of 18-19 March 1945 on Japan. Although the carriers were damaged and there were some American casualties, the enemy lost 161 aircraft. Most of this damage, strangely enough, was not caused by Kamikazes. An important result of this raid was the destruction, while still on the ground on Kyushu, of many of the Japanese planes scheduled to be employed in the defense of the Ryukyus. This disaster forced the Fifth Air Fleet to reevaluate its plans. Moreover, a Tenth Army landing relatively unharassed by enemy air raids was guaranteed, for Toyoda's squadrons were unable to mount a major air offensive until after the beginning of April.

Scattered conventional and Kamikaze flights from Japan and Formosa carried the attack to the Western Islands Attack Group of the ICEBERG force first; later these planes began swarming all over the transports and picket line off Okinawa. During the first few days of April, the toll of ships damaged and sunk grew at a steady rate while naval casualties mounted in consequence. By 6 April, Admiral Toyoda was prepared to launch from Kyushu the first of ten carefully planned Kamikaze attacks, which were to be flown over a period ending 22 June. A total of 1,465 sorties emanated from Kyushu to sink 26 American ships and damage 164 others. Not included in these loss figures are the victims of small-scale Kamikaze efforts by another 250 planes which rose from Formosa air bases, and the 185 additional sorties flown from Kyushu, independent of the mass attacks. The Japanese decision to turn to large-scale air operations was arrived at after Toyoda had studied both his and the Thirty-second Army situations and had found that "it would be futile to turn the tide of battle with present tactics." He therefore dispatched the first and largest coordinated suicide attack—Kikusui Operation No. 1 52--against ICEBERG forces on 6 April. Spearheading the Kamikazes were 14 planes sent to bomb and strafe Okinawa airfields before dawn in order to destroy Allied aircraft suspected of being there. Apart from their nuisance value, the raids did little damage to the runways and none to TAF planes, for the squadrons had not yet flown ashore. Following the first group of enemy hecklers were more than 100 fighters and bombers sent to engage TF 58 off Amami-O-Shima in order to draw American carrier-based planes away from the suiciders heading for Okinawa.

For a 36-hour period, 6-7 April, the Japanese flew 355 suicide sorties, which were accompanied by nearly an equal amount of conventional cover, reconnaissance, and bombing planes. As these aircraft bore in to crash, torpedo, and bomb the ships at anchor in Hagushi transport area, crewmen in exposed positions and troops on the beaches were subjected to a deadly rain of antiaircraft artillery shell fragments. Friendly fighters were not immune from the effect of the hundreds of guns firing from the beaches and ships; three American pilots were shot down when they followed Japanese planes too closely into the murderous barrage.

The main attack, which began about 1500 on 6 April, spread out all over the combat zone with the outer ring of radar pickets and patrol craft—lacking a protective smoke-screen cover—catching the full fury of the battle. Ships of all types, however, were fair game for the Kamikazes. Before the Okinawa landing, the Japanese confined the direction of their suicide attack efforts to American carrier task forces. After 1 April, the attacks were mounted against convoys, and, just prior to the first Kikusui, the enemy began hitting all surface forces. After the time of the 6-7 April attack, the Japanese reserved the carrier forces for Kamikaze attention while their conventional bombers and fighter craft were directed to hit other American vessels and transports around Okinawa. In this first mass suicide attack, Admiral Turner's forces claimed to have shot down at least 135 Japanese planes, while the pilots from the Fast Carrier Task Force reported splashing approximately 245 more, bringing the total American claims of enemy losses to nearly 400 pilots and planes. Contemporary Japanese sources place the losses in Kikusui No. 1 at 335. As a sidelight to the air battle over the land fighting on Okinawa, the Japanese mounted their only real surface threat to the success of the American invasion. Intending to attack Allied shipping at Okinawa, the 69,100-ton battleship *Yamato* and a covering group steamed out of the Tokuyama Naval Base, on Honshu, at 1500 on 6 April. Less than two hours later, the enemy vessels were sighted by two U.S. submarines in the screen lying off the east coast of Kyushu. Within 24 hours, TF 58 pilots had administered death blows to the *Yamato* and a part of her group, and had forced the remainder to scurry home.

Since TAF pilots had not yet begun operations from Okinawa when Kikusui No. 1 struck, the four Marine squadrons on board the carriers *Bennington* (VMF-112 and -123) and *Bunker Hill* (VMF-221 and -451) carried the ball for Marine aviation during the time that General Mulcahy's planes and pilots were still on board their carrier transports. Until late in April, as much as 60 percent of the ground support missions flown for Tenth Army units were carried out by Navy and Marine carrier pilots, while the primary concern of TAF flyers was to blunt the Kamikaze menace. To at least one TAF air group commander, "it seemed strange for planes off the carriers to come in for close-support missions, passing [Okinawa-based] Marine pilots flying out for CAP duty. . . ." Almost as soon as Colonel Munn's MAG-31 squadrons touched down at Yontan, a 12-plane combat air patrol was organized and launched to remain airborne until dark. Prior to the time that TAF joined the fighting, CAPs had been flown by planes from both the Support Carrier Group and TF 58. Originally, a large CAP, varying from 48 planes in relatively quiet periods to 120 or more during critical times, was flown to protect the surface forces from air attacks. Basically, the aircraft were deployed "in a circle in depth" over the invasion and picket craft.

Generally, TAF planes were airborne from dawn to dusk on CAP flights, and they flew special early morning and twilight CAPs as well. On 14 April, the commander of the ICEBERG operation transferred the responsibility for flying night

CAPs from TF 58 to TAF. In addition, TAF was to maintain another four planes constantly on patrol during the hours of darkness. This last mission was assigned alternately to the night fighters of VMF(N)-542 and -543 commanded by Majors William C. Kellum and Clair "C" Chamberlain, respectively. In order to guard the radar picket ships—special objects of the Kamikaze attacks—General Wallace's fighter command was ordered on 14 April to maintain a continuous two-plane daylight CAP over each of the three picket ships that were stationed offshore northeast of TAF airfields. Each flight leader was to report directly to the captain of the ship he was guarding. In turn, the naval officer would control the flight and ensure that its planes were kept out of range of the ship's antiaircraft guns. Two days after this mission was first initiated, the number of ships protected by this CAP was increased by two.

By the time that TAF had been established ashore, the three Marine Landing Force Air Support Control Units, commanded overall by Colonel Vernon E. Megee, had landed also. Although they were shore-based representatives of CASCU and outside of the TAF chain of command, by the very nature of their functions the LFASCUs worked closely with the Marine aviation units. Once air support operations began, coordinating agencies relayed all orders concerning aircraft missions directly to General Mulcahy's command in a smoothly functioning system. At Tenth Army headquarters, Megee's LFASCU-3 screened all requests for air support received from LFASCU-1 (Colonel Kenneth H. Weir) and -2 (Colonel Kenneth D. Kerby) which were working with IIIAC and XXIV Corps respectively. If a review of TAF and carrier aircraft commitments indicated that an air support request was consistent with priority requirements, the mission was approved. At that time, if Marine planes were assigned, LFASCU-3 relayed the order for the mission directly to the TAF operations section. Frontline control of the ground support missions flown by both land- and carrier-based aircraft was provided by Air Liaison Parties (ALPs) from the Joint Assault Signal Companies attached to each division. Ground unit requests for air support were reviewed first with respect to the capabilities and availability of the other supporting arms to fulfill a specific mission, and then passed on to the LFASCU at corps headquarters. If the request was approved here, the LFASCU would requisition the necessary number and types of planes, and stipulate the armament they needed for successful completion of the mission. In addition., the LFASCU provided strike direction and supervised the scheduling of all air support in unit fire support plans.

Not all close air support missions were ground controlled in this campaign. Employed at Okinawa was an air coordinator, or airborne traffic director, who spotted and marked the ground target for the planes flying the mission. The coordinator would direct the flight to the best target heading, observe attack results, and correct subsequent runs if he decided that they were needed. At times when smoke and weather conditions over the target denied the airborne controller suitable visibility, the support mission would be run nevertheless, but directed by the ALP.

It took time to establish land-based radar reporting, control, and homing stations on Okinawa and the outlying islands. In addition to the problems involved in getting the Air Warning Squadrons (AWSs) and their equipment ashore rapidly, initially it proved difficult to net the ground-to-ground communications systems with the overall ship-to-shore warning system. Prior to the establishment of the ADCC, the individual radar stations had reported directly to CASCU aboard the Eldorado. After 8 April, the day on which the control center first began to provide shore-based operational homing facilities, AWS early warning teams began reporting directly to the ADCC which, in turn, passed on to Navy control the reported enemy and friendly plots.

Early warning teams were also assigned temporarily to each assault division and corps headquarters. They then operated in coordination with the AAA units already assigned to the defense of corps and division sectors. Here, the teams monitored ships' radar telling circuits and local air warning and interfighter director nets, from which air raid warning information was obtained and passed on to the ground units. In addition to radar coverage, the air warning squadrons provided radio monitoring services, the results of which figured prominently in and assisted the operation of the Air Defense Command.

The AWSs also worked very closely with and were, in fact, supervised by the senior Marine AAA officer, Colonel Kenneth W. Benner, commanding the 1st Provisional Antiaircraft Group. He was responsible for coordinating the disposition and operation of his organic radar with that of the AWSs in order to ensure maximum surface and low-angle electronic surveillance for defense against enemy air attacks. Because theirs was a vital role in the overall air defense of the ICEBERG forces, land-based AAA units, although attached to the assault corps, were directly under the operational control of General Wallace's ADCC. On 20 April, the antiaircraft units reverted to the Tenth Army which then assigned the 53d Antiaircraft Artillery Brigade the mission of coordinating all AAA activities. At the same time, the brigade became the TAF agency for providing the ground forces with early air raid warning services while continuing to fulfill its AAA defense mission.

Initially, the 1st Provisional Antiaircraft Artillery Group was assigned to support IIIAC during Phases I and 11 of the operation by providing AAA defense for corps units, installations, and beaches, and the captured airfields in the corps zone. Additionally, the group was to provide anti-boat defense of corps beaches, supplement field artillery units in both direct and general support mission, and be prepared to fire seacoast artillery missions.

The assault elements of the group were the 2d (Lieutenant Colonel Max C. Chapman) and 16th (Lieutenant Colonel August F. Penzoll, Jr.) Antiaircraft Artillery Battalions, which supported the 6th and 1st Marine Divisions respectively. Scheduled to land on order at later dates, the 5th (Lieutenant Colonel Harry O. Smith, Jr.) and 8th (Lieutenant Colonel James S. O'Halloran) AAA Battalions were to reinforce the group and extend antiaircraft defenses already existing.

Because of the rapid progress of the infantry and the assignment of higher priority to items needed ashore immediately, the landing of the Marine AAA battalions was delayed. Group and battalion reconnaissance parties landed on L plus 2 to select sites, and beginning on 5 April, the units themselves were given an unloading priority. By 12 April, the battalions were in position ashore.

Initially, one heavy and two light AAA batteries of the 2d Battalion were assigned a defense sector on 6th Marine Division beaches; the 16th Battalion supported the 1st Division with two heavy and two light batteries. The remaining five 90mm gun batteries of the group defended Yontan air field.

When the 53d Antiaircraft Artillery Brigade assumed control of Tenth Army AAA units, it found that the defenses in the IIIAC and XXIV Corps zones were unbalanced. On 27 April, the brigade adjusted the dispositions and, in addition, extended AAA defenses across the island to the east coast in order to break up enemy raids coming from that direction. The lst Provisional Group continued the Yontan area defense, but was made responsible for defense of the entire Yontan-Kadena sector also. To aid in this last mission, Colonel Benner's group was augmented by two Army AAA-Automatic Weapons battalions. Lieutenant Colonel O'Halloran's 8th Antiaircraft Battalion landed at Nago Wan on 17 April to defend IIIAC units and supply dumps in that area. Its most immediate problem in view of the tactical situation on the Motobu Peninsula, was achieving ground security. For that reason, battalion .50-caliber heavy machine guns and some .30-caliber light machine guns obtained locally were assigned a primary mission of ground defense.

Enemy air attacks on shore installations were directed at Yontan and Kadena airfields mainly, and usually took place at night. The only firing opportunities afforded shore-based antiaircraft artillery during daylight occurred when Japanese aircraft, with the obvious intention of attacking the transport area, made their approaches from the landward side of the anchorage. Usually, the illumination or visual sighting of an enemy plane, and sometimes even an American one, was the signal for a wave of wild uncontrolled firing both from shipboard and the island. "Carbines, rifles, and even .45 caliber pistols enthusiastically joined the fun on occasion." Under these conditions, casualties and materiel damage resulted from falling shell fragments and wild shots until the Tenth Army insisted upon the enforcement of greater fire discipline by all unit commanders.

From the beginning of ADCC operations, there was no satisfactory communications and control system linking the fighter command and the antiaircraft artillery units. When ADC was heavily engaged with enemy air attacks, liaison with AAA units weakened or broke down completely. At times, permission for the guns to fire on unidentified or enemy planes was withheld, even when the area was definitely under attack. On several occasions, air raid warning flashes were not relayed to the AAA command until after the infantry and shore party units had been informed. Of necessity, an efficient control system was soon initiated. By the end of the month, Marine AAA units were credited with the destruction of 15 planes and 8 assists, 5 probably destroyed, and 6 damaged.

It was noted that, during enemy air attacks, Japanese aviators showed an increasing knowledge of radar evasion measures, and frequently used "window" in both conventional and Kamikaze attacks. In commenting on the enemy failure to mount air attacks on the ground forces, one observer stated that "it was difficult to understand why they had not resorted to formation bombing from low altitudes," since low-angle radar detection of approaching aircraft was almost impossible. He concluded that the concentration on suicide attacks was too great; he might have added that the Japanese just did not have enough planes by this time to divert their air strength to missions other than the Kamikaze attacks. While TAF fighter pilots added to the expanding bag of downed enemy planes, other types of air missions in support of the Tenth Army were performed at the same time by General Mulcahy's command. Upon its arrival, the Army Air Forces' 28th Photo Reconnaissance Squadron rephotographed the entire Okinawa Gunto area to obtain more accurate and complete coverage than had been available for the maps used on L-Day. The squadron also provided infantry commanders with enlarged aerial photographs of masked terrain features to their zones. As soon as Major Allan L. Feldmeier's VMTB-232 arrived on 22 April, it was given tasks other than its original mission of antisubmarine warfare. During the remainder of the month, the squadron flew numerous artillery observation missions daily, bombed and strafed enemy lines and installations in southern Okinawa, and conducted heckling raids in the same areas almost nightly.

The second mass Kamikaze attack took place during 12-13 April. Although as frenzied and almost as destructive as the first attack, it was mounted by only 392 planes, on both conventional and suicide missions, as opposed to the 699 total in the first attack. As in Kikusui No. 1, TF 58 pilots downed most of the enemy, but carrier-based Marine flyers were active also. Flying Leathernecks from the *Bennington* shot down 26, and *Bunker Hill* Marines downed 25. Okinawa-based TAF pilots accounted for 16 more.

During the interval between the first and second mass raids, the Japanese command had recognized the threat presented to their air attacks by American land-based aircraft, so Kadena was bombed early on the 15th by planes that preceded the Kamikazes. TAF personnel and airplanes were endangered further when both of the fields occupied by Tenth Army squadrons were fired upon by an artillery piece, or pieces, nicknamed "Kadena Pete" in not-too-fond memory of "Pistol Pete" at Henderson Field on Guadalcanal. TAF reports evaluating Kikusui No. 2 noted that the evasive tactics employed by the enemy "do not tend to indicate that the flyers were top-flight fighter pilots," and that "a definite lack of aggressiveness" seemed "to confirm the belief that the pilots were green."

A third mass raid of 498 aircraft (196 suiciders) occurred 15-16 April. As the furious air battle carried over into the second day, TAF planes began to score heavily. The largest bag made by land-based aircraft to that date was accomplished by VMF-441 (Major Robert O. White) pilots, who had shot down 17 of the 270 Japanese pilots and planes allegedly splashed on these two days.

In this attack, a TAF pilot made the first sighting of the so-called "Baka" bomb in its maiden appearance over Okinawa, This small, single-engined, wooden craft, powered by rockets, carried a one-man crew and over a ton and a half of explosives. Carried by a twin-engined bomber to a point near the target, the Baka was released when its pilot had verified the weapon's target and position, oriented his own position, and started the rocket motors. Although the destructive powers of the Baka were real, its employment was erratic and it appeared too late in the war to be influential.

TAF operations for the rest of April tended to fall into a routine of CAPs and support missions. On 22 April, the dusk air patrol was vectored to a point over part of the radar picket line then being attacked by enemy aircraft. When the half-hour battle had ended, Marine pilots claimed 333 Japanese planes. Five days later, during the fourth mass Kamikaze attack (27-28 April), 115 suicide-bent Japanese pilots were launched against friendly shipping and the steadfast radar pickets. On the second day of the attack, at about 1600, the airborne TAF CAP and an additional 36 Corsairs were vectored out 40 miles northwest of Okinawa to intercept an approaching Kamikaze formation. After dark, when the two-hour fight was over, the Marine fighters were credited with downing 351 enemy planes. Upon being congratulated by the Tenth Army commander on the accomplishments of his pilots, General Mulcahy Sent a message to the ADC: "Not only brilliant work by fighter pilots but excellent command control and most efficient reservicing by ground personnel were admiration of and inspiration to all." By the end of April, TAF pilots had flown 3,521 CAP sorties and shot down or assisted in the downing of 1433 enemy aircraft.

Chapter 6. The Defense Stiffens

Approach To Shuri

In the days immediately following the facing movement of the XXIV Corps and the beginning of its drive to the south, increasingly stiff and bitter resistance gave proof that the prepared enemy defenses were being uncovered. The nature of the contacts with the Japanese also heralded the end of the relatively easy and fast-moving XXIV Corps advance. By the morning of 6 April, it was evident that the Japanese "lines were drawn for a full-scale battle." What the 7th and 96th Divisions had encountered was a strong enemy position that extended the width of the island and roughly followed the line through Machinate, Kakazu, Kaniku, Minami-Uebaru, and Tsuwa. With flanks anchored on the East China Sea and the Pacific Ocean, the Japanese barrier was the outermost of a series of defense rings centering about Shuri, headquarters of the Thirty-second Army. The veteran troops of the 62d Division were entrenched in this outpost sector, which was composed of well-prepared positions on high ground that was liberally studded with machine guns and mortars, and surrounded by barbed wire, antitank ditches, and minefields. Unknown to the Americans, the enemy was prepared to fight a "prolonged holding action" here.

Limited gains through highly developed defenses in the Nakama-Kakazu-Ouki area were made on 7 April. In the 96th Division zone, Army troops advanced over broken ground and wooded ridges to reach the approaches of Kakazu. By 1600, after a furious struggle, one infantry battalion—supported by three air strikes, four artillery battalions, and the 14-inch rifles of the *New York*—managed to penetrate to a point within 500 yards of the northern limits of Kakazu.

To break through the increased resistance, General Hedge had concluded that additional artillery support was essential, and on 5 April he had requested that Tenth Army give him whatever battalions were available. Because III Amphibious Corps Artillery could not be employed with maximum effect in the north, General Buckner ordered most of the 155mm units of IIIAC Artillery to be attached to XXIV Corps. On L plus 6 and 7, the 8th and 9th 155mm Gun Battalions and the 1st, 3d, and 6th 155mm Howitzer Battalions were detached from IIIAC and displaced south to support the attack there.

The howitzer battalions were assigned to the 419th Field Artillery Group and paired off with Army artillery battalions to form three firing groupments, which were controlled by the Army battalion commanders. The Marine gun battalions, a IIIAC Artillery headquarters detachment, and the 749th Field Artillery Battalion (8-inch howitzers) were formed into a provisional group, named The Henderson Group after its commander, Lieutenant Colonel Frederick P. Henderson, IIIAC Artillery Operations Officer. Brigadier General Josef R. Sheetz' XXIV Corps Artillery could now support the drive against the Shuri defenses with four 155mm gun battalions, one 8-inch and six 155mm howitzer battalions, and two 155mm gun battalions from the 420th Field Artillery Group. During the night of 7-8 April, XXIV Corps units repulsed minor enemy infiltration attempts. The Japanese had planned that their first major counterattack against Tenth Army troops would coincide with the Kikusui attack on 6 April, but when aerial reconnaissance reported the presence of a more lucrative target for aircraft, a large American convoy steaming south of Okinawa, the Kamikaze and ground attacks were rescheduled for the night of 8 April. This attack was cancelled indefinitely when another large convoy was spotted off the west coast of Okinawa just prior to the jumpoff. Because the situation was not favorable in either case, cooler heads amongst the Thirty-second Army staff prevailed and were able to stave off the launching of an unsupported Army counterattack. It was only a question of time, however, before the advocates of an all-out offensive would have their day.

When it could no longer be employed profitably in the north, the 11th Marines was also sent south to provide additional Marine artillery in answer to Hedge's request of 5 April. The three 105mm howitzer battalions of Colonel Brown's regiment displaced southward on 9 April to reinforce the direct support battalions of the 7th and 96th Divisions. This reinforcement was in addition to the IIIAC artillery dispatched earlier. The 2d and 3d Battalions of the 11th Marines were attached to the 96th Division, and the 4th assigned to the 7th Division. On 12 April, the remaining battalion of the 11th Marines, 11/1, (75mm pack howitzers) was also attached to the 96th Division.

Moving south at the same time as the Marine artillery were elements of the 27th Infantry Division (less RCT 105), which had landed at noon that day.

Released from Tenth Army reserve, the division moved to a bivouac area just east of Kadena airfield, where it awaited a combat assignment. Heavy enemy opposition and torrential rains driven by strong winds hampered the efforts of XXIV Corps when it resumed the attack on the 10th. On the corps front overall, the 7th Division was able to advance approximately 400 yards in its zone, but an antitank ditch and a minefield near Ouki, and mutually supporting eaves and pillboxes on the right flank, seriously limited the division attack.

The 96th Division, which had begun the battle for Kakazu Ridge on the previous day, continued its attack against this key feature in the enemy's Shuri defense system. On 9 April, the division had attempted to take the position with two battalions in a predawn surprise attack. Frequent Japanese counterattacks and withering fire caused heavy casualties and forced the soldiers to relinquish their gains at 1630 and withdraw to positions from which the attack was launched. Nothing was left to chance on L plus 9, as all three regiments attacked after an intense artillery and naval gunfire bombardment lasting 30 minutes was placed on previously located positions. Air cover was not available because of the continuing bad weather, which turned the ground into a quagmire and bogged down the tanks scheduled to support the advancing infantry. When the day's fighting ended, the division had made an average gain of 300 yards along the entire front.

As night fell and the fighting died down all along the XXIV Corps lines, the Thirty-second Army issued orders for a counterattack to be mounted on 12 April. Encouraged by the overly optimistic reports of the success of Kikusui No. 1 during the 6-7 April raids, the Japanese planned the counterattack to coincide with the second mass Kamikaze raid. Although the suicide flights began to pour into the skies above Okinawa at 1300 on 12 April, it was not until more than nine hours later that the ground effort was launched. The mission of the enemy assault units was to inflict as much damage as possible in rear areas, where their close proximity to Tenth Army troops would protect them from the devastating fire of American naval guns and artillery.

Under the cover of a mortar barrage, Japanese troops attempted the penetration of American lines. They were thrown back as artillery and small arms fire caught them fixed in the light of star shells thrown up by gunfire support ships. The enemy made several more attempts, but XXIV Corps units repulsed each one. On the night of 13-14 April, two lesser attacks occurred, but these also were driven off. In the two days' action, XXIV Corps reported 1,584 Japanese troops killed and four captured.

A partial explanation for the failure of the counterattacks is found in the strength of American reaction to them. In addition, Japanese sources offer another approach:

"When the Army chief of staff, after the opening of the offensive, visited the headquarters of the 62d Division, he learned that the senior staff officer [of the Thirty-second Army], Colonel Yahara, after the issuance of the Army order for the attack, personally communicated to the responsible operational officers of both the 24th and 62d Divisions that commitment of a few shock troops would suffice for the attack instead of employing a major force, since the attack was bound to fail. Colonel Yahara's opposition to the attack sprung from his belief that it was not in keeping with the defensive mission of the Thirty-second Army and that it would result in a sheer waste of manpower." He was right, for, in effect, the attack was very costly to the Japanese, who concluded that "the night assault resulted in a complete failure."

Although XXIV Corps estimated that its troops had destroyed 6,883 of the enemy by 14 April, its order of battle maps still indicated that the 12th, 13th, and 14th Independent Infantry Battalions of the 62d Division's 63d Brigade opposed the corps advance. Although Tenth Army intelligence agencies knew that elements of four new battalions had been added to the enemy line after the 12-13 April counterattack, the Americans were unable to explain the continued identification of those infantry units that had received enough casualties to be considered destroyed. Actually, the inability of the Tenth Army to maintain a current order of battle file stemmed directly from the replacement system of the Thirty-second Army. The Japanese gradually fed individuals and small groups coming from service and support assignments into forward units. At the same time, entire companies and battalions—as yet uncommitted—were absorbed temporarily, or permanently in some cases, into the existing defensive lineup, and were given the designation of the unit into which they had been incorporated.

The first reorganization of the 12th Independent Infantry Battalion on 23 March serves as an excellent example of this practice. At that time, its organic strength was 1,043; attached special guard, labor, and naval elements raised the total to 1,333. The battalion was armed with 49 light and 9 heavy machine guns, 42 grenade launchers, and 2 75mm guns. On 12 April, after more than a week of continuous fighting against the XXIV Corps, 12th Independent Infantry Battalions strength was listed by the Japanese as 1,257. Only 414 men remained of the original battalion and 61 from the unit attached originally, but the battalion had been strengthened by the addition of the 2d Battalion, 22d Regiment (less one rifle company) and the entire 1st Light Mortar Battalion. Surprisingly enough, the battalion was more heavily armed than it had been before L-Day, for it now had 45 light and 13 heavy machine guns, 45 grenade launchers, 19 90mm mortars, and 3 75mm guns.

By the end of the second week of April, Tenth Army intelligence officers had obtained a fairly accurate picture of Japanese defense plans from captured enemy maps and documents. The Americans were forced to revise their L-Day estimate of enemy strength upward by 7,000 to a total of 72,000, which was "deemed a conservative minimum." It was apparent that the bulk of the Thirty-second Army had not yet been met. As the Tenth Army prepared for this encounter, it became evident that the ammunition supply chain could not keep up with the demand, and it was necessary to apply command restrictions on ammunition expenditure as early as

9 April. Concerning this shortage, the Marine Deputy Chief of Staff of the Tenth Army noted: "The artillery, in fact, was used too freely. For a considerable period, artillery ammunition was being unloaded over the beaches at the rate of 3,000 tons per day. . . . It was considered normal to fire a concentration of four or five battalions. A good bit of TOT [time on target] firing was done."

The nature of the Shuri defenses demanded the fullest employment possible of all available weapons. Artillery, especially, was needed to reduce prepared positions and denude them of their skillfully prepared camouflage, to seal off the firing ports, and to collapse the labyrinth of interconnecting tunnels that housed and protected the defending troops. Since their operations were not subject in the same degree to the restrictions of inclement weather and enemy air attacks, as were air and naval gunfire, corps and divisional artillery, of necessity, served as the support workhorses for assaults.

Because General Hedge knew that a maximum effort would be needed if Thirty-second Army lines were to be penetrated, he scheduled a corps attack, three divisions abreast, for 19 April. Beginning 15 April, four days were spent in preparation for the attack. While guns and howitzers steadily hammered at enemy forward positions and troop concentration areas, artillery ammunition reserves were stockpiled both at the batteries and distribution points. In the pre-attack period, planes from TAF and Task Forces 51, 52, and 58 flew a total of 905 sorties in direct support missions for XXIV Corps. The pilots dropped 482 tons of bombs and expended 3,400 rockets and over 700,000 rounds of .50 caliber and 20mm ammunition on Japanese installations. Added to this firepower was that coming from the strong force of TF 51 battleships, cruisers, and destroyers that remained offshore both day and night.

Prior to the attack, the frontline units attempted to improve their positions with small local attacks, while patrols were sent forward in order to pinpoint enemy positions and weapons emplacements. When the 27th Division entered the line on 15 April, a general reshuffling of the XXIV Corps front took place. On that date, General Griner assumed responsibility for the corps right flank and, on the following day, regained his 105th Infantry, which had been released from army reserve following the capture of Tsugen Shima. All initial XXIV Corps assault deployments were completed two days before the jump-off. The support provided by air, naval gunfire, and artillery prior to the 19 April attack might seem pallid in comparison with the destructive potential of the nuclear weapons of a later era. To the assault force leaders and their troops, however, the immensity of the preparatory and supporting fires was awesome. The firepower of 6 battleships, 6 cruisers, and 9 destroyers was assigned to direct support of the attacking corps, and 650 Navy and Marine aircraft were directed to hit enemy defenses, assembly areas, and supply points.

Beginning at 0600 on 19 April, 27 battalions of artillery, covering the five-mile front with a density greater than one weapon to every 30 yards, fired in their pre-attack bombardment everything from 75mm to 8-inch howitzers. Regarding this massing of battalions, one observer remarked: "Not many people realize that the . . . artillery in Tenth Army, plus the LVT(A)s [mounting 75mm howitzers] and NGF equivalent gave us a guns/mile of front ratio on Okinawa that was probably higher than any U.S. effort in World War II. We look with awe on the Russian doctrine of 300 guns/mile of front for an attack. But if you take our Okinawa figures, and apply a reasonable multiplication factor for our flexible fire direction system that rapidly enabled us to mass all guns within range on a target, we equalled or exceeded the Russians in effective available fire support."

Equally impressive was the air support provided the ground troops during this offensive. At one time alone during 19 April, "we had 375 aircraft on station, and . . . LFASCU-2, controlling seven simultaneous air strikes on a ten-mile front, had literally reached the point of saturation." Commenting on this, the commander of the LFASCUs stated that "I do not believe that we have ever exceeded, or since equalled, this magnitude of close air support on any given day."

To the troops poised for the attack, it seemed incredible that anyone could survive in that terrible downpour of steel, yet it soon became apparent that almost all of the enemy did. The Japanese were hidden in eaves and protected by solid limestone walls deep within the hill-ridge complex astride the XXIV Corps route of advance,

Initially, the assault infantry made moderate gains, but when the enemy remanned his positions, the attack slowed and then halted under the resumption of intense mortar, machine gun, and artillery fire. Generally, all along the line, advances were negligible to nonexistent as enemy resistance stiffened. Kakazu Ridge, the formidable bastion opposing the 27th Division, proved to be as difficult to take at this time as it had been when the 96th Division made the attempt. The 27th mounted a battalion-size infantry attack, supported by a reinforced tank company, in an attempt to bypass the ridge through a cut between Kakazu and Nishibaru. Anticipating the probable use of this route, on the night of 18 April the Japanese had emplaced mortars, machine guns, antitank guns, and antiaircraft cannon to cover the Ginowan-Shuri road, which crossed through the cut. The enemy cut off the tank company from its covering infantry by planned protective fire. The tanks were able to get behind the ridge to shoot up the village of Kakazu, but without infantry support, they were forced to withdraw to their own lines. Only 8 of the original 30 tanks in the foray made it back through the cut; the remaining 22 fell victim to the fire of antitank and antiaircraft guns, mines in Kakazu village, and satchel charges borne to the tanks by suicide-bent enemy soldiers.

By the end of the day, on the corps right flank, the 27th Division was halted at the western end of the Urasoe-Mura escarpment; the 96th Division, in the center, had pushed through Kaniku to gain positions on the forward slopes of Nishibaru Ridge; and the 7th Division, on the left, was held up by fanatic opposition and heavy fire, with the net result that it made no progress at all.

As the XXIV Corps ground out the second day of its offensive, the pattern of future fighting emerged—little yardage gained at a high cost in lives to both sides. Heavy casualties were sustained by all the attacking divisions, but the Japanese frontline units also were punished and considerably reduced in size. Only the sheer courage and fanatic determination of the enemy and the strength of his natural defenses kept the XXIV Corps at bay. Action during the period 20-23 April consisted of heavily supported local attacks against key strongpoints.

When General Hedge renewed the XXIV Corps attack on 24 April, he was ready to throw the full weight of its power against the forces holding Shuri's outer defense ring. During the night of 23-24 April, however, unknown to the Americans and under cover of "the most intensive artillery fire yet experienced on the XXIV Corps front," General Ushijima had withdrawn his defending units from the line that had held up the 7th and 96th Divisions for two weeks. All along the front, American forces now made sweeping and significant gains, and the heretofore-difficult Kakazu Ridge was taken with little effort.

After the 27th Division had entered the lines on the corps right flank in mid-April, 2/11 and 3/11 were reassigned from support of the 96th Division to reinforce the fire of 27th Division artillery. This change was made because "General Sheetz thought, even then, that the 1st Marine Division would be needed in the south, on the coast." At this time, the 11th Marines commander, Colonel Brown, heavily reinforced his three 105mm battalions with regimental headquarters personnel so that as many men as possible could gain battle experience.

Firing battery crewmen were not the only Marines in the 11th to gain on-the-job training in the south, for regimental communications personnel were kept exceptionally busy. Although radio was depended upon primarily, wiremen laid telephone wires from Army fire direction centers to the Marine units supporting XXIV Corps after frequent interference in 11th Marines radio circuits had made reliance on wire communications necessary. Owing to a shortage of trained wiremen in the Army battalions, these same Marines in addition had to lay and maintain all lateral wire communications for three Army divisional artillery headquarters. This communication system permitted the rapid massing of all XXIV Corps and attached artillery fire whenever all other means of communication broke down. Forward observer teams of the 11th Marines also gained valuable experience when they went forward to the XXIV Corps infantry units their artillery battalions were supporting. The knowledge gained by the teams supporting the 27th Division was especially useful later when the 1st Marine Division relieved the 27th in the same general area.

Indications that greater Marine participation in the Shuri battle would be forthcoming occurred on 21 April when Tenth Army ordered General Geiger to make the 1st Tank Battalion available for attachment to the 27th Division. Although the IIIAC commander had no compunction about his Marines fighting in the south, he was not happy at the prospect of their being committed piecemeal. If Marine assistance was needed in the south, it was Geiger's opinion that the entire 1st Marine Division should be committed. Although a warning order for the tank battalion displacement had been dispatched to the 1st Division, the actual movement orders were never issued and the matter was apparently dropped by Tenth Army.

General Buckner acknowledged the need for a substantial infusion of fresh troops into the main battleline, and directed General Geiger, on 24 April, to designate one IIIAC division as Tenth Army reserve. One regiment of that division was to be ready to assemble and move south on 12 hours' notice. General Geiger selected the 1st Marine Division, and General del Valle placed the 1st Marines on alert status.

At this point, the question arises why the 2d Marine Division, in Tenth Army reserve, was not committed in action on Okinawa when it was apparent that it was needed. On 9 April, Admiral Nimitz authorized General Watson's division to return and debark at Saipan; on the 14th, the division was released from Tenth Army reserve and reverted to IIIAC control, although it remained on Saipan. Both at this time, and in later critiques of the fighting on Okinawa, there was a strong body of senior officers who felt that there was no sound reason why the 2d Marine Division could not have been employed to make an amphibious assault on the southeastern coast of Okinawa. Possibly, a second landing could have succeeded in cracking the Shuri barrier where the attack of the XXIV Corps in mid-April failed. General Vandegrift suggested that the 2d Division be employed when he visited Okinawa on 21 April with Brigadier General Gerald G. Thomas, Admiral Nimitz, and Nimitz' chief of staff, Rear Admiral Forrest P. Sherman. When, during a meeting at Geiger's CP, Buckner stated that he was going to commit IIIAC divisions in the south shortly, Vandegrift "did not object to the Marines being committed to the main fight—they were on Okinawa for this purpose. But I did question Buckner's tactical plan. Instead of trying to slug it out with the enemy, Geiger, Thomas, and I argued for an amphibious landing in the rear or anyway on the flank of the enemy by Buckner's reserve, the 2d Marine Division on Saipan. Forrest Sherman, among others, objected to a landing on the far east coast as impractical. We replied that the bay of our choice was the alternate landing area for the original operation, so apparently Buckner had thought it quite practical. Having been shot down on this point, Sherman claimed it would take too long to load out the 2d Division from Saipan. We promised him it could be underway in six hours. Despite these and other arguments Sherman refused to back us, nor did Buckner seem impressed. I learned later that General Bruce, commanding the 77th Army Division which had fought so well on Guam, proposed a similar plan as did Kelly Turner, whose transports were being hurt by the kamikaze tactic."

Although General Bruce had also pressed for a second landing, for his troops had all but captured Ie Shima, Buckner refused because his G4 had told him that food but not ammunition could be supplied for this project. In addition, the site of the proposed 77th Division landing was so far south of the main Tenth Army line at that time, neither XXIV Corps artillery nor troops could support it. Besides, at the time that the 77th was available, it was needed in the line, as the 7th, 27th, and 96th Divisions were in bad shape because of casualties and fatigue. Nor did Buckner want to use the 2d Marine Division for a second landing, for it was scheduled to invade Kikai Shima, north of Okinawa, in July.

The Tenth Army commander was evidently convinced that the greater need was for fresh troops on the Shuri front and that a landing on the southeastern beaches was logistically infeasible. Despite the arguments presented by General Vandegrift in favor of such a tactic, he was not supported by either Nimitz or Sherman, and Buckner remained unmoved in his decision. He faced the basic alternatives of a two-corps frontal attack against Shuri or an envelopment of the enemy forces facing his troops. Having decided against the landing in the enemy rear, his next step was to commit IIIAC in the south. On 26 April, General Buckner was informed that Phase III of the plan, the projected invasion of Miyako Shima in the Sakashima Group east of Taiwan, was cancelled. This high-level decision by the JCS freed IIIAC from the Miyako operation and permitted Buckner to insert that corps into the southern Okinawa line. The next day, the army commander declared his intent to attach the 1st Division to XXIV Corps at an early date in order to relieve the understrength and badly battered 27th Division for garrison duty under Island Command. Also on 27 April, the 77th Infantry Division completed its move from Ie Shima to Okinawa, and its leading elements moved into position to relieve the 96th the next day. Matters concerning the future employment of IIIAC units were discussed at a conference held at Tenth Army headquarters on 28 April. Colonel Walter A. Wachtler, General Geiger's G-3, was informed that the 1st Marine Division was to be attached to XXIV Corps on the last day of April. General del Valle's troops would begin moving south to relieve the 27th Division on that same day. Upon its relief, the 27th was to move north to relieve the 6th Marine Division, which would then move to an assembly area near Chibana to await further orders for the movement south. It was planned that, on or about 7 May, the IIIAC was to take over the zone held at that time by the 1st Marine Division and, simultaneously, Tenth Army would then assume tactical control of the two-corps front. A coordinated army attack would be made soon thereafter.

1st Marine Division Joins XXIV Corps

While the XXIV Corps made preparations to relieve two of its frontline divisions, the attack to the south continued. The enemy reacted savagely to the grinding advance of the 96th Division, throwing counterattacks, repeated artillery and mortar barrages, and never-ending infiltration attempts in the soldiers' path. The division objective was the Maeda Escarpment. Retention of this position was vital to Thirty-second Army defense plans, because the terrain offered a commanding view of all of the Japanese positions as far as the Shuri foothills, and at the same time guaranteed continued enemy observation into American lines. The region surrounding Maeda, therefore, became the focus of ferocious fighting when the enemy attempted to retain the dominating ground of the second Shuri defensive ring. On 29 April, units of the 77th Division began relief of the 96th Division and immediately took up the attack. The soldiers of the 77th were very tired from the fighting they had just experienced on Ie Shima and the division was far understrength because of casualty losses. As a result, it could make but slight gains against the highly developed defenses. The 27th Division lines on the 29th had been pushed through Kuwan and Miyagusuku during a daylong drive, which exposed deeply dug-in, heavily mined Japanese positions. These extended throughout the rugged hills and ridges that bordered the east and southeast sides of Machinato airfield. At 0600 on the following day, the 1st Marine Division was attached to XXIV Corps. Immediately thereafter, march serials of the 1st Marines and 1st Tank Battalion began moving to the 27th Division area in the south. The Army division, meanwhile, continued its attack south of Machinato airfield. At 1000, the first of the Marine units began moving into 27th Division lines even as it halted its forward progress and disengaged its advance patrols, which had been caught in a heavy fire fight.

On the extreme right of the corps line, beginning at Kuwan, 1/1 took up positions, which made a half-circle around the south of Machinato and joined up with 3/1 just to the northeast of Nakanishi. No orders were issued for the resumption of the attack in this area, so the Marines spent the rest of 30 April digging in, improving existing defenses, and registering defensive fires.

The commander of 3/1 had been informed by the commander of the relieved Army battalion that some Japanese were still holed-up in Miyagusuku. Marines, dispatched to mop up, moved towards the village, whereupon enemy artillery and mortar fire began falling on them. Under this cover, Japanese troops began infiltrating back into Miyagusuku in some strength. After being pinned down in the village ruins by the concentrated fire, the Marines were forced to withdraw; they set up north of the village for the night. At dusk, the 3/1 reserve was committed on the left of the line, where it tied in with the one yet-unrelieved unit of the 27th Division.

The 77th Division completed the relief of the 96th at the same time the 1st Marines took over the right of the 27th Division lines. At noon, General Bruce assumed command of the zone from General Bradley and, throughout the day, 77th Division troops attempted to improve their positions on the escarpment. Despite heavy supporting fires, the sheer fury and fanatic determination of the defenders forced the attackers back to defensive positions of the previous night.

By midafternoon of 1 May, two of the 1st Division assault regiments, the 1st Marines on the right and the 5th Marines on the left, had relieved the 27th Division; General del Valle assumed command of the former Army zone at 1400. Although this action marked the official entry of the 1st Division into the southern front, the 11th Marines had been in the vanguard when it supported the 7th, 27th, and 96th Divisions throughout most of the fighting in April. The artillery battalions of the 27th Division remained in position to continue supporting the 1st and 77th Divisions in their attack to the south. Even before completing relief of the 27th Division on 1 May, General del Valle's Marines saw clearly the results of combat in southern Okinawa, and soon learned of the tenacity of the defenders. When the 5th Marines relieved the remaining Army regiments during the afternoon of the 1st, they learned how hard these units had been hit. Each 2/5 infantry company replaced one depleted battalion of the 105th, and 3/5 took over the area held by the 106th. At 1400, while consolidating their positions south of Awacha, 2/5 Marines observed about a platoon of Army tanks moving south in the town. As soon as the tanks had emerged from the town, they were hit by 47mm AT fire within 20 yards of the Marine line. Perhaps even more disturbing to the Marines was the news that their unit identification and the location of their front had already been noted on an enemy map captured just that day.

General del Valle's men continued their defensive activities on their first day in the south. By 1700, all lines had been tied in, and 1/5 had taken up positions in a reserve area. As the frontline Marines dug in, preparations were made for a fully supported division attack scheduled for the following day, with the north bank of the Asa Kawa River as the objective. The corps commander instructed General del Valle to exert constant pressure against the enemy and to support the 77th Division attack with fire and maneuver. Because it flanked the Army division, the 5th Marines was assigned this task.

In order to prevent an American penetration after the 27th Division had taken Gusukuma, the Japanese had been forced to reform their west coast battleline. It now was held by a major portion of the 62d Division, which was positioned along a line that ran generally from Jichaku and Uchima through the ridges north of Dakeshi to Awacha. In addition, there were "powerful elements of the Division scattered and remaining in the cave positions within the [American] lines still offering resistance." It was these forces with which the 1st Marines would have to contend. The 1st of May brought cloudy and cooler weather, and sporadic showers heralded the Okinawa rainy period, which, in itself, serves as a harbinger of the approaching typhoon season (July-November). During the previous night, all 1st Marines battalions had received intermittent mortar and artillery fire. The day was devoted by 1/1 to patrolling its front and attempting to readjust its lines. A reconnaissance patrol discovered that a deep L-shaped ravine cut across the entire battalion front and that it formed a natural barrier to the next logical objective. The Marines also found that the retreating enemy had blown out the fill where the main north-south highway crossed this chasm. Added to the enemy artillery and antitank guns registered on the area, this obstacle obviously would prohibit an armor-supported infantry penetration.

A patrol sent from one of the Marine rifle companies to the west of the ravine to scout out other approaches was taken under extremely heavy fire that came from the steep cliffs along the far side of the declivity. It was apparent that the enemy, from positions on the high ground to the south and southeast of the Asa Kawa, had excellent observation of the battalion approach route and that the Marines were going to have a difficult time reaching and crossing the river.

On the left of the regiment, meanwhile, 3/1 prepared for a second attempt to secure Miyagusuku, this time with the support of seven tanks from the 1st Tank Battalion, four of them mounting flamethrowers. The flat trajectory tank cannon fire blasted the houses and walls still standing, and 300 gallons of flaming napalm set the entire pyre aflame. At 1045, when the fires had died down, a small patrol passed through without enemy opposition. Approximately two and a half hours later, the rest of the battalion followed, and, as it cleared Miyagusuku, there was a step-up in the intermittent Japanese mortar and artillery fire that had been falling since before dawn. Added to this fire was that of enemy riflemen and machine gunners. Increased casualties and the difficulties encountered in evacuating them forced the assault companies to withdraw under a smoke screen and mortar barrage once the battalion commander had given permission for such a move. By 1900, the battalion returned to the positions it had occupied on 30 April.

The 1st Division attack to the Asa on 2 May began in driving rain which seriously limited visibility and reduced the amount of effective air support supplied that day. The two frontline Army divisions in XXIV Corps attacked enemy-held ridge positions containing pillboxes and mutually supporting small arms and automatic weapons emplacements. Added to these barriers and the destructiveness of Japanese artillery fire was the foe's determined and ferocious refusal to yield any ground. When the 5th Marines jumped off at 0900, following artillery, naval gunfire, and some air preparation, 2/5 on the extreme left came under flanking fire from positions in front of the 307th's lines. Within an hour, the 2d Battalion was pinned down, and, by 1100, heavy casualties forced its withdrawal under a smoke cover to its original positions. As soon as the 3d Battalion crossed its line of departure, it too came under the frontal and flanking fire that had driven 2/5 back. "The advance was untenable and had to be withdrawn to initial positions." Because the 5th Marines was unable to advance, Company L of 3/1 (on the battalion left) was stopped in its attempt to move beyond Miyagusuku with Company K. The latter, however, was not pinned down and was able to progress beyond the edge of the ruins that were once a village. At 1446, the 1st Marines commander, Colonel Chappell, was ordered to change the axis of the regimental attack from due south to the southeast. General del Valle had reasoned that the new attack direction, which would hit the flank of many of the positions holding up the 5th Marines, would enable both Company L and his left regiment to continue the advance.

After new attack orders had been issued, battalion boundaries adjusted, and a 10-minute artillery barrage laid, the 1st Marines attack was resumed at 1630 against very heavy fire. By dark, 3/1 had fought its way to a small series of hills approximately 300 yards south of Miyagusuku. Pouring rain, machine gun fire, and grenades began falling on the leading elements of the assault as the troops gained this ground. Here they began digging in at 2000 for the night. Almost immediately, the enemy began the first in a series of infiltration attempts which were to mark the hours of darkness. The violence of the hand-to-hand clashes on the hill held by Company K was reflected in a comment the next morning by one of the Marines, who said that this had been the grimmest night he had spent so far on Okinawa.

On the extreme right of the division, 1/1 ran into equally heavy resistance in its effort to cross the ravine facing it. Although one company had already passed through Nakanishi, and was in position by 1000 to plunge into the ravine where it angled north towards Miyagusuku, the slowness of the attack to the left of the 1st Marines presaged caution, and the 1/1 commander was told to be wary of exposing his troops to enfilade fire.

Despite all precautionary measures, including the blasting of enemy positions by self-propelled assault guns at the beginning of the attack, Japanese fire continued to pour from the caves and heights overlooking the defile to catch the advancing troops.

Disregarding this fusilade and the casualties resulting from it, Company B managed to gain a defiladed position just short of the initial objective. At this point, however, the Marines were cut off both front and rear by enemy fire. At 1300, orders for a general withdrawal were issued, and the company disengaged and pulled back to high ground under the cover of smoke. At 1630, when the attack was resumed in the new direction, the 1st Battalion attacked straight across the ravine in order to ensure flank protection before making the southeasterly move. The impetus of the drive carried Company A to the outskirts of Jichaku, where it dug in. By the end of a quiet but wet night, the assault units had established a firm line where the division awaited the joining of RCT-7.

The 7th Marines had displaced south on the morning of the attack, its battalions moving to the vicinity of Uchitomari. On the following day, 3 May, the regimental CP displaced forward to a point about 200 yards north of Gusukuma, while the 1st and 2d Battalions took up beach defense positions in the vicinity of Machinato airfield. The 3d Battalion was attached to the 5th Marines to assist the advance of that regiment.

Continuing the attack on 3 May, the division assigned intermediate and final objectives to the 1st Marines. The first began at the railroad spur bridge crossing the Asa River between Asa and Uchima, and extended northeast, generally following the spur initially and then the main line itself, to a point just east of Miyagusuku. The second began at the same bridge, but ran generally east along the high ground between Dakeshi and Wana to the division boundary. The line between the attacking regiments, bent back to reflect the assignment given the 1st Marines, gave to the 5th the thankless task of clearing out the confused terrain that soon would be called Awacha Pocket.

Although the 5th Marines gained about 500-600 yards in its zone, the 1st became heavily engaged in fire fights all along the line and was restricted to limited gains. Forward elements of 1/1 ran into difficulty in every direction; Company F, attacking Jichaku, was held up by a stubborn defense, and Company A was cut up in its attempt to reduce the ravine position that had stymied the battalion on the previous day. Neither company was able to move forward and both were forced to withdraw under the cover of smoke late in the morning, carrying with them the large number of casualties they had sustained. Because it appeared that the attack would not succeed without armor support, plans were made to use tanks after the road south of Kuwan had been cleared of mines. After dark, an engineer mine-clearing team, protected by infantry, began reconnoitering the proposed armor attack route. Company L, on the left of the 1st Marines line, was unable to move until 3/5 had seized a high hill to the left front of the company. After it took the hill, the battalion was driven off at 1555 by a heavy enemy artillery concentration. Company L was ordered to retake the objective, and, following a 10-minute 81mm mortar barrage, gained the hilltop 20 minutes later. Here, the company was pinned down by Japanese fire coming from high ground to the front and on its flanks. When Company K was unable to close in on L and had to fall back, Company I was committed on the right of K to close a gap that had developed along the battalion boundary. The regiment then assigned Company G of 2/1 to back-up the 1,200-yard front of 3/1.

To escape the furious machine gun and mortar fire that had followed it after it was driven off the hill on the right of 3/1, 3/5 was forced to fall back another 100 yards; its advances on 3 May were limited to 200-300 yards. Passing through 2/5 that morning to begin its attack with two companies in the assault, the 1st Battalion, 5th Marines, was able to gain some 500-600 yards, but was forced in late afternoon to bend its lines back to tie in with 3/5. Immediately upon being relieved, 2/5 swung over to its left to take over part of the 307th Infantry lines on the outskirts of Awacha.

Once its 2d Battalion was relieved by 2/5, the 307th Infantry moved it to the left and, with all three of its battalions on line, mopped up the top of the escarpment—and the upper part of its reverse slope—during the day. By nightfall, the Army regiment held positions commanding the Japanese defensive alignment all the way back to the Shuri foothills. Despite having been pushed back, the enemy still determinedly refused the Americans further gains and fanatically resisted from reverse-slope caves, sometimes counterattacking in company and platoon strength to regain critical terrain.

The ferocity of Japanese resistance continued unabated all along the XXIV Corps line, for as veteran units were annihilated, they were quickly rebuilt with fresh rear area troops, or replaced with new infantry elements. General Hedge's dire prediction at the beginning of the 19 April attack that "it is going to be really tough . . . and that I see no way to get [the Japanese] out except blast them out yard by yard" was being all too grimly substantiated.

The Japanese Counterattack

During the grueling see-saw battle in the south, both sides suffered heavily. The slow but perceptible American gains were costly, but the Japanese paid the higher price. The 62d Division bore the brunt of the April attack and by the end of the month its combat strength was less than half of what it had been originally. Although many Thirty-second Army officers viewed the Japanese cause on Okinawa as hopeless, they were buoyed up by the fact "that after thirty consecutive days of systematic fighting the main body of [our] fighting forces should remain intact. . . ." Not yet bloodied in the fight for Shuri were most of the units of the 24th Division, 44th IMB, and 5th Artillery Command. An attitude favoring the offense permeated General Ushijima's command, whose members considered that commitment of these fresh troops in one major effort would effectively blunt the American drive. Prior to the landings on the west coast, the expectation of an American amphibious assault at Minatoga had caused the Thirty-second Army commander to deploy a considerable portion of his strength in that area. But, by the end of April, the steady attrition of the forces manning the Shuri outer defense ring caused General Ushijima to reappraise his situation and reexamine his mission. Since he had been ordered to prolong the battle as long as possible and inflict heavy casualties on the invaders, Ushijima decided to utilize the units immobilized in the southeast to reinforce the Shuri positions.

Implementing this decision, the 24th Division and the 44th IMB were ordered to begin a movement north on 22 April. The 24th, recovering control of its 22d Regiment from the 62d Division, was to occupy defensive positions in a line from Gaja on the east coast to Maeda at the eastern end of the Urasoe-Mura escarpment. The depleted battalions of the hard-hit 62d Division were to concentrate in the area from Maeda to the west coast near Gusukuma. Taking up blocking positions behind the 62d on the high ground to the south and east of the Asa River, the 44th IMB was to cover Naha and the ridges and draws flanking to the west of Shuri.

To protect the area south of the Naha-Yonabaru valley, and to forestall further American landings on the west coast, both Admiral Ota's force and a provisional guard group, formed to guard the Chinen Peninsula, were kept in place. The Chinen units were not to make a last-ditch stand, but were to make a fighting withdrawal to Shuri if the southeastern beaches were invaded.

In less than a week, by 27 April, the new enemy defensive setup had been established. But even small local Japanese counterattacks failed, despite the reconstitution of the frontlines and the infusion of fresh troops. Steadily XXIV Corps units encroached upon enemy positions and forced their defenders back. In the Thirty-second Army headquarters deep below Shuri Castle, General Cho led other firebrands in an attempt to convince the army commander that conditions were favorable for an all-out, army-sized counterattack, employing the relatively intact 24ththh Division as the spearhead. Colonel Yahara was a lone dissenter to the plan. His belief that the Japanese attack would end in abject failure and certain defeat was based on several factors. He noted that the Americans, positioned on commanding ground, were materially and numerically superior. Fatalistically prophesying an inevitable Japanese defeat no matter what, the colonel reasoned that the army should "maintain to the bitter end the principle of a strategic holding action." Any other course of action would doom the army, be detrimental to its mission, and open the way for an otherwise earlier invasion of the Japanese homeland.

Despite Colonel Yahara's impassioned and reasoned arguments, General Cho, backed by other proponents of the offensive—the division and brigade commanders—swayed Ushijima to their way of thinking, and, in the end, prevailed. In scope and desired objectives, the attack plan was exceedingly ambitious; it called for nothing less than the destruction of XXIV Corps and capture of Futema and its environs.

The counterattack was to begin at 0500 (Y-Hour) on 4 May (X-Day). The Japanese believed it would be successful because they knew a relief of the American lines was then taking place. At Y-Hour, the 89th Regiment (on the right) would begin a penetration of the 7th Division front to gain its objective, the Minami-Uebaru foothills, by sunset. In the center, the 22d Regiment was to hold its positions near Kochi and Onaga, where it would support the assaulting units with fire. When the 89th Regiment formed an east-west line at Tanabaru, the initial objective, the 22d would move out, destroying any American unit remaining to its front, and follow up in rear center of the division main effort to be made by the 32d Regiment. At Y-Hour, the 32d would drive forward to seize 77th Division positions southeast of Maeda, and then continue on to gain the heights west of Tanabaru by sunset also.

Armored support of the attack was to be supplied by the 27th Tank Regiment, after it had moved from positions near Ishimmi to penetrate the 77th Division lines west of Kochi. Here, the tanks would take up new positions to assist the 22d and 32d Regiments. The day before the attack, the 44th IMB was to move to the area northwest of Shuri, where the brigade would provide left flank security until the initial objective was taken. Immediately thereafter, the 44th would swing north to Oyama and the coast just beyond, to isolate the 1st Marine Division from the battle. This task would be supported by the heretofore-uncommitted 62d Division. To make certain that the Marines would be cut off, the Japanese planners had reinforced the 44th IMB with a considerable number of armored, artillery, and antitank elements. On the night of 3-4 May, the guns, mortars, and howitzers of the 5th Artillery Command were to move out of their hidden positions into the open to provide the Japanese attack with full gunfire support. The Thirty-second Army also called upon Admiral Ota to participate in the massive counterattack, for he was directed to form from his naval command four infantry battalions to be used as army reserve in exploiting the breakthrough. The Japanese attack plan provided also for hitting the open flanks of the XXIV Corps. Embarking from Naha on the night of 3-4 May, a makeshift navy of landing barges, small craft, and native canoes was to land a major portion of the 26th Shipping Engineer Regiment behind 1st Marine Division lines at Oyama. Concurrently, elements of the 26th, 28th, and 29th Sea Raiding Squadrons were to wade the reef on the Marine flank, go ashore in the vicinity of Kuwan, and move inland to support the counterlanding of the 26th. Committed to the west coast attack was a total of approximately 700 men.

Another envelopment was to be attempted on the east coast where about 500 men from the 23d Shipping Engineer Regiment and the 27th Sea Raiding Squadron would land behind the 7th Division at Tsuwa. The mission of both regiments was to infiltrate American rear areas in small groups and to destroy equipment and harass CPS with grenades and demolitions. No concerted attacks were to be made unless assault groups numbered more than 100 men. If all went according to plan, the two countermanding elements would join up near the center of the island to assist the 24th Division advance.

A never-changing assumption in ICEBERG intelligence estimates was an enemy capability to mount a large-scale counterattack. As of the evening of 3 May, however, an analysis of recent enemy tactics indicated that he was more likely to continue fighting a series of delaying actions from successive positions, defending each one "until the troops on the position are nearly annihilated." Since the American order of battle of enemy elements facing XXIV Corps was then current, and each enemy move and countermove had been viewed with respect to the related tactical situation, indications of an imminent major attack were not perceptible. Local counterattacks and stiffened resistance were merely attributed to the infusion of new strength into Japanese lines. XXIV Corps troops were not caught off-guard, however, when the attack was finally mounted.

Preceding the two-day struggle—called by Colonel Yahara "the decisive action of the campaign"—the fifth mass Kamikaze attack struck at dusk on 3 May. Tokyo had notified the Fifth Air Fleet on 30 April of the impending Thirty-second Army attack. The Japanese air command then issued orders for a mass suicide raid to be launched on 3 May, prior to the beginning of the ground assault. Kikusui No. 5 targets were to be American supply areas, airfields, and the ever-suffering radar pickets. Although they were to have played only a secondary role in the overall attack, the Kamikaze pilots were more destructive and successful in what they did than was the Japanese infantry. In two hours, however, 36 of the 125 suiciders in this raid were shot down according to the claims of antiaircraft gunners ashore and afloat, and those of carrier- and land-based American pilots. Japanese sources note that a total of 159 planes of all types participated in the 34 May raid.

Although a barrier of antiaircraft fire kept the conventional bombers at such heights over the airfields and the anchorage that they could cause only superficial damage, the suiciders bore in to inflict wide-spread havoc on the radar pickets. A destroyer and an LSM were sunk; two minelayers and a support landing craft (LCS) were damaged. Enemy bombers again appeared over the island shortly after midnight to hit Tenth Army rear area installations, but as before, accurate AAA fire kept them high over their potential targets and caused the bombing to be erratic. A string of bombs fell near Sobe, however, and crashed through the overheads of IIIAC Evacuation Hospital No. 3, destroying two dug-in surgery wards, killing 13 and wounding 36 patients and medical personnel. Radar-directed TAF night fighters were unable to close with the enemy bombers because American electronic early-warning equipment was disrupted by "window" that had been dropped by four Japanese reconnaissance aircraft.

Beginning on 4 May at 0600, and for four hours thereafter, the Kamikazes pushed a murderous onslaught against the radar pickets to coincide with the Thirty-second Army ground effort. By the time that the morning forays and the one later at dusk against the escort carrier group were over, the number of naval casualties and ships damaged and sunk was sobering. There were 91 Americans killed, 280 wounded, and 283 missing on the 4th, and on the picket line, two destroyers and two LSMs were sunk; two other destroyers, a minesweeper, a light minelayer, and an LCS were damaged. A turret on the cruiser *Birmingham* was hit by a suicider in the morning attack, and another enemy pilot succeeded in crashing the flight deck of the carrier *Sangamon* in the afternoon, causing an explosion which damaged both elevators and destroyed 21 planes.

Enemy air did not go unpunished on the 4th, for American pilots claimed to have destroyed a total of 95 Japanese aircraft. ADC flyers had their second most successful day, next to 12 April, for their claims totalled 603/4 kills, bringing TAF claims overall to 206 in less than a month of operations. The Navy was not concerned solely with helping to beat off the aerial attacks, for Admiral Turner alerted his surface force to the possible threat accruing from suiciders in the enemy Sea Raiding Squadrons. He cautioned his "flycatcher" screen of cruisers, destroyers, and gunboats on both coasts to be especially watchful. It was this screen that discovered the shipping engineer regiments attempting to slip behind American lines and assisted the ground forces in combating the counterlandings by illuminating and shelling them. When daylight of 4 May revealed the extent of the Japanese ground effort, the two battleships, five cruisers, and eight destroyers assigned as daytime gunfire support for XXIV Corps joined with artillery and air to blunt the Japanese infantry advance and silence its weapons support.

The Japanese ground offensive began shortly after dark on 3 May with a steadily accelerating rate of artillery fire placed mainly on the frontlines of the 7th and 77th Divisions. As American guns replied in kind, the normal battlefield sounds became an almost unbearable cacophony. In a comparatively less noisier sector near Machinato airfield, LVT(A) crews on guard opened up on unidentified individuals they heard on the beach, and shortly thereafter, support craft were seen firing at targets in the water just offshore. Less than an hour after this outbreak of firing, the 1st Marines reported enemy barges heading in for shore at Kuwan.

The landing took place here, instead of at Oyama as originally planned, because the landing craft carrying the bulk of the attack force had trouble negotiating the route through the reefs and lost their way. This error was further compounded by the fact that the troops went ashore at the exact point where Company B, 1/1, had anchored its night defense position.

The stealthy enemy approach went undetected by beach sentries and became known only when a clamorous babble signalled the opening of the Japanese attack. This alert resulted in an immediate response from the Marines; they opened up immediately at the overcrowded barges with fire from machine guns and mortars, previously sited to cover the reef. A combination of burning barges, flares, and tracers soon gave the battle scene an infernal glow. This illumination over the reef revealed Japanese heads bobbing in the water and provided the Marine riflemen and machine gunners with targets which they raked unmercifully, blunting the raid. The 1st Marines commander immediately reinforced the threatened area, and LVT(A)s from the 3d Armored Amphibian Battalion took up blocking positions on the reef above Kuwan. By 0245, those survivors of the ill-fated landing attempts who had gained the beach were being pounded steadily by all available weapons. Despite the immediate Marine reaction to the attempted Japanese envelopment from the sea, some enemy troops managed to infiltrate to the rear of 1/1 before the fighting began on the beach. These raiders were engaged by Company F, 2/1, in an intense fire fight, which ended with 75 enemy dead lying where they had fallen around the Marine positions.

Because he was left with but one rifle company as his regimental reserve, Colonel Chappell requested the attachment of a 7th Marines battalion to his regiment. Division approved the request and ordered 2/7 to move south to report to 1/1 for orders. Preceding the rest of his battalion, Lieutenant Colonel Berger and his staff arrived at the 1/1 CP at 0500 to find all in order and the Japanese threat contained. With the exception of scattered enemy remnants holed up in Kuwan, most of the 300-400 Japanese who had attempted the landing were dead, and were seen either lying on the beach or floating aimlessly in the water amidst the flotsam of the early-morning battle. Lieutenant Colonel Berger's battalion, assigned to mop up the countermanding area, began relieving the right flank elements of 1/1 at 0645 so that the 1st Battalion could continue the attack to the south.

Other enemy landings were attempted before dawn behind 1st Division lines farther up the west coast. Most of these Japanese efforts were doomed to failure either when the combined fire of naval vessels, LVT(A)s, infantry, and service troops caught the boats in the water or when, by light of day, the few Japanese able to reach shore were hunted down and killed. An estimated 65 enemy landed near Isa in the vicinity of the division CP; some who hid in the cane fields survived until dawn, only to be tracked down by 1st Reconnaissance Company scouts accompanied by war dogs and their handlers.

On the east coast, the countermanding met with the same lack of success, for the "flycatchers" and 7th Division troops cut the shipping engineers to pieces, killing an estimated 400. Thus, the Thirty-second Army gambit failed; there was little indication that the rest of Ushijima's counterattack plan could be fulfilled.

Japanese artillery fire continued through the night of 3-4 May, reaching a deafening thunder at 0430, when a half-hour cannonade was fired in preparation for the 24th Division attack. Added to the bursting fragments of the high-caliber shells were those of many thousands of mortar projectiles which fell on the frontlines when the attackers attempted to breach XXIV Corps defenses. The Japanese assault units suffered heavily as they moved through their own fire to gain the American lines. The attack was blunted, however, under a blanket of steel laid down by naval gunfire, air, and 16 battalions of divisional artillery, backed up by 12 battalions of 155mm guns and 155mm and 8-inch howitzers from XXIV Corps artillery. Beginning at daybreak, the first of 134 planes to fly support for XXIV Corps made its initial bombing run. By 1900, 77 tons of bombs, 450 rockets, and 22,000 rounds of machine gun and cannon ammunition had been expended on Japanese troop concentrations and artillery positions. Even in the face of the Kamikaze attacks, gunfire support vessels, from battleships to patrol and landing craft, ranged the coastal waters delivering observed and called fire on enemy targets.

The heavy smoke that Thirty-second Army had ordered laid on American lines obscured from the Shuri heights the enemy's view of the progress of the battle. Despite the fact that it was a bald-faced lie, good news, telling of "the success of the offensive carried out by the 24th Division," poured into the army command post at the opening of the attack.

The initial impetus of the attack on the Tenth Army left flank by the 89th Regiment was blunted by 7th Division troops, who had begun mopping up isolated pockets by noon. In the center, the 22d Regiment, unable to maintain attack momentum by following up what were to have been "successful" advances by right flank units, spent the day locked in a violent fire fight with 7th Division infantry in the Kochi-Onaga region.

The major drive of the 24th Division, mounted by the 32d Regiment, was towards the Urasoe-Mura escarpment, where the 44th IMB was to exploit and pour through the break it made to hit the rear of the 1st Marine Division. A day-long series of enemy attacks in strength all along the line fell far short of General Ushijima's goals, and darkness found Tenth Army units still in firm control of the escarpment. An inescapable conclusion was that the Japanese push had failed. Not only had XXIV Corps troops securely retained their original positions, but in some cases, even in the face of withering enemy fire and stubborn Japanese resistance, the Americans had attacked and captured some enemy territory.

The 1st Marine Division attack on 4 May was delayed twice, from 0800 to 0900 and then to 1000, owing to the need for its units to be reorganized and resupplied. As soon as the assault battalions of the 1st and 5th Marines resumed their advance, heavy and well-placed fire from the 62d Division pinned down the left flank company of 1/1 east of Jichaku, and caused heavy casualties. The left flank of 3/1 received machine gun fire from both its front and from its flanks, and was unable to advance. By 1700, however, except for a short stretch of enemy territory extending from the gap in the left center of 3/1 lines to the eastern edge of Jichaku, the leading elements of the 1st Marines were only a few hundred yards away from the final regimental objective, the north bank of the Asa Kawa. In midafternoon, division attached 3/7 to the 5th Marines, and Colonel Griebel moved the battalion into blocking positions behind his 3d Battalion. As darkness fell on the evening of 4 May, its gloom was no greater than that already pervading Thirty-second Army headquarters. As the shambles of the thwarted counterattack were surveyed by the staff, it was quite apparent that the effort was a failure. The commander of the 24th Division, General Amamiya, nonetheless, ordered the 32d Regiment to try again after dark what it had failed to accomplish earlier that day. Following an extremely heavy artillery and mortar barrage, the regiment hit the frontlines of the 77th Division at 0200 on 5 May in an attempt to penetrate the 306th Infantry positions. Despite the blunting of its initial attack by American artillery, the 32d returned at dawn, this time with armored support. The assaulting force received the same reception it had been given earlier; six tanks were destroyed and the remnants of the regiment forced to withdraw. In the course of these attacks, 3/32 had suffered crippling casualties and the 1st and 2d Battalions of the regiment had been wiped out.

The survivors of the several counterattacks were hunted down by Tenth Army troops at the same time the frontline divisions consolidated their positions and prepared to resume the advance. Only in the 1st Marine Division zone was the pattern of enemy opposition consistent with that occurring before the counterattack of the 4th. Desperation arising from the failure of the major 24th Division effort further spurred the shaken troops of the 62d Division to make a more steadfast stand against Marine advances. Japanese strength was concentrated on the left of the 1st Division zone, where last-ditch attempts were made to guard the vital western approaches to Shuri. Attacking platoons were hit from all sides by fire emanating from caves, pillboxes, and fortified tombs.

Overcoming this opposition with difficulty, General del Valle's troops made substantial gains during the day. On the left flank, the 5th Marines registered encouraging progress, advancing up to 600 yards in some parts of its zone. Following close behind the 1st Marines, the 7th filled the gap on the right flank which resulted from the eastward swing of the division. In the course of the day's action, the 1st Marine Division succeeded in reaching the Asa Kawa; and by evening, frontline units began digging in on the commanding ground overlooking the river line, awaiting new enemy counterattacks which never materialized. Casualty figures following these two days of battle revealed that the 7th and 77th Divisions, which had felt the full fury of the counterattack, lost a total of 714 soldiers killed, wounded, and missing in action. The 1st Marine Division, which had continued its southerly drive in the same period, suffered corresponding losses totalling 649 Marines. Reflecting the fury with which the enemy had fought and the punishment that he had sustained, the Japanese losses were at least 6,227 men, all dead and almost all of them irreplaceable veteran infantry troops.

Checked by the tremendous firepower of the Tenth Army, each Japanese division in the attack had been chopped down to approximately 20 or 25 percent of its original strength, and enemy artillery strength was halved. In addition to these losses, Ushijima lost 59 artillery pieces destroyed in American air-naval gunfire-artillery bombardments. As a result, never again in the Okinawa campaign did Tenth Army troops receive such intensively destructive Japanese artillery fire as that which had preceded the doomed enemy counterattacks. The net result of this two-day Japanese effort was that the Thirty-second Army was compelled to abandon the offensive on the evening of the 5th and to return to its old positions.

In the end, the decisive defeat of the Japanese counterattack bore out the dire predictions of Colonel Yahara. The senior operations officer also won a tearful promise from his army commander that his, Yahara's, counsel would be followed in the future. The defensive pattern then in effect in the 62d Division zone was to be duplicated across the entire army front. Additionally, the 24th Division and the 5th Artillery Command were to reorganize; their tactics would be revised to consist of holding actions in previously prepared and strongly fortified positions. This revision would force the Americans to advance in the face of withering fire, gaining little. The final judgment on the worth of the Japanese counterattack was given by its strongest proponent, General Cho. "After this ill-starred action," Ushijima's chief of staff was reported by a reliable observer as having "abandoned all hope of a successful outcome of the operation and declared that only time intervened between defeat and the 32d Army."

Chapter 7. Forging Ahead

IIIAC On The Lines

On 5 May, Tenth Army ordered the attack to the south continued on the 7th with two corps abreast; IIIAC on the right, XXIV Corps on the left. With two corps now poised for the assault, Tenth Army assumed direct command of the southern front. The day before the attack, 6 May, General Geiger's CP opened at a new location near Futema, where the operation order was received. Effective at 0600 on the 7th, the 1st Division would revert to IIIAC control and the latter would then take over the zone of action for which General del Vane had been responsible previously. The 7 May attack was a prelude to a second and major assault to be launched on 11 May. The objective of the first attack was to gain favorable jump-off positions for the second one, which was to be directed against the Shuri defenses. Before IIIAC units could get into position for the scheduled 7 May attack, the Marines had to get across the Asa River estuary. General Geiger ordered the 1st Division to attack south on the 7th, with the main effort on its left. The 6th Division was to relieve the 1st on the right of the corps zone with one regimental combat team before 1600 on 8 May. Both Marine divisions spent 6 May readying for the next day's work; General Shepherd's division moved to assembly areas preparatory to its commitment, and the 1st maintained pressure on the enemy. During the course of this day, as 2/74 stood fast along the Asa River estuary line, other elements of the division were unable to budge virtually a stonewall defense. Despite accurate counterbattery fire, enemy artillery activity increased noticeably. Two tanks working in front of the 5th Marines lines were knocked out by well-placed Japanese antitank fire as they blasted enemy cave positions at close range.

The 1st Marines attack zone was narrowed considerably when new regimental boundaries were established. A concentration of the force of the Marine attack against enemy positions in the western approaches to Dakeshi hill defenses was necessary because the 1st Marines line cut back sharply from the Asa Gawa to the 5th Marines positions north of the Awacha Pocket. This situation subjected attacking units of the 1st Marines to punishing frontal and flanking fire from a well-organized maze of hills and ridges protecting Dakeshi. In a downpour which lasted two days, 3/1 attacked on 6 May. Its attempts to breach the Dakeshi defenses were unavailing and easily fended off by 62d Division troops. Similarly, the efforts of 2/1 were stymied. Fierce enemy fire held up the attacking Marines and forced elements that had been able to gain even a little ground to withdraw. Despite an intense four-battalion artillery preparation, and air and naval gunfire bombardment, the 5th Marines could penetrate only slightly into the Awacha Pocket, then held by 23d Independent Infantry and 14th Independent Machine Gun Battalions.

On the left, 2/5 moved its lines forward about 200 yards to tie in with the 307th Infantry, after which the Marines coordinated their advance with that of the soldiers. When 2/5 resumed the assault, it called for mortar and artillery fire on enemy reverse slope positions impending the advance of the units on the regimental right flank.

At 0600 on 7 May, General Geiger assumed IIIAC command responsibility for the 1st Marine Division zone and regained control of his corps artillery battalions which had been attached to XXIV Corps up to this time. General Nimmer then reorganized his command into three groups: the IIIAC artillery battalions comprised the first; XXIV Corps Artillery made up the second; and the third group consisted of the 27th Infantry Division Artillery (104th, 105th, and 106th Field Artillery Battalions), which had remained in position when the rest of the division headed north to relieve the 6th Marine Division. The purpose behind Nimmer's action was to provide IIIAC divisions with maximum effective tactical support.

Commanded by Lieutenant Colonel Custis Burton, Jr., the 2d Provisional Field Artillery Group (3d and 6th 155mm Howitzer Battalions and XXIV Corps 145th Field Artillery Battalion) was given the mission of providing general support to the 1st Division and reinforcing the fires of the 11th Marines. Similarly, the 27th Division Artillery under Brigadier General William B. Bradford, USA, was to support the 6th Marine Division and the 15th Marines. Lieutenant Colonel Ernest P. Foley commanded the third group—named after him—consisting of the 7th, 8th, and 9th 155mm Gun Battalions, which were to deliver long-range reinforcing, counterbattery, interdiction, and harassing fires in support of IIIAC generally. The Marine 1st 155mm Howitzer Battalion remained under XXIV Corps Artillery control until 23 May, when it reverted to its parent unit, IIIAC Corps Artillery. During the period that Marine artillery units had supported XXIV Corps (7 April to 6 May), they fired 53,988 rounds in a total of 2,344 missions. As the 1st Marine Division once again came under IIIAC control, it could look back on the six difficult days of combat it had been with XXIV Corps. During this period, the division sustained 1,409 battle casualties, including 199 men who were either killed or subsequently died of wounds in the fighting to gain the northern bank of Asa Kawa and the outer reaches of the Dakeshi defense system.

The attack of the 1st Marines, scheduled to begin at 0900 on 7 May, was held up because muddy terrain prevented supporting armor from arriving on time. In the meanwhile, Colonel Arthur T. Mason, the 1st Marines new commander, ordered his 3d Battalion to support the attack of 2/1 on Hill 60--a height commanding the battalion front—by bringing all available fire to bear on the reverse slope positions of this enemy-held hill. The supporting fires continued until 1400, when tanks arrived at the front to assist in the attack.

As mortars and assault guns pounded the top and reverse slope of the hill, and artillery fire covered the foot of the objective, the coordinated tank-infantry assault was launched against determined, fanatic, and well dug-in Japanese troops. In less than half an hour, Company E, spearheading the attack, swept to the hilltop in a practical application of "the effect of properly massed supporting fires in front of the assault troops." A hand-grenade duel ensued when the enemy defenders emerged from their caves after the fires supporting the attack were lifted. Almost immediately, the volume of Japanese fire of all types "grew noticeably stronger and progressively more intense so that it was evident that the enemy was receiving large reinforcements." In view of this potential threat, the position was adjudged untenable by the battalion commander, who withdrew his company to their lines of the previous night.

It had become apparent by the morning of 7 May that the deep draw cutting across the front of 1/5 and to the right of 2/5 positions contained the bulk of the enemy's Awacha defenses. At 0900, General del Valle and Colonel Griebel conferred with the commanders and staffs of the two assault battalions, and discussed the methods by which the Japanese positions rimming the draw and studding its steep slopes were to be reduced. It was decided that an extensive air, artillery, and rocket preparation would precede the infantry jumpoff scheduled for 1200; a reinforced tank company was moved up in time to support the assault.

The fighting that afternoon was marked by tactics which "General Buckner, with an apt sense of metaphor, called . . . the 'blowtorch and corkscrew' method. Liquid flame was the blowtorch; explosives, the corkscrew." Marine flamethrower and demolition teams burnt out and sealed many of the enemy cave installations in their zone. By 1700, the time the battalions dug in for the night, 1/5 had gained 300-400 yards in the center, but 2/5 and 3/5 could do little more than attempt to straighten their lines. Even though 62d Division troops holding this area gave way slightly during the day, it was obvious that Awacha Pocket was not going to be taken quickly or easily. News of the collapse of Nazi Germany and the announcement of V-E Day on 8 May, the day of the Allied victory in Europe, drew little response of any sort from either side on Okinawa. Most of the cold, rain-soaked Americans and Japanese in the frontlines were concerned only with that very small but vital part of the war where their own lives were at stake. Still, V-E Day did not go unnoticed. The Americans conducted Thanksgiving services on board many of the ships off Okinawa. In addition, the voices of naval guns and artillery pieces helped in the celebration. At exactly noon, every available fire support ship directed a full-gun salvo at the enemy; in addition, three battalions from IIIAC Artillery massed fire on a suspected Japanese CP. The results of the noontime shoot were not ascertained, but, in the words of one observer, "It made one hell of a big noise."

Heavy, driving, and cold rains on the 8th continued to immobilize Tenth Army troops. The attack was bogged down in the 1st Marine Division zone; but in the area directly in front of the lines, numerous caves and pillboxes were destroyed in a general mop-up. The 1st and 5th Marines each received a battery of 75mm pack howitzers that were manhandled up to the front in an unsuccessful attempt to place direct fire on enemy dispositions.

General Shepherd's 22d Marines, selected to lead his 6th Division drive in the south, moved out from Chibana on 8 May, and by 1530 the same day its 1st and 3d Battalions had relieved the 7th Marines along the Asa Kawa. At 1600, the 6th Division commander assumed responsibility for his zone in the corps front. Once in position opposite the Asa Kawa estuary, the 6th spent 9 May in patrolling and reconnoitering before the crossing was attempted. A patrol from 3/22 (on the division right) inspected a ruined bridge crossing the river and later reported that it was not passable to either foot or vehicular traffic, that the water in the estuary was four feet deep at high tide in its most shallow portion, and that the river bed had a thick mud cover. Other patrols, also from 3/22, were sent out at noon to discover possible crossing sites and to determine enemy strength and dispositions. These patrols drew fire from positions across the river, but noted that other caves and pillboxes farther south appeared to be unmanned. The Marines also reported that the soft stream bed could not support a tank ford. To the left of 3/22 was the 2d Battalion in positions near Uchima. Its only enemy contact during the day took place when a patrol that crossed the river drew heavy enemy fire. Before withdrawing, the Marines rescued both the pilot and observer of an artillery spotting plane that had been shot down in enemy territory. As a result of the information collected by the patrols, both the division and regiment were better able to plan for an effective exploitation of a beachhead following the crossing of the Asa River.

The 6th Engineer Battalion moved light bridging material up to the 22d Marines line in daylight, and under the cover of darkness began constructing a footbridge near the site of a ruined bridge. At 0300, 10 May, 3/22 was to cross the river with 1/22 in support, and then attack the high ground overlooking the south bank of the Asa at dawn. The 2d Battalion was to provide tire support from a strongpoint set up on high ground southwest of Uchima. This river crossing was only a part of the all-out army attack scheduled for 11 May. Envisioned in the objectives of the plan were the envelopment and destruction of enemy forces occupying the Shuri bastion, and finally, the total annihilation of General Ushijima's command.

General del Valle's division made fairly substantial gains on 9 May, even in the face of miserable weather conditions which prevented the attack from being launched until 1200. When armor support became available and was able to move forward over the muddy terrain, the troops advanced 200-300 yards and generally straightened the division line. Until this attack, Colonel Mason had kept 1/1 in reserve where the battalion took in 116 replacements for the 259 casualties it had sustained in the period between 30 April and 6 May.

On 9 May, the immediate objective of 1/1 was to penetrate and destroy enemy defenses on Hill 60. Just before the attack began, the assault battalion moved behind 2/1, which was to exploit the successful penetration by seizing and consolidating the captured positions; 3/1 was to support all of this action with fire.

Because there was no contact with the 5th Marines on the left, a general shift was made into its zone to wipe out the sources of enemy fire that were taking a heavy toll of troops in 1/1. As a result of a combination of heavy casualties and exhaustion occurring in the ranks of 1/1, its attack almost bogged down, but was revitalized at 1600, when the Marines swept forward over the difficult final 150 yards to gain the initial objective line. Following a thorough air, artillery, naval gunfire, and mortar preparation, the 5th Marines attacked the mouth of Awacha Draw at noon on the 9th, with 3/5 and 3/7 in the assault; 1/5 and 2/5 furnished fire support from positions facing the draw. Initially, the attack moved rapidly and the first objective—the same ridgeline that had faced 1/1--was soon reached, but fire in large volume on 3/7 from the left of its exposed flank held up the attack. At 1515, 1/7, which had moved up from Gusukuma that morning, was committed in the line to fill the gap that had appeared between 3/7 and 1/5.

To overcome the determined stand of Awacha's defenders, and spurred on by the need to continue the division attack to gain the objectives assigned by Tenth Army, General del Valle issued a new operation order late in the afternoon of the 9th. Assigned a limited zone on the left of the division front, the 5th Marines (less 3/5) was to reduce the Awacha Pocket beginning with an attack the next morning. New boundaries were given the 1st and 7th Marines (with 3/5 attached) which placed them in jump-off positions across the division front for the planned 11 May attack. Colonel Snedeker assumed responsibility for the new 7th Marines zone at 1855, relieving the 5th, and placed 3/5, 3/7, and 1/7 on line for the 10 May attack.

As an aftermath to the unsuccessful 4-5 May counterattack, the Japanese attempted to readjust and reinforce their lines against expected American reprisals and a continuation of the Tenth Army onslaught. To gain the time and breathing space needed to rebuild the 62d Division somewhat, General Ushijima gradually withdrew the division from the tangled Maeda-Asa Kawa complex toward Shuri where replacements from the Naval Base Force, service and supply troops, and Boeitai could join. Remaining in front of the 96th Infantry Division in positions extending from Dakeshi to Gaja were the 22d and 89th Regiments of the 24th Division, which had been reinforced in the second week of May by division troops and the now-defunct sea raiding base battalions.

IIIAC forces were opposed by the 44th Independent Mixed Brigade, which was built around a nucleus composed of the 15th IMR, now at full strength, and fresh replacements from the 3d Battalion, 2d Infantry Unit, 7th Independent Antitank Battalion, 1st and 2d Independent Battalions, and the 26th Shipping Engineer Regiment. Although American forces were in close contact with the enemy and fully engaged by them at Dakeshi, it was difficult to determine Japanese troop strength in the area because the core of this strength was screened by outposts and scattered strong defensive positions still held by remnants of the 62d Division. During the night of 9-10 May, the enemy was particularly active in the 1st Marine Division zone, and he made numerous attempts to infiltrate the 5th Marines area. Between 0200 and 0300, 1/5 fought off two counterattacks in which the Japanese had closed to bayonet range; enemy troops were driven off only after an extended hand-to-hand battle. After daybreak, upwards of 60 enemy bodies were found in front of the battalion lines. Despite this early-morning action, the division continued the attack at 0800, following a heavy artillery and smoke preparation, with three infantry regiments abreast.

Although General del Valle's troops encountered stiff opposition all along the line, the 5th Marines, on the corps left, received the most violent enemy reaction from positions centered around the Dakeshi Ridge and the high ground running generally along the corps flank. Armor assigned to support the 5th Marines attack did not arrive in time for the jumpoff; poor roads had again bogged down the tanks and prevented them from aiding the infantry.

Less than an hour after the attack began, 1/5 was pinned down by heavy enemy machine gun and mortar fire that skyrocketed casualty figures. At 1700, the battalion was withdrawn under the cover of smoke. Although 1/5 was unable to move forward, the rest of the regiment made inroads into enemy positions. Supported by artillery and flamethrower tanks, 2/5 overran all enemy resistance in that portion of Awacha Draw which lay in its zone. This action placed the regiment in the heart of the Awacha defenses; it did not account for the many other remaining Japanese pockets which the 5th Marines was to meet in the next few days.

As the 5th fought its battle, the 7th Marines attacked with the 1st and 3d Battalions in the assault, 2/7 and 3/5 in reserve. On the right, 3/7 was immobilized at its line of departure by accurate mortar and artillery shelling, and heavy small arms fire from pillboxes and caves to its front. The 1st Battalion, however, attacked on time; by noon, its forward elements were on the low ground north of the Dakeshi Ridge, where visual contact was reestablished with 1/5. Japanese fire on this advanced position increased as the morning wore on, and shortly before noon, machine gun fire from a draw in the 5th Marines zone began hitting the 1/7 assault company. This fire continued unabated and finally halted the attack. When 1/5 was forced to withdraw, 1/7, exposed on both flanks, found its position untenable. The 7th Marines assault units were pulled back to their original lines at 1754.

For the 10 May attack, Colonel Mason's 1st Marines was given the task of gaining the road leading west out of Dakeshi. Although 3/1 jumped off and reached its planned intermediate objective on time, it was forced to hold up and wait for the 1st Battalion, which did not begin its scheduled advance because of the late arrival of its supporting armor. At 1020, both battalions resumed the attack, now supported by armor, and reached a low ridge overlooking the Dakeshi road at 1600. All attempts by assault companies to move beyond this point were met by extremely heavy machine gun fire from Dakeshi ridge, driving back the combat patrols attempting to bypass the nose of the ridge. It soon became painfully evident that no further advance would be possible until the ridge was taken.

While the 1st Division set in its defenses for the night, the 6th Division remained active. As soon as it became dark on 9 May, the 6th Engineer Battalion began building a footbridge for the planned infantry crossing over the Asa Kawa estuary. At 0530, two and a half hours after 22d Marines assault elements had crossed over to the south bank of the river, a Japanese two-man suicide team rushed out of hiding to throw themselves and their satchel charges onto the south end of the footbridge; both the bridge and the enemy soldiers were destroyed. Prior to this destructive act, however, 1/22 and 3/22 each had succeeded in moving two assault companies across the river under the cover of darkness, and to positions for a continuation of the attack to the south. The loss of the bridge, therefore, posed no great hardship; included in the attack plans were contingency provisions that were to go into effect if this, in fact, took place. Therefore, when the bridge was blown up, engineer demolition teams with the assault elements breached the seawalls on the south bank of the river to permit immediate access to the frontlines to supply- and troop-laden LVT(A)s.

At 0520, under the cover of a protective smoke screen and an artillery preparation, the attack south of the Asa began. The assault companies were at first hampered by fog and the smoke of battle. During the early morning hours, enemy resistance was moderate and limited to small arms and machine gun fire. Soon, however, Japanese artillery shells began falling on the bridgehead area.

By noon, the Marines had succeeded in driving only 150 yards into enemy defenses, while, at the same time, the volume of both small arms and artillery fire increased steadily. Under the cover of heavy supporting fire, each assault battalion brought its reserve company across to join the attack. Even with continuous artillery and naval gunfire support, the ground troops could not crack the Japanese line.

The only weapons capable of breaching these defenses—tank-mounted flat trajectory cannon—were not available because supporting armor was unable to ford the mud- and silt-bottomed stream despite its numerous attempts to do so. The tanks were then forced to withdraw to the northern bank of the Asa, there to await the construction of a Bailey bridge, which the 6th Engineers were to begin building after dark on the night of 10-11 May. The 22d Marines advanced along their entire front during the afternoon; the 1st Battalion made the greatest gain, 350 yards. As darkness fell, the division halted and forward companies dug in for the night. The engineers began work on the Bailey bridge at 2200, stopping only when the crossing site was shelled. This intermittent shelling successfully delayed completion of the bridge by six hours. The first Marine tanks did not cross the river until 1103 on 11 May, some four hours after the coordinated, two-corps Tenth Army attack had begun.

Air Operations In May

A mass Kamikaze raid on 10-11 May, the fifth of the campaign, unintentionally served to preface the 11 May ground attack of the Tenth Army. There was no indication that the Japanese had prior knowledge of the impending attack or that their air assault had been planned to forestall the American push. An enemy air raid should have been anticipated, however, because the first relatively clear weather since the previous Kikusui attack appeared at this time. Between midnight of 10 May and 0420 on the following day, the Air Defense Control Center plotted 19 enemy raids approaching Okinawa, each one ranging in size from one to nine aircraft. Most of the planes orbited over the water about 40 miles northwest of the island, where they formed up for a furtive pass at American targets. None, however, approached any closer than 10 miles to Okinawa.

This situation soon changed on the 11th, when, at 0630, TAF pilots intercepted the first in a series of suiciders attempting to crash targets in the Ie Shima and Hagushi anchorages. By the time of this mass raid, enemy air tactics generally followed the pattern previously observed during the major landings in the Philippines, but with an increased emphasis on the use of the Kamikaze. Like the tactics employed at Leyte, at Okinawa attacking groups approached at altitudes ranging from 9,000 feet to sea level; the low-level approach was usually made during periods of limited visibility. Japanese pilots also would approach a target at low altitudes if their attack was covered by clouds and poor visibility, or when they felt that American radar units could not detect their planes. While this indicated some training in low-level evasive tactics, it did not show that enemy pilots had a proper appreciation of the range and coverage of American radar. At Okinawa, enemy air activity usually began when the final night CAP had withdrawn to home fields, and ended when the early morning patrol flight approached. As successful as the alert American air patrols had been in protecting assault shipping and radar picket vessels, it was impossible to prevent losses as long as even a single Japanese plane penetrated the ICEBERG air screen. In at least five instances in May, Kamikazes that had been so seriously damaged by fighter aircraft that they could not have possibly returned to home bases—and conceivably could not have even recovered level flight—managed to remain on course, break through the American screen, and hit their targets.

On-station planes from TF 51 and TAF fended off the raids of 11 May, but not before a Dutch merchantman, two American destroyers, and an LCS had been hit. A total of 217 Japanese planes were employed in Kikusui No. 6; 104 of these were suiciders. The claims of opposing sides regarding the number of planes their pilots had downed conflict similarly in this particular engagement as they did in others. Uniquely enough, the number the Japanese admitted losing in this air battle was in excess of the number that the Americans claimed that they had shot down. A Japanese source lists 109 of their planes shot down or missing, while ICEBERG forces claimed only 93. Of this number, the two destroyers that were under attack have been credited with blasting 34 enemy aircraft out of the sky; ships' AAA and defending air patrols claimed the remainder. TAF pilots downed 19 planes of this last portion in slightly more than two hours of fighting in the morning, and increased the score of the Tenth Army air arm to 234.

A sidelight of the 11 May raid occurred when USS *Hugh W. Hadley*, a radar picket, was under direct attack from Kamikazes. Protecting the destroyer overhead was a two-plane CAP maintained by VMF-323 pilots. The conduct of these Marine flyers is best described by the ship's action report: "One very outstanding feat by one of these two planes . . . was that, though out of ammunition, he twice forced a suicide plane out of his dive on the ship, and the third time forced him into such a poor position that the plane crashed through the rigging but missed the ship, going into the water close aboard. This was done while all guns on the ship were firing at the enemy plane . . . His wingman also stayed at masthead height in the flak and assisted in driving planes away from the ship."

On the day before, Captain Kenneth L. Reusser and First Lieutenant Robert R. Klingman of VMF-312 destroyed an enemy plane in a manner described as "one of the most remarkable achievements of the war." Several times earlier in the month, extremely fast Japanese reconnaissance craft—apparently on photographic missions—had been encountered at high altitudes, usually 30,000-38,000 feet. Klingman was flying wing on Reusser, division leader of a four-plane CAP, which was then at an altitude of 10,000 feet. Reusser noticed the presence of vapor trails at about 25,000 feet, and obtained permission to investigate. He led his division in a climb to 36,000 feet, where two of the planes were forced to disengage after reaching their maximum altitude. Klingman and Reusser continued to climb and close with the

Japanese intruder only after they had fired most of their ammunition to lighten their aircraft. At 38,000 feet, they intercepted the enemy and Reusser opened fire first. Expanding all of his remaining ammunition in one burst, he scored hits in the left wing and tail of the enemy plane. Klingman then closed in, but was unable to fire because his guns had frozen at this extreme altitude. After a two-hour air chase, he finally downed the Japanese plane by cutting off its tail control surfaces with his Corsair's propeller. Although Klingman's plane had holes in the wing and engine, and the propeller and engine cowling were damaged, he managed to land the plane intact and without injury to himself.

An almost tragic aftermath to this encounter occurred two days later, when Klingman was flying another mission. His plane's hydraulic system failed and he chose to bail out over the water rather than attempt a crash landing on one wheel. A destroyer escort recovered the lieutenant from the water and carried him to the *Eldorado*, where he had dinner with the Expeditionary Force commander, Admiral Turner. Marine and Navy night fighter aircraft came into their own during May, especially with the arrival at Okinawa on the 10th of Lieutenant Colonel Marion M. Magruder's VMF(N)-533 following its long over-water flight from Engebi, Eniwetok Atoll, in 15 F6F-5Ns (radar-equipped Grumman Hellcats) and 5 transport planes.

Prior to the Okinawa operations, the quality of the direction and conduct of night CAPS was poor and the results of most operations negligible. As an example, in the first year of night fighter operations—November 1943 through October 1944--Navy and Marine pilots accounted for only 39 enemy aircraft; in less than two months of the Okinawa campaign, night fighters shot down 35 Japanese planes, and VMF(N)-533 fliers claimed 30 of them. Noteworthy is the fact that, with six enemy planes to his credit, Captain Robert Baird of 533 was the only Marine night fighter ace in the war. The drastic change for the better in night fighter squadron operations resulted from improved electronic equipment, techniques, and performances of both pilots and the ground director crews. The new Hellcats also were a large factor in this improvement. With the arrival of additional air warning squadrons and their radar equipment on Okinawa, and their establishment on outlying islands as they were captured, the intricacies of guiding night fighters to targets were overcome. Within a short time after their appearance in the Okinawa battle zone, fighter directors could bring a pilot to within 500 feet of an enemy plane, at which point the flyer could establish visual contact with the intruder aircraft and down it.

One of the most spectacular, unique, and perhaps the only air-to-air rocket kill in the war occurred in the early-morning darkness of 17 May, when VMTB-232 pilot First Lieutenant Fred C. Folino spotted an unidentified plane while flying his TBM (Avenger) on a night heckling mission. He radioed an ICEBERG control ship for information and identification of the stranger, all the while climbing to gain altitude to get into attack position. Assured by the controller that there were no friendly planes in the area, and having requested and received permission to attack, the Marine pilot dove on the now-fleeing enemy. Folino expended all of his ammunition as the torpedo bomber strained to close the gap. He then began firing his rockets. The first was short of the target, the next one struck the plane, and a third tore off a large portion of the wing. "Momentarily lost to the TBM, the plane next appeared on the beach below, a blazing wreck." Acknowledging this act, Admiral Spruance sent his personal congratulations to Lieutenant Folino.

After dark on 17 May, TAF pilots extended the range of their operations to Japan for the first time. The arrival of AAF fighter squadrons and their Thunderbolts (P-47s) on Ie Shima in mid-May provided General Wallace's ADC with a long-range strike capability. This was demonstrated when a pair of Thunderbolts rocketed and strafed three airfields on southern Kyushu on this first extended mission, and then added to the insult by strafing the brightly lit streets of Kanoya before returning to home base unchallenged by enemy pilots. Following this night run, AAF pilots began making daylight runs over southern Japan. Judging by the quality of the opposition they received, it became apparent that the Japanese had been holding back their more skillful pilots and newer and faster aircraft for the close-in defense of the Empire. The American pilots reported that they were encountering "pilots who were . . . skillful and aggressive. . . ." The majority of the enemy planes rising to meet the Army Air Force's flyers were Zekes (Zeros), but some were the newer single-seat fighters, the faster Jacks and Franks, which had just begun to appear in the air war over Okinawa and Japan. In the final analysis, the AAF Thunderbolts outperformed the Japanese aircraft without exception. They outclimbed and outturned the enemy planes and especially excelled in the high altitudes, where Japanese aircraft performance had been superior earlier in the war. If nothing else, these performance factors and the raid on Kyushu further dramatized the complete ascendancy of American air power. This evidence, however, did not convince the Japanese that continuation of the mass Kamikaze raids was merely an exercise in futility.

American planes rising from crowded fields on Yontan and Ie Shima successfully blunted the suicide attacks, and as a result, Special Attack Force aircraft and pilot losses mounted all out of proportion to the results achieved. IGHQ then decided that the only way to reverse the situation was by destroying the U.S. planes at their Okinawa fields. A surprise ground attack mission was therefore assigned to the Giretsu (Act of Heroism) Airborne Raiding Force. Armed with demolition charges, grenades, and light arms, the commandos of this unit were to land on Kadena and Yontan fields, where they would make one desperate effort to cripple American air operations—even temporarily—by destroying or damaging planes and airfield facilities. The men undertaking this raid were to be flown to Okinawa on the night of 24 May in planes that would accompany those in the formation of Kikusui No. 7.

The Giretsu, consisting of 120 men, was divided into five platoons and a command section, and was transported to the assigned target in 12 twin-engine bombers. The general attack began at about 2000, when Yontan and Kadena fields were bombed as a prelude to the airborne raid. Approximately two and a half hours later, antiaircraft artillerymen and aviation personnel based at Yontan were surprised to see several Japanese bombers purposely but rashly attempting to land. With one exception, the planes that were shot down over the field either attempted to crash ground facilities and parked aircraft or went plummeting down in flames, carrying entrapped troops with them. The plane that was the one exception made a safe wheels-up landing, and troops poured out even before it had come to a halt. As soon as the raiders deplaned, they began to throw grenades and explosive charges at the nearest parked aircraft, and sprayed the area with small arms fire. The confusion which followed this weird gambit is difficult to imagine. Uncontrolled American rifle and machine gun fire laced the airfield and vicinity, and probably caused most of the ICEBERG casualties. TAF pilots and ground personnel, as well as the men in the units assigned to airfield defense, took part in the general affray, which saw the death of 2 Marines and the wounding of 18 others.

When the attack was over, no prisoners had been taken and 69 Japanese bodies were counted. Despite his losses, the enemy accomplished one part of his mission: he had destroyed 8 planes (including the personal transport of Major General James T. Moore, Commanding General, AirFMFPac, who had arrived that morning), damaged 24 others, and set fire to fuel dumps, causing the loss of some 70,000 gallons of precious aviation gasoline.

Meanwhile, approximately 445 aircraft, of which nearly one-third were suiciders, struck at the American naval forces, concentrating on the radar pickets. The first phase of the attack was broken off about 0300 on the 25th, only to resume at dawn with a renewed fury that continued during the day. At the end, the enemy planes had damaged an APD and a LSM, both so severely that the former capsized later and the latter had to be beached and abandoned. Eight other vessels, generally destroyer types, were also damaged, but in varying degrees. In this action, the Japanese pilots exacted a toll of 38 Americans killed, 183 wounded, and 60 missing in action. The raiders suffered also, for friendly air claimed the shooting down of over 150 enemy planes. Of this number, ADC planes claimed an all-time high to date, 75 destroyed in this 24-hour period, to bring the total of TAF claims to 370. High scorer during the 24-25 May raid was the 318th Fighter Group with 34 kills listed, followed by MAG-31. Postwar Japanese sources dispute these statistics, stating that only 88 planes failed to return to base. Regardless of this conflict in numbers, enemy air continued to suffer.

The last mass Kamikaze attack in May began just two days later, 27 May, and lasted until the evening of the 28th. The raid caused TAF to establish the longest single enemy air alert of the campaign thus far — 9 hours and 16 minutes. Japan sent up 292 aircraft, of which nearly one-third again were suiciders. Heavy antiaircraft artillery fire and combat air patrols fought off the invaders, but not before a destroyer had been sunk and 11 other ships damaged in varying degrees. As before, personnel losses to the fleet were great: 52 men killed, 288 wounded, and 290 missing. The enemy did not escape unscathed, for ICEBERG forces claimed to have splashed more than 100 intruders, and of these, TAF fliers claimed 40. Japanese sources again show figures that differ from those in American records, and show losses of only 80 planes for Kikusui No. 8.

By the end of May, ADC fighter pilots had added 279 claimed kills to April figures. This gave TAF a total of 423 enemy aircraft destroyed in the air in 56 days of operations. In this same period, 7 April through 31 May, only three American planes were shot down by Japanese pilots out of the 109 aircraft lost to such other causes as pilot error, aircraft malfunctions, and cases of mistaken identity by friendly AAA units.

Prevailing bad weather during most of May had limited air activity, although both sides flew a number of missions even under minimal flying conditions. TAF records for this period indicate that its planes were grounded nine days in May, while cloud cover of varying degree existed during the other 22 days. In addition, the continuing rain that bogged down wheeled and tracked vehicles also turned fighter strips into quagmires. On Ie Shima, for example, a total of 20.82 inches of rain fell from 16 May to the close of the month, causing one Marine air unit to note that "the resultant mixture of water and Ie Shima soil produces mud of a character that surpasses description." Towards the middle of May, TAF strength was increased when pilots and planes of Marine Aircraft Group 22 and the Army Air Forces' 318th Fighter Group arrived and began operations.

Although the ground troops showed a partisan interest in the aerial dogfights high above them and the vivid pyrotechnical displays occurring during the air raids at night, the infantry was more vitally concerned with winning its own battle and with the assistance the air units could give in the drive southward. Out of a total of 7,685 sorties flown by TAF pilots in May, 716 (against an April figure of 510) were in support of the ground forces. Included in the May figure were night heckler and intruder missions flown away from Okinawa. The majority of the ground support sorties were directed against enemy troop concentrations, caves, and truck parks. As the campaign progressed, and as the pilots gained experience with their planes and improved ordnance and a greater familiarity with the area, the ground support effort became increasingly effective. By the middle of May, TAF had reached the state where it was fully prepared to assist the forces of the Tenth Army, then poised to strike the heart of the Shuri defenses.

On Shuri's Threshold

Although the enemy chose 11 May to mount a mass Kamikaze attack and many Japanese planes were, in fact, then diving on American surface forces off Okinawa, both corps of the Tenth Army launched a coordinated assault at 0700. Two and a half hours earlier, enemy infantry units had attempted a counterattack following a heavy mortar and artillery barrage on the center of the 1st Marine Division line. Unfortunately for the attackers, the barrage lifted too soon and they were caught by American prearranged defensive fires while still forming. Though the enemy force sustained heavy casualties, the remnants attempted to reform and continue the assault, only to be wiped out by Marine close-range small arms fire. The 6th Engineers had not yet bridged the Asa Kawa when the attack was to begin; nevertheless, the 6th Division jumped off on time before this vital support route was completed. With the 22d Marines in the lead, the assault troops advanced slowly against a stubborn and well-organized defense built around machine guns and mortars concealed in cave mouths. In early afternoon, enemy troops hidden in a particularly formidable coral hill formation held up the movement of 1/22 on the left. All attempts to envelop the position from either flank failed. The battalion then halted to permit a heavy naval gunfire shelling of the Japanese defenses, after which the Marines resumed the advance under the cover of armor support which had crossed the now-completed bridge shortly before noon. Flamethrowers, demolitions, and direct tank fire were employed when the attack again began; the position was reduced after a bitter close-in fight. Upon inspection, this hill proved to be a key feature of the Asa Kawa defense system, and contained a vast network of headquarters and supply installations within a large tunnel and cave complex. Continuing on, the 22d Marines took nearly 1,000 yards of strongly defended enemy territory by 1800, after which mopping up operations continued well into the night. All during the day, the Bailey bridge had remained under continuous enemy artillery and sniper fire, in the face of which reinforcements and supplies poured over the crossing to support forward elements and maintain the momentum of the advance.

To the left of the 6th Division, the 1st Marine Division attacked following an intense air, artillery, and naval gunfire preparation. Substantial gains were made all along the line against a defiant enemy who contested every inch of the advance. Behind the continuing bombardment, the 1st Marines pushed forward along the railroad near the division right boundary, while the 7th Marines made slower progress in the center and left of the line as it reached positions west of the high ground protecting Shuri.

As 2/1 attacked towards its objective, the high ground west of Wana, it began receiving some of the heaviest enemy resistance experienced in the division zone that day. When the battalion passed the nose west of Dakeshi, troops on the left came under heavy flanking machine gun fire from the village. Unable to continue the advance in the direction of the objective, the battalion attacked in column down the west side of the railroad, taking advantage of the cover furnished by the high embankment. At 1600, 2/1 had advanced about 900 yards and was partially on its goal, but held up so that the 22d Marines could come up on the right. Here, the 2d Battalion became subject to accurate long-range flanking artillery fire which soon took a heavy toll in casualties. The situation became more difficult when supply and evacuation were prevented because all possible routes of approach were covered. It finally became necessary for the companies to dig in for the night where they stood.

The 3d Battalion jumped off at about the same time as 2/1, and moved out to cover a gap that had occurred between the latter and the 7th Marines, which was still fighting in the middle of Dakeshi. As the foremost elements of 3/1 reached the point where 2/1 was first fired upon, they were likewise hit and their supporting tanks were unable to get past the draw because of heavy and accurate 47mm antitank fire. Finally, the 3d Battalion negotiated the gap and took up positions just east of the railroad embankment, where it was subjected to frequent artillery and mortar shelling for the rest of the afternoon and all through the night. Meanwhile, the 7th Marines continued the attack on Dakeshi, where enemy reaction to all forward movement proved costly to both sides. Because 3/7 had been held up throughout most of 10 May, the regiment jumped off the next day with 1/7 and 2/7 in the assault to envelop the strong positions in front of the 3d Battalion. While 3/7 contained the enemy to its front and the regimental reserve, 3,/5, protected the rear, attacking forces pushed forward to gain troublesome Dakeshi Ridge.

On the right of the 7th's zone, 2/7 advanced in the face of Japanese mortars, grenades, and automatic weapons fire—the latter coming from pillboxes and coral caves—to gain approximately 800 yards and seize the ridge overlooking and running through Dakeshi. At 1800, the battalion attack was halted on the positions then occupied. As the men dug in for the night, some of the veterans of the Peleliu campaign were reminded of how much the fight for the ridge that day resembled the action at Bloody Nose Ridge. Throughout the night of 11-12 May, the new defenders of Dakeshi Ridge fought off numerous Japanese attempts to infiltrate under cover of the constant artillery and mortar barrages coming from enemy emplacements on Wana Ridge.

The fall of aggressively defended and vital Dakeshi Ridge, and its occupation by Marines, meant that one more barrier to the heart of the Shuri defenses had been raised. In addition, the Japanese were now denied the use of commanding ground from which the terrain from Shuri and Naha to Machinato Ridge, and the entire coastal area in between, could be covered by observation and fire. The taking of Dakeshi Ridge effectively and decisively breached the enemy's Naha-Shuri-Yonabaru line, and raised some question as to how much longer he could hold it before Shuri itself was threatened.

Dakeshi was further endangered by the manuever of 1/7, which swung towards the town from the northeast and placed the fanatically defended village in between a rapidly closing pincers. Although Dakeshi was now ripe for capture, positions on the reverse slope of the ridge, in the village itself, and a pocket of resistance to its north continued to be held by soldiers who were determined to defend to the death.

In the 1st Division rear, 2/5 eliminated the last remaining organized resistance in the Awacha Pocket, and 1/5 moved up behind 1/7 to wipe out scattered enemy remnants bypassed during the day. At 1800, 3/5 reverted to parent control.

Tanks providing close-in fire support to the 7th Marines on 11 May had been pressed into service to evacuate casualties. Some wounded were taken up into the tanks through the escape hatches; others rode on the rear deck of the tracked vehicles, which backed out of the battle area in order to provide an armored shield between the stretcher cases and enemy fire.

By nightfall, 1/7 was positioned and linked on its left with the 305th Infantry of the 77th Infantry Division to form a solid line at the division boundary. The major effort of XXIV Corps was made in the left center of its zone by the 96th Infantry Division, which had completed the relief of the 7th the previous day. While the 77th pressed the enemy through central Okinawa towards Shuri, the 96th approached a hill mass directly northwest of Yonabaru. This terrain feature controlled the eastern reaches to Shuri, completely dominated the east-central coastal plain, and was the easternmost anchor of the enemy's main battle position. All natural routes to the hill were constantly under observation and thoroughly covered by Japanese fire. Conical Hill, as this bastion was soon named, commanded a series of ridges and other lesser hills, whose capture was to be costly and time-consuming. Murderous fire during the 11 May attack forced the frontline units of the 96th Division to relinquish whatever gains were made that day, although the 383d Infantry on the division left had battled forward 600 yards to establish a foothold on the northwest slopes of Conical. On the same day, assault battalions of the 77th Division gained but 400-500 yards. Strongly entrenched enemy took advantage of the broken terrain to take the flanks, and at times the rear, of the advancing soldiers under fire. At nightfall, the division halted, consolidated its gains, and dug in to the accompaniment of sporadic mortar and artillery fire.

Enemy small-boat activity during the night of 11-12 May increased noticeably over that of previous nights. American patrol boats reported making many radar and visual contacts off Naha, and some enemy craft were spotted apparently heading for the Hagushi transport area. The "flycatchers" remained vigilant, however, and efficiently thwarted these Japanese surface ventures. Seven enemy boats were sunk between midnight of the 11th and 0400 the next day. Several other Japanese craft were fired upon with unknown results.

These coastal skirmishes were tame in comparison to the bloody land battle which continued with unabated violence. When the Tenth Army attack resumed on the 12th, Marine assault elements found Japanese resistance undiminished. On the right of the 6th Division zone, 3/22 moved out in the face of small arms fire pouring down from positions in rocky cliffs overlooking its route of advance, and from the mouths of Okinawan tombs dug in the hillsides that lined it. By 0920, the battalion reached its objective, the high ground commanding a view of Naha below, and sent out patrols through the suburbs of the city to the banks of the Asato Gawa. Here, the Marines found the bridge demolished and the river bottom muddy and unfordable. Patrols from 1/22 also were sent down to the river bank after the battalion had reached the heights in its zone at 1400. Both battalions dug in for the night in firm control of the terrain on the northern outskirts of Naha.

The 2d Battalion was unable to keep pace with or match the advances of the troops coming down the west coast; for, in addition to fighting the enemy in its path, 2/22 was forced to contend with the telling effect of Japanese fire coming out of the

1st Division zone from positions on the dominating terrain standing between the division boundary and the Shuri hill mass. Nevertheless, at 1400 Company G reached the battalion objective, the high ground overlooking Naha. Because the left flank of 2/22 was overextended, at 1350 General Shepherd attached 3/29 to the 22d Marines and alerted the rest of the regiment for commitment into the lines. By the end of the day, 6th Division troops occupied positions from which they were to fight for pretty much the rest of the month. After first having repulsed a counterattack, at 0730 on 12 May, 1/7 together with 2/7 launched a converging attack aimed at closing a 400-yard gap existing between the two battalions. As this assault force moved into the ruins of Dakeshi village, the enemy mortar and artillery fire that had been falling steadily since the Tenth Army advance had begun increased sharply. At 1522, however, the adjacent flanks of the two units made contact, and the battalions consolidated their positions for the night along the northern outskirts of the village and on the high ground to its east and west.

The 1st Marines attack to improve positions west of Wana was held up for three hours, while 2/1 was given an airdrop of rations, water, ammunition, and medical supplies. During the interim, this battalion came under extremely heavy and accurate mortar and small arms fire, which caused many casualties. At 1030, the battalion jumped off, but all companies reported that they had run into a swarm of sniper and heavy machine gun fire coming from positions in the vicinity of Wana. Casualty evacuation and resupply soon became increasingly difficult because all routes were exposed to enemy observers located on the heights to the left of the 2/1 advance. As the day wore on, the assault companies were forced to dig night defenses on ground then held, not too many yards ahead of their 11 May positions.

Attacking to the southeast on the left of 2/1, the 3d Battalion was partially protected by the overhanging bank of an Asa Kawa tributary, and penetrated 300 yards towards the mouth of Wana Draw. Forward movement ceased at 1630 and the 1st Division dug in for the night, 2/1 tying in with 3/29 on the right. All the while, 2,/1 remained in an isolated forward position. An undetermined number of the enemy counterattacked the Marines at 2230, causing General del Valle to alert the 5th Marines for possible commitment in support of the 1st, but 3/1 contained the attack without need of reinforcement.

Enemy small boats were again active on the night of 12-13 May. An attempted counterlanding on the coast between the Asa and Asato Rivers was broken up by American patrol craft. The approximately 40 surviving Japanese were eliminated by 3/22 at the edge of the reef.

When the 6th Division attack resumed at 0730 on the 13th, the task of 3/22 was to reconnoiter the northern outskirts of Naha. As one patrol approached a village that another patrol had passed through safely on 12 May, it was turned back by enemy fire. Battalion 81mm mortars were laid on the settlement's houses, and an infantry platoon accompanied by a tank platoon was sent in at 1400 to overcome all resistance. Well-concealed and determined defenders, however, stymied this attack. One tank was disabled by a satchel charge placed by a suicidally inclined Japanese soldier and the rest of the Shermans were forced to turn back. Another infantry and tank platoon teamed up, this time attacking from the north of the village, but this effort, too, was thwarted by the combination of heavy machine gun fire, an enemy determination to hold, and the narrow village streets which restricted tank movement. Regiment then ordered the enemy blasted out and the village burned. After levelling the buildings, and killing approximately 75 defenders, the Marine tanks and troops withdrew at

1630. In its zone, 1st Battalion Marines met resistance from enemy outposts holed up in houses on the north bank of the river.

The main division effort was made on the left by 2/22, with 3/29 assigned to clear high ground overlooking the Asato River from which the enemy fired into the left flank elements of 2/22. Because of the difficulty in getting essential supplies and the rocket trucks scheduled for preparation fires forward to the front, the attack was delayed until 1115. Despite the heavy rocket and artillery preparation, intense enemy resistance grew yet more determined as the day wore on, making the tank-infantry assault teams' way difficult. By the end of the day, the two assault battalions had gained no more than 200-300 yards. Just before dark, Company H, 3/29, rushed and seized the troublesome hill on the left quieting the heavy flanking machine gun fire that had been coming from that sector.

At the close of the day, it was clear that the 22d Marines had been worn out and its battle efficiency sapped in the fighting that brought the division down to the outskirts of Naha. During the 2,000-yard advance south from the Asa Kawa, the regiment had suffered approximately 800 Marines killed and wounded. Therefore, General Shepherd ordered the attack resumed on 14 May with the 29th Marines making the main effort on the left, supported by the 22d Marines on the right. The 3d Battalion, 29th Marines, reverted to parent control at 1800, at which time the regiment officially assumed responsibility for its new lines. To take over the positions vacated by the 29th, the 4th Marines—IIIAC reserve—moved south, where it would guard the division rear and back up the LVT(A)s guarding the open seaward flank of the 6th Division.

In the 1st Marine Division zone on 13 May, the 1st Marines was forced to repel two predawn counterattacks in platoon to company strength before launching its own attack. The Marine assault was first delayed until supporting tanks got into positions, and then held up again until the 7th Marines had cleared Dakeshi. Organic crew-served weapons of the 1st Marines fired upon observed enemy positions in the village in support of the 7th. The 1st Marines attack finally began at 1230, when 3/1 jumped off to extend the battalion line to the right into the 2/1 sector and to clean up bypassed enemy positions. Primarily, the 3d Battalion objective was the high ground at the mouth of Wana Draw. Heavy machine gun fire from three sides and a deadly hail of mortar, grenade, and rifle fire greeted the tank-infantry assault teams as they gained the hill. Finding the position untenable, the attackers were forced to withdraw under the cover of smoke and fire furnished by the tanks, which also evacuated casualties. The same formidable obstacle of flying steel that met 3/1 forced 2/1 back and prevented the latter from moving its left flank up to extend its hold on the high ground west of Wana. After first blunting a predawn enemy attack on 13 May, Colonel Snedeker's 7th Marines jumped off at 0730 with 2/7 in the assault, 1/7 and 3/7 in reserve. The 2d Battalion cleaned out Dakeshi, the 1st Battalion eliminated snipers and sealed caves on the ridge overlooking the village, and the 3d Battalion protected the rear of the regiment. Despite the employment of tanks, self-propelled 75mm guns, and 37mm antitank guns, the enemy was not subdued until late in the afternoon.

Opposing 2/7 on the reverse slope of Dakeshi Ridge was a honeycomb of caves centering around one which was later found to be the command post of the 64th Brigade. These positions were discovered late in the afternoon and taken under close assault; so close, in fact, that Japanese postwar records note that even the brigade commander and his CP personnel took part in the fighting. After dark, the enemy ordered survivors of the last-ditch stand to attempt to infiltrate American lines in order to reach Shuri and reform.

In the XXIV Corps zone, assault elements of the 96th Infantry Division executed a flanking maneuver west of Conical Hill and gained a foothold from which the stronghold could be reduced. On 13 May, the division captured the western and northern slopes of Conical, thus opening the way for the capture of Yonabaru and the unlocking of another door to Shuri's inner defenses.

Both corps of the Tenth Army attacked at 0730 on 14 May to clear the eastern and western approaches to Shuri and to envelop the flanks of that bastion. Fighting was especially bitter in the IIIAC zone, where the Marine divisions were unsuccessful in their attempts to break through the enemy line west of Wana and northwest of Naha. It soon became apparent that the Marines had run into the Japanese main line of resistance. This assumption was borne out by the heavy losses sustained by attacking infantry units and the number of tanks, 18, in the two Marine tank battalions destroyed, disabled, or damaged by enemy antitank, mortar, and artillery fire, mines, and suicide attackers.

General Shepherd's troops had jumped off at 0730 on the 14th to seize the high ground running generally along the north bank of the Asato Gawa. From the very beginning of this attack, the assaulting forces met strong, well-coordinated, and unremitting opposition. Attacking in conjunction with the 29th Marines, the 22d succeeded in seizing approximately 1,100 yards of the bank of the Asato, despite the presence of numerous machine gun and sniper positions in the path of the advance. It was on the regimental left, however, that the going was roughest and the fighting most savage. In the face of mounting casualties during the day, the attack of 2/22 finally ground to a halt at 1500, when the battalion ran into a system of strongly defended and thoroughly organized defenses. These guarded a rectangularly-shaped hill, dominating and precipitous, that was quickly dubbed "Sugar Loaf." This hill itself was at the apex of an area of triangularly shaped high ground that pointed north. A concentration of Japanese power here had turned back 2/22 in the two previous days. Enemy dispositions on Sugar Loaf were so organized that the defenders could cover the front, rear, and flanks of any portion of the position with interlocking bands of automatic weapons fire and devastating barrages from mortar, artillery, and grenade launchers.

Although the intensity of Japanese resistance increased proportionally as assault troops approached this bastion—already recognized as a key defensive position—it was not realized at first that this bristling terrain feature and its environs constituted the western anchor of the Shuri defenses. At the time that the 22d Marines reached Sugar Loaf, the regimental line was spread thinly and excessive casualties had reduced combat efficiency to approximately 62 percent.

Nonetheless, despite the factors which forced the halt, 2/22 received direct orders from division at 1515 to seize, occupy, and defend the battalion objective— including Sugar Loaf Hill—this day at any cost. In answer to the battalion commander's earlier request for reinforcements, Company K, 3/22, was attached to back up the attack. Moving out at 1722 behind a line of tanks and an artillery-laid smoke screen, Company F attacked Sugar Loaf for the second time on the 14th. In a little more than two hours later, some 40 survivors of Companies F and G were in position at the foot of the hill under the command of the battalion executive officer, Major Henry A. Courtney, Jr.

Snipers were everywhere, and the group also came under fire from mortars on the flanks as well as the reverse slopes of Sugar Loaf. To carry supplies and much-needed ammunition up to the exposed Marines, and to reinforce Major Courtney's pitifully small force, Lieutenant Colonel Horatio C. Woodhouse, Jr., 2/22 battalion commander, sent 26 newly arrived replacements forward. All during this time, the Japanese were rolling grenades down on the Marine position from the heights above, and Courtney saw no other alternative to remaining where he was than to attack up the hill to seize its crest. All American illumination of the area was stopped when Courtney and his 40-odd Marines stormed the hill at 2300, throwing grenades as they scrambled up the slopes. As soon as they carried the crest, they dug in to wait out a night of expected counterattacks and the enemy's customarily heavy mortar fire. On the left of 2/22, enfilade fire from flanking hills in the zone of the 29th Marines undoubtedly contributed to the battalion's hard going during this day. After 3/29, the regimental assault battalion, had jumped off at 0730 on the 14th, it tried to bypass Japanese strongpoints on its left to draw abreast of 2/22 on its right. The 3d Battalion was forced to halt and fight around this center of resistance the rest of the morning and part of the afternoon, when Japanese fire on its rear proved troublesome. At about 1630, the 29th Marines' commander regrouped his assault elements and moved 1/29 into the line on the left of 3/29. The attack was renewed with Companies A and H working over the flanks of the enemy position, slowly compressing and neutralizing it. Company G, in the meanwhile, continued the attack southward, and, after fighting its way 200 yards across open ground, gained the forward slopes of a hill northwest of Sugar Loaf, where it tied in with the lines of 2/22.

In the 1st Division zone, the objective of the 2d Battalion, 7th Marines, on 14 May was Wana Ridge. The battalion jumped off at 0730, with 1/7 prepared to pass through and continue the attack if 2/7 was unable to continue. As soon as the left element of 2/7 cleared past Dakeshi village and entered open terrain, it was pinned down by Japanese fire. While Company E was held up, Company G, followed by F, swung through the zone of 1/1 to approach a point within 100 yards of Wana Ridge. Before they could take cover, concentrated enemy machine gun and mortar fire inflicted heavy casualties upon these leading elements of 2/7, and they were ordered to hold their positions until relieved by 1/7.

At 1107, Colonel Snedeker ordered the relief of the 2d Battalion by the 1st, which was ready to effect the relief at 1252. At that time, however, the commander of 1/7 requested that all supporting arms under the control of 2/7 be transferred to him, and before the transfer had been completed the renewed attack was delayed until 1615. When this designated H-Hour arrived, and following an intensive naval gunfire, artillery, rocket, and 4.2-inch mortar preparation, 1st Battalion assault units moved out behind tanks and under the cover of a protective smoke screen. The main effort was made by Company B, which advanced through Dakeshi to the south into open terrain. Immediately upon coming into this clearing, these Marines were taken under the same fire that had pinned down Company E earlier.

When enemy fire from Wana and Shuri prevented the company from advancing further, it was ordered to withdraw to Dakeshi to set up a night defense. In the meanwhile, moving south in unfamiliar territory to take over the positions of Company G, Company A ran into numerous enemy groups attempting to penetrate Marine lines. The relief was finally effected at 1900, but not before the commander and executive officer of Company A had become casualties. Coordinated with the attack of the 7th Marines against Wana Ridge was the one launched that same day by the 1st Marines. The regiment's major effort was made by 1/1, with the western tip of the ridge as the initial objective; the 2d and 3d Battalions supported the assault by fire. By noon, Company C secured the objective and began digging in and consolidating the newly won position despite heavy enemy fire. There was no contact on the left with the 7th Marines, which was moving up slowly against bitter opposition. Meanwhile, the portion of the ridge to have been occupied by the 7th soon was swarming with Japanese soldiers forming for a counterattack. Because he could not be reinforced in time, the commander of Company C requested and received permission to withdraw. After doing so in good order, the company set up a strong line for night defense on the battalion left, where contact was made with the 7th Marines. Units of the 5th Marines began relieving assault companies of the 1st at 2200, so that the 1st Division could renew its attack against Wana the next morning with a relatively fresh regiment.

With the coming of darkness on 14 May, Tenth Army assault troops were probing deeply into the Japanese main line of resistance all along the island. Almost flying in the face of indisputable evidence indicating that nearly half of the enemy garrison had been killed—the heaviest losses consisting of first-rate infantrymen—was the undeniable fact that there were no signs of Japanese weakness anywhere along the Tenth Army front. Conversely, the nature of operations in the south promised that enemy defenses were not going to be breached without grinding, gruelling, and unrelenting tank-infantry combat.

Logistical Progress

All ICEBERG assault and first echelon transports and landing ships had been unloaded by the end of April and released for other assignments.

As stated earlier here, the complexities of logistical support operations were compounded by several factors, not the least of which was the disrupted unloading schedule. Additionally, the jammed condition of the beach dumps and the shortage of shore party personnel and transportation gave the Tenth Army supply problems, also. The primary concern, however, was with the inability of the Tenth Army to maintain an adequate artillery ammunition reserve on the island. This situation arose because of the rapid expenditure of shells of all calibers and types needed in the drive to reduce the positions protecting Shuri. Beginning with the major XXIV Corps attack on 19 April, the initial Tenth Army ammunition support was quickly expended and replenishment shipments were gobbled up as soon as they arrived.

Although "ammunition resupply had been based on an estimated 40 days of combat," it was necessary to revise shipping schedules upwards drastically in order to meet the increased demands. On 17 April, General Buckner made the first of many special requests for ammunition in short supply. Specifically, he asked CinCPOA to load five LSTs at Saipan with 155mm howitzer and gun ammunition for arrival at Okinawa by 27 April. The fulfillment of this request was a stop-gap measure and in no way guaranteed that the critical artillery ammunition shortage would be alleviated for the rest of the campaign.

Kamikazes played a large part in creating this shortage by sinking a total of three ammunition ships in April with a loss estimated at being well in excess of 22,000 tons of vitally needed cargo. Even after the release of a considerable amount of ammunition late in April, when contingent operations for Phase III of ICEBERG were cancelled, the shortage remained critical throughout the fighting. Artillery commands were never able to maintain more than a minimally satisfactory reserve level of shells in their ammunition points.

Although initial shipments consisted of "balanced loads" of ammunition, as the supply requirements of the Tenth Army became clearer it also became apparent that there would be a greater demand for artillery shells than for small arms ammunition. Accordingly, logistics officers were able to schedule resupply shipments that more suitably filled the needs of the ground forces on Okinawa. But even as L-Day ended, unloading facilities on the Hagushi beaches were already overtaxed. Because some of the assault beaches were not capable of sustaining heavy and continuous shore party operations, and other sites selected for eventual use were either not suitable or not uncovered on schedule, the program of beach unloading as set up in the logistics plan proved totally unrealistic. The most satisfactory tonnage unloading figure that could be attained under the then-present conditions was reached on 5 May, and the figures never equalled the planned goals thereafter.

Four new beaches were opened up between 17 April and 17 May on the east coast of the island in Chimu and Nakagusuku Wan to support the southern drive of XXIV Corps and base development activities. Unfortunately, the gap between actual and planned unloading tonnage was never closed, even with the addition of these new points.

Because Phase III was cancelled and the mission of IIIAC changed, General Buckner could mount a four-division attack on Shuri. This increased ground activity vastly accelerated the consumption of all classes of supplies, and caused more supply ships to be called up than could be handled efficiently. In essence, this move was a calculated risk in the face of numerous mass and individual Kamikaze attacks on the transport areas. Nonetheless, the risk had to be taken if an adequate reserve of essential supplies was to be maintained in the immediate area.

As the insatiable appetites of the ground units for supplies increased in late April and early May, quartermaster and shore party units made extensive efforts to speed the unloading and processing of all goods. To help ease the situation, Rear Admiral John L. Hall, Jr., Senior Officer Present Afloat at Hagushi, and General Wallace, the Island Commander, recommended to General Buckner that more cranes, transportation, and personnel be employed to empty beached landing ships and craft; that more LVTs and crane barges be used at the reef transfer line; that intermediate transfer dumps be established to prevent excessively long hauls by shore party vehicles; and that the requirements for ammunition and fuel oil dispersion be modified somewhat to conserve personnel and transport. The admiral made one other recommendation: that the beach at Nago Wan be transferred from the control of IIIAC to that of the Island Command, General Buckner approved these recommendations almost immediately, but any gains made by these improvements were quickly minimized by the increasing size and variety of logistics tasks. At no time after the landing was there any prospect that the Tenth Army had not come to Okinawa to stay, but the problem of sustaining the momentum of the ground offensive became quite acute in late April and early May. In addition to his tactical responsibilities as commander of the Joint Expeditionary Force, during this early phase of the campaign Admiral Turner also had a logistic responsibility for maintaining adequate levels of all classes of air, ground, and naval replenishment stocks needed to support a successful Tenth Army operation.

Admiral Spruance, acting in accordance with the ICEBERG operation plan, announced that the amphibious phase of the Okinawa landing was ended on 17 May.

At 0900 on that day, Vice Admiral Harry W. Hill, Commander, V Amphibious Force, relieved Admiral Turner as Commander, Task Force 51, and took over the control of his naval activities, and of air defense. In the shift of command responsibilities, Admiral Hill was directed to report to General Buckner, who took command of all forces ashore and assumed Turner's former responsibility to Admiral Spruance for the defense and development of captured objectives. At this time, all of Turner's former logistics duties were taken over by a representative of Commander, Service Squadron Ten, the Navy logistical support force in forward areas.

Admiral Turner's successful period of command responsibility at Okinawa was marked by his direction of the largest amphibious operation of the Pacific War. Forces under his command had killed 55,551 and captured 853 Japanese troops in ground action, and had claimed the destruction of 1,184 enemy aircraft. During the first 46 days of the campaign, i.e., until 16 May, 1,256,286 measurement tons of assault, garrison, maintenance, and ground ammunition cargo had been unloaded over island beaches. Gunfire support force guns, from 5- to 16-inch in caliber, had fired over 25,000 tons of ammunition while covering Tenth Army ground troops and protecting the ships of TF 51.

In the course of six weeks of incessant fighting, the enemy had exacted a terrible price for every inch of ground he yielded. On 17 May, Tenth Army casualty figures included 3,964 men killed, 18,258 wounded, 302 missing, and 9,295 non-battle casualties. Of these casualties, hospital ships had evacuated 10,188; APAs 4,887; and air transport, 5,093. The hard-hit naval forces had lost 1,002 men killed, 2,727 wounded, and 1,054 missing. Air defense units, both TAF and carrier-based squadrons, lost 82 planes to all causes, while TF 51 had 156 ships sunk or damaged in action with the enemy. Despite the fact that a major portion of Okinawa had been taken, and Tenth Army ground units had punished the enemy unmercifully, all evidence pointed to a continuation of the hard fighting. Nevertheless, the tactical situation on the fringes of Shuri almost imperceptibly showed signs that the Japanese defenses were slowly giving way.

Chapter 8. Reduction of the Shuri Bastion

As conceived in Tenth Army plans, the object of the full-scale attack beginning on 11 May was to destroy the defenses guarding Shuri. In the end, this massive assault took the lives of thousands of men in two weeks of the bloodiest fighting experienced during the entire Okinawa campaign. For each frontline division, the struggle to overcome enemy troops on the major terrain feature in the path of its advance determined the nature of its battle. Facing the front of the 96th Infantry Division was Conical Hill; the 77th Division fought for Shuri itself. Marines of the 1st Division had to overcome Wana Draw, while Sugar Loaf Hill was the objective of the 6th Marine Division.

Battle For Sugar Loaf Hill

Sugar Loaf Hill was but one of three enemy positions in a triangularly shaped group of hills which made up the western anchor of the Japanese Shuri defense system. Sugar Loaf was the apex of the triangle, which faced north, its flanks and rear well covered by extensive cave and tunnel positions in Half Moon Hill to the southeast and the Horseshoe to the southwest. The three elements of this system were mutually supporting. In analyzing these defenses, the 6th Marine Division pointed out that: "the sharp depression included within the Horseshoe afforded mortar positions that were almost inaccessible to any arm short of direct, aimed rifle fire and hand grenades." Any attempt to capture Sugar Loaf by flanking action from east or west is immediately exposed to flat trajectory fire from both of the supporting terrain features. Likewise, an attempt to reduce either the Horseshoe or the Half Moon would be exposed to destructive well-aimed fire from the Sugar Loaf itself. In addition, the three localities are connected by a network of tunnels and galleries, facilitating the covered movement of reserves. As a final factor in the strength of the position it will be seen that all sides of Sugar Loaf Hill are precipitous, and there are no evident avenues of approach into the hill mass. For strategic location and tactical strength it is hard to conceive of a more powerful position than the Sugar Loaf terrain afforded. Added to all the foregoing was the bitter fact that troops assaulting this position presented a clear target to enemy machine guns, mortars, and artillery emplaced on the Shuri heights to their left and left rear.

Following its successful charge to seize the crest of Sugar Loaf, Major Courtney's small group had dug in. An unceasing enemy bombardment of the newly won position, as well as the first in a series of Japanese counterattacks to regain it, began almost immediately. At midnight, 14-15 May, there were sounds of enemy activity coming from the other side of the crest, signifying an impending *banzai* charge to Courtney. He forestalled the charge by leading a grenade-throwing attack against the reverse slope defenders, in the course of which he was killed. At 0230, only a handful of tired and wounded Marines remained on the top of Sugar Loaf, and Lieutenant Colonel Woodhouse ordered his reserve, Company K, to reinforce the depleted group. With the coming of dawn, the forces on Sugar Loaf had been reduced again by enemy action and fire, while 2/22 itself had been hit by numerous Japanese counterattacks and attempts at infiltration all along the battalion lines. At 0630, Company D of 2/29 was attached to the 22d Marines to help mop up the enemy in the rear of 2/22.

There were less than 25 Marines of Courtney's group and Company K remaining in the 2/22 position on Sugar Loaf when daylight came; at 0800, the seven survivors of the Courtney group were ordered off the hill by the battalion commander. Within a short time thereafter, the enemy launched another attack against the battered position. During the height of this attack, a reinforced platoon of Company D arrived on the hilltop and was thrown into the battle. Suffering heavy casualties while en route to the position, the Company D platoon was hit even harder by the charging Japanese as soon as it arrived at the top of the hill. At 1136, the few survivors of Company K and the 11 Marines remaining of the Company D platoon were withdrawn from Sugar Loaf. The Company D men rejoined their parent unit, which was manning a hastily constructed defensive line organized on the high ground just in front of Sugar Loaf.

The enemy counterattack was the beginning of a series which soon reached battalion-sized proportions, and which, by 0900, had spread over a 900-yard front extending into the zones of 1/22 and 3/29. An intensive naval gunfire, air, and artillery preparation for the division assault that morning temporarily halted the enemy attack, but it soon regained momentum. By 1315, however, the Japanese effort was spent, though not before the 22d Marines in the center of the division line had taken a terrific pounding. In an incessant mortar and artillery bombardment supporting the enemy counterattack, the battalion commander of 1/22, Major Thomas J. Myers, was killed, and all of his infantry company commanders—and the commander and executive officer of the tank company supporting the battalion—were wounded when the battalion observation post was hit.

Major Earl J. Cook, 1/22 executive officer, immediately took over and reorganized the battalion. He sent Companies A and B to seize a hill forward of the battalion left flank. When in blocking positions on their objective—northwest of Sugar Loaf—the Marines could effectively blunt counterattacks expected to be mounted in this area. Because the possibility existed of a breakthrough in the zone of 2/22, the regimental commander moved Company I of 3/22 into position to back up the 2d Battalion. At 1220, Lieutenant Colonel Woodhouse was notified that his exhausted battalion would be relieved by 3/22 as soon as possible, and would in turn take up the old 3d Battalion positions on the west coast along the banks of the Asato. The relief was effected at 1700 with Companies I and L placed on the front line, and Company K positioned slightly to the right rear of the other two. Company D, 2/29, reverted to parent control at this time. During the ground fighting on the night of 14-15 May, naval support craft smashed an attempted Japanese landing in the 6th Division zone on the coast just north of the Asato Gawa. Foreseeing the possibility of future raids here, General Shepherd decided to strengthen his beach defenses. In addition to a 50-man augmentation from the regiment, 2/22 was also reinforced by the 6th Reconnaissance Company to bolster its night defenses. To further strengthen Lieutenant Colonel Woodhouse's command, he was given operational control of 2/4, which was still in corps reserve.

The objective of the 29th Marines on 15 May was the seizure of Half Moon Hill. The 1st and 3d Battalions encountered the same bitter and costly resistance in the fight throughout the day that marked the experience of the 22d Marines. A slow-paced advance was made under constant harassing fire from the Shuri Heights area. By later afternoon, 1/29 had reached the valley north of Half Moon and became engaged in a grenade duel with enemy defenders in reverse slope positions. Tanks supporting the Marine assault elements came under direct 150mm howitzer fire at this point. Several of the tanks were hit, but little damage resulted. At the end of the day, the lines of the 29th Marines were firmly linked with the 22d Marines on the right and the 1st Division on the left.

Facing the 6th Marine Division was the 15th Independent Mixed Regiment, whose ranks were now sadly depleted as a result of its unsuccessful counterattack and because of the advances of 1/22 and the 29th Marines. More than 585 Japanese dead were counted in the division zone, and it was estimated that an additional 446 of the enemy had been killed in the bombardments of supporting arms or sealed in caves during mopping-up operations. Expecting that the Americans would make an intensive effort to destroy his Sugar Loaf defenses, General Ushijima reinforced the 15th IMR with a makeshift infantry battalion comprised of service and support units from the 1st Specially Established Brigade.

The success of the 6th Division attack plan for 16 May depended upon the seizure of Half Moon Hill by the 29th Marines. Once 3/29 had seized the high ground east of Sugar Loaf, 3/22 was to make the major division effort and capture the hill fortress. Immediately after the attack was launched, assault elements on the regimental left flank encountered heavy fire and bitter opposition from enemy strongpoints guarding the objective. The 1st Battalion was spearheaded by a Company B platoon and its supporting armor. After the tank-infantry teams had passed through the right flank to clear the reverse slope of the ridge held by Company C, devastating small arms, artillery, mortar, and antitank fire forced them to withdraw. The fury of this fire prevented Company C from advancing over the crest of the ridge and the other two platoons of Company B from moving more than 300 yards along the division boundary before they too were stopped by savage frontal and flanking fire. The night defenses of the battalion remained virtually the same as the night before; however, the units were reorganized somewhat and their dispositions readjusted. At 1400 that afternoon, Lieutenant Colonel Jean W. Moreau, commander of 1/29, was evacuated after he was seriously wounded by an artillery shell which hit his battalion OP; Major Robert P. Neuffer assumed command.

Continuously exposed to heavy enemy artillery and mortar bombardment, 3/29 spent most of the morning moving into favorable positions for the attack on Half Moon. Following an intensive artillery and mortar preparation, tanks from Companies A and B of the 6th Tank Battalion emerged from the railroad cut northeast of Sugar Loaf and lumbered into the broad valley leading to Half Moon. While Company A tanks provided Company B with direct fire support from the slopes of hills just north of Sugar Loaf, the latter fired into reverse slope positions in the ridge opposite 1/29, and then directly supported the assault elements of the 3d Battalion.

At about the same time that their armor support appeared on the scene, Companies G and I attacked and quickly raced to and occupied the northern slope of Half Moon Hill against slight resistance. The picture changed drastically at 1500, however, when the Japanese launched a violent counteroffensive to push the Marines off these advanced positions even while they were attempting to dig in. The enemy poured machine gun, rifle, and mortar fire into the exposed flanks and rear of the Americans, who also were hit by a flurry of grenades thrown from caves and emplacements on the south, or reverse, slope of the hill. As evening approached, increasing intense enemy fire penetrated the smoke screen covering the digging-in operations of the troops and they were ordered to withdraw to their earlier jump-off positions to set in a night defense.

On the right of the division, when the 22d Marines attack was launched at 0830 on the 16th, assault elements of the 1st Battalion were immediately taken under continuous automatic weapons fire coming from the northern edge of the ruins of the town of Takamotoji, just as they were attempting to get into position to support the attack of 3/22. The fact that this previously quiet area now presented a bristling defense indicated that the Japanese had reinforced this sector to confound any American attempt to outflank Sugar Loaf from the direction of Naha. In the end, because of the criss-crossing fires coming from the village, Half Moon Hill, and the objective itself, the 3d Battalion was unable to fulfill its assignment.

The battalion commander, Lieutenant Colonel Malcolm "O" Donohoo, had planned to attack Sugar Loaf from the east once the flank of the attacking unit, Company I, was safeguarded by a successful 3/29 advance. Company L, 3/22, was to support the attack by covering the south and east slopes of Sugar Loaf with fire, while 1/22, in turn, would take the high ground west of Sugar Loaf, where it would support the Company L movement by fire. The success or failure of the attack on the hill hinged on the success or failure of 3/29. At 1500, despite the fact that 3/29 had not fully occupied the high ground, Company I moved out with its tank support and reached Sugar Loaf without serious opposition. Once the troops in the van attempted to gain the crest, however, they began receiving heavy enemy mortar and machine gun fire. In an effort to suppress this fire, the tanks began flanking the hill, but ran into a minefield where one tank was lost. Company I, nevertheless, gained the top of the hill at 1710 and began digging in. The situation was in doubt now, because both 1/22 and Company L were pinned down and 3/29 was forced to withdraw from Half Moon. Company I, therefore, was in an exposed position and its precarious hold on Sugar Loaf had become untenable. With both flanks exposed and its ranks depleted by numerous casualties, the company had to be pulled back from the hill under the cover fire of both division and corps artillery. As 3/22 reorganized for night defense, enemy batteries bombarding the Marine lines wounded Lieutenant Colonel Donohoo, who was replaced by Major George B. Kantner, the battalion executive officer.

This day was categorized by the 6th Division as the "bitterest" of the Okinawa campaign, a day when "the regiments had attacked with all the effort at their command and had been unsuccessful." One infantry regiment, the 22d, had been so sorely punished that, in assessing his losses for the day, Colonel Schneider reported that the combat efficiency of his unit was down to 40 percent. Because the fighting of the preceding eight days had sapped the offensive capabilities of the 22d Marines and reduced the regiment to a point where its continued employment was inadvisable, it became apparent that the 29th Marines would have to assume the burden of taking Sugar Loaf. On 17 May, the regimental boundary was shifted west to include the redoubt in its zone and thereby lessen control problems in the attacks on both it and Half Moon.

In an effort to neutralize the seemingly impregnable Japanese defenses here, the attack of 17 May was preceded by an intensive bombardment of 29th Marines objectives by all available supporting arms. In this massive preparation were the destructive fires of 16-inch naval guns, 8-inch howitzers, and 1,000-pound bombs. Following this softening up, and spearheaded by a heavy and continual artillery barrage, the 29th Marines launched a tank-infantry attack with three battalions abreast. The 1st and 3d Battalions on the left had the mission of taking Half Moon, while 2/29, with Company E in assault, was to take Sugar Loaf.

Company E made three attempts to take its objective, and each proved costly and unsuccessful. The first effort, involving a wide flanking movement in which the railroad cut was utilized for cover, was stymied almost immediately when the troops surged onto open ground. A close flanking attack around the left of the hill characterized the second effort, but the steep southeastern face of the height precluded a successful climb to the top. The axis of the attack was then reoriented to the northeast slope of Sugar Loaf, and the lead platoon began a difficult trek to the top, all the while under heavy mortar fire coming from covered positions on Half Moon. Three times the assaulting Marines reached the crest, only to be driven off by a combination of grenades and bayonet charges. Almost all fighting was at close range and hand-to-hand. After quickly reorganizing for a fourth try, the now-fatigued and depleted company drove to the hilltop at 1830, when it was met again by a determined Japanese counterattack. This time, however, the Marines held, but heavy casualties and depleted ammunition supply forced the battalion commander to withdraw the survivors of the company from Sugar Loaf. Thus, the prize for which 160 men of Company E had been killed and wounded on that day fell forfeit to the Japanese. Some small sense of just retribution was felt by Company E Marines when the enemy foolishly and boldly attempted to reinforce Sugar Loaf at dusk by moving his troops to the hill along an uncovered route. Artillery observers immediately called down the fire of 12 battalions on the unprotected Japanese, decisively ending their reinforcement threat.

So well integrated were the enemy defenses on Half Moon and Sugar Loaf, capture of only one portion was meaningless; 6th Division Marines had to take them all simultaneously. If only one hill was seized without the others being neutralized or likewise captured, effective Japanese fire from the uncaptured position would force the Marines to withdraw from all. This, in effect, was why Sugar Loaf had not been breached before this, and why it was not taken on the 17th.

A combination of tank fire, flame, and demolitions had temporarily subdued the Japanese opposing the 1/29 approach on the 17th and enabled Companies A and C to advance swiftly across the valley and up the forward slopes of Half Moon. While Company C mopped up remaining enemy defenders, Company A renewed its attack across the valley floor and raced to the forward slopes of Half Moon. When Company B attempted to cross open ground to extend the battalion lines on the left, it was stopped cold by accurate fire coming from the hill, Sugar Loaf, and Shuri. At this time, the positions held by the exposed platoons of Company A became untenable. The battalion commander authorized their withdrawal to a defiladed area approximately 150 yards forward of their line of departure that morning.

By 1600, 3d Battalion companies had fought their way to Half Moon under continuous fire and begun digging in on the forward slope of the hill. They were not able to tie in with 1/29 until 1840, two hours after Company F had been ordered forward to fill in the gap between the battalions. Following a crushing bombardment of these hastily established positions on Half Moon and the exposure of the right flank of 3/29 to direct and accurate fire from enemy-held Sugar Loaf, the entire battalion was pulled back when Company A was withdrawn from its left. Strong positions were established for night defense — only 150 yards short of Half Moon. The gaps on either side of 3/29 were protected by interlocking lanes of fire established in coordination with 1/29 on its left flank and 2/29 on its right. On 18 May at 0946, less than an hour after the 29th Marines attacked, Sugar Loaf was again occupied by 6th Division troops. The assault began with tanks attempting a double envelopment of this key position with little initial success. A combination of deadly AT fire and well-placed minefields quickly disabled six tanks. Despite this setback and increasingly accurate artillery fire, a company of medium tanks split up and managed to reach and occupy positions on either flank of Sugar Loaf, from which they could cover the reverse slopes of the hill. In a tank-infantry assault, Company D, 2/29, gained the top of the heretofore-untenable position, and held it during a fierce grenade and mortar duel with the defenders. Almost immediately after subduing the enemy, the company charged over the crest of the hill and down its south slope to mop up and destroy emplacements there. Disregarding lethal mortar fire from Half Moon that blanketed Sugar Loaf, Company D dug in at 1300 as well as it could to consolidate and organize its newly won conquest.

All during the attempts to take Sugar Loaf and Half Moon, the enemy on Horseshoe Hill had poured down never-ending mortar and machine gun fire on the attacking Marines below. To destroy these positions, Company F was committed on the battalion right. Supported by fire from 1/22 on its right and Marines on Sugar Loaf, the company pressed forward to the ridge marking the lip of the Horseshoe ravine. Here it was stopped by a vicious grenade and mortar barrage coming from the deeply entrenched enemy. Because of this intense resistance, the company was forced to withdraw slightly to the forward slope of the ridge, where it established a strong night defense.

Implicit in the 6th Marine Division drive towards the Asato Gawa was a threatened breakthrough at Naha. To forestall this, General Ushijima moved four naval battalions to back up the 44th Independent Mixed Brigade. Few men in the rag-tag naval units were trained for land combat, much less combat at all, since the battalions were comprised of inexperienced service troops, civilian workers, and Okinawans who had been attached to Admiral Ota's Naval Base Force. The commander of the Thirty-second Army thought that the lack of training could be compensated in part by strongly arming the men with a generous allotment of automatic weapons taken from supply dumps on Oroku and the wrecked aircraft that dotted the peninsula's airfield.

Despite their lack of combat experience, the naval force was to perform a three-fold mission with these weapons: back up the Sugar Loaf defense system, hold the hills northwest of the Kokuba River, and maintain the security of Shuri's western flank in the event that the defenses of the 44th IMB collapsed. The furious Japanese defense of the buffer zone stretching from the Naha estuary of the Kokuba to the western outskirts of the town of Shuri indicated their concern with the threat to the left flank of the Shuri positions. The coming of darkness on 18 May was not accompanied by any noticeable waning in the furious contest for possession of Sugar Loaf, a battle in which the combat efficiency of the 29th Marines had been so severely tested and drained. In the nearly nine days since the Tenth Army had first begun its major push, the 6th Marine Division had sustained 2,662 battle and 1,289 non-battle casualties, almost all in the ranks of the 22d and 29th Marines. It was patently obvious that an infusion of fresh blood into the division lines was a prerequisite for the attack to be continued with undiminished fervor. Accepting this fact, General Geiger released the 4th Marines to parent control effective at 0800 on 19 May, at which time General Shepherd placed the 29th Marines in division reserve, but subject to IIIAC control.

At 0300 on the morning of the scheduled relief, a strong Japanese counterattack hit the open right flank of Company F, 2/29, poised just below the lip of the Horseshoe depression. The fury of the enemy attack, combined with an excellently employed and heavy bombardment of white phosphorous shells, eventually forced the advance elements of Company F to withdraw to the northern slope of Sugar Loaf. At first light, relief of the three exhausted battalions of the 29th began, with 2/4 taking up positions on the left, 3/4 on the right.

Despite the difficult terrain, constant bombardment of the lines, and opposition from isolated enemy groups which had infiltrated the positions during the night, the relief was effected at 1430 at a cost to the 4th Marines of over 70 casualties—primarily from mortar and artillery fire. At approximately 1530, a counterattack was launched against 2/4, which then was in a precarious position on Half Moon Hill, on the division left flank. After nearly two hours of fighting, the attack was broken up. The advance Marine company was then withdrawn from its exposed point to an area about 150 yards to the rear, where the battalion could reinforce the regimental line after tying in with 3/5 and 3/4.

The area from which the attack had been launched against Company F, 2/29, was partially neutralized during the day by the 22d Marines. Under its new commander, Colonel Harold C. Roberts, the regiment pushed its left flank forward 100-150 yards to the high ground on the left of Horseshoe. Disregarding heavy artillery and mortar fire as well as they could, the Marines dug in new positions which materially strengthened the division line. After a night of this heavy and accurate enemy bombardment, the two assault battalions of the 4th Marines jumped off at 0800 on 20 May. Preceded by a thorough artillery preparation and supported by the 6th Tank Battalion, the 5th Provisional Rocket Detachment, and the Army 91st Chemical Mortar Company, the Marines moved rapidly ahead for 200 yards before they were slowed and then halted. The determined refusal of the Japanese infantry entrenched on Half Moon and Horseshoe Hills to yield, and fierce machine gun and artillery fire from hidden positions in the Shuri Hill mass, where enemy gunners could directly observe the Marine attack, blocked the advance.

It soon appeared as though the fight for Half Moon was going to duplicate the struggle for Sugar Loaf. To reinforce the 2/4 assault forces and to maintain contact with the 5th Marines, Lieutenant Colonel Reynolds H. Hayden, commander of 2/4, committed his reserve rifle company on the left at 1000. In face of a mounting casualty toll, at 1130 he decided to reorient the axis of the battalion attack to hit the flanks of the objective rather than its front. While the company in the center of the battalion line remained in position and supported the attack by fire, the flank companies were to attempt an armor-supported double envelopment. At 1245, when coordination for this maneuver was completed, the attack was renewed.

Company G, on the right, moved out smartly, and, following closely behind the neutralizing fire of its supporting tanks, it seized and held the western end of Half Moon. While traversing more exposed terrain and receiving fire from three sides, the left wing of the envelopment—Company E—progressed slowly and suffered heavy casualties. Although subjected to a constant barrage of mortars and hand grenades, the company reached the forward slope of its portion of the objective, where it eventually dug in for the night. The night positions of 2/4 were uncomfortably close to those of the Japanese, and separated only by a killing zone along a hill crest swept by both enemy and friendly fire. Nonetheless, the battalion had made fairly substantial gains during the day and it was set in solidly.

Earlier that day, as 3/4 attacked enemy positions on the high ground forming the western end of Horseshoe, it had received fire support from the 22d Marines. The 4th Marines battalion employed demolitions, flamethrowers, and tanks to burn and blast the honeycomb of Japanese-occupied caves in the forward (north) slope of Horseshoe Hill. When the regiment halted the attack for the day at 1600, 3/4 had gained its objective. Here, the battalion was on high ground overlooking the Horseshoe depression where the Japanese mortars, which had caused so many casualties that day, were dug in. To maintain contact with 2/4 and to strengthen his line, Lieutenant Colonel Bruno A. Hochmuth, 3/4 commander, had committed elements of his reserve, Company I, shortly after noon. Anticipating that a counterattack might possibly be mounted against 3/4 later that evening, Colonel Shapley ordered 1/4 to detail a company to back up the newly won positions on Horseshoe. Company B was designated and immediately briefed on the situation of 3/4, routes of approach, and courses of action to be followed if the Japanese attack was launched.

The sporadic mortar and artillery fire that had harassed 4th Marines lines suddenly increased at 2200, when bursts of white phosphorous shells and colored smoke heralded the beginning of the anticipated counterattack. An estimated 700 Japanese struck the positions of Companies K and L of 3/4. As soon as the enemy had showed themselves, they were blasted by the combined destructive force of prepared concentrations fired by six artillery battalions. Gunfire support ships provided constant illumination over the battlefield. Company B was committed to the fight and "with perfect timing," moved into the line to help blunt the attack.

Star shells and flares gave a surrealistic cast to the wild two-and-a-half hour fracas, fought at close quarters and often hand-to-hand. The fight was over at midnight; the few enemy who had managed to penetrate the Marine lines were either dead or attempting to withdraw. The next morning, unit identification of some of the nearly 500 Japanese dead revealed that fresh units—which included some naval troops—had made the attack. The determination of the attackers to crush the Americans reemphasized the extremely sensitive and immediate Japanese reaction to any American threat against Shuri's western flank.

On 21 May, the main effort of the 6th Division attack was made by the 4th Marines, with the 22d Marines pacing the attack and giving fire support. The objective was the Asato River line. Under its new commander, Lieutenant Colonel George B. Bell, 1/4 attacked in the center of the line. Forward progress down the southern slopes of Sugar Loaf towards the easternmost limit of Horseshoe was slowed by both bitter fighting and the rain that fell during the morning and most of the afternoon. This downpour turned the shell-torn slopes into slick mud-chutes, making supply and evacuation over the treacherous footing almost impossible. But the fresh battalion overcame the combination of obstacles placed in its way by the weather, terrain, and numerous remaining enemy pockets all along the river front, to advance 200 yards. Demolition and flamethrower teams blasted and burned the way in front of 3/4 as it drove into the extensive and well-prepared enemy positions in the interior of Horseshoe. By midafternoon, Companies K and L had destroyed the deadly mortars emplaced there, and were solidly positioned in a defense line that extended approximately halfway between Horseshoe Hill and the Asato Gawa.

Intensive mortar and artillery fire from the heights of Shuri combined with the rugged terrain within the 2/4 zone of action restricted the use of tanks and prevented that battalion from advancing appreciably on 21 May. After five days of furious fighting and limited gains in the Half Moon area, General Shepherd concluded that the bulk of enemy firepower preventing his division from retaining this ground was centered in the Shuri area, outside of the division zone of action.

Thoroughly estimating the situation, he decided to establish a strong reverse slope defense on the division left, to concentrate the efforts of the division on a penetration in the south and southwest, and to make no further attempts at driving to the southeast, where his troops had been meeting withering fire from Shuri. The division commander believed that this new maneuver would both relieve his forces of a threat to their left flank and at the same time give impetus to a drive to envelop Shuri from the west.

The sporadic rain which fell on the 21st, came down even more heavily and steadily that night. Resupply of assault elements and replenishment of forward supply dumps proved almost impossible. The unceasing deluge made southern Okinawa overnight a veritable mudhole and a greater obstacle to all movement than the unrelenting enemy resistance.

The Battle For Wana Draw

When the 1st Marine Division smashed the Japanese outpost line at Dakeshi, the battleground for General del Valle's Marines shifted to the foreboding Wana approaches to the Shuri hill mass. All evidence now signified that the main Japanese defenses in southern Okinawa consisted of a nearly regular series of concentric rings whose epicenter was protected by some of the most rugged terrain yet encountered in the drive south. The mission of breaching the Wana defenses fell to the 1st Marine and 77th Infantry Divisions at the same time that the 6th Marine and 96th Infantry Divisions attempted to envelop enemy flanks. A somewhat crude Japanese propaganda attempt appeared in a leaflet discovered on the body of an infiltrator in the rear of the 1st Division on 14 May. Purportedly a letter from a wounded 96th Division soldier in enemy hands, it warned in fractured English that "the battles here will be 90 times as severe as that of Yusima Island [Iwo Jima]. I am sure that all of you that have landed will lose your lives which will be realized if you come here. The affairs of Okinawa is quite different from the islands that were taken by the Americans."

An analysis made of the Wana positions after the battle showed that the Japanese had "taken advantage of every feature of a terrain so difficult it could not have been better designed if the enemy himself had the power to do so." Utilizing every defense feature provided by nature, General Ushijima had so well organized the area that an assault force attacking to the south would be unable to bypass the main line of resistance guarding Shuri, and would instead have to penetrate directly into the center of the heretofore unassailable defenses of the Thirty-second Army.

The terrain within and immediately bordering the division zone was both varied and complex. The southernmost branch of the Asa Kawa meandered along the gradually rising floor of Wana Draw and through the northerly part of Shuri. Low rolling ground on either side of the stream offered neither cover nor concealment against Japanese fire coming from position along the reverse slope of Wana Ridge and the military crest in the southern portion of the ridge. Approximately 400 yards wide at its mouth, Wana Draw narrowed perceptibly as the stream flowing through it approached the city. Hill 55, a dominating piece of terrain at the southern tip of the ridge, guarded the western entry into the draw. Bristling with nearly every type of Japanese infantry weapon, the positions on the hill had clear fields of fire commanding all approaches to the draw. Manning these guns were troops from the 62d Division's 64th Brigade, and an ill-assorted lot of stragglers from remnants of the 15th, 23d, and 273d Independent Infantry Battalions, the 14th Independent Machine Gun Battalion, and the 81st Field Antiaircraft Artillery Battalion, all under command of the Brigade.

By 0400 on 15 May, elements of the 5th Marines had relieved 2/1 and most of 3/1. At 0630, the relief was completed and Colonel Griebel assumed command of the former 1st Marines zone west of Wana. The 5th Marines commander placed 2/5 in assault with the 3d Battalion in support and the 1st in reserve. Acting on the recommendations of battalion and regimental commanders of both the 1st and 5th Marines, General del Valle decided to neutralize the high ground on both sides of Wana Draw. Tanks and self-propelled 105mm howitzers were to shell the area thoroughly before 2/5 tried to cross the open ground at the mouth of the draw.

Fire teams from Company F protected nine Shermans of the 1st Tank Battalion against possible attacks from suicide-bent enemy soldiers as the tanks worked over the Japanese positions in the mouth of the draw during the morning. Because tanks invariably drew heavy artillery, mortar, and AT fire, the Marines guarding them were forced to take cover. Nevertheless, the open ground of the battle area permitted the infantry teams to cover the tanks with fire from protected positions at long range. The mediums received heavy and intense fire from the sector to their front and from numerous cave positions on both sides of the draw. Some respite was gained when naval gunfire destroyed a 47mm AT gun which had hit three tanks at least five times each. About midafternoon, the tanks withdrew to clear the way for a carrier-plane strike on the draw. Following this attack, the nine original tanks, now reinforced by six others, continued the process of neutralizing the draw. Another 47mm AT gun opened up late in the afternoon, but it was destroyed before it could damage any of the tanks.

After a day spent probing the mouth of Wana Draw, 2/5 infantry companies set up night defenses east of the railroad, dug in, and established contact all along their front. At the CP that night, the 5th Marines commander observed that "Wana Draw was another gorge like the one at Awacha. It was obvious that the position would have to be thoroughly pounded before it could be taken," and ordered the softening-up operations of the 15th repeated the next day.

Colonel Snedeker's 7th Marines spent the 15th in reorganizing its infantry companies, improving occupied positions, and mopping up in the vicinity of Dakeshi. During the day, air liaison parties, gunfire spotters, and forward observers were kept busy directing concentrated artillery and naval gunfire bombardments and air strikes on known enemy strongpoints on Wana Ridge. At 2100, 1/7 was ordered to prepare a feint attack on 16 May, when all supporting arms were to fire a preparation and troops were to concentrate as though preparing to jump off in an assault.

The battalion was already positioned for the feint when preparatory fires began at 0755. At this time, 4.2-inch and 81mm mortars smoked the area immediately in front of 1/7 to heighten the deception. Fifteen minutes after it had begun, the barrage was lifted for another fifteen-minute period in an attempt to deceive the Japanese. The Marines believed that the enemy, fooled into thinking that an attack was imminent, would rush from covered caves to reoccupy their battle positions, where they would again be blasted. When there was no apparent reaction to the feint, supporting arms resumed firing at 0825 with undetermined results.

At 0950, regiment notified Lieutenant Colonel John J. Gormley, the 1/7 commander, that an air strike on Wana Ridge was scheduled for 1000, immediately following which he was to send patrols forward to determine what remaining enemy resistance existed on the target. Having learned that the strike was delayed, at 1028 Lieutenant Colonel Gormley requested that the mission be cancelled and sent the patrols out after he had ordered a mortar barrage placed on the ridge. The Company C patrols moved forward unopposed until they reached the western end of Wana Ridge. Here they received intense grenade and machine gun fire which was answered by their battalion 81mm mortars and supporting fire from the 5th Marines. Rushing forward when this fire had been lifted, the patrols carried and occupied the troublesome objective.

Lieutenant Colonel Gormley then ordered the newly won position held and reinforced by troops he sent forward for this purpose. Once leading elements began to move out again, enemy troops lodged in burial vaults and rugged coral formations showered grenades down upon the advancing Marines. Unsuccessful in halting the advance, the enemy tried but failed to mount a counterattack at 1605. Although supporting arms of 1/7 blunted this attempt, enemy resistance to the Marine attack continued.

Nightfall forced the battalion commander to withdraw the troops spearheading the assault and move them to more secure positions on a plateau almost directly north of the ridge for night defense. Contact was then established on the right with

2/5 and on the left with 3/7. At 2400, 3/7 effected a passage of the lines to relieve the 1st Battalion, which then went into regimental reserve.

During the 16th, 15 tanks, two of them flamethrowers, had supported the attack of 1/7 from positions on Dakeshi Ridge, while a total of 30 tanks—including 4 flamethrowers—supported 2/5 by burning and blasting enemy strongpoints in Wana Draw. At 0900, the 2/5 armored support drew antitank, mortar, and artillery fire that disabled two tanks, and damaged two others, which withdrew after evacuating the crews of the stalled cripples. Two of the AT positions which had been spotted in the morning were destroyed that afternoon when the main battery of the USS *Colorado* was brought to bear on them. Generally, when a Marine tank was damaged and abandoned temporarily, efforts to retrieve it later were usually stymied by enemy fire. Disabled tanks remaining in the field overnight usually were either destroyed by enemy demolition teams or occupied by snipers, who converted them into armored pillboxes.

Before retiring at nightfall on 16 May, the 1st Tank Battalion had expended nearly 5,000 rounds of 75mm and 173,000 rounds of .30 caliber ammunition, and 600 gallons of napalm on targets on Dakeshi Ridge and in Wana Draw that day. Following the two-day process of softening up provided by all supporting arms, the 5th Marines prepared to run the gantlet of Wana Draw on 17 May.

"Under the continued pounding of one of the most concentrated assaults in Pacific Warfare," cracks appeared in the Shuri defenses on 17 May. On that day, 2/5 made the main regimental effort, sending tank-infantry teams to the mouth of Wana Draw, where they worked over the caves and pillboxes lining its sides. The 2/5 attack was made in conjunction with a 7th Marines effort to gain the pinnacle ridge forming the northern side of the draw. When a terrific mortar and artillery barrage drove the 7th back at 1200, 2/5 assault troops—also under heavy fire—were forced back to their original positions, where they could protect the exposed flank of the 7th Marines battalion.

On the right of 2/5, Company E finally succeeded in penetrating the Japanese defenses. After having been driven back earlier in the day, the company established a platoon-sized strongpoint on its objective, the west nose of Hill 55. Because the low ground lying between this point and battalion frontlines were swept by heavy enemy fire, tanks were pressed into use for supply and evacuation purposes.

Having relieved 1/7 at 0600, 3/7 attacked towards Wana Ridge from Dakeshi Ridge with two companies in assault: Company I on the right, K on the left. A total of 12 gun and 2 flamethrower tanks supported Company K as it attempted to secure the low ridge crest northwest of Wana. Meanwhile, Company I gained and held a plateau that led to the western nose of the Wana Ridge line.

Extremely heavy resistance plagued Company K efforts to move forward, as the enemy concentrated his fire on the leading infantry elements. Attempting to lessen the effectiveness of the Marine tank-infantry tactics, the Japanese employed smoke grenades to blind the tanks and drastically restricted their supporting fire. Before the tanks could be isolated in the smoke and cut off from their infantry protection, and when the flanks of Company K became so threatened as to make them untenable, both tanks and infantry were withdrawn—the latter to Dakeshi to become 3/7 reserve. Late in the afternoon, the 3/7 commander ordered Company L forward to reinforce I for the night and to assist in the attack the next morning.

Following a period of intermittent shelling from enemy mortars and artillery during the night 17-18 May, 3/7 again attacked Wana Ridge. Supporting arms delivered intense fire on the forward slopes and crest of the ridge all morning; the attack itself began at noon. Reinforced by a platoon from L, Company I succeeded in getting troops on the ridge, but furious enemy grenade and mortar fire inflicted such heavy casualties on the assault force that Lieutenant Colonel Hurst was forced to withdraw them to positions held the previous night, where he could consolidate his lines. An abbreviated analysis by the division fairly well summarized that day's fighting: "Gains were measured by yards won, lost, then won again."

Pinned down by heavy enemy fire on the reverse slope of its position on Hill 55, the isolated platoon from Company E, 2/5, could neither advance nor withdraw. Tanks again supplied ammunition and rations to the dug-in troops. Six mediums initially supported the early-morning operations of 2/5 by firing into caves and emplacements in the terrain complex comprising the draw. This tank fire was coordinated with that coming from Shermans in the Wana Draw sector. In addition to this daylong tank firing, the artillery battalions expended over 7,000 rounds of 105mm and 75mm artillery ammunition on selected point targets. Under the cover of tank fire, at 1200 Company F sent one infantry platoon and an attached engineer platoon with flamethrowers and demolitions into the village of Wana to destroy enemy installations there. The party worked effectively until 1700, when it was recalled to Marine lines for the night because Wana Ridge, forming the northern side of the draw behind and overlooking the village, was still strongly infested by the enemy. Before leaving Wana, Marines destroyed numerous grenade dischargers, machine guns, and rifles found in the village and in the tombs on its outskirts.

The 1st Marine Division's bitter contest for possession of Wana Draw continued on 19 May along the same bloody lines it had run on the four previous days. Colonel Snedeker's regiment again made the major effort for the division, and the 5th Marines continued to punish the mouth of Wana Draw. As before, attacking Marines were sorely beset by enemy fire, which answering artillery, tank, mortar, and regimental 105mm howitzer concentrations had failed to neutralize.

The 3d Battalion, 7th Marines, attacked that afternoon in a column of companies, Company I in the lead, followed by Companies L and K in that order. Resistance to the attack was immediate, although the vanguard managed to reach the nose of the coral ridge to its front under a blanket of mortar shells falling all about. Then, because 3/1 was to relieve 3/7 and it was too risky to effect a relief right on the ridge under the conditions then prevailing, the leading elements withdrew about 75 yards to the rear.

Earlier in the day, 1/7 and 2/7 had been relieved in position near Dakeshi by 1/1 and 2/1 respectively. With the relief of the 3d Battalion, the 7th Marines relinquished the responsibility for the capture of Wana Ridge to Colonel Mason's 1st Marines, and Colonel Snedeker's regiment went into division reserve. In the five-day struggle for Wana, the 7th Marines had lost a total of 44 men killed, 387 wounded, 91 non-battle casualties, and 7 missing. Of this number, the 3d Battalion sustained 20 Marines killed and 140 wounded. In a supporting and diversionary role for the five-day period, the 5th Marines suffered 13 men killed and 82 wounded.

Despite the punishment they had received from the 5th Marines and its supporting tanks, the Japanese built new positions in Wana Draw daily, and reconstructed and recamouflaged by night old ones that Marine tank fire had exposed and damaged by day. As the assault infantry plunged further into the draw, and as the draw itself narrowed, an increasing number of Japanese defensive positions conspired with the rugged terrain to make passage more difficult.

Dominating the eastern end of Wana Ridge, on the northwestern outskirts of Shuri, was 110 Meter Hill, commanding a view of the zones of both the 1st Marine and 77th Infantry Divisions. Defensive fire from this position thwarted the final reduction of Japanese positions in Wana Draw and eventual capture of the Shuri redoubt. Tanks, M-75 (self-propelled 105mm howitzers), 37mm guns, and overhead machine gun fire supported the attacks which jumped off at 0815. The assault troops moved rapidly to the base of the objective, tanks and flamethrowers clearing the way, while enemy mortar and machine gun fire inflicted heavy casualties in the ranks of the onsurging Marines.

Initially, 3/1 moved to the southeast and up the northern slope of Wana Ridge, where it became involved in hand grenade duels with Japanese defenders. The Marines prevailed and managed to secure approximately 200 yards of this portion of the ridge. By 1538, 2/1 reported to regiment that it was on top of the objective and in contact with 3/1, and had secured all of the rest of the northern slope of the ridge with the exception of the summit of 110 Meter Hill. A considerable gap between the flanks of 2/1 and the 305th Infantry on the Marine left was covered by interlocking bands of machine gun fire and mortar barrages set up by both units. Confronted by intense enemy fire from reverse slope positions, 2/1 riflemen were unable to take the hillcrest and dug in for the night, separated from the enemy by only a few yards of shell-pocked ground.

After it tied in with 2/1 for the night of 19-20 May, Lieutenant Colonel Stephen V. Sabol's 3d Battalion moved out at 0845, and was again within grenade-throwing range of Wana Ridge defenders. Burning and blasting, tanks supported the assault by destroying enemy-held caves and fortified positions blocking the advance. When 3/1 had gained the northern slope of the ridge and could not budge the Japanese troops in reverse-slope defenses, Colonel Mason decided to burn them out by rolling split barrels of napalm down the hill into Japanese emplacements in Wana Draw, and then setting them afire by exploding white phosphorous (WP) grenades on top of the inflammable jellied mixture.

Working parties began manhandling drums of napalm up the hill at 1140, and had managed to position only three of them by 1500. At 1630, these were split open, sent careening down the hill, and set aflame by the WP grenades. An enemy entrenchment about 50 yards down the incline halted the drums; in the end, the Japanese sustained little damage and few injuries from this hastily contrived field expedient. The proximity of the combatants that night led to considerable mortar, hand grenade, and sniper fire, as well as the usually lively and abusive exchange of curses, insults, and threats of violence that often took place whenever the protagonists were within shouting distance of each other. On the division right, 2/5 jumped off in attack on 20 May at 0900, supported by artillery and M-7 fire and spearheaded by tanks. The battalion objective was the area running roughly from Hill 55 southwest to the Naha-Shuri road. A continuous artillery barrage was laid on Shuri Ridge, the western extension of the commanding height on which Shuri Castle had been built, as assault units quickly worked their way towards the objective. At 0930, lead elements were engaged in close-in fighting with enemy forces in dug-in positions bordering the road. Under constant and heavy enemy fire, engineer mine-clearing personnel preceded the tanks to make the road safe for the passage of the mediums. Working just in front of the advancing troops, the Shermans flushed a number of enemy soldiers from their hidden positions and then cut them down with machine gun fire. Close engineer-tank-infantry teamwork permitted the Marines to secure the objective by noon.

Heavy small arms and mortar fire poured into the advance 2/5 position, which Company E held all afternoon. The sources of this fire were emplacements located on Shuri Ridge. Continued artillery and pointblank tank fire, and two rocket barrages, finally silenced the enemy weapons. By 2000, Company E had established contact all along the line and dug in for the night. Except for the usual enemy mortar and artillery harassment, there was little activity on the front. Just before dawn, 1/5 relieved the 2d Battalion in place; 2/5 then went into regimental reserve.

Once in position, 1/5 was ordered to patrol aggressively towards Shuri Ridge and on the high ground east of Half Moon Hill. It maintained a sufficient force in the vicinity of Wana Ridge and Hill 55, at the same time, to assist the 1st Marines attack. Tank-infantry teams again reconnoitered the area south of the division line against a hail of machine gun and mortar fire. In addition to providing the tanks protection from Japanese tank-destroyer and suicide units, Marine ground troops directed the tank fire on targets of opportunity. Tank commanders in vehicles that were sometimes forward of foot troops often called down artillery fire on point targets at extremely close ranges. In spite of fierce resistance that became most frenzied as Marines closed in on Shuri, the 5th Marines positions on Hill 55 were advanced slightly in order to give the division more favorable jumping off points for a concerted effort against General Ushijima's headquarters.

At dawn on 21 May, 2/1 moved out against heavy opposition to secure the summit of 110 Meter Hill and the rest of Wana Ridge. Although some small gains were made, the objectives could not be reached. Tank support, which heretofore had been so effective, was limited because of the irregular and steep nature of the ground. Though armor could provide overhead fire, the vehicles were unable to take reverse slope positions under fire because a deep cleft at the head of the draw prevented the Shermans from getting behind the enemy. Reconnaissance reports indicated that as the draw approached Wana, its walls rose to sheer heights of from 200 to 300 feet. Lining the wall faces were numerous, well-defended caves that were unapproachable to all but the suicidally inclined. It was readily apparent that no assault up the draw would be successful unless preceded by an intense naval gunfire, air, and artillery preparation. Included also in the reports was the fact that the steep terrain forward of Wana did not favor tank operations. On the left of 2/1, Company G mopped up opposition in the small village on the northern outskirts of Shuri. Resisting the attempts of the company to turn the flank of 110 Meter Hill were elements of the 22d Independent Infantry Battalion, the sole remaining first-line infantry reserve of the Thirty-second Army—thrown into the breach to hold the area around the hill. Advancing down the draw were two companies abreast, E and F, whose attack was initially supported by the massed fires of battalion mortars and then by all other supporting arms.

Darkening skies and intermittent rain squalls obscured the battle scene to friendly and enemy observers alike. Although it was apparent that 2/1 was right in the middle of a preregistered impact area, judging from the accuracy of enemy mortar and artillery fire, the battalion held its forward positions despite mounting casualties. A gap existing between 2/1 and the 77th Division was covered by fire, and Company F, linked with Company C of 1/1, had been temporarily attached to 3d Battalion for night defense.

Under its new commander, Lieutenant Colonel Richard F. Ross, Jr., 3/1 attempted to clear out reverse slope positions on Wana Ridge in a concerted tank-infantry effort. According to the plan, Company L and the tanks—each to be accompanied by one fire team—would attack up Wana Draw. Supporting this assault from the crest of the ridge would be the other two infantry companies in the battalion, prepared to attack straight across the ridge on order. Their objectives were Hill 55 and the ridge line to the east.

Company C, 1/1, was ordered to take over the 3d Battalion positions, when Lieutenant Colonel Ross' men jumped off in the assault. At about 1415, Company L began the slow advance against bitter opposition. Almost immediately, several of the escorting tanks were knocked out by mines and AT guns. Company K moved across the draw to Hill 55 at 1500, followed by I, which was pinned down almost immediately by extremely heavy mortar and machine gun fire and unable to advance beyond the middle of the draw. By 1800, Company K was on Hill 55 and tied in with 1/5, but could not push further east towards Shuri.

Because the rampaging enemy fire prevented Companies I and L from reaching the ridgeline and advancing up Wana Draw, they were withdrawn to that morning's line of departure positions. Company C of 1/1 was placed under the operational control of 3/1 for the night and occupied the positions held by Company I on 20 May. Here, it tied in with Company L on the right and on the left with Company F, 2/1. The miserable weather prevailing all day on 21 May worsened at midnight when the drizzle became a deluge and visibility was severely limited. Taking advantage of these conditions favoring an attacking force, an estimated 200 Japanese scrambled up Wana Ridge to strike all along the Company C line. In the midst of a fierce hand grenade battle, the enemy managed to overrun a few positions. These were recaptured at dawn, when the Marines regrouped, reoccupied the high ground, and restored their lines. In the daylight, approximately 180 enemy dead were counted in front of Marine positions.

Torrential rains beginning the night of 21-22 May continued on for many days thereafter. This downpour almost halted the tortuous 1st Division drive towards Shuri. Seriously limited before by terrain factors and a determined stand by the enemy in the Wana area, tank support became nonexistent when the zone of the 5th Marines, the only ground locally which favored armored tactics, became a sea of mud. Under these conditions aiding the Japanese defense, the 1st Division was faced with the alternatives of moving ahead against all odds or continuing the existing stalemate. To make either choice was difficult, for both presented a bloody prospect.

The Army's Fight

For IIIAC, the period 15-21 May was marked by the struggles of its divisions to capture two key strongpoints—Wana Draw and Sugar Loaf Hill. During this same seven days, XXIV Corps units fought a series of difficult battles to gain the strongly defended hills and ridges blocking the approaches to Shuri and Yonabaru. These barriers, incongruously named Chocolate Drop, Flat Top, Hogback, Love, Dick, Oboe, and Sugar, gained fleeting fame when they became the scenes of bitter and prolonged contests. But, when XXIV Corps units had turned the eastern flank of Shuri defenses and anticipated imminent success, the Army attack—like that of the Marines—became bogged down and was brought to a standstill when the rains came. On 15 May, the 77th Division continued its grinding advance in the middle of the Tenth Army line against the hard core of Thirty-second Army defenses at Shuri; 96th

Division troops, in coordination with their own assault against Dick Hill, supported the 77th Division attack on Flat Top Hill. Fighting on the left of the 96th, the 383d Infantry found it difficult and dangerous to move from Conical Hill because of overwhelming fire coming from a hill complex southwest of their location. In addition, the 89th Regiment tenaciously held formidable and well-organized defenses on the reverse slope of Conical, and prevented the soldiers from advancing farther south. On 16 May, 2/383 attacked down the southeast slope of the hill, but murderous enemy crossfire again prevented the soldiers from making any significant gains. A supporting platoon of tanks, however, ran the gantlet of fire sweeping the coastal flat and advanced 1,000 yards to enter the northwestern outskirts of Yonabaru, where the Shermans lashed the ruins of the town with 75mm and machine gun fire. Heavy Japanese fire covering the southern slopes of Conical prevented the infantry from exploiting the rapid armor penetration, however. After having exhausted their ammunition supply, the tanks withdrew to the line of departure.

On the division right flank, the 382d Infantry attempted to expand its hold on Dick Hill. In a violent bayonet and grenade fight, American troops captured some 100 yards of enemy terrain, but heavy machine gun fire from Oboe Hill--500 yards due south of Dick—so completely covered the exposed route of advance, the soldiers were unable to move any farther.

Fire from many of the same enemy positions which had held back 96th Division forces, also effectively prevented the 307th Infantry from successfully pushing the 77th Division attack on Flat Top and Chocolate Drop Hills. Both frontal and flanking movements, spearheaded by tanks, were held up by extremely accurate and vicious Japanese machine gun fire and mortar barrages.

Somewhat more successful on the 16th was the 305th Infantry, which threw the full weight of all of its supporting arms behind the attack of the 3d Battalion. Flamethrower tanks and medium tanks mounting 105mm howitzers slowly edged along the ridges leading to Shuri's high ground. Barring the way in this broken terrain were Okinawan burial vaults which the Japanese had occupied, fortified, and formed into a system of mutually supporting pillboxes. At the end of a ferocious day-long slugging match, this armored vanguard had penetrated 200 yards of enemy territory to bring the 77th Division to within 500 yards of the northernmost outskirts of Shuri.

A very successful predawn attack by the 77th Division on 17 May surprised the Japanese, forcing them to relinquish ground. Substantial gains were made and commanding terrain captured, including Chocolate Drop Hill and other nearby hills. Advancing abreast of each other, 3/305 and 2/307 dug in at the end of the day only a few hundred yards away from Shuri and Ishimmi. Although outflanked by 3/307, Flat Top defenders sent down a heavy volume of machine gun and mortar fire on the soldiers as they attempted to move across exposed country south of the hill. Troops following the assault elements spent daylight hours mopping up, sealing caves and burial vaults, and neutralizing those enemy strongpoints bypassed in the early-morning surprise maneuver.

Practically wiped out that day was the enemy 22d Regiment, which had defended Chocolate Drop, and whose remnants were still holding the reverse slopes of Flap Top and Dick Hills. Reinforcing these positions was the 1st Battalion of the 32d Regiment. On 17 May, this regiment was ordered by the 24th Division commander, Lieutenant General Tatsumi Amamiya, to take over the ground formerly held by the 22d Regiment, and to set in a Shuri defense line that would run from Ishimmi to Dick and Oboe Hills. Taking advantage of the natural, fortress-like properties of the region which they were to defend, the depleted 32d Regiment and survivors of the 22d were disposed in depth to contain potential American penetrations. Few reserves were available to the defenders should the Americans break through. On 17 May, the 96th Division ordered the 382d Infantry to attack and capture the hill mass south of Dick Hill and centering about Oboe. The failure of this effort indicated that the ground here needed to be softened up further before the infantry could advance. In the sector of Conical Hill held by the 383d, steady pressure from reverse slope defenders forced the division to commit into the line a third regiment—the 381st Infantry—to maintain the positions already held by the 96th. At this time, 3/381 assumed control of the left portion of the 2/383 sector on the eastern slope of the hill, and brought up its supporting weapons in preparation for a new attack.

While the remainder of 96th Division assault battalions held their lines and tank-infantry, demolition, and flamethrower teams mopped up in their immediate fronts, 3/381 made the division main effort. Operating to the west of the coastal road, medium tanks supported the attack by placing direct fire on machine gun positions on Hogback Ridge, a terrain feature running south from Conical Hill. Hogback's defenders disregarded the tank fire to place heavy machine gun and mortar barrages against the battalion attacking up finger ridges sloping down to the ocean. Although this heavy resistance limited the advance to only 400 yards, the division commander believed he could successfully attack through Yonabaru to outflank Shuri.

Both frontline divisions of XXIV Corps progressed on 18 May. Units of the 77th penetrated deeper into the heart of Shuri defenses by driving 150 yards farther south along the Ginowan-Shuri highway and advancing up to 300 yards towards Ishimmi. On 19 May, the 77th Division began a systematic elimination of Japanese firing positions in 110 Meter Hill, Ishimmi Ridge, and the reverse slopes of Flat Top and Dick Hills. All of these positions provided the enemy with good observation and clear fields of fire, commanding terrain over which the American division was advancing. Every weapon in the 77th arsenal capable of doing so was assigned to place destructive fire on the enemy emplacements. While these missions were being fired, the infantry fought off a series of counterattacks growing in size and fury as darkness fell. The enemy was finally turned back at dawn on 20 May when all available artillery was called down on them.

In the 96th Division zone on the 19th, the left regiment again made the main effort while the center and right regiments destroyed cave positions and gun emplacements in the broken ground between Conical and Dick Hills. Hogback Ridge and Sugar Hill, which rose sharply at the southern tip of this ridge to overlook Yonabaru, were bombarded by two platoons of medium tanks, six platoons of LVT(A)s, artillery, and organic infantry supporting weapons. The attack following this preparation failed, however, in the face of overwhelming enemy fire. Destruction of enemy positions spotted the day before did serve, however, to weaken further the faltering 89th Regiment defense. Returning to Hogback Ridge on 20 May, the attacking infantry made a grinding, steady advance down the eastern slopes of the ridge and finally reached Sugar Hill. Other 96th Division units also registered some significant gains that day; 383d Infantry assault battalions fought to within 300 yards of Love Hill, destroying those strongpoints that had blocked their progress for a week. The 382d Infantry finally reduced all enemy defenses on the southern and eastern slopes of Dick Hill, while it supported a successful 77th Division attack on Flat Top at the same time.

On gaining Flat Top Hill, the 307th Infantry was then ready to continue the attack south to Ishimmi Ridge and then on to Shuri. Coordinating its attack with the 1st Marines on its right, the 305th advanced down the valley highway 100-150 yards or to within 200 yards of the outskirts of Shuri. As a result of these gains, the 77th Division commander planned another predawn surprise attack, only this time on a coordinated division-wide level across the front.

Assault troops of the 307th Infantry jumped off at 0415 on 21 May in the zone of the 305th, advancing 200 yards without opposition. An hour later, leading elements had entered the northern suburbs of Shuri and were fighting their way up the eastern slopes of 110 Meter Hill. The 306th Infantry, which relieved the 305th later that morning, sent its 2d Battalion to the right of the line where visual contact was made with the 1st Marines. By nightfall, having spent most of the day mopping up bypassed positions, the 306th set up a night defense on a line running from the forward slopes of Ishimmi Ridge, through the outskirts of Shuri, to 110 Meter Hill.

The assault battalions of the 307th Infantry, the other 77th Division frontline regiment, jumped off at 0300 to take the regimental objective, a triangularly shaped mass consisting of three hills located in open ground about 350 yards south of Flat Top. The lead elements reached the objective at dawn, but following units were unable to exploit the successful maneuver when they were discovered by the enemy and pinned down by his frontal and flanking fire. Any further move forward was prohibited by this continuous and accurate fire, and the battalion was forced to dig in at nightfall on the ground then held.

Overall, the most important advances on 21 May in the XXIV Corps zone were made by 96th Division units. As 1/383 moved out against moderate opposition to take Oboe Hill, 2/383 paced the advance by attacking over exposed terrain to its southeast to take a hill approximately 400 yards from Shuri. At 1130, when enemy elements were noticed pulling out of their positions in front of the attacking infantry, the Japanese were fired upon as they retreated towards higher ground. Despite this withdrawal of the enemy, American forces were prevented from advancing any further during the day by isolated enemy counterattacks along the regimental lines. On Love Hill, enemy defenders who had successfully refused to yield ground during the past week again steadfastly maintained their positions on the 21st. They called down heavy and accurate artillery concentrations on American tank-infantry teams reaching the base of the hill and forced them to turn back.

The western slopes of Hogback Ridge were secured by 2/383 as the 3d Battalion, 381st Infantry, fought its way up the eastern slopes to the top of Sugar Hill. Every yard acquired during the day came because of the individual soldier's efforts in the face of fanatic enemy determination to hold. Nevertheless, advance elements of 3/381 were in position about 200 yards from the Naha-Yonabaru highway by nightfall. As a result of this hard-won success, a 700-yard-long corridor down the east coast of Okinawa was secured, giving promise that the final reduction of the Shuri redoubt might be launched from this quarter.

To strengthen the attack on Shuri, which General Hedge believed could be outflanked when he viewed the progress of the 96th Division, he alerted the 7th Infantry Division and ordered it to move to assembly areas immediately north of Conical Hill on 20 May. Two days later, the division was committed in the line and attacked to take the high ground south of Yonabaru.

Intermittent rain beginning on 21 May increased steadily to become soaking torrents before the assault infantry of the 7th Division was in jumpoff positions. In no time at all, "the road to Yonabaru from the north—the only supply road from established bases in the 7th Division zone . . . became impassable to wheeled vehicles and within two or three days disappeared entirely and had to be abandoned." Like the Tenth Army divisions on the west coast, those on the east were effectively stymied by the mud and the rain, which now seemed to be allied with General Ushijima and his Thirty-second Army.

Fighting The Weather

The Naha-Yonabaru valley served as a funnel through which American forces could pass to outflank Shuri. A major obstacle blocking the entrance to this route is the Ozato Hills, a rugged and complex terrain mass paralleling Nakagusuku Wan and lying between Yonabaru and the Chinen Peninsula. Since strong blocking positions were needed in the Ozato Hills to safeguard the left flank and rear of the force assigned to assault Shuri, the 184th Infantry of the 7th Division was ordered to take Yonabaru on 22 May and secure the high ground overlooking the village. In a surprise attack at 0200, 2/184 spearheaded a silently moving assault force which passed through Yonabaru quickly, and was on the crest of its objective—a hill south of the village — by daylight. When the enemy arose at dawn and emerged from cave shelters to man gun and infantry positions, he met sudden death under American fire. The Thirty-second Army was completely taken aback, for an American night attack was totally unexpected in this sector, much less an attack unsupported by armor. When the commander of the 184th saw that his initial effort was successful, he committed a second battalion and drove forward to secure other key points in the zone. By the end of the day, the regiment had advanced 1,400 yards and gained most of its objectives, even though rain and mud drastically hampered all phases of the operation. While the 7th Division scored for the Tenth Army on the east coast, IIIAC units pushed forward on the west. In the 6th Marine Division zone, the 4th Marines attacked to gain the northern bank of the Asato Gawa. The 1st and 3d Battalions advanced as 2/4 maintained positions on Half Moon Hill and kept contact with the 1st Marine Division. Assault troops seized the objective by 1230, when patrols crossed the shallow portion of the Asato and moved 200 yards into the outskirts of Naha before drawing any enemy fire. Frontline Marines dug in reverse slope positions along the northern bank of the river under the sporadic fire of heavy caliber artillery weapons and mortars. At 6th Division headquarters, plans were drawn for a river crossing on 23 May.

Although the flank divisions of the Tenth Army were making encouraging progress, the three divisions in the center of the line found success to be an elusive thing during the week of 22 May, A fanatic Japanese defense compounded the difficulties arising because of the steady rain. Supply, evacuation, and reinforcement were all but forestalled by the sea of mud, which caused the troops to wallow rather than maneuver. Under these conditions, infantry units could only probe and patrol ahead in their immediate zones.

The rain continued for nine days, and ranged from light, scattered showers to driving deluges. In the end, the entire southern front became a morass that bogged down both men and machines. Footing was treacherous in the mud swamps appearing in valley floors, and all slopes—from the gentlest to the most precipitous— were completely untrafficable. Because TAF planes had been grounded and could not fly airdrop missions, all supplies had to be manhandled to the front. Tired, wornout foot troops from both frontline and reserve units were pressed into action and formed into carrying parties.

Despite the unrelenting round-the-clock efforts of engineers to keep the road net between forward supply dumps and the frontlines in operating condition, continued use by trucks and amtracs finally caused the roads to be closed, but only after the mud itself had bemired and stalled the vehicles. As a result, division commanders found it impossible to build up and maintain reserve stocks of the supplies needed to support a full-scale assault. With the movement of American forces all but stopped, the entire front became stalemated. During the advance to the south, responsible Tenth Army agencies had reconnoitered both the east and west coasts of Okinawa behind the American lines in an attempt to find suitable landing and unloading sites. When discovered and found secure from enemy fire, they were developed and LSTs and other landing vessels were pressed into use to bring supplies down the coasts from the main beaches and dumps in the north. The two divisions deriving the major benefits from use of the overwater supply routes were the 6th Marine and 7th Infantry Divisions anchored on the open coasts. Behind the 1st Marine and 77th and 96th Infantry Divisions, in the center of the Tenth Army line, was a mired road net which prevented any resupply effort by vehicles coming both from the north and laterally from the coasts.

A sanguine outlook for continued advances by the Tenth Army flanking divisions was dispelled when they ran into resistance of the same type and intensity offered to the center units. A combination of this increased resistance and the appalling weather forestalled the potential envelopment and isolation of the main forces of the enemy, and forced the two coastal divisions into the same sort of deadlock the rest of the Tenth Army was experiencing.

Attacking to the west on 23 May, the 7th Division immediately ran into heavy resistance in the hills just north of the Yonabaru-Naha road. Both division assault regiments met increasingly stiff opposition during the day, because: "The Japanese realized that this advance along the Yonabaru-Naha road threatened to cut off the Shuri defenders. . . ." Even in the midst of the American attacks, the enemy attempted to infiltrate and counterattack.

At the same time that the 184th Infantry moved into the Ozato Hills and towards the mouth of the valley leading to Shuri, the 32d Infantry struck out to the west and southwest through Yonabaru to isolate the forces protecting the Thirty-second Army redoubt. Units spearheading the regimental drive were slowed and unable to advance in the face of the considerable machine gun and mortar fire coming from positions in the low hills east of Yonawa. Here, a mile southwest of Yonabaru, the regiment was forced to halt and dig in a line for the night because tanks, urgently needed to sustain the drive, had become immobilized by the mud.

On the west coast, despite the continuing rain during the night of 22-23 May, 6th Division patrols crossed and recrossed the Asato almost at will to feel out the enemy. Scouts from the 6th Reconnaissance Company patrolled the south bank of the upper reaches of the river, and reported back at 0718 that the stream was fordable at low tide, resistance was light, and no occupied positions had been found. Because the patrol reports of this and other units indicated "that it might be feasible to attempt a crossing of the Asato without tank support," early that morning General Shepherd ordered the 4th Marines to increase the number of reconnaissance patrols south of the river, and to be ready to cross it if enemy resistance proved light.

Between dawn and 1000 on the 23d, Marine lines received long-range machine gun and rifle fire from high ground near Machisi, but the patrols met no determined resistance at the river bank. General Shepherd decided to force a crossing here with two assault battalions of the 4th wading through ankle-deep water to the other side. At 1130, a firm bridgehead was established against only light resistance; 1/4 was dug in and prepared to continue the attack on the right, 3/4, on the left.

The regimental objective was a low ridge, running east to west, about 500 yards south of the river in the vicinity of Machisi. The attacking Marines approaching this point began to meet sharply increased opposition. Previous suspicions concerning the nature of the defenses here were confirmed when the infantry neared the height. In addition to reverse-slope mortar emplacements, the face of the height was studded with many Okinawan tombs that had been fortified. Darkness halted the attack 100 yards short of the objective, where the troops were ordered to organize and defend the high ground they held.

Although the Asato could be waded at the time of the assault crossing, strong, steady rain had turned it into a chest-high raging torrent by the next day. Supply and evacuation, difficult enough over the muddy terrain, now became almost impossible. At least 12 men were required to carry a stretcher case safely across the river to the rear. Supplies were sent forward under the same conditions; men stood in the water hour after hour under intense artillery and mortar fire, forming a human chain in a successful attempt to supply the advance companies. By midnight, the 6th Engineer Battalion had constructed two footbridges and was to have begun building a Bailey bridge, but heavy enemy fire during the afternoon prevented the engineers from bringing the components of the bridge forward.

General Geiger shifted the boundary between the two IIIAC divisions slightly to the right (west) to concentrate the corps attack on the right flank. At the same time, 2/4 could both contract its overexpanded lines and better protect the left flank and rear of the regimental bridgehead. As a result of this change, 3/5 relieved 2/4 at 1400, and the latter moved laterally to its right to ease the tension on the strained lines of 1/4.

No forward progress was marked in the center of the Tenth Army line on 23 May by the assault regiments of the 1st Marine and 77th and 96th Infantry Divisions. Activity in the immediate front of each division was limited to patrol action. Assessing the threat to Shuri by the American advances down both coasts, General Ushijima, his commanders, and his staff believed that the Thirty-second Army was "still able to halt the collapse of all positions by holding positions in depth to the line of Shichina and Kokuba" even though Marines "had broken into the city of Naha." This evaluation was tempered somewhat by the realization that Thirty-second Army troops would "be unable to maintain their Shuri front" if the American spearhead in the Naha-Yonabaru valley was not blunted. To stem the tide of the XXIV Corps attack against his positions north and east of Shuri, General Ushijima threw every available man into a defense line that began on the southwest slopes of Conical Hill, ran through Yonawa, and was anchored at the road junction in the village of Chan.

When the 7th Division attempted to expand its hold on the valley and the high ground to the south, the soldiers received ample proof of the presence of enemy reinforcements. Following increased and determined Japanese stands, which reach a climax in a series of counterattacks on the night of 24-25 May, the 7th Division ground to a halt, unable to push any further west. In sharp contrast to the stubborn and immediate reaction aroused by these efforts to gain the road net east of Shuri, a few

American patrols progressed slightly towards the Chinen Peninsula against only sporadic interference.

A break in the weather on 24 May was too short-lived to enable the Tenth Army to build up supply reserves, repair roads, or to attack in any great force. The enemy, however, took advantage of the brief respite to counterattack the 7th Infantry Division. In support of this ground action was Kikusui No. 7 and the airborne attack against Yontan airfield on 24-25 May.

Although their participation in the air defense of Okinawa was often more glaringly spectacular than destructive, on the night of 24 May, Marine and Army antiaircraft artillery battalions guarding Yontan and Kadena airfields scored heavily against Kamikaze raiders over the island. Marines manning 1st Provisional Antiaircraft Artillery Group guns were credited with destroying five planes, damaging six, downing one probable, and assisting in the destruction of another plane during this action.

In the entire month of May, Marine AAA gunners destroyed 8 planes, damaged 15, scored 5 probables, and had 1 assist. For the same period, the 53d AAA Brigade was alerted to 53 air raids in which 88 planes were tracked by its radar, gun directors, and guns. The May score of the brigade overall was 24 planes destroyed, 15 damaged (all by Marine AAA units), and 5 probables.

The clear weather permitting the flurry of enemy air activity held for a brief time only. The rains came again. Gravely concerned over the effects the weather was having on his division supply system, General Shepherd believed it necessary to establish firm vehicular and foot crossings over the now-rampaging Asato if 6th Division assault battalions were to be provided with adequate rations, ammunition, and medical supplies. In addition to replenishing Marine forces at the bridgehead, a well-stocked supply reserve would be required to support a continued attack to the south. At the same time that the 4th Marines sent probing patrols south to the vicinity of Machisi on the 24th, the regimental objective was bombarded by a heavy artillery concentration and an air strike—one of the first to be flown in clearing skies that day in support of ground forces. The 6th Engineer Battalion bridge builders who had labored throughout the night to erect some sort of crossing over the Asato, began putting together a Bailey bridge at dawn. Working all morning and part of the afternoon under enemy artillery and mortar shelling, the Marine engineers finished the bridge at 1400 and opened it for traffic 45 minutes later. A pile bridge, to be utilized as a tank bypass, was completed at 1840. Informing the division commander that the passage was open, the commanding officer of the engineer battalion matter-of-factly added: ". . . tanks should cross as soon as possible as arty [artillery] is falling in area."

To intensify 4th Marines efforts south of the river, 3/22 moved into the line on the division left, relieving 2/4 at 1000 on the 24th. Once in position, Lieutenant Colonel Clair W. Shisler's battalion tied in with 3/5 and 1/4. At this time, the 2d Battalion moved across the river "to relieve the battered 3/4 on the right" of the 4th Marines line. The 3d Battalion became regimental reserve and moved to an assembly area in the rear where it held muster; none of its companies had over 90 men. Major Walker's 6th Reconnaissance Company, which had been attached to the 4th Marines on 23 May as regimental reserve, reverted to division control when the 1st Battalion, 29th Marines, was ordered to an assembly area just south of the Asato. In order to beef up Colonel Shapley's reserve for the continuation of the drive south, 1/29 was attached to the 4th in place of the scouts.

With the rain beating down once again, the 4th Marines attacked on 25 May to capture that part of the regimental objective near Machisi not taken on the 23d. Although severely restricted by the deep mud and limited visibility, assault infantry seized the greater part of the north-south ridgeline lying west of the village. At 1030, the 4th overcame determined Japanese defenders entrenched on the reverse slope and occupied the objective. Once the captors had reorganized their forces and consolidated the newly won positions, they prepared to carry on further. The attack now progressed slowly as assault troops forged ahead against a storm of frontal and flanking fires. When the regiment halted for the day at 1630, the battalions established firm contact along the line and dug in night defenses. During the preinvasion rehearsal phase 6th Division training had emphasized village and street fighting. This training was first put into practical use on the 25th when attacking troops entered the eastern outskirts of Naha and came under fire from Japanese-defended houses. The heavy fire from these as well as from the many burial vaults along the ridges in this area inflicted numerous casualties in the Marine units.

Effectively dividing this section of Naha into two separate zones of action was a canal connecting the Asato River and the estuary of the Kokuba. The waterway was 20 yards wide, had a thick mud bottom, and stone banks 3 to 5 feet high.

As the 4th Marines fought in the eastern portion of Naha, the 6th Reconnaissance Company crossed the Asato to enter the once-urban, now-razed, area of Naha west of the canal. Major Walker's men quickly cleared a sector of snipers and a few disorganized troops, and set up defenses for the night. At 1900, the engineers completed construction of a footbridge across the mouth of the Asato. The bridge was anchored on the southern bank behind the defense perimeter of the scouts, and on the northern bank in front of 2/22, which manned the lines of the 22d Marines. Company G of the battalion was assigned as a clutch unit to relieve or support the reconnaissance company upon order.

Although the reconnaissance company had experienced a relatively quiet night, the two assault battalions of the 4th Marines spent the hours of darkness in fighting off counterattacks. At 2000, 1/4 reported that the enemy was forming up approximately 200-250 yards in front of its positions and had begun smoking Marine lines. A Japanese mortar barrage preceded the counterattack, which was broken up almost immediately under a mixed artillery and mortar shelling that continued on for another two hours without letup. Later, at midnight, when Company E, 2/4, was hit by a counterattack, it was immediately reinforced by a platoon from 1/29. After a two-hour-long hand grenade duel, in which the Marines suffered only light casualties, the enemy was successfully repelled.

Across most of the rest of the Tenth Army front on the 25th, high water and mud limited activity to patrol actions. The 7th Infantry Division, however, which had forced the enemy from commanding terrain features and inserted an opening wedge into the southeastern defenses of Shuri on 24 May, continued its vigorous drive on the 25th. Additional key positions were secured against ever-stiffening resistance and under conditions of terrain and weather that favored the enemy. Limiting the 7th Division attack was the problem of getting supplies forward, after its only supply route to the front sank in a sea of mud under the ravages of continuous use. In the 96th Division zone, troops holding positions south and west of Conical Hill were all but isolated from rear area facilities of the division. Suffering serious losses under a rash of small counterattacks and continual attempts by the enemy to infiltrate, the depleted infantry companies holding the line were forced to utilize all available manpower from battalion and regimental service and support units. The frontline units put these soldiers into the line as riflemen or assigned them to the tremendously wearing task of hand-carrying supplies forward over the muddy ground. Descriptive of these agonized efforts is a comment made by one of the 96th's officers, who said: "Those on the forward slopes slid down. Those on the reverse slopes slid back. Otherwise, no change."

A happy change in these gloomy reports of a bogged-down campaign—and possibly a favorable portent for the future—occurred on 26 May, when it appeared as though the enemy was pulling out of Shuri. Observers at the 1st and 5th Marines regimental observation posts (OPs) reported that there was a good deal of enemy movement south, and thus prompted the 1st Marine Division G-2 to request air observation of the suspected area at 1200.

Despite hazardous flying conditions in rain and poor visibility, which in themselves would limit the value and amount of information gained, a spotter plane was catapulted from the *New York* almost immediately after receipt of the G-2 request. Upon arrival over the target area, the airborne observer confirmed the presence of a large number of Japanese troops and vehicles clogging the roads leading south from Shuri.

Within 13 minutes after this sighting, the USS *New Orleans* had fired the first salvo in a continued devastating barrage that was brought to bear on the withdrawing enemy by artillery, mortars, the main and secondary batteries of gunfire support ships, and the machine guns and bombs of Marine aircraft that had risen from rain-sodden fields to harry the enemy from above. Commenting on the part played by gunfire support ships at this point, the naval gunfire officer in the IIIAC staff recalled: "the *New York* was some distance from the beach but the *New Orleans* was close in. The *New Orleans* heard the report of the *New York's* plane and asked the spotter for coordinates. She positioned herself and began adjustment by full salvos of main battery. . . . Other firing ships and support craft with H&I [Harassing and Interdiction] missions or otherwise in the area, noticed the increased activity, sent up planes, and got into the act. Ships without planes asked to be cut in with ships that did have them and often a plane spotter was firing two or more ships at the same time." Enemy hopes for a successful withdrawal under the inclement weather conditions were shattered by the massed fires which caught and blasted some 3,000-4,000 Japanese troops with their tanks, vehicles, and artillery pieces in the open. The pilots of observation planes zoomed through the overcast to treetop height and lower to count and report back an estimated 500 enemy killed.

The continuing stubborn reluctance on the part of some Japanese to give way to the Americans seemed to belie the fact that General Ushijima's forces were indeed withdrawing. The Tenth Army found that only local attacks and patrols could be accomplished in the rain against enemy resistance. Even limited forward movement directed towards the heart of Shuri aroused heavy and immediate response, and indicated that Japanese inner defenses were holding firm. Light resistance was found only along the coasts; in the IIIAC zone on the right, where the 6th Reconnaissance Company held the levelled and deserted Naha, and in the east, where patrols of the 184th Infantry approached Chinen Peninsula.

Following the discovery of the enemy withdrawal and the initial bombardments placed on his movements, artillery batteries and gunfire support ships fired continuous harassing and interdiction missions on all routes, road junctions, and crossroads in the area leading south from Shuri. To keep the enemy disorganized and unable to make a stand, and to exploit the implications inherent in the Japanese withdrawal, General Buckner sent the following message to his two corps commanders on 27 May: "Indications point to possible enemy retirement to new defensive position with possible counteroffensive against our forces threatening his flank. Initiate without delay strong and unrelenting pressure to ascertain probable intentions and keep him off balance. Enemy must not repeat not be permitted to establish himself securely on new position with only nominal interference."

Continued rains and their subsequent effect on the terrain precluded a full-scale attack all along the front. Therefore, the Tenth Army settled for aggressive patrol action against the remaining Japanese strongpoints facing its lines. Apparently contradicting what influence the previous day's withdrawal should have had on the tactical situation, patrol reports reading "Does not appear that resistance has lessened," or "No indication of Japanese withdrawal," implied that Shuri would not yet, if ever, fall easily. Assault units of the 7th Infantry Division, driving west from Yonabaru, ran into 62d Division elements hastily committed by General Ushijima to shore up his threatened right flank. On the far left flank of the Tenth Army, advance patrols of the 184th Infantry reached Inasomi, approximately two miles southwest of Yonabaru, without meeting any organized resistance. To contain the overall threat this potentially deep penetration posed to Japanese defenses in the south, the Thirty-second Army moved additional troops of the 62d Division down from Shuri.

On the opposite flank of Tenth Army, early on the 27th, Company G, 2/22, moved across the Asato, passed through reconnaissance company lines, and pressed well into Naha against only slight resistance. At the same time, patrols from the 4th Marines moved 200-300 yards ahead of regimental lines to take advantage of the apparent enemy weakness here. Lieutenant Colonel Woodhouse was ordered at 0915 to move the rest of his battalion across the river, and nearly two hours later 2/22 was directed to attack and seize the high ground approximately 100 yards north of the Kokuba estuary. The 4th Marines received the same order to seize the rest of Naha. Colonel Shapley attacked with 1/4 on the left, 2/4 on the right; 3/4 filled in on the left flank between 3/22 and 1/4.

Following a pre-attack nine-battalion artillery preparation, 6th Division forces advanced abreast at 1230 against light opposition, reached the objective at approximately 1700, and dug in for night defense at 1900, when regimental lines were tied in all around. Actually, occupation of the objective in force amounted to the same thing that had been accomplished by patrols that morning. Badly in need of rest after a 10-day tour in the lines, the 4th Marines was alerted that it would be relieved by the 29th Marines; the changeover was scheduled to begin at 0630 the next morning.

Another important change in the ICEBERG command structure occurring in May took place on the 27th, when the Fifth Fleet once again became the Third Fleet and Admiral Halsey took over the responsibility for supporting the ICEBERG campaign from Admiral Spruance. As in February, when the latter had taken over from Halsey, the ships and men of the fleet remained the same, only the numerical designations of the task groupings changed (i.e., TF 58 became TF 38, etc.). At the same time that this command change was effected, General Buckner became directly responsible for CinCPOA for the defense and development of captured positions in the Ryukyus.

Large-scale movements were still impracticable on 28 May because of the mud, although: "The morning . . . was clear with no rain." Despite the limited trafficability of both roads and terrain, local commanders hewed to the concept of General Buckner's directive of the previous day and maintained constant and continuous pressure on enemy forces, In the XXIV Corps zone, the 184th Infantry deepened the 7th Division salient in the Ozato Hills by moving to within 1,000 yards of Shinzato, a village located where Chinen Peninsula joined the mainland. Less satisfactory progress was registered for the units driving west, as 62d Division blocking forces held up other 7th Division troops. Strongly held positions southwest of Conical Hill frustrated 96th Division attempts altogether, and the 77th Division made little or no headway against a determined defense of Shuri heights. At the end of the day, XXIV Corps gains were negligible and inconclusive. Despite reports of increased troop withdrawals, the enemy's obstinate reluctance to yield indicated that General Ushijima either had established a strong rearguard to protect the withdrawal or that he was in fact not abandoning Shuri.

In the IIIAC sector, Marines were no more successful in prosecuting their portion of the war and had no easier time of it than had the Army units. In its attack on 110 Meter Hill, 2/1 was covered by the fires of 3/1 and 3/306. Once 2/1 had gained its objective, 3/1 was to advance down Wana Draw. The 2d Battalion gained the hilltop twice, only to be thrown back by mortar barrages coming from reverse slope emplacements and vicious machine gun fire raking positions on the crest from three directions. Lieutenant Colonel James C. Magee, Jr., believed that, even if his battalion succeeded in carrying the hill, "it could not possibly hold it against a strong counterattack." Heavy casualties had depleted the size of the battalion to a point where its total effective strength was 277 men; no rifle company could muster more than a total of 99 Marines.

At first glance, it would appear as though reinforcement of the battalion at this time might possibly have tipped the scales of victory in favor of the Marines and enabled them to capture 110 Meter Hill. Replacements were available; the 1st Marine Division had received a total of 53 officers and 1,255 enlisted men in the three-day period of 27-29 May, when the 57th, 59th, and 63d Replacement Drafts arrived at Okinawa. The division was precluded by IIIAC orders, however, from inserting these fresh troops into the line during a battle situation, the course of which depended upon close teamwork by experienced veterans. Only after several days of indoctrination and training in reserve areas could the men be sent forward. Infantry replacements were at a premium in any case because of the heavy losses sustained by the rifle regiments. This condition existed even though over 350 emergency replacements had been assigned from division special and service troops to the infantry regiments in mid-May and the regular "flow of Marine replacements was beyond expectations." Nonetheless, despite this constant infusion of new Marines, at no time during the drive to the south were 1st Division infantry regiments able to exceed more than 85 percent of effective T/O strength. To the commanders of undermanned companies and battalions in this period of the campaign, immediate reinforcement was not only desirable—it was of paramount importance. From the point of view of senior commanders, such as the regimental commander of the 1st Marines: "the existence of a replacement pool which could not, at the moment, be used for combat proved to be extremely valuable. At the end of May, when the rainy period had rendered the roads and the countryside impassable to anything on wheels or tracks, the supply of forward troops became most critical. Something like 500 replacements, if any recollection is correct, were available to the 1st Marines; these men were formed into man-pack trains, under the direction of the executive officer. Their exhausting struggles, heavily laden, through mud which even an unburdened man found difficult to negotiate were the solution to the supply problem at this time, though with no margin to spare."

Even though 2/1 and other assault units could not be reinforced, supply support from non-committed elements permitted them to concentrate on the immediate problem of fighting the enemy. Late on the 28th, after being withdrawn to that morning's jump-off position, organic crew-served weapons of 2/1 worked over the reverse slopes of 110 Meter Hill as the battalion lines were themselves raked by the continual fire of Japanese flat-trajectory cannon. With unabated fury and determined fanaticism, the enemy stood his ground and even sought to infiltrate 2/1 lines after dark when many Japanese soldiers were killed.

Also on 28 May, patrols from 3/1 penetrated some 300 yards into Wana Draw under intense machine gun and rifle fire. At 1600, Colonel Mason ordered the battalion to clear all Japanese troops from the draw, but the battalion commander's request that the attack be delayed until the following morning instead, in order that he might organize and concentrate his forces for the drive, was approved.

The 1st Division concluded that: "The beginning of the end for Shuri came on the 28th." Although rear-guard action continued unrelentingly in the high ground north of the city in the 77th Division zone, the 5th Marines attacked at 0730, captured the village of Asato, and 1/5 patrolled 300 yards beyond that without appreciable opposition. During the same day, the 306th Infantry managed to mop up the area approximately 150 yards in front of its lines. On the corps boundary, 3/306 sent strong patrols forward, coordinating their movements with those of 2/1. By dark, 1/307--to the left of the 306th—attacked the high ground east of Shuri against determined opposition. Despite the fact that it was bitterly opposed and repulsed by heavy mortar fire initially, the battalion inched forward under the cover of smoke and managed to dig in for the night. While the 1st and 77th Divisions were moving slowly forward, the 29th Marines began relieving the 4th in position. Enemy shelling during the relief added to the more than 1,100 casualties already sustained by Colonel Shapley's regiment. Beginning at daylight, 3/29 relieved 1/4 and 3/4, the elements on the left of the 4th Marines line, 1/29 moved into the western portion of Naha relieving 2/4, and 2/29--in regimental reserve—moved to an assembly area near Colonel Whaling's CP. Upon its relief, the 4th Marines marched and motored to beach areas near Machinato airfield, where it became 6th Division reserve.

Continuing to advance after passage of the 2/4 lines, 1/29 moved abreast of and then paced the attack of the 22d Marines. The direction of the battalion attack changed to the southwest when Company C pivoted on Company A—on the right boundary—and gained 250 yards through the rubble of Naha. Heavy small arms fire and a scattered mortar and artillery shelling followed the Marines, who finally set in a night defense along a line 800 yards from the Kokuba. Here visual contact was established with the 22d Marines across the canal on the right, and with 3/29 on the left flank.

The 22d Marines had moved out on the 28th before dawn, At that time, 1/22 passed through the lines of the 2d Battalion to take up the assault in the direction of the banks of the Kokuba estuary, west of the canal running through Naha. Moving rapidly against only slight resistance, its flanks and rear protected by 2/22, the battalion captured its objective by 0845.

General Shepherd then assigned the task of defending western Naha to his reconnaissance company in order to release the 22d Marines for further offensive action to the east against Japanese positions in the Kokuba hills. Major Walker was first notified of the scouts' new assignment at 1030, when he received the following message from the division G-3, Lieutenant Colonel Victor H. Krulak: "Reposing great confidence in your integrity and political ability you are hereby named acting mayor of Naha. The appointment effective 1600 carries all pay and emoluments accruing to office. To be collected from Imperial Treasury."

Shortly after midday, the 6th Engineer Battalion was ordered to reconnoiter all bridge crossings over the canal. Also, it was to install a jeep crossing and at least two foot bridges over the canal prior to 0400 on the 29th to facilitate the 22d Marines attack east of the Kokuba. The engineers worked in the dark in front of Marine lines under a constant downpour of rain and shells, as they manhandled the bridge construction material up to the various bridging sites. The task was completed at 0420. At 0430, elements of 1/22 were across the canal and organized on the eastern shore. This was the division's third opposed river crossing in 20 days. The attack began a half hour later and the Marines made some immediate progress against scattered machine gun and rifle fire. Supporting the assault was 2/22, while the 3d Battalion followed in reserve. At 0845, 1/22 made contact with 1/29 and the two infantry battalions pushed on abreast of each other. As spearhead elements approached the hills north of Kokuba, increased resistance indicated that the enemy was positioned there in strength. Because of the hard fighting and numerous casualties experienced by 1/22, at 1500 2/22 was alerted to relieve it, when the situation permitted, on the ground then held. Since the 1st Battalion was heavily engaged at the time, its commander advised against the relief being effected then. Instead, Companies E and G were committed into the line at 1800 to reinforce the night defenses of the regiment.

Until darkness fell the 6th Division assault regiments continued the attack in an effort to reduce the strong enemy position encountered earlier that afternoon. Aggravating the situation was the fact that the routes of approach to these Japanese emplacements were across open ground that afforded the attacking Marines little or no cover from the fire of well-dug-in machine guns and mortars. The position itself was centered on a small group of hills on which were located several radio towers that had been demolished in air raids when the rest of Naha was razed earlier. Rain and mud precluded the use of vital armor support. It still remained an infantryman's war.

On the same day, 29 May, the 29th Marines attacked to the south and then cut east in order to come abreast of the 22d Marines; the 29th's objective was the high ground immediately northwest of Shichina. Like the 22d Marines approach route, that of the 29th was over low and open ground, causing the regimental commander to comment that the terrain was "about as suitable to fighting as a billiard table." The 1st Battalion maintained a slow, steady pace against moderate resistance, and dug in at dark slightly to the left rear of 3/22, on the regimental boundary. The 3d Battalion of the 29th paced the advance of 1/29, but 3/5 on the left had advanced so rapidly during the day that 3/29 was forced to bring its lines forward some 600 yards at the end of the day to maintain firm contact with the 5th Marines.

Tuesday, 29 May 1945, is a significant date in the history of the Okinawa campaign, for it was on this day elements of the 1st Marine Division captured Shuri Castle. This ancient redoubt, once the seat of the rulers of Okinawa, had served as General Ushijima's center for controlling the defense of the island.

The 5th Marines attack began at 0730; 1/5 on the left, 3/5 on the right. The 3d Battalion jumped off with Company L in assault. Enemy machine gun, mortar, and small arms fire was placed on the attacking Marines but was unable to prevent them from advancing a total of 600 yards at day's end. Following Company L, Companies I and K moved out later in the morning in an attempt to strengthen and protect the left of the battalion line, but enemy mortars positioned west of Shuri fired a furious barrage that seriously limited forward movement. Despite the efforts to destroy them by bazooka fire, the mortars remained active and held the companies back. The battalion night defense set up at dusk showed 3/5 lines cutting back sharply from the left of Company L's exposed position to tie in with 1/5 at Shuri Ridge. The 1st Battalion moved rapidly over muddy terrain against little opposition and immediately occupied Shuri's ridge crest in close proximity to the castle. From this position, at approximately 0930, Lieutenant Colonel Charles W. Shelburne, the battalion commander, requested permission to send one of his assault companies to storm the apparently lightly manned fortification. Despite the fact that the castle itself was within the zone of the 77th Infantry Division, General de Valle granted the request when it was forwarded to him for approval. He believed that the capture of this enemy strongpoint would favorably effect and shorten the campaign; this opportunity, therefore, had to be seized at once. Shortly after the island was secured, General del Valle offered the opinion that "at that time the position of the 77th Division was such that it would have taken several hard days' fighting through enemy resistance," if he had waited for the tactical situation to unfold normally.

Bowling over the few Japanese that were in their way, Marines from Company A, 1/5, drove east along the ridge and right into the castle itself, securing it at 1015. The 77th Division had programmed an air strike and a heavy artillery bombardment on the bastion for 29 May and had received warning of the attack of the 5th Marines only a few short minutes before it was mounted. Fortunately for the Marines, General Bruce and his staff worked frantically to contact all supporting arms and were just "barely able to avert called strikes in time."

The air and artillery preparation of Shuri by the 77th Division resulted from General Bruce's decision on the 28th to attack the next day, weather permitting. The 1st Marine Division had given him no indication that it planned to enter the zone of the 77th, for: "Had timely notice been given and the move been properly coordinated," the Army commander believed "the 77 Div could have rendered adequate support to the Marines."

Overshadowing this near tragedy was the fact that Company A success resulted from the close teamwork of Tenth Army support and assault troops who had not permitted the enemy to relax for an instant. Without this unrelenting pressure, the breakthrough would not have been possible.

To profit from the 1/5 gain, General del Valle quickly revised his attack plan and sent 3/1 through the lines of the 5th Marines to relieve 1/5. At 1400, the relief had been effected and 1/5 continued the attack south. The commander of 3/1 immediately set up his battalion in perimeter defense around the battered walls of the castle. Augmenting this defense were two companies from 1/1 which fought their way into assigned positions that faced north, and tied in with the lines of 3/1. Upon the 5th Marines sweep into Shuri, the 1st Marines was ordered to follow the attack closely; 3/1 was to relieve 1/5, and 1/1, tailing 3/1 around Hill 55, was to attack east into the yet-unoccupied sector north of Shuri. Moving out in a column of companies, the battalion crossed the line of departure in front of Hill 55, where the leading element came under intensive fire from a heavy machine gun hidden in a deep and rugged cut a few hundred yards south of bypassed Wana Draw. Unable to either silence the weapon or attack through its curtain of fire, the battalion axis of advance was angled to the right and the troops eventually made contact with 3/1 south of Shuri. While 1/1 and 3/1 hit Shuri from the west, the 2d Battalion was ordered to hold Wana Ridge, from which it was to provide fire support to regimental assault elements. To augment and increase this effort, "all battalion headquarters personnel, cooks, wiremen, and stretcher bearers were sent forward to help man the lines."

At no time after the capture of Shuri Castle was there any indication that the Japanese defenders of the hills north of the city were either being worn down or concerned with the Americans positioned in their rear. Reports from Tenth Army units all along the line gave proof that Japanese resistance remained undiminished. Only in a goodly portion of Chinen Peninsula, scouted by 7th Division troops during the day, was there little or no opposition.

Offsetting the relatively unhindered advance down the coasts by Tenth Army flanking divisions, a vividly contrasting picture was presented by the massive struggle down the center of the island. Despite the efforts of General Buckner's forces to execute a mass double envelopment successfully and encircle the bulk of General Ushijima's troops at Shuri, all signs pointed up the fact that the Japanese rear guard had accomplished its mission well; the greatest portion of the units defending Shuri had indeed escaped to the south.

Chapter 9. Breakout to the South

Japanese Withdrawal

Threatened by an American frontal encroachment upon their Shuri defenses and an envelopment of their flanks by the Tenth Army divisions driving down the east and west coasts of Okinawa, the Japanese were forced to reevaluate thoroughly the battle plans adopted in March. On the night of 22 May, General Ushijima convened at his headquarters a conference of his principal commanders and staff officers. The major and only item on the agenda of this momentous meeting was a discussion of how best to prevent—or at least to postpone—the disaster engulfing the Thirty-second Army. Contingency plans calling for a massive defense centering about Shuri had been included in final battle preparations completed before 1 April 1945. All Japanese units located elsewhere on Okinawa and still able to fight would withdraw on order for a last-ditch stand in the vicinity of the Thirty-second Army headquarters. Tactical conditions at the time of this conference indicated that, to hold Shuri, approximately 50,000 Japanese soldiers would have to be compressed into a final defense sector less than a mile in diameter. These close quarters would not permit an effective defense, but would, in fact, make the defenders "easy prey" for the massive American fire which would undoubtedly seek them out from all directions. Although many Japanese long-range artillery pieces were still in firing condition, the constricted space factors around Shuri prevented their proper emplacement and subsequently efficient employment.

In a discussion of the alternatives to remaining at Shuri, Ushijima's staff considered two other defensive areas—Chinen Peninsula, and the Kiyamu Peninsula at the southern tip of Okinawa. The hills, cliffs, and lack of roads on Chinen presented a group of formidable natural defenses, especially against tank-infantry tactics. Militating against a choice of this area were the lack of sufficient caves and prepared positions to hold the entire Thirty-second Army and the inadequacy of ammunition supplies that had been stockpiled there. Another disadvantage ruling out Chinen was the poor road net, which would equally hamper the Japanese and the Americans. Finally, in face of these considerations and the route that would have to be taken to the peninsula, Thirty-second Army units would find it difficult to reconcentrate and reorganize speedily at the same time that they would undoubtedly be waging a hard fight during disengagement and withdrawal. The weight of the evidence against Chinen ruled it out quickly. It appeared to the Thirty-second Army staff that Kiyamu Peninsula was the best area in which to develop a solid defense for prolonging the battle. This area, dominated by the Yaeju Dake-Yuza Dake Escarpment, contained a sufficient number of natural and manmade caves in which to store supplies and protect troops against American bombardments. The terrain on the peninsula had been defensively organized earlier by the 24th Division, which also had cached a large store of ammunition and weapons there before it was ordered north into the Shuri defenses. As opposed to the poor road net into Chinen, all roads south led directly to the proposed new positions and would permit the army to make a rapid mass movement. On the other hand, Tenth Army tanks also could move south quickly over these roads, but only to the outpost defenses of the sector. American tanks would be denied passage beyond this point by the sheer cliffs, steep hills, and deep ridges of the region. In this broken terrain, the infantry would be on its own.

Not all of the senior Japanese leaders approved the planned withdrawal. One dissenter was General Fujioka, commander of the 62d Division. His objection was based on a compassion for the thousands of severely wounded men who could not be taken south. General Fujioka felt most strongly about this point because it was his division that had originally been assigned to defend Shuri, and it was his officers and men who had taken the brunt of American attacks on the city. He contended, therefore, that their desire to fight to the last in their present positions should be fulfilled.

Supporting the anticipated withdrawal was General Suzuki, commander of the 44th Independent Mixed Brigade, who tempered his approval with the stipulation that the army move into the Chinen Peninsula positions that his forces had previously developed. Fully supporting the move to Kiyamu were Generals Amamiya and Wada, commanders of the 24th Division and 5th Artillery Command, respectively. General Amamiya reinforced his argument with information that his 24th Transportation Regiment had been able both to salvage and to preserve enough trucks to transfer the army ammunition reserve in five nights' time if weather conditions permitted.

Not long after weighing all of these arguments, General Ushijima ordered the move to Kiyamu. The first transportation to head south left Shuri at midnight, 23 May, carrying wounded and a portion of the ammunition supply. The main body of the Thirty-second Army was scheduled to begin the trek southward on 29 May.

According to the army plan, the new defensive dispositions would be as follows:

The 44th IMB was to move from positions on the westernmost flank of the Shuri front to take up defense positions on a line running from Hanagusuku on the east coast to Yaeju Dake.

The 24th Division would occupy the commanding heights of the Yaeju Dake-Yuza Dake escarpment, the ridges of Mezado and Kunishi, and Nagusuku, on the west coast.

Elements of the above two units would establish and defend an outpost line—and the zone forward of it—which would run from Itoman through Yunagusuku to Gushichan.

The heavily depleted forces of the 62d Division would occupy defenses along the coast in the rear of the main battle line; at these positions the division could reorganize, and, at the same time, be prepared to reinforce threatened sections of the line.

The firing batteries of the 5th Artillery Command were to be emplaced within the confines of a triangularly shaped area formed by Kunishi, Makabe, and Medeera, in direct support of the defense line.

Admiral Ota's Okinawa Naval Base Force was assigned as reserve and would move on order to an assembly area in the center of the Kiyamu defense sector.

Each unit breaking contact with the Americans on the Shuri line was to leave a sufficiently strong force in position to keep the Americans occupied long enough to permit a successful withdrawal. Posing a threat to this plan was the penetration of 7th Infantry Division elements through Yonabaru. To oppose them, remnants of the 62d Division were to disengage and pull out of the Shuri front on the night of 25 May, and then move through Tsukasan to counterattack the Tenth Army spearhead. Replacing the 62d in the line was the comparatively strong and rested 22d Independent Infantry Battalion, which had been in reserve during the fighting in April and May. The orders to General Fujioka were both explicit and simple: "Annihilate the enemy rushing from the Yonabaru area." In addition, a secondary mission laid on, should the primary fail, was to slow or stop the American advance for a period long enough to permit the main body of the Thirty-second Army to escape.

To give General Ushijima time to organize his new dispositions on Kiyamu, the force remaining on the Shuri front was to hold until 31 May. Behind it, withdrawing units would leave other rear guard elements to hold a strong defense line running along the Kokumba River to the hills north of Tsukasan and Chan until the night of 2 June. At that time, the line would then cut south through Karadera to the east coast. Approximately 2,000 yards further south, another temporary line—this one centered on Tomusu—would be established and held until the night of 4 June. Thirty-second Army staff planners believed that the time gained during holding actions along these lines would permit the organization and manning of the final outpost zone. Before beginning its own retreat south, the composite naval unit on Oroku Peninsula was to guard the western flank of the withdrawal route.

All available replacements were thrown in the disintegrating Shuri front on 23 May, when the onsurging Tenth Army forced the enemy to bolster his defenses. On 24 May, the first Japanese walking wounded began leaving caves that passed as hospitals. Many terminal cases, too seriously wounded to be moved, were either killed with a lethal injection of morphine, or—less mercifully—left behind to suffer a more lingering end without the relief-giving drug. Limited medical care of the wounded, because of circumstances rather than willful neglect, appears to have been commonplace, judging from the following description of conditions: "At one time there were almost 90 men in the cave, lying on the ground in the mud in pitch darkness, except when a doctor or corpsman would come around with a light and ask them how they felt. Medical supplies were very low, so very little could be done to care for the wounded. Men died on all sides. Filth accumulated. In the heavy rains, water poured into the cave and the wounded almost drowned. The smell was so bad that they could hardly breathe."

In accordance with the schedule of the withdrawal plan, on the night of 25 May some 3,000 men remaining in the 62d Division moved into positions blocking the drive of the 7th Infantry Division. The enemy expected that the continuing bad weather would aid their efforts in this sector considerably. This expectation was valid, but only to the degree that the rain put greater obstacles in the way of the successful American drive than did the Japanese infantry. Reinforcing the 62d and coming under its command were the 7th Heavy Artillery and 23d Shipping Engineer Regiments, which left their defenses on Chinen Peninsula to occupy holding positions on the right of the division. Owing to the failure of the 62d Division to accomplish its mission, General Ushijima was convinced that it was necessary to evacuate Shuri while he still had the time. On 28 May, he ordered that the withdrawal was to begin on the following evening. The Naval Base Force, misinterpreting the order, jumped the gun by withdrawing to Kiyamu ahead of time. Admiral Ota's force was intercepted and sent back to Oroku Peninsula to take up its assigned positions west of the Japanese escape route.

On the night of 29 May, the 24th Division moved out of the lines in orderly fashion, leaving one-third of the 32d Regiment and the 22d IIB as a covering force. While the division evaded the Tenth Army and headed south, the 44th IMB remained in blocking positions outside of Naha and the 62d Division was likewise defensively disposed near Chan and Karadera.

With the arrival of dawn on Wednesday, 30 May 1945, the greater portion of the Thirty-second Army had successfully postponed its final reckoning at the hands of the Tenth Army by withdrawing from Shuri and out of the grasp of General Buckner's flanking divisions. Having taken advantage of the heavy rains and the accompanying poor visibility, General Ushijima had executed a "properly deft withdrawal" to establish new army headquarters outside of Mabuni, 11 miles south of Shuri, in a cave deep within Hill 89. By then, his covering forces were in position to slow down a Tenth Army pursuit and thereby give the Thirty-second Army a bit more time to organize the defense of Kiyamu Peninsula.

The Pursuit

American attempts to exploit the successful breakthrough at Shuri and maintain incessant pressure on the reeling Thirty-second Army were frustrated on 30 May by an electrical storm accompanied by torrential rains on an already-saturated landscape. Movement of all Tenth Army units was effectively halted by the mud. Amphibious craft and vehicles were employed on both coasts to give logistic support to the two corps and enabled the ground commanders to maintain at least minimum supply levels. Out of a total of 916 missions of all sorts flown by VMTB-232 in May, 74 were supply air drops in support of frontline troops and advance patrols. In spite of the submarginal flying conditions and limited visibility on 30 May, the squadron flew 12 air drop missions to the 1st Marine Division. General del Valle expressed his appreciation to Major Feldmeier's pilots in a message which read in part: "Those pilots have guts!" This congratulatory message could have been repeated just as well the next day, when the squadron's Avengers flew 37 missions over southern Okinawa to drop water, medical supplies, rations, and ammunition to the ground forces.

The weather situation changed so abruptly at the end of the month that "For the first time no enemy planes were detected in the area for the 24-hour period" ending at midnight, 30 May. The heavy rain, however, did not completely stop ground activity on the 30th, for attacks were made all along the Tenth Army front. In the XXIV Corps zone, the 96th Division and the right flank regiment of the 7th Division—the 17th Infantry—attacked west and captured the high ground in the rear of the Shuri positions, one and a half miles west of Yonabaru. Other elements of the 7th Division passed through Shinzato and Sashiki against little opposition, and moved deeper into the Chinen Peninsula. The 77th Division ran into determined holding action by the 32d Regiment, but managed nevertheless to capture all of the high ground and key defensive positions occupied by the enemy immediately to the northeast and east of Shuri.

In the 1st Marine Division zone, a grave situation confronting 3/1 on 30 May was rooted in events that had occurred the day before, when the battalion broke off contact with the enemy in Wana Draw and headed for Shuri Castle. At the time of the disengagement, all battalion assault companies badly needed food, water, and ammunition. An air drop scheduled at 1800 on the 29th at the castle was not made, with the result that the frontline troops were without food and water for 36 hours. Commenting on this later, the battalion commander noted: "During this period the battalion was operating under the worst imaginable conditions, no food, water, little ammunition, the battalion CP 2500 yards to the rear of the lines, battalion dump 1000 yards to the rear of the CP and all transportation hopelessly mired, with the results that no food of any type was available and the men had resorted to drinking water from shell-holes due to their extreme thirst."

Early in the morning of the 30th, Lieutenant Colonel Ross was informed that an air drop was scheduled for 0600, and shortly thereafter he learned that a very low ceiling had grounded the planes. The battalion's Marines had now been without food and water for two days and a night. This situation and an inadequate ammunition supply forced the battalion commander to tell Colonel Mason that unless this logistics problem was solved, it would be most difficult for the battalion to undertake any extensive operations. Finally, at 1335 an air drop was made, but another one had to be scheduled since most of the first had fallen outside of the drop zone and in enemy territory. Enough of the supplies were recovered, however, to issue each man one-third of a K-Ration and one canteen of water.

While attempting to locate the headquarters of the Thirty-second Army at Shuri Castle, representatives from the 1st Division G-2 Section had discovered numerous caves containing many enemy documents of intelligence value. Together with these intelligence people, General del Valle had sent the division colors to Lieutenant Colonel Ross with a request that they be raised over the castle. After locating the remnants of a Japanese flagpole, the battalion commander had it erected near the southern wall, raised the American flag, and then ordered all observers to evacuate the area rapidly because he expected the Japanese to use the flag as an aiming point and to fire an artillery concentration on the position almost immediately.

Continuing supply problems prevented the 1st Marines from making any concerted attack on 30 May until the 1st and 2d Battalions had received supply air drops. On the left of the 1st Marines, the 306th Infantry extended to the right, allowing Colonel Mason's left battalion, 2/1, to move its left company to the right, relieving Company C, 1/1. Patrols from 1/1 ventured into the ruins of northern Shuri, but were forced back by machine gun and 47mm AT fire from well-entrenched positions in a ravine southwest of Wana Draw. On the right of the division zone, the 5th Marines was also limited to local patrol action by its need to bring supplies forward over muddy routes. On 30 May, in torrential rains, the 22d and 29th Marines pressed the 6th Division attack east to clear the north bank of the Kokuba. Heavy enemy resistance, built around a framework of mutually supporting machine guns emplaced in the mouths of Okinawan tombs, was made even more effective by the fact that the Marines had no armor support for the greater part of the day. Jump-off time was advanced one hour to 1000 to permit division interpreters and cooperative prisoners to broadcast surrender inducements over loudspeakers to enemy holdouts in front of the 22d Marines. A barrage of small arms and mortar fire signified a negative response to this effort. After a 15-minute artillery, rocket, and naval gunfire preparation, the division attack began at 1010.

On the right of the division line, Lieutenant Colonel Woodhouse was killed by sniper fire while in the van of 2/22 controlling its attack. The battalion executive officer, Major John G. Johnson, assumed command and maintained unit pressure against the caves and the improvised tomb-pillboxes thwarting the Marine advance. By nightfall, after a series of costly local attacks and mopping-up activities, the battalion possessed hill positions overlooking the Kokuba estuary and the trans-island rail line between Naha and Yonabaru.

The 3d Battalion passed through 1/22 and then jumped off abreast of 2/22, meeting the same heavy resistance along the way. Blocking the 3/22 path to the Kokuba was commanding terrain in which Knob Hill, Hill 27, and a number of radio towers were located. At approximately 1530, 3/22 secured this area, but only after the ground troops had fought a number of small arms and grenade-throwing duels while clearing the enemy out of an intricate system of tunnel-connected caves. Following the seizure of this high ground, Lieutenant Colonel Clair W. Shisler reorganized his 3d Battalion and continued the advance to the high ground north of and overlooking the Kokuba. As his troops dug in for the night, they were subjected to intense mortar and artillery fire.

Advancing alongside of 3/22, 1/29 made the main regimental effort. During the attack, a Marine threw a satchel charge or a grenade into one of the tombs along the advance route, setting off an estimated ton of explosives and causing approximately 25 casualties in Company C; B immediately passed through to maintain the attack. Although machine gun and small arms fire from the numerous caves and fortified tombs in the battalion zone slowed the progress of the attack, 1/29 was able to advance under the cover of fire support from 3/29. The latter also advanced slowly, meanwhile maintaining contact with the 5th Marines on its left. At the end of the day, both 6th Division assault regiments had gained 800 yards and were in firm possession of the key high ground overlooking the Kokuba from the south. During the night of 30-31 May, the volume of enemy artillery and mortar fire on Tenth Army positions was noticeably lighter in comparison to that which had fallen previously in the battle for Shuri. When assault troops surged towards troublesome Japanese pockets remaining about Shuri on the morning of the 31st, they were pleasantly surprised by the almost complete lack of opposition. Only sporadic sniper and machine gun fire broke the weird silence in an area that had just recently been filled with the din and crackle of battle. Adhering to the Thirty-second Army withdrawal plan, rearguard forces from the 44th IMB, 32d Regiment, and 22d IIB had pulled out of their positions during the night to occupy the second holding line north of Tsukasan. Another aspect of the completely reversed situation was the break in weather, which changed the seemingly unending period of rain and solid overcast into a day of sunshine and high scattered clouds.

American ground units moved into Shuri, later described as "a perfect final defensive position," and found it to be nearly abandoned. Soldiers from XXIV Corps quickly advanced and occupied assigned objectives, and spent most of the time thereafter mopping up isolated pockets of resistance. Only on the extreme left of the 96th Division line, where attack elements encountered the Tsukasan line defenses, was the corps objective not taken. The encirclement and occupation of Shuri became a reality at 1255 on the 31st, when patrols from 3/383 and 1/5 made contact south of the city.

In a coordinated sweep with the 77th Infantry Division, the 1st Marine Division cleared out the enemy-infested areas immediately surrounding Shuri. Mopping up of bothersome pockets in the northern outskirts of the city and in the stubborn Wana Draw was completed by noon. Later in the day, the 1st Marines was ordered into division reserve and given a primary mission of patrolling Shuri.

Despite supply and evacuation problems, the 5th Marines continued its southeasterly advance towards the hills just north of Shichima, overlooking the Naha-Yonabaru highway. The 3d Battalion made the main effort for the regiment, jumping off at 1445--15 minutes after it had received an air drop of water and ammunition. Upon reaching the hills, rifle and machine gun fire from Japanese blocking units forced the battalion — on the corps boundary — to dig in for the night. A gap existing between the 1st and 3d Battalions was plugged by Company F of 2/5.

The heretofore steady progress of Tenth Army flanking units was slowed on 31 May when enemy resistance to the 6th and 7th Divisions became stronger. General Shepherd's assault regiments jumped off at 0730 and rapidly moved forward for several hundred yards before encountering unyielding Japanese positions in the hill mass west of Shichima and Kokuba. These were occupied by Admiral Ota's ragtag naval troops and units of the 32d Regiment. The Marine advance was held up until about 1300, when a coordinated assault was launched under the cover of long-range support fire furnished by a company of tanks situated as close to the line of departure as a minefield and a sea of mud would permit. Although the division had some evidence that the enemy defense was crumbling here, the Marines had gained only 400 yards by nightfall and were still short of their objective. In night defense lines that were consolidated along a series of low hills immediately west of the objective, the assault battalions made preparations for a coordinated attack on 1 June. All through the night, artillery batteries fired concentrations on suspected Japanese gun positions in an attempt to destroy them.

On the left flank of the Tenth Army, the 7th Division continued its two-pronged attack. One assault force drove up the Naha-Yonabaru valley against a chain of well-defended hills to reach the corps boundary at Chan; the second sent strong combat and reconnaissance patrols into the hills and valleys guarding the neck of Chinen Peninsula. Little opposition was met there.

By the end of May, the Tenth Army had overcome the seemingly impregnable Shuri redoubt, only to run into newly organized defenses positioned along the Kokuba River and north of Tsukasan. Since the initial landings on L-Day, General Buckner's forces had killed an estimated 62,548 Japanese soldiers and captured 465 others in 61 days of bloody endeavor. The Tenth Army had seized all but eight square miles of the island, and that parcel was becoming a pocket of doom into which the remnants of General Ushijima's army were being driven. The battle so far had cost the Americans 5,309 men dead, 23,909 wounded, and 346 missing in action.

On 1 June, as though in anticipation of an imminent end to the fighting but in fact on the date stipulated in the ICEBERG logistics plan, unloading operations off Hagushi changed from the assault to the garrison phase. This same day, the second consecutive clear one, the direction of the attack was reoriented in the XXIV Corps zone. In the 96th Division zone, the 381st and 383d Infantry Regiments relieved the 32d Infantry north of Chan on the line paralleling the corps boundary, where it turned east to end at a point 1,100 yards north of Karadera. A day later, General Griner's two regiments were to attack to the south; their objective, the hill complex approach to the Tomui-Araguuku-Meka area. Guarding the right rear of the corps advance was 2/305, which had moved out to the boundary when the 77th and 96th Divisions had exchanged zones of responsibility.

With its 32d Infantry in reserve, the 7th Division attacked to the south in a much narrower zone than it had been assigned before. During the previous two days, combat patrols had thoroughly scouted and prepared the way, enabling the division to gain an average of 1,100 yards against steadily rising opposition. Facing the Americans were elements of the 7th Heavy Artillery and 23d Shipping Engineer Regiments, which slowly pulled back towards Itokazu during the day.

Maintaining constant pressure, both IIIAC assault divisions made substantial gains on 1 June in a coordinated attack, which resulted in the capture of all the high ground commanding the cross-island highway running through the Kokuba River valley. The 1st Division attack was made by 1/5 and 3/5, which overran enemy positions in the hills east of Shichina to advance 1,500-1,800 yards before halting for the night. In the 6th Division Zone, the 22d and 29th Marines broke through the defenses that had held them up the day before and advanced swiftly in a smoothly functioning tank-infantry attack. By late afternoon, the assault regiments possessed the high ground on the northern bank of the Kokuba, and sent patrols across the northern fork of the river to select suitable crossing sites. Having accomplished their mission of slowing the American advance, Japanese holding forces in the second defense line had withdrawn the previous night. Their action paved the way for the Tenth Army to continue the pursuit and to make an unopposed tactical river crossing.

According to oral instructions General Geiger gave him in the early morning of 1 June, General Shepherd was given 36 hours to prepare his division for an amphibious operation. For as complex an operation as this, considerably more preparation time was usually allotted. Nevertheless, division planners were "to study the practicality of a shore-to-shore landing on Oroku."

Major Walker's 6th Reconnaissance Company was to reconnoiter the peninsula after dark on the lst. The company was to move out at 2100 and cross Naha harbor in rubber boats to the northern part of Oroku. At 1110 that morning, General Shepherd received a IIIAC warning order alerting him that the 6th Division axis of attack would probably be reoriented in the direction of Oroku Peninsula, where the division would land to secure the harbor and seize the air field. To prevent disclosure of the presence of the reconnaissance company Marines on Oroku, all IIIAC units were directed to restrict the use of illuminating and parachute flares between 2030 and 0300, 1-2 June.

Four scouting teams of four men each spent six hours on enemy-held Oroku, where they heard considerable Japanese activity and were fired upon. On their return, the reconnaissance teams reported that the peninsula was Japanese-occupied, but that the enemy was not there in great strength.

Besides ordering the Oroku attack, General Geiger directed the 1st Division to assume responsibility for and occupy the zone of the 6th, excluding Naha, on 2 June. Colonel Snedeker's 7th Marines relieved the 22d and 29th Marines shortly after noon of this date, and General del Valle assumed control of the overall zone at 1215. On the left, 2/7 took over the 22d Marines line along the north bank of the Kokuba, and 3/7 replaced the 29th Marines in hill positions west of Kokuba village.

Immediately after arriving at the Kokuba, 2/7 was ordered across the river and into the hills bordering its south bank. Company E was the first to cross. Utilizing a damaged but still standing bridge in the battalion zone, the company gained the heights north of Tomigusuku and fought off an estimated 50 to 100 Japanese who tried to turn the Marine right flank while Company G was filing over the bridge. By nightfall, Company F had joined the other two companies in establishing a firm bridgehead south of the river, and thus safeguarded the crossing site. Early in the morning of 2 June, the 5th Marines crossed the north branch of the Kokuba over a railroad bridge that the retreating Japanese had neglected to blow up. While attempting to advance beyond a seized ridge guarding the approaches to the village of Tomigusuku, the 5th Marines assault units were pinned down by intense frontal and flanking rifle and machine gun fire, which prevented their making even limited gains for the rest of the day. Despite this bitter enemy reaction here, the 5th Marines advance put the final segment of the Naha-Yonabaru highway into Tenth Army hands. Just before midnight, the enemy launched a determined counterattack—the first since his withdrawal from Shuri against Marine lines. The Japanese were driven back, but left behind 20 dead.

To the left of the IIIAC zone, XXIV Corps units made large gains all along the line. In the process of cleaning out Chan, seizing the high ground north of Tera and Kamizato, and penetrating through Japanese defenses to the west of Kamizato and Karadera, 96th Division assault regiments advanced 800-1,200 yards. Farther west the 7th Division succeeded in pushing forward 2,400 yards against slight opposition from retreating Japanese garrison troops. At the end of 1 June, Army infantry troops were positioned for a final drive to close off Chinen Peninsula entirely. Rain during the night of 1-2 June again resulted in the mud and supply problems experienced by all Tenth Army units earlier, and forced them to accommodate their operations more to the obstacles posed by the rain and mud than the enemy.

By noon of 2 June, the 6th Marine Division had received final instructions regarding the Oroku operation, and General Shepherd's staff had already begun detailed planning. After examining possible courses of action and schemes of maneuver for the landing—and eliminating those that seemed least likely to be successful—the division commander decided to land on the Nishikoku beaches on the northeast coast of the peninsula and drive south, generally following an axis of attack astride the high ground in the center of the peninsula.

Governing the acceptance of this landing plan was the fact that Nishikoku had low rolling ground leading from the most suitable beaches on Oroku to the airfield and Naha harbor. In addition, an attack inland from this beachhead would be angled in the best direction for comprehensive, massed artillery support from the mainland. Other landing sites on Oroku under consideration were rejected because the high seawall ringing the peninsula would have to be breached, which time limitations prohibited. Also the enemy had direct observation of these other prospective beachhead sites from high ground inland. Owing to a shortage of amphibious tractors then existing at Okinawa, General Shepherd could count on having only 72 LVTs available for the landing. Most of the other amtracs were in poor condition as a result of continued extensive employment during the heavy rains in ship-to-shore supply operations and in coastal runs supplying the flanking divisions of the Tenth Army, and an almost-complete reliance on the LVTs for overland supply of frontline units. Nevertheless with the LVTs he was given, General Shepherd planned to land his division in a column of regiments, the 4th Marines in assault. Colonel Shapley in turn, chose his 1st and 2d Battalions to spearhead the attack. The regiment was to drive rapidly inland to seize dominating terrain near Kagamisui, just north of the airfield, from which it was to cover the movement ashore of the rest of the division. As soon as the 4th Marines had moved beyond the beachhead area onto its objective, and when LVTs had made the return trip and were available, the 29th Marines would land. After this phase of the assault had been completed, tanks and supplies would be unloaded from landing craft.

The 6th Division assault forces were to mount out from assembly areas near the mouths of the Asato and Asa Rivers, and supplies and tanks would be loaded at a point that had been developed near Machinato and named Loomis Harbor after Colonel Francis B. Loomis, Jr., the G-4 for III Amphibious Corps. Because it would be difficult to maintain a waterborne resupply operation continuously during the peninsular fighting, General Shepherd decided to seize Ono Yama concurrently with the Oroku assault. This small island in the middle of Kokuba Channel, across from the southern end of the Naha Canal, served as an anchor for bridges from the mainland and the peninsula. Once a task force of reconnaissance company Marines reinforced by a company of LVT(A)s had taken the island, it would provide security for an engineer detachment that was to repair the damaged bridges. After its capture, Ono Yama served the 6th Division as a logistic support base that was located fairly close to the fighting.

Both logistical and personnel preparations for the assault were increasingly complicated by the almost-complete breakdown of the road net as a result of the resumption of heavy rain. Therefore, all division tactical and support movement had to be made over water. "Even the division CP, deploying to a forward location near Amike was required to move entirely by DUKWs." Despite these handicaps, all 6th Division assault and support units made ready for the amphibious landing on K-Day, 4 June; the reinforced reconnaissance Marines were to land at 0500 on Ono Yama, and the main assault force 45 minutes later on Oroku. While the 6th Division was temporarily out of the fighting and preparing for the Oroku invasion, the attack south increased in impetus and force. By late afternoon of 3 June, the 7th Infantry Division had reached the east coast of Okinawa below Kakibana and cut off the Chinen Peninsula completely. The 32d Infantry then moved into the hill complex of the peninsula to destroy any members of the Japanese garrison still remaining. General Arnold consolidated the lines of the 17th and 184th Infantry in the hills overlooking Itokazu and Toyama, where the soldiers poised for an attack to the southwest against Kiyamu Peninsula positions.

To the right of the 7th, the 96th Division also scored gains on 3 June. Kamizato, Tera, and then Inasomi fell after only a perfunctory enemy defense. Before halting the attack to setup night defenses, General Bradley's assault regiments had taken 1,400 yards of enemy territory, even though the combination of continuing bad weather and almost insurmountable supply problems seemed to conspire against further

American successes. At sunset, 96th Division troops overwhelmed determined enemy defenders to seize commanding terrain in the hill mass north of the road and rail junction at Iwa. Because an already-existing gap between Marine and Army units had been widened by the accelerated pace of the XXIV Corps, the 305th infantry continued its role of guarding the exposed flank of the corps at the boundary between it and IIIAC.

To the right of the 305th, from midnight, 2 June, to dawn the next day, the 5th Marines frustrated persistent enemy attempts to infiltrate its lines. After sunrise, the Marines spent the morning probing the front with patrols, which soon were pinned down by scattered but well-placed enemy fire from positions south of Tsukasan and west of Gisushi. When the 1st and 3d Battalions could move forward no further, 2/5 was alerted to its possible commitment to ease the situation.

At 1230, Lieutenant Colonel Benedict was ordered to circle around the left battalion—1/5—by moving in a wide arc through the XXIV Corps zone, and to outflank and come up behind enemy strongpoints on the high ground near Tomusu and Gishusi. Taking only equipment that it could carry, the battalion moved out at 1330. At 1800, after having trekked over a difficult, muddy, and circuitous route, it arrived at a jump-off position 400 yards east of its objective. Twenty minutes after arriving here, 2/5 attacked with Companies E and G in the assault and quickly secured the target against only slight enemy resistance. As 2/5 Marines began to dig in, they found that the entire ridge contained a well-organized cave defense system, and began blowing up cave entrances to seal them. A white phosphorous grenade thrown into one cave set off what apparently was a Japanese ammunition dump; the resulting explosion blew up the entire side of the hill in the Company E sector, killing 3 Marines and wounding 17. The exposed 2/5 position ahead of the 1st Division line presented the battalion with a most difficult task of evacuating casualties, which was accomplished only "by invaluable assistance" provided by 2/383 on its right.

While 2/5 was outflanking the Gisushi position, at 1530 the 1st and 3d Battalions resumed the regimental attack under enemy fire which had lessened considerably since the morning. When these two battalions halted at 1900, they had advanced 1,500 yards and through Tsukasan, placing the 5th Marines south of the former rear command post of the Thirty-second Army. The relative ease with which the 1st Division had advanced on 3 June indicated that the Japanese rear guard had once again withdrawn towards fixed positions on Kiyamu.

Spearheaded by 1st Reconnaissance Company patrols, assault units of the 7th Marines rolled up 200 yards in the division right. This advance established Marine control of virtually the entire hill mass south of Kokuba. Scattered enemy holding groups constantly harassed advancing Marines on the right flank during the day, however, with mortar, machine gun, and machine cannon fire from emplacements in the hills guarding the entrance to Oroku Peninsula. This steady enemy fire constantly menaced supply and evacuation parties traveling a well-worn route into the regimental zone from the only bridge over the Kokuba River. A combination of this harassment and the difficulty of negotiating over rain-damaged road nets again forced the Marines to depend upon air drops as a source of supply for rations and ammunition.

To fulfill the logistic requirements of the ground forces, the Avengers of VMTB-232 were kept as busy in June as they had been in May air dropping prepackaged loads to IIIAC and XXIV Corps units that could not be replenished through normal supply channels. The squadron made 24 drops on 1 June; 32 on 2 June; 24 on 3 June.

Having received a supply replenishment from planes during the day, both assault battalions of the 7th Marines were across the Kokuba by nightfall of the 3d and solidly set in the hill mass south of the river; 3/7 was in contact with 1/5, and the regiment was tied in across its front.

Well within the period it had been allotted, the 6th Division completed arrangements for its shore-to-shore operation by the end of 3 June. Beacon lights to mark the line of departure were set in place 1,200 yards north of the Nishikoku beaches at 1215 that day, and division assault forces were en route to board the LVTs at embarkation points on the west coast. The 22d Marines were placed in IIIAC reserve in and around Naha; its regimental weapons company moved to the shore of the Kokuba estuary, where it set up its 37mm and self-propelled assault guns in position to support the 4 June landing. Supplementing the massive fire support provided by artillery, naval gunfire, air, and its own organic weapons, the 4th Marines would have the additional fire support of a company of LVT(A)s, a company of tanks, and a mobile rocket launcher detachment. All preparations were completed at 2300, and the 6th Marine Division stood poised for the Oroku Assault.

The Capture Of Oroku Peninsula

As directed in the landing plan, the 4th Marines were to land on beaches designated Red 1 and Red 2 with 1/4 on the right, 2/4 on the left. The total length of the beaches was approximately 600 yards. Offshore, a rough coral shelf about 200 yards long was a not-insurmountable barrier to the landing site. The assault wave was to be followed by the other waves in LVTs. As envisioned, the shore-to-shore movement would be a comparatively simple operation. In addition to the beacon lights marking the line of departure, the only other control measure was to be the normal radio communication between the assault units. In the early morning darkness of 4 June, troops and equipment loaded aboard the tracked amphibians according to plan. An intense prelanding bombardment was laid down on the target for an hour's duration before H-Hour; over 4,300 rounds of high explosive shells ranging in caliber from 75mm to 14-inch blasted suspected enemy positions on the high ground immediately behind the Nishikoku beaches.

Once loaded, the invasion flotilla headed south towards the target in two columns, 400 yards apart; 1/4 in the seaward column since it was to land on Red 2, the westernmost beach. Almost simultaneously with the beginning of the bombardment of Oroku, 3/5 began blasting Ono Yama, and 15 minutes later the 6th Reconnaissance Company landed on schedule, supported by LVT(A)s of the Army 708th Amphibious Tank Battalion.

During their approach to the line of departure, assault Marines were treated to the spectacle of the furious lashing given the beach area by the guns of 1 battleship, 2 heavy cruisers, 1 destroyer, and 15 battalions of artillery which joined in the cannonading. At the line of departure, the lead LVT(A) of each column signalled a column left, whereupon the following LVTs executed the movement, formed up into seven waves, and headed towards the beach. Four LCTs carrying 20 tanks and 10 LCMs carrying elements of the 4th Marines Weapons Company followed in the wake of the assault waves.

Before they had reached the line of departure, mechanical failures forced all of the tractors carrying 1/4 to slow down and some to fall out of the formation. Radio communication as well as overall contact was lost. By the time that the battalion had reached the line of departure, nine tractors had dropped out and only six were able to make the final run into the beach. Some of the cripples got underway again, but troops in the other amtracs had to be picked up by spare LVTs in the wave carrying the regimental headquarters. The battalion commander's request for a delay of H-Hour was refused by Colonel Shapley, who ordered the attack to proceed according to schedule. As a result, only two platoons of the right assault company of 1/4 and one from the left landed on time. The 2d Battalion experienced no difficulty during its approach and landing. Intelligence estimates had indicated that the peninsula was defended by 1,200-1,500 enemy troops. At 0600, when the first Marines went ashore they saw no Japanese defenders on the beach, however, and were able to rush inland 300 yards to high ground against only scattered machine gun fire. All 2d Battalion units were ashore and reorganized in little more than a half hour after the first elements had landed.

By 0650, all tanks of Company A, 6th Tank Battalion, in support of 2/4, and attached engineer mine removal teams were ashore. Four self-propelled 105mm howitzers of the regimental weapons company also landed at this time. Except for one tank lost in a pothole, Company C tanks landed at 0800 and began supporting those troops of 1/4 already on the peninsula. The rest of the infantry battalion came ashore during the remainder of the morning.

Once ashore, the assault forces found the terrain very open and generally flat, with several 50 to 100-foot tall hillocks breaking up the landscape. As the attack moved inland to the central, southern, and western portions of the peninsula, the Marines encountered many ridges and steep hills—the highest of which was some 183 feet in height. The small hills initially captured were unoccupied by the enemy, but close inspection showed that the terrain was honeycombed with tunnels and numerous firing ports, which, when manned, had given the defenders commanding all-around views of the area.

Following its surge beyond the beachhead, 2/4 met mounting resistance on the left. Extensive minefield on the plateau immediately adjoining the landing site and the rain-soaked ground held up the tank-infantry advance as well. Both obstacles restricted tank operations and forced the Shermans to remain road-bound. Many sections of the roads had been blown up by the enemy and the mediums were unable to bypass these spots over the bemired fields; the ground troops were thus threatened with having their armor support severely curtailed. The job of filling in the cratered roads soon surpassed the capabilities of the tank dozers.

Although the 1/4 reserve, Company B was the only element of the battalion to land in near-full strength. It was then committed at once on the right of 1/4 and ordered to take the high ground overlooking Kagamisui. The company promptly overran the objective maintaining the momentum of the battalion attack and permitting 1/4 to gain its objective, 1,000 yards inland, at 1100. In regimental reserve, 3/4 was nevertheless committed to the right of 1/4 at approximately 0905, within 20 minutes after it had landed. The 3d Battalion immediately pushed forward to the edge of Oroku airfield. Observers noted that the field was overgrown with rough grass, was swampy, and appeared in very poor condition overall. Large revetments were ranged along the edges of the three runways. Even though they provided excellent concealment and some cover, it would have been dangerous to use them since the enemy seemed to have had them well ranged in with mortars. The wreckage of several planes, apparently strafed and bombed earlier by American aircraft, was strewn over the field. Running along the right (west) edge of the field was a seawall, heavily overgrown with palmetto and brush. On the eastern edge of the airdrome was a series of foothill ridges that were crisscrossed with caves and aircraft revetments.

An hour after 3/4 had landed, General Shepherd believed that the beachhead had been sufficiently enlarged to the point where it could accept the landing of a second regiment. Accordingly, he ordered the 29th Marines to begin moving to Oroku immediately. Two of Colonel Whaling's battalions were quickly transported to the peninsula and moved into the lines on the left of the 4th Marines. The 2d Battalion was ashore and relieving left flank units of 2/4 by 1300; 3/29 took over the rest of the zone at 1430, whereupon 2/4 went into regimental reserve.

At 0900, 6th Division wiremen ferried a four-trunk cable across the mouth of Naha Harbor in rubber boats, strung it over the mast of a sunken ship, and had it tied at the terminals of assault unit switchboards on Oroku at 1100. At the same time that this task was underway, division engineers worked rapidly to repair the bridges between Naha, Ono Yama, and the peninsula. Bridging operations began immediately after the harbor island had been secured at 0600. After 30 minutes of sharp fighting during which it killed an estimated 25 enemy soldiers, the 6th Reconnaissance Company deployed to positions where the scouts could protect engineers who were assembling the Bailey bridge.

Elsewhere on Ono Yama, other engineers inflated rubber pontoons that were to be placed into the water to support a bridge spanning the wide estuary between the island and Oroku. It was not possible to establish this link until Marines on the peninsula had neutralized heavy enemy machine gun fire aimed at puncturing and sinking the pontoons.

By nightfall, 1/29 was landed and in regimental reserve, 2/4 was set up in an assembly area as its regiment's reserve, and the attack had halted for the day. At this time, the invasion force had pushed inland 1,500 yards against steadily increasing resistance. In addition to this Japanese opposition, the attack had been slowed in the afternoon by very heavy rain storms as well as numerous minefields, whose neutralization and destruction taxed overworked mine-disposal teams.

During the first day on Oroku, the assault forces had received a considerable amount of fire from a variety of automatic weapons ranging up to 40mm in caliber. It was later learned that these weapons had been stripped from the damaged aircraft on and around Oroku airfield and distributed to the ground defense force, which then was able to offer a more formidable response to the Marine invasion. From early evening and on through the night of 4-5 June, Marine lines were subjected to sporadic enemy artillery and mortar fire. A startling new Japanese weapon met by Marines on Iwo Jima was brought into the Okinawa campaign when the 6th Division was introduced to the enemy's 8-inch rocket. Dubbed a "Screaming Mimi" or "Whistling Willie" by the troops, because of the noise it made while tumbling through the air end over end, the projectile was more a source of annoyance than danger and caused few casualties. Its explosion was loud and concussion great, but this rudimentary missile's fragmentation was ineffectual and its accuracy was poor. "It was launched from a pair of horizontal rails about 15 feet long, aiming was strictly hit or miss, a process of sandbags, guesswork, and luck." The rockets continued to fall in rear areas during the night, while enemy snipers and would-be infiltrators were active.

Troops on Ono Yama received machine gun and spigot mortar fire in the darkness. These 320mm mortar shells, nicknamed "flying ashcans" by Americans, had been employed only briefly earlier in the Okinawa campaign and had not appeared again until this time.

At 0700 on 5 June, 1/22 reverted to the 6th Division from corps reserve, and, as division reserve, then was deployed on the division boundary in the right (west) flank of the 7th Marines attacking south. At 0730, the Oroku assault resumed and moved slowly against determined stubborn opposition until noon, when the 4th Marines was halted by an enemy strongpoint near Toma.

Muddy ground on the right of the 4th Marines zone made it impossible to employ tanks, so a platoon of the tracked vehicles skirted the seawall to come up on the airfield behind 3/4--in whose zone Toma lay—to assist the infantry attack. As the armor drew near open terrain on the field, it began receiving enemy artillery fire. The 15th Marines was called upon to provide counterbattery fire against suspected enemy positions revealed by gun flashes; a tank officer adjusted this artillery fire from his forward position. An inspection later disclosed that the 15th Marines had silenced four 120mm dual purpose, one 6-inch, and several field guns of smaller caliber. Blown roads and bridges in the 3/4 zone, not yet repaired by the engineers, forced the battalion to attack Toma without accompanying tanks, which provided direct fire support, however, from positions in the rear of the lines.

The enemy was well dug in in this sector and located in deep, strongly fortified caves that were impervious to all but pointblank fire. Since tanks were bogged down and not available, 37mm guns were brought to the front and employed to good advantage against the enemy positions. After having been stymied through most of the day, 3/4 finally overran the Japanese defenses late in the afternoon with the aid of the fire from M-7s in the 1/4 zone and the support of tanks that had rumbled into position behind the 3d Battalion earlier. By nightfall, the battalion held 75 percent of the airfield and favorable jumpoff positions for the resumed attack on the next day. In the right center of the 4th Marines zone, 1/4 became pinned down by frontal and flanking fire almost immediately after it attacked the morning of the 5th. When 3/4 cracked open the Toma defenses, the 1st Battalion was able to take up the attack again. As it did so, 1/4 moved forward over terrain that was broken by a number of steep hills containing many extensive tunnels in the mouths of which machine guns were emplaced and sited for all-around defense. The 4th Marines' commander noted that the heavy resistance met all along his line was reminiscent of that encountered in the battle for Naha. When the attack for the day ended at 1700, 1/4 held positions on high ground overlooking Ashimine and Toma on the right, and an unnamed village, designated "Oroku Mura," on the left.

Overcoming both bitter enemy resistance and problems of supply and evacuation, the 4th Marines advanced the division line 1,000 yards on the 5th. Frontline units experienced considerable small arms and automatic weapons fire as well as many grenade launcher barrages, "but very little heavy mortar and no artillery fire, which was a relief to all hands." The enemy placed the artillery and mortar concentrations on rear areas instead, however, preventing LVTs from using the tank route leading to 3/4 positions to give that battalion supply and evacuation support. A 50-man working party, organized at regimental headquarters to replace the amphibious tractors, hand-carried urgently needed supplies up to 3/4, and took out evacuees on its return to Colonel Shapley's CP.

The 29th Marines made slow but steady progress on 5 June against enemy opposition that was moderate to heavy. By 1400, the regimental advance was slowed when assault units encountered a strong center of resistance near Hill 57, at the southeast outskirts of Oroku Mura. This strongpoint gave trouble to left flank elements of the 4th Marines also. A Japanese counterattack launched against 3/29 before the battalion had moved forward 1,000 yards was easily blunted, but fire from enemy positions located in the areas of adjacent battalions finally forced the 3rd Battalion to hold up.

The 2nd Battalion continued to push its left flank southeast along the banks of the Kokuba, and finally secured a bridgesite area opposite Ono Yama. This permitted the engineers to float a 300-foot pontoon bridge into position. Pausing only to leave security detachments at the bridge as a guard against enemy attempts to destroy it, the battalion continued the attack. At 1810, the first LVT crossed over the bridge to Oroku from Ono Yama, opening a direct ground supply line to the assault troops. In the course of their operations on 6 June, the two assault regiments of the 6th Division uncovered major enemy defenses that were centered along the axial ridge running northwest-southeast along the length of Oroku Peninsula. The terrain of this hilly region favored the defenders, not only by its complexity but also by a heavy overgrowth of tangled vegetation. Immediately after they had resumed their attacks on the 6th, both the 4th and 29th Marines were held up by determined enemy opposition from concealed and well-camouflaged defenses.

A platoon of tanks supported the attack of the 2/29 with overhead fire at ranges of up to 1,200 yards from a high ridge overlooking the battalion objective—the village of Oroku. Left flank elements of the 2d Battalion pushed forward and captured the high ground in the village itself, but were unable to advance much farther in the face of heavy enemy fire. A second platoon of tanks moved along the river bank and attempted to get into position to subdue this fire, but it was unable to bypass a destroyed bridge in its path.

On the right of the 29th Marines zone, 3/29 moved over terrain that "consisted of a series of small temple-like hills, each of which had been converted into a fortress by construction of innumerable caves, from which mutually supporting automatic weapons could cover adjacent positions and deny the open ground between the hills [to the Americans]." Naval personnel from Admiral Ota's force manned the machine guns and 20mm cannon guarding the sector. After a day of bitter fighting without armored support—the narrow roads in the battalion zone were heavily mined and cratered, and impassable to tanks—the gains of 3/29 were limited to a scant 150 yards.

Immediately fronting the 1/4 line of attack was a hill the Marines called "Little Sugar Loaf," that 3/29 had been unable to take earlier. Lieutenant Colonel George B. Bell planned for his infantry to capture it by means of a double envelopment coordinated with a tank drive up the center of the valley leading to the objective. Assault companies forming the wings of the envelopment were pinned down as soon as they jumped off. The attack did not begin until 1530, when support tanks arrived and were in position. Although the advance began to gain momentum, the battalion commander thought that night would fall before the objective was taken and ordered his assault elements back to the lines occupied that morning, with little to show for the day's efforts. Although 1/4 had demonstrated how the enemy defenses could be breached in this sector, it was not to have the satisfaction of doing it itself; early the next day it was relieved by 2/4.

To the right of 1/4 on 6 June, Lieutenant Colonel Hochmuth's 3d Battalion attacked following an air strike on the many ridges in front of the battalion. As Company I on the right prepared to move out, its right flank was subjected to some 20mm and heavier caliber fire from Senaga Shima, a small rocky island flanking the Marine lines and lying approximately 1,000 yards off the southern coast of the peninsula. Tenth Army artillery and naval gunfire support ships blasted the island, silencing all but the 20mm weapons. An air strike was urgently called for and arrived a half hour later. "As rack after rack of bombs fell," scoring direct hits on the Japanese emplacements, "the troops stood up and cheered." Disregarding the 20mm fire from Senaga as best they could, Marines from 3/4 moved rapidly forward as soon as the last plane in each of a series of air strikes made its final run over a target in front of the battalion. Scattered small arms fire paced the troops attacking over comparatively flat terrain, but 3/4 succeeded in securing the rest of the airfield by the end of the day.

Engineer road-construction crews and mine-disposal teams worked on 6 June in warm and clearing weather. Discovered and disarmed on the main north-south road bisecting the peninsula were 83 mines of all types. At noon, Company B of the tank battalion landed from LCTs with the rest of the battalion's tanks and immediately went into reserve. Also on 6 June, the 22d Marines as a whole reverted from corps reserve; 3/22 joined the 1st Battalion on the division east boundary, adjoining the west flank of the 7th Marines driving south; and 2/22 was alerted to move to a new defense position elsewhere on the division boundary.

Considerable resistance continued to plague the 6th Division as it unrelentingly swept across the peninsula on 7 June. The 4th Marines again made the most satisfactory progress of the day, but its right flank, which had advanced against only slight opposition on the previous day, was confronted with a much stronger defense in the vicinity of Gushi. As 3/4 tried to take the last section of high ground on the west coast, its leading company came under a deadly machine gun and rifle crossfire at the same time that extremely accurate and heavy mortar barrages fell on the only route of approach to the battalion goal. Both direct and indirect supporting fires bombarded Japanese positions to no avail. At the end of the day the battalion commander, faced with the prospect of sustaining heavy casualties if he pushed on, decided to pull his forwardmost elements back and hold the ground already taken.

Colonel Shapley's 2d Battalion passed through 1/4 at 0730, and began its attack on Little Sugar Loaf with the supporting fires of 37mm guns, tanks, and self-propelled 105mm howitzers. Left flank elements of 3/4 also supported the attack as Company G maneuvered around to the right of the enemy position and took it at 1100.

Following its capture of Little Sugar Loaf, the 4th Marines pushed ahead slowly against machine gun fire coming from all directions and ever-stiffening enemy opposition. Frontline Marines, already expert in the technique of sealing caves, furthered their expertise while closing the many caves on Oroku with a deadly combination of direct fire, flame, and demolitions. Unit commanders soon surmised that the peninsula was being defended by an enemy force greater than the 1,500-2,000 soldiers and naval troops previously estimated. Captured documents and POWs substantially confirmed the fact that the Oroku defense had been reinforced by a number of naval troops, which had originally moved south to Itoman and then had been ordered back to the peninsula. This information also indicated that the original American strength estimate of naval personnel was faulty and now had to be revised upward because many Okinawan conscripts had been dragooned into the ranks of Admiral Ota's force. Although many of the Japanese on Oroku had been killed after three days of fighting on the peninsula, the stubborn opposition of those still alive caused casualty figures in the 4th Marines to mount. Frontline units could only be supplied after dark because of the lethal fire covering approach routes. By nightfall, the lines of 3/4 extended in a southeasterly direction and faced north, while on the left, 2/4 still attacked towards the southeast. The boundary between the 4th and 29th Marines ran in a southeasterly direction down the middle of the peninsula.

Just to the left of the 4th Marines, 3/29 began the first of three days of extremely vicious fighting by a grenade and bayonet assault without armored support on the hill to its immediate front. During the period following these three days, the battalion gained little ground, but killed an estimated 500 troops, destroyed a large variety of weapons, and sealed many caves containing enemy soldiers, supplies, and equipment.

Two factors served to restrict the progress of the 29th Marines on 7 June. Hostile enemy concealed in the rocky outcropping of the coastal ridge paralleling the Kokuba pinned down the attackers with a drumfire from automatic weapons. Secondly, the positions of the enemy in a confined area and the proximity to the 29th of adjacent friendly troops severely limited the employment by the regiment of its supporting fires. To destroy the Japanese weapons positions and the soldiers manning them, gun crews from 2/29 manhandled their 37mm weapons up steep slopes to the ridge overlooking the enemy emplacements and effectively raked them with murderous direct fire.

In the zone of the 2d Battalion, tank-infantry teams made satisfactory progress towards their village objective. The boggy, steep, and difficult terrain and heavy concentrations of minefield that limited tank employment elsewhere on the peninsula were not in evidence in the east coastal zone, where the Shermans proved their worth. After crossing the newly constructed bridge at the site where a destroyed one had held up the tanks on the previous day, and rolling along the southern shore of Naha harbor, the tank platoon attached to 2/29 assisted the infantry in capturing Oroku village. Without pause, the battalion continued its attack and seized the high ground in the immediate vicinity of the village. Accurate and heavy enemy artillery fire and an extensive minefield then held the tanks up. Along the division boundary, on 7 June the 22d Marines continued sending patrols out into the high ground immediately east of Chikuto. Having fixed the approximate center of enemy strength in this area, 3/22 moved two companies into position to attack the high ground designated Hill 103. By 1400, the Japanese stronghold was overrun, which effectively eliminated fire from that area on the 1st Division west flank, and gave it an additional measure of security.

Hill 103 proved to be an important enemy observation post occupied by a large number of Japanese troops. By choosing to remain in their caves, these soldiers sealed their own doom since this ineffectual defensive tactic confined their fields of fire and permitted the Marine attackers to outflank the position over covered routes of approach.

According to the original scheme of maneuver established for the Oroku invasion, the 4th and 29th Marines would drive towards the base of the peninsula in a southeasterly direction. But, the rapid pace of the division attack during its first four days on the peninsula had forced the enemy to withdraw to the south of Oroku village and, with his back to the Kokuba Gawa, into the hills which were honeycombed with strong defensive positions. General Shepherd's order on 8 June reorienting the axis of attack to the northeast was a formal recognition of the course that the battle was taking. By this time, the 4th Marines on the right had advanced much further than the stalled 29th had in its zone on the left. Colonel Shapley's regiment was in the process of pivoting on the right flank elements of the 29th

Marines in a counterclockwise movement that, when ended, would head the 4th in the direction of the hard core of Japanese resistance. In effect, the elements on the right wing of the 4th would sweep in front of the 22d Marines and continue on to the northeast. Neither the 22d nor the 29th Marine lines would remain static, however, for at this point all three infantry regiments were moving and inexorably tightening the circle around Admiral Ota's hapless force.

During the evening of 7 June, 1/4 was alerted and prepared to enter the line the next morning on the right of 3/4. For the 8 June attack, battalion boundaries were changed to reflect the new direction in which these two units were to head. Early on the 8th, Marine mortars laid a smoke screen over the route 1/4 was to take as it skirted along the eastern edge of the airfield while getting into jump-off positions. The 1st Battalion's objective was the high ground located approximately midway between Uibaru and Gushi. At 1030, the assault elements attacked and immediately were pinned down by a hail of fire from rifles, machine guns, and mortars.

Bitter enemy reaction to the Marine assault was unallayed despite the massive fires of American tanks, M-7s and organic infantry crew-served weapons. The attacks of the 1st and 3d Battalions were so coordinated that one could aid the other at any given time. Because the tanks were unable to deliver direct support fire from their masked positions, they lumbered forward into the open shortly after midday and blasted the 1/4 objective for 20 minutes. After this preparation, Company A again attacked the high ground, this time overrunning enemy machine gun and mortar emplacements. At 1430, Company C jumped off to the south with armor support and proceeded to clean the enemy out of the high ground in its sector and down to the seawall. Meanwhile, Company B entered the battalion line to the left of Company A and swung north, tying in for the night with 3/4. After clearing the ground in the battalion rear, Company C moved into position on the right rear of A to cover the exposed battalion flank overlooking the north-south Itoman road. Thus, the 1st Battalion commander had the unique experience of having his three infantry companies make successful attacks in as many different directions. While the 1st Battalion headed for the seawall, 3/4 began a cross-peninsular attack over extremely rugged terrain that was marked by a maze of interlacing ridges. "Every slope had its allotment of caves, each covering the other from flank and rear." Many of these caves were filled with enormous stores of explosives, which created a hazardous condition for the demolition teams attempting to seal them. Nonetheless, the indomitable teams set off hundreds of pounds of demolitions to destroy the honeycomb of cave entrances.

At 1300 on 8 June, an hour and a half after it had resumed its attack, 2/4 was just 200 yards short of that day's objective. Taking time out only to regroup, the battalion continued its advance, but was slowed by ever-increasing Japanese fire from well-constructed positions in the mouths of caves. Nevertheless, by 1530, 2/4 assault elements had captured the objective and began organizing for night defense. Before dark, patrols were sent back to mop up bypassed positions in the battalion rear.

To effect a junction with the 4th Marines, the 22d Marines pivoted on its right flank unit, while the 3d Battalion on the left moved in a clockwise direction to tie in with 3/4. A 3/22 patrol moved to the seawall and made contact with the right flank element of the 4th at 1550. Shortly thereafter, another battalion patrol scouted potential LVT landing beaches on the East China Sea coast north of Itoman, Reinforced by an infantry company from the 2d Battalion, 1/22 sent out strong combat patrols to take two hills. One, Hill 55, was approximately 500 yards east of

Chiwa, and the other, designated Hill 55-1, was almost the same distance east of the first. Throughout the day, the patrols received light small arms fire which increased in intensity as the hill objectives were neared. At 1800, the easternmost height, Hill 55-1, was in possession of the Marines, who were forced to withdraw under cover of darkness because of an ammunition shortage coupled with heavy incoming enemy mortar fire.

Originally scheduled to jump off at 0830, on 9 June, the 22d Marines attack was delayed until 0900. The 1st Battalion was to retake Hill 55-1, 2/22 was to seize Hill 55, while 3/22 was ordered to capture Hill 28 on the outskirts of Chiwa. The plan of attack called for the 1st Battalion to seize its objective, and for the 2d Battalion to pass through and capture its target. Not until late afternoon was 1/22 able to complete its mission, and the few daylight hours remaining did not give 2/22 enough time to capture its objective. As a result, Colonel Harold C. Roberts concurred in the battalion commander's recommendation to postpone the attack. Intense fire coming from Hill 55 prevented Lieutenant Colonel Shisler's 3/22 from outposting Hill 28 until after dark. But Hill 26, just south of the primary battalion objective, was secured and occupied at 1000 by Company I, which soon made firm contact with 4th Marines patrols after the latter had cleaned out Chiwa.

In the course of its fighting on 9 June, the 4th Marines found little that was different from previous days' experiences on the peninsula, for: "The advance was still slow and tedious against bitter resistance. Every Jap seemed to be armed with a machine gun, and there was still some light and heavy mortar fire. Casualties continued to mount and the number of Japs killed soared over the maximum of 1500 which were supposed to have been defending, and there were still plenty left."

The 1st Battalion was ordered to seize high ground near Hill 55-2, the third hill so designated in the 6th Division zone, in the vicinity of Uibaru. The Marine attack was delayed until supporting armor could get into firing positions on the road paralleling the right flank of 1/4. Once ready to fire, the tanks were driven off by a bombardment from an enemy rail-mounted 75mm gun, firing from cave ports on the side of a cliff near Chiwa.

Despite the temporary loss of its supporting armor, 1/4 attacked in the face of intense machine gun and mortar fire. Progress was slow and casualties increased steadily as the battalion advanced over ground that was honeycombed with caves, all of which had to be blown before they could be passed. At dusk, the right flank of 1/4 was anchored on a ridge northwest of Chiwa, while the battalion left flank extended to the outskirts of Uibaru, which had been taken earlier that day by 3/4.

A rocket barrage preceded the morning attack of 3/4 on 9 June. After the 3d Battalion moved out, difficult terrain prevented the battalion commander from maintaining unit control as his men worked closely with 2/4 to take the latter's objective, Uibaru. Upon occupying the village, the 3d Battalion received 20 casualties when a heavy enemy mortar concentration blasted its positions.

As the three infantry regiments of the 6th Division converged on the Oroku garrison from different directions and completely isolated it from the main body of the Thirty-second Army at Kiyamu, Admiral Ota's mixed defense force was slowly compressed into a small pocket in the southeast region of the peninsula. On all levels, Marine commanders found it increasingly difficult to maintain unit control and to coordinate the employment of their supporting fires with those of adjacent friendly units because of the limitations imposed by restricted zones of action. These conditions conspired with the stubborn terrain and the no-less yielding defense to slow to some degree all of the attacking Marine battalions. One of these units, 2/4, was ordered to capture the last remaining Japanese-held high ground in its zone. To complete this mission, the 2d Battalion was required to mount a frontal attack up a 400-yard wide valley over terrain that offered little cover or concealment. After the battalion jumped off at 1145 on 9 June, supported by tanks, M-75, and 37mm guns, its initial progress was slow. Further inhibiting the advance was the fact that a lack of tank approaches to the objective lessened the amount of close armor support given to the infantry. Also, 2/4 had to move ahead cautiously, for it was attacking in the direction of its own artillery and across the front of the 29th Marines.

Supplementing the natural tank obstacles in this sector, the Japanese had constructed a tank trap in front of their well-prepared ridge position and further safeguarded the area by a liberal sprinkling of mines. Since the Marines had no armored bulldozers or tank dozers immediately available, they were unable to construct a bypass in time to permit tanks to move ahead to support 2/4. At 1530, therefore, the battalion commander decided to halt the attack for the day.

Late in the afternoon, after 1/4 had pushed through Gushi, a tank managed to move through the now-demolished village and on to the road leading south to Itoman. Once in position on the flank of the cliff-emplaced enemy 75mm gun, it knocked the Japanese field piece out of commission. Only two shots were fired—one from the enemy gun, which missed, and one from the tank, which didn't.

On 10 June, the momentum of the 6th Division attack was accelerated. Early that morning, heavy construction equipment began clearing all tank approaches to the 2/4 frontlines, and by 0815 tanks and self-propelled howitzers were moving into position to support the infantry attack. In coordination with the 29th Marines on the left, 2/4 jumped off at 0945 with three companies abreast in assault. Less than an hour later, all attack elements were on the objective and organizing defensive positions from which they were to support the attack of the 29th Marines for the next two days.

From all appearances, the end of the battle for Oroku was near. At the same time that 2/4 had broken through the Japanese lines, the 1st and 3d Battalions advanced against lessening resistance. By 1400 on 10 June, the battalion boundaries of the 4th Marines had converged to squeeze 3/4 out of the line, and it went into regimental reserve.

While the 4th Marines pressed eastward, the 22d Marines drove northeast towards Tomigusuki, with 2/22 making the main regimental effort. This 1st and 3d Battalions provided fire support from positions they then held. When 2/22 had seized its objective, 3/22 was ordered forward and coordinated its attack with that of 1/4 on the left. The 4th and 22d Marines made slow but steady progress on 10 June, but 29th Marines battalions continued to meet stubborn resistance and could report only limited gains. Moving slowly through Oroku village behind flame tanks, 2/29 was held up and its way blocked when the lead tank was destroyed by a direct hit from a Japanese 8-inch shell. The regiment, therefore, was unable to reach the last major enemy defense pocket in the sector, which was located on the high ground west of Oroku village. The Japanese troops trapped here began a number of frantic attempts to break out. During the night 10-11 June, a series of local counterattacks hit all along the front. The heaviest of these took place in the sector of 1/4, which counted over 200 enemy dead in front of its lines after dawn. In reaction to the unfaltering and determined opposition of the Japanese defenders, General Shepherd launched an all-out armor-supported attack, committing the greater portion of eight infantry battalions to destroy the last vestiges of enemy resistance on Oroku.

In the 4th Marines zone, 3/4 resumed its attack at 0730, passing through the right elements of 1/4; the latter along with 2/4 remained in position to support the attack by fire. As the leading company began moving forward over a route that ran between Hill 58 (east of Uibaru) and Tomigusuki, it was held up by a hail of fire coming from Hill 62, on the right front. Covered by sniper fire from 1/4 on the left and tank supporting fire from the rear, Company I spent the better part of the day attempting to overcome the fortified hill blocking its path, and captured it before dark. By this time, Company K on the battalion right still was 300 yards short of establishing contact with 3/22.

The 22d Marines, led by 2/22, attacked Hill 62--north of Tomigusuki — following an intense 30-minute artillery preparation fired by six battalions of 105mm and one battalion of 155mm howitzers. Once 2/22 had seized Hill 62, 3/22 was to support the 4th Marines until the latter masked its fire, after which it would pass through 2/22 and capture Hill 53, overlooking Kokuba Estuary. The 2d Battalion was unable to carry the hill in its first attempt and did not, in fact, seize the hilltop until 1220, after a heavy fire fight.

At 1300, 3/22 effected a passage of the 2d Battalion lines and was in position to attack 45 minutes later. Despite the lack of an artillery preparation on the objective, the assault elements attacked, following a heavy mortar concentration. One factor preventing the tanks from gaining more favorable firing positions or even advancing with the infantry was the presence of well-concealed minefields along the route they were to travel. A mine-removal team worked under direct enemy fire and finally cleared a lane through which the tanks could pass to provide limited support. At 1450, Company L occupied Hill 53, giving the 6th Division high ground that overlooked not only the Kokuba Estuary, but also the entire Oroku area to the north where the 29th Marines had been unable to make any headway. That regiment attacked to seize the commanding terrain west of Oroku village repeatedly throughout the day, but was unable to find a way to overcome the series of small, mutually supporting hill positions that comprised the defense system here. Undoubtedly aware that his end and that of the Oroku garrison force was not far distant, Admiral Ota had sent the following communique to his superiors in Tokyo on 6 June: "More than two months have passed since we engaged the invaders. In complete unity and harmony with the Army, we have made every effort to crush the enemy. Despite our efforts the battle is going against us. My own troops are at a disadvantage since all available heavy guns and four crack battalions of naval landing forces were allocated to Army command. Also, enemy equipment is superior to our own."

"I tender herewith my deepest apology to the Emperor for my failure to better defend the Empire, the grave task with which I was entrusted."

"The troops under my command have fought gallantly, in the finest tradition of the Japanese Navy. Fierce bombing and bombardments may deform the mountains of Okinawa but cannot alter the loyal spirit of our men. We hope and pray for the perpetuation of the Empire and gladly give our lives for that goal."

"To the Navy Minister and all my superior officers I tender sincerest appreciation and gratitude for their kindness of many years. At the same time, I earnestly beg you to give thoughtful consideration to the families of my men who fall at this outpost as soldiers of the Emperor."

"With my officers and me I give three cheers for the Emperor and pray for the everlasting peace of the Empire."

"Though my body decay in remote Okinawa, My spirit will persist in defense of the homeland."

"Minoru Ota

"Naval Commander"

Four days after the transmission of the above, Admiral Ota released his last dispatch to his immediate commander, General Ushijima: "Enemy tank groups are now attacking our cave headquarters. The Naval Base Force is dying gloriously at this moment. . . . We are grateful for your past kindnesses and pray for the success of the Army."

Marine artillerymen killed or dispersed a group of Japanese soldiers attempting to break out of their entrapment during the night 11-12 June, and the 22d Marines dispatched 51 of the enemy attempting to infiltrate the regimental line. Obvious signs of a break in the enemy's stubborn and well-coordinated defense appeared on 12 June, when the 4th and 29th Marines compressed an already compact enemy pocket west of Tomigusuki, while the 22d pressed to the north in the direction of Oroku village.

The 4th Marines advanced slowly under heavy machine gun fire from positions in the hills and draws surrounding Hill 62 and from well-concealed caves on the hill itself. At 1225, the hill was captured and the attack continued with the Marines systematically cleaning out all pockets of resistance as they advanced. Three hours later, 3/4 tied in with the 22d Marines for the night, 500 yards from Naha Bay and with only one more large hill to be seized. The same day, the 29th Marines cracked open the firm enemy defenses that had held it up for almost a week. Oroku village was cleaned out by 2/29, as 1/29 began the first in a series of coordinated attacks at dawn to neutralize the enemy's mutually supported positions west of Oroku. By late afternoon, Easy Hill—the last Japanese strongpoint in the zone of the 29th Marines—was taken. Having lost this key terrain feature, enemy troops were forced to flee to the alluvial flatlands along the river coast between Hill 53 and Oroku. At this time, they "began displaying flags of surrender. Language officers equipped with loudspeaker systems were dispatched to the front line areas to assist in the surrender of those Japanese who desired to [do so]. The attempt was partially successful, 86 enemy soldiers voluntarily laid down their arms."

The 6th Division made a final sweep of the remaining Japanese-held area with 3/29, which relieved the 1st Battalion, and 2/29 jumping off to destroy all enemy still existing in their zone. Advancing rapidly to the southeast, the 29th Marines battalions swept past the 1st and 2d Battalions of the 4th Marines, pinching them out of the line; 3/4 also raced to the beach. As they approached the river flats, the attackers formed into skirmish lines, flushing the routed Japanese from the marshy grasslands along the river bank. A number of enemy soldiers gave themselves up, some committed suicide, others fought to the bitter end, and a few stoically awaited their deaths.

During the liquidation of this pocket, Colonel John C. McQueen, 6th Marine Division Chief of Staff, and Colonel Roy N. Hillyer, Tenth Army Chaplain, viewed the fighting from the north shore of the Naha Estuary at a point approximately 1,000 yards across the water from Oroku. "They saw the Marines come up over the high ground from the south and close in on the Japanese . . . The last survivor was a Japanese officer who calmly walked over to the seawall, sat down, lit a cigarette, and waited for the Marines to kill him."

Marine assault troops reached the seawall at noon and spent the rest of the day ferreting out small enemy groups attempting to evade death or capture by hiding in the cane fields and rice paddies near the river. At 1750, General Shepherd reported to General Geiger that all organized resistance on Oroku Peninsula had ended. During the day, 6th Division troops had killed 861 enemy soldiers and captured 78 prisoners.

The 6th Reconnaissance Company received orders at noon on 13 June to seize troublesome Senaga Shima — the island that had been scouted the night of 10 June — at 0500 on 14 June. To accomplish the task, a company from 1/29 was attached. For four days preceding the assault, the island had been subjected to a heavy and continuous bombardment. At the scheduled time, the LVT(A)-borne attack was launched and proceeded according to plan. There was no resistance to the landing. As the reconnaissance Marines combed the island, they found only dead bodies and silenced guns — all victims of the intense prelanding preparation. The battle of Oroku ended on 14 June. General Shepherd noted that: "The ten-day battle was a bitter one, from its inception to the destruction of the last organized resistance. The enemy had taken full advantage of the terrain which adapted itself extraordinarily well to a deliberate defense in depth. The rugged coral outcropping and the many small precipitous hills had obviously been organized for defense over a long period of time. Cave and tunnel systems of a most elaborate nature had been cut into each terrain feature of importance, and heavy weapons were sited for defense against attack from any direction."

Despite the powerful converging attack of three regiments, the advance was slow, laborious, and bitterly opposed. The capture of each defensive locality was a problem in itself, involving carefully thought out planning and painstaking execution. During ten days' fighting, almost 5,000 Japanese were killed and nearly 200 taken prisoner. Thirty of our tanks were disabled, many by mines. One tank was destroyed by two direct hits from an 8" naval gun fired at point blank range. Finally, 1,608 Marines were killed or wounded.

A most noteworthy aspect of the Oroku operation was the ability of the Tenth Army to exploit the amphibious capability of one of its Marine divisions during a critical phase of the Okinawa campaign despite the extremely limited time available for assault preparations. Overcoming most obstacles and discounting others, the 6th Marine Division planned and launched an amphibious assault within the 36-hour period allotted to it. In an after-action analysis of the operation, General Shepherd stated that "with trained troops and competent staffs in all echelons, the amphibious landing of a division is not of excessive complexity."

Chapter 10. Battle's End

On To Kunishi Ridge
At the same time the 6th Marine Division was landing on Oroku Peninsula, the 1st Marine Division was rolling up gains totalling 1,800 yards in its drive south from the Naha-Yonabaru valley. General del Valle's regiments made this advance while a faltering division supply system behind them threatened to break down completely because of the mud and the rain. The roads had become such quagmires that even tractors and bulldozers became stalled when they attempted to drag division vehicles out of or over the mud. Tanks and trucks were unable to cross the Kokuba; the

approaches to the bridge at the mouth of the river were untrafficable for a distance of over 500 yards. In an effort to facilitate resupply and evacuation operations, tanks were ordered off the roads. In general, forward units were logistically supported by Marines who hand carried supplies up to dumps behind the lines; the "trails were only negotiable for foot troops—vehicles could not have been used if we [2/7] could have gotten them across the inlet." On the division right on 4 June, the 7th Marines pushed forward to close off the neck of Oroku Peninsula and further entrap Japanese forces there. The hill mass at the base of Oroku in the division zone held the commanding terrain feature of the area, Hill 108. This height overlooked the East China Sea and the next major division objective, Itoman. Although the exposed right flank of the 7th Marines came under constant harassing fire from high ground to the right of the division boundary, the division left flank was generally secure since the adjacent 96th Infantry Division had moved forward steadily since its advance from the Kokuba River line.

After the Japanese defenses at Shuri had collapsed, the 1st Marines remained behind in the vicinity of the city to patrol and mop up, and the 5th Marines pursued the fleeing enemy. Before the dawn of 4 June, the 1st joined in the pursuit; 3/1 made a wide swing through the zone of the 96th Division in order to take the high ground north of Iwa and Shindawaku while 1/1 passed through the lines of the 5th Marines and took up positions in front of Hills 57 and 107.

By 0930, 3/1 had reached the small village of Tera, just north of Chan. At 1300, the battalion point was pinned down by fire coming from high ground just west of the Tomusu-Iwa road, and the advance guard attempted without success to clean out the enemy position. Just before 1400, the time scheduled for 3/1 to make its coordinated attack with 1/1, a cloudburst occurred. The supply problems here were further aggravated by the rain, and because of a communications blackout between the battalion and its artillery and naval gunfire support, 3/1 broke contact with the enemy and withdrew to a bivouac area in a draw behind the 383d Infantry. At 1730, Lieutenant Colonel Ross' entire battalion was in defilade, protected from enemy artillery fire. Contact with the artillery battalions and naval gunfire support ships was still lacking at this time and a mortar ammunition shortage existed. The afternoon downpours had turned the roads into morasses and the fields into calf-deep mud wallows in which the suction of the ooze pulled the soles off of the shoes of men walking in it.

Since food as well as mortar ammunition was in short supply, the 383d Infantry generously supplied the battalion with enough K-rations to enable 3/1 to issue two meals to each Marine. It was the general consensus of the members of 3/1 that "taking all things into consideration, this day probably was the most miserable spent on Okinawa by the men of this battalion." In addition, 3/1 found itself all but isolated from its regiment, since there was neither communication with nor a supply route to the 1st Marines CP, some 11,000 yards to the rear.

The 1st Battalion, 1st Marines, passed through the lines of 2/5 at approximately 1000 on the 4th. This was nearly three hours after Company F of 2/5 had attacked and seized Hill 107 without opposition, and completed its occupation of the high ground across the entire front of the regiment. When 1/1 took over from 2/5 at noon, the latter passed into corps reserve with the rest of the 5th Marines, but maintained its positions as a secondary line.

Although the downpour on 4 June had forced General del Valle to cancel the attack of 1/1 scheduled for 1400 that afternoon, the 7th Marines on the right had already jumped off. An hour later, the cancellation order was rescinded, and Lieutenant Colonel Shofner's battalion was again ordered to attack, to contact the 7th Marines, and to seize its original objective—the high ground north of Iwa and Shindawaku.

At 1630, the assault companies of 1/1 moved out to secure their target, some 1,500 yards away. The route of attack was up a valley floor, at the end of which a number of lesser hills rose in front of the objective. A creek that ran east to west across the valley was not visible from the LD; but a map reconnaissance indicated that the assault forces would be able to cross it with little difficulty. The Marines met no opposition after jumping off until reaching the "creek," now swollen into a raging torrent by the day's rains. It presented a formidable barrier to further progress. A reconnaissance of the stream banks uncovered a rudimentary bridge for carts to the left of the battalion position. The assault troops were ordered to move upstream, cross the bridge, and redeploy on the other side. As soon as the first Marine elements had crossed and were wallowing in mud towards firm ground, the heretofore-silent Japanese opened up with mortars and point-blank machine gun fire, sweeping the ranks of the onsurging troops. The Marines pushed on, nonetheless, and two platoons made it across to the south bank of the creek, only to become pinned down.

The 7th Marines on the right was unable to negotiate the swiftly flowing waters and was held up on the north bank, and the bridge-crossing site was fully covered by enemy defensive fires coming from a 200-foot-high ridge in front of 1/1. Therefore, the battalion commander ordered his troops to withdraw to the sector of 2/5 for the night. Because 1/1 had sustained a number of casualties, a covering force remained behind to evacuate the wounded after dark. The next morning, the 1st Battalion was ordered to bypass the enemy strongpoint by swinging into the zone of the 96th Division and follow closely in the trace of the 3/1 attack on Iwa.

Colonel Mason anticipated the problem of maintaining radio and wire contact with his battalions as they raced south. His movement order provided that, in case of a complete communications breakdown between regiment and the assault battalions, the most senior battalion commander of the committed units would assume tactical command overall until contact was established with regiment once more. Following a mud-slogging and wearying march south on 5 June, 50 men from 1/1 dropped out of ranks from exhaustion. During the trek, the battalion lost contact with regimental headquarters for a brief time and temporarily came under control of Lieutenant Colonel Ross.

Out of contact with regimental headquarters from the time he had led his battalion south from Shuri, and with the battalion objective yet uncaptured, Lieutenant Colonel Ross decided to complete his mission nevertheless. He took his command group forward early in the morning of 5 June to make a visual reconnaissance of the target. While this inspection was taking place, the Marines of 3/1 built fires in an attempt to warm themselves and dry as much of their clothing as possible before mounting the attack. Prior to the jumpoff, 3/1 received 19 supply air drops from VMTB-232 aircraft. In between the day's intermittent showers, the squadron flew a total of 41 resupply sorties; its all-time high to that date. The battalion departed its bivouac area at 1030 and arrived at the assembly area shortly thereafter; Lieutenant Colonel Ross then issued his attack order for the capture of the Iwa-Shindawaku ridge. Before jumping off at 1230, 3/1 learned that patrols from 2/383 had passed through Iwa without opposition. As soon as the Marine attack began, lead elements were held up for a short time by sporadic machine gun and sniper fire, but took the ridge before dark. In the two days spent to envelop the objective, the battalion had travelled more than 3,000 yards. By this time, the advance CP of the regiment had moved far enough forward to enable Colonel Mason to issue attack orders personally to his battalion commanders.

The plan for the next day's attack called for 3/1 to continue the advance and seize Shindawaku. The 1st Battalion would destroy all bypassed enemy pockets in the regimental zone and to the rear of 3/1, and would backtrack to the stream where the 4 June attack had been stymied.

To the relief of all, the rain stopped during the night of 5-6 June. At dawn of the 6th, 1/1 moved out of its bivouac east of Iwa, swung down to the village and then turned north. At this point, all three of its infantry companies formed a battalion skirmish line over an extremely wide front. The Marines then swept northward and past the zone where 3/7 was preparing to attack in a southwesterly direction. Lieutenant Colonel Shofner's troops accomplished their sweep at 1400 and then attacked and seized the ridge overlooking the stream. The few enemy soldiers still manning positions on this objective, not expecting an attack from the rear, were surprised while changing into civilian clothes. After taking the position with little effort, 1/1 went into reserve near Tomusu.

Because 3/1 had not been resupplied before its attack at 0900 on the 6th, the 383d Infantry again issued the Marines K-rations; this time, enough to provide each man in the battalion with one and a half meals. After jumping off, 3/1 advanced west and reached the outskirts of Shindawaku at 1030, when enemy troops were discovered occupying commanding ground on the ridge running northwest from the village. By 1800, however, the battalion had secured the ridge after a brief fight and 2/1 had moved to an area northwest of Iwa. Although the left flank of 3/1 was tied in with 2/383 for the night, the Marine battalion had not been able to contact the 7th Marines on the right. Early the next morning, 2/1 was moved into position to plug this gap.

During its drive south, the 1st Marine Division was sporadically halted for brief periods before a number of blocking positions organized and manned by small enemy groups. Each of these groups was generally the size of a company, and all of them together comprised a force equaling no more than two battalions. The Japanese holding units had been ordered and were determined to delay the Tenth Army as long as possible. The tactical situation and the nature of their mission, however, prohibited their setting up anything more permanent and stronger than hastily contrived defensive positions, which were unable to hold back the aggressive Marine offensive for long. When reconnaissance patrols uncovered these strong points, infantry commanders deployed their forces to take the objective by a combination of fire and maneuver. In most cases, the major attack force maneuvered into position to assault the objective from its flank or rear. At this time, Marine elements in front of the target supported the attack by firing on the objective to keep the enemy fixed in position. At times, the enveloping force provided fire support for a frontal attack. Regardless of the methods employed, the weather situation, and the condition of the terrain, General del Valle felt that "it was refreshing to be able to maneuver again, even on a modest scale."

On the critical right flank, the 7th Marines paced the division advance on 5 June with the 2d and 3d Battalions attacking against increasing opposition; 1/7 followed behind, mopping up the rear area. Acting as a screen to the right of 2/7 along the division right boundary, the 1st Reconnaissance Company dispatched patrols far ahead of the battalion advance, which sent back invaluable information. The company, however, found that its operations were severely restricted by its limited communications system and supply organization.

Like the 1st Marines, the 7th found the enemy less difficult than such other problems as those caused by the weather and the terrain. Marine wounded were evacuated in the rain over a five-mile sea of mud; sniper fire generally harassed the 8 to 10 litter bearers required for each casualty during the entire trip to the rear. Each day's attack was usually delayed until the weather was clear enough for land- and carrier-based planes to make a supply drop; so many sorties were flown for the 7th Marines as it trekked southwards that the trail of the regiment was blazed with brightly colored cargo parachutes.

The initial attack of the 7th Marines southwards from the Kokuba River bridgehead on 4 June gained the regiment approximately 1,100 yards. That same day, 2/7 captured Takanyuta. On the next day, the formerly raging torrent in front of 3/7 had receded to uncover a causeway over which part of the battalion crossed; the remainder moved to the zone of the 2d Battalion and crossed the stream from there. Once beyond the south bank, the assault battalions of the 7th drove forward 1,000 yards to a point just north of Hanja village. When furious machine gun and mortar fire from a hill mass in the zone of the 6th Division held up the 7th Marines, General del Valle received permission from IIIAC to lay the artillery fire of the 11th Marines on the suspected enemy positions. General Shepherd was authorized to cancel the fire when it threatened his troops. As the 1st Division continued its drive past the neck of the Oroku Peninsula, expanding the already-lengthy right flank of the division, 1/22 was ordered into defensive positions along this flank.

On the next day, 6 June, the 22d Marines battalion had not yet occupied its assigned flank security positions. It became necessary, therefore, to order 1st Division troops into the 6th Division zone to capture Hill 103 and destroy the enemy automatic weapons and mortars harassing the right flank of the 7th Marines. Lieutenant Colonel Berger's battalion had already attacked and was, in fact, within a few yards of the crest of the hill when elements of the 22d Marines arrived. Reorienting the direction of its attack to the south towards Hill 108, 2/7 advanced 1,000 yards before encountering stiff opposition near Dakiton, where it dug in for the night. On the left, the 3d Battalion pushed to the high ground southeast of the same town and likewise dug in.

Clearing skies on 7 June heralded a 1st Division success in breaking through to the coast that day and isolating Admiral Ota and his ill-fated troops on Oroku from the rest of the doomed Thirty-second Army in the south. Following up a thorough combined arms preparation, 2/7 overran Hill 108 to command a view of the island south to Kunishi. The former defenders of 108 were seen fleeing south in small groups ranging in size from 10-20 men each. The fire of Marine support weapons and machine guns relentlessly pursued the Japanese troops, killing many. After receiving an air drop of supplies, 3/7 attacked at 1430, overran Hanja, made contact with 2/1 on its left, and dug in for the night on a ridge just north of Zawa.

Following receipt of still another supply air drop early on 8 June, 3/7 resumed its attack with a sweep through Zawa as advance elements of 2/7 probed the Japanese positions guarding Itoman. Besides positioning the division for a final drive south, the breakthrough to the seacoast uncovered beaches on which LVTs could land when a waterborne supply system was established. When the first LVTs touched down on the coast approximately 500 yards north of Itoman shortly after noon on 8 June, General Hedge congratulated General del Valle "for cutting the island in two." Use of this new water route brought in enough rations to permit distribution of the first full issue to 7th Marines troops in more than a week. As the weather improved, some vehicular traffic appeared over slowly drying roads in the south. A few new bridges were constructed across the once-swollen streams in the north to help speed supplies of all sorts to assault troops driving to the southern tip of the island.

Advancing abreast of and pacing the march of the 7th Marines to the sea on 7 June, the 1st Marines also reported substantial gains. Early in the morning, 2/1 filled the gap existing on the right between 3/1 and 3/7, while 3/1 maintained contact with 3/383. By 1800, 2/1 was in possession of the height overlooking Zawa, and the 3d Battalion had moved 1,200 yards along the corps boundary to occupy the high ground 1,000 yards north of Yuza; 1/1 had moved to Iwa preparatory to relieving 3/1. All infantry battalions had been plagued by the supply situation, but it seemed to members of 2/1 that they had been especially dogged since leaving Shuri. Their only source of supply had been the air drops, and by the time that one could be made, the assault companies were several thousand yards forward of the drop zone. The supplies then were recovered by headquarters personnel, who carried them to forward dumps. At this point, Marines from the reserve company would pick up the supplies and carry them to assault units.

Sustained by supplies brought ashore by the LVTs, in the continuing good weather of 8 June, 1st Division troops pushed ahead against perceptibly stiffening resistance. The 1st Marines rolled forward; 3/1 secured its objective near Yuza at 1600, when it was relieved by 1/1 and went into regimental reserve near Shindawaku. Slightly later that day, 2/1 secured the high ground overlooking the Mukue River. On 9 June, division assault units spent the day probing enemy positions to their front in preparation for a major attack on the 10th.

Improved weather conditions and correspondingly better road nets over which supply convoys could travel served to release the VMTBs for other assignments. Following 6 June, when VMTB-232 made 49 drops, ground units requested paradrop missions on only eight other days in the rest of the month. By this stage of the campaign, the Marine pilots had become quite proficient and accurate in paradrop operations. In reference to a drop Major Allen L. Feldmeier's VMTB-232 had made on 8 June to its soldiers, the 383d Infantry sent him the following message: "Your drops have excellent results. We received 95 of the 97 packs which you dropped." Later in the month, VMTB-131 flew 3 missions totalling 20 sorties in which 70 packs—each averaging 1,000 pounds of food and ammunition—were dropped. Ground units receiving the supplies reported that they had recovered 90 percent or more of the packs. Increased enemy opposition arose on 9 June as 1st Marine Division units approached the Tera-Ozato area, which had been outposted by the Thirty-second Army. Patrols from both the 1st and 7th Marine received heavy rifle and machine gun fire while attempting to cross to the south bank of the Mukue Gawa. Small infiltration groups finally forded the stream, but were unable to advance beyond the bank. The 2d Battalion, 1st Marines, sustained moderate casualties during this day's fighting, but was unable to evacuate them until after dark because accurate enemy fires covered evacuation routes.

In the 7th Marines zone, 1/7 relieved 3/7, which then went into regimental reserve. No appreciable gains were made as 1/7 companies mounted two unsuccessful attempts to seize high ground overlooking Tera. The second effort was repulsed by extremely heavy small arms fire, which forced the assault elements to withdraw under the cover of a smoke screen. On the extreme right of the division,

2/7 patrols crossed the Mukue Gawa and attempted to seize the ridge north of Itoman, but were thwarted by enemy fire coming from emplacements fronting the 1st Battalion zone. One platoon of Company E was able to get to the far side of the river where it was pinned down immediately by accurate frontal and flanking fire.

Operating a combination CP-OP while aboard an LVT(A) floating 100-200 yards offshore of the battalion flank, Lieutenant Colonel Berger had a grandstand view of the fighting. When he saw that the advance platoon was pinned down, he went ashore to order the rest of the company to cross at the river mouth and reinforce the stricken unit. Steady Japanese machine gun fire prevented the Marines from wading across and shortly thereafter denied passage to troop-laden LVTS attempting the same route. At nightfall, the battalion commander ordered the exposed units to withdraw to the northern bank of the Mukue River under the cover of LVT(A) fire.

The 2d Battalion jumped off on the 10th with Companies F and G passing through the night defenses of Company E, dropping onto the beach from the top of a 10-foot-high seawall, and wading 400 yards across the stream mouth to a point on the south bank opposite the ridge. Shells from LVT(A)s pounded this high ground and Itoman beyond it. Following this preparation, the assault troops scaled the seawall to attack these two objectives. Although the battalion lost five officers in the first seven minutes of fighting, the onsurging Marines swept over the ridge, through the ruins of Itoman, and on to the high ground beyond the southern edge of the town.

At the same time that the 2d Battalion had crashed through Itoman, 1/7, spearheaded by Company A, made a rapid and unopposed rush to the crest of the hill north of Tera, where the Japanese strongpoint that had opposed the 7th Marines on the previous day was located. From this newly gained height, the battalion called for an artillery concentration on the high ground immediately east of Tera. Battalion 81mm mortars blistered the village with a barrage of white phosphorous shells, burning to the ground all buildings still standing. Although few Japanese troops were found in the area, numerous dazed civilians, who had miraculously escaped death in the bombardment, were discovered wandering aimlessly among the ruins. After sending the Okinawans to stockades in the rear, 1/7 prepared night positions and organized for the scheduled 11 June attack on Kunishi Ridge. By 10 June, the rains had ended and the transportation problem, although not so critical as it had been previously, was still not completely alleviated. The ground was drying and once-overflowing streams had lowered to a point where the road-construction and bridge-building efforts of the engineers could open the way to tracked and wheeled vehicles. Division engineers had converted oil drums into culverts and built tank fords over the fire-swept Mukue Gawa. In addition, the engineers provided round-the-clock maintenance for these fords so that the heavy traffic south could continue unabated. One especially important ford was built at the point where the Zawa-Tera highway crossed the Mukue.

The task assigned to 1/1 was the capture of Yuza Hill, the high ground approximately 700 yards west of Yuza and about 450 yards directly north of Ozato; 2/1 was to support the attack by fire, while units of the 96th Division were to provide security to the left flank of the 1st Marines. When the tank fords over the Mukue were opened on 10 June, Shermans also moved forward to support the 1st Marines attack.

Another support element, the 11th Marines, assisted the infantry assault. Following a rolling barrage, tank-infantry teams from 1/1 swept onto the western nose of the hill and Company C swarmed up to its crest in the face of blazing enemy machine gun and artillery fire. The company lost 70 of its 175 men in this charge.

Lieutenant Colonel Shofner's attack plan called for Company B to follow in the left rear of the lead elements and then to attack straight up the hill after first having worked its way through Yuza into jump-off positions. Upon reaching the crest, B was to tie in with Company C on its right and with the Army units on the left. Although the latter had begun the attack abreast of 1/1, Japanese troops entrenched in the extremely well-fortified Yuza Dake escarpment prevented the soldiers from advancing beyond their line of departure. Company B was unable to move forward because of the intense artillery and mortar fire coming from the front of the Army zone, and could not help Company C, which was isolated in an exposed and extremely tenuous position.

Late in the afternoon, Shofner sent Company B around to the right to join the company on the hill. Both assault companies had sustained heavy casualties in the fighting, but C was hit hardest; all of its officers were either dead or wounded. More Marines were lost during the night, 10-1 1 June, as a result of the constant deluge of enemy mortar and artillery fire placed on the hill. Added to this heavy toll were the casualties caused by grazing machine gun fire coming from weapons emplaced on Yuza Dake. Twenty more men were wounded in the dawn of 11 June, when at 0400, the Japanese mounted an unsuccessful counterattack. For the next two days, 1/1 waited on Yuza Hill for the 96th Division infantry to reduce the escarpment to the east. The Marine battalion had little trouble in maintaining its hill position despite the persistent Japanese artillery fire harassing it the entire time. While the 1st Battalion fought to gain its objective on the 10th, 2/1 with the help of armor support successfully cleaned the enemy out of the commanding ridge between Tera and Yuza. The next day, because 1/1 had been stymied on Yuza Hill, Lieutenant Colonel Magee's battalion was ordered to capture Hill 69, the commanding terrain feature directly west of Ozato. At 1030, the closely coordinated tank-infantry-artillery attack began when the battalion moved out in a column of companies. Initial progress was rapid, but when the infantry vanguard entered the valley leading to Ozato, well-placed Japanese mortar and artillery concentrations caused many Marine casualties. As the left flank of the spearhead approached Ozato, enemy machine gun and rifle fire began mowing down the attackers.

These mounting losses gradually slowed the momentum of the Marine assault, which the battalion commander attempted to revive by placing a second company in the line of attack to the right of the first. Despite the increasing volume of the massed fires provided by 2/1 supporting arms, enemy fire continued unabated. Disregarding their slowly ebbing strength and the loss of three supporting tanks, the assault units surged forward to capture the objective shortly before sundown. By dark, the battalion had consolidated the position and set in night defense lines from which it repulsed numerous infiltration attempts and blunted one counterattack before 11 June dawned.

In preparation for the many casualties anticipated during the fighting yet remaining, a light plane landing strip was placed into operation approximately 2,000 yards north of Itoman on 11 June. It was noted at the time that, for maintaining morale and obtaining immediate medical treatment for critical cases, "the value of this means of evacuating casualties cannot be overstressed." Now casualties were flown almost directly from medical clearing stations immediately behind the front to hospitals in the rear, a distance of 12 miles, in an average time of 8 minutes. This brief flight obviated a long and often body-racking haul in an ambulance jeep over roads that were practically nonexistent. From 11 to 22 June, VMO- 3 and -7 flew out 641 casualties from this strip.

On the same day the landing strip became operational, Colonel Snedeker's 7th Marines advanced 400 to 1,000 yards against ever-stiffening enemy opposition. The 1st Battalion, having cleared Tera, attacked to gain the high ground immediately south of the village. After mopping up in Itoman, 2/7 pushed 500 yards southward. Confronting the regiment now, approximately 800 yards equidistant from the outskirts of Tera and Itoman, was Kunishi Ridge, to be "the scene of the most frantic, bewildering, and costly close-in battle on the southern tip of Okinawa."

Battle For Kunishi Ridge

Running from the northeast to the southwest for a distance of perhaps 1,500 yards, the sheer coral escarpment of Kunishi Ridge held Japanese positions which comprised the western anchor of the last heavily defended line in front of Kiyamu. Both the forward and reverse slopes of the ridge were replete with caves, weapons emplacements, and fortified tombs, all of which reinforced natural defenses provided by the complex and difficult terrain features of the ridge itself. In front of the 7th Marines line, a broad valley containing grassland and rice paddies led to this crag and afforded the defenders unobstructed lanes of fire and the attackers little cover and concealment. Approaching tanks would fare no better than the infantry since they were restricted to two routes leading into the objective area—both covered extremely well by Japanese antitank guns. One road followed the coast line; the second cut across the center of the ridge at a right angle, dividing it. Having pushed through Itoman and Tera during the morning of 11 June, 2/7 and 1/7 prepared to continue on to Kunishi Ridge. Immediately after midday, tank-infantry teams from both assault battalions moved out towards the objective. Two hours later, withering frontal fire from the ridge, enfilade fire from the yet-uncaptured Hill 69, and accurate artillery concentrations on the tanks forced the attack to a halt. Because of these fires, and more coming from Japanese-held Yuza Dake, the commander of the 7th determined that it would be too costly to continue the attack in the daylight, so at 1447, he ordered the assault forces to withdraw. After making an aerial reconnaissance of the ridge in a low-flying observation plane, Colonel Snedeker concluded that a night attack would be the course of action most likely to succeed.

That afternoon, as the battalions dug in a night defense and prepared to continue the attack on the following day, the two assault battalion commanders were thoroughly oriented on the general scheme of maneuver at the regimental CP. Colonel Snedeker decided to attack straight across the valley, using the road leading into the ridge as the boundary separating the battalion zones and the telephone poles bordering the road as a guide. The assaulting battalions were to penetrate the enemy defenses at the point where the road entered the ridge. There the battalions were to peel off to their zones of attack and roll up the enemy's line. Until the hour of attack, 0330, on 12 June, normal artillery fires would be placed alternately on Kunishi Ridge and then Mezado Ridge (500-600 yards southwest of Kunishi), and thereafter only on the latter. In order to maintain deception and guarantee that the enemy would be surprised, the division issued an order prohibiting the use of flares and illumination of any kind—except in emergencies—after 0245. Before the night attack began, however, the Tenth Army decided to employ another type of weapon. Prior to and following the 1 April assault landings, the Japanese on the island had been subjected to a massive psychological warfare effort in which propaganda leaflets were delivered by aircraft and artillery shells. Also, Japanese-language broadcasts were directed at the enemy over loudspeakers placed near the front lines. For a period of several days preceding 11 June, this war of paper and words had been accelerated and an emphasis placed on the hopelessness of the Japanese position and the futility of continued fighting. Both the leaflets and the broadcasts called upon General Ushijima to surrender.

On the afternoon of 11 June, General Buckner sent a Tenth Army reception party, fully empowered to negotiate with any Japanese parley group, to the 2/7 observation post overlooking Itoman. At 1700, all American firing ceased in the 7th Marines zone in dubious but hopeful anticipation of an enemy party bearing white flags. No such group appeared, although six Japanese soldiers did surrender about an hour later to Marines in the lines. The battlefield's unnatural silence was shattered at 1804 when hostile mortar fire fell on the surrender point and American artillery resumed fire on Kunishi in answer.

Both battalions were poised to attack Kunishi Ridge with one company leading the assault. At H-Hour minus 1 (0230), Companies C and F proceeded to assembly areas and contacted each other on the line of departure. At 0500, when reinforcing Companies B and G moved out in their trace, the two assault units had already reached the crest of the ridge, achieving complete surprise. Company C, for example, destroyed several small enemy groups in the act of preparing their breakfasts.

At daybreak, while en route through the valley to reinforce the Marines digging in on the ridge, intense enemy fire caught the two follow-up companies and pinned them down. It became painfully apparent that the Japanese defenders had quickly recovered from their initial setback. In no mood to relinquish their hold on Kunishi Ridge without a last-ditch fight, they began lobbing hand grenades on the Marines situated in the forward positions. Here, Company F was consolidating at a point approximately 400 yards due north of Mezado village and was tied in on its left with Company C, whose line was extended some 450 yards to the northeast. Under the cover of smoke and with the assistance of tanks, the companies stalled in the valley made three attempts to reach the ridge during daylight on the 12th. Meanwhile, the troops already there needed rations, medical supplies, ammunition, and reinforcements; there were wounded to be evacuated also. Tanks attempting to get into firing positions south of Tera to silence the enemy weapons and relieve the companies pinned down were themselves fired upon, and in fact were unable even to leave the cover of the village.

In midafternoon, the Shermans were pressed into service to carry rations and personnel up to the ridge. At 1555, concealed in Tera from enemy observation, the tanks were loaded with supplies and Marines for the trip forward. Before dark, a total of nine tankloads in three runs had carried a reinforced platoon of 54 Marines and critical replenishment items up to the line. By displacing the assistant driver of each tank, it was possible to cram six riflemen inside instead. On arrival at the ridge, men and supplies were unloaded through tank escape hatches and casualty evacuees embarked in their place.

No further trips to the ridge were possible because of approaching darkness. In addition, the road leading to the front lines had caved in under the last tank in the column returning from the third trip. This tank bellied up, and neither the crew nor the casualties inside could leave through the escape hatch. After Marine mortars had fired a smoke cover for the tank, another came alongside to evacuate the troops it held. The disabled tank was then disarmed and abandoned for the night. In all, 1st Tank Battalion vehicles evacuated 22 wounded from the ridge.

The darkness precluding further tank operations enabled the remainder of the 1st and 2d Battalion of the 7th Marines to move to the ridge without incident. In regimental reserve, the 3d Battalion patrolled to the rear and guarded the flanks of the other two. With three companies now up front, each of the two forward battalions extended its lines further. By midnight, the battalion commanders were convinced that their positions were reasonably secure, and reassured that "the large amount of artillery support available could destroy any enemy counterattack which might be made against the initial ridgehead. . . ." As General del Valle described it, "The situation was one of the tactical oddities of this peculiar warfare. We were on the ridge. The Japs were in it, both on the forward and reverse slopes." Patrols from the 1st Marines ranged south along the corps boundary and into the outskirts of Ozato on 12 June. Although furious fighting was then going on in the 7th Marines zone, the 1st encountered relatively little opposition except for sporadic fire from Kunishi Ridge that was placed on cave-sealing and mopping-up teams working in the vicinity of Hill 69. On the following day, combat patrols began reconnoitering towards Kunishi Ridge in preparation for a predawn attack scheduled for the 14th.

Throughout the division zone, all efforts on 13 June were concentrated on preparing for this large-scale operation. The incessant cannonading of artillery pieces and naval rifles gave the forces of General Ushijima in the southern part of the island no respite. Two rocket launching craft took positions off the southern tip of Okinawa to rake reverse slope defenses of the Thirty-second Army. More than 800 5-inch rockets ripped into the towns of Makabe and Komesu in an hour's time alone.

In the four days following its seizure of Kunishi Ridge, the 7th Marines was somewhat isolated from other friendly ground units by "No Man's Valley," the 800-yard approach to its positions. This broad expanse was thoroughly covered by the fire of Japanese soldiers infesting the lower slopes and crests flanking the ridge. Supplies were either paradropped or brought in by tanks. Some air drops fell in the valley, "but they were in the minority." The rest were right on target and fell into a drop zone under Marine control. Sometimes it was even dangerous for the Marines to recover supply containers in these supposedly safe areas because of the many enemy snipers awaiting such targets of opportunity. One Japanese sharpshooter alone killed and wounded 22 Marines before he was finally located and eliminated.

Despite the inviting target their sheer bulk offered, tanks had to be used and did yeoman work in hauling supplies forward to the ridge. On their return trip, they evacuated casualties, some of whom were strapped to the side of the Shermans and then sandbagged as protection against enemy fire. In the morning of the 13th, a tank dozer constructed a bypass around the place where the road had caved in on the previous day. Upon completion of the detour, the lumbering mediums began shuttling back and forth to the ridge. Some of the tanks placed point-blank fire on enemy ridge positions covering the supply route in the 1/7 zone, and other tanks operated in the 2/7 zone, working over the western end of Kunishi Ridge. On the supply/evacuation runs, tanks lifted some 50 Marines from Company A to reinforce the rest of 1/7 on the ridge, and took out 35 casualties on the return trip.

During the course of the day, the assault battalions continued consolidating their holdings on Kunishi, and 1/7 sent patrols east along the ridge to contact the enemy and uncover his positions. The battalion advanced only slightly. When a Japanese smokescreen obscured Kunishi village to friendly observation, 81mm mortars hammered the area to disrupt enemy activity suspected there. Shortly after twilight, a group of enemy troops was sighted on Mezado Ridge and was quickly dispersed by a heavy concentration of mortar and small arms fire. Marines from 2/7 patrolled along the west coast but were soon pinned down by long-range enemy fire coming from the eastern part of the ridge; they had to be withdrawn under the cover of smoke. An increasing number of tanks became disabled by the accurate fire of AT guns well hidden in the ridge. A salvo from the main battery of a supporting battleship scored four observed direct hits on enemy emplacements, but did little to subdue other Japanese positions in the area. This particular barrage exploded on targets within 250 yards of friendly troops.

During the night of 13 June, the 1st Marines was ordered to attack the front of Kunishi Ridge in its zone before dawn the next day; H-Hour was set for 0330. Following a 30-minute artillery preparation, 2/1 jumped off with two companies in assault. Despite an earlier division order prohibiting the use of flares by units adjacent to the assaulting force before and during an attack at night, the attack area and the attackers were nonetheless illuminated. Many urgent calls to higher echelons for an immediate ban placed on the firing of flares proved fruitless. Fortunately, the Marines advanced undiscovered by the enemy and initial progress was unopposed. By 0500, two platoons from Company E had reached the topographical crest of the ridge; the support platoon and company headquarters were stopped well below this point by extremely severe enemy fire.

Half an hour later, Company G had worked one of its platoons up to a point on the ridge where it tied in with the left flank of Company E. At daybreak, increasingly active enemy sniping and intense fire on the flanks and rear of the assault companies served to isolate these platoons from the rest of their battalion. Tanks then rumbled forward to support the beleaguered Marines, whose casualties were mounting rapidly. One company lost six of its seven officers. Because routes to the advance positions were under accurate and direct enemy fire, the mediums were again pressed into action to haul supplies up to the line and carry casualties to the rear, much in the same manner as they had for the 7th Marines elsewhere on Kunishi Ridge. At the end of the day, an estimated 110 wounded Marines had been evacuated by the tanks.

Even though the enemy attempted to dislodge them, the Marines held onto their tenuous position. After dark, the reserve company was moved up and a perimeter defense was established for the night. Japanese small arms, mortar, and artillery fire, and recurring showers of hand grenades poured on the Marine positions throughout the hours of darkness. In addition, the enemy made many attempts to infiltrate all along the line. As the sun rose on 15 June, 2/1 found enemy pressure to be as constant as it had been the day before, and battalion casualties reaching alarming proportions. Although the tanks continued to carry supplies and evacuate the wounded, 2/1 critically needed ammunition and rations. A requested air drop scheduled for 0900 was delayed until the middle of the afternoon, and then more than two-thirds of the packs dropped into enemy territory and could not be recovered. The efforts of 2/1 assault companies notwithstanding, Kunishi Ridge was far from secured when 2/5 relieved 2/1 after dark on the 15th.

Earlier that day, 3/555 had relieved 1/1 on Yuza Hill, following which, the latter moved to an assembly area near Dakiton; 3/1 had already set up in the vicinity of

Shindawaku. With 2/5 on the line, Colonel Griebel had complete responsibility for the zone formerly held by the 1st Marines.

During the afternoon before 2/5 was to go into the lines, its company commanders were taken by tank to the front lines to make a personal reconnaissance of the area they were to take over. When they arrived at the positions of 2/1, they discovered that the tactical situation precluded a daylight relief. They also found that 2/1 held only a 75-yard section on the crest of Kunishi Ridge, with a portion of the battalion occupying a small pocket on the forward slopes of the ridge. As a result of this situation, the commanders of 2/1 and 2/5 agreed that the relief should begin only after it had become dark. In order to maintain tight control over the move and prevent matters from becoming confused in the restricted area where the relief was to take place, Lieutenant Colonel Benedict decided to commit only one of his companies initially. The relief of 2/1 was completed at 2030, a half hour after it had begun. The 1st Marines as a whole went into division reserve at 2300, after having been in the division line for 12 straight days during which it suffered nearly 500 casualties.

On the day before fresh troops had joined in the fight for Kunishi, the 7th Marines resumed its grinding advance by "the slow, methodical destruction of enemy emplacements on the ridge, to which the descriptive word 'processing' had come to be applied." The 2d Battalion was ordered to seize the rest of the ridge in its zone and to be prepared to continue the attack to Mezado Ridge. Company A attacked east to seize the remainder of the reverse slope of Kunishi Ridge within the 7th Marines zone, while B and C provided fire support and mopped up behind the assault company. Despite difficult terrain and an unrelenting enemy opposition, Company A succeeded in closing to the outskirts of Kunishi village.

At 1247, Company B was ordered to continue the advance through Kunishi, and then to attack north to secure the forward slope of the easternmost sector of Kunishi Ridge. Although the company passed through the village and began heading for the high ground with only slight interference, withering machine gun fire soon pinned down all but two rifle squads, which were able to climb the height, Once the Marines had gained the crest of the ridge, the Japanese launched a strong counterattack, forcing the squads from their temporary holding. The company as a whole then withdrew to lines held the previous night. To the right of 1/7, the 2d Battalion was subjected to increasingly intense enemy fire despite suppressive American counter-barrages; 2/7 reported only limited gains that day. At 1530, the logistic and tactical support of the 7th Marines by tanks ended when the armor began assisting the 1st Marines. On the 14th, the tracked vehicles had carried 48 men of the 7th Marines forward and evacuated 160.

During the following two days, 2/7 was supported by naval gunfire, artillery, air, rockets, and 81mm mortars, which mercilessly pounded the enemy. Both gun and flame tanks furnished direct close-in support, but could make no appreciable dent in Japanese defenses. A stubborn enemy notwithstanding, 2/7 moved its lines some 500-700 yards to the right and in front of the first high ground leading to the Mezado Hill mass, the division objective after Kunishi.

The 1st Battalion fared no better in its attempt to seize the rest of Kunishi Ridge in its zone on 15 June than it had on the 14th. Notified that 15 artillery battalions were on call for supporting fires, 1/7 moved out at 0945 following an artillery preparation and preliminary patrolling. Company C attacked directly east along the ridge while B moved through Kunishi village and then turned north towards the high ground again.

Heavy Japanese fire from prepared emplacements prevented the Marines from advancing across the open ground between the village and the ridge line, and Company C was unable to relieve the pressure on B. At 1600, the two units were withdrawn once again to positions held 13-14 June.

During the night 15-16 June, small enemy groups were active in front of 1/7 lines harassing the Marines with small arms fire and lobbing hand grenades into their foxholes. Before dawn on 16 June, the troops on the left (east) flank were pulled back to the west approximately 200 yards to permit a massive artillery preparation on the objective which had stymied 1/7 the preceding two days. An extremely heavy concentration of artillery, mortar, and rocket fire drummed that day's target for nearly three hours before the assault forces jumped off. By 1345, 1/7 had completely seized the rest of the ridge in its zone and immediately began mopping up and consolidating its newly won ground. Shortly thereafter, battalion troops "repeatedly encountered and destroyed numerous groups of the enemy wandering through the town of Kunishi in a confused, disorganized, and bewildered state. It was evident that the end was not far off."

One other major accomplishment that afternoon was the capture by Company A of "The Pinnacle," a particularly difficult enemy strongpoint situated so that it could be neither destroyed nor neutralized by any type of support weapon immediately available. It was in this area that the enemy sniper who had shot 22 Marines earlier was hunted down and killed. Approaches to The Pinnacle were swept by Japanese fire, and its seizure by the infantry was slow, tortured, and costly. To the right of 1/7, the 2d Battalion lines were extended some 400 yards further west to where the battalion held the first high terrain approaching the Mezado hills. This progress was accomplished even while the battalion had sustained heavy casualties and lost its valuable armored support, which fell victim to Japanese land mines and 47mm AT guns. Expert employment of its supporting arms enabled 2/7 to make slight gains on the 16th. For example, salvos from the main battery of USS *Idaho* were called down on targets located within 400 yards of frontline troops. In addition, air liaison parties controlled air strikes, often consisting of 25-30 planes each, which successfully destroyed stubborn pockets holding up the advance.

No longer was Kunishi Ridge a major obstacle in the way of the 1st Marine Division, for the terrain that the Japanese had so doggedly defended here, including the approaches to Mezado, had been virtually cleaned out by the end of 16 June. Only that portion of the ridge on the far left of the division, in the 5th Marines zone, still presented some problems. With the reduction of enemy opposition on The Pinnacle, the 7th Marines was able to make physical contact with the 5th.

As 1st Division troops prepared for the final drive south, mopping up operations on Oroku Peninsula neared an end. Concurrently, General Shepherd's staff drew up plans for the eventual commitment of the 6th Division in the southern front. Initially, the 22d Marines was to pass through right flank elements of the 7th Marines on 17 June to relieve 2/7; 3/7 would come out of reserve to relieve the 1st Battalion.

In the 5th Marines zone on 16 June, 2/5 attacked at 0730 and spent the day working over that portion of the regimental area that lay between Kunishi Ridge and Hill 69. At approximately 1800, a reinforced company reached the crest of the ridge and tied in with the left flank unit of the 7th Marines. Bitter, close-quarter fighting had been the order of the day for 2/5, whose assault companies had received continuously heavy small arms fire. Rising casualty figures again required tanks to be employed as evacuation vehicles; this task was in addition to their shuttling ammunition and rations forward. In face of Japanese holding action to its front, 2/5 made slow but steady progress.

Although enemy infiltrators attempted to breach 5th Marines lines during the night 16-17 June, they were thoroughly discouraged. As 2/5 resumed the attack on the 17th, oppressive enemy small arms fire coming from the vicinity of Aragachi in the XXIV Corps zone punished the front and flank of the battalion. Its task was to seize that portion of Kunishi Ridge still held by the enemy. Attacking with a two-company front, the 2d Battalion faced the problem of coping with Japanese reverse-slope positions and destroying them. To smooth the way somewhat, a rocket barrage was laid on the objective. A short time later, at 1030, tanks moved out and clambered over the ridge route, which had been opened earlier by an armored bulldozer. Murderous enemy fire criss-crossed the crest of the ridge as 2/5 grimly pushed on. All tanks were pressed into action as armored ambulances once again, but only the walking wounded could be taken inside of the vehicles and evacuated. Stretcher cases presented a serious problem because they could not be taken up through the tank escape hatches, but had to be lashed to their rear decks. Often, wounded were hit a second and third time on their trip to the aid station.

Throughout the afternoon, the volume and intensity of enemy fire as well as the ferocity of the enemy opposition remained undiminished. Tank, artillery, and mortar fire, and the ripple fire of several rocket barrages were directed at suspected Japanese strongpoints and weapons emplacements in an attempt to open the way for Marine tank-infantry teams. At 1700, Lieutenant Colonel Benedict decided to commit his reserve company and further strengthen the assault companies by sending forward 133 replacements, which had been assigned to the battalion three days earlier.

With this infusion of fresh troops in its line, 2/5 surged eastward along the ridge; by nightfall, the battalion held approximately three-fourths of the 1,200 yards of Kunishi Ridge in the regimental zone. Because the position of the battalion was somewhat precarious, at dusk Colonel Griebel attached Company K, 3/5, to the 2d Battalion with a mission of protecting the battalion rear. At 2315, an estimated company-sized counterattack hit 2/5 positions, but was thoroughly blunted; Company K troops killed the few Japanese that succeeded in penetrating the lines.

On the coastal flank of the IIIAC zone, 6th Division Marines had become fully involved in the drive to the south by the end of 17 June. Moving forward during the afternoon of the previous day to relieve 2/7, the 1st and 3d Battalions of the 22d Marines attempted to cross the valley between Itoman and Kunishi, but were forestalled by the severe enemy fire covering this route. Forced to turn back to their previous positions, the two battalions waited until dark to begin the relief. The uneventful passage of the lines began at 0300, 17 June, and by dawn assault elements were in jump-off positions at the base of the northern slope of Mezado Ridge, prepared to attack at 0730 in coordination with 3/7 on the left.

An artillery, naval gunfire, and air bombardment of Mezado Ridge, and of Hill 6964 and Kuwanga Ridge beyond it, preceded the attack. Once the fire had lifted, the 22d Marines moved out with two assault battalions abreast--3/22 on the left. Machine gun and intermittent mortar fire paced the advance up the slope of the ridge, but as the morning wore on, the Marine progress became increasingly difficult in the face of stiffening resistance. To support the attack of 1/22, 6th Division tanks moved around the right flank of the regiment and through the water towards an off-shore reef to gain firing positions commanding direct observation of the caves on the western tip of Mezado Ridge. As one armored platoon began to negotiate the route, the unexpected depth of the water prevented it from working its way forward far enough to enfilade the ridge, and its tanks were forced to deliver supporting fire from the most advanced points that they had been able to reach. Tank weapons could not suppress the heavy machine gun fire coming from the reverse slope of the hill mass holding up 1/22. As a result, the battalion was unable to gain more than a foothold on the forward slope of Mezado Ridge until 1700, when it positioned two companies on the crest of the ridge for night defense.

Inadequate maneuvering room to the front also limited the employment of supporting armor. Besides the flank route through the water, the only other suitable tank road ran through a rice paddy which had been cratered in four places and heavily mined as well. Once the mines were removed or neutralized, tanks lumbered up to these craters and dumped into them bundles of large logs that had been attached to their front slope plates. Tanks and logs instead of dump trucks and fill dirt were used to plug the craters because only armored-plated vehicles could weather the severe enemy fires.

After two craters in the road had been filled, it was discovered that the approaches to a small bridge further up the road had been mined. Sniper and machine gun fire prevented engineer clearing teams from neutralizing the mined area, and the road project was abandoned temporarily. Nonetheless, the tanks advanced as far forward as possible to deliver overhead supporting fires.

By noon, 3/22 had secured the highest point on the ridge and maintained the momentum of its attack to clean out the town of Mezado as well. Before dusk, the battalion had captured the key terrain around Hill 69 and was in command of the ground overlooking the next objective, Kuwanga Ridge. With the exception of an attempted enemy counterattack in the sector of 1/22 at 2210, a generally quiet night was passed by the 22d Marines.

When 1st Division troops jumped off on the 17th, 3/7 attacked in a column of companies, Company K leading, to take the Hill 69 east of Mezado. Company I maintained contact with the 22d Marines, and Company L took up positions to protect the left flank of K. Following an unopposed 1,400-yard drive across the plateau just east of Mezado to seize Hills 69 and 52, 3/7 halted for a short time to reorganize, and then attempted to continue the drive to the crest of Hill 79--the last remaining barrier before Makabe. Heavy Japanese fire from positions on the high ground commanding the Kuwanga-Makabe road forced the battalion to dig in for the night before it could gain the hill. Once dug in, 3/7 Marines quickly organized to blunt all enemy attempts to infiltrate and counterattack in the darkness. When the Japanese 22d Regiment did launch its counterattack, it was directed against 1/22. This determined effort born of despair was doomed from its inception because that portion of the enemy regiment scheduled to exploit the counterattack had been almost completely destroyed that afternoon. In effect, the near annihilation of the 22d Regiment meant that the left flank of the Japanese outpost line had all but collapsed, and that the 32d Regiment, holding positions near Makabe, was faced with the threat of having its left flank rolled up.

The Marines were prepared to turn this threat into reality by exploiting the successes of 17 June with the commitment of fresh troops into the battle on the next day. While the 7th Marines finished "processing" Kunishi Ridge, the 8th Marines (Reinforced), commanded by Colonel Clarence R. Wallace, prepared to relieve 3/7 to continue the attack southward. Before the dawn of 18 June, this 2d Marine Division infantry regiment, now attached to the 1st Division, entered the lines.

Iheya-Aguni Operations

After its feint landings on the southeastern coast of Okinawa on L-Day and L plus 1, the 2d Marine Division remained on board its transports which steamed in the vicinity of the target area until 11 April. On that date, the Demonstration Group set out for Saipan, arriving there four days later. On 14 May, CinCPac ordered the division (less one RCT) detached from the operational control of the Tenth Army and designated it as the area reserve under control of CinCPOA. In addition, General Watson received an alert for his division to conduct Phase III(d) of the ICEBERG Plan, the landing on Kikai Jima. Once captured, this small island north of Okinawa was to be utilized as a northern outpost for the Ryukyus area, and was to base four fighter groups, two night-fighter squadrons, and one torpedo-bomber squadron. The 8th Marines (Reinforced) remained under the control of General Buckner for the impending landings on Iheya and Aguni Shimas, and was ordered to reembark immediately. For the entire month after its arrival at Saipan, the division remained on board the transports. A warning order for the Kikai invasion had been issued on 6 May, but this alert was reduced in urgency four days later by a message that indicated that Phase III(d) might not be conducted. With the arrival of the 14 May message releasing the division from Tenth Army control, the Marines began unloading and rehabilitating their equipment ashore in preparation for the time when it was to be ordered to mount out for Kikai. On 3 June, the landing was deferred for an indefinite period, and on the 19th, the 2d Marine Division (less RCT 8) was released from its role as Ryukyus area reserve and reverted to the control of FMFPac. Once again, on 24 May, the 8th Marines departed Saipan headed for Okinawa; its eventual target, the islands of Iheya and Aguni. Because of the heavy damage that had been sustained by the fleet and especially the radar pickets during Kamikaze raids, early in May Admiral Turner asked General Buckner to begin a study of outlying islands to determine where long-range radar and fighter director facilities could be installed. Resulting from this study was the decision that Tori, Aguni, Iheya, and Kume Shimas could be captured in that order. A special landing force, a reinforced company from the 165th Infantry, made an unopposed landing on Tori on 12 May and a detachment from Air Warning Squadron 1 began operations almost immediately.

Since the Okinawa campaign was now reaching a crucial stage, General Buckner believed that the forces already committed in the fight southward should not be diverted to such secondary actions as the proposed landings on the other outlying islands noted above. He requested, therefore, that the reinforced 8th Marines be returned to Okinawa to effect the Iheya-Aguni landings. Brigadier General LeRoy P. Hunt, ADC of the 2d Marine Division, was designated the landing force commander for these operations. Flying to Okinawa with key members of his staff on 15 May, General Hunt spent the 16th and part of the 17th conferring with Tenth Army staff officers about the proposed operation plan. By 30 May, when the 8th Marines arrived at Okinawa, a complete naval gunfire and air support schedule had already been established, and detailed contingency plans drawn up to meet any situation that might arise from enemy sea or air action.

The attack force, commanded by Admiral Reifsnider, steamed from the Hagushi transport area early on 2 June and set a course for the target, located 15 miles northwest of Hedo Misaki. The bombardment prior to the H-Hour of 1015 proceeded as scheduled; 2/8 and 3/8 landed on Iheya 27 minutes later. Neither enemy opposition nor enemy troops were encountered. The Marines only found some 3,000 confused but docile natives who were taken under tow by military government teams supplied by the Tenth Army Island Command. Late in the afternoon of the 3d, the troops began general unloading and the island was officially declared secure the next day.

The landing on Aguni Shima, 30 miles west of Okinawa, was delayed until 9 June by inclement weather. On that day, 1/8 went ashore under circumstances similar to those found at Iheya. The only Marine casualties of the two amphibious assaults were sustained at Iheya; 2 Marines were killed and 16 wounded by aerial rockets and short rounds of naval gunfire. In accordance with the instructions it had received from Tenth Army before the operation, the 8th Marines stood ready for immediate commitment on Okinawa upon completion of the two landings. When fresh units were needed for the final thrust against the Japanese dug in on Kiyamu Peninsula. Colonel Wallace and his troops were available.

The Final Push

By 4 June, the remnants of the Thirty-second Army had fully manned the outpost line of Kiyamu Peninsula. Concentrated in this area were approximately 30,000 Japanese troops, distributed as follows: 24th Division and attachments, 12,000; 62d Division and attached units, 7,000; 44th IMB and attached units, 3,000; 5th Artillery Command and attached units, 3,000; and troops attached directly to Thirty-second Army Headquarters, and the command itself, 5,000. "Attrition during retirement operations," was the official Japanese explanation for the 20,000-man differential between their estimated strength figure of 50,000 in late May and the total number of effective available at the beginning of June. Of General Ushijima's remaining forces, approximately 20 percent were survivors of the original, first-rate infantry and artillery defense garrison; the rest were either untrained rear-echelon personnel or Boeitai. Leading this motley force at battalion level and above were many of the original senior commanders who had remained alive and were still capable of arousing a fighting spirt in their men.

Their unflagging belief in a final Japanese victory was unrealistic in view of the alarming losses of weapons and equipment that the Thirty-second Army had sustained since the American landing on 1 April. Hand grenades and explosives either were in short supply, or in the case of some units, non-existent. Only 20 percent of the original number of heavy machine guns owned by the army remained, and few of its heavy infantry cannon and mortars were still firing. Although the army ammunition supply along with 2 150mm guns, 16 150mm howitzers, and 10 antiaircraft artillery pieces had been transported south to Kiyamu when Shuri was abandoned, the stock levels of artillery ammunition precluded more than 10 days of sustained firing.

Despite these outward signs of its imminent defeat and impoverished condition, the belief held by General Ushijima's army in ultimate victory was derived from deep-seated tradition, strongly enforced discipline, and the historically pervasive influence of Japanese military doctrine throughout the Empire. These intangibles, almost completely alien and incomprehensible to Americans, promised that Kiyamu Peninsula was not to fall and the battle for Okinawa was not to end before a final, violent climax.

Influenced by the location and relative strength of enemy strongpoints facing the Tenth Army, and the availability and status of his assault forces, General Buckner had shifted the corps boundary west on 4 June. In the now-narrower IIIAC zone, General Shepherd's division sought to capture the Oroku Peninsula while the 1st Marine

Division was to cut off the peninsula from the rest of the island, capture Itoman, seize both Kunishi and Mezado Ridges, and drive to Ara Saki, the southernmost point of the island. The assignment given XXIV Corps included the capture of the Yuza Dake-Yaeju Dake Escarpment as a primary objective. On line facing this foreboding terrain were the 96th and 7th Divisions. Nearly two weeks of punishing and brutal fighting were to ensue before the two army divisions could eliminate all enemy resistance in this Thirty-second Army defense sector. XXIV Corps units spent the period 4-8 June in regrouping and attempting to gain favorable jump-off positions for the attack on the escarpment on the 9th. All supporting arms were employed to soften the well-organized enemy defense system. Armored flamethrower, tank, assault gun, and artillery fires were added to the point-blank blasts of experimental 57mm and 75mm recoilless rifles in an effort to reduce the natural bastion.

The defense of the Yuza Dake-Yaeju Dake outpost line had been assigned to two units. Guarding the escarpment from Hill 95 on the east coast to Yaeju Dake was the 44th IMB; the remainder of the high ground, including Yuza Dake, was the responsibility of the 24th Division. Added to the tenacious determination of the foe was the natural, fortress-like quality of the terrain he guarded. This combination enabled the Japanese to defend the Yuza Dake area with only one regiment, the 89th.

Facing the 7th Division were enemy troops who compared unfavorably with the veterans defending Yuza Dake. Coming from miscellaneous shipping engineer, sea raiding, mortar, and line of communication units, the soldiers were loosely organized into provisional infantry regiments and put into the 44th IMB line. The vital Hill 95-Nakaza Valley area was held by survivors of the 15th Independent Mixed Regiment, which first began to give way under the repeated pounding of the 7th Division attack. General Arnold's soldiers relentlessly pushed forward on 11 June, the second day of the all-out corps assault on the escarpment, and threatened the rest of the Thirty-second Army line by breaking into the 44th IMB defenses. An attempt by General Ushijima to shore up this section of his rapidly crumbling outpost by committing jerry-built infantry units comprised of service and support troops proved to be "as ineffective as throwing water on parched soil."

The 89th Regiment continued to withstand the inroads of 96th Division infantry on 12 June, but this day marked the beginning of the end for the 44th Independent Mixed Brigade. Although it had been reinforced with two battalions from the 62d Division as a result of the brigade commander's urgent pleas, the time for decision was already past, as was the chance for these newly committed units to affect the ultimate course of the battle. Clear weather on 13 June, following a night of abortive enemy counterattacks, permitted General Hedge to employ fully all of his supporting arms. Units of the 62d Division attempting to reach and revive the hapless 44th IMB were themselves blasted by American air, artillery, and naval gunfire. Although the 89th Regiment—reinforced by the 24th Reconnaissance Regiment—still maintained its hold on Yuza Dake, its rear and flank were threatened this day by the impending penetration south of Yaeju Dake. Further advances on 14 June forced General Ushijima to commit the 13th Independent Infantry, which was almost immediately smashed by 7th Division troops. Also committed and destroyed on the 14th were the remaining reserve battalions of the 62d Division.

Elsewhere, as Japanese positions began to give way under the pressure of the American onslaught, Thirty-second Army headquarters lost all contact with the 15th IMR—the last infantry element of the 44th IMB able to maintain unit integrity. To stave off the last stages of a crushing defeat, General Ushijima ordered the 62d

Division into the deteriorating Japanese line from reserve positions southwest of Makabe, but a savage lashing from American artillery, naval guns, and air-delivered napalm and bombs thoroughly disrupted the deployment. Few, if any, of the enemy troops arrived at their destination.

The 96th Division took advantage of this confused situation to rush its infantry through the Yuza Dake perimeter. On the left, the 7th Division surged down the coast. By the end of 17 June, XXIV Corps regiments held firm control of all commanding ground on the Yuza Dake-Yaeju Dake Escarpment. Compressed between the front lines of the corps and the southern tip of Okinawa were the remnants of the Thirty-second Army—a hodge-podge of units and individuals from the 62d Division, 44th IMB, and 24th Division. Before the island had been secured by the Tenth Army, most of these Japanese troops would die violently in a forlorn attempt to protect the headquarters of General Ushijima.

Death Of An Army

The death throes of the Thirty-second Army became even more obvious as the Tenth Army advanced against steadily lessening resistance on 18 June. Although most sections of the Japanese line proved softer than before, two isolated centers of opposition developed during the day—one around Medeera and the other in the area of Mabuni. The first was held by the remnants of the 24th Division, and the second, around Hill 89, was defended by elements of the headquarters and troops of the remaining Thirty-second Army units. Leading the 1st Marine Division attack was the 8th Marines, which had relieved the 7th Marines the previous night. At 0730, 2/8 (Lieutenant Colonel Harry A. Waldorf) jumped off from Mezado Ridge to head south and occupy a line west of Makabe from which it could launch a "quick decisive thrust" to the sea. Light machine gun and rifle fire, later mixed with sporadic mortar and artillery rounds, hit the left front and flank of the battalion as it made a rapid 1,400-yard advance to cap its first day in the lines. By dark, the battalion had secured its objective and began digging in for the night. Since its left flank was well forward of 1/5, Company B, 1/8, was attached to fill the gap.

Early on 18 June, General Buckner had gone forward to witness the fighting, and "probably chose the 1st Division front on this date because he wanted to see the 8th Marines in action," as he thought well of the regiment. As General Oliver P. Smith recalled: "On his way to the front [to the 3/8 OP], General Buckner met Bob Roberts (Colonel Harold C. Roberts, commanding Officer of the 22d Marines). Roberts urged General Buckner not to go to the front at this particular point as the rapid advance had bypassed a good many Japanese, and, further, there was considerable flanking fire coming from the high ground in front of the 96th Division. General Buckner did not heed this advice. (Roberts was killed an hour or so later on another part of the front.) The General got up on a ridge where Lieutenant Colonel Paul E. Wallace [commanding 3/8] had an OP. Tanks and infantry were operating ahead. A rifle company was on the ridge preparing to move forward. General Buckner took position behind two coral boulders separated by a slit through which he could look. His position was slightly forward of the crest. He had not been in this position long when a Japanese 47mm shell hit the base of the boulders. The first shell was followed by five more in rapid succession. Either a fragment of the first shell or a piece of coral rock thrown out by the detonation hit General Buckner in the chest. This wound was mortal. Hubbard [General Buckner's aide], with the assistance of others in the vicinity, dragged General Buckner over the crest to a defiladed position. A Navy hospital corpsman was there and a doctor arrived within three minutes. Plasma was available, but the General had lost blood so rapidly that plasma could not save his life."

Upon being informed of General Buckner's death, Brigadier General Elwyn D. Post, Tenth Army Chief of Staff, sent a message to CinCPOA reporting the death. In addition, General Post, knowing General Buckner's expressed desires concerning the succession of command, recommended in the message that General Geiger be designated the new Tenth Army commander. On 19 June, General Geiger was appointed a lieutenant general and was officially designated Commanding General, Tenth Army, the same day, making him the senior officer present on Okinawa. This was the first time that a Marine officer had commanded a unit of this size. General Joseph W. Stilwell, U. S. Army, former deputy commander of the Southeast Asia Command, arrived on the island at 0700, 23 June, succeeding General Geiger the same day, after the Marine general had successfully directed the final combat operations on Okinawa. Early in the morning on which General Buckner died, the 5th Marines was to take Hill 79, northwest of Makabe. At dawn, 1/5 moved out around the western nose of Kunishi Ridge and then south through the 8th Marines zone in order to get into positions to jump off at 0730. As soon as the attack began, the assault units were pinned down by fire coming from the objective and unable to move until 1100, when tanks arrived and rumbled into support positions. A coordinated tank-infantry assault was launched soon after, and the Marines were on the hill by noon. Following in the wake of the attack was 3/5, up from reserve, which moved into support positions behind the 1st Battalion for night defense.

Enemy AT fire forced the Marine tanks to operate cautiously, but did not slow them down. Artillery-delivered smoke on a suspected antitank gun position on Hill 81 just north of Makabe blinded the enemy gunners and permitted the Shermans to operate without being fired upon. Other AT guns were destroyed during the day after having been spotted from the air by an experienced tank officer, who was flown over the battlefield for that purpose. By dark, 1/5 had gained the lower slopes of Hill 79 with armored assistance, but could not advance beyond that point because of heavy enemy fire from high ground in the 96th Division zone and Hills 79 and 81. At the end of the day, tank-infantry teams from 2/5 eliminated the last large pockets of enemy resistance on Kunishi Ridge, and dug in on commanding ground for the night. In the 6th Marine Division zone, 2/22 passed through the lines of 3/22 on 18 June to attack Kuwanga Ridge. Moving rapidly ahead despite steady automatic weapons fire, the battalion gained a foothold on the high ground and began simultaneous drives to the east and west to clear the ridge of enemy. Although fired upon by rifles, machine guns, and mortars, the battalion possessed the greater part of the ridge before midafternoon. At this time, General Shepherd saw that the understrength 2/22 was spread too thinly over the 1,800-yard-wide ridge to withstand a concerted enemy counterattack, so he ordered the 4th Marines to attach one battalion to the 22d for night defense; Colonel Shapley ordered 3/4 forward.

The other two battalions of the 22d Marines spent the day hunting down and destroying numerous enemy groups infesting the reverse slopes of Mezado Ridge. Forward observation posts became especially plagued by all sorts of fire coming from these bypassed Japanese soldiers. Colonel Roberts, the regimental commander of the 22d Marines, was killed at his OP by sniper fire at 1430. The regimental executive officer, Lieutenant Colonel August Larson, assumed command.

Assault forces of XXIV Corps also made important gains on the 18th. The 96th Division push on Medeera positions from the east was coordinated with the 1st Division attack on the same objective from the west. The 7th Division continued its drive with a two-pronged attack. One assault element dashed down the reverse slope of Hill 153 to sweep past Medeera and ended its attack at the corps boundary near Komesu. Three battalions abreast spearheaded the second prong of the attack, advancing slowly down the coast towards Mabuni. During the night of 18-19 June, at least 340 Japanese soldiers were killed in attempted infiltrations and scattered attacks all along the Tenth Army front.

With the realization that "his Army's fate had been sealed," General Ushijima began spiritual and physical preparations for a Samurai's death. On 16 June, he sent the first of his farewell messages, this a report to IGHQ in Tokyo, which read:

"With a burning desire to destroy the arrogant enemy, the men in my command have fought the invaders for almost three months. We have failed to crush the enemy, despite our death-defying resistance, and now we are doomed."

"Since taking over this island our forces have, with the devoted support of the local population, exerted every effort to build up defenses. Since the enemy landing, our air and land forces, working in concert, have done everything possible to defend the island."

"To my great regret we are no longer able to continue the fight. For this failure I tender deepest apologies to the emperor and the people of the homeland. . . . I pray for the souls of men killed in battle and for the prosperity of the Imperial Family."

"Death will not quell the desire of my spirit to defend the homeland."

"With deepest appreciation of the kindness and cooperation of my superiors and my colleagues in arms, I bid farewell to all of you forever."

"Mitsuru Ushijima"

Three days later, he sent a last message to all Thirty-second Army units with which he still had contact, congratulating the survivors on having performed their "assigned mission in a manner which leaves nothing to regret" and calling upon them "to fight to the last and die for the eternal cause of loyalty to the Emperor." General Ushijima then directed most of his staff officers to leave the Mabuni command post, to disguise themselves as island natives, and to infiltrate the American lines in order to escape to northern Okinawa. Some of his key advisors, like Colonel Yahara, were assigned the mission of reaching Japan in order to report to Imperial General Headquarters; others were ordered to organize guerrilla operations in the rear of Tenth Army tactical units and the Island Command. Despite their having been thoroughly indoctrinated with the tenets of Japanese military tradition, there were some enemy soldiers who did not particularly wish to die for Emperor and Homeland. Psychological warfare teams had interpreters and cooperative prisoners broadcast surrender inducements in Japanese over loudspeakers mounted on tanks operating at the 7th Division front and on LCIs cruising up and down the southern coast. These broadcasts successfully convinced 3,000 civilians to surrender.

A more significant result of these messages occurred on 19 June, for instance, when 106 Japanese soldiers and 283 Boeitai voluntarily laid down their arms and gave up in the face of the 7th Division advance. At this stage of the campaign, the broadcasts influenced increasing numbers of the enemy to surrender as the conviction that all was lost and their cause was hopeless sank into their war-weary minds.

Their forward progress now slowed by fleeing civilians as well as the entrenched enemy, 7th Division troops, nonetheless, advanced to within 200 yards of the outskirts of Mabuni by nightfall of 19 June. Tanks accompanying the assault infantry placed direct fire on caves fronting Hill 89, not knowing that at that very time, General Ushijima was giving a farewell dinner for his departing staff officers.

Farther inland, on the right of the division zone, 184th and 381st Infantry units drove towards Medeera from the south and east against considerably lessened fire and resistance. Nevertheless, small fanatic groups, defending the complex terrain protecting the 24th Division headquarters, had to be overcome before the major objective could be seized. To the northwest of Medeera, 96th Division soldiers pushing towards Aragachi from the north found the same enemy reluctance to withdraw, encountered elsewhere along the Tenth Army front, before they could reach the high ground overlooking the village. While observing the 384th Infantry fighting to gain these heights, the ADC of the 96th Division, Brigadier General Claudius M. Easely, was killed by enemy machine gun fire. The advance of IIIAC assault forces on 19 June was highlighted when the 8th Marines completely penetrated Japanese defensive positions to reach the sea. Less successful, however, were the efforts of the 5th Marines in a day-long attack on Hills 79 and 81. With a company of tanks in support, 1/5 jumped off at 0730 to take Hill 79 first and then 81. Despite the direct fire placed on the initial objective by the Shermans and M-7s, the battalion was unable to take Hill 79 and was forced to return to positions held the previous night.

As he observed the course of the fighting and judged that neither Hill 79 nor 81 were going to be taken, Colonel Griebel ordered 2/5 to take the latter from the south in order to lift some of the enemy pressure on 1/5. Lieutenant Colonel Benedict's 2d Battalion, which had been relieved on Kunishi Ridge at 1315 that day by 3/7, moved out in a march column at 1515, made a wide swing to the southwest through the 8th Marines zone, and halted at a point some 300 yards southwest of Hill 79 at 1700. Moving out some 15 minutes later, the battalion headed towards Makabe preparatory to attacking Hill 81. As the battalion cleared the southern slope of Hill 79 and began to maneuver across the 1,000 yards of exposed flat terrain lying between that hill and Makabe, the entire column was taken under sniper fire from the hill. Company G, in the lead, was forced to double time over the entire route in order to reach some cover in Makabe. During this race for life, the company sustained some casualties from the fire as well as 20 exhaustion cases.

To maintain the momentum of the attack, the battalion commander passed Company F through G at 1950 and he himself accompanied the assault platoon, which was pinned down as soon as it attempted to move up the slope of Hill 81. The condition of his men, the lateness of the hour, and the intensity of the enemy fire compelled him to call off the attack and organize his battalion into a defense perimeter near Makabe.

More satisfactory progress in the 1st Division advance was made by the 8th Marines. After moving through 2/8 at 0800, 3/8 continued south to attack Ibaru Ridge following an hour-long artillery preparation and a 15-minute smoking of the target. At 1024, the battalion was on the ridge. Quickly it reorganized and resumed its drive by passing Company K, 3/8 reserve, through the initial assault elements more "for the experience rather than for any tactical necessity." By 1634, the entire battalion line was in place on the seacoast in its zone. The 3d Battalion, 5th Marines, which had taken Makabe that morning, kept pace with the rapid 2,500-yard advance of 3/8 and reached the coast in its zone at approximately the same time. With 3/5 attached,

Colonel Wallace's regiment took charge of the night defense of the coastal zone, and tied in with the 5th Marines and the 4th Marines along a curving line reaching from Komesu to the boundary between the Marine divisions. The 4th Marines made the major effort of the 6th Division on 19 June, with the 22d Marines mopping up behind. Colonel Shapley's battalions kept pace with the 8th Marines most of the day, but strongly defended enemy positions in the Kiyamu-Gusuku hill mass prevented the 4th from reaching the coast on the 19th. Mortar fire from defiladed emplacements behind the hill, and machine gun fire as well, increased in volume as the 1st and 3d Battalions moved into the low ground leading from Ibaru Ridge to the Kiyamu-Gusuku plateau. With the approach of night, the two battalions dug in at the foot of the steep rise leading to the hilltop. At 1845, 2/4, which had covered the open right flank of the regiment and had taken part in the attack on the ridge, was relieved by 1/29.

Before moving into the 6th Division line on 20 June, the 29th Marines began marching south from Oroku Peninsula at 0800 on the 19th. Its former sector was then occupied by the 6th Reconnaissance Company. At 1415, Colonel Whaling received orders to attack immediately in coordination with the 4th Marines. The regiment jumped off from Kuwanga Ridge at 1705 with 1/29 on the left, 2/29 on the right. Moving rapidly against light enemy resistance, the troops reached the Kiyamu-Gusuku Hill mass before dark and immediately tied in with the 4th Marines for the night.

Unperturbed by night-long disorganized enemy infiltration attempts all along its front, the 6th Division jumped off with four infantry battalions abreast--3/4, 1/4, 1/29, and 2/29 from left to right—to take the hill complex on 20 June. Again making the division main effort was the 4th Marines, in whose zone lay Hills 72 and 80, the key terrain features on the objective. Directly in front of 1/4 line of departure was Hill 72, but the battalion could not place enough men on the crest of that height at one time to maintain a solid foothold. Japanese defenders hidden among the brush and boulders lining the narrow approach to the top frustrated all efforts to gain the hill. Tanks attempted to cut a road to the crest from the flank of the position, but this scheme was foiled when an armored dozer was completely destroyed by a satchel charge thrown from a distance of 15 feet. After a day of bitter fighting at hand-grenade range, the battalion dug in for the night at the same place it had been the night before, less than 20 yards away from the enemy on the ridge above steep rock cliffs, ranging from 50 to 200 feet in height and covered with heavy undergrowth, faced 3/4. Since a frontal attack was clearly infeasible, the battalion commander sent a company to the left through the 8th Marines zone to take the ridge by attacking up its nose on the east; this sector appeared to be the one most susceptible to attack. Clearing out several bunkers and numerous caves to make way for Company L following in its wake, Company I mopped up the eastern slope while Company L tied in with the 8th Marines in order to extend the battalion's hold on the ridge. By late afternoon, 3/4 held strong positions on the left flank of Hill 72 and was ready to close in on that strong point. Although it was in regimental reserve when the attack had begun, 2/4 was alerted to support either of the other two assault battalions. At 1040, it was committed on the right of 1/4 with orders to take Hill 80. Attacking with two companies abreast, the battalion reached its objective at approximately 1230, when Company G fought its way to the top against only moderate resistance. Company E, the other assault element, was held up at the base of the hill by an enemy pocket, which the battalion commander decided to bypass, leaving a

Company E platoon behind to guard it. At 1520, the two-platoon company passed through the right element of Company G to seize the remainder of Hill 80 from the west. By 1645, all units of the battalion were on the hill and digging in. Possession of Hill 80 gave the battalion terrain commanding the right flank of the stubbornly held Hill 72.

On the extreme right of the division, the 29th Marines advanced to the coast on 20 June against little opposition except for heavy fire received on the left flank of 1/29 from enfiladed positions on the reverse slope of Hill 72. Later in the afternoon, when General Shepherd decided to envelope the Kiyamu-Gusuku sector from the left (east), he shifted the boundary of the 29th Marines to the east to include all of Ara Saki. The regimental line was then tied in with the 4th Marines for the night. The 29th Marines positions barred escape to the sea from the tip of the island.

On 20 June, psychological warfare detachments on board a LCI equipped with a loudspeaker broadcast surrender inducements to the many civilian and military personnel hiding in inaccessible cave refuges lining the coastal cliffs. A feeling that further resistance was futile as well as a sense of impending doom impelled over 4,000 island natives and some 800 soldiers to heed the message and to surrender. These POWs were then herded through the front lines before dark to stockades in the rear.

By 20 June, 1st Marine Division action centered about Hills 79 and 81. While 1/5 and 2/5 concentrated their efforts in this area, extensive mopping up operations were conducted by the 7th Marines at Kunishi Ridge, the 8th Marines along the coast north of Ara Saki, and 3/5 around Komesu. These exercises added approximately 50 military and 2,000 civilian POWs to those already captured by IIIAC forces. After 3/5 gave fire support to the 7th Division from positions on Komesu Ridge, its patrols linked up with 1/184 at 1520. Physical contact was not maintained for the night, but both battalions occupied high ground near Komesu and Udo and were able to cover the gap between battalions by fire.

A brief but soaking downpour before dawn turned the roads around Makabe into knee-deep quagmires, and the tanks and M-7s supporting 2/5 were prevented from moving into position until shortly before noon. A more favorable situation existed in the 1/5 zone, where tanks lumbered forward at 0730 to join the infantry in the attack on Hill 79. The battalion commander swung the axis of attack from the northwest to the southeast and assaulted the objective with three companies abreast. By 1300, Company C on the right flank was 75 yards from the hillcrest, while the other two companies, A in the center and B on the left, were destroying snipers and machine gun nests on the hillside with the aid of flame and gun tanks. At 1635, Company A announced that some of its troops were on the hill, but less than two hours later it reported that heavy small arms fire had prevented it from consolidating its slight hold with the few men available; it was forced, therefore, to withdraw. In possession of most of Hill 79, 1/5 dug in for the night, fully expecting to secure the entire objective the next day.

At 1230, when the 2/5 tank-infantry assault on Hill 81 began, the tracked vehicles reported that road blocks in Makabe denied them passage to the hill. An armored dozer cleared the way by 1400, and tanks moved along the road on the corps boundary to positions where they could fire into the right of Hill 81. The infantry battalion moved to and jumped off from the northern edge of Makabe at 1520 with Companies E on the right, F on the left, and G in reserve. Twenty-five minutes later, Company F was pinned down in the low ground south of the hill; a smoke screen was required to cover the evacuation of casualties. Company E, attacking from the southeast, pushed forward for about 100 yards along the eastern slope of the hill before it too was pinned down. First Company F, and then G was ordered to pass through E and continue the attack. Enemy machine gun and mortar fire pinned down these two companies also. When tanks supporting the attack ran out of ammunition at 1910 and withdrew, the assault companies attempted without success to garner more ground on their own. His troops stymied, the battalion commander pulled them back to more favorable positions for night defense.

To the left, in the XXIV Corps zone, only two strong enemy pockets remained at the end of 20 June. One was centered about the caves containing the Thirty-second Army headquarters in Hill 89, and the other was in Medeera and west of the village on Hills 79 and 85, which together with Hill 81 in the 1st Marine Division zone formed the Makabe Ridge defenses. The last courier contact between the two strongpoints was made on the night of 20 June, after the commander of the 24th Division, Lieutenant General Amamiya, urged his soldiers "to fight to the last man in their present positions." This exhortation fell on deaf ears, for the general had few live men remaining to defend the Medeera sector at the time of proclamation. The 1st Marine Division had just about annihilated the 22d and 32d Regiments during its march to the coast, and the 96th Division had destroyed the 89th Regiment and its reinforcements when taking Yuza Dake and Aragachi. The only troops left to General Amamiya were a motley conglomeration of artillerists, drivers, medical attendants, engineers, Boeitai, and personnel from almost every headquarters unit of the forces that had made up the island garrison on L-Day. Despite the growing numbers of the enemy which surrendered and others who committed suicide, the Tenth Army still had to contend with some Japanese who fought to the last with fanatic determination. An attack to destroy these soldiers holding the Makabe Ridge defenses was scheduled for noon of 21 June.

At 1027 that day, General Shepherd notified the Tenth Army commander, General Geiger, that organized resistance had ended in the 6th Marine Division zone of action. Beginning this last official day of the Okinawa campaign, the 4th Marines enveloped troublesome Hill 72. While 2/4 and 3/4 worked around to the south of the ridge, 1/4 held its position to support the attack by fire. Linking up at 0930, the two assault battalions and supporting armor worked north to the objective, and then drove over its top and down the reverse slope. By 1020, the Marines and both flame and gun tanks were mopping up the last vestiges of enemy resistance on the hill. At the tip of the island, the 29th Marines met only light opposition during its sweep of Ara Saki; Company G, 2/22, attached to 1/29, raised the division colors on the southernmost point of the island later in the day.

Both the 7th and 8th Marines were assigned the task of flushing out enemy holdouts in the IIIAC zone and of accepting the surrender of an ever-increasing number of soldiers and civilians. Hill 79 was finally taken by 1/5 at 1735; more difficult, however, was the capture of Hill 81.

Although scheduled to jump off at 0900, the attack of 2/5 was delayed until 1104 in order that tank routes could be prepared and so that the battalion could take immediate advantage of a blistering rocket barrage on the hill objective. The attack plan called for Company E to lead the assault on the hill, and to be followed successively by Companies F and G, which were to be fed in from the left until Hill 81 was taken. Company E encountered only light and scattered small arms fire as it jumped off, and finally fought to and occupied its assigned objective after having destroyed two machine gun positions that had halted it on the way up. Almost immediately, Company F began fighting its way up the slope to the hilltop, burning out and sealing caves along the route. Shortly thereafter, Company G made its tortuous trek up the incline to join the other two at the top, all companies received heavy fire from caves, which honeycombed the enemy position. The effort to secure the objective was spurred on by information received at the battalion CP of that Hill 81 was the last organized enemy position on Okinawa; this story later proved untrue. After having made several unsuccessful requests for reinforcements, and been ordered in turn to continue the attack with the forces at hand, at 1430 Lieutenant Colonel Benedict was relieved and ordered to report to the regimental commander. He then turned over command of the battalion to his executive officer, Major Richard T. Washburn. At 1500, the commander of 3/5 reported in at the 2/5 OP and assumed joint command of the two battalions; his Company L began moving to Makabe soon after to support the attack on Hill 81.

All companies advanced slowly during the afternoon, and as 2/5 reached the crest of the hill, enemy fire slackened noticeably. At 1700, all companies reported their portion of the objective secured; all organized enemy resistance in the IIIAC zone had ended.

In the XXIV Corps zone, a heavy 4.2-inch mortar concentration on Hill 79 preceded the attack of 305th Infantry elements at 1200. The crew-served weapons organic to the infantry battalions supported the tank-led attack. At 1630, following an afternoon of withering rifle and machine gun fire coming from caves and pillboxes on Makabe Ridge, the infantry launched a final, successful surge to the top of the hill. Before XXIV Corps units could report the end of organized resistance in the army zone, they had to come to grips with a bitter, last-ditch Japanese defense; objectives were captured only after enemy defenders had been killed to the last man. The soldiers first secured Mabuni and then Hill 89. General Buckner's doctrine of "corkscrew and blowtorch" was employed effectively by flame tanks and demolition teams burning and blasting the "palace guard" defending the cave entrances leading to General Ushijima's headquarters. By the end of the day, Hill 89 had been secured, and its inhabitants were frantically attempting to escape a death by entombment.

After 82 days of bloody and bitter fighting, the rapid advance of the Tenth Army in the final stages of the campaign brought about irrevocable collapse of all major Japanese opposition. General Geiger could thus announce at 1305 on 21 June that the island of Okinawa had been secured by American forces. The official end of the Okinawa campaign was marked by a formal flag-raising ceremony at Tenth Army headquarters at 1000, 22 June, attended by representatives of all units in that command. As described by General Smith: "A large metal flagpole had already been erected at Army Headquarters. . . . The only band available was that of the 2d Marine Aircraft Wing. Prior to playing the National Anthem, the band played 'Anchors Aweigh,' 'The Marines Hymn,' and an appropriate Army tune." Brigadier General Lawrence E. Schick, USA, Tenth Army Deputy Chief of Staff, read the official dispatch declaring the end of organized resistance, and General Geiger then gave the signal for the flag to be raised. Following the official announcement on 21 June of the ending of organized resistance on Okinawa, Tenth Army headquarters began receiving congratulatory messages from statesmen and military commanders throughout the world. Though heartfelt and sincere, none of these commendations to the men who had fought the Battle of Okinawa could match the simple accolade bestowed on Marines of the IIIAC by the commander who had led them, for as

General Geiger wrote: "This has been a hard campaign. The officers and men have simply been marvelous. They have carried on day and night, mud and battle, without a murmur and could have continued had it been necessary. They have carried out every mission assigned by the Tenth Army and have broken through every position of the Japanese defenses which stood in their way in a minimum of time. The Marine Corps can ever be proud of the two divisions which fought on this island. The cost has been high, but the time element was essential and I am sure you will be happy to know that the Marines required no urging to attack, attack, and again attack, until the Japanese were completely annihilated. You will never know how I regret leaving the III Corps."

Chapter 11. ICEBERG Dissolves

Mopping Up

With his defenses overrun and forces shattered, there was little hope of diverting or lengthening the path leading to the inevitable fate of his Thirty-second Army. Lieutenant General Mitsuru Ushijima decided, therefore, to end his life according to the dictates that governed his living of it, the traditional way of the Samurai. Joining him in fulfilling his obligation to the Emperor and dying in the symbolic way of *bushido* was the army chief of staff, Lieutenant General Isamu Cho. Following a meal late on the night of 21 June, Cho and Ushijima composed their last farewell messages and the following valedictory poems written in the classic Japanese style:

> The green grass of this isle
> Withers untimely before fall,
> Yet it will grow again
> In the warm spring of the Empire
>
> Smearing heaven and earth with our blood,
> We leave this world with our ammunition gone,
> Yet our souls shall come back again and again
> To guard the Empire forever.

At noon on 22 June, Ushijima dressed himself in his full field uniform and Cho donned a white kimono on which he had written "The offering of one's life is to fulfill the duties towards the Emperor and the Country. Cho, Isamu." As the two led a party of aides and staff officers out to a ledge at the mouth of the cave headquarters, Cho was quoted as saying, "Well, Commanding General Ushijima, as the way may be dark, I, Cho, will lead the way." Ushijima replied, "Please do so, and I'll take along my fan since it is getting warm."

Ten minutes after leaving the cave, first Ushijima and then Cho died in the Japanese time-honored ritual of *harakiri*. Each in turn bared his abdomen to the knife used in the ceremonial disembowelment and thrust inward; as each did so, there was a simultaneous shout and flash of a sword as the headquarters adjutant decapitated first one general and then the other. The bodies were then secretly buried in graves prepared earlier. Three days later, 32d Infantry patrols discovered them at the foot of the cliff of Hill 89 where it faced the sea. On the white bedding cover which served as his winding sheet after death, General Cho had written:

"22d Day of June, 20th Year of Showa, I depart without regret, fear, shame, or obligations. Army Chief of Staff, Army Lt. Gen. Cho, Isamu Age at departure, 51 years.

"At this time and place, I hereby certify the foregoing."

On 25 June also, the Imperial General Headquarters in Tokyo announced the end of Japanese operations on Okinawa, and, in effect, of the Thirty-second Army. IGHQ then put all of its efforts into preparations for the defense of the Home Islands against an anticipated American invasion.

Although the commander and chief of staff of the Thirty-second Army were dead, and many Japanese officers and enlisted men were surrendering, other enemy soldiers both in groups and individually continued a fanatic, last-ditch stand until they were destroyed. General Stilwell believed it necessary to eliminate these isolated Japanese pockets to safeguard the Island Command forces that were developing the additional supply, training, airfield, and port facilities required to convert Okinawa into a massive base for further operations against Japan. He ordered, therefore, the Tenth Army to begin an intensive, coordinated mop-up of southern Okinawa on 23 June; 10 days were allotted to this task.

The 1st Marines and 307th Infantry were deployed in a line of blocking positions paralleling the Naha-Yonabaru highway to bar the way to enemy soldiers who were attempting an escape to northern Okinawa. The American sweep northwards was mounted by the five assault divisions that had made the final drive in the south and had been on line when the war ended; they began the sweep by merely making an about-face in position. As the soldiers and Marines drove towards the Tenth Army blocking positions, they smashed all remaining enemy opposition, blew and sealed Japanese caves, buried all Japanese dead, and retrieved all salvageable enemy and friendly equipment along the way. To coordinate and pace the 10-day sweep, three phase lines were established. Flanking divisions were to guide on the 96th Division as it progressed up the center of the island. General Stilwell retained control of the entire operation.

On 30 June, in less than the time allotted, the mop up was successfully completed. Elements of the 77th Division reduced the final defensive positions of the 24th Division near the ruins of Medeera; the 96th Division thoroughly cleaned out enemy pockets in the Medeera-Aragachi sector; the 1st and 6th Marine Divisions worked over Japanese survivors in the Kiyamu-Gusuku and Komesu Ridges; and the 7th Division did the same to the Hill 89-Mabuni area. Several brief but bloody fire fights flared during the methodical, workman-like sweep of the objective area when strongly armed enemy bands tried futilely to break through the American line and were smashed.

Results of the sweep indicated that an estimated 8,975 Japanese had been killed and 2,902 military prisoners and 906 labor troops had been added to those already in Tenth Army stockades. Enemy losses for the entire Okinawa campaign, were placed at 107,539 counted dead and an estimated 23,764 more which were assumed to have been sealed in caves or buried by the Japanese themselves. In addition, a total of 10,755 of the enemy had been captured; some of this number had surrendered. As the overall Japanese casualty total of 142,058 was "far above a reasonable estimate of military strength on the island," Tenth Army intelligence agencies presumed that approximately 42,000 of these casualties were civilians that had been unfortunately killed or wounded in American artillery, naval gunfire, and air attacks on enemy troops and installations while the natives had been in the proximity. American losses were heavy also. The total reported Tenth Army casualty figures were 7,374 killed or died of wounds, 31,807 wounded or injured in action, and 239 missing. There were 26,221 nonbattle casualties in addition. The combat divisions alone reported a total of 38,006 casualties of all types. Between 1 April and 30 June, Army units received 12,277 replacements; Marine units joined 11,147 Marines and naval corpsmen in the same period.

Both British and American naval forces took heavy casualties while supporting and maintaining the Tenth Army. During the 82 days of ground operations, 34 ships and craft were sunk and 368 damaged; 763 carrier-based aircraft were lost to all causes. In addition, 4,907 sailors were killed or missing in action and 4,824 were wounded. At the time that these losses were sustained, ships and ground antiaircraft artillery and planes controlled or coordinated by the Navy claimed the destruction of 7,830 Japanese aircraft and 16 combatant ships.

In accordance with the planned succession of operational control established for ICEBERG, Headquarters, Ryukyus Area superseded the Tenth Army on 1 July 1945. At that time, General Stilwell became a joint task force commander directly responsible to Admiral Nimitz for the defense and development of all captured islands and the defense of the waters within 25 miles of Okinawa. Concurrently, after CinCPac had dissolved Task Force 31, Admiral Hill and his staff departed for Pearl Harbor and Rear Admiral Calvin H. Cobb took over as Commander Naval Forces, Ryukyus, under General Stilwell. TAF at this time came under the Ryukyus command. All of these forces, and others that were to be sent to Okinawa, were to be commanded by General Stilwell. He was to coordinate and control the massive effort supporting the impending operations against the center of the Japanese Empire. Slated to become a major force in carrying the air war to Japan was the Tactical Air Force.

TAF Fights On

Only five days had intervened between the eighth mass Kamikaze raid of 27-28 May—Kikusui No. 8—and the ninth, which began on the evening of 3 June and lasted until 7 June. As before, TAF fighter aircraft rose from fields on Okinawa and Ie Shima to meet approximately 245 Japanese planes coming from the Home Islands. American pilots and antiaircraft artillery units claimed a total of 118 enemy planes downed during Kikusui No. 9; the Marine pilots of TAF claimed 35 of this number. At the same time that Generals Cho and Ushijima began their suicide preparations, Japanese pilots flying the final mass Kamikaze raid of the Okinawa campaign arrived over the island, prepared to die according to the philosophy of the Samurai, but in a more modern fashion. Approximately 68 of the 257 aircraft launched in Kikusui No. 10 were suiciders. The first group of raiders appeared over Kerama Retto on 21 June at 1830, and correctly replied to friendly recognition signals. One Kamikaze dived headlong into the seaplane tender *Curtis* to start night-long fires that severely damaged the ship. Shortly after, planes from this flight attacked LSM-59 as it was towing the hulk of decommissioned *Barry* away from the Kerama anchorage to act as a Kamikaze decoy, and both vessels were sunk.

On 22 June, Marine pilots from MAG-22 were flying a barrier combat air patrol over Amami O Shima, when they were jumped by approximately 60 enemy planes heading for Okinawa along the well-travelled Kamikaze air route from Kyushu. The skies immediately buzzed with a frenzy of darting and diving aircraft. One pilot was later heard to say over the radio, "Come on up and help me, I've got a Frank and two Zekes cornered." No further word was heard from him, and he was later listed as missing. During the debriefing after this engagement, the MAG-22 fliers reported that the enemy had tried to decoy them into unfavorable positions. Four of the Japanese planes were first sighted at 20,000 feet, and as a division of Corsairs went after them, the decoy planes made a run for safety, but pulled up "and dropped their belly tanks in front of and above the Marine planes. Our pilots had to [maneuver violently] in order to evade the falling tanks. The F4Us turned to press home their attack when the larger force of enemy planes jumped in and a general melee resulted." In evaluating the enemy, the Marines reported that the Japanese pilots flew a good, tight division formation of four planes abreast, and "they seemed to be good pilots but maneuvered poorly." Of the 51 planes Americans claimed to have shot down in this encounter, TAF pilots listed 44.

Although MAG-14 (VMF-212, -222, -223), commanded by Colonel Edward A. Montgomery, did not arrive on Okinawa until 8 June, too late to participate in the "turkey shoots" against the Kamikaze attacks, once the group began operations on the 11th, its pilots and planes took part in the stepped-up tempo of TAF strikes on such scattered targets as Sakashima Gunto to the south of Okinawa, Kyushu to the north, and the coast of China to the west. On 22 June, Captain Kenneth A. Walsh, an ace at Guadalcanal and winner of the Medal of Honor for achievements during the same campaign, shot down his 21st enemy plane. In its brief combat tour in the Ryukyus, the group as a whole claimed nine kills.

Whenever the weather permitted in June, TAF greatly expanded its offensive operations and strikes on outlying targets. The primary mission of the far-ranging American planes was to seek out and destroy enemy planes and support installations. These operations involved flights of large numbers of single engine aircraft over water for distances nearly equalling their maximum ranges. Because of their long-range capability, the P-47 Thunderbolts of the AAF fighter squadrons attached to TAF18 performed a dual role as both fighters and bombers. On some missions, the P-47s bombed and strafed targets of opportunity as well as assigned targets; they escorted light, medium, and heavy bomber missions after Bomber Command joined TAF in June and July. At this time, existing airfields on Okinawa were expanded, and new ones built at Awase on the east coast and Chimu in the north in accordance with base development planning. The influx to these and the other fields of newly joining squadrons increased ADC aircraft strength from 432 planes at the beginning of June to 711 at the end. With these additional aircraft, TAF mounted increasingly stronger air attacks against the Japanese Home Islands. Marine fighter planes from ADC hit Kyushu installations for the first time on 10 June, the day before Major General Louis E. Woods relieved Major General Mulcahy as TAF commander.

There was little change in the missions of TAF, Ryukyus Command, from those it had fulfilled as an agency of the Tenth Army. On 1 July, when the command change occurred, ADC assumed complete responsibility from TF 31 for the air defense of the Ryukyus. At this time, TAF aircraft strength was substantially increased, especially by the bomber squadrons, and General Woods could send his planes to better objectives further away from Okinawa than those attacked previously. In its first raid under TAF, on 1 July the 41st Bombardment Group sent its Mitchell bombers to blast Kyushu. On that same day, TAF inaugurated a combat air patrol over Kyushu in hope that Japanese pilots would take off from island airdromes to engage the American planes. Few enemy pilots rose to the occasion.

In another phase of TAF operations, Thunderbolts began hitting Japanese installations on the China coast near the Yangtze Estuary on 1 July. A landmark in TAF operations occurred on the 9th, when B-24s attacked Japan from Okinawa. All together, the 47 heavy bombers—and the 25 Mitchells and 32 Thunderbolts acting as bombers accompanying them—spread 1,880 clusters of fragmentary bombs and 280 clusters of incendiary bombs over dispersal areas and field installations of Omura airfield on Kyushu. Another 92 Thunderbolts escorting the mission acted merely as spectators; no enemy interceptors appeared. In accordance with orders from CinCPOA, TAF, Ryukyus was dissolved on 14 July. On that date, all Marine air units reported to the 2d MAW, which was then designated Task Group 99.2, and assigned to the Ryukyus Command. AAF squadrons and groups that had been temporarily assigned to TAF were transferred to the Far East Air Forces (FEAF), which assumed control of the mounting number of air attacks against Japan.

Under the Ryukyus Command, Marine squadrons continued flying the types of missions they had flown previously, but they now ranged much further away from the island than when they had been committed to the air defense of ICEBERG forces. On 19 July, ADC flyers made their first visit to the China coast, when 59 F4Us flew cover for TF 95, then operating off the enemy-held littoral. At 0001, 1 August, the 2d MAW and all of its squadrons with the exception of VMTB-131 and -232, and VMB-612, passed to the operational control of FEAF; the three other squadrons were assigned to the control of Fleet Air Wing 1.

In the period 7 April through 13 July, TAF amassed a creditable record. A Marine aviator himself, General Geiger wrote General Woods that the air support provided by TAF pilots was "outstanding and contributed materially to a speedy and successful completion of the campaign." By the end of 13 July, TAF claimed a total of 625 Japanese planes destroyed in the air and 29 probables; MAG-33 pilots were the high scorers with claims of having shot down 214 enemy aircraft. Of particular interest is the fact that Marine night fighters came into their own in the air above Okinawa; VMF(N)-533 registered claims of 35 enemy planes downed, while VMF(N)-542 claimed 17, and -543, 11. Some overwhelming statistics appeared in the course of the Okinawa air operations. For example, while flying 118,982 hours and 38,192 sorties, TAF pilots expended 4,102,559 rounds of .50 caliber ammunition and 445,748 rounds of 20mm. In addition, the flyers released 499 tons of napalm, 4,161 tons of bombs, and 15,691 rockets.

The pilots and planes of VMTB-131 and -232 recorded some amazing statistics during their supply drop operations to ground troops. In addition to the 70 supply sorties carrier-based aircraft flew in support of IIIAC ground units, the two TAF squadrons flew 760 sorties for the Tenth Army—80 of these went to XXIV Corps, the rest to IIIAC. The total weight that the TBMs carried on these missions was 668,984 pounds; the supplies weighed 495,257 pounds, cargo parachutes and air delivery containers took up the rest of the weight. Handling these supplies on the carriers first and at the airfields on Okinawa later was the IIIAC Air Delivery Section. Consisting of 1 officer and 82 enlisted Marines, the section was attached to Tenth Army and worked very closely with the TAF squadrons.

Although seemingly prosaic when compared to combat air patrols, supply drop missions were very often just as hazardous. For optimum results, the Avenger pilot had to maintain an air speed of 95 knots, very close to a stall, at an altitude of about

250 feet while trying to spot a drop zone that was supposedly marked by colored smoke, WP grenades, or panels, either separately or together. At the same time, he was being fired upon by Japanese weapons of all sorts—antiaircraft guns as well as small arms. Some pilots had to fly under an arc of friendly artillery and naval gunfire.

In attempting to drop supplies on targets, Marine aviators often found that the drop zone had not been properly marked or correctly identified, or that the Japanese were using the same color of smoke that Tenth Army ground units were supposed to have employed. As a result, the drop mission either was aborted until the zone could be properly identified, or the pilots made an educated guess—in which case, the supplies sometimes were dropped into enemy territory.

When the drop zone was particularly difficult to spot, Air Liaison Parties from the Joint Assault Signal Companies attached to frontline infantry units coached the TBM pilots to their target by radio. The primary mission of the ALPs was to direct TAF and carrier-based aircraft to the target. Coordinating the requests from lower echelons were the three Marine Landing Force Air Support Control Units (LFASCUs) commanded by Colonel Vernon E. Megee. Colonel Megee wore two other hats: he was representative ashore of the Navy Close Air Support Control Unit (CASCU) that was on board *Eldorado*, and he commanded LFASCU-3 which was the control unit at Tenth Army headquarters. LFASCU-3 coordinated the air requests forwarded from the IIIAC infantry regiments by LFASCU-1, and from XXIV Corps units by LFASCU-2. Each of these control units operated at the headquarters of the corps to which it was attached. Although close air support techniques and the methods for their control were rudimentary at the beginning of World War II, during the latter stages of the war and especially on Okinawa, improved aircraft, proven control procedures, and pilots skilled in providing close air support served together to make this supporting arm one of the most powerful that was available to the infantry. On Okinawa, ground troops developed great trust and confidence in the ability of close air support to strengthen attacks on particularly stubborn enemy strongpoints and to clear the way for assaults in general. Surprisingly enough in view of the many support sorties flown, there were but few instances when friendly troops were bombed, strafed, or rocketed by accident, even though strikes were often conducted less than 100 yards away from friendly lines. After getting their first taste of what close air support could do for them, Army units were soon "insatiable in their demands."

Throughout the course of the war in the Pacific, senior Marine commanders became and remained staunch adherents to and supporters of the close air support doctrine. As it developed, they became convinced that more extensive use of the ALPs at the division, regimental, and battalion levels would increase the quality and quantity as well as the effectiveness of air support.

After the Okinawa campaign, the consensus of the Marine commanders present there was that, with proper communications equipment and more intensive and complete training, ALPs could easily take over control of strike missions from LFASCUS and "talk" the pilots directly to their targets. This procedure of direct air-ground control between ALPs and the planes above them had been developed by the Marine Corps prior to the Okinawa invasion and was used in the 1st and 6th Marine Division training cycles. Colonel Megee later explained that this system was not used at Okinawa because: "to have permitted each battalion air liaison party to control striking aircraft on a corps front of only ten miles, when many simultaneous air strikes were being run, would obviously have led only to pandemonium and grave hazard for all those concerned. On the other hand, where conditions approximated those in the Philippines, i.e., battalion or regimental actions in an uncrowded area, actual control of aircraft was frequently delegated to the air liaison party."

After having read the comments and recommendations of both Army and Marine commanders concerning the air support they received in the Okinawa campaign, Major General James T. Moore, commander of Aircraft, Fleet Marine Force, Pacific, forwarded them to the Commandant of the Marine Corps. In a covering letter, General Moore recommended "that Marine Air and Ground be organized and combined under one command with the primary mission of Marine Air being the support of Marine Ground Forces." This might very well be interpreted as the first definitive recommendation made by a senior Marine general for the establishment of the balanced air-ground amphibious force in readiness which has become the hallmark of the present-day Marine Corps.

That the ready acceptance of Marine aviation by Marine ground forces as an equal or supporting partner in amphibious operations was not an immediate thing is indicated by General Woods, who said: "All senior ground generals in World War II believed in the air-ground team but when in the combat area, they were never able to keep aviation under their command. Maybe it is because they gave only lip service to the doctrine. Even as early as Guadalcanal, the First Wing was not under the command of General Vandegrift, and when the First Division left the combat area, all [Marine] aviation units were left behind!"

A review of Marine air activities is not complete without mention of the Marine observation squadrons, the VMOs. Although their exploits were not so spectacular as those of the fighter and torpedo bomber squadrons, nor their planes so swift and deadly, the VMOS attached to IIIAC performed as vitally important a role in the successful prosecution of the Okinawa campaign. Assigned to the Marine components of the ICEBERG forces as artillery spotters, VMO-2, -3 and -6 and their OY "Grasshoppers" were ashore and operating from Okinawa fields by 3 April. The squadrons were soon flying other types of missions, however, and not necessarily for the Marine artillery regiments. Within two days, for example, both VMO-2 and -3 were serving a total of 11 Army and Marine artillery battalions—the equivalent of nearly three full regiments. As soon as VMO-7 arrived in early May, it, too, was kept busy. In addition to spotting missions, Grasshopper pilots and their aerial observers flew photographic and reconnaissance missions. Sometimes, line routes for ground communications were selected after the observers had reported the number and location of telephone poles still standing. In early June and until the end of the campaign, the VMOS made many evacuation flights. During the 12-day period from 11-22 June inclusive, VMO-7 made a total of 369 evacuation flights from the strip behind 1st Division lines; these were in addition to the 243 spotting and 17 photo-reconnaissance missions flown in the same period.

By the end of the Okinawa battle, the four VMOS had flown 3,486 missions. The most valuable of these, in the view of artillery commanders, were the spotting missions. As the G-3 of IIIAC Artillery noted later: "If there was any group of indispensable officers in IIIAC Artillery on Okinawa, it was our air spotters. The nature of the terrain in southern Okinawa seriously limited ground observation—especially while we were fighting our way uphill on the Shuri massif. Without our AOs [Aerial Observers], IIIAC Artillery would have been blind."

Colonel Henderson continued: "The courage and daring of our AOs and the VMO pilots was an outstanding feature of the campaign. I think that VMO pilots are the unsung heroes of Marine Aviation. . . .When they wanted to really investigate something . . . they would go right down on the deck. Often they would fly past cave openings at the same level so they could look in and see if there was a gun there."

This tactic was most important because of the difficulty that often arose in locating Japanese artillery positions, especially those sited in cave mouths.

Considered more a hindrance than a safeguard by both artillery and air support units, restrictive fire plans NEGAT and VICTOR greatly diminished the effect of artillery and naval gunfire bombardments during the early part of the campaign. Colonel Henderson noted that "They were supposed to protect our own close air support planes from friendly artillery fire, but more often served to protect the Japanese from our fire." In addition, the plans were invoked too often, and then remained in effect far too long. Colonel Kenneth H. Weir, commander of LFASCU-1, agreed in principle with this complaint. He said that "if air support units could have been given the maximum ordinates and azimuths of the artillery and naval gunfire falling into an area in which air strikes were to be made," in many instances the aircraft could have attacked or continued an attack without invoking the restrictive fire plans. This controversial point was settled on 16 May when Tenth Army cancelled the use of Plans NEGAT and VICTOR, except in unusual circumstances.

Island Command Activities

The tasks to be carried out by Island Command during both the combat and the garrison phases of the Okinawa campaign were more complex and staggering in many ways than those assigned to other Tenth Army combat organizations. Major General Fred C. Wallace was responsible for providing administrative and logistic support to combat units, executing the CinCPOA base development plan, and assuming—when directed by Tenth Army—the responsibility for the garrison and defense of Okinawa and its outlying islands. To achieve the objectives required in these various assignments, Island Command had been organized so that it would direct, control, and coordinate a joint task force comprised of a large portion of the service and support troops in the Tenth Army. As Tenth Army noted later: "In effect, Island Command [served] as a combined Army Service Area and advance section of a Communication Zone." The degree and scope of the functions delegated by Tenth Army to General Wallace increased in an almost direct proportion to the decrease in fighting and subsequent narrowing of the combat zone. Before the beginning of July, Island Command controlled some 153,000 men and had become responsible for the defense and development of every major island in the entire Okinawan chain of islands. Subordinate and reporting to General Wallace were the commanders of Naval Operating Base, Ryukyus; Joint Communication Activities; Hydrographic Survey; Army and Navy Air Bases; Construction Troops; Military Government; and Ground Defense Forces. Additionally, General Wallace exercised control over a large number of service troops which had been assigned directly to his headquarters.

When ICEBERG Plan Phase III operations against Miyako and Kikai were cancelled in late April, all base development efforts, and troops scheduled for employment on these and other islands of the Ryukyus, were reassigned to Okinawa. In the planned revisions, the number of airfields originally scheduled for development on the island was doubled, and a corresponding increase in supply installations and troop staging, rehabilitation, and training areas was envisioned. All of these impending developments, however, were held in abeyance until remnants of the Thirty-second Army had been destroyed. As an example of his single-minded determination to pursue the basic objective, General Buckner had ordered all airfield construction units to concentrate on maintaining and reconstructing supply roads to frontline organizations when the heavy rains and resultant mud of late May and early June threatened to bog down but failed to halt the Tenth Army attack. In spite of the weather and incident delays, the first American-built airstrip on Okinawa—a 7,000-foot runway at Yontan—was completed by 17 June. Before the end of the month, 5 airfields were operational on the island, and 8 of the 18 proposed fields were sited and were in the midst of being rehabilitated or constructed to meet the needs of the increased numbers of newly arriving B-29s.

Besides air base development and road maintenance, the Island Command engineering troops fulfilled other important tasks. They widened over 160 miles of existing native roads into two-, three-, and four-lane highways to accommodate the burgeoning load of supply and troop traffic. Island Command also opened new beaches, constructed piers, and cleared dump areas to handle the influx of supplies to be used in the impending operations against Japan proper. Engineers developed a massive water system capable of answering the needs of hundreds of thousands of soldiers and civilians. Other pipelines were laid and tank farms built to handle the tankerloads of aviation fuel necessary to maintain current and act as a reserve for projected air operations. Construction of the hundreds of storage, administration, and hospital buildings to be used by invasion-bound troops paced the buildup elsewhere on the island.

As the end of organized resistance on Okinawa neared, Island Command shifted the weight of its logistical support from Tenth Army to preparations for approaching operations. One base development phase influenced by planned future operations resulted in the preemption of vast areas of arable land in southern Okinawa and on the Motobu Peninsula. Not only was the topography of the island altered, but the way of life, means of subsistence, and sources of sustenance of island natives were irrevocably changed. Ejection of the natives from generations-old family holdings and removal of other islanders from more populated areas meant that they became, in effect, wards of the Island Command.

The agency responsible to Island Command and taking over its role as guardian for the displaced Okinawans was Military Government. Like so many of the other agencies directed by General Wallace, this one was a joint service effort. Even during the initial stages of the battle, military government teams functioned as though they were conducting a "disaster relief operation," in which they had to clear the islanders out of the way of the course of the fighting for reasons of mercy as well as for the purpose of keeping them from hampering Tenth Army operations. In this period, as the native population became concentrated in stockades and resettlement areas in northern Okinawa, the Americans gave assistance to the Okinawans as the natives reconstituted the normal functions of civil government and developed a self-sustaining local economy. Primary emphasis was on increased Okinawan participation in both areas. An idea of the magnitude of the job that was performed by a relatively small group of military government personnel is reflected by the fact that it was in charge of 261,115 civilians on 30 June, and 100,000 more by the end of the war. Complementing the sweep that Tenth Army forces made in the south after the end of organized resistance, Island Command garrison forces in occupied areas of northern Okinawa conducted mopping-up operations, which lasted well into August and assumed the proportion of pitched battles at times. The majority of the flare-ups occurred north of the Ishikawa Isthmus, garrisoned by the 27th Infantry Division on 2

May. Army forces on Kerama Retto also felt the backlash from survivors of Japanese units that had been defeated but did not know it.

Upon passing to Island Command control and moving to the areas in northern Okinawa formerly occupied by the 1st and 6th Marine Divisions, the 27th Division began patrolling extensively, assisting the military government collection teams, and blowing caves as well as fortified and prepared positions found in its assigned zone of responsibility. When the toll of enemy dead rose from an average of 3 or 4 to 15 a day and Army troops found evidence of increasing numbers of recently occupied and prepared bivouac positions, General Wallace decided to make a thorough sweep of northern Okinawa to kill or capture the Japanese remaining there.

On 19 May, the division began a sweep northwards from the base of Ishikawa Isthmus with three regiments abreast. Within five days, the soldiers met heavy resistance at Onna Take, the heavily forested hill mass rising to 1,000 feet from the center of the isthmus. Here, 1st Division Marines had fought guerrillas in April while the 6th Division was fighting the battle on Motobu Peninsula. Since that time, the enemy had added to the natural defenses of the area and extensively fortified the region. The soldiers fought a 10-day pitched battle here without benefit of air or artillery support. After it was over, there was evidence that a sizable number of Japanese had escaped the trap and headed further north. The 27th Division continued its sweep and followed the Japanese. The mop up was finally completed on 4 August, when Army troops reached Hedo Misaki. The division reported at the end of the nearly three-month drive that it had killed over 1,000 Japanese and captured 500.

As the fighting on Okinawa drew to a climax, preparations for another off-island operation began. Like Tori, Ibeya, and Aguni Shimas, Kume Shima had been one of the targets originally selected for capture during Phase III(d) of the ICEBERG operations. The priority of these targets was downgraded later as the ground campaign unfolded, and this phase of the ICEBERG operation was finally cancelled. A Tenth Army study in late May resulted in the choice of these islands as radar and fighter director sites. The first three were captured in early June, and Kume was targeted for seizure during the mop up phase on Okinawa. Largest of the outlying islands selected for early-warning facilities—some 40 square miles in size—it is approximately 55 miles west of Naha. Assigned to capture the island was the FMF Amphibious Reconnaissance Battalion, which had been attached to Island Command for garrison duty in the Eastern Islands after the Marines had seized them. On 21 June, the battalion was released to Tenth Army control for the Kume Shima assault landing.

Kume was scouted in the night of 13-14 June by Company B patrols. Information received from captured civilians indicated that only a 50-man enemy garrison held the island. This intelligence proved correct after the landing on 26 June, but Company A and the 81mm Mortar Platoon from 1/7 were attached to Major Jones' 252-man battalion in case the Japanese force encountered was larger than expected.

Leaving the company from 1/7 behind to guard the beachhead, Major Jones and his battalion set out to contact the enemy. After five days of intensive patrolling, no Japanese were found and no opposition was developed. On 30 June, Jones declared the island secure.

Although the Kume assault force had encountered no enemy in the late June operation, the garrison troops only several days later became involved in two fire fights with Japanese soldiers. Six of the enemy were killed and three of their four machine guns were captured. Constant aggressive patrolling forced the survivors to scatter into the hills in the interior of the island, where they offered no threat to the successful operation of air warning facilities. Air Warning Squadron 11 arrived at Okinawa on 4 July, and its units were set up on Kume Shima two days later. By 12 July, the radar and fighter director sections of the squadron had begun operations and been integrated into the system controlled overall by the Air Defense Control Center on Okinawa.

Evaluation Of Operations

As some scholars in the field of military history and tactics have noted, the Okinawa operation represents "the culmination of amphibious development in the Pacific war." Shortly after the initial landings, British observers accompanying the ICEBERG force reported that "This operation was the most audacious and complex enterprise which has yet been undertaken by the American Amphibious Forces." And they were undoubtedly right, for "more ships were used, more troops put ashore, more supplies transported, more bombs dropped, more naval guns fired against short targets" than in any previous campaign in the Pacific. Despite the immensity of all of the factors involved in the ICEBERG operation, the Okinawa landing realistically demonstrated the soundness of the fundamental amphibious doctrine that the Navy and the Marine Corps had developed over the years and had tempered in the Pacific fighting. This thesis was amplified by General Geiger, who pointed out that the battle for Okinawa "reemphasized most clearly that our basic principles of tactics and technique are sound, 'in the book,' and need only to be followed in combat." The touchstone to success at Okinawa was interservice cooperation, where "Army artillery supported Marine infantry and vice versa," and "Marine and Army planes were used interchangeably and operated under the same tactical command," and "each contiguous infantry unit was mutually supporting and interdependent," and finally, when "the Navy's participation was vital to both throughout." The target information center (TIC) was the primary Tenth Army agency that coordinated the request for and assignment of supporting arms. In the TICs existing at division, regimental, and battalion levels throughout the Tenth Army, a centralized target information and weapons assignment system gave unit commanders the ability to mass the maximum amount of firepower on both assigned targets and targets of opportunity.

At each infantry echelon down to battalion level, the artillery liaison officer was also in charge of the TIC and worked very closely with the operations officer. Utilizing previously collated intelligence pinpointing enemy positions and screening support requests, the TIC section head — an artillery liaison officer — and the naval gunfire and air liaison officers allocated fire missions to each of the three support elements which they represented. A primary consideration in making each assignment was the capability of the weapon or weapons to be employed.

The target information center at IIIAC headquarters was controlled by the Corps Artillery commander — who made it one of his special staff agencies — and its mission was to provide supporting arms with target information. Colonel Henderson, the operations officer of IIIAC Corps Artillery, described the TIC as General Nimmer's 2 Section: "expanded to meet the needs of artillery, NGF and CAS [close air support] on a 24 hour basis. The Corps Arty S-2 was the IIIAC TIO [target information officer]. The working responsibility for coordinating arty, NGF and air lay with the Corps Arty S-3 for both planned fires and targets of opportunity. The Corps Arty S-3, S-2 (TIO) and Corps AirO and NGFO were allocated in a big hospital tent adjacent to

IIIAC headquarters most of the time. The S-3 and S-2 (TIO) had 'hot line' phones to Corps G-3 and G-2. The Corps Arty FDC [fire direction center] and the Corps fire support operations center were one and the same facility—with NGF and air added.The TIC was given radio jeeps and operators from the Corps Signal Battalion and Corps Artillery to man the Support Air Request, Support Air Observation, and Support Air Direction (SAD) radio nets. As all division and corps commanders commented favorably on the TIC system, Tenth Army recommended that it be adopted for all future operations."

In writing about the fire support functions of the TIC, the commander of the 11th Marines noted: "For the first time in the Pacific, coordination of naval gunfire and air support with artillery was prescribed in army orders, a forerunner of the present FSCC [Fire Support Coordination System]. Examination of the record will show that each division and corps, Army and Marine, used a different modification of it. It is worthy of note that the system used by the First Marine Division was most like what we have today."

Until the Kamikaze threat waned in late May and early June, most of the close air support missions were flown by carrier-based planes rather than the TAF aircraft on Okinawa. The latter were too fully committed flying combat air patrols and intercepting Japanese planes to fly strike missions until the later stages of the campaign; Marine-piloted Avengers on supply drops were an exception. The majority of the close support missions in the Okinawa campaign were pre-planned; strike requests were submitted to the LFASCUS, which assigned them well enough in advance so that the strike pilots could be thoroughly briefed before the mission was flown. When a ground element urgently needed close air support, its air liaison party submitted a request through the chain of command to the LFASCU at corps headquarters, which approved the request or turned it down, if, in fact, this action had not taken place earlier at regimental or division level.

Tenth Army unit commanders were favorably impressed also by the aerial supply drop system that was of such vital assistance to the attackers when supply routes had become bogged down. They recommended that a unit similar to the IIIAC Air Delivery Section be formed to work with each field army or independent corps. Tenth Army also recommended that the JASCOs assigned to each combat division be disbanded. Motivating this proposal was the feeling that when the marked dissimilarity in the training and functions of the various components of the JASCOs were taken into account, separate air liaison, shore fire control, and shore party communications parties would operate more efficiently.

The naval gunfire spotting and liaison teams were specially commended for competently handling the staggering volume of naval shells fired in support of the land forces. The shore bombardment of Okinawa on L-Day was "the heaviest concentration of naval gunfire ever delivered in the support of the landing of troops." Some 3,800 tons of shells poured in from battleships, cruisers, and destroyers, and from the rocket racks and mortars of the support vessels to explode on enemy shore targets. During most of the campaign, each frontline regiment was assigned one call fire ship and one illumination ship. In certain instances, such as during the 6th Marine Division drive to the Motobu Peninsula, each assault battalion had a destroyer on call, Most fire support ships remained on station for the entire campaign and were not rotated to other duties. As the operation progressed, the quality and results of their shooting improved immeasurably.

On certain occasions, however, the ground units encountered intricately sited and deeply dug-in enemy positions which were impregnable to even the weight of naval gunfire salvos. At these times, the Japanese positions would withstand the fires of individual supporting arms or all of them together. Then, assault forces began a wearing-down process involving the employment of flame and gun tanks, demolitions, and infantry all together in what General Buckner referred to as "the corkscrew and blowtorch" method. Although artillery utilized every expedient conceivable, including the use of antiaircraft artillery guns and LVT(A) howitzers to supplement their regular fires, the Shuri and Kiyamu defenses remained invulnerable for long periods at a time.

One artillery weapon that was organic to the infantry regiments and immediately available for employment under optimum frontline conditions was the 105mm self-propelled howitzer, the M-7. This field piece was found in the 105mm howitzer (self-propelled) platoon containing four gun sections, which replaced the 75mm howitzer (self-propelled) platoon, in the regimental weapons company when it was reorganized on 1 May 1945 according to the G-series Table of Organization (T/O). The 1st and 6th Marine Divisions had received the T/O change, revamped their weapons companies, and were supplied with the M-7s before embarking for Okinawa.

No other Tenth Army units remained continuously on line so long a period as the artillery battalions of both Marine and Army divisions during the battle in southern Okinawa. In this period, the artillery of all six infantry divisions supported the attack. Marine and Army corps artillery units supplemented the fires of the 24 divisional battalions with 12 of their own in general support.

Augmenting the Marine artillery were the guns of two LVT(A) battalions, which had been organized and trained as field artillery before the landing. Because of its organization, each LVT(A) battalion had the fire support capability of a four-battalion regiment of 75mm howitzers. Prior to Okinawa, General Geiger had become convinced that the armored amtracs could be trained as field artillery and used as such immediately after landing on L-Day at H-Hour and until direct support battalions arrived ashore. Thereafter, the LVT(A)s would reinforce corps and divisional artillery. After landing on L-Day, the LVT(A)s had their "batteries laid and ready to shoot for forward observers as early as H plus 30 minutes — but the Japanese wouldn't accommodate us with targets."

A total of 2,246,452 rounds were fired in support of the infantry by tanks, LVT(A)s, M-7s, and field artillery pieces; this was more than triple the 707,500 rockets, mortars, and rounds of 5-inch shells or larger fired by the gunfire support ships. In either case, the figure is staggering. Because Tenth Army had established a centralized system of target assignment and fire direction, unit artillery commanders were able to mass the fires of all their guns that were within the range of a specific target with little effort in a minimum of time.

In an analysis of Marine artillery operations on Okinawa, General Geiger discovered that there had been instances when 155mm guns and howitzers were unable to destroy certain well-built Japanese defenses when called upon to do so. Further, both corps and division artillery often found it difficult to reduce natural cave positions, which fell only under the direct fire of self-propelled guns or when artillery of a larger caliber than that found in Marine artillery battalions were employed.

The expectation that the invasion of Japan would require a vastly increased fire potential in the existing Marine artillery organizations led General Geiger to recommend changes in its makeup. Accordingly, he proposed a new setup consisting of a field artillery observation battalion and four group headquarters and headquarters batteries, and the following firing batteries: one 105mm howitzer (self-propelled); three 155mm howitzer; two 155mm gun; one 155mm gun (self-propelled); two 8-inch howitzer; one 8-inch howitzer (self-propelled); and one 240mm howitzer.

General Geiger was particularly impressed by the penetrating and destructive power of the 200-pound shell of the 8-inch howitzer when compared with the results achieved by the 95-pound projectile fired by 155mm guns and howitzers, the largest caliber pieces organic to Marine artillery units. The Marine commander asked that some of these 8-inch battalions be included when task organizations were formed for future scheduled Marine operations against Japan scheduled for the future. Teamwork was a most important ingredient in the formula for reduction of heavily fortified Japanese positions. During the course of the Okinawa campaign, the work of supporting arms, infantry-engineer, air-ground, and tank-infantry teams played a vital role in the defeat of the enemy. Ground assault operations, however, were the especial province of the tanks and the infantry. Concerning the armored support of 6th Division Marines on Okinawa, General Shepherd wrote that "if any one supporting arm can be singled out as having contributed more than any others during the progress of the campaign, the tank would certainly be selected." In a battle lesson issued to the Thirty-second Army, General Ushijima supported this opinion, stating that "the enemy's power lies in his tanks. It has become obvious that our general battle against the American forces is a battle against their M-1 and M-4 tanks."

In comparison with the factors limiting armored support during some of the other Pacific island battles, tanks were more widely employed on Okinawa because its terrain, for the most part, favored armored operations. Tenth Army units lost a total of 153 tanks to accurate enemy AT fire, vast and thickly sown minefields, and demolitions-laden Japanese soldiers who attempted to destroy both the tanks and themselves, but who failed in their efforts for the most part, however, because of the accurate fire of the infantrymen protecting the tanks. Individual Japanese damaged seven tanks from the five Army battalions, disabled one from the 6th Marine Division, and none in the 1st Marine Division where "the alertness of the covering infantry and the tank crews prevented the successful completion of these attacks."

Tanks from the Army 713th Armored Flamethrower Battalion, the first unit of its type to be formed and take part in sustained action, supported Army and Marine units alike. After the campaign, the battalion was highly praised for "a consistently outstanding record of performance."

While covered by infantrymen and standard tanks, flame tanks were particularly successful in burning the enemy out of rocky outcroppings, reverse slope positions, and ruins. The commanders of both the XXIV Corps and the IIIAC favored the increased employment of flame tanks. General Hedge suggested the addition of two battalions to each corps in future operations; General Geiger recommended that one company of these tanks be made organic to each Marine tank battalion. Both Marine combat divisions had Army 4.2-inch chemical mortar companies attached for the campaign. The division commanders reported that they were very satisfied with the performance of the large-caliber mortars, which could furnish high angle fire on targets not otherwise suitable for 81mm mortars and artillery howitzers. After noting the successful results that had followed employment of the 4.2-inch mortars attached to his division, General del Valle was convinced that their accuracy, long range, and tremendous destructive power were such that he recommended the inclusion of this type of company in the T/O of a Marine division.

Two other new Army support weapons impressed Marine leaders for the same reasons as had the heavy mortars; they were the 57mm and 75mm recoilless rifles. Although neither had been issued for testing by Marine units, nor were the rifles employed extensively by the Army, after viewing a combat demonstration of the effectiveness of the new weapons, IIIAC observers reported that the recoilless rifles held considerable promise for tactical employment. General Geiger acted on this information and recommended that the Marine Corps thoroughly field test both weapons with a view of adopting them in place of the 37mm guns and 2.36-inch bazookas in the infantry regiments at that time.

Few startling innovations to accepted infantry tactical methods appeared out of the Okinawa fighting. Concerning this, General Geiger commented: "No new or unusual features of infantry combat were disclosed or developed during the campaign on Okinawa which would tend to modify or annul current standard principles or doctrines." Those facets of the battle sometimes cited as having reflected the emergence of new concepts in the Pacific war—such as the employment of night attacks and refinement of tank-infantry tactics—were actually just the logical outgrowth of existing tactical doctrine that evolved after the Americans had become familiar with the enemy and his way of fighting.

For the most part, in the early years of the war, there was little inclination toward night offensive action; Marines were too intent on tying in their lines before darkness in order to blunt inevitable Japanese counterattacks and infiltration of the lines. During the Okinawa campaign, however, Marine units took part in night operations more extensively than ever before, and with a great degree of success. Approximately 21 patrols and attacks were mounted at night by Marines; 13 of this number were conducted by the Amphibious Reconnaissance Battalion. In commenting on this aspect of Marine tactics on Okinawa, General Geiger said: "All night operations were characterized by the fact that they were performed in an orthodox manner. Previous training in such maneuvers and existing doctrines on the subject were employed and proved sound. Daylight reconnaissance, a limited objective of a prominent terrain feature, explicit orders for all echelons, noise discipline, and contact were as prescribed in the training manuals. In every case surprise was achieved and the night attack or movement was successful."

Regarding the American night attacks, Colonel Yahara commented that they were "particularly effective, taking the Japanese completely by surprise. The Japanese had so accustomed themselves to ceasing organized hostilities at nightfall, and . . . reorganizing and relaxing during the night that attacks in these hours caught them both physically and psychologically off-guard."

In general, a study of the Marine conduct of night operations on Okinawa revealed no new, startling doctrine, for it indicated the following:

Orthodox methods are good methods.

A correct estimate of the situation is a major contributing factor toward success.

Night operations need not be confined to highly specialized units.

Such operations afford echelon commanders with an excellent tactical device.

Present doctrine is quite satisfactory for the training and indoctrination of troops. In reviewing the success of those night attacks launched during the Okinawa campaign, it seems surprising that American commanders did not employ this offensive tactic more often.

Immediately after the fighting for Shuri had intensified, severe gaps appeared in the ranks of the assault elements. Although replacements were fed to Tenth Army continually during the course of battle, they were often too poorly or incompletely trained to go into the frontlines immediately. Yet, they were needed to beef up the strength of the hard-hit units. Nevertheless, Tenth Army issued an order to the corps commanders directing that newly arriving personnel were to be indoctrinated and oriented before assignment to frontline units. It was very often difficult to adhere to this directive, especially when the situation demanded that the replacements be committed into the lines before they were completely "shaken down." General Geiger "had only two divisions to fight" on Okinawa and found it impossible to guarantee the "relief of front line divisions for rest and assimilation of replacements." To remedy this, he suggested that a corps on extended operations should have a triangular organization much like that of the Marine divisions to provide for an "automatic reserve." Without this, his two Marine divisions had to remain constantly on line until the end of the operation. Based on the knowledge gained at Okinawa, a corps of at least three divisions was considered a must for future joint operations of a similar nature.

Some serious personnel problems arose before and during the campaign for Army and Marine divisions alike. Most deeply concerned was XXIV Corps, which had been deeply involved in the Philippines operation during the time that preparations for ICEBERG were underway. General Hedge favored the Marine replacement system in which Marine replacements were attached to and trained with infantry units during the preinvasion phases, and then travelled with these units to the target area, where they worked as shore party labor units until needed in the lines to replace infantry casualties.

Including the replacements they had received before departing Pavuvu and Guadalcanal respectively, the 1st Marine Division landed at Okinawa approximately 10 percent over T/O strength, and the 6th Marine Division arrived at the target with a 5 percent overage. Because they had participated in the training and rehearsal phases of ICEBERG, the replacements could be assigned to line regiments when required. Most of the replacements who arrived at Okinawa during the later stages of the battle had come directly from Stateside. Since they were not so well trained as the earlier replacements, the infantry units to which they were assigned had to divert some of their efforts to indoctrinate and train the new arrivals for battle rapidly.

Possibly influenced by the Marine replacement system, Tenth Army recommended that, in future operations, a large-sized replacement company should be assigned to and train with an infantry division before an invasion, and then accompany that division to the target area. General Hedge suggested that infantry battalions be permitted to carry a 25-percent-strength overage to the target, and that balanced infantry replacement battalions, each consisting of 1,000 men, be attached to and loaded out with every invasion-bound infantry division.

Both the 1st and 6th Marine Divisions contained a large number of combat veterans who had participated in two or more campaigns in the Pacific. As of 30 June 1945, the 1st Marine Division had 205 officers that had served overseas 24 months or more; over half of these had been in the Pacific area for more than 30 months. Nearly 3,200 enlisted Marines had been in the field for two years or more; almost 800 of these had been in a combat zone for 30 or more months. General del Valle considered that these facts reflected the approach of a serious personnel and morale problem in the division. By the fall of 1945, 1st Marine Division personnel already in or entering the two-year category "will have spent their entire time in a coconut grove or jungle with not a single opportunity for leave or liberty." Steps were taken later, however, which alleviated the situation before it reached a crucial point. The immediate replacement of infantry losses was a problem common to commanders of all assault echelons. They believed that the solution was to be found in the establishment of a smoothly working replacement system, wherein replacements would be attached to and train with an infantry unit before an invasion. Experienced troop leaders knew that long hours of closely coordinated training were needed before assault and replacement organizations could be considered combat ready. Arduous hours of team training served as the basis of American successes at Okinawa. The final action report of the Tenth Army noted: "The support rendered the infantry by naval gunfire, artillery, air and tanks was adequate in every respect. Without such magnificent support, little progress could have been made by the infantry in their advance against the heavily organized enemy positions in southern Okinawa. Supporting fire enabled the infantry to carry out the tremendous task of repeated assaults against strongly fortified positions."

Logistical planning too required teamwork, and the problems facing the logistics planners reflected the magnitude of the Okinawa operation. Consider for example, that in Phase I of ICEBERG alone, a total of almost 183,000 troops and 746,850 measurement tons of cargo had to be loaded into 433 assault transports and landing ships by 8 different subordinate embarkation commands at 11 widely separated ports from Seattle to Leyte over a distance of some 6,000 miles.

The Joint Expeditionary Force alone contained 1,200 ships of all kinds. By the time that the island was secured, "About 548,000 men of the Army, Navy. and Marine Corps took part, with 318 combatant vessels and 1,139 auxiliary vessels exclusive of personnel landing craft of all types." These figures coupled with the long distances over which supplies had to travel, created logistics problems of an immense nature beyond all that which had transpired in earlier Pacific operations.

Some concept of the size of the unloading job at Okinawa may be seen in the amounts of assault and first echelon cargo unloaded in all the Central Pacific campaigns from the Gilberts through Okinawa. This dramatically indicates that in the overall tonnage of supplies and equipment unloaded, the total for Okinawa was almost double that for the entire Marianas operation and three times that for the Iwo Jima campaign. Errors of omission and commission in the logistics program seemed critical at the time that they appeared, but none was grave enough to effect the fighting for long. Some problems arising from the nature of operations began before L-Day and continued thereafter; they were important enough however, to cause unit commanders to comment on them and make recommendations for improvement in their action reports. In the logistics planning phase, embarkation officers too often found that ships' characteristics data for assigned ships was incorrect or out of date; at times, it was either not furnished or unavailable. When division staffs began completing loading plans, they found that, for the uninitiated and non-specialist, there were too many forms. These were too complicated and often repetitive. During the loading phase, ships' captains often received confusing and contradictory orders, which on several occasions resulted in their ships arriving in loading areas or appearing at places other than those to which they were to have gone. In most cases, the confusion arose from poor coordination between Marine and Navy staffs.

A sequel to this liaison gap at times appeared in the improper loading of assault transports. The commander of the transport group that lifted the 1st Marine Division to the target from the Russells reported that plans for loading some of his ships were not even begun until the vessels were alongside waiting to take a load. In reference to the loading of his entire group, he also said: "It can be fairly stated that these ships were not combat loaded. It is true that cargo was landed according to priority. However, the 60 percent combat load as expressed in Transport Doctrine was greatly exceeded. All ships were, in the opinion of the squadron 'commercial loaded, according to a definite priority.' This was due to the fact that an inadequate number of vessels were assigned by higher command to lift the First Marine Division."

During the preinvasion preparatory period, Marine divisions, especially the 6th, found the Marine Corps supply system on the Pacific overly cumbersome. Two basic factors aggravated the situation. One was the fact that the relations of the Marine Supply Service, FMFPac, to the several combat and service commands in the Guadalcanal area—where the greater portion of IIIAC strength was based—caused many delays because of the many agencies through which supply requisitions had to pass before the requestor received the items requisitioned. In addition the 6th Division was located too far away from the stocking agency, which in this case was the 4th Base Depot on Banika in the Russells.

General Shepherd believed: "Supply problems, many requiring written correspondence and decisions by high authority, were not simplified by the addition of another senior echelon, the South Pacific Echelon, Fleet Marine Force, Pacific. The recent change in the concept of operations of the Corps, by which administration of divisions is theoretically divorced from the Corps, has not benefited the Division. Supply and administration cannot, in practice, be separated from command." A built-in problem, inherent in the nature of the organization and equipment of a Marine division, appeared on L-Day, The initial lack of resistance beyond the beachhead permitted the landing of many Marines who would otherwise not have gone ashore until scheduled. This caused a shortage of landing craft slated to move cargo to the beaches and in turn brought about a delay in the landing of such selected items of division cargo as motor transport and prime movers, which were ticketed for unloading on L-Day.

The truth is that neither Marine division ever had enough motor transportation either to supply itself adequately or to move its artillery. An allotment of motor vehicles and prime movers which might have been sufficient to the normal small island type of fighting to which Marines were accustomed was insufficient for a long operation such as Okinawa.

At the end of the campaign, General del Valle recommended that each infantry regiment be furnished five prime movers with trailers to supplement motor transport already organic to the division. He also recommended that the infantry regiments be given in addition two bulldozers for "initial road, trail, dump clearance. . . ." The 1st Division commander noted that motor transport, tractors, and engineering equipment, urgently needed for combat operations were often deadlined for lack of spare parts. To alleviate this situation, he recommended that, in future logistical planning, provisions should be made for the inclusion of an ample supply of spare parts in resupply shipments.

According to an officer who was deeply involved in shore party and supply operations at Okinawa: "Logistically, the touchstone of success was . . . interservice cooperation. In many instances, shortages of . . . supplies suffered by one service was made up by another service." It was a unique example of the unification that was developed throughout the campaign through the Central Pacific.

In the end, hasty field expedients and the overwhelming superiority of American matériel strength, as well as the interservice collaboration, overcame any obstacle to the capture of Okinawa that logistical problems may have caused.

The story of the Okinawa campaign is incomplete without a brief investigation of enemy tactics. Contrary to the Japanese beachhead defense doctrine encountered in earlier Pacific landings, when the enemy strongly defended his beaches or ferociously attacked the invader before he could organize the beachhead, at Okinawa, the Tenth Army met a resistance in depth similar to that experienced by Americans in the Philippines invasion. IGHQ had ordered General Ushijima to fight a long holding action to buy the time necessary for Japan to complete Homeland defenses. If the Americans sustained a high attrition rate while attempting to batter down the Thirty-second Army defenses, so much the better; there would be that fewer Americans in the anticipated invasion of Japan. From the time that the Tenth Army landed over the Hagushi beaches until it encountered the northern outposts of the Shuri line, it was harassed, harried, and delayed by small provisional units and somewhat stronger blocking forces, the latter comprised of veteran regulars. The fall of Saipan in 1944, if nothing else, brought home to IGHQ the military potential of the United States. This loss caused the Japanese command to accelerate the construction of defense positions in Japan as well as on Iwo Jima and Okinawa. The fast carrier task force air raids on Okinawa beginning in October 1944 spurred General Ushijima's Thirty-second Army on to strengthen Okinawa defenses further. Beginning in mid-April, when the Tenth Army encountered the maze of concentric defense rings encircling Shuri, Americans became painfully aware of the results of these efforts.

The rugged and complex ridgelines in the Shuri area were defended from vast entrenchments, from a wide variety of fortified caves employed as pillboxes, and from elaborate, multi-storied weapons positions and gun emplacements that had been gouged out of the ridges and hills and connected by tunnels, which usually opened on the reverse slopes. "The continued development and improvement of cave warfare was the most outstanding feature of the enemy's tactics on Okinawa."

Among other outstanding features of Thirty-second Army defense tactics was the use of a considerable amount of reinforcing artillery, mortar, and machine gun fire. Also, the Japanese made mass *Banzai* charges only infrequently, but with a hopeful view either of exploiting a successful attack or of just keeping the Americans off-balance. The enemy did, however, fritter away his strength and dwindling forces in small-sized counterattacks, which had little chance of success and which were, in most cases, blunted easily by the Americans.

Despite the obvious fact that his Thirty-second Army was decisively beaten, General Ushijima must be credited with having successfully accomplished his assigned mission. He did provide Japan with valuable time to complete the homeland defense.

The final act of the Okinawa story unfolded on 26 August 1945, when General of the Army Douglas MacArthur—appointed earlier as Supreme Commander for the Allied Powers (SCAP)—authorized General Stilwell to negotiate the surrender of enemy garrisons in the Ryukyus. Responding to orders issued by Stilwell, top enemy commanders reported at the headquarters of the Ryukyus command on 7 September to sign "unconditional surrender documents representing the complete capitulation of the Ryukyus Islands and over 105,000 Army and Navy forces." Witnessing the ten-minute ceremony in addition to those officiating were Army and Marine infantry units and tank platoons, while above it all hundreds of planes flashed by.

In a report to the Secretary of the Navy, Fleet Admiral Ernest J. King, CominCh, stated that "the outstanding development of this war, in the field of joint undertakings, was the perfection of amphibious operations, the most difficult of all operations in modern warfare." As the next to last giant step leading to the defeat of Japan, the Okinawa invasion was a prime example of a successful amphibious operation, and the culmination of all that Americans had learned in the Pacific War in the art of mounting a seaborne assault against an enemy-held land mass. This knowledge was to serve well in preparing for the invasion of Japan.

CPSIA information can be obtained
at www.ICGtesting.com
Printed in the USA
LVHW04s1615100618
580230LV00032B/1927/P

9 781934 941829